the Unofficial Guide® to Having a Baby

Second Edition

*Ann Douglas and
John R. Sussman, M.D.*

WILEY

Wiley Publishing, Inc.

To my family.
— John Sussman

To Julie, Scott, Erik, and Ian, for the wonderful
times we've shared both before and after your births;
and Laura, the baby I never got to take home.
— Ann Douglas

Acknowledgements

A book of this scope requires the behind-the-scenes efforts of a lot of people.

In addition to our editors at Wiley and our research assistants Suzanne Boles and Lisa Clarke, who assisted us with the revisions to the second edition, we would like to thank the following individuals who generously shared their expertise with us while we were working on the first edition of the this book: Barbara Hotelling, BSN, RN, Richard Whatley, MD, CCFP, and Lisa Mandelbaum, RD, who served as the book's technical reviewers; Winston Campbell, M.D., Professor of Obstetrics/Gynecology and Director of Maternal-Fetal Medicine at the University of Connecticut Health Center; Miriam DiMaio, Senior Genetic Counselor, Department of Genetics, Yale University School of Medicine; James X. Egan, M.D., Vice Chairman, Department of Obstetrics and Gynecology at the University of Connecticut Health Center; Janet Estes, founder of the online Infant Loss Mailing List; Siobhan Furst, pediatric nurse, Hospital for Sick Children; Robert Greenstein, M.D., Ph.D., Professor in Pediatrics and Director of the Division of Human Genetics at the University of Connecticut Health Center; Sara Grimes, founder and co-administrator of the Subsequent Pregnancy After Loss online mailing list; Elizabeth Hawkins-Walsh, nursing professor, Catholic University of America; Susan Hays, Director of the Health Sciences Library at New Milford Hospital; Herman Hein, Professor of Obstetrics at the University of Iowa Hospitals and Clinics; Tracy Keleher, Producer, Canadian Parents Online; Michael Nettleton, co-administrator of the Subsequent Pregnancy After Loss online mailing list; Linda Omichinski, Registered Dietitian; John Rodis, M.D., Associate Professor of Obstetrics/Gynecology and Pediatrics and Director of Perinatal Genetics at the University of Connecticut Health Center; and Jennifer Zint, expert on surrogacy.

We would also like to thank the parents who shared the most intimate details of their lives with us while serving on our parent panel or by participating in individual interviews: Nicole Alexander, Wilma Anderson, Laura Augustine, Jennie Baird, Heidi Barrett, John Beck, Krista Beck, Leila Belhadjali, Serene Blascovich, Melissa Bolton, Andrea Brenton, Susan Breuker, Michelle Brown, Laura Buren, Charlene Busselaar, Noel C. Kurtz, Sue Cain, Anne Cavicchi, Dawnette Chadwick, Catie Chi Olson, Nancy Clanton, Debbie Clanton-Churchwell, Dawn Clapperton, Melanie Clark, Holly Clawson, Helena Cright, Debby David, Molly Davies, Jennifer Dawson, Joanna Delavan, Bob Dony, Cherisa Duncan, Cindy Durrett, Erin Dwyer, Susan Erhardt, Jennifer Fariel, Amy Fessler, Janet Flach, Deirdre Friedrich, Robin Frojen-Andersson, Tanya Frojen-Andersson, Danielle Gardiner, Jim Gastle, Laura Gazley, Olivia Gerroll-Kelley, Angela Goldie, Stacy Graham, Victoria Grandy, Stephanie Griffin, Lou Guimond, Jennifer Hanskat, Lori Harasem-Mitchell, Heather Harms, Elaine Harper Nugent, Barbara Hennelly, Mary Hernandez-Froment, Sarah Hetherington, Steve Hiller, Marilyn Copley Hilton, Troy Hilton, Anne Hoover, Johnna Horn, Toni Howard, Marie Hughes, Vidya Iyer, Tracy Myers Janevic, Bridget Kelley, Aricka Krier, Grace Lacson, Therese Lafferty, Joanna Lasiter, Erika Lingo, Marcie Longstaff, Karen Lyall, Rhona Lyons, Allison Martin, Marie Martorella, Randa McBride, Jacqueline McKenzie, Heather McKinnon, Wendy McWilliams, Rhonda Melanson, Michele Minietta, Janna Skura Mintz, Cindy Mount, Lisa Mullen, Olivia Mundahl, Debbie Myers, Christa Newbold, Ellen Newlands, Ashley Ocampo, Jennifer Ogle, Vicki Paradine, Jackie Patrick, Allison Peck, Sandra Pendak, Jane Pendergast, Carrie Petersen, Heather Petit, Tola Plusnick, Brenda Pressler, Suzi Prokell, Diana Quin-Conroy, Kathi Rawnsley, Charity Reed, Lisa Reed, Kseniya Reinoehl, Karen Rolfe, Amie Rossini, Marianne Salas, Debbie Saltrick, Kimberley Sando, Kim Schrader, Colleen Shortall, Nicola Shute, Collette Smith, Julie Snyder, Destiny Sparks-McAffrey, Andrea Stalnecker, Beth Starks, Terrie Tarnowski, Jane Tracogna,

Thomas Viano, LeeAnn Volle, Linda Wacht, Lisa Wagley, Jodi Walker, Ruth Ann Wallace, Tina Walsh, Trina Walsh, Kama Warner, Meredith Webb Feinberg, Jessica Lauren Weiss, Lori Wells, Jennifer Welter, Lynne Whitman, Helen Williams, Margaret Williams, Leslie Wilson, Ginny Wood, Jeffrey Wooten, Christy Young, Susan Yusishen, Suzanne Zavesky, Beth Zerbest, and Melissa Ziegler.

We would also like to thank acquisitions editor Jennifer Farthing, who invited us to write the first edition of this book; acquisitions editor Roxane Cerda, who adopted our "baby" and enthusiastically made the case for a second edition; developmental editor Suzanne Snyder, who was unwaveringly cheerful from the first page of the manuscript to the last; the countless unsung heroes in the production, sales, and marketing departments at Wiley who worked so hard to make the first edition of this book such a success; and our agent Ed Knappman of New England Publishing Associates, who first brought the two of us together as a pregnancy book-writing team.

Finally, we would like to thank our families for sharing us with our computers during the first edition and second edition writing marathons. We couldn't have done it without your support.

Thanks to you all!

Contents

About the Authors

Ann Douglas is one of North America's most popular pregnancy and parenting writers. An award-winning journalist and the mother of four children, ages six through fifteen, Ann is the author of 24 books, including *The Mother of All Pregnancy Books* and *The Mother of All Baby Books*. The next three books in Ann's best-selling "Mother of All Books" series — *The Mother of All Toddler Books, The Mother of All Parenting Books,* and *The Mother of All Pregnancy Organizers* — are scheduled for publication in 2004.

Known for her lively anecdotes and real-world advice, Ann makes regular radio and television appearances and is frequently quoted in such publications as *Parenting, Parents, Fit Pregnancy, American Baby,* and *Working Mother.* She teaches online pregnancy and parenting courses for WebMD.com and Netscape's Online Learning Center as well as through her own web sites, BellyUniversity.com™ and MomUniversity.com™

You can download copies of Ann's pregnancy and parenting tip sheets, access her online archive of parenting articles, join her parenting book club, sign up for her monthly parenting newsletter, or inquire about her speaking and consulting services by visiting her Web site at www.having-a-baby.com.

Dr. John R. Sussman has practiced obstetrics and gynecology for 20 years and is the Chief of Obstetrics and Gynecology at New Milford Hospital. He is Assistant Clinical Professor in the Department of Obstetrics and Gynecology at the University of Connecticut Health Center. Dr. Sussman is the co-author (with B. Blake Levitt) of *Before You Conceive: The Complete Prepregnancy Guide* (Bantam, 1989) and (with Ann Douglas) *Trying Again— A Guide to Pregnancy After Miscarriage, Stillbirth, and Infant Loss* (Taylor, 2000). He is a frequent guest instructor at WebMD

University (WebMD.com) and maintains his private practice's Web site at newmilfordobgyn.com.

During his career, Dr. Sussman has delivered more than 2,000 babies. He is the father of two children, one of whom he delivered.

One of the most exciting and important decisions you'll ever be faced with is whether or not to have a child. Assuming you decide to take the plunge, you're in for a wild and exciting ride.

First there's the business of trying to get your body in the best possible condition to support a pregnancy: eating properly, staying active, and avoiding substances that could be harmful to your baby.

Then there are the joys and frustrations of trying to conceive: struggling to distinguish between the symptoms of early pregnancy and those of PMS; running to the bathroom every half hour on the day that your period is due in an effort to determine whether that month's Baby Olympics have paid off; and spending an obscene amount of money on home pregnancy tests in an effort to get the answer you want.

If you don't manage to conceive as quickly as you would like, you will have to find some way of coming to terms with the fact that this is one aspect of your life over which you have only a limited amount of control. You could, like 10 percent of American couples, be experiencing fertility problems. If you and your partner are unable to conceive naturally, you may decide to consider other avenues to becoming pregnant — assisted reproductive technologies, surrogacy, adoption, and so on — or you may decide to abandon your dream of having a child altogether. We discuss each of these options in this book.

Assuming that you do manage to conceive fairly quickly — and the odds of this happening are, by the way, decidedly in your favor — you will still have a lot of heavy-duty physical and emotional adjustments to make. Starting long before the pregnancy test comes back positive, your body will begin to undergo a remarkable metamorphosis that will allow it to grow a baby.

And then there are the emotional changes of pregnancy. During the months between conception and birth, you'll likely experience the full gamut of emotions — euphoria, worry, joy, depression, and everything in between. It's the emotional changes of pregnancy that are, for most women, both the most difficult and the most wondrous aspect of being pregnant. One moment you may be feeling totally euphoric about the miracle that is taking place in your very own body, convinced that deciding to have a baby is the best thing you've ever done. The next moment you may be making yourself totally crazy, worrying about all the 1,001 ways that having a baby is going to change your life — and your partner's life — forever.

And then there's the whole idea of giving birth — a process that is simultaneously miraculous and terrifying to many women. Preparing for your baby's birth means learning to trust that your body will know what to do when the big moment arrives, and then coming to terms with any fears you may have about what may happen during the birth.

While first-time mothers tend to focus their attention on the hours leading up to the birth, experienced mothers know that the rollercoaster ride doesn't end when your baby arrives. If anything, it is just beginning. While you may initially view this new littler person in your life with more curiosity than love, the emotions of motherhood don't take long to set in. The feelings you experienced when you fell in love for the first time may seem almost insignificant as compared to the love that will blossom between you and your baby over time.

Made in America

The road to parenthood may not be the easiest of journeys, but it's certainly one of life's most rewarding. If you're thinking about having a baby in the near future, the news is good: the odds of having a healthy baby are decidedly in your favor. Consider the numbers for yourself:

- Eighty-five percent of couples who are trying to conceive will be pregnant within one year. Even those couples who don't manage to conceive right away have a good chance of becoming parents through either fertility treatments, adoption, or surrogacy.

- While the rate of early miscarriage is high, 90 percent of women whose pregnancies are confirmed will carry their babies to term.

- According to the Centers for Disease Control and Prevention, only 2 percent to 3 percent of babies are born with any major congenital anomaly.

While there are no guarantees that everything will go perfectly during pregnancy (Mother Nature doesn't hand out those kinds of guarantees), there is plenty of good news for couples who are eager become parents. New methods of preventing or treating infertility, miscarriage, and stillbirth are making parenthood a possibility for couples who might not otherwise have been able to achieve that dream. (See Chapters 4 and 17.) For couples facing above-average challenges on the reproductive front, there's never been a better time to have a baby.

While there's plenty of good news to report on the childbearing front, we'd be guilty of whitewashing the facts if we tried to pretend that everything is rosy. There are still a few rather significant blemishes on America's childbearing record: the country's infant mortality rate is higher than that of many other industrialized nations, and, despite all the advances in obstetrical care, nearly as many American women today give birth to low birthweight babies as did some 20 years ago.

Statistics also help to illustrate how the whole nature of giving birth in America is changing, both for better and for worse. Here are some other noteworthy trends you'll want to take into account as you go about planning your pregnancy:

- After declining steadily for much of the early 1990s, the cesarean rate has been climbing steadily since 1998. In 2001 — the last year for which statistics are available — it stood at 24.4 percent, an all-time high.

- Women are waiting longer than ever to start their families. The average age of a first-time mother today is 25 years old — about three years older than the average age of a first-time mother back in the 1970s.

- The rate of triplet and other higher-order multiple births is now in decline, after increasing by more than five times between 1980 and 1998.

As helpful as the numbers may be in understanding what your childbirth experience may be like, they don't tell you everything. You have to dig a little deeper to find out what it's really like to have a baby in America today. And that, in a nutshell, is what this book is all about.

The smart guide to pregnancy

If you've spent much time in bookstores lately, you already know that most pregnancy books fall into one of two basic categories: those that manage to scare you to death by piling on details about every conceivable pregnancy-related problem, and expect you to follow a prenatal diet and fitness regime that would have even boot camp recruits begging for mercy; and those that are so full of new-age warm-and-fuzzies that you couldn't find a cold hard medical fact to save your life.

Then there's this book, *The Unofficial Guide to Having a Baby* — a book that is overflowing with facts, tips, and resources galore — to say nothing of pages. While most Unofficial Guides come in at approximately 400 pages, we knew we needed at least

800 pages to do this subject justice. Fortunately, the editors at Wiley agreed with us and gave us carte blanche to write a pregnancy book that is packed with the very types of information that expectant parents both want and need. They even gave us some extra pages when we sat down to write the second edition because — like us — they wanted the second edition to build on the first edition's reputation as America's definitive pregnancy reference book.

What you'll find in this book

At the heart of this book is something that most pregnancy books tend to neglect: firsthand accounts of what it's *really* like to have a baby. You'll hear real parents talk about the joys and frustrations of trying to conceive, the raging hormones of early pregnancy, the wonder of feeling your baby's first kick, the legendary (some would say infamous!) discomforts of the third trimester, the experience of coping with a pregnancy that doesn't end when your due date rolls around, the challenge of trying to decide whether or not you're really in labor, and the wondrous experience of giving birth to a child and becoming a parent.

If some of this material sounds like the kind of information you might share with a friend over a cup of coffee, it's certainly for good reason. There were a lot of real-life parents involved in the planning of this book. We pulled together a panel of 150 new and expectant parents and asked them to share their pregnancy wisdom. As you will see as you get into the heart of the book, the parents on our panel were surprisingly frank about their experiences, baring their souls about such highly intimate aspects of their lives as the sexual positions they used while trying to conceive their babies, how they and their partners really felt about being pregnant, and what it was really like to give birth. Time and time again, *they* thanked *us* for giving them the opportunity to pass along the very types of pregnancy wisdom that they wished someone else had told them when they were embarking on their own journeys to parenthood.

The panel came up with practical tips on every pregnancy-related situation imaginable: keeping the fun in sex when you're trying to conceive, coping with morning sickness on the job, convincing your boss to agree to the best possible maternity leave package, choosing a caregiver and a place to give birth, weathering the physical and emotional highs and lows of pregnancy, and getting the best possible value for your dollar when it comes to health insurance, maternity wear, baby gear, and much more.

The result of all their input is the book that you're holding in your hands — one that is unlike anything else you're likely to find on the bookstore shelf because it's drawn from the experiences of real parents like you.

The book is also far more comprehensive than most pregnancy books. Rather than spouting a few clichés about prenatal nutrition, uttering some reassuring words about pregnancy complaints, and insisting that you'll be "just fine" when it comes time to deliver, we delve into the nitty-gritty, boldly going where no other pregnancy book has gone — at least until now. You'll find facts drawn from the latest medical journals and statistical databases and lists of resources that you can use to follow up on points that we raise in the text. The text is also liberally sprinkled with the URLs of Internet sites that you'll want to check at some point during your pregnancy, including leads on online support groups that can help to make the experience of having a baby a little more real.

Like any complex issue, the facts about pregnancy are often more gray than black and white. In situations in which the data conflict or an issue is particularly controversial, we present you with the facts on both sides of the argument and allow you to make up your mind for yourself.

Since pregnancy can also be a fun time in your life, we've thrown in a bit of less serious stuff too — like information about all those old wives' tales you've probably heard by now. (After all, where is it written that pregnancy books have to be deadly serious — and deadly boring, to boot?)

We've got plenty of other goodies in store for you, including the following:

- A frank discussion of the pros and cons of having a baby — everything from physical and emotional concerns to financial matters and the potential career fallout of stepping on to the Mommy or Daddy Track.

- The inside scoop on getting pregnant fast, and tips on coping with the emotional rollercoaster ride that you can find yourself on if you don't conceive as quickly as you'd like. We allow you to step inside the bedrooms of the members of our parents panel and find out what worked for them, and why. We also give you valuable information designed to help you find your way through the infertility maze, providing you with clear definitions of the fertility-related lingo you'll need to understand, as well as practical advice on choosing a fertility clinic — information that we hope you won't need, but that can be valuable to have if your path to parenthood proves to be a little rockier than average.

- The inside scoop on what's going on with your baby, what's going on with your body, and what's going on with your head on a week-by-week basis, as well as "The Hot List" — must-ask questions for each of the 40 weeks of pregnancy.

- Detailed information on the symptoms of early pregnancy, advice on coping with your partner's reaction (good, bad, or ugly), and tips on breaking the news to your boss.

- Advice on choosing a doctor or midwife and a place to give birth.

- A discussion of the pros and cons of prenatal testing and the facts you need to consider when deciding whether or not you're prepared to hop on this particular medical merry-go-round.

- The facts you need to make healthy choices throughout your pregnancy, especially when it comes to nutrition, medication, sex, exercise, spa treatments, and staying on the job.

- A detailed examination of topics that other books tend to gloss over or ignore completely: coping with a high-risk pregnancy; preparing for a multiple birth; coping with miscarriage or stillbirth; being pregnant and single, pregnant and gay, and so on.

- Comprehensive information on the physical and emotional changes you may experience during your pregnancy, including how your body is changing, how your baby is growing, what you need to be concerned about, and important issues that you might want to think about as your pregnancy progresses. We provide you with helpful tips on coping with such common pregnancy complaints as morning sickness, backaches, urinary tract infections, yeast infections, and more.

- The facts about important decisions you will need to make before, during, or after the birth: whether or not to be induced if you go past your due date, the pros and cons of various types of pain relief during labor, and what you need to know about circumcision.

- A sneak preview of labor and delivery (i.e., what labor really feels like, how to distinguish between true and false labor, when to call your caregiver, why you may or may not want to invite others to the birth, and what to expect during both a vaginal and cesarean delivery).

- The truth about life after baby (i.e., what babies are really like and how to survive the postpartum period!).

- A set of appendices that are packed with information designed to help you to make the best possible health-related choices for yourself and your baby. You'll find a detailed glossary of fertility, pregnancy, childbirth, and baby-related terms; as well as leads on other books you might want to check out in order to round out your pregnancy research.

As you can see, we've packed a lot of useful information into *The Unofficial Guide to Having a Baby.* So toss this book in your handbag, put it on your night table, or stash it in your desk drawer at work so that we'll be there when you need us during the exciting months ahead.

A note about the second edition

If you read the first edition of this book, you'll notice that we've added a lot of new material to the second edition and that we've changed the method of organization quite dramatically. Instead of being organized on a topic-by-topic basis, the book is now organized on a week-by-week basis, with groups of weeks being clustered into a series of monthly chapters. (Chapter 5 contains information on Weeks 1 to 4, for example.)

We decided to go this route after receiving numerous letters from readers asking us to consider organizing the book in a way that would allow them to find out what they should expect to experience during each week of pregnancy. We hope you enjoy the new format and, as always, would welcome your comments on the book. You can write to us via www.having-a-baby.com.

Special Features

Every book in the Unofficial Guide series offers the following four special sidebars that are devised to help you get things done cheaply, efficiently, and smartly.

1. **Moneysaver:** Tips and shortcuts that will help you save money.

2. **Watch Out!:** Cautions and warnings to help you avoid common pitfalls.

3. **Bright Idea:** Smart or innovative ways to do something; in many cases, the ideas listed here will help you save time or hassle.

4. **Quote:** Anecdotes from real people who are willing to share their experiences and insights.

We also recognize your need to have quick information at your fingertips, and have provided the following comprehensive sections at the back of the book:

1. **Glossary:** Definitions of compluicated terminology and jargon.

2. **Further Reading:** Suggested titles that can help you get more in-depth information on related topics.

3. **Index**

More Information Online

In additon to the Special Features listed above, we have posted additional useful information online at www.wiley.com/go/anndouglas.

1. **Your Next Pregnancy:** The latest news on contraception and some advice on spacing your family and preparing an older child for the birth of a new baby.

2. **Resource Directory:** Leads on the hottest Internet sites and the names, addresses, and phone numbers of the pregnancy and parenting-related organizations that every parent needs to know about. The latest news on contraception and some advice on spacing your family and preparing an older child for the birth of a new baby.

3. **Important Documents:** A sample birth plan; a sample contract for hiring a doula; and valuable information on emergency childbirth procedures, including tips on what to do while you wait for the ambulance to arrive.

The Truth About Getting Pregnant

Chapter 1

GET THE SCOOP ON. . .
Your emotional readiness for pregnancy ▪ The
career costs of having a baby ▪ How having a
baby affects your financial picture ▪ The five
biggest tax breaks for parents with young
children ▪ Confronting the age issue

PART I

Is This the Right Time to Have a Baby?

Scarlett O'Hara said it best: "Death and taxes and childbirth. There's never any convenient time for any of them." If Margaret Mitchell had written her famous novel *Gone With the Wind* today rather than in an era when family planning was even less of an exact art than it is now, she might have noted that there's *never* a good time to have a baby.

There is, after all, always a good reason not to have a baby: too much is happening at work, you don't have enough money in the bank, you want to lose the extra weight you've been carrying around since your freshman year at college, and so on.

The biological clock waits for no woman, however — a point economist Sylvia Ann Hewlett hammered home in a recent article in the *Harvard Business Review.* "Media hype about advances in reproductive science. . . [gives] women the illusion that they can delay childbearing until their careers are well established. . . . Too many career women put their private lives on the back burner, assuming that children will eventually happen for them courtesy of high-tech reproduction — only to discover disappointment and failure."

Pamela Madsen, executive director of the American Infertility Association, echoed those thoughts in an interview with *Time* magazine: "Those women who are at the top of their game could have had it all, children and career. The problem was, nobody told them the truth about their bodies."

The truth, of course, is that there's still no "miracle cure" for the age-related decline in fertility that is part and parcel of being female (and male, too, for that matter). While stories about celebrity mamas giving birth in their late 40s — thanks to the Herculean efforts of highly skilled fertility doctors — seldom fail to make headline news, what these news stories neglect to point out is that these high-tech successes are the exception rather than the rule: only 3 percent to 5 percent of women who attempt in vitro fertilization in their 40s end up with the fairy-tale happy ending they and other women of their generation have been led to expect.

Of course, that's not to say that the biological clock is the only factor that warrants consideration when you're deciding whether or not to have a baby — that you should rush off and have a baby at age 20 or 25 just because you can. You're more than just a baby-making machine, after all! You'll also want to take into account how you feel about becoming a mother, how your partner feels about becoming a parent (assuming, of course, that you have a partner), how having a baby may impact your career, and whether your budget can handle the added costs associated with having a baby.

That, in a nutshell, is what this chapter is designed to do: to arm you with the facts so that you can decide whether or not you're ready to sign yourself up for the most exciting but perilous adventure there is — parenthood!

A question of timing

If you're waiting for some magical signal to tell you that it's time to switch into baby-making mode, you could find yourself in for a serious disappointment. That signal may or may not come.

Sure, there are couples who report that their biological clock suddenly starts acting like a biological time bomb when "the time is right." After years of being relatively low-key about the whole parenthood thing ("Yeah, sure, we're planning to have kids. . . someday"), they're suddenly hit with a powerful urge to go forth and multiply — *right now.*

That was certainly how things played out for Karen, a 34-year-old mother of three. "My husband and I had been together for 10 years before we married," she recalls. "We met in high school. We traveled, enjoyed ourselves, bought and renovated a house, and then thought that a child was the next logical step. As soon as we started thinking about it, I suddenly couldn't wait."

Of course, the drama doesn't necessarily play out this way for everyone. Some couples never experience that "We have to start trying right now" sense of biological urgency. For them, starting a family is much more of a business decision — a surprisingly cool-headed weighing of the pros and cons. "I just had this sense that

> 66 We had been married for three years and purchased the house that we wanted kids in. More and more frequently, my husband and I were asking [one another], 'What do you want to do tonight?' The clincher came when I was carrying my sister's very tired two-year-old son. For the first time, he snuggled his head into my neck for a rest. I knew then that I wanted that on an ongoing basis. I told my husband that I was ready and to let me know whenever he was. A few months later he said, 'Okay, let's go for it.' 99
>
> — Jacqueline, 34, currently pregnant with her second child

we were missing out on something really important," recalls John, a 39-year-old father of two. "And I knew that if we waited much longer (my partner's the same age as me), we were likely to miss out for good. We sat down one night and carefully considered what parenthood had to offer, for better and for worse. Then we decided to take the plunge."

Of course, sometimes there's a mix of logic and emotion at play — a deep-rooted desire to have children mixed with old-fashioned practicality.

"I hate to admit it, but our main consideration was my age," confesses Susan, a 33-year-old mother of one. "I was 31 when we got married, and I knew I wanted to have more than one child. I suppose in reality I had many years still to start trying, but my mother died of breast cancer at 32 and my grandmother died of breast cancer when she was very young also. I was scared that I would get breast cancer and die without being able to have a child — or get cancer and not be able to have a child. So although we'd been married less than a year and weren't really financially ready yet, we started trying."

> 66 When I decided to have my first baby, it was purely an emotional decision. We did not plan our finances, buy a new house, build our careers, or do anything most other couples do to prepare for their first baby. We simply felt we wanted to bring a child into our family, so we went for it! I think there is really something to be said about women and the urge to have children. It's so hard to explain, but you just 'feel' like you want to have a baby, so you go for it. 99
>
> — Suzi, 27, mother of two

While there isn't any official "parenthood preparedness test" you can take (biological or otherwise!) that will tell you for certain whether you're ready to become a parent, sociologists and psychologists have identified a few factors that can predict whether or not your timing is likely to be on or off. As a rule of thumb, you have better odds of enjoying the experience of being a parent if

- you have a realistic idea of what parenthood is really like (in other words, you don't have romantic ideas about it always playing out like something you might see on a diaper commercial!);

- you are willing to make the sacrifices required to be a parent, such as putting someone else's needs before your own on a daily — even hourly — basis (you know, giving up your once-sacred Sunday-morning coffee-and-newspaper reading marathon because some Pablum-encrusted cutie wants to go for a walk in her stroller);

> 66 My husband and I decided to try to become pregnant after my father passed away from cancer in 1996. I regretted not having given him more grandchildren and I was faced with my own mortality, since he was only 65 years old. My husband and I had been married 10 years by that time. 99
>
> — Janet, 33, mother of one

- you and your partner are equally committed to the idea of having a child;

- you and your partner are used to sharing responsibility for a variety of household tasks and intend to share the responsibilities of child-rearing, too.

Things can get sticky if one partner feels fully ready to have a baby, but the other partner is anything but. If you're the one who is eager to go into baby-making mode, you may feel frustrated — even hurt — by your partner's reluctance to start a family. Here are some tips on weathering this particular storm as a couple.

- Keep the dialogue going. While it may be difficult to hear your partner talk about why he's not ready to start a family, it's important to listen to what he has to say. You need to find out whether he's saying "no for now" or "no forever" and you need to find out if there's anything you can do to help address his concerns about having children. (It could be that he's worried that starting a family will force him into the provider role whether he's ready or not — something that men who are not quite finished sowing their wild oats can view as a life sentence!)

- Talk about other things other than your baby-making plans. Don't let this one trouble spot become the focal point of your entire relationship or you could be headed for trouble. Instead, try to find ways of staying connected as a couple while you find ways to navigate this relationship rough spot.

- Refuse to play the blame game. Rather than getting angry and trying to pin the blame for your partner's lack of enthusiasm about starting a family on his job, his mother, or other things in his life, simply accept the fact that he's not yet ready. You'll simply end up muddying the waters (and possibly alienating your mother-in-law to boot!) if you insist on pinning the blame on something or someone.

- Accept the fact that you can't force anyone to have a baby with you any more than you can force him (or her) to fall in love with you. It can be disappointing — heartbreaking even — to discover that you and your supposed soul mate are not on the same page (or even in the same book) when it comes to something as fundamental as starting a family, but that doesn't mean you have the right to bully him into giving in. Remember, you want your baby to have a father who is going to be a Dad in the truest sense of the word, not just someone who felt blackmailed into helping the woman he loves conceive.

If you're patient, and lucky, you may find that your partner will eventually become less resistant to the whole idea of having a baby. (Some women find that the moment they back off and stop forcing the issue, their partner surprises them by suddenly becoming more open to the possibility.) If it continues to be a source of major difficulty in your relationship, you could be wise to seek some outside help from a couple's therapist.

Of course, the whole question of timing can become a moot point overnight if Mother Nature has other plans for the two of you — something Jim, a 37-year-old father of three, discovered when his first child was born nine years ago: "I was not as 'ready' as Sue," he confesses. "My preference was to wait for a time until I had established my career a bit more. But in the end the Final Decision was really quite simple. It happened."

The career costs of having a baby

Wondering what having a baby might mean for your career? This next section of the chapter gives you the facts about both the Mommy Track and the Daddy Track — corporate America's "pink and blue" ghetto.

The Mommy Track

You've no doubt heard all the whispering about the Mommy Track — the idea that having a baby can wreak havoc on your career. The argument goes as follows: Women who work and raise children can find themselves being forced to settle for fewer opportunities for career advancement than their childless colleagues.

While the situation has improved a great deal since the term Mommy Track was first coined in the late 1980s, you can still expect your career to take a bit of a hit if you decide to try to juggle a family and a career. If your employer feels that you're less committed to your job than your childless counterparts because you're not willing or able to attend after-hours meetings with the rest of your work team, you could find yourself being passed over when plum assignments are being handed out or being stuck with a real bare-bones increase at salary review time.

Watch Out!

You don't necessarily have to be a mommy to find yourself stuck on the Mommy Track. A 2002 Haverford College study, entitled *Sex, Kids, and Commitment to the Workplace: Employers, Employees and the Mommy Track,* found that women are typically paid 8 percent to 10 percent less than their male counterparts, regardless of whether or not they actually plan to have children. "Women often are given lower salaries and fewer responsibilities even when they're first hired, because most employers believe the stereotype that women are less committed and will leave to marry and have children," economics professor Anne E. Preston told the *Chicago Tribune*.

What's wrong with this picture?

Although the National Center for Health Statistics reports that approximately 80 percent of working women will become pregnant at some point during their working lives, the American workforce still hasn't quite come to terms with this simple biological fact. Some companies still penalize "nine to fivers" — employees who must attend to other responsibilities at the end of the working day rather than putting in a few extra hours at the office — for having a life outside of work.

There's even been a bit of a backlash in the workplace against working parents — a backlash that's been orchestrated by childless colleagues who resent being asked to pick up the slack for colleagues with kids every time the co-worker's nanny calls in sick or baby comes down with the flu. (Of course, if these supposedly put-upon childless workers were to take a broader view of things, they'd realize that they're likely to need to call in their fair share of favors when the time comes to provide care to an aging parent or other relative. Studies have shown that the vast majority of workers face some sort of childcare or eldercare crisis at some point during their working lives. It's simply a matter of time.)

If you work for a less-than-enlightened organization that values "face time" (the amount of time you spend on the job) over productivity (what you actually accomplish while you're on the job), the onus is on you to blow your own horn on a regular basis (the whole idea of acting as your own publicist being so that you won't be overlooked when promotions and other perks are being passed around). If you plan to job-share or work part-time hours after the birth of your baby, it will be particularly important for you to maintain a high profile at the office on the days when you're in. That way, co-workers can bring you up to speed on developments that have occurred on your days off.

Given these deep-rooted workplace prejudices, it's not hard to see why some women are drawn to self-employment. According to the National Foundation for Business Owners, over half of women leaving corporate life to start their own businesses do so because they are seeking more flexibility in their working arrangements.

Of course, an increasing number of women are opting for a more traditional alternative — taking a break from the workforce while their children are young. The percentage of American households with a stay-at-home parent increased from 38.9 percent in 1995 to 41.3 percent in 2002. Economists credit tough economic times for the increase: rising daycare costs, stagnant wages, and increased competition for jobs (and hence increased pressure to work longer and longer hours), meant that it simply didn't make economic sense for some families to have two parents working. Hence the decision of a growing number of mommies (and some daddies, too) to exit stage left.

The Daddy Track

Here's another development you need to know about: According to *Fortune* magazine, some working fathers are being penalized for their involvement with their families. This is what writer Betsy Morris had to say in an article on the subject: "Well-educated men with working wives are paid and promoted less than men with stay-at-home wives, probably because they can't clock as much face time. . . . Corporate manuals would do well to carry a warning: Ambitious, beware. If you want to have children, proceed at your own risk. You must be very talented, or on very solid ground, to overcome the damage a family can do to your career."

Some fathers find that they are expected to put in incredibly long hours, but that if they resist working those kinds of hours because they aren't prepared to settle for being a dad in name only, they're immediately pegged as being less than a team player — the career kiss of death in some corporate circles. While fathers who end up getting switched to the Daddy Track may not be in for quite as rough a ride as their Mommy Track counterparts, it can be a frustrating experience nonetheless. After all, they somehow neglect to point out in business school that, when push comes to shove, you could be asked to choose between your career or your family (although, of course, no employer would ever be quite that blunt about it).

But it's pretty hard to play the part of the dad if you head off to work before the kids get up and you don't get home until long after they're in bed — something the previous generation of fathers might have accepted as business as usual, but today's generation of dads typically sees as an increasingly raw deal.

Double income, no life?

Fortunately, the situation isn't totally bleak for parents with young children. Having a baby doesn't have to spell doomsday for your career. It may not be easy to balance the needs of your family against the demands of your job, but it can be done.

A more important issue to consider on the career front is what it's like to juggle your family with your career. Most working couples admit to being incredibly busy and constantly tired. It just seems to go with the turf. Some couples are lucky enough to work for companies that see the benefits of introducing such family-friendly workplace policies as telecommuting, job sharing, and flextime. Here's what you need to know about each.

Telecommuting

Telecommuting is corporate lingo for working from home. Although only a handful of companies allow their employees to work from home on a full-time basis, a significant number have proven willing to allow their employees to telecommute on an occasional or part-time basis. Simply knowing that your boss will be okay with the idea of having you work from home on a day when your child is running a fever can take a lot of the stress out of being a working parent.

Job sharing

Job sharing means splitting a full-time position with another person. Along with the hours, you split the salary and, in some companies, the benefits as well. If you're interested in cutting back on your hours, you might want to consider job sharing. Because most job-shared positions start out as full-time jobs, job sharers have a better chance of holding on to status and benefits and of keeping a leg-hold on the corporate ladder than their part-time counterparts. The secret to successful job sharing is to find a reliable job-sharing partner — someone who is willing to keep up his or her end of the bargain. You don't want to get saddled with someone who can't be counted on or you'll end up picking up the slack.

Flextime

Flextime means working flexible hours. Although most companies put some types of controls in place (they may require that you be at the office during certain core hours, for example), when you're given the option of working flexible hours, you can adjust your hours of work so that they mesh better with your child-care arrangements, your partner's schedule, and so on.

Unfortunately, despite all the talk about the need for employers to be more family friendly, a 2002 study conducted by The Center for Designing Work Wisely found that only one-third of American workers have access to flexible work schedules, and that the number of employers offering flexible work arrangements has been relatively stagnant since 1997. (While the proportion of full-time workers with flexible schedules jumped from 15.1 percent in 1991 to 27.6 percent in 1997, the rate of growth slowed considerably after that, increasing to just 28.8 percent in 2002.)

And here's another stat that's worth noting on the flextime front: fathers with young children are far more likely to have access to flexible scheduling than mothers with young children; while 33.6 percent of dads had access to such an arrangement, only 27.9 percent of moms can make the same claim.

Although these programs all sound terrific on paper, there's just one downside to these types of work and family programs — one that no one likes to talk about. Although many organizations pay lip service to the whole idea of supporting working families, in some companies, those employees who *do* decide to take advantage of these types of opportunities are labeled as being less dedicated to the job than their more workaholic counterparts. A study by the Catalyst research group in New York found, for example, that about 50 percent of women working flextime hours have experienced some ill will from their co-workers. And, what's more, about a quarter of the 45 women who participated in the study had to take a demotion in order to switch to part-time or flextime hours. So it can be a bit of a two steps forward, one step back kind of experience.

When you're trying to decide how to balance the needs of your family with the demands of your career, don't just go by what's written in the company benefits manual. Get the lowdown from other working parents. Find out what benefits are available, who's taking advantage of them, and what fallout — if any — there has been for their careers. Then you'll be in a better position to decide whether you wish to stick with the status quo, change jobs, start your own business, become a stay-at-home mom, or possibly even rethink your timing when it comes to having a baby.

Watch Out!

Make sure you know what you're getting yourself into before you try to sell your employer on the idea of a reduced work week. You may find that you are expected to cram the same amount of work into a reduced number of hours — but for a smaller paycheck, of course. (Some deal!)

Just remember that if having a baby is important to you, you don't want to let it slip too far down your to-do list or it could be the one item that gets missed. And that's a huge price to pay for any career.

Dollars and sense

Prenatal classes don't touch upon it and financial planning books generally choose to ignore it: just how dramatically your financial situation can change when baby makes three.

If you're wondering what kind of financial roller-coaster ride you may be in for should you decide to proceed with Operation Baby, this next section of the book is for you. We talk about how much that little bundle of joy is likely to cost you over the next 18 years and then we alert you to some tax breaks that will help to ease the pain. (Well, at least a little.)

But before we get into all that, we're going to start out by talking about why you and your partner (assuming you have a partner) might want to give yourselves a bit of a prebaby financial checkup (the financial equivalent of the preconception health checkup we're going to recommend to you in the next chapter!)

The prebaby financial checkup

If you're serious about starting a family in the foreseeable future, there's no time like the present to get your financial house in order — to consider how starting a family is likely to impact on your financial situation over both the short-term and the long-term. Here are the key issues you and/or your partner will want to zero in on as you prepare to embark on Operation Baby:

- **Are you carrying an excessive amount of debt?** If you're juggling student loans and car loans, and carrying balances on more credit cards than you're prepared to admit, this is the time to focus on debt reduction. Pay off your debts as aggressively as possible and consider getting rid of all but one "emergency" credit card (ideally a no-fee, no-frills credit card that charges a rock-bottom interest rate).

- **Are you paying an excessively high rate of interest on any outstanding loans?** If you're paying an exorbitantly high rate of interest on some of your loans — or, even worse, carrying a huge outstanding balance on your credit card — you might consider refinancing some of your loans at a more attractive rate and/or applying for a lower-interest debt consolidation loan to save yourself some money on interest charges.

- **Do you have an emergency fund that is equivalent to three to six months worth of net income?** While you might have been willing to fly by the seat of your pants in your pre-baby days, now that you're assuming responsibility for another human being, you will want to start building up a small nest egg. That way, you won't be caught totally off guard if you happen to lose your job or find yourself faced by some other unexpected financial crisis.

- **Are you at least breaking even on a month-to-month basis?** There's no doubt about it — this is the most painful part of the financial tune-up process: the financial world's equivalent of paying a visit to the dentist. But it's really important to get a handle on whether or not you're managing to balance your budget each month. The only way to do this is to pull out your financial paperwork (bills, statements, etc.) and analyze your income and expenses on a month-by-month basis. (Table 1.1 will assist you in doing these calculations.) Then, after you tally up your income and expenses, you'll have a sense of whether or not you're keeping your head above water financially. You will also want to consider what budgetary modifications may be in order when baby makes three. (If your income is going to drop significantly, you're likely going to have to have to tighten things up on the expense side of the ledger, too.)

■ **Do you have an up-to-date will (or any will at all, for that matter)?** If you've been making like Scarlett O'Hara and postponing that will-writing exercise until tomorrow, we've got news for you: tomorrow is officially here! You see, once you have dependents, you are responsible for ensuring that they will be taken care of should anything untoward happen to you. If you were to die without a will, you would give up your right to designate a guardian for your child — reason enough to set up an appointment with your attorney today.

■ **Do you have enough life and disability insurance?** You should also plan to review your life and disability insurance coverage to ensure that your coverage is going to be adequate to meet the needs of your growing family. You may be surprised to discover just how much coverage is required to replace your contributions to the family. In addition to replacing any income you generate, your life and disability insurance needs to cover your share of all current and future household expenses, including mortgages, loans, and unpaid debts; the cost of your child's education; childcare expenses; and — in the case of life insurance — such final expenses as funeral and burial costs, taxes, probate fees, and so on. If you discover that you don't have adequate coverage, you'll want to get in touch with an insurance agent so that you can crank up your coverage sooner rather than later.

Moneysaver

Plan to start saving for your baby's education as soon as possible. The experts estimate that it will cost approximately $250,000 to put a kid through college by the time the current crop of babies is ready to start hitting the books.

- **Is your health coverage adequate?** The basic health coverage that met your needs so well in your prebaby days may not be quite so ideal as you switch into mother mode, so you'll want to size up your health coverage as well. Basically, you'll need to decide whether you're looking for a *health maintenance organization* (an HMO is a nonprofit cooperative that provides medical care to individuals for a fixed fee each month provided that you choose a health care provider or healthcare institution from within the network); a *point of service plan* (a healthcare plan that provides you with the built-in service guaranteed by an HMO plus the flexibility of seeing a doctor outside the network); *a preferred provider plan* (a network of doctors that provides discounted care to members of a sponsoring organization such as an employer or a union); or an *indemnity plan* (crème de la crème health coverage that allows you to choose your own doctor and hospital, but that tends to be prohibitively expensive). Note: You'll find some tips on sizing up a health insurance plan further on in this chapter.

Table 1.1. The Baby Bottom Line: How Having a Baby Affects Your Budget

	Before Baby	After Baby
Income		
Your salary	_____	_____
Your partner's salary	_____	_____
Bonuses	_____	_____

	Before Baby	After Baby
Income *(cont.)*		
Investment income	_____	_____
Rental income	_____	_____
Spousal support	_____	_____
Child support	_____	_____
Other sources of income	_____	_____
Expenditures		
Taxes and other income deductions	_____	_____
Federal income tax	_____	_____
State income tax	_____	_____
401(k) contributions	_____	_____
Social Security	_____	_____
Medicare	_____	_____
Federal/state unemployment tax	_____	_____
Union dues	_____	_____
Other deductions	_____	_____
Insurance		
Life insurance	_____	_____
Disability insurance	_____	_____
Medical insurance	_____	_____
Business/professional insurance	_____	_____
Other insurance	_____	_____
Household expenses		
Rent or mortgage	_____	_____
Property taxes	_____	_____

(continued)

Table 1.1. (continued)

	Before Baby	After Baby
Household expenses (cont.)		
Homeowner's insurance	_____	_____
Utilities (heat, electricity, water)	_____	_____
Service contracts (cleaning, lawn care, etc.)	_____	_____
Telephone	_____	_____
Internet	_____	_____
Household equipment	_____	_____
Household repair	_____	_____
Other	_____	_____
Food		
Groceries	_____	_____
Restaurant meals	_____	_____
Takeout food (including drive-thru coffee)	_____	_____
Other	_____	_____
Health care		
Unreimbursed medical expenses	_____	_____
Drugs	_____	_____
Dental care	_____	_____
Eye care	_____	_____
Other	_____	_____
Transportation		
Car loan payments	_____	_____
Gasoline	_____	_____

	Before Baby	After Baby
Transportation *(cont.)*		
Maintenance/repairs	_____	_____
License fees (vehicle and driver's license)	_____	_____
Tolls and parking fees	_____	_____
Bus, subway, or commuter train fees	_____	_____
Taxis	_____	_____
Other	_____	_____
Personal care		
Clothing	_____	_____
Cosmetics	_____	_____
Dry cleaning	_____	_____
Hair salon or spa	_____	_____
Health club membership	_____	_____
Credit, debts, loans		
Debt repayment	_____	_____
Credit cards	_____	_____
Line of credit	_____	_____
Student loans	_____	_____
Other debts	_____	_____
Entertainment		
Cable TV	_____	_____
Movies	_____	_____
Concerts	_____	_____
Vacations	_____	_____
Gifts	_____	_____

(continued)

Table 1.1. *(continued)*

	Before Baby	After Baby
Entertainment *(cont.)*		
Books	_____	_____
Music	_____	_____
Video rentals	_____	_____
Computer games/software	_____	_____
Hobbies	_____	_____
Wine, beer, and alcoholic beverages	_____	_____
Other	_____	_____
Professional services		
Accountant	_____	_____
Lawyer	_____	_____
Financial advisor	_____	_____
Personal trainer	_____	_____
Career/life coach	_____	_____
Other	_____	_____
Educational expenses		
Tuition	_____	_____
Books	_____	_____
Other	_____	_____
Other expenses		
Child care	_____	_____
Charitable donations	_____	_____
Other	_____	_____

Adapted from *Family Finance: The Essential Guide for Parents* by Ann Douglas and Elizabeth Lewin (Dearborn Publishing, 2001).

Can I really afford to have a baby?

Now we get down to the real nitty-gritty part of our discussion: what it actually costs to have a child.

As an expectant parent, you need to be concerned about two basic types of costs: the long-term costs of raising a child to age 18 (or later, if your late bloomer takes a little longer to fly the coop) and the short-term costs of giving birth to a child.

What it costs to raise a child

Government statistics about the costs of raising children are enough to send you sprinting to the doctor's office for a refill on your birth control prescription. According to the latest numbers from the U.S. Department of Agriculture, for example, you can expect to spend somewhere between $127,080 and $254,400 raising a child from birth to age 18, depending on your household income (see Table 1.2).

But before you resort to such drastic measures, you might want to bear in mind that you're not required to have the entire lump sum saved in advance and that there are always ways to cut corners if you have to. (Hey, where there's a will, there's a way!)

If, for example, you decide to shop second-hand for baby clothes or you're lucky enough to be on the receiving end of a lot of hand-me-downs from an older sister who is finished having her family, you could very well whittle that $380 first-year clothing expenditure down to virtually nil. And if you put some of the bargain-hunting tips that are discussed in Chapter 11 to good use, you'll be able to trim a lot more than that out of your budget.

 Moneysaver

If you're worried about the financial hit you will take when it comes time to set up the nursery, start putting money aside as early on in your pregnancy as possible. Have your bank transfer a small amount of money per week into a separate savings account, and you'll have a nice nest egg to draw upon when it comes time to start shopping for baby equipment.

Table 1.2. The Cost of Raising a Child From Birth to Age 18: 2002

Age of Child	Total	Housing	Food	Transportation	Clothing	Healthcare	Childcare/Education	Miscellaneous
Before-Tax Income for Your Household: Less Than $39,700								
0–2	$6,620	$2,550	$930	$770	$360	$480	$890	$640
3–5	6,780	2,520	1,030	750	350	460	1010	660
6–8	6,860	2,440	1,330	870	390	530	600	700
9–11	6,850	2,200	1,590	950	440	580	360	730
12–14	7,670	2,450	1,670	1,060	730	590	250	920
15–17	7,580	1,980	1,810	1,430	650	620	420	670
Total	$127,080	$42,420	$25,080	$17,490	$8,760	$9,780	$10,590	$12,960
Before-Tax Income for Your Household: Between $39,700 and $66,900								
0–2	$9,230	$3,450	$1,110	$1,150	$420	$630	$1,470	$1,000
3–5	9,480	3,420	1,280	1,120	410	610	1,630	1,010
6–8	9,470	3,340	1,630	1,250	460	700	1,040	1,050
9–11	9,370	3,100	1,920	1,320	510	750	680	1,090

12–14	10,110	3,350	1,940	1,440	850	760	500	1,270
15–17	10,300	2,880	2,150	1,820	760	800	860	1,030
Total	$173,880	$58,620	$30,090	$24,300	$10,230	$12,750	$18,540	$19,350

Before-Tax Income for Your Household: More Than $66,900

0–2	$13,750	$5,490	$1,470	$1,610	$560	$730	$2,220	$1,670
3–5	14,050	5,460	1,660	1,580	540	700	2,420	1,690
6–8	13,860	5,370	2,000	1,710	600	800	1,660	1,720
9–11	13,670	5,130	2,330	1,780	650	860	1,160	1,760
12–14	14,520	5,390	2,450	1,900	1,080	870	890	1,940
15–17	14,950	4,910	2,580	2,300	980	920	1,560	1,700
Total	$254,400	$95,250	$37,470	$32,640	$13,230	$14,640	$29,730	$31,440

The figures shown in each age line indicate the expenditure for each year that the child falls within a particular age range. For example, a child will be under the age of two for two years (age birth to one and age one to two), so if your income is under $39,700 you would need to count on having two years of expenditures in the $6,620 range.

The figures represent the estimated expenses for a child in a two-child family. To calculate the expenses for an only child, multiply the expenditures for each category by 1.24. To estimate expenses for a child in a family with three or more children, multiply the expenditures for each category for each child by 0.77.

Source: U.S. Department of Agriculture

So while it's only sensible to arm yourself with the facts, you don't want to drive yourself totally crazy worrying about money or — even worse — convince yourself that you can't afford to have a baby because you don't have Junior's Harvard tuition socked away just yet. (If that were the criteria for becoming a parent, there would only be a handful of babies born in the United States each year, after all.)

What it costs to give birth

While there's no such thing as an "average cost" of giving birth in America, a typical hospital birth can run anywhere between $11,000 and $20,000, depending on whether your baby was delivered by a doctor or a midwife, whether you required the services of an anesthesiologist, and whether your baby was delivered vaginally or via cesarean section. Fortunately, the only one who is likely to see the final tab for your baby's birth is your health insurance company. Assuming you have adequate health insurance coverage, you're only likely to find yourself out-of-pocket for a small percentage of these costs.

And speaking of health insurance, if both you and your spouse have access to health insurance plans at work or through the government (because you're on Medicaid), go with whichever one offers the most bang for your buck. You might want to use the following checklist to help you decide which health insurance plan will best meet the needs of your growing family.

 Bright Idea

Ask to have a sneak peak at a prospective health insurer's welcome booklet and its list of health-care providers before you agree to sign up for the plan. Not only should you plan to evaluate the coverage: you'll also want to make a few phone calls to ensure that the doctor or midwife you prefer is, in fact, accepting new patients.

Checklist 1.1. Questions to Ask When Shopping for a Health Insurance Plan

_____ Is the health insurance plan registered with the American Association of Health Plans (www.aahp.org) or the National Committee for Quality Assurance (www.ncqa.org; 202-955-3500)? (Note: The National Committee for Quality Assurance Web site allows you to create online report cards for any health plan or plans you're considering. This Web site is definitely worth checking out.)

_____ Is the plan you're considering suited to the needs of young families?

_____ How long do you have to add your newborn to the plan? (Most health insurance companies only give you 30 days to add your baby to your plan. If you miss this window of opportunity, you have to wait until the next open enroll-ment period — something that likely means your baby will go uninsured until then.)

_____ Are all of the hospitals covered by the plan accredited by the Joint Commission on Accreditation of Healthcare Organizations (www.jcaho.org/; 630-792-5000)?

_____ Does at least one of the hospitals covered by the plan have an extensive department in any specialty you or your baby might require (for example, a neonatal intensive care unit)?

_____ How many of the physicians within the plan are board certified?

_____ Are the physicians or midwives who are covered by the health insurance plan experienced and highly respected pro-fessionals? Do they have specialized training in such areas as infertility and high-risk pregnancy?

_____ Are there enough physicians or midwives for you to choose from? (You should think twice before joining a plan that has fewer than 3 specialists in any specialty or fewer than 10 primary care physicians.)

_____ What is the rate of turnover among physicians or midwives?

_____ Do the physicians or midwives covered by the plan have offices that are conveniently located?

_____ If you decide to use the services of a physician or midwife outside the plan, what percentage of the cost of their ser-vices, if any, will be covered by the health insurance plan?

(continued)

Checklist 1.1. *(continued)*

_____   How are treatment decisions made?

_____   Which drugs and treatments are and are not covered by the plan?

_____   If experimental treatments are not covered, how does the health insurance plan go about defining what's experimental and what's not?

_____   Are there any restrictions on medical coverage? For example, does your primary-care doctor or the health insurance plan administrator have to give the go-ahead before you show up at an emergency room?

_____   What type of nonemergency care, if any, is available to you when you travel?

_____   Are the doctors within the plan required to sign a "gag clause" that prohibits them from telling patients about expensive or experimental treatments that aren't covered by the plan?

_____   Does the health insurance plan dictate standardized procedures for certain diseases or medical conditions (for example, what is its policy regarding vaginal births after cesareans)?

_____   Is there a cap on the number of referrals to specialists or for expensive tests that a physician can order in a year (or other financial disincentives to utilize services)?

_____   Does the plan cover the cost of obtaining a second opinion?

_____   What types of infertility-related services are covered by the plan? How many sessions or treatments are covered?

_____   Are alternative therapies, such as the services of chiropractors and acupuncturists, covered by the plan?

_____   Are prenatal visits, well-baby care, and immunizations covered by the plan?

_____   What is the co-pay (that is, the amount of money you're required to pay out of your own pocket) for prenatal visits, a vaginal or cesarean birth, ultrasounds, prenatal testing, and other types of services?

_____   What is the deductible you are required to pay for a particular time period (usually per person/per year)?

Watch Out!

Before you cancel your existing insurance or managed-care coverage, make sure that the other provider is willing to take you on. Difficult as it may be to believe, some companies treat pregnancy as a preexisting medical condition (the label that's typically slapped on bonafide diseases) and will not cover maternity costs for pregnant applicants.

You can find out more about the ins and outs of managed-care plans at some of the health care Web sites listed in the "Resource Directory" (see www.wiley.com/go/anndouglas).

The top five tax breaks for new and expectant parents

Our discussion of the costs of raising children would not be complete without a mention of the top five tax breaks that every expectant parent needs to know about:

- the medical expense deduction
- the Child and Dependent Care Tax Credit
- Dependent Care Assistant Accounts
- the Child Tax Credit, and
- the earned income credit.

To find out more about these and other tax breaks that may be available to you, call 800-TAX-FORM (800-829-3676) or visit the IRS Web site, www.irs.gov.

Medical expense deduction

Here's some good news if you're about to take a stroll down Maternity Avenue: You are entitled to deduct the portion of your medical and dental expenses that exceeds 7.5 percent of your adjusted gross income from your taxable income. Medical care expenses include the premiums you pay for insurance that covers the expenses of medical care, as well as expenses you pay in getting to and from medical care. Note: You must have records to substantiate your claim and you cannot deduct expenses for which you were reimbursed by a third party (that is, an insurance company or your employer).

If you expect to have significant medical expenses that straddle two tax years — that is, you conceive in September and your baby is due in June — you might consider deferring your initial payments until the new year or prepaying for all of your pregnancy-related services in the first year. This can help to push you over the magic 7.5 percent threshold. (Of course, you'll want to run this particular scenario by your tax advisor before you get too carried away. We specialize in babies, not bookkeeping!)

Child and Dependent Care Tax Credit

If you need to pay for child care so that you can go to work, you may be eligible for another hefty tax break: the Child and Dependent Care Tax Credit.

The Child and Dependent Tax Credit provides up to $3,000 in federal tax relief per child to a maximum of $6,000 per family for families who have to pay for the care of a child or other dependent in order to hold down a job or look for work. (Note: These were the figures that applied in 2003. You'll want to double-check with the IRS on a year-to-year basis to find out how much the Child and Dependent Care Tax Credit is worth in future years or if it still exists. After all, the juiciest tax breaks have a tendency to go the way of the dodo bird over time!)

 Moneysaver

Make sure you're fully up to speed on childcare tax credits in your particular state. Some states allow families to deduct some or all of their childcare expenses from their taxable income. Others offer childcare tax credits that are either set as a flat percentage or sliding-scale percentage of the federal childcare tax credit amount, or as a flat or sliding-scale percentage of the actual childcare expenses paid by the family.

Watch Out!

Don't forget to subtract the assistance you receive through your Dependent Care Assistance Program at work from the childcare expenses that you claim under the Dependent Care Tax Credit on your return or you will be essentially claiming the same tax break twice — not exactly a way to stay on the good side of the friendly folks at the IRS.

To qualify for this particular tax credit, you and your spouse must each have earned income through your employment (unless one of you was either a full-time student or was physically or mentally incapacitated during the tax year in question).

Of course, there's plenty of other fine print that you need to know about before you can bank on qualifying for this particular tax credit. Fortunately, you can find out everything you could ever want to know about this particular tax credit by visiting the IRS Web site at www.irs.gov. (Of course, if you'd prefer to read a slightly friendly version of the childcare tax rules, you might want to consider picking up a copy of *Choosing Childcare for Dummies* by Ann Douglas — one of the authors of this book.)

Dependent Care Assistance Program

A Dependent Care Assistance Program is a tax break that allows employers to provide up to $5,000 in tax-free income to employees in order to help offset the cost of child and dependent-care services. The income is exempt from federal income and payroll taxes and — depending on where you live — it may be exempt from state taxes, too. Your employer can either decide to give you this income on top of your regular wages or in lieu of a portion of your wages; it's a win-win situation for you either way provided you actually use the funds in your Dependent Care Assistance Program Account. (If you don't end up using the money, you lose it. You can't get the money back. What Uncle Sam giveth, Uncle Sam can taketh away.)

Child Tax Credit

The Child Tax Credit can help put a bit of extra cash back in your pocket by allowing you to reduce any federal tax you owe by up to $1,000 for each qualifying child under the age of 17. (Of course, you might not get the entire amount: the credit is phased out at higher income levels, beginning at an adjusted gross income level of $55,000 for married single filers, $75,000 for head of household, and $110,000 for married joint filers.)

Here's something you may not know about the child tax credit: Low-income families may qualify for an unexpected windfall if the amount of their child tax credit is more than their taxes. Uncle Sam allows you to claim an "additional" child tax credit for as much as 10 percent of your earned income greater than $10,000. Or, if you have three or more qualifying children, you may be able to claim an additional child tax credit up to the amount of Social Security you paid during the year, less any earned income credit you receive. Of course, you still can't receive more than $1,000 for each qualifying child. Hey, we're talking Uncle Sam, here — not your Fairy Godmother!

Earned Income Credit

The Earned Income may not have the word "child" attached to it, but it is one of the biggest tax breaks available to lower-income families with young children. While the size of the Earned Income Credit and the income cutoffs vary from year to year, this particular tax credit can put thousands of dollars back in your pocket, so it's definitely worth finding out if you qualify.

 Watch Out!

Don't miss out on the Child Tax Credit simply because you failed to provide the IRS with all the information it needs to assess your eligibility for this particular windfall. You must provide Social Security numbers for all dependent children who are being claimed as dependents, including those born at the end of the tax year. Otherwise your credit will be disallowed.

MONEYSAVER

Plan to download a copy of *Credit Where Credit is Due: Using Tax Breaks to Help Pay for Child and Dependent Care* from the National Women's Law Center Web site: www.nwlc.org. If you don't have access to the Internet, you can call to request a free copy by calling (202) 588-5180.

The age issue

While you might be tempted to hold off on starting a family until you have your financial house in order, it might not be the wisest move from a biological standpoint. According to the American College of Obstetricians and Gynecologists, postponing motherhood indefinitely isn't necessarily in the best interests of mother or baby. Not only do you risk missing out on the experience of motherhood entirely (the biological clock waits for no woman, after all), you face an increased risk of experiencing reproductive or other health problems, or of giving birth to a baby with health problems. Here's what you need to know in order to be fully informed on the age issue:

- **Older mothers are less fertile than younger mothers.** According to the American Society for Reproductive Medicine, a woman over age 40 has just a 5 percent chance of conceiving during any given cycle as compared to the 20 percent odds enjoyed by a woman in her early 20s. (See Chapters 2 and 4 for more on the age-fertility link.)

- **Older mothers face an increased risk of miscarriage.** According to a study reported in the *British Medical Journal,* by the time a woman reaches age 45, her odds of having a pregnancy end in miscarriage are roughly 75 percent.

- **Older mothers face an increased risk of giving birth to a baby with a chromosomal abnormality.** While a 25-year-old woman faces 1/476 odds of giving birth to a baby with a

chromosomal abnormality such as Down syndrome, a
45-year-old woman faces 1/21 odds.

- **Older mothers are more likely to conceive twins or other
  multiples than younger mothers.** Because complications
  are more common in multiple pregnancies and multiples
  are more likely to be born prematurely, the rate of loss in
  multiple pregnancies tends to be higher than when a
  woman is carrying a single baby.

- **Older mothers are more likely to develop complications
  during their pregnancies.** Preeclampsia (extremely high
  blood pressure), placenta previa (when the placenta
  blocks the exit to the uterus), placental abruptions (the
  premature separation of the placenta from the uterine
  wall), gestational diabetes (a form of diabetes that is triggered during pregnancy), premature birth (birth before
  the 37th completed week of pregnancy), and intrauterine
  growth restriction (when the baby ends up being significantly smaller than what would be expected for a baby of a
  particular gestational age) are all more common in order
  mothers than in younger mothers. Women over the age of
  40 are also more likely to have preexisting health problems such as coronary artery disease that may complicate
  their pregnancies — yet another reason to keep an eye on
  the biological clock.

- **Older mothers are more likely to require an operative
  delivery.** Forceps, vacuum extractions, and inductions are
  more common among older mothers, and, what's more,
  older mothers are more likely to require a cesarean delivery than their younger counterparts. (A study reported
  in the medical journal *Obstetrics and Gynecology* noted that
  mothers over the age of 44 are 7.5 times as likely to require
  a cesarean delivery as younger mothers.)

If you decide to put your baby-making plans on hold for the foreseeable future, but you're still hoping to become a mother someday, it's important that you take steps now to safeguard your future fertility. Here are the key points to keep in mind:

- **Choose a birth control method that is fertility enhancing.** The birth control pill (a.k.a. "the Pill") gets top marks from fertility experts because it changes the consistency of your cervical mucus, making it more difficult for bacteria to pass through the mucus and into your uterus and tubes. The Pill also serves up some added benefits on the fertility front: it helps to prevent ovarian cysts, halt the progression of endometriosis (a condition that can lead to fallopian tube scarring), to decrease the incidence of ovarian and uterine cancer, and to restore a normal hormonal balance in women who don't ovulate. Of course, it doesn't provide you with protection against sexually transmitted diseases, so that's something you'll want to keep in mind if you haven't quite settled upon Mr. Right yet. A birth control method you might want to steer clear of until your baby-making days are behind you is the intrauterine device (IUD): it has been linked to an increase incidence of pelvic inflammatory disease — a major cause of infertility in women. Note: You can find out more about the pros and cons of all the major methods of birth control in "Your Next Pregnancy" (www.wiley.com/go/anndouglas).

- **Pay attention to any gynecological red flags.** If you notice an unusual discharge from your breasts or detect any unusual menstrual bleeding, see your gynecologist sooner rather than later. The sooner you seek treatment for any hormonal imbalances or other gynecological health problems, the less likely these problems are to take a toll on your future fertility.

- **Get the scoop on your family's reproductive history.** Find out if you have close female relatives who have had difficulty conceiving or who have had trouble with endometriosis, uterine fibroids, early menopause, or uterine abnormalities. Some of these conditions tend to run in families, so you'll want to know upfront what you may be dealing with so that you can either seek treatment or fast-forward your baby-making schedule if it looks like you may be facing greater-than-average challenges on the reproductive front.

- **Choose your sexual partners with care.** Sexually transmitted disease (STDs) are just plain bad news for the female reproductive system, so take steps to protect yourself and your future baby-to-be. (Some STDs can be harmful — even deadly — to the developing baby, so you can't be too careful on this front.)

- **Quit smoking.** While you're no doubt aware of the terrible toll that smoking can take on your heart, lungs, and other organs, you might not realize that it can do a real number on your reproductive system, too. Studies have shown that women who smoke are 30 percent less fertile than other women. And, what's more, they're at increased risk of developing pelvic inflammatory disease. So smoking is just plain bad news for you and the baby you hope to have some day. (See Chapter 2 for more on the harmful effects of tobacco smoke on both mother and baby.)

 WATCH OUT!

Sperm counts are on the decline worldwide. A recent study reported in the *British Medical Journal* found that sperm counts in Scottish men have been declining at a rate of 2.1 percent per year while an earlier study of Parisian men pointed to a decline of 2.1 percent per year. That amounts to a drop of approximately 25 percent over the course of a single generation — a development that scientists attribute to increased levels of such environmental toxins as dioxins, pesticides, and environmental estrogens.

▪ **Encourage your partner to safeguard his fertility, too.**
Future fathers are sometimes guilty of assuming that fertility is "a girl thing" that they, as guys, don't have to pay
much attention to. That kind of thinking is dangerously
outdated and could rob a guy of his chance to be a dad.
In fact, in recognition of the fact that sperm quality does
tend to deteriorate over time, The American Society of
Reproductive Medicine is now recommending an age limit
of 50 for sperm donors. But, of course, that's not all a
guy needs to think about on the fertility front. A man's
reproductive system can be damaged by sports injuries,
exposure to toxic chemicals or radiation, the use of ana-
bolic steroids, the use of certain types of medications that
can hamper sperm production and/or reduce sperm
counts — even by something as simple as carrying around
too much weight. (Men who are significantly overweight
tend to have excessively high levels of the female sex hormone estrogen, something that can affect a man's fertility.) And any dad who is actively trying to father a child
should be laying off the alcohol, drugs, and cigarettes, too:
these vices can interfere with a man's ability to ejaculate
and/or affect his overall fertility. (Just tell your guy the
true high in life comes from being a dad!)

Just the facts

▪ There's no such thing as "the perfect time" to have a baby.
There are always pros and cons to be weighed.

▪ Having a baby can take its toll on your career. Both women
and men can find themselves relegated to the Mommy
Track or the Daddy Track if they are perceived as being less
committed to their careers than their childless co-workers.

▪ Raising a child is an expensive proposition. You can expect
to spend between $127,080 and $254,400 raising a child
from birth to age 18.

- The biological clock waits for no woman. You risk missing out on the experience of becoming a parent if you postpone parenthood for too long.

- Be sure to take steps to safeguard your fertility so that it will be there for you if and when you need it. (This advice applies to both men and women, by the way. Remember, baby-making is a team sport!)

GET THE SCOOP ON. . .
Lifestyle changes you might want to make before
you start trying to conceive ▪ Genetic testing
and carrier testing ▪ Why it's a good idea to
schedule a preconception visit with your doctor
or midwife before you start trying to conceive

Conception Countdown: Planning for a Healthy Pregnancy

Chapter 2

You've weighed the pros and cons of parenthood and you've decided to take the plunge. But before you stampede toward the bedroom, ovulation predictor kit in hand, there's still one more issue you'll want to consider: whether you're in the best possible physical condition to embark on a pregnancy.

Now before you hit the panic button and assume that we're suggesting that only men and women in peak physical condition should consider becoming parents, we want to reassure you that we're nowhere near that extreme in our views. After all, if the bar were set that high for parenthood, there would only be a handful of babies born each year!

What we're suggesting is that you consider whether there's room for improvement when it comes to your overall health and well-being and that you commit to giving yourself a bit of a lifestyle makeover before you start trying to conceive. (Hint: If you've been look-ing for an excuse to kick your cigarette habit or to break out of your six-cups-of-coffee-a-day rut, you've just found it!)

In this chapter, we give you a crash course on preconception planning, identifying the key issues that you and your partner will want to zero in on so that you can increase your odds of giv-ing birth to a healthy baby. (You'll notice that we say "increase your odds." That's because there are no guarantees in the reproductive world. You can play by the rules and still have dif-ficulty conceiving, experience a miscarriage, or give birth to a baby with a health problem. But at least at the end of the day you will have the satisfaction that comes from knowing you did everything within your power to give your baby the healthiest possible start.)

We also give you the facts about genetic counseling and car-rier testing so that you can decide whether you would like to pursue either of these options. (Some prospective parents like to have as much information as possible about their reproduc-tive odds. Others feel that too much information can, in fact, be a bad thing, and prefer to take a much more low-tech approach to pregnancy planning. Hopefully, reading this chapter will help you to decide which camp you fall into and which approach will work best for you.)

Finally, we wrap up the chapter by talking about the advan-tages of scheduling a preconception checkup with your doctor or midwife — your final "system check" before embarking on Operation Baby.

Getting ready to get pregnant

There's no denying it — the time to start taking care of your body is before you get pregnant. Studies have shown that you increase your odds of having a healthy baby if you are in the best possible physical condition before you conceive.

Your answers to the questions in our Preconception Health Checklist that follows should give you an idea of how physically ready your body is to support a pregnancy. These are also the types of questions your caregiver is likely to ask at your preconception visit, so you might as well start considering your answers right now.

Checklist 2.1. Preconception Health Checklist

_____ Are you at a healthy weight?

_____ Have you been dieting recently?

_____ Do you skip meals regularly?

_____ Are you on any type of special diet?

_____ Do you smoke?

_____ Do you drink alcohol?

_____ Do you drink coffee?

_____ Are you using any prescription medications or using any other types of drugs?

_____ Are you currently using any herbal products?

_____ Are you taking any vitamins?

_____ Do you currently have or have you ever had any sexually transmitted diseases, such as genital herpes, gonorrhea, chlamydia, syphilis, venereal warts, or HIV/AIDS?

_____ Do you have any chronic health conditions, such as epilepsy, lupus, diabetes, high blood pressure, heart disease, PKU, or kidney disease?

_____ Have you been immunized against rubella (German measles)?

_____ Have you been screened for Hepatitis B?

_____ Have you had your flu shot?

_____ Have you had a dental checkup recently?

_____ Is your workplace free of hazards that could jeopardize the well-being of your baby?

_____ Are you anemic?

_____ Are you in the habit of douching?

_____ Have you been diagnosed with endometriosis?

(continued)

Checklist 2.1. *(continued)*

_____ Have you ever had problems with your uterus, tubes, or cervix? Have these problems required surgery?

_____ Did your mother take a drug called DES when she was pregnant with you?

_____ Have you had two or more abortions during or after the 14th week of pregnancy?

_____ Have you had three or more miscarriages?

_____ Have you had five or more pregnancies?

_____ Have you given birth within the previous 12 months?

_____ Have you ever given birth to a baby who was either less than 5½ pounds or more than 9 pounds at birth?

_____ Have you ever given birth to a stillborn baby?

_____ Have you ever given birth to a baby who died within the first month of life?

_____ Have you ever given birth to a baby with a birth defect?

_____ Have you given birth to a baby who required care in an intensive-care nursery?

_____ Have you experienced vaginal bleeding late in pregnancy?

_____ Do any of the following medical problems run in your family: high blood pressure, diabetes, hemophilia, birth defects, mental retardation, cystic fibrosis, Tay-Sachs disease, sickle-cell anemia, or thalassemia?

Now let's consider what a "yes" answer to any of these questions could mean in terms of your ability to conceive and carry a baby.

Are you at a healthy weight?

It's always best to try to embark on pregnancy at a healthy weight, if you can manage it. Here's why:

■ Seriously underweight or overweight women don't tend to ovulate as often as other women, something that can wreak havoc on a woman's efforts to conceive.

WATCH OUT!

Recent studies involving sheep have indicated that even modest nutritional deficiencies in a mother's diet at the time of conception may increase the odds that she will give birth prematurely. While no one is suggesting that you're a sheep — that would be a *baaaaad* assumption on our part! — you might want to err on the side of caution and ensure that you're on nutritionally solid ground before you start trying to conceive.

- Seriously underweight women are at increased risk of giving birth to a low-birthweight baby (a baby who weighs less than five pounds at birth and who may be at increased risk of experiencing some potentially serious health problems).

- Seriously overweight women face a higher-than-average risk of experiencing preeclampsia, gestational diabetes, of requiring a labor induction and/or a cesarean section, and of giving birth to extremely large babies, babies with neural tube defects, babies with heart defects, or babies who are at increased risk of developing diabetes later in life.

- If you're not an ideal weight, you might want to try to lose weight or gain weight so that you reach a healthy range before you start trying to conceive. Just don't try to lose a ton of weight overnight: that's not healthy for you or the baby and may throw a wrench in your baby-making plans anyway by disrupting ovulation.

Have you been dieting recently?

Going on a crash diet right before you start trying to conceive is just plain bad news. While your objective may be noble — getting to a healthy weight before you embark on a pregnancy — you risk depleting your body of important nutrients at the very time when those nutrients are needed to grow a healthy baby. In fact, if the Fad Diet Du Jour that you've been following is overly strict, you may even stop ovulating entirely — your body's way of switching into self-preservation mode in the face of a perceived "famine." (See Chapter 6 for more on nutrition during pregnancy.)

Note: If you're struggling with an eating disorder such as anorexia nervosa or bulimia nervosa, or if you have battled with such an eating disorder in the past, you'll want to be upfront with your doctor or midwife about the situation. Studies have shown that women with eating disorders face an increased risk of miscarriage, obstetrical complications, of giving birth to a low-birthweight baby, and of developing postpartum depression. That's not to say that these problems are unavoidable, of course: you may simply require some added psychological support (and possibly some nutritional counseling as well) during your pregnancy.

Do you skip meals regularly?

If you're in the habit of skipping meals, your body could be missing out on such important nutrients as folic acid, iron, and calcium.

It's particularly important to ensure that your diet contains adequate quantities of folic acid. Studies have shown that women who consume at least 0.4 mg of folic acid each day reduce their chances of giving birth to a child with a neural tube defect (for example, anencephaly or spina bifida) by 50 percent to 70 percent. Other studies have indicated that folic acid may help to reduce the risk of miscarriage as well as the odds that you will develop high blood pressure during pregnancy. There's even some evidence that, when combined with an adequate intake of iron, folic acid may offer your baby-to-be a measure of protection against childhood leukemia.

To increase your intake of this important nutrient, you should consume foods that are naturally high in folic acid, such as oranges, orange juice, honeydew melon, avocados, dark green vegetables (broccoli, Brussels sprouts, romaine lettuce, spinach), asparagus, bean sprouts, corn, cauliflower, dried beans, nuts, seeds, bran cereals, whole-grain products, wheat germ, and fortified breakfast cereals. You should plan to talk to your doctor or midwife about whether it would be a good idea for you to take a folic acid supplement as well. (Most women find that it is difficult to get enough folic acid through diet alone.)

Because neural tube defects can occur very early on in pregnancy, it's important to ensure that you have adequate levels of folic acid in your diet before you start trying to conceive. That's why most doctors recommend that you consume adequate amounts of folic acid throughout your childbearing years. After all, nearly half (49 percent) of pregnancies are unplanned.

It's also important to ensure that your diet contains sufficient quantities of iron. During pregnancy, a woman's iron needs double. The extra iron is required to create additional red blood cells that carry oxygen from your lungs to all parts of your body as well as your growing baby.

If you find that you are tired all the time, it could be because you're low on iron. Try boosting your iron intake by consuming iron-rich foods, such as whole-grain and enriched cereals, lean meats, dried peas and beans, dark green vegetables, and dried fruits. Because vitamin C helps your body absorb iron, consume these iron-rich foods with a glass of orange juice or other foods that are high in vitamin C, such as melons, strawberries, grapefruits, raspberries, kiwi, broccoli, tomatoes, sweet potatoes, and so on.

 Bright Idea

While you're loading up on the folic acid in your diet, be sure to pass the folic acid-rich foods your partner's way, too. Studies have shown that men whose diets are rich in folic acid are less likely to have problems with poor sperm counts and poor sperm quality.

Bright Idea

Your mother was right. Breakfast is the most important meal of the day. If you tend to skip breakfast because you're not hungry first thing in the morning, stop eating after 6 p.m. If, on the other hand, your reason for missing your morning meal is because you're in too much of a rush in the morning, throw a banana, a cup of yogurt, and a couple of ice cubes into the blender and make a breakfast shake you can sip in the car on the way to work.

Finally, you'll also want to ensure that your diet contains an adequate amount of calcium. A woman who is calcium-deficient prior to and during pregnancy may end up giving birth prematurely to a calcium-deficient baby. Just don't go overboard in the calcium department: consuming more than 2,500 mg of calcium per day from supplements and food sources (e.g., milk, yogurt, cheese) puts you at increased risk of developing a urinary tract infection and it can make it more difficult for your body to absorb other important nutrients such as iron, zinc, and magnesium.

See Chapter 6 for more detailed information about nutrition during pregnancy.

Are you on a special diet?

If you are on a special diet to control diabetes or some other type of medical condition, be sure to consult with a nutritionist before you start trying to conceive. It's possible that your body may be lacking some important nutrients that it needs to support a healthy pregnancy.

This advice also applies if you're on a very strict vegetarian or vegan diet, by the way. If you don't eat meat, you may have to make a special effort to ensure that you're obtaining adequate quantities of vitamins B12, B2, and D; calcium; iron; and zinc. See Chapter 6 for more about the unique challenges that vegetarians and vegans face during pregnancy.

Do you smoke?

Looking for a reason to quit smoking? Pregnancy is the best excuse you'll ever have. Not only is smoking harmful to your health: it is harmful to the health of your developing baby. And it also decreases your odds of conceiving and being able to carry a pregnancy to term. In other words, it's just plain bad news for mothers and mothers-to-be. (See Table 2.1.)

As a rule of thumb, you should stop smoking before you stop using birth control. This will allow your body to be nicotine-free by the time you conceive. Note: Nicotine replacement therapy (e.g. patches, bum, or Zyban — a mild, low-dose antidepressant that is designed to ease some of the mood changes that can accompany nicotine withdrawal) is not recommended for use during pregnancy, so if you're intending to use these products as quit-smoking aids, you'll want to make sure they have a chance to clear your system as well before you go into baby-making mode.

If you're not sure how to go about quitting, you might want to visit the Centers for Disease Control's How to Quit Page: www.cdc.gov/tobacco/how2quit.htm. You'll find links to all kinds of great online resources for "quitters" just like you.

Table 2.1. Fifteen Reasons to Quit Smoking Before You Start Trying to Conceive

1. **Smoking makes you less fertile.** Women who smoke are 30 percent less fertile than other women.

2. **Smoking increases the odds that you will experience a miscarriage.** Smokers are almost twice as likely to miscarry as nonsmokers.

3. **Smoking increases the likelihood that your baby will be stillborn.** Babies of smokers are twice as likely to be stillborn as babies of nonsmokers.

(continued)

Table 2.1. *(continued)*

4. **Smoking causes birth defects.** Smoking 10 cigarettes per day increases the odds that you will give birth to a baby with cleft palate and cleft lip by 50 percent.

5. **Smoking disrupts the flow of oxygen to the baby.** Your baby receives less oxygen because nicotine restricts the flow of blood through the blood vessels in the placenta.

6. **Smoking can harm the lungs of your developing baby.** Exposure to secondhand smoke while in the womb can leave your baby more susceptible to respiratory disorders and infections during early childhood.

7. **Smoking increases the odds that you will give birth prematurely.** Babies who are born prematurely tend to experience more health problems than those who are carried to term.

8. **Smoking increases the odds that you will experience certain types of pregnancy-related complications.** Women who smoke during pregnancy are also more likely to experience placental abnormalities and bleeding.

9. **Smoking reduces the likelihood that you will eat properly during pregnancy.** Smoking acts as an appetite supressant, and if you're less hungry, you're less likely to seek out the nutrient-rich foods that your body needs to grow a healthy baby.

10. **Smoking interferes with the absorption of vitamin C.** Because vitamin C plays an important role in iron absorption, smoking can indirectly contribute to iron-deficiency anemia.

11. **Smoking can interfere with breastfeeding.** Because smoking can decrease the quantity and quality of breast milk, smoking can lead to early weaning.

12. **Smoking is linked to a number of childhood health problems.** Children who are exposed to secondhand smoke are more likely to develop asthma, bronchitis, and ear infections. And, according to some brand-new research, they are also more likely to be obese.

13. **Smoking increases the odds that your baby will experience serious, even fatal, health problems during infancy.** Babies who are exposed to secondhand smoke are more likely to die of SIDS and to develop certain types of childhood brain cancers.

14. **Smoking is linked to childhood behavioral problems.** A recent study found that the toddlers of mothers who smoked during pregnancy were four times as likely to be diagnosed with behavioral problems as the toddlers of nonsmokers.

15. **Smoking increases the odds that your baby will develop lung cancer later in life.** Children who are exposed to secondhand smoke are at greater risk of developing lung cancer than children who are not exposed to secondhand smoke.

Do you drink alcohol?

According to the Centers for Disease Control and Prevention, approximately 12.8 percent of pregnant women admit to drinking during pregnancy — this despite the fact that babies who are exposed to alcohol prenatally can be born with serious medical problems including fetal alcohol syndrome.

But that's not the only risk you face by drinking during pregnancy. A seven-year study involving nearly 25,000 pregnant women found that drinking the equivalent of a bottle of wine a week increases the risk of miscarriage by 3.7 times. Researchers at Denmark's University of Aarhus believe that alcohol may lead to miscarriage by either causing chromosomal defects in the developing baby or by triggering the release of prostaglandins (the same hormones that are involved in triggering labor contractions).

Why take the chance? You'll save yourself nine months of worry if you stop consuming alcohol before you start trying to conceive. (There's enough to worry about when you're pregnant, after all.)

 WATCH OUT!

Here's another reason to lay off the booze once you start trying to conceive: A study conducted at the University of Washington in Seattle found that maternal drinking during pregnancy significantly increases the risk of alcohol-related problems in offspring at age 21.

Do you drink coffee?

Coffee may be your early-morning beverage of choice right now, but it's best to give it up or switch to decaf once you start trying to conceive. Caffeine is thought to restrict the growth of a developing baby by constricting blood vessels and reducing blood flow to the uterus. What's more, a few studies have indicated that excessive consumption of caffeine (that is, more than three cups of drip coffee per day) may contribute to fertility problems and possibly miscarriage as well. While the jury's still out on this one (some experts say you're perfectly fine enjoying caffeinated beverages in moderation), if you're going to worry unduly about downing that occasional cup of coffee, tea, or caffeinated soda pop, why not simply switch to decaf for the duration of your pregnancy? It'll give you one less thing to stress about between now and delivery day.

Are you using any prescription medications or any other types of drugs?

Both prescription and nonprescription drugs can affect your developing baby. That's why it's important to ask your doctor to review the list of drugs you use on a regular basis and to let you know if you should be discontinuing any of them once you start trying to conceive. Note: Acne medications such as Acutane (isotretinoin) have been proven to cause birth defects. To increase your chances of having a healthy baby, you should stop taking the drug at least one month before you start trying to conceive. (You'll find a detailed discussion of medication use during pregnancy in Chapter 5.)

Be sure to be upfront with your doctor if you're in the habit of using recreational drugs such as marijuana, cocaine, and heroin. These drugs can be extremely harmful to the developing baby. Babies born to mothers who smoke marijuana during pregnancy typically weigh less than other babies and are more prone to respiratory infections and other health problems.

Babies born to women who abuse cocaine during pregnancy face an increased risk of being born prematurely, having lower birth weights, suffering neonatal seizures and brain bleeds, and dying of Sudden Infant Death Syndrome. And babies born to mothers who used heroin during pregnancy frequently suffer from a variety of health problems at birth, including respiratory problems, developmental problems, and heroin withdrawal. The bottom line here is pretty clear: Drugs and babies don't mix. You owe it to your future baby-to-be to kick your drug habit before you start trying to conceive. Note: You can get the support and information you need to tackle your drug problem by getting in touch with Narcotics Anonymous: www.na.org.

Are you currently using any herbal products?

Herbal products may be "natural," but that doesn't mean they can't be harmful to the developing baby. Some herbal products contain highly active ingredients that pack a powerful pharmacological punch. So make a list of the herbal products that you're using (or — better yet — bring the bottles with you to your preconception appointment so that you can check with your doctor about which products are — and aren't — safe for use during pregnancy).

Just don't be surprised if your doctor can't give you a definitive answer about the safety of every herbal product you happen to pull out of your handbag: there's not a lot of research about the use of herbal products during pregnancy (an issue we'll be discussing at greater length in Chapter 5). If you don't get a definite thumbs-up from your doctor, you'll want to err on the side of caution. Your baby's long-term health and well-being is too important to gamble on any product, "natural" or not.

Are you taking any vitamins?

Large doses of vitamins can be harmful to your baby. This is one of those cases when too much of a good thing can be a bad thing. Your best bet is to stick with a vitamin that has been specially formulated for use during pregnancy. That way, you can feel confident that you're receiving safe amounts of the recommended vitamins and minerals.

Do you currently have or have you ever had any sexually transmitted diseases?

Your sexual past can come back to haunt you when you start trying to conceive, so tell your doctor if you have or have had any STDs (sexually transmitted diseases) such as genital herpes, gonorrhea, chlamydia, syphilis, venereal warts, or HIV/AIDS. Here's why:

- Unrecognized genital herpes can be harmful — even fatal — to your baby.

- Gonorrhea and chlamydia can scar your fallopian tubes and either make it difficult for you to conceive or increase your chances of having an ectopic (tubal) pregnancy.

- Syphilis, if uncured, can cause birth defects. Note: some types of genital warts can be a symptom of syphilis.

- If you are HIV positive or have full-blown AIDS, your pregnancy will have to be carefully managed to reduce the risk of infecting your baby.

Your doctor can provide you with information on ways of treating or controlling these diseases both prior to and during pregnancy. You'll find additional information on sexually transmitted diseases in Chapter 16.

 Bright Idea

Ask your doctor to test you for chlamydia at your next pelvic exam. Five percent of American women are infected with the disease, which can cause infertility, ectopic pregnancy, and recurrent pelvic pain. You should be particularly vigilant about being tested if either you or your partner have had sex with someone else at any time.

Do you have any chronic health conditions?

Women who suffer from serious medical conditions — such as epilepsy, lupus, diabetes, high blood pressure, heart disease, PKU (phenylketonuria), or kidney disease — require special care during pregnancy. Here are some examples of the types of issues that women with these types of conditions must confront during pregnancy:

- Women with poorly controlled insulin-dependent diabetes are four to six times more likely to give birth to a baby with birth defects than nondiabetic women. That's why it's so important for diabetic women to ensure that their blood sugar is well controlled both prior to and during pregnancy.

- Women who are epileptic need to carefully consider the risks of taking antiseizure medications during pregnancy. Although some medications increase the chances of birth defects, seizures can themselves be harmful to the developing fetus.

- Women with lupus — an autoimmune disorder in which the body attacks its own tissues — are at increased risk of experiencing miscarriage or preterm labor. As a rule of thumb, women who have been symptom free for six months prior to conceiving are likely to have a healthy pregnancy.

- Women with chronic high blood pressure are at increased risk of developing pregnancy complications, including placental problems and fetal growth restriction. A change in medications may make it possible for a pregnant woman with chronic high blood pressure to manage her condition without harming her baby.

- Women with heart disease or kidney problems may require a change of medications as well as careful monitoring throughout their pregnancies.

■ Women with phenylketonuria (PKU) — an inherited body-chemistry disorder in which the body is unable to process a particular type of amino acid (a building block of protein) — must follow a special diet in order to prevent mental retardation and birth defects in their babies.

You can learn more about high-risk pregnancy in Chapter 16.

Have you been immunized against rubella (German measles)?

The American College of Obstetricians and Gynecologists advises pregnant women to check with their doctors to find out if they are immune to rubella before they start trying to conceive. Rubella — also known as German measles — is an infectious viral disease that, if acquired during pregnancy, is known to cause blindness, heart defects, deafness, and other birth defects in the newborn. The risk to the developing baby is greatest during the first month of pregnancy, when the risk that the baby will be affected by exposure is 50/50. By the third month of pregnancy, the risk of the baby being affected by such exposure drops to just 10 percent.

Note: The U.S. Centers for Disease Control recently reduced the recommended waiting period before attempting to conceive after a rubella shot. Instead of having to put your baby-making plans on hold for three months — the previous recommendation — you can now start trying to conceive 28 days after your shot.

 Watch Out!

If you're planning to travel to Third World countries during your pregnancy, you should plan to be immunized against the following infections, which are thought to cause miscarriages: variola (smallpox), vaccinia (cowpox), and typhoid fever (Salmonella typhi infection). See Chapter 9 for more about travel during pregnancy.

BRIGHT IDEA

While you're asking your doctor if you're immune to rubella, find out if you're in need of any other vaccinations. It's important to ensure that your measles, mumps, tetanus, polio, hepatitis, and chickenpox shots are up to date, too.

Have you been screened for Hepatitis B?

The Centers for Disease Control and Prevention recommend that pregnant women be screened for Hepatitis B — a disease that commonly results in liver disease and cancer in adulthood. Untreated infants of infected mothers have a 50 percent chance of contracting the virus. Women who are considered to be at high risk of developing the disorder (that is, health-care workers who handle blood) are advised to be vaccinated against Hepatitis B prior to becoming pregnant.

Have you had your flu shot?

A full-blown case of influenza can lead to miscarriage or premature labor. The Centers for Disease Control and Prevention and the American College of Obstetricians and Gynecologists recommend that pregnant women who will be more than three months pregnant during the winter months consider getting a flu shot. (Of course, if you're allergic to eggs, a flu shot would not be an option for you. In this case, you'll just have to keep your fingers crossed that you won't get sideswiped by a major flu bug while you're pregnant.)

Have you had a dental checkup recently?

If you're overdue for a dental checkup, you might want to schedule a visit to your dentist before you start trying to conceive. Since gum disease tends to get worse during pregnancy due to the hormone changes of pregnancy (increased estrogen levels, to be specific), you'll want to seek treatment for any pre-existing periodontic problems before you start trying to conceive. Researchers at the University of North Carolina recently

Bright Idea

While your dentist won't insist that you do without an X-ray in the event of a dental emergency, it's generally best to avoid all but the most essential X-rays during pregnancy. (Of course, if you happen to become pregnant a little sooner than you anticipated and realize to your horror that you had a dental X-ray the week after you conceived, there's no need to hit the panic button: The current generation of X-ray aprons have been designed to ensure that there is virtually no radiation leakage to the baby.)

discovered a link between severe periodontal disease and preeclampsia, and earlier studies have indicated that women with periodontal disease may be at increased risk of giving birth to a premature, low-birthweight baby. You can find out more about the effects of periodontal disease during pregnancy by visiting the American Academy of Periodontology Web site at www.perio.org or by calling 800-FLOSS EM.

Is your workplace free of hazards that could jeopardize the well-being of your baby?

If you or your partner is regularly exposed to hazardous substances in the workplace, you may want to consider a job change or job modification before you start your family. Hazardous substances in the workplace can affect both the quality of sperm and the development of the embryo.

Here are some of the types of substances and procedures you should avoid while you're trying to conceive and throughout your pregnancy:

- chemicals such as paints, lacquers, wood-finishing products, industrial or household solvents, and darkroom chemicals
- nuclear medicine testing procedures; X-rays; and anesthesia, which you might be exposed to while working in a hospital, laboratory, or dental office
- lethal and teratogenic gases used in fire-fighting and so on.

You can find a chart in Chapter 5 detailing some of the types of toxins you might encounter.

Are you anemic?

If you are anemic, the hemoglobin in your blood is insufficient to carry the amount of oxygen required to reach all of the cells in your body. This can cause serious problems during pregnancy by reducing the amount of oxygen your baby receives. If your anemia is significant, there is an increased risk for intrauterine growth restriction and also fetal hypoxia during labor. In addition, the mother will be less able to handle the blood loss associated with delivery (vaginal or cesarean) if she's already significantly short on blood. Also, anemia that hasn't been adequately evaluated may turn out to be a symptom of a more serious genetic or systemic disease.

Are you in the habit of douching?

Douching is just plain bad news on the reproductive front. Women who douche are at increased risk of developing pelvic inflammatory disease, acquiring HIV, being diagnosed with cervical cancer, and experiencing a preterm delivery. And, according to a recent study in *Obstetrics and Gynecology,* women who douche at least twice a month have higher rates of bacterial vaginosis (BV) infections than women who don't douche (infections that have been linked to preterm labor). So if there's a baby in your future, you might want to kick this particular habit right now.

Have you been diagnosed with endometriosis?

Endometriosis is the name given to a medical condition in which tissue similar to the tissue that lines the inside of the uterus grows outside the uterus, typically on the surfaces of organs in the pelvic and abdominal regions.

Endometriosis is one of the top three causes of female infertility. Approximately 30 percent to 40 percent of women with the condition experience fertility problems.

Researchers are unsure why endometriosis affects fertility, but they think that the condition may interfere with the uterus's ability to accept an embryo, change the egg in some way, or prevent the fertilized egg from making its way to the uterus in its normal fashion.

Because endometriosis often goes undiagnosed, it's important to be aware of the key symptoms of this medical condition so that you can seek treatment sooner rather than later if you suspect you may be affected:

- extremely painful (even disabling) menstrual cramps
- heavy menstrual periods
- premenstrual spotting
- bleeding between periods
- chronic pelvic pain (including pain in the lower back and pelvic region)
- pain in the intestinal region
- painful bowel movements or painful urination during menstruation
- gastrointestinal symptoms (especially the urge to evacuate or pain with bowel movements)
- fatigue
- difficulty becoming pregnant.

Note: In vitro fertilization (IVF) has proven to be quite effective in treating infertility in women with endometriosis. You can find out more about this and other assisted reproductive technologies (ART) in Chapter 4.

Have you ever had problems with your uterus, tubes, or cervix? Have these problems required surgery?

A history of uterine or cervical problems or surgery increases your chances of experiencing a miscarriage or giving birth to a premature baby. Make sure that your doctor is aware of these problems so that he or she can suggest some possible treatments (for example, a cerclage procedure to prevent an incompetent cervix from opening prematurely).

Uterine surgery may increase your likelihood of experiencing a uterine rupture during pregnancy or delivery, and tubal surgery may increase your odds of experiencing an ectopic (tubal) pregnancy — a condition, which is potentially life-threatening and should ideally be ruled out as early as possible in the first trimester.

Did your mother take a drug called DES when she was pregnant with you?

Diethylstilbestrol (DES) was a drug given to many pregnant women in the 1950s and 1960s. It has since been found to be linked to breast cancer and cancer of the vagina in the daughters of women who took the drug. What's more, 90 percent of these so-called DES daughters have experienced abnormalities of the cervix, vagina, and uterus that may make it difficult for them to conceive and carry a pregnancy to term. Approximately 20 percent of these women are infertile, and 20 percent experience repeated miscarriages; but 60 percent of them are able to carry a pregnancy to term.

Just one additional footnote before we move on: The sons of women who took DES also have genital abnormalities, including smaller-than-average testicles and penis, undescended testicles, low sperm counts, poor motility of sperm, cysts, and possibly even testicular and prostate cancer.

Have you had two or more abortions during or after the 14th week of pregnancy?

Although the majority of women who have previously had elective abortions do not have difficulty going on to have children, some women do experience problems. As a rule of thumb, the earlier in your pregnancy the abortion was performed, the better your odds of avoiding future problems. If, however, your abortion was poorly done or you developed a subsequent pelvic infection, you could experience problems conceiving or carrying a subsequent pregnancy to term. Specifically, abortions after the 14th week are more likely to have been associated with cervical trauma and a subsequent increased risk of cervical incompetence (a medical condition in which the cervix opens up very early on in pregnancy, resulting in miscarriage).

Have you had three or more miscarriages?

If you have had a large number of miscarriages, you are at increased risk of experiencing another. What's less important than how many miscarriages you've experienced, however, is the number of miscarriages as compared to the number of live births. Consider the numbers for yourself: Women who have had two or more miscarriages and have never given birth to a child have a 40 percent to 45 percent chance of experiencing another miscarriage. Women who have had as many as four miscarriages and yet have successfully given birth to a live baby have only a 25 percent to 30 percent chance of experiencing another miscarriage. (Note: We will be discussing the issue of pregnancy loss in far greater detail in Chapter 17.)

Have you had five or more pregnancies?

Women who have had five or more pregnancies are at increased risk of developing problems during pregnancy, such as placenta previa (where the placenta partially or fully covers the cervix, sometimes necessitating a cesarean delivery), postpartum hemorrhage (excessive loss of blood after delivery), intrauterine growth restriction (if the pregnancies are closely spaced and nutrition is not optimal), and rapid labor. That's not to say that it will happen for sure (chances are it won't, in fact): it's simply something that you and your doctor or midwife need to keep in mind when you're making plans for the birth.

Have you given birth within the previous 12 months?

If your pregnancies are spaced too closely together, your body may not have had a chance to replenish its stores since you gave birth to your previous child. This puts your baby at increased risk for stillbirth, low birthweight, prematurity, and sudden infant death syndrome (SIDS) — although these conditions are thought to be more of a problem in economically disadvantaged groups where nutrition and access to appropriate health care are less than ideal.

Have you ever given birth to a baby who was either less than 5½ pounds or more than 9 pounds at birth?

If you've previously given birth to a very small or very large baby, you should see your doctor right away to discuss ways of preventing history from repeating itself. Your doctor will make an attempt to identify the underlying cause of the problem (for example, gestational diabetes) and take steps to try to minimize its effects during subsequent pregnancies.

Have you ever experienced a stillbirth?

If your baby was stillborn because of a problem that was preexisting or you developed during your pregnancy (for example, diabetes), careful prenatal management may increase your odds of delivering a healthy baby the next time around. You may want to consider testing for autoimmune disease, reviewing the records relating to your previous pregnancy and birth (including the autopsy and placental pathology reports), having chromosome testing performed, if warranted, and so on. Note:

You can learn more about pregnancy after stillbirth by reading Chapter 17.

Have you ever given birth to a baby who died within the first month of life?

You and your doctor will want to know whether there was a preventable cause of death and, if there was, take action to prevent a repeat of this tragedy. See Chapter 17 for more about the most common causes of infant death.

Have you ever given birth to a baby with a birth defect?

Some birth defects are genetically caused; others result from unknown causes. If the birth defect was genetically caused or you're not sure what caused it, you may wish to go for genetic counseling before contemplating a subsequent pregnancy.

Have you given birth to a baby who required care in an intensive-care nursery?

Once again, you'll want to discuss your previous experience with your doctor so that your situation can be reviewed and steps can be taken, if possible, to avoid a similar outcome to this pregnancy. In many cases, your doctor will be able to reassure you that the problems your first baby experienced are unlikely to be experienced by your next child.

Have you experienced vaginal bleeding late in pregnancy?

Bleeding in late pregnancy may indicate problems with the position or adherence of the placenta. Women who have experienced a full or partial placental abruption (that is, premature separation of the placenta) or placenta previa (when the placenta implants over the cervical opening) are at increased risk of experiencing similar problems in a subsequent pregnancy.

Bright Idea

Create a detailed health record for yourself and bring it with you to each medical appointment. Start by compiling a complete family medical history. Then, keep a chronological record of information worth noting about your own health: symptoms and illnesses, results of any medical tests you take, a record of prescriptions, and so on.

Do certain medical problems run in your family?

If any of the following — high blood pressure, diabetes, hemophilia, birth defects, mental retardation, cystic fibrosis, Tay-Sachs disease, sickle-cell anemia, or thalassemia — run in your family, you could be at an increased risk. For high blood pressure or diabetes, you are at risk of developing pregnancy-induced hypertension or gestational diabetes during your pregnancy — conditions that, if left unmanaged, could affect your baby's well-being as well as your own health.

Genetic disorders such as hemophilia, birth defects, some forms of mental retardation, cystic fibrosis, Tay-Sachs disease, sickle-cell anemia, and thalassemia can be passed from one generation to the next. If these types of medical problems run in your family (see Table 2.2), you might want to meet with a genetic counselor to discuss your odds of having a child with one of these problems.

Note: It is possible to have a genetic disorder or to carry a gene for a particular disorder without even knowing it. That's why genetic counseling plays an important role in preconception health planning.

As you may recall from your high-school biology class, there are various types of gene disorders:

- Dominant gene disorders (Huntington's disease, for example) are caused by a single abnormal gene from either parent.

- Recessive gene disorders (for example, cystic fibrosis) occur when both parents carry an abnormal gene for a particular disorder.

- X-linked or sex-linked gene disorders (hemophilia, for example) are caused by an abnormal gene on the X chromosome.

- Chromosomal disorders (such as Down syndrome) are caused by problems with the fetus's chromosomes. Chromosomal disorders are sometimes inherited but are more often caused by an error that occurred when the sperm or egg was being formed.

- Multifactorial disorders (such as congenital heart defects) are disorders that are believed to be caused by a mix of genetic and environmental factors. (See Figure 2.1.)

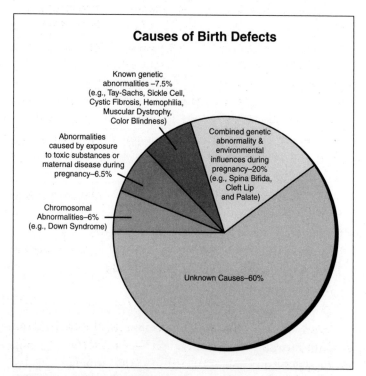

Figure 2.1: Causes of birth defects

Table 2.2. Genetic Disorders for Which Prenatal Diagnosis Is Available

Disorder	Incidence	Inheritance	Method of Prenatal Diagnosis
Cystic fibrosis	1 in 2,500 in white population	Recessive	Chorionic villus sampling (CVS); amniocentesis
Congenital adrenal hyperplasia	1 in 10,000	Recessive	CVS; amniocentesis
Duchenne-type muscular dystrophy	1 in 3,300 male births	X-linked recessive	CVS; amniocentesis
Hemophilia A	1 in 8,500 male births	X-linked recessive	CVS; amniocentesis; fetal blood sampling, rarely
Thalassemia	1 in 1,600 in Mediterranean or Indian population	Recessive	CVS; amniocentesis
Huntington's disease	4–7 in 100,000	Dominant	CVS; amniocentesis
Polycystic kidney	1 in 3,000 by clinical disease (adult type)	Dominant	CVS; amniocentesis diagnosis
Sickle-cell anemia	1 in 484 of African Americans in the U.S.	Recessive	CVS; amniocentesis
Tay-Sachs disease	1 in 3,600 Ashkenazic Jews; 1 in 400,000 in other populations	Recessive	CVS; amniocentesis

Some of these diseases — for example, Tay-Sachs disease, sickle-cell anemia, and thalassemia — tend to be particularly problematic for members of certain ethnic groups:

- Tay-Sachs — a disease that causes fatal brain damage — is more common in people of Central and Eastern European Ashkenazi Jewish descent and in certain French-Canadian subpopulations. It occurs in about 1 in 3,600 infants born to members of these ethnic groups.

- Sickle-cell anemia — a blood disorder — is more common in African Americans and individuals of Mediterranean, Arab, and Asian Indian origin. Approximately 1 in 484 infants of African-American descent are born with the disorder.

- Thalassemia — a blood disorder — is more common in people of Mediterranean and Indian origin. Approximately 1 in 1,600 children born to these ethnic groups is affected by the disease.

If you belong to one of these ethnic groups, you may wish to consult with a genetic counselor to assess your risk of giving birth to a child with one of these diseases.

A genetic counselor will

- provide you with the facts about a particular disease or condition, describe its probable course, and inform you about any available treatments;

- explain how a disease or condition is passed from one generation to the next;

- assess your chances of passing on a serious medical condition to your child;

- advise you whether carrier identification tests are available at genetic clinics within the United States or abroad to detect the types of diseases or conditions you're most likely to pass on to your child;

- advise you whether prenatal diagnostic tests are available at genetic clinics within the United States or abroad to test for these particular diseases or conditions (see Table 2.2);

- let you know if preimplantation diagnosis is available for this disorder (that is, when in vitro fertilization produces several embryos, the one with the best DNA is chosen for implantation — a procedure that costs up to $20,000);

■ put you in touch with other families who are dealing with similar conditions;

■ refer you to health-care practitioners who specialize in a particular disease or disorder.

What follows is a partial list of genetic disorders for which prenatal diagnosis is available. Because breakthroughs are constantly being made in the field of genetic testing, be sure to ask your genetic counselor whether prenatal testing is available for the particular disease or condition you may be carrying.

There are many other reasons why couples go for genetic counseling prior to attempting a pregnancy. You can find out if you're a good candidate for genetic counseling by answering the questions in our Genetic Counseling Checklist below.

Checklist 1.2. Is Genetic Counseling for You?

Wondering if you and your partner might be good candidates for genetic counseling? If you answer yes to one or more of the following questions, it's an option you might wish to consider.

_____ Do you have a genetic disorder?

_____ Does your partner have a genetic disorder?

_____ Are you and your partner close relatives (for example, first cousins)?

_____ Do you, your child, or a close family member have a birth defect?

_____ Do you, your child, or a close family member have a medical condition that has not been thoroughly diagnosed?

_____ Are you concerned that you may be a carrier of a genetic disorder which runs in your ethnic group (for example, Tay-Sachs, sickle-cell anemia, or thalassemia)?

_____ Have you had three or more miscarriages and/or a stillbirth of unknown cause?

_____ Would you and your partner like more information about your chances of giving birth to a baby with a genetic disorder or birth defect?

There have been some remarkable advances in the field of genetic testing in recent years. Here are just a few examples of what genetic testing can do for you if you are thinking about starting a family:

- Preimplantation testing: Genetic technologies at the molecular level allow the identification of specific mutations known to cause genetic disease. These technologies now make it possible to detect genetic diseases in offspring even as early as before implantation (such as when used as an adjunct to IVF). If multiple embryos are conceived in the laboratory, tests can allow only the embryo(s) without the disease to be implanted. This is a better alternative than delaying the diagnosis until CVS or amnio is done and then facing the potential need for abortion.

- Carrier testing for members of a particular ethnic group: Couples of Jewish descent may wish to undergo an Ashkenazi DNA carrier test panel, an all-in-one test that costs approximately $2,300 per person and that can predict with 95 percent to 99 percent accuracy whether a particular person is a carrier for diseases such as Tay-Sachs, cystic fibrosis, Gaucher's disease, Niemann-Pick (Type A), Bloom Syndrome, Familial Dysautonemia, Fanconi Anemia Group C, Mucolipidosis Type IV, and Canavan disease, all of which tend to be problematic for Jews of Eastern European descent. The chances that a particular person of Jewish descent carries a gene for one of these diseases ranges from 1 in 15 for Gaucher's disease to 1 in 122 for Mucolipidosis Type IV. The chances of being a carrier of at least one of these mutations are approximately 10 percent for Ashkenazi Jews.

- Carrier testing for cystic fibrosis: A case can be made for giving all couples the option of being tested for cystic fibrosis — not just those of certain ethnic groups or who have one or more family members with the disease. Cystic fibrosis is carried by 1 in 25 Caucasians and 1 in 65 African

Americans. What makes this disease so challenging to predict is the fact that there are more than 600 different mutations worldwide that are known to cause the disease. Although it's not yet possible to test for all of these mutations, couples considering pregnancy can be tested for 87 different mutations for just $300 per person. Depending on the person's ethnic background, this test will detect 72 percent to 97 percent of carriers of this relatively common genetic disorder.

■ Carrier testing for fragile X syndrome: A similar case can be made for offering to test all women who are planning a pregnancy for fragile X syndrome — a significant cause of mental retardation. Fragile X is carried by 1 in 250–400 women, making it about as common as the risk of a 35-year-old woman having a baby with Down syndrome. Fragile X syndrome affects 1 in 1,000–1,200 males and 1 in 1,500–2,000 females. At this point, testing for both female carriers (fragile X is almost always inherited from the mother) and affected fetuses is possible. Though traditionally considered routine only for those with family histories of fragile X or mental retardation in which the fragile X status was unknown, carrier testing is now available to all individuals and costs approximately $350 per person. Considering the relative frequency with which the fragile X chromosome is carried in the general population, you might want to talk to a genetic counselor or your ob/gyn about being tested. (See Table 2.3 for detailed information on DNA carrier testing for genetic diseases, and see Table 2.4 for a list of the pros and cons of carrier testing.)

 Bright Idea

You can find a directory of genetics centers, clinics, university departments of genetics, and associations of geneticists at www.kumc.edu/gec/prof/genecntr.html.

Table 2.3. DNA Carrier Testing for Genetic Diseases

Disorder	Symptoms	Prognosis	Carrier Frequency & Disease Incidence	Genetic Testing for Carrier Status
Genetic disorders for which testing is available to all individuals				
Cystic fibrosis	Causes thick secretions that lead to chronic lung disease, gastrointestinal tract problems, and sterility in men. People with cystic fibrosis are of normal intelligence.	Varies considerably. Average life span is now over 30 years.	1/25 whites (Jews and non-Jews) carries the gene; 1/2,500 have the disease. 1/80 African Americans carries the gene; risk of affected child 1/25,000. Both the mother and the father must be a gene carrier for a child to be affected with cystic fibrosis.	DNA tests can detect 97% of European Jewish gene carriers, 90% of northern European non-Jewish gene carriers; 70% or less of carriers from other ethnic groups.
Fragile X syndrome	Causes moderate-to-severe mental retardation in males; autistic-like behavior may be present. 60% of females with the disorder have borderline-to-mild retardation, and 40% have intelligence in the normal range without any recognizable symptoms of the disorder.	Moderate-to-severe retardation may be recognizable during early childhood. Milder cases may not be detected until the child reaches school age.	1/400 women of any ethnic background carries the fragile X premutation (an abnormal gene that predisposes her to having children with fragile X syndrome). 1/1,200 males and 1/2,000 females are affected. Only the mother needs to be a carrier in order for a child to be affected.	A DNA test detects virtually all carriers of the common fragile X mutation.

Recessive gene carrier testing options for individuals of Central/Eastern European Jewish ancestry (Ashkenazi Jewish ancestry)

Tay-Sachs disease	Causes brain cells to die, leading progressively to severe retardation, seizures, and blindness starting at four to six months of age.	Death usually occurs by age six. No effective treatment is currently available.	1/30 Jews carries the gene. The risk of having an affected child is 1/3,600. 1/300 non-Jews carries the gene. Both parents must be gene carriers for a child to be affected.	DNA tests detect 94% of Jewish gene carriers. Enzyme testing detects almost all carriers of common Tay-Sachs mutations.
Canavan disease	Similar to Tay-Sachs disease.	Death usually occurs by age 10, although survival into adulthood occasionally occurs. No effective treatment is currently available.	1/40 Jews carries the gene. The risk of having an affected child is 1/6,400. 1/500 non-Jews in the U.S. carries the gene. Both parents must be gene carriers for a child to be affected.	DNA tests detect 97% of Jewish gene carriers. Carrier testing in other ethnic groups is less accurate.
Niemann-Pick disease, Type A	Causes severe feeding problems and failure to grow with progressive and severe degeneration of brain function in early infancy.	Death usually occurs by age 3. No effective treatment is currently available.	1/90 Jews carries the gene. The risk of having an affected child is 1/32,000. Very rare among non-Jews. Both parents must be gene carriers for a child to be affected.	DNA tests detect 95% of Jewish gene carriers. Carrier testing in other ethnic groups is less accurate.

(continued)

Table 2.3. *(continued)*

Disorder	Symptoms	Prognosis	Carrier Frequency & Disease Incidence	Genetic Testing for Carrier Status
Recessive gene carrier testing options for individuals of Central/Eastern European Jewish ancestry (Ashkenazi Jewish ancestry)				
Gaucher disease	Causes anemia, bone pain, enlargement of the spleen and liver. People with Gaucher disease are of normal intelligence, and the nervous system is rarely affected.	Disease is usually mild and often not diagnosed until adulthood, if ever. Some suffer from chronic disability starting in childhood or early adulthood. Enzyme treatments are available for those with severe symptoms.	1/15 Jews carries the gene. 1/900 is affected by Gaucher disease. 1/200 non-Jews carries the gene. Both parents must be gene carriers for a child to be affected.	DNA tests detect 97% of Jewish carriers.
Recessive gene carrier testing options for individuals of African, Hispanic, Mediterranean, Asian, and Middle Eastern Ancestry				

Sickle-cell disease	Causes severe anemia, bone pain, damage to major organs, and susceptibility to infection. Individuals with sickle-cell disease are of normal intelligence. Treatments include drugs and transfusions.	Varies considerably. Severe disease can lead to frequent hospitalization; mild disease may allow for survival to adulthood. Both parents must be gene carriers for a child to be affected.	1/11 African Americans carries the gene. Risk of having an affected child is 1/484. Less than 1/50 individuals of Mediterranean, Arab, Asian, or Indian ancestry carries the gene.	Hemoglobin electrophoresis finds all carriers of sickle-cell gene.
Thalassemia	Severe anemia, transfusion dependency, and organ damage. Individuals with thalassemia are of normal intelligence.	Varies. (Depends on specific mutations in family.) In severe cases, complications of disease and treatment lead to death during third and fourth decades. Treatments include transfusions, drugs, and bone-marrow transplants.	1/20 individuals of Mediterranean or Indian ancestry carries the gene. The risk of having an affected child is about 1/1,600. 1/75 African Americans carries the gene. 1/10 Southeast Asians carries the gene. Both parents must be gene carriers for a child to be affected.	Hemoglobin electrophoresis and complete blood count find almost all carriers of common inherited anemias.

Note: Carrier frequencies above refer to individuals without a family history of the disorder.

Source: Department of Genetics, Yale University School of Medicine.

Table 2.4. Pros and Cons of Carrier Testing

Pros:

Carrier testing involves a simple blood test.

You'll have your results in one to two weeks.

You will know with certainty what the chances are for having a baby with the disease and what the options are for diagnosing the condition prenatally.

Cons:

Learning that you are a carrier for a particular disease may be a source of worry to you and your partner.

These tests can cost hundreds of dollars per person and may not be covered by your medical insurance.

Although it is unlikely, finding out that you are a carrier of a potentially harmful gene may influence insurance decisions about you or members of your family or influence the way you or others view yourself.

As you might expect, the testing of general populations rather than just high-risk populations for carrier states is sometimes a touchy political issue, as can be the testing for disease in the not-necessarily-at-risk fetus or in the preimplantation cell mass in that it can resemble a negative eugenics approach to some. Nevertheless, these technologies are becoming a fact of life for a growing number of couples. Like it or not, "designer babies" are here to stay.

 Bright Idea

If you aren't already doing so, start keeping a menstrual calendar. Note the date when your period starts, the number of days it lasts, and anything else your doctor might want to know about. This information could prove helpful if you experience problems in conceiving. It can also prove invaluable in pinpointing the date of conception — and consequently your due date.

Now that you have an idea of how physically ready you are for pregnancy, it's time to take the next important step by visiting your doctor.

What's up, doc? Things to talk about with your doctor

Fifteen years ago, women didn't show up on their doctors' doorsteps until they had missed their second period and were 99 percent sure they were pregnant. Today, most doctors recommend that their patients come in for a checkup before they start trying to conceive.

The reason for the change in thinking is obvious. Recent studies about the benefits of preconception health have served to hammer home an important message: It's not enough to quit smoking, improve your eating habits, and start popping prenatal vitamins the moment the pregnancy test comes back positive. To give your baby the best possible start in life, you need to ensure that you are in the best possible health before you start trying to conceive.

Here's why.

Even though today's pregnancy tests are highly sensitive and allow women to test for pregnancy sooner than ever before, you probably won't know for sure that you're pregnant until at least four weeks after the date of your last menstrual period — perhaps even longer if your cycles are particularly lengthy or irregular. During this time when you're wondering whether you're pregnant, your baby's major organs are being formed — a process that medical science refers to as either organogenesis or embryogenesis. (See Table 2.5.) That's why it's so important to be as healthy as possible before you start trying to conceive. This means setting up an appointment to see your doctor for a preconception checkup.

Watch Out!

You and your doctor will have a harder time pinning down your due date if you become pregnant immediately after you stop taking the Pill. That's why most doctors suggest that you wait until after your first spontaneous postpill period before you start trying to conceive. (You may be told that you should wait three or more months after stopping the Pill. This advice is medically unfounded and may result in a pregnancy sooner than you planned.)

Table 2.5. What Happens When

Here's the scoop on some key milestones in your baby's development. Note: The time frames referred to here are postconception rather than postmenstrual. In other words, the key period of development for your baby's heart is three to seven weeks after conception or five to nine weeks after the first day of your last menstrual period (assuming, of course, that you have "textbook" 28-day menstrual cycles).

neural tube: days 19 to 27

heart: weeks 3 to 7

gastrointestinal tract: weeks 4 to 10

kidneys: weeks 5 to 8

limbs: weeks 5 to 8

lungs: weeks 5 to 8

genitals: weeks 7 to 10

hair: weeks 10 to 16

During the preconception checkup, your doctor will

- talk with you about your plans to start a family and answer any questions you might have about fertility, pregnancy, and childbirth;

- tell you what you can do to improve your odds of having the healthiest baby possible (that is, quit smoking, abstain from alcohol while you're trying to conceive and through-out your pregnancy, and so on);

▪ discuss whether you should attempt to lose or gain weight prior to becoming pregnant;

▪ provide you with information about how any chronic health conditions you may have — diabetes; cardiac problems; high blood pressure; epilepsy; lung, liver or kidney disorders, and so on — might best be managed before and during pregnancy (see Chapter 16);

> 66 It was really important to me to find a doctor who would give me objective information about how being about 100 pounds overweight might affect my preg-nancy. I didn't want to end up with a doctor who would make me feel bad or guilty for being overweight. 99
>
> – Carla, 33, mother of one

▪ review which medicines you're currently taking (that is, both prescrip-tion and over-the-counter medications) and let you know which ones you should stop taking or change once you start trying to conceive (see Chapter 5);

▪ provide you with some basic information on the time it may take you to conceive, given your age — according to the American Society for Reproductive Medicine, you have a 20 percent chance of conceiving in any given cycle if you're under 30 but only 5 percent if you're over 40 (see Chapter 4);

▪ talk with you about your overall reproductive health and let you know whether it makes sense for you to monitor your basal body temperature (that is, your temperature first thing in the morning — before you even get out of bed), identify changes in cervical mucus, purchase an ovulation predictor kit, and so on, in order to increase your chances of predicting ovulation (see Chapter 3);

- discuss how any previous miscarriages, abortions, still-births, sexually transmitted diseases, and/or venereal infections might impact on either your chances of conceiving or your ability to carry a pregnancy to term (see Chapters 4, 16, and 17);

- determine whether you should have preconception genetic counseling or testing (that is, if there's a family history of mental retardation, cerebral palsy, muscular dystrophy, cystic fibrosis, hemophilia, or spina bifida; if you are at increased risk of having a child with Tay-Sachs disease, thalassemia, or sickle-cell anemia because of your ethnic background; or if you are over 35);

- review the importance of healthy eating (see Chapter 6) and/or prescribe a prenatal vitamin supplement so that your body will have the vitamins and minerals it needs during the first few weeks of pregnancy;

- discuss the role of physical fitness during pregnancy (see Chapter 6);

- talk about the importance of minimizing stress both when you're trying to conceive and after you become pregnant (see Chapters 4 and 7);

- inform you about hazards to avoid while you're trying to conceive (that is, exposure to X-rays, toxins, and other substances that could be harmful to your baby — a topic we'll be discussing in greater detail in Chapter 5);

 Bright Idea

Try to book the last appointment of the day for your preconception checkup (as opposed to earlier in the day, when there could be a waiting room full of people). That's when your doctor or midwife is most likely to be able to take the time to answer your questions and address your concerns without feeling rushed to go on to the next patient.

- do a pelvic exam and Pap smear to check for symptomless infections, ovarian cysts, and other conditions that might be difficult or risky to treat during pregnancy;

- do a blood test to determine if you are anemic or carrying any sexually transmitted diseases;

- do a urine test to screen for symptomless conditions such as diabetes, urinary tract infections, kidney infections, and other asymptomatic infections that may pose a problem during pregnancy;

- do a rubella test (German measles test) to determine whether you are immune to the disease;

- check that your immunizations are up-to-date, and screen you for Hepatitis B;

- provide your partner with information about lifestyle modifications he might want to make to give the baby you hope to conceive together the healthiest possible start in life.

By the time you walk out of your doctor's office, you should have a clear idea of what you can do to increase your chances of conceiving quickly and having a healthy baby.

Just the facts

- Don't wait until the pregnancy test comes back positive to start leading a baby-friendly lifestyle. The time to get rid of any unhealthy lifestyle habits is before you start trying to conceive.

- Talk to your doctor about genetic counseling and carrier testing so that you and your partner can make an informed decision about whether of these options is for you.

- Schedule a preconception checkup with your health-care practitioner so that you can ensure you have a clean bill of health before you embark on Operation Baby.

GET THE SCOOP ON. . .
The biggest lies about fertility and infertility
■ Fertility awareness and other methods of
increasing your chances of conceiving ■ "Trying"
versus letting nature take its course

The Overachiever's Guide to Getting Pregnant Fast

If you've spent the past 10 years or more of your life running to the drugstore at regular intervals in an effort not to get pregnant, it can feel a bit odd to find yourself suddenly engaged in the business of baby-making. Even if you are trying to take a rather laid-back approach to conceiving — that is, you're letting passion rather than an ovulation predictor kit determine when you have sex — you probably can't help but think of sex in a whole new way. Rather than merely being an intimate expression of love and passion between you and your partner, it has now become a biological process that is capable of producing the ultimate miracle — another human being.

If, like many couples, you and your partner have been reading up on the art of conception, you've probably stumbled across all kinds of contradictory information about getting pregnant. One book will

tell you that you can conceive during the days before and immediately after you ovulate; another will tell you that you've missed
your chance if you haven't hopped in the sack by the time ovulation occurs. Similarly, one magazine article will suggest that
you stand on your head after sex so that you can give the sperm
a bit of a boost as they begin their quest to fertilize an egg;
another will tell you that you can get up out of bed and do jumping jacks if you'd like; since the sperm are designed to find their
way to the egg, gravity be damned.

So why is there such a glut of misinformation about this all-
important topic? Because there's so much interest in the topic!
As a result, the media tend to give massive amounts of coverage
to every new study that promises to shed a bit more light on the
mysteries of conception. It doesn't matter if the research sample
is overly small, the results are tentative and require further
examination, or that the researchers are practicing bad science:
news stories about pregnancy make good copy, period.

Because there's so much misinformation, we start out this
chapter by debunking some of the more convincing myths
about fertility and conception. Then we talk about the length of
time it takes to conceive, what you can do to increase your odds
of conceiving quickly, and the pros and cons of "trying" versus
letting nature take its course. Along the way, we evaluate the
latest (but not necessarily greatest) home tests available to
would-be parents who are eager to do whatever they can
to increase their odds at winning at baby roulette.

The biggest misconceptions about fertility and infertility

How many of these "conception misconceptions" have you
come across since you started reading up on the art of baby-
making? More than a few, we're sure. These misconceptions are
so deep rooted that many people are convinced they're nothing
short of pure fact. Here's what you need to know to avoid making that mistake yourself.

MYTH: You are most fertile on day 14 of your cycle.

This rule holds true only if your menstrual cycle length happens to be 28 days. However, many women have cycles that are either shorter or longer than this, or that are highly irregular. (Just a reminder: The length of your cycle is defined as the length of time between the first day of one period and the first day of the next.) Since ovulation occurs approximately 14 days before the onset of your next period, if your cycle is 35 days long, you can expect to ovulate on or around day 21.

On the other hand, if your cycle is highly unpredictable — that is, your cycle ends up lasting for 28 days during one cycle and 35 days during the next — you are likely to find it much more challenging to try to pinpoint your fertile days since history rarely, if ever, repeats itself.

MYTH: Taking your temperature every morning will tell you when to have intercourse.

Many women who are trying to conceive make a point of taking their temperature each morning so that they can track their basal body temperature (BBT), or resting temperature. Although tracking your BBT can provide plenty of valuable information, it won't tell you when to have sex. The reason is simple: By the time your temperature starts to rise, ovulation has already occurred and you've missed the window of opportunity for conception. (Well, for this cycle at least!)

 Bright Idea

If you're not already in the habit of keeping track of your menstrual cycles, you might want to start keeping a menstrual calendar. You can either purchase a journal or calendar specifically for this purpose or you can simply note details about your menstrual cycle in your personal organizer. Having detailed records about the length of each menstrual cycle, your patterns of bleeding, and any menstrual symptoms you happen to experience could prove invaluable down the road if you have difficulty conceiving and you need to go for fertility treatment.

You can still pick up a lot of valuable information from tracking your BBT, however. By studying your temperature graph and your related fertility signals, you can often determine

- whether you are ovulating at all (if your temperature remains relatively flat over the course of your entire cycle, chances are you're not);

- whether your luteal phase (the second half of your cycle) is long enough for implantation to occur;

- whether your progesterone levels (the hormone needed to sustain a pregnancy) are sufficiently high during your luteal phase;

- whether you are already pregnant (a likely scenario if you have more than 18 consecutive high temperatures during the luteal phase of your cycle);

- whether you are in danger of having a miscarriage (if your temperature suddenly drops, this could be an indication that a miscarriage is imminent); and

- whether you were pregnant before you had what you might otherwise have deemed a "late period."

The only way you can use a BBT chart to predict your most fertile days is to look at a few months' worth of charts and try to determine whether your cycle conforms to any repeatable patterns. For example, if your temperature always shoots sky-high on day 14, you'll know that you have a good chance of ovulating in that same time frame during your next cycle.

But, of course, even that is an inexact science. Your cycle can be thrown off by illness, stress, jet lag, and life's other curveballs. We're human beings, not robots, after all!

MYTH: To maximize your chances of conceiving, you should make love during the days leading up to and following ovulation.

Although *part* of this statement is correct, the rest of the statement contains a false assumption — proof positive a little bit of knowledge can be a dangerous thing. While it's a good idea to time intercourse on the days prior to ovulation, you've missed your opportunity if you try to conceive more than a day after ovulation has occurred. The reason is simple: The egg is capable of surviving for only 12 to 24 hours after ovulation, so if it hasn't been romanced by a sperm cell by then, it's too late.

A study conducted by researchers from the National Institute of Environmental Health Sciences confirmed the importance of timing intercourse prior to or at the time of ovulation: all of the 192 pregnancies that occurred in the 625 couples participating in the study resulted from intercourse the day of ovulation or within five days before it.

Researchers from the University of Utah reached a similar conclusion. They found that the odds of conceiving are greatest if intercourse occurs one to two days prior to ovulation rather than on the actual day of ovulation.

MYTH: There's something wrong with you if you don't conceive within the first three months of trying.

This is a particularly nasty bit of misinformation because it causes a lot of couples a tremendous amount of anxiety and grief for no good reason. Although some couples do manage to conceive within the first three months of trying, a large number of other highly fertile couples take considerably longer than that. Consider the numbers for yourself:

- Your odds of conceiving in any given cycle are approximately 20 percent to 25 percent.

> ❝It took us about six months to get pregnant, but we weren't actually making love on the days we were supposed to until about four months after we stopped using birth control. I think my husband was purposely avoiding the 'right' day because he was feeling ambivalent about the whole thing.❞
>
> — Susan, 33, mother of one

- Approximately 60 percent of couples who are actively trying to conceive (having intercourse two to three times a
  week) will conceive within the first 6 months of trying, 75
  percent within 9 months, 80 percent within a year, and
  90 percent within 18 months.

So, as you can see, those couples who manage to hit a reproductive home run the first time up at bat are the exception
rather than the rule. Most couples require a bit more batting
practice than that.

MYTH: Your fertility declines dramatically after age 35.

Although it's true that your fertility declines as you age, you still
have an excellent chance of having a baby even if you're past
the reproductive world's magic age of 35.

According to the National Center for Health Statistics, you
have a 96 percent chance of conceiving within one year if you're
under 25, an 86 percent chance if you're between 25 and 34, and
a 78 percent chance if you're between the ages of 35 and 44.

What you may require, however, is a bit more patience. The
older you get, the longer it takes to achieve a pregnancy. (See
Table 3.1.)

Table 3.1. The Odds of Conceiving and Average Number of Months It Takes to Conceive for Women of Various Ages

Age	Odds That You'll Conceive in Any Given Cycle	Average Number of Months It Takes to Conceive
Early 20s	20% to 25%	4 to 5 months
Late 20s	15% to 20%	5 to 6.7 months
Early 30s	10% to 15%	6.7 to 10 months
Late 30s	8.3% to 10%	10 to 12 months

Adapted from a similar chart in *How to Get Pregnant* by Sherman J. Silber, M.D. (New York, Warner Books, 1980). Note: The data reported by Silber is supported by more recent data from the National Center for Health Statistics.

MYTH: You can increase your chances of having a boy or a girl by timing intercourse a particular way.

Although theories like this abound, there is no scientific evidence to link the timing of conception and the sex of the baby. A 1995 study conducted by the National Institute of Environmental Health Sciences concluded that there's no connection between the timing of intercourse and the ability to conceive a baby of a particular sex. (Just in case you're wondering what we're talking about, one popular theory claims that you can increase your odds of conceiving a baby girl by making love no closer than two to three days prior to ovulation, and that you can increase your odds of conceiving a baby boy by timing intercourse as close to ovulation as possible.)

Even high-tech methods of sex selection aren't able to offer couples much better than 75–25 odds, so you've got to be dreaming in technicolor (or at least pink and blue!) if you expect some of these low-tech sex selection techniques to deliver up a baby of the "right" sex.

MYTH: Just relax and you'll get pregnant.

If you haven't had anyone pass along this little gem yet, consider yourself blessed. It's one of most pervasive fertility myths out there. Although it's true that a lot of stress can cause your reproductive system to shut down (it's part of the "fight or flight" survival mechanism we all possess), there's no firm evidence that moderate amounts of

> ❝ If I had a nickel for every time someone told me to relax and not think about it, I'd be a millionaire. ❞
>
> — Rhonda, 30, mother of two

stress (that is, the running-to-the-bathroom-to-see-if-you're-pregnant-yet kind of stress) affects your chances of conceiving.

Of course, this implies that only totally relaxed would-be-mamas can count on hitting the reproductive jackpot —

something that would dramatically reduce the number of babies born each year. So this is one conception worry you can, well, relax about!

MYTH: Women are the only ones who have to worry about declining fertility. Men can father children well into their 70s.

Although it's common knowledge that women are capable of bearing children during only the first half of their adult lives, many people don't realize that men also experience a decline in their fertility as they age. Studies have shown that a man's fertility begins to decline from his late teens onward, and that pregnancy rates for couples in which the man is 40 or older are only one-third those of couples in which the man is 25 or younger. Scientists believe that it's an age-related decline in the production of sperm that is responsible for this decrease in male fertility. (See Chapters 1 and 4 for more about age and fertility.)

The moral of the story?

Even guys have a "best before date."

MYTH: You need to have sex every single day if you want to get pregnant.

Although you do boost your odds of conceiving if you have sex every day rather than every other day, you only boost your odds of conceiving minimally.

Researchers at the National Institute of Environmental Health Sciences recently concluded that couples who had intercourse every other day during their fertile period had a 22 percent chance of conceiving in any given cycle, as compared to 25 percent for couples who had intercourse every day. On the other hand, couples who had intercourse only once a week reduced their odds of conceiving in a given cycle to 10 percent.

If your partner's sperm count is low or marginal, you may be advised to have intercourse every other day in order to give his sperm count a chance to build up. Your doctor may even recommend that your partner refrain from ejaculation entirely during the days leading up to your most fertile period. He won't recommend that you limit your sex life to just a few days a month, however: studies have shown that abstaining from sex for more than seven days can decrease your fertility. Any gain in sperm count is more than offset by the increased number of aged sperm cells with lower fertilization potential.

> 66 Do not have sex every day. If you're trying to maximize your chances of conceiving, it's better to go every other day around the time you are ovulating. You are also more fresh, and therefore you can put your heart into making sex as pleasurable and romantic as possible. 99
>
> — Rhonda, 30, mother of two

MYTH: To give the sperm a chance to make it through the cervix, you should stand on your head.

Although it's not a good idea to dash off to the bathroom and allow all of the semen to dribble into the toilet, you don't have to go to extreme measures (standing on your head or lying on your back with your knees to your chest for a half an hour after making love) to ensure that the sperm make their way past the cervix. For the most part, they know where they're headed and what they're supposed to do when they get there. "Sperm are like salmon," says Mark Sauer, M.D., a professor of obstetrics and gynecology at the College of Physicians and Surgeons at Columbia University. "They always seem to swim upstream. A couple shouldn't be concerned about what position they use — the sperm know what direction to head in."

MYTH: Your left ovary releases an egg one month, and your right ovary the next.

It's a great theory, but there's very little truth to it. Ovulation is a random event each month, with both ovaries vying for the honor on a first-come, first-served basis. If you have only one ovary, it wins the draw by default.

Fertility awareness and other methods of increasing your chances of conceiving

You can use various methods to increase your odds of conceiving in any given cycle. What they all boil down to, however, are ways of monitoring your fertility signs in order to pinpoint your most fertile days.

Before we get into a detailed discussion of fertility-awareness methods, however, let's quickly review the science behind the process of conception.

The science of sex

During the first half of your menstrual cycle — the so-called follicular, or proliferative, phase — approximately 20 eggs (or ova) begin to ripen and occupy fluid-filled sacks called follicles. At the same time, the level of estrogen in your body continues to rise, causing the endometrial lining in your uterus to thicken, thereby readying it for the possible implantation of a fertilized egg and boosting the production of cervical mucus, the substance that helps the sperm to make their way to the egg.

Just prior to ovulation, rising levels of estrogen trigger a brief but intense surge of lutenizing hormone (LH) from the pituitary gland that causes the dominant follicle to rupture and release its egg. Some women experience pain in the lower abdomen as this is occurring, a sensation the Germans call "mittelschmerz" or "pain in the middle."

During the second half of your cycle — the luteal or secretory phase — the ruptured ovarian follicle (now known as the corpus luteum, or "yellow body") begins to produce progesterone, one of the key hormones that is required to sustain a pregnancy. It continues to produce progesterone until the placenta assumes this function some three months down the road.

The rising levels of progesterone cause the endometrial glands to ready the uterus for the arrival of a fertilized egg, which happens some five days later, if conception actually occurs.

When pregnancy occurs, your progesterone levels remain high. If it doesn't occur, the corpus luteum begins to regress; progesterone levels fall; and 12 to 14 days after ovulation, the uterus begins to shed the endometrial layer and your menstrual period begins. (See Figure 3.1.)

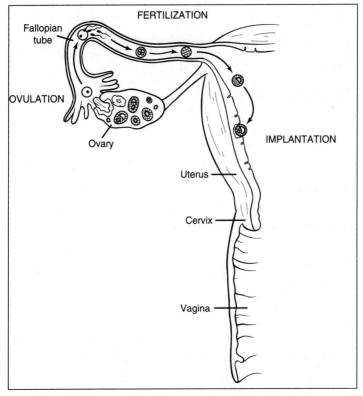

Figure 3.1: The fertilized egg implants itself on the uterine wall. *Figure created by Articulate Graphics.*

Now that we've completed this brief refresher course on the female reproductive system, let's consider some of the methods you can use to pinpoint the days on which you are most fertile.

Basal body temperature

One of the best ways to figure out what's happening with your menstrual cycle is to take your temperature (with an oral thermometer) at the same time each morning before you get out of bed and record this information on a temperature graph — a reading that is known as your *basal body temperature* (BBT) chart or resting temperature chart (see Table 3.2).

Table 3.2. Using a BBT Chart

Instructions (see figures 3.2 and 3.3)

Starting with the first day of your menstrual period, write the month and day across the top of the graph and keep the chart and thermometer on your night table.

Each morning, as soon as you wake up, place the thermometer in your mouth and take your temperature. Do not eat, drink, smoke, or get out of bed before taking your temperature. Note: If you're a shift worker, take your temperature after awakening from your longest, most restful stretch of sleep.

If you are using a digital thermometer, it will beep when it's time to read your temperature. If you're using a mercury thermometer, you should wait a full five minutes before reading your temperature.

Record the temperature reading on your BBT chart by placing a dot in the middle of the appropriate horizontal line in the column underneath the date. (If you forget to take your temperature one day, simply leave that day's column blank.)

If you think your reading may be off because you're ill, you're taking a particular medication, or because of a change in your sleep schedule, be sure to note the reason on your chart. You should also note the days on which you have sexual intercourse by checking off the appropriate boxes in the "coitus" section of the graph and the days on which you are menstruating by checking off the appropriate boxes in the "menses" section of the chart.

Note: Remember to start a new chart whenever you start a new menstrual cycle.

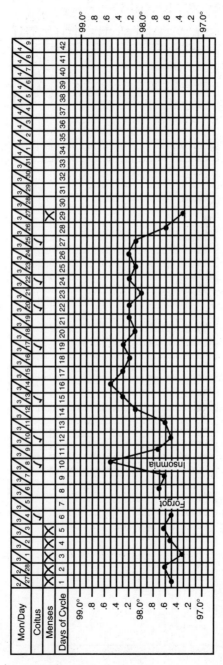

Figure 3.2. A filled-out BBT chart.

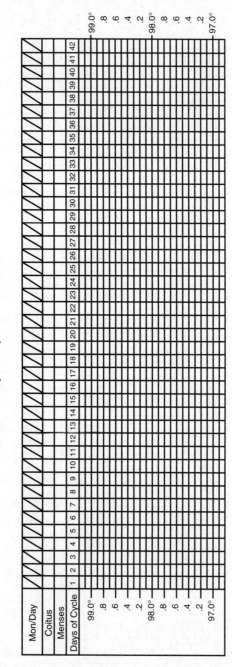

Figure 3.3. A BBT chart you can use.

If you are ovulating normally, your temperature may dip slightly just prior to ovulation and then shoot upward once you have ovulated. Just bear in mind that this is not a reliable indication of impending ovulation. Not everyone experiences this dip and, even if you do experience it, by the time you've "dipped" and your temperature has rebounded, baby-making season has come and gone. Your temperature will typically range from 97.0 to 97.5 degrees Fahrenheit prior to ovulation, and from 97.6 to 98.6 after ovulation. If you are pregnant, your temperature will remain elevated for the next nine months. If you're not, it will start to drop either close to or on the day your period starts as the level of progesterone in your body drops.

You will probably want to include information on your chart about the days on which you had intercourse. A simple checkmark or circle on the appropriate day is all that is required.

Many women find it useful to include some other types of information on their BBT charts as well, such as any changes to their routines that might have influenced their temperature reading on a particular morning. Something as simple as having a cold or fever, drinking alcohol the night before, getting less than three consecutive hours of sleep before you take your temperature, taking your temperature at a significantly different time than usual, or sleeping under an electric blanket if you don't usually do so can throw your readings out of whack.

Although BBT charts are a source of much useful information, they aren't a useful tool for everyone. Some women who are ovulating normally don't experience the classic temperature rise upon ovulation. Instead, their basal body temperature

Bright Idea

Use a digital oral thermometer rather than an old-style mercury thermometer. It's easier to read, it requires no shaking (which can cause your body temp to go up for no good reason), and it even beeps to remind you to record your reading if you accidentally go back to sleep.

remains constant throughout their menstrual cycle. These women often have more luck monitoring the quantity and quality of their cervical mucus.

Cervical mucus

Over the course of your menstrual cycle, hormonal fluctuations cause both the quantity and the quality of your cervical mucus (the substance secreted by your cervix) to change. As ovulation approaches, your secretions change from a thick, opaque texture to a thin, clear, and slippery texture that many women compare to egg white. According to Toni Weschler, author of *Taking Charge of Your Fertility,* there's a logical reason for these cervical mucus changes: "Women are only fertile the few days around ovulation, and therefore only produce the substance necessary for sperm nourishment and mobility during that time."

It's possible to monitor the quality and quantity of cervical mucus by inserting one or two fingers into your vagina daily and noting the characteristics of your cervical mucus on your fingers when you remove them from your vagina. If you notice that you suddenly have an abundance of "egg white" — the type of mucus that is best suited to carrying sperm — you can bet that your fertile time has arrived.

Because you want your vaginal environment to be as sperm-friendly as possible, you will want to avoid

- vaginal sprays and scented tampons (because they can cause a pH imbalance in your vagina);
- artificial lubricants, vegetable oils, and glycerin (because they can kill off sperm);
- using saliva as a lubricant (because saliva can also kill sperm);
- douching (because it alters the normal acidity of the vagina; can cause vaginal infections and/or pelvic inflammatory disease; and may wash away the cervical mucus that is required to transport the sperm).

Watch Out!

Showering, bathing, and swimming may all temporarily alter the quantity and quality of your cervical mucus, so do your checks before you shower, bathe, or swim. You can run into similar difficulty if you attempt to do your checks after you've had intercourse, so it's important to plan ahead.

Position of your cervix

As your body approaches ovulation, your cervix tends to rise up in your vagina, soften, and open slightly. Although it generally feels firm at the beginning of your cycle, like the tip of your nose, it can feel as soft and fleshy as your lips by the time you're ready to ovulate. After ovulation, the cervix changes position, dropping lower in your vagina as estrogen levels fall and progesterone levels rise.

You can check the position of your cervix by washing your hands thoroughly with soap and rinsing well, squatting slightly or sitting on the toilet, and then inserting one finger deep into your vagina and feeling for your cervix. You should try to check your cervix at roughly the same time each day, for the sake of consistency. Just one quick note about this fertility sign: It can take a bit of time to get a sense of what your cervix is like at various times in your cycle. Don't assume that you're hopelessly inept when it comes to predicting your fertility if you can't master this particular technique. It's not an easy maneuver to perfect!

Secondary fertility signs

Some women also get some additional "clues" that ovulation is fast approaching, including the following:

- Spotting around the time of ovulation (sometimes called midcycle spotting or peri-ovulatory bleeding)
- Ovarian pain or achiness
- Abdominal bloating
- Water retention ("puffiness")
- An increased interest in sex

- Fuller vaginal lips
- A swollen vulva
- Increased breast sensitivity and/or breast tenderness
- Increased skin sensitivity
- Heightened sensory awareness (particularly smell, taste, and vision).

Because these symptoms aren't experienced by all women or by the same woman in every cycle, fertility experts classify them as *secondary fertility signs* rather than as *primary fertility signs.* (The primary fertility signs consist of changes to the basal body temperature, changes to the quantity and quality of the cervical mucus, and changes to the position of the cervix.)

Ovulation predictor kits (OPKs) and related products

There's no doubt about it: ovulation predictor kits are big business in America today — amounting to approximately $40 million in sales each year. In fact, the range of products available has undergone a population explosion of its own since the first edition of this book was published back in 1999.

Here's the lowdown on the "classic" ovulation predictor kit (OPKs) that uses urine to test for peak fertility days as well as some of the new kids on the fertility block.

Ovulation predictor kits (OPKs) (urine-based)

Ovulation predictor kits are home test kits that are used to predict ovulation. They work by detecting the LH surge in your urine that typically indicates that ovulation is fast approaching. (See Table 3.3.)

Although ovulation predictor kits (OPKs) can be expensive — you can expect to pay $21 for a kit with six days' worth of tests and you may need more than six days' worth of tests if your cycles are irregular — they are considered to be a reasonably effective method of predicting ovulation because they are able to detect the LH surge that typically appears 24 to 36 hours before ovulation. They're not, however, considered to be as reliable as high- and

Moneysaver

If your cycle is irregular and you think you're going to need to purchase more than one ovulation predictor kit per cycle, ask your pharmacist if you can return any unopened kits for a refund or credit if you don't end up needing them after all.

low-tech ovulation prediction methods that either detect estrogen in the urine or monitor changes to the cervical mucus — the current "gold standard" of ovulation prediction.

What they can't do, however, is tell you when to start having sex. Ideally, you should be doing that before the LH surge appears. (You'll recall from our earlier discussion that a recent study indicated that the best time to start trying to conceive is three to five days prior to ovulation.)

One other word of caution before we move on: The fact that you have an LH surge does not necessarily mean you're ovulating. LH can surge with or without the release of an egg. To make matters worse, it's possible to have a series of LH surges prior to the "real" one — something that can throw your timing way out of whack (unless, of course, you're willing to make a lot of OPK company shareholders very happy by loading up on truckloads of tester kits each month).

Table 3.3. The Big Three: How the Three Major Types of Ovulation Predictor Tests Work and What They Cost

Type of Test	What It Tests For	What It Costs
Ovulation predictor kits	Lutenizing hormone (LH) levels in urine	$21 for six days' worth of tests
Fertility monitor (urine test type)	Lutenizing hormone (LH) and estrogen levels in urine	$200 for the monitor plus $50 for each package of 30 test strips
Saliva ovulation tests	Estrogen levels in saliva	$60 for the kit (including microscope)

Fertility monitors

Fertility monitors rely on the same basic technology as urine-based ovulation predictor kits, but they typically test for the presence of two hormones rather than just one: LH and estrogen. (See Table 3.3.) Note: One company has brought out a fertility monitor that relies on saliva tests rather than urine tests, but that product is still unique to the marketplace.

What really distinguishes fertility monitors from ovulation predictor kits, however, is the fact that the fertility monitor (sometimes referred to as a fertility "computer") stores the fertility information for you. (Most models will actually store a couple of months' worth of fertility data for you so that you can go back and look for patterns.)

The fertility monitor tells you which days you need to test your urine. Based on the hormone levels detected in the test, it will tell you when you're at your most fertile so that you can time intercourse accordingly.

While fertility monitors can be very useful in helping to pinpoint your most fertile days, they come with a rather hefty price tag. You can expect to pay approximately $200 for the actual fertility monitor plus $50 for each box of 30 test strips. (You'll need a new test strip each time you test, so you could go through most of a box each month. And since the manufacturer of one of these systems advises that you throw away all remaining test strips at the end of each cycle if you find that you have fewer than 10 left — it's apparently important that the test strips that you use during each cycle come from the same box, to minimize the possibility that the results could be affected by slight differences in test strip quality from box to box — you could find yourself in the market for a new box of test strips each month.)

Saliva ovulation tests

Saliva ovulation tests are home test kits that are designed to detect the increased salt content in a woman's saliva — something that occurs when estrogen levels peak around the time of ovulation. (See Table 3.3.)

Moneysaver

Fertility monitors don't come cheap, so you'll want to make sure you're a good candidate for one before you fork over your hard-earned cash. One major manufacturer of fertility monitors advises that its product may not be able to accurately predict ovulation in women who have recently been pregnant, who have just stopped breastfeeding or who have just stopped using a hormonal method of contraception; and that certain medical conditions and medications can interfere with the performance of the product: e.g., menopausal symptoms, breastfeeding, liver and kidney disease, polycystic ovarian syndrome, antibiotics containing tetracyclines (not oxytetracycline or doxycycline), and treatments that affect your cycle (e.g., hormonal contraception, certain fertility treatments and hormone replacement therapy).

To use a saliva ovulation test, you simply take a small sample of saliva and apply it to one of the test slides. (Note: You're supposed to do the test first thing in the morning, before you eat, drink, or brush your teeth.) You then allow the slide to dry and view it through the microscope eyepiece. If you can only see a small amount of salt on the slide, you know that ovulation is still a ways off. If there are a lot of little dots that are starting to cluster into chainlike formations, you know that ovulation is approaching. And if there is a clear fern pattern on the slide, you know that ovulation is imminent. (When the salt in the woman's saliva dries, it leaves a crystal pattern that resembles a fern plant, which is why this type of saliva pattern is described as "ferning.")

According to the manufacturers of these tests, saliva tests are 98 percent accurate in predicting ovulation. It's also a whole lot less messy, which is one of the reasons why saliva ovulation tests are becoming an increasingly popular option. (The other key advantage to these types of tests is that they tend to give you a bit more advance warning that ovulation is approaching, because you can gradually observe changes to the pattern of the saliva.)

Saliva test kits are moderately priced. They're more expensive than traditional OPKs, but less expensive than fertility monitors. A reusable kit (including microscope) typically sells for around $59.

Watch Out!

If having a computer or other ovulation predictor tests telling you when you're supposed to have sex is a bit too Big Brotherish for you and is causing your libido to go AWOL, you might want to consider switching to a more low-tech baby-making approach. You don't want your baby to destroy your sex life before he or she is even conceived! Besides, if you're making love at least three times per week, you don't need a computer or other high-tech device to tell you when Ovulation Season has begun. You're pretty much maximizing your chances of conceiving as it is.

Sperm count home testing kits

You knew it was only a matter of time before some enterprising company brought a home sperm test kit to market. Well, that day arrived back in 2001, when the Food and Drug Administration approved a male fertility test that allows men to determine whether or not their sperm concentrations meet or exceed the 20 million sperm per milliliter of ejaculate the World Health Organization uses as the definition of male fertility.

While the test has proven to be about 87 percent reliable when compared to lab tests, the test is not without its critics, most of whom are quick to point out that the test only measures one dimension of male fertility. While it is capable of measuring sperm counts, it isn't able to provide information about any of the other factors that can affect male fertility: pH and white blood cell counts, speed and motility, and the size and shape of the sperm.

The test also isn't much of a bargain. For the same $40 that a guy could expect to fork over for the test, he could have a basic semen analysis done at a doctor's office. (As a point of comparison, a thorough lab workup that assesses 10 or 15 different attributes of sperm well-being costs approximately $100 — roughly two-and-a-half times as much as the home sperm count test.)

And the winner is. . .

Obviously, sperm count tests aren't attracting rave reviews from fertility experts. But how do low-tech methods like fertility awareness stack up against high-tech methods like fertility monitors?

According to an article published in the December 2002 issue of *Obstetrics and Gynecology,* you're better off placing your faith in commercial fertility monitors or in techniques that chart fertility based on changes in vaginal discharge than you are in relying on traditional methods of fertility awareness that involve monitoring basal body temperature and using menstrual calendar calculations alone. (According to the University of Utah researchers who conducted the study in question, such methods are not as reliable when it comes to predicting the fertile days before ovulation.)

Bedroom gymnastics: Positioning 101

No chapter on conception would be complete without at least a few words on sexual positioning.

As a rule of thumb, the sexual positions that enable the sperm to be deposited high up in the vagina right next to the cervix are thought to provide the best opportunity for baby-making. This is why some doctors suggest that couples who are having difficulty conceiving use the so-called missionary position for intercourse (that is, male partner on top) and that they tuck a pillow under the woman's hips to ensure that the maximum amount of semen reaches her cervix.

This position may be the most conducive to sperm placement, but it can be less than orgasm-friendly for the female partner. Although you might be tempted to forgo your own orgasm for the sake of baby-making, don't. Scientists believe that the evolutionary purpose of the female orgasm is to cause the uterus to contract, thereby causing sperm to be drawn up into the reproductive tract.

And here's another reason not to let your eagerness to conceive get in the way of your ability to enjoy yourself in bed: a single orgasm is thought to be 22 times as relaxing as the average tranquilizer. So if you're finding the process of trying to get pregnant more than a little stressful, an orgasm could very well be just what the doctor ordered.

Some doctors recommend that the female partner remain in bed for at least half an hour following intercourse to provide the sperm with the necessary window of opportunity to make their way past the cervix. Others argue that sperm are designed to make this very journey, and that they don't need this sort of reproductive head start. Our advice is to refrain from hopping out of bed right away, but not to feel obligated to watch the clock for the full 30 minutes. There's no need to be completely obsessive about things, after all. Right?!!!

> 66 I hated hearing, 'Just relax. You're trying too hard.' How can you not try hard when you want a child so badly? 99
>
> — Randa, 23, mother of one

"Trying" versus letting nature take its course

Some couples pull out the thermometers and temperature charts right away. Others prefer to give nature a chance rather than making a conscious effort to time intercourse around the woman's most fertile days.

Which route you decide to go will depend on such factors as

- your age (that is, is your biological clock ticking away nicely or is it about to go off?);

- your eagerness to start a family (that is, how important is it for you to get pregnant right away as opposed to a few months down the road?);

- your personalities (that is, are you a Type A who wants to be in control of everything or a Type B who tends to take things a little more in stride?);

- the likelihood that you or your partner might have an underlying fertility problem and consequently might need a little extra help in conceiving.

As you might expect, there are pros and cons to each alternative.

If you decide to let nature take its course, you don't have to feel obligated to make love just because the ovulation predictor kit gives you the green light. On the other hand, sheer bad luck (for example, one or the other partner working late at the office for too many nights in a row during the woman's most fertile period) could delay your efforts to conceive.

If you decide to make a conscious effort to try to conceive by planning intercourse around your most fertile days, you might manage to conceive sooner. Unfortunately, this particular approach can be hard on both your sex life and your relationship with your partner. "We had to try for a year to get our daughter," says Randa, a 23-year-old mother of one. "To say the least, trying took all the fun out of sex. Between thermometers, pillows under my hips, and reading every fertility book at Barnes and Noble, the honeymoon was over!"

> 66 Try to keep sex fun, even if you are scheduling it. Use rooms other than the bedroom, or schedule your rendezvous for an odd time of day. 99
>
> — Tracy, 31, mother of one

Suzi, a 27-year-old mother of two, also found that having "reproductive sex" rather than "recreational sex" started to take its toll on her sex life. "When I wasn't pregnant the first month, I started taking my temperature so I would be sure we were timing things as well as possible," she recalls. "It took some of the romance out of it when I would announce to my husband that it was time to 'do the deed.' He had a hard time concentrating. My suggestion is that if you do have to use ovulation predictor kits or you're taking your temperature, when you do know that it's 'the time,' consider keeping this information to yourself. Enjoy the moment. Be romantic. Seduce your husband. Don't make it such a stressful chore. Relax and have fun."

> 66 It's a good time to get creative with your sexual routines — whether that means using massage oils or props or your own fantasies. This is probably good practice for the rest of your pregnancy. There will be times in the coming months that you or your partner have a hard time getting in the mood. 99
>
> — Jennie, 30, eight months pregnant with her first child

By the way, don't make the all-too-common mistake of assuming that Herculean baby-making efforts are necessarily in order just because you've decided that you're ready to have a baby. If you and your partner regularly have sex at least three times a week, you probably won't have to do anything different when you start trying to conceive. You've already done your bit by ensuring that there's an ample quantity of sperm in your fallopian tubes, ready and waiting for an egg to pass by. You can leave the rest up to Mother Nature.

Just the facts

- There are a lot of fertility myths out there. Make sure you're clear on the real facts of life before you start trying to conceive.

- You're better off relying on commercial fertility monitors or in techniques that chart fertility based on changes in vaginal discharge than you are in relying on traditional methods of fertility awareness that involve monitoring basal body temperature and using menstrual calendar calculations alone.

- Ovulation predictor kits (OPKs) can alert you to the fact that your body has experienced an LH surge — a biological event that typically precedes ovulation by approximately 24 to 36 hours.

- Saliva ovulation tests are designed to detect the increased salt content in a woman's saliva that occurs as estrogen levels peak around the time of ovulation.

- Although the jury is still out on the issue, certain sexual positions maybe more baby friendly than others. This is one time in your life when you might want to forgo anything that requires truly extraordinary gymnastics in the bedroom in favor of the missionary position.

- There are both advantages and disadvantages to "trying" versus "letting nature take its course." The factors to consider when you're trying to decide which route to take include your age, your eagerness to start a family right away, your personality, and the likelihood that you or your partner might have an underlying fertility problem.

GET THE SCOOP ON. . .
Whether you have a fertility problem ▪ Choosing
a fertility specialist ▪ The fertility workup ▪ The
causes of infertility ▪ The types of treatments
available ▪ The stress of infertility ▪ The truth
about surrogacy ▪ The facts about adoption

When Plan A Fails

If things haven't gone according to plan and you
have not yet been able to conceive, you may feel
that you are the only person living through the
nightmare of infertility. If friends and family members seem to be able to conceive at the drop of a hat,
while you continue to try and try and try, you may
feel particularly discouraged and alone.

The fact of the matter is that there are far more
people with fertility problems than you realize. The
problem is that no one wants to talk about it.
Because many couples feel embarrassed by their
inability to conceive, the subject of infertility tends to
get brushed under the carpet. Although it's easy to
conclude that you're the only one who's having difficulty getting pregnant, chances are that someone
you know is currently going through or has gone
through a similar experience.

Consider the numbers for yourself:

- According to the American Infertility Association,
  infertility affects approximately 10 percent of
  Americans of reproductive age — approximately
  6 million men and women.

- The rate of secondary infertility (defined as the inability to conceive or carry a child after a successful earlier pregnancy) is on the rise. A recent Cornell University study found that while just 10 percent of infertility patients in the mid-1990s had been diagnosed with secondary infertility, by 2001, most fertility specialists were spending one-third of their time treating couples struggling with secondary infertility.

- According to the Centers for Disease Control and Prevention, each year approximately 1.2 million American women go for infertility-related medical appointments and, what's more, approximately 13 percent of American women report having gone for some sort of infertility consultation or treatment at some point in their lives.

In this chapter, we give you the facts about infertility. We tell you how to determine if you have a fertility problem, how to choose a fertility specialist, what to expect from your initial fertility workup, what causes infertility and how it can be treated, how to cope with the stress of infertility, and what you need to know about two other routes to parenthood: surrogacy and adoption.

Do you have a fertility problem?

If you and your partner have been having unprotected intercourse for more than a year yet still haven't managed to conceive, it's possible that you, your partner, or the two of you have some sort of fertility problem.

The American Society of Reproductive Medicine defines infertility as the inability to conceive after one year of unprotected intercourse. Although it recommends that most couples under age 35 give themselves a full year before seeking treatment, it suggests that couples over 35 as well as those who have some underlying cause of infertility (for example, endometriosis, fibroids, irregular periods, prior abortion, DES mothers, varicoceles, or significant health problems) seek the help of a specialist sooner.

Choosing a fertility specialist

If you suspect that you and your partner may have a fertility problem — or if you're a woman in a lesbian relationship or a single mother considering pregnancy — it's time to start shopping around for a fertility specialist.

You have three basic options when it comes to choosing a doctor:

- an obstetrician/gynecologist (ob/gyn) Note: Not all ob/gyns specialize in the treatment of infertility;

- a urologist (that is, a medical doctor who specializes in the treatment of disorders of the kidneys, urinary tract, bladder, and male reproductive organs);

- a reproductive endocrinologist (that is, an obstetrician/gynecologist who has completed extra training in the medical and surgical treatments of reproductive disorders).

You'll find a list of questions you'll want to ask a prospective fertility specialist in Checklist 4.1.

Checklist 4.1. Finding the Right Specialist

_____ What percentage of your practice focuses on the treatment of infertility?

_____ Are you board-certified in reproductive endocrinology?

_____ What types of treatments do you provide? Do you conduct the full range of infertility tests and treatments yourself, or will you need to refer us to other specialists?

_____ What are the fees for those treatments? What percentage of these fees is my health insurance plan likely to cover?

_____ What are your success rates for couples with our type of fertility problem? Does that rate refer to the number of pregnancies achieved or the number of live births?

_____ Will you be available to answer our questions by phone, or will we need to come in and set up an appointment whenever we have any concerns?

_____ Will our questions be answered by you or another person?

_____ How would you react if, at any point in our treatment, we decided that we wanted to get a second opinion?

Watch Out!

If you or your partner is out of town a lot on work-related matters, it could take you a little longer than average to conceive. The reason is simple: It's hard to get the egg and the sperm to meet if you're on two different continents. Be sure to take these absences into account when you're calculating the length of time you've been trying to conceive. Otherwise, you could find yourself embarking on a series of invasive and costly fertility treatments when you don't really have a fertility problem.

Now let's consider what types of answers may indicate that you've found the right specialist.

What percentage of your practice focuses on the treatment of infertility?

Look for a specialist whose practice focuses on the treatment of infertility. Wherever possible, choose specialists who are associated with reputable university medical schools or teaching hospitals, since they are most likely to be on top of the latest developments in the field. If you do decide to go this route, however, make sure that you're comfortable with the "team approach" to treatment. You're likely to encounter an ever-changing parade of medical students and physicians-in-training.

Are you board-certified in reproductive endocrinology?

Since many ob/gyns treat infertility and their expertise varies widely, it will probably be difficult for you to assess the ob/gyn's qualifications. If a specialist has been certified in reproductive endocrinology by the American Board of Obstetrics and Gynecology, you can be certain that this physician has the training and expertise to deal with most, if not all, of your fertility treatment needs.

What types of treatments do you provide?

There are an unbelievable number of fertility treatments available: drug therapy, surgery, and an ever-growing number of methods of assisted reproduction. (We'll be discussing some of these so-called "assisted reproductive technologies" — or ART — later on in this chapter.) Make sure you're clear from the outset which types of procedures this particular specialist provides — and which he doesn't. Also ask him if he conducts the full range of infertility tests and treatments himself, or will he need to refer you to other specialists. Otherwise, you could find yourself having to hop from one doctor to another over the course of your treatment.

Because you're already comfortable with your obstetrician/gynecologist, he's probably as good a starting point as any. Depending on his experience and expertise, you may, in fact, be able to undergo the majority of tests and treatments for infertility while still under his care.

What are the fees for those treatments?

Also: What percentage of these fees is my health insurance plan likely to cover? Although you'll have to check your plan brochure's list of covered services — or, to be sure, call your health insurer directly to get the specifics on coverage — the specialist who you're considering should be able to give you a rough idea of the types of services that most patients are required to pay for out of their own pockets.

 Watch Out!

The expertise of general obstetrician-gynecologists varies widely when it comes to infertility. Unfortunately, some doctors fail to either recognize or admit to their own limitations. If your doctor doesn't seem to have a clear idea of what may be causing your fertility problems, perhaps it's time to get a second opinion. Your biological clock is ticking. Don't let anyone waste your valuable time.

What are your success rates for couples with our type of fertility problem?

Also: Does that rate refer to the number of pregnancies achieved or the number of live births? There is a lot of double-speak when it comes to success rates for fertility treatments. Some fertility specialists consider the achievement of pregnancy to be a measure of success — whether that pregnancy results in a live birth or not. That's why it's important to make sure that you and the specialist are speaking the same language when it comes to the concept of success.

Will you be available to answer our questions by phone?

Make sure that the specialist or another member of the medical team will be available to speak with you by phone or meet with you in person if you experience unusual side effects to any treatments or have any questions or concerns.

Will our questions be answered by you or another person?

Make sure that your questions will be answered by the specialist himself, or at the very least, by an equally qualified person. You'll want to find out in advance if you are going to be dealing with the physician himself or a nurse or other staff member when you have questions. Some practices have qualified nurses who can address many of your concerns adequately, but others rely on receptionists to relay answers from the busy physician — a process that can make it cumbersome to obtain answers to any follow-up questions.

 Bright Idea

Ask the specialist to give you the billing code and diagnostic code for any procedures you may require. That way, you can find out in advance which ones are covered by your health insurance plan — and which ones aren't.

How would you react if we wanted to get a second opinion?

Look for a specialist who will not be threatened by your need to research your options thoroughly, and who will be willing to discuss in advance how your desire to obtain a second opinion will be handled, should it arise.

If you need some help in tracking down a doctor who specializes in infertility, contact RESOLVE Inc., 1310 Broadway, Somerville, MA 02144, phone 888-623-0744, e-mail info@resolve. org; Web: www.resolve.org; or the American Society for Reproductive Medicine, 1209 Montgomery Highway, Birmingham, AL 35216-2809, phone 205-978-5000, e-mail: asrm@asrm.org, Web: www. asrm.org. RESOLVE can put you in touch with gynecologists who have additional training in infertility, reproductive endocrinologists, and urologists who specialize in male factor infertility. The American Society for Reproductive Medicine can put you in touch with one of its members who is in practice in your area.

> ❝I experienced a lot of stress while we were trying to conceive. I felt abnormal. . . . I cried frequently when I learned of a friend or acquaintance who was expecting, and it seemed that everywhere I went there were tons of women who were either pregnant or carrying newborns around.❞
>
> — Christy, 25, former infertility patient, now four months pregnant with her first child

The infertility workup

An infertility evaluation is designed to answer four basic questions:

- Is the female ovulating regularly?
- Is the male producing healthy, viable sperm?
- Are the egg and the sperm able to unite and develop normally?

- Is anything preventing the fertilized egg from implanting and developing properly?

Because it's almost impossible to gather all this information in a single session, you will likely to be asked to come for a series of appointments, typically two or more.

During your initial visit, the doctor will take a medical history of both you and your partner. Because you might not have been entirely open with your partner about details of your sexual history, these histories can be taken separately. It's important to level with the doctor and give him information that could be helpful in making a diagnosis: that is, whether you have been treated for an STD (sexually transmitted disease) or had an abortion. If you don't want the doctor to inadvertently share this information with your partner when he is meeting with the two of you together, be sure to let him know that what you have told him is, in fact, privileged information. Your doctor will then conduct a detailed physical examination. The results of that examination and the medical history will help to determine what comes next.

If your doctor recommends further testing, noninvasive tests such as bloodwork for you and a semen analysis for your partner will be the likely first steps. There is, after all, little point in subjecting the female partner to surgical investigations if the male partner is, in fact, sterile or what is referred to as "subfertile." If the male partner's test comes back abnormal, a referral to a urologist usually follows. If the semen analysis is normal, a series of tests is then generally performed on the female partner. Here's what you and your partner can expect from a typical fertility workup.

The female partner's infertility workup

Although the fertility workup includes many of the same components as the preconception checkup, it touches on some new areas as well.

Medical history

The specialist will start by taking a detailed medical history that focuses on

- your menstrual history (for example, the age at which you started menstruating, the length of your cycles, your pattern of bleeding, whether you suffer or have suffered from either endometriosis or pelvic inflammatory disease, whether you've had any previous pregnancies including those that resulted in miscarriages or abortions, and whether there's a family history of reproductive difficulties in your family);

- your sexual history (for example, what type of contraception you were using before you started trying to conceive, how long you've been trying, how you've been timing intercourse, whether you've had a large number of sexual partners in the past, and whether you and your partner are using sexual techniques or practices [for example, using lubricants or douching after intercourse] or experiencing sexual difficulties [for example, premature ejaculation or inadequate penetration] that may not be conducive to fertilization);

- your lifestyle (for example, whether you smoke or drink heavily; whether you suffer from any eating disorders such as anorexia or bulimia; whether you exercise heavily);

 Watch Out!

Exercising to excess can take its toll on your fertility. Studies have shown that compulsive overexercise (for example, running or jogging long distances every day) can stimulate the release of endorphins that can interfere with the normal production of FSH and LH. This can result in a condition known as luteal phase deficiency — a hormone imbalance that can interfere with embryo implanatation and increase the odds of a first-trimester miscarriage. This is definitely one of those situations where you *can* get too much of a good thing.

Bright Idea

If your doctor orders baseline testing for follicle stimulating hormone (FSH) and lutenizing hormone (LH), try to schedule your initial appointment during the first week of your cycle so that you don't have to wait until the following cycle to do the necessary blood work or start treatment.

- your general health (for example, whether you are taking any prescribed or over-the-counter medications, whether you have had any major illnesses in the past, and whether you have had any surgery that might have affected your fertility).

Your doctor will also ask you to share any information you have about your mother's reproductive history, including

- how long it took her to conceive her first child;
- whether she had any miscarriages (and, if so, how many);
- whether she ever experienced an ectopic pregnancy;
- whether she suffered from menstrual irregularities or severe cramping;
- at what age she started menstruating and at what age she started menopause;
- whether she ever took DES to prevent miscarriage.

The answers to these questions may help to shed some light on your current reproductive difficulties.

Physical examination

Once the doctor has gathered information about your medical history, she will conduct a detailed physical examination. She will

- note your general health and physical appearance;
- record your height, weight, and blood pressure;
- check the results of a urinalysis test;

- listen to your heart and lungs with a stethoscope;

- note secondary sex characteristics such as breast development, fat distribution, and hair growth around your nipples, on your face, and on your abdomen;

- feel your thyroid gland to see if it is enlarged or of abnormal consistency;

- examine your breasts and squeeze your nipples to see if a milky discharge is extruded;

- check your abdomen by applying pressure and feeling the different areas to check for lumps and painful spots or growths such as uterine fibroids;

- examine your vagina and outer genital organs for structural problems, as well as unusual sores or infections;

- examine your cervix and vaginal walls, looking for signs of infection, sores, growths, or abnormal narrowing or erosion of the cervix;

- do a Pap smear to screen for cancer and sexually transmitted diseases;

- manipulate your reproductive organs so that she can determine the size, shape, and texture of your uterus, uterine ligaments, and ovaries;

- feel for any unusual lumps, bumps, or enlargements in your reproductive organs;

- examine your rectum for any usual growths, bulging, or pocketing.

> 66 If you don't get a diagnosis from one doctor, keep looking. It took us two doctors and two years to find a doctor who recognized I had polycystic ovarian syndrome. 99
>
> — Therese, 31, mother of one

Fertility tests

If your partner's semen analysis comes back normal (see below), the doctor may order one or more tests to determine whether ovulation is taking place, whether there are adequate quantities of the hormones required to produce a healthy endometrial lining and healthy cervical mucus, and whether the reproductive tract is free of any scar tissue and anatomical defects that might otherwise prevent fertilization and implantation.

Here's a brief description of the types of tests your doctor might order:

- **Serum progesterone blood test:** This test is done to confirm that you are ovulating. Blood samples are drawn in the middle of the luteal phase (that is, on day 21 of a 28-day cycle). If the progesterone level is significantly elevated, it's likely that you're ovulating. Note: If your cycles are irregular, you may have to go in for weekly blood tests starting at day 20 and continuing until you menstruate. More often, however, your doctor will assume that your irregular cycles indicate an ovulation problem, and will order a more extensive blood test (that is, one to check a number of your hormone levels) instead.

- **Prolactin blood test:** Prolactin is a hormone that inhibits ovulation in nursing mothers. If you have excessively high levels of prolactin, you may have a benign (that is, non-cancerous) pituitary tumor, in which case your doctor may refer you for further tests, such as a CAT scan.

- **Thyroid hormone blood test:** Abnormal amounts of thyroid hormone can indicate that you have problems with your thyroid. Women with underactive thyroid glands (hypothyroidism) are prone to menstrual and ovulatory disorders. Those with overactive thyroids (hyperthyroidism) have more variable menstrual patterns but can become seriously ill if the condition is not recognized and treated during pregnancy.

- **Blood tests for other reproductive hormones:** Depending on the results of your medical history and your physical examination (your degree of menstrual irregularity, if any, or any problems with excessive body hair growth, for example), your doctor may need to obtain specific hormone levels to uncover a variety of endocrinologic conditions. This may involve testing at specific times of the cycle or testing after receiving certain medications.

- **Hysterosalpingogram (HSG):** A hysterosalpingogram is used to determine whether any damage has occurred to your fallopian tubes. It involves filling your reproductive tract with a special type of dye that shows up on X-rays. The test — which is conducted during the follicular phase — involves inserting dye into your uterus through a tube that is placed through your cervix. If one or both of your tubes are blocked, the dye will outline where the obstruction lies. If only one tube appears to be blocked, it may simply be due to the fact that the open tube provided the pathway of least resistance to the dye. (Pregnancy rates aren't very different between women whose HSGs show one tube open to the passage of dye as opposed to both tubes.) An HSG can also be useful in identifying the locations of any scarring or growths such as fibroids in your uterus (see following). Some women — particularly those with blocked tubes — find this procedure to be quite painful, so you might want to talk with your doctor about the advisability of taking a pain medication prior to the procedure. Note: The value of HSG as a diagnostic tool is clear. What is more controversial is whether the procedure can actually enhance fertility. There has long been an anecdotal claim among doctors treating infertile patients that there is a blip in the fertility curve in the months following HSG. Studies have demonstrated, however, that this enhancement is seen only with the use of oil-based dyes and not with water-soluble dyes.

Watch Out!

If you have a history of pelvic infection, pelvic surgery, or pelvic tenderness, you may be at risk of developing an infection after the HSG. Ask your doctor if it would be advisable for you to take a course of antibiotics before you go in for the procedure.

- **Endometrial biopsy:** An endometrial biopsy can confirm whether you're ovulating and indicate whether your endometrial tissue is sufficiently hospitable to allow a fertilized egg to implant. The biopsy is taken within several days of when you are expected to start menstruating. The doctor inserts a speculum in your vagina and cleanses your cervix, and then a tissue sample is removed from the uterine lining through a combination of suction and gentle scraping. If you're concerned that this procedure may cause a miscarriage in the event that you have managed to conceive, you may find it reassuring to know that the odds of having an endometrial biopsy cause a miscarriage are extremely small. If you are worried about this possibility, you might choose to use some sort of contraceptive during the cycle in which the endometrial biopsy will be taken or plan to undergo a sensitive blood pregnancy test the day before the procedure to determine whether you are, in fact, pregnant.

- **Laparoscopy:** Like an HSG, a laparoscopy is a test designed to detect obstructions in your fallopian tubes. It's considerably more high-tech and risky than an HSG, however, and can provide more detailed information. The test involves inserting a fiber-optic scope into your abdomen to look for damage caused by endometriosis, pelvic inflammatory disease, or adhesions from any pelvic surgery, and to look for physical evidence that you are ovulating. You need to go under general anesthetic to have the procedure, and you may experience some soreness in your abdomen and shoulders afterward. Note: If your doctor suggests that you have a D & C done at the same time as your laparoscopy as part of your infertility workup, get a second opinion. Studies have shown that such D & C procedures provide no more information than what can be obtained through a less-expensive and less-hazardous endometrial biopsy. You should also be prepared to put the brakes on if your doctor wants you to undergo a laparoscopy right away: As a rule of thumb, you should be prepared to wait for six months after your HSG — assuming, of course, that it was normal — so that you can take advantage of the fertility-enhancing effects of HSG. Obviously, if your doctor suspects that you have endometriosis or significant pelvic adhesions — or if you are over 40 — a waiting period may not make sense.

■ **Hysteroscopy:** A hysteroscopy also involves inserting a fiber-optic scope into the body, but in this case, it is inserted into the uterus through the cervix. It is used to detect abnormal growths or anatomical defects in your uterus when your HSG suggests that these may play a role in your fertility problems. (We'll be discussing these problems elsewhere in this chapter.)

 Bright Idea

If you're scheduled to undergo an endometrial biopsy, take some Tylenol or ibuprofen about 45 minutes before the test, and plan to have someone available to drive you home afterward just in case you don't feel up to driving yourself. Because the biopsy can be momentarily painful, you may experience a brief bout of nausea and dizziness — not enough to debilitate you by any means, but enough to make you feel rather crummy.

- **Postcoital test:** The postcoital test is used to assess what happens once the sperm make it inside the vagina. You are asked to have sexual intercourse just before you expect to ovulate (when your cervical mucus is at its best) and to show up at your doctor's office at a designated time some 2 to 16 hours later. The doctor then uses a syringe or pipette to extract at least two samples of cervical mucus from the cervical canal, and examines it under a microscope to determine how many sperm are alive and swimming. The test can show whether your mucus is inhospitable to your partner's sperm; it can also suggest whether there are antibodies in either your body or your partner's body that are interfering with sperm production or killing sperm; and whether the root of the problem is the fact that sperm is not being deposited closely enough to the cervix (as can be the case if the male partner experiences premature ejaculation). As you might expect, many couples dislike having to have sexual intercourse upon demand and then rush off to the laboratory. That's why many doctors encourage couples to make love the night before and then come into the laboratory the next morning. Note: It's possible to fail the postcoital test because you've inadvertently missed your most fertile period (that is, the days prior to ovulation when your cervical mucus is most abundant). If you fail the postcoital test, you will likely be asked to repeat it to ensure that the problem lies with you and your partner, not with the timing.

 Bright Idea

Use an ovulation predictor kit to time your postcoital test. You will ensure that it is the optimal time for the test, and you just might find yourself pregnant as a result.

- **Ultrasound:** Ultrasound is used during the basic infertility evaluation only if the internal or pelvic exam is inconclusive or significant abnormalities are suspected. Sometimes a saline solution is injected into the uterus in order to get a better look at the uterine interior, where problems such as polyps (an overgrowth of tissue that is similar to a wart or skin tag) and fibroids (noncancerous tumors of the uterine muscle) may be seen. When this is done, the procedure is known as sonohysterography or hysterosonography.

The male partner's infertility workup

If your doctor feels that your partner may have a problem with his reproductive functioning, she will refer him to a urologist, ideally one who has particular experience and expertise with fertility-related issues. The urologist will then take a detailed medical history, paying particular attention to

- **his sexual and developmental background** (whether both of his testicles were descended into his scrotum when he was born, at what age he went through puberty, how many partners he's had, whether he has had any problem with impotence or ejaculatory problems, whether he has ever fathered a child with someone else, whether he's ever been treated for a sexually transmitted disease, etc.);

- **his lifestyle** (whether he smokes cigarettes or marijuana, whether he takes frequent saunas or hot tubs, whether he has gained or lost more than 20 pounds recently, etc.);

- **his general health** (whether he has been sick or had a fever in the past three months, whether he has ever had the mumps [can result in inflammation of the testes], whether he has had any surgery to the pelvic area, whether he is taking any medications that could be interfering with his fertility, etc.).

Once the urologist is finished asking the male partner a series of questions, he will conduct the physical examination. He will

- note the male partner's general appearance, paying particular attention to such secondary sex characteristics as facial, chest, and pubic hair; deepness of voice; and physical build;

- record his height and weight;

- note whether he has fat deposits around his breasts (that is, gynecomastia);

- check his blood pressure;

- listen to his chest;

- check his urine;

- check his reflexes;

- examine his head and neck, and check his thyroid for enlargement;

- examine his penis (check the location of the opening of the urethra, note any discharge, investigate any tenderness or unusual firmness, and so on);

- examine both of his testes, noting both their size and their firmness;

- check the epididymis for tenderness or swelling that could indicate an infection;

- search for varicoceles around the testes (similar to varicose veins);

- palpate the prostate and seminal vesicles while he is sitting and then check the prostate gland for any swelling or inflammation by inserting a gloved finger into his rectum;

- check to ensure that he has full sensation throughout his external genital area.

Once the physical checkup has been conducted, the man will be asked to provide a sample of semen, which will then be

analyzed in the lab. Because many men feel uncomfortable producing this sample on demand in a clinical setting, most doctors
will allow the man to collect the sample at home and then bring
it into the lab. He can collect the sample by masturbating or by
having intercourse using a special lubricant-free and spermi-
cide-free condom. (If the man decides to go this route, he
should ask the doctor to recommend a specific brand of condom. What's more, he should make a point of telling the lab
technician how the sample was collected because some of the
sample will inevitably be lost as it is poured into the specimen
jar — something that could inadvertently skew the results of
the test.)

To ensure that the semen analysis provides accurate information about the man's fertility, the man should

- abstain from ejaculating during the two to three days prior
  to giving the sample,
- collect the sample in a clean container,
- keep the sample at body temperature,
- deliver it to a designated lab within one hour of collection.

Once the sample has been received at the lab, it will be subjected to a number of different tests. Here are the major ones:

- **Coagulation and liquification:** If a man's semen doesn't
  coagulate at the time of ejaculation, there could be an
  underlying problem with the seminal vesicles. If it doesn't
  reliquify (that is, turn back into liquid approximately
  30 minutes after ejaculation), there could be a problem
  with the man's prostate.

 Watch Out!

Make sure that the technician at the lab knows that you're dropping off a sample of semen, not urine. The test results won't be accurate if the sample is
allowed to sit around for longer than an hour because the sperm begin to
deteriorate rather quickly.

- **Color and appearance:** Semen should be whitish-grey upon ejaculation, and translucent once it has had the chance to reliquify (something that happens approximately 30 minutes later). A yellow hue can indicate infection. A reddish or brownish tinge may indicate the presence of blood.

- **Odor:** An unpleasant odor may indicate infection. A total absence of odor can indicate a prostate problem.

- **Volume:** The normal amount of ejaculate is 2 to 5 milliliters (that is, one-half to a full teaspoonful). If there's too little semen, it's possible that some of the semen has been ejaculated backward into the bladder, that the seminal vesicles are missing, that there's an obstruction in a duct, that there's a problem with semen production, or that the man has ejaculated too frequently. Too much semen can indicate a problem caused by overactivity of the seminal or prostate glands — a condition that can affect the quality or motility of the sperm.

- **pH:** Normal semen is just slightly alkaline, ranging between 7.2 and 7.8. If the pH level is too high or too low, it's possible that the prostate or seminal vesicles are infected or inflamed.

- **Viscosity:** If the sample is too thick and sticky, an infection may be suspected, in which case antibiotics may be prescribed.

- **Sperm concentration:** The average sperm count for fertile men is anywhere between 40 and 120 million per milliliter. The World Health Organization (WHO) defines a normal sperm concentration as 20 million/mL or more. There is substantial variation between lab technicians' reading of the same semen specimen and also from one semen sample to the next. As a result, it is often necessary to check two or three semen samples to get a more accurate reading. Note: Sperm counts appear to be declining worldwide.

A study in 1951 revealed that only 5 percent of fertile men had sperm counts under 20 million, whereas today 20 percent to 25 percent have counts below this level. In Denmark average sperm counts went from 113 million/mL in 1940 to 66 million/mL in 1990. (Scientists believe that toxins in the environment may be to blame.) But before you panic, consider this fact: Fertility rates among couples over similar time spans have not declined to the same degree, a finding that suggests that this decreasing sperm count is not being reflected in a similarly dramatic decrease in fertility.

- **Motility:** The motility test measures the sperm's ability to swim. The lab technician estimates both the percentage of sperm that are moving (for example, 50 percent to 60 percent) and the quality of that movement (for example, on a scale of one to four, with grade two or higher being considered normal).

- **Morphology:** Although sperm can have slightly different shapes and appearances, in general, a healthy, mature sperm has an oval head, a cylindrical middle, and a long, tapering tail. If more than 50 percent of the sperm are abnormal, there may be a fertility problem.

- **Sperm antibodies:** If the sperm clump together, there could be either an infection or antibodies in the semen. Antibodies prevent the sperm from swimming, acting in much the same way as an anchor does to a boat.

- **Cultures:** The sample can be cultured and checked for bacteria and sexually transmitted diseases such as chlamydia, gonorrhea, HIV, and so on if infection is suspected.

- **White blood cells:** The presence of significant numbers of white blood cells may indicate inflammation such as prostatitis.

- **Mucus penetration:** If there are concerns about the ability of the man's sperm to make their way through his partner's cervical mucus, a mucus penetration test (sometimes called a sperm invasion test) may be performed as well. In this test, a column of cervical mucus from a cow is placed into a reservoir of sperm. The idea of the test is to see how well the sperm can make it through the mucus.

- **Crossover sperm invasion test:** This test is performed when there's reason to suspect that there's a problem with one partner or another, but it isn't clear whom. In this case, the male partner's sperm is combined with the egg of a donor female, and the female partner's egg is fertilized with semen from a donor male. The results can help to determine where the fertility problem lies.

- **Hamster egg penetration test:** Although this test sounds like something out of a bad science fiction novel, it's for real. In an egg penetration test — sometimes called a sperm penetration assay — a laboratory technician observes how well the sperm are able to penetrate a hamster egg. Although the test is not standardized from lab to lab and its usefulness is widely debated, it may help to identify sperm abnormalities not revealed by the usual measures of count, motility, and morphology in couples with unexplained infertility. It also may be useful in assessing the effects of various sperm treatments and as a preparatory step for in vitro fertilization.

If the results of the semen analysis are abnormal, the test should be repeated at least twice. Fevers, infections, and viruses can affect a man's sperm count for months. If the next round of tests comes back abnormal, he may need to undergo a sperm antibody test (to determine whether his body is producing antibodies to his own sperm), hormonal blood tests (to measure the levels of both male and female hormones in his body), and an exam to check for varicocele. Less frequently, he may need to undergo a testicular biopsy (to determine if his fertility problems are caused by a lack of sperm-generating cells in his testicles, in which case he is permanently sterile), vasography (to check the structure of his duct system and locate any obstructions), and a fructose test (to see if seminal vesicles are adding fructose to semen as they should be).

The causes of infertility

Here are some fast facts on the causes of infertility:

- Approximately 35 percent of fertility problems are caused by male problems, 35 percent by tubal and pelvic problems, 15 percent by ovulatory dysfunction, 5 percent by unusual causes such as immunological, anatomic, or thyroid problems, and 10 percent by unknown causes.

- When the problem rests with the female partner, it's likely to be caused by either the scarring of the fallopian tubes — caused by endometriosis, pelvic inflammatory disease, gonorrhea, chlamydia, and intrauterine devices (40 percent) — or irregular ovulation accompanied by poor cervical mucus (40 percent). The other 20 percent of female fertility problems result from either unexplained infertility (10 percent) or other causes (10 percent).

- Approximately 10 percent of couples experience infertility problems for which there is no obvious explanation. Nearly half of these couples will, however, go on to conceive within a three-year period.

Problems with the female partner

Two main types of fertility problems can affect the female partner: (1) hormonal and ovulation problems and (2) structural problems.

Abnormal amounts of FSH, LH, estrogen, and other related hormones can

- prevent a woman from ovulating,
- make the vaginal environment inhospitable to sperm, or
- interfere with the implantation of the fertilized egg.

Bright Idea

If you are experiencing fertility problems caused by uterine fibroids, ask your doctor if you are a good candidate for uterine fibroid embolization (UFE) — a radiology technique that cuts off the blood supply to the fibroids, causing them to shrink. A Canadian study found that a group of women who had previously been advised to have hysterectomies in order to manage their fibroid symptoms were able to become pregnant and give birth to healthy babies after undergoing UFE treatment.

Common fertility problems that fall within the category of hormonal and ovulation problems include

- **polycystic ovary syndrome** (in which the ovaries develop small cysts that interfere with ovulation and hormone production),

- **hyperprolactinemia** (in which the secretion of an excessive amount of the hormone prolactin interferes with ovulation),

- **deficiencies in gonadotropin-releasing hormone** (the hormone responsible for triggering the release of FSH and LH from the pituitary gland),

- **a luteal phase deficiency** (when insufficient levels of progesterone prevent the fertilized egg from implanting properly).

Structural problems are also a cause of infertility in the female partner. In order for conception and implantation to occur, both the uterus and the fallopian tubes must be in good working order.

If you have experienced an ectopic pregnancy, have had a surgical procedure that could have damaged your tubes, or have had an infection such as pelvic inflammatory disease or a sexually transmitted disease, your tubes could be damaged.

Similarly, if you were born with a congenital uterine abnormality (for example, septum) or have developed adhesions (bands of scar tissue), polyps, fibroids (noncancerous tumors of the uterine muscle), or endometriosis (a disease in which tissue normally found in the uterine lining grows on nearby surfaces, including the fallopian tubes, ovaries, and inside of the abdomen), your fertility could be similarly compromised.

Problems with the male partner

Various problems can impair fertility in the male partner. Here are some of the most common causes of male infertility:

- **Undescended testicles:** One out of every 200 baby boys is born with one or more undescended testicles. The condition can be treated with either hormone therapy or micro-surgery before the child is two. If, however, the condition is not treated, sterility can result.

- **Varicocele:** A varicocele is a varicose vein in the spermatic cord. It impairs fertility by increasing the amount of blood circulation to the area, and consequently the temperature, a situation that can kill off sperm.

- **Medications:** Certain medications have been proven to affect fertility. These include corticosteriods (anti-inflammatory agents used to treat ailments including aller-gies, arthritis, asthma, skin disorders, and chronic athletic injuries such as tennis elbow), certain antidepressants and antihypertension drugs, large doses of aspirin, 6-mercaptopurine (used in the treatment of inflammatory bowel disease), and drugs used in chemotherapy. These drugs can affect libido, reduce sperm production, destroy normal DNA production, and alter the hormonal balance, all of which can affect fertility.

- **Sexual problems:** Impotence, premature ejaculation, inability to ejaculate, and sexual problems that restrict full penetration are all problems that can prevent a couple from conceiving.

- **Hypospadias:** Hypospadias is a congenital anomaly in which the urethral opening is found on the underside rather than the tip of the penis. It causes the ejaculate to be deposited too low in the vagina to facilitate conception.

Watch Out!

Certain types of herbal products may be harmful to sperm. One high-profile study indicated that would-be fathers would do well to steer clear of St. John's wort, ginkgo biloba, and echinacea while they are trying to help their partners to conceive. Not everyone agreed with the study methodology, however, so there's definitely a need for further research in this area. In the meantime, however, you might want to err on the side of caution and stop using as many herbal products as possible until your fertility problems have been resolved. If nothing else, doing so will help to rule out one possible cause of your reproductive difficulties.

- **Retrograde ejaculation:** Retrograde ejaculation is a neurological problem that causes the male partner to ejaculate backward into his bladder rather than forward out through the urethra. It is caused by poor neurological functioning in the nerves that control the muscle at the base of the bladder — a muscle that is supposed to block passage to the bladder during ejaculation. It can be seen in rare, severe cases of diabetes, with some neurologic disorders, and as a complication following prostate surgery.

- **Hormonal problems:** Low sperm counts can result when the male partner's pituitary, thyroid, or adrenal glands are not functioning properly.

- **Immunological problems:** When antibodies in a man's body attack his own sperm, a low sperm count can result.

- **Testicular failure:** Testicular failure occurs when semen is produced but contains no sperm. It can be caused by a blow to the testes, exposure to the mumps, or a birth defect.

Fertility treatments

An ever-growing number of fertility treatments are available today: everything from hormone and drug therapy to surgery to the most high-tech conception procedures imaginable.

Let's briefly consider "traditional" fertility treatments for both the female and the male partner, and then take a peek inside the Brave New World of assisted reproduction.

Treatments for female infertility

As you know, female infertility can be caused by two basic types of conditions:

1. hormonal and ovulation problems, and,
2. structural problems.

These conditions can be treated through drug or hormone therapy and surgery.

Drug and hormone therapy

Drug and hormone therapy is used to treat such conditions as

- polycystic ovary disease
- elevated levels of prolactin (the hormone that inhibits ovulation in breastfeeding women)
- an excess of adrenal androgens (male-type hormones)
- amenorrhea (lack of menstruation)
- anovulation (lack of ovulation) or oligo-ovulation (infrequent ovulation)
- pituitary failure
- endometriosis
- certain glandular disorders
- premature menopause

Moneysaver

Certain pharmaceutical companies have programs in place to help couples experiencing genuine financial hardship. Be sure to ask your doctor if he knows of any such programs for which you might qualify.

Watch Out!

If you experience severe abdominal pain during a cycle in which you are using fertility drugs, contact your doctor immediately. You could be experiencing hyperstimulation syndrome — a condition in which the ovaries become enlarged, causing lower abdominal pain and distention, nausea, vomiting, diarrhea, weight gain, cardiovascular and pulmonary disturbances, damage to the ovaries, and even death. Hospitalization may be required.

Clomid

Clomiphene citrate (Clomid) is one of the most commonly prescribed fertility drugs. Though usually used to stimulate ovulation in women with highly irregular, nonovulatory cycles, it also is frequently used in cases of luteal phase deficiency (as an alternative to progesterone supplementation) or in cases of unexplained infertility (to give the ovaries a slight "boost" and tip the scales in favor of conception).

Women using the drug typically take Clomid for five consecutive days starting anywhere from day three to day five of their cycle.

Clomid causes ovulation in approximately 75 percent of women who take the drug, but only about 35 percent to 40 percent actually become pregnant and carry a baby to term. This has been commonly attributed to adverse effects of Clomid on the uterine lining, cervical mucus, or the ovaries' ability to produce progesterone, but, in fact, it is more likely due to either other causes of infertility or a lack of persistence. Pregnancy rates in patients who ovulate while taking Clomid are the same per cycle and cumulatively as those of fertile patients. In other words, about 60 percent to 75 percent are pregnant within six months of cumulative treatment if no other infertility factors are present.

Possible side effects of the drug include hot flashes, bloating, midcycle pain or other abdominal discomfort due to the stimulation of the ovaries, breast tenderness, nausea, dizziness,

headaches, depression, increased anxiety, insomnia, and tired-
ness. There is also an increased chance of multiple birth:
women who take the drug are five times more likely to conceive
multiple fetuses, the vast majority of which are twins.

Treatment with Clomid is relatively inexpensive and usually
does not require significant monitoring with blood tests and
ultrasound.

Pergonal/ Human Menopausal Gonadotropins

Another widely used fertility drug — Pergonal — consists of
purified FSH and LH obtained from the urine of post-
menopausal women. It is used to stimulate the development of
follicles in the ovaries. Pergonal is used when anovulatory
women don't respond to Clomid or when there are reasons to
induce the ovulation of multiple eggs, such as when used in
assisted reproductive technologies and as an adjunct to artificial
insemination in cases of unexplained infertility (see following).

Pergonal is injected daily until the follicles reach an opti-
mum size, at which point an injection of human chorionic
gonadotropin (hCG) is given to trigger ovulation. Women who
take the drug must be monitored carefully to ensure that hyperstimulation does not occur. Other side effects include pain,
rash, or swelling at the injection site. About 20 percent of
women who take Pergonal will have a multiple birth.

Other fertility medications

While Clomid and Pergonal are perhaps the most commonly
used fertility medications, they aren't the only drugs used to
treat infertility.

Newer alternatives to Pergonal consist of purified FSH and
genetically engineered FSH, both of which can make the treatment of ovulatory disorders safer, more convenient, and
cheaper. (Treatment with Pergonal may cost upward of $1,500
per cycle for the drugs alone, not to mention the considerable
costs of frequent blood tests and ultrasound exams.)

Other drugs commonly used to treat infertility in women are bromocriptine (Parlodel), a drug that suppresses the pituitary gland's production of prolactin; gonadotropin-releasing hormone (GnRH), which induces ovulation; and Lupron, a drug that enhances the response to Pergonal in selected patients, and is also commonly used to treat endometriosis either instead of or in addition to surgery. A midcycle injection of human chorionic gonadotropin (hCG) is often used in conjunction with human menopausal gonadotropins and clomiphene citrate. For women with polycystic ovary disease and those who are found to be borderline insulin diabetic or "insulin resistant," metformin (Glucophage) is often used to help induce ovulatory cycles.

Surgical treatment

Surgery — the second method of treating infertility in women — is used to repair structural problems and damage to the female reproductive system. It is used to address fertility problems caused by

- pelvic inflammatory disease,
- endometriosis,
- tubal damage and adhesions,
- fibroids,
- endometrial polyps,
- Asherman's Syndrome (when bands of scar tissue in a woman's uterus join one part of the endometrium to another, in some cases cementing the walls together),
- congenital uterine abnormalities (for example, a double uterus, bicornuate uterus, septate uterus, and rudimentary horns),
- uterine abnormalities in DES daughters (that is, daughters of women who took diethylstilbestrol during their pregnancies).

Repairs can often be made to the fallopian tubes, the uterus, and the other female sex organs to increase a woman's chances of conceiving and carrying a baby to term.

Just a few words of caution before we conclude our discussion of surgical solutions to infertility. Some gynecologists — particularly those who don't specialize in the treatment of infertility — are quick to suggest surgery for conditions that are abnormal, but not necessarily the cause of infertility. Three classic cases of this overzealousness are surgeries for pelvic adhesions, fibroids, and mild endometriosis. Not only are some of these procedures unnecessary and inherently risky, but in some cases, they can create additional adhesions, which can add to your fertility problems. Adhesion prevention is the creed of the true infertility specialist, and he will employ surgical techniques to minimize adhesion formation. So before you check yourself into the hospital and sign that patient consent form, make sure you understand what your doctor is doing — and why.

Treatments for male infertility

As you know from our earlier discussions, male infertility problems are also caused by a number of structural and hormonal problems. These conditions can be treated through drug and hormone therapy and surgery.

- **Drug and hormone therapy:** Drug therapy can be used to correct such conditions as antibody problems, retrograde ejaculation, infections of the prostate or seminal vesicle, and low sperm counts. Hormone therapy can be used to treat such conditions as hypogonadotropic hypogonadism (a condition in which low levels of FSH and LH result in a lack of normal testicular function and a lack of masculine characteristics), congenital adrenal hyperplasia (a lack of an enzyme required for the production of male hormones), and hyperprolactinemia (a condition in which there is too much prolactin in the blood).

- **Surgery:** Conditions such as varicoceles, obstructions in the epididymis, and blockages in the ejaculatory ducts can be repaired through surgery.

- **Artificial insemination:** Artificial insemination (AI) refers to the introduction of sperm into the female reproductive tract by means other than sexual intercourse. It can be either intracervical (which can use freshly ejaculated semen) or intrauterine (which requires a sperm-washing process prior to depositing sperm into the uterus). AI is typically used when there are problems delivering adequate numbers of sperm high into the vagina (as is the case with premature ejaculation or other ejaculatory dysfunction, hypospadias, and impotence); when there are problems with mucus abnormalities or marginal sperm counts or motility (in which case intrauterine insemination [IUI] may be a better option); in cases of unexplained infertility (where it may be combined with fertility drugs); or in situations when a woman chooses to initiate a pregnancy without a male partner and requires donor insemination.

The facts about assisted reproductive technologies

Now we move into the Brave New World of modern fertility treatment — the world of assisted reproductive technologies (ART). A few decades ago, technologies such as in vitro fertilization (IVF), Gamete Intrafallopian Transfer (GIFT), and Zygote Intrafallopian Transfer (ZIFT) were simply the stuff of which science fiction novels were made.

Today, they're a fact of life for a growing number of American families. According to the Centers for Disease Control and Prevention, the number of ART cycles performed in the United States increased by 54 percent between 1996 and 2000.

The success rates for ART procedures have also improved during that time: the percentage of ART cycles resulting in live births increased from 22.5 percent in 1996 to 25.3 percent in 2000.

Watch Out!

Fertility centers measure success in a number of different ways: pregnancy per cycle rates, live birth per egg retrieval rates, live birth per embryo transfer rates, and live birth per cycle rates. The last statistic — the so-called "take-home baby rate" — is the most meaningful one to couples who are trying to start families. It shows the percentage of cycles started that have resulted in a live birth.

The bottom line

According to the 2000 Assisted Reproductive Technology Success Rates study conducted by the Centers for Disease Control and Prevention, 99,639 cycles of ART were carried out in the United States in 2000. These cycles resulted in 19,042 live births (that is, deliveries in which at least one infant is born alive).

While thousands of American couples end up with story-book happy endings to their baby-making dreams each year as a result of ART treatments, it's important to go into ART with your eyes wide open. Here are some of the key facts that you'll want to keep in mind when you're trying to decide whether or not ART is the right choice for you:

- Assisted reproductive technologies are more likely to be successful on younger women than on older women. While the live birth rate for women under the age of 35 undergoing ART procedures is 33 percent, that rate drops to just 4 percent for women over the age of 42. (See Table 4.1 at the end of this list.)

- Couples who conceive through ART are more likely to become pregnant with multiples. In 2000, 35 percent of all live births resulting from ART were multiple births (that is, twins, triplets, or higher-order multiples) as compared to 3 percent in the general population. Although many infertile couples might initially be delighted at the thought of having two or more babies, multiple pregnancies are much riskier than singleton pregnancies, particularly when three or more fetuses are involved. What's more, health-care costs can go through the roof if the mother requires hospitalization during her pregnancy or the babies require weeks — if not months — of care in a neonatal intensive care unit.

- The costs of ART treatments can be prohibitive (see Table 4.2 at the end of this list). Unless you have access to exceptionally comprehensive health insurance coverage, you may find it difficult to finance ART treatments on your own.

- A Centers for Disease Control and Prevention study found that ART may increase the risk of low birthweight. The researchers found that 3 percent of low birthweight and 4 percent of very low birthweight infants born in 1997 were conceived using ART procedures — a rate that is roughly six times higher than expected, given the frequency of these procedures.

- A study conducted by Australian researchers concluded that birth defects are much more common in children conceived through ART than in other children. The researchers found that 8.6 percent of children conceived through ICSI and 9 percent of children conceived through standard IVF had been diagnosed with at least one major birth defect, as compared to 4.2 percent of children who had been conceived naturally. After the

 Bright Idea

The *Assisted Reproductive Technology Success Rates* report — which is published annually by the Centers for Disease Control and Prevention — contains details on the success rates of fertility clinics throughout the United States. You can download a copy of the report online at www.cdc.gov/nccdphp/drh/.

Watch Out!

Because the odds of ending up with a live baby can be discouragingly low, many fertility clinics offer some sort of money-back guarantee or shared-risk guarantee (in other words, the clinic picks up the tab for all or part of your treatment costs if you don't manage to conceive) to couples who don't get pregnant. Although these offers sound like a win-win venture, as with anything else, you need to read the fine print. Most of these offers don't extend to the cost of diagnostic tests or drugs, nor do they cover patients with extremely poor prognoses. So make sure you find out upfront what the guarantee does and doesn't cover.

researchers controlled for factors such as the mother's age that might have influenced the rate of birth defects, ICSI and IVF children were found to be twice as likely to be born with a birth defect as other children. Drugs taken to stimulate ovulation or to sustain the pregnancy, the ART procedure itself, and/or the underlying cause of the infertility may help to explain the increased rate of birth defects, according to the researchers.

Table 4.1. The Outcomes of ART Cycles Using Fresh, Nondonor Eggs or Embryos for Women of Various Ages

Age	Pregnancy Rate	Live Birth Rate
Under 35	38%	33%
35 to 37	32%	27%
38 to 40	25%	18%
41 to 42	16%	10%
Over 42	8%	4%

Table 4.2. ART and Other High-Tech Fertility Methods at a Glance

The Procedure	What It Involves	What It Costs	Your Odds of Success (Live Birth Rate)
In Vitro Fertilization (IVF)	An egg and sperm are combined in the lab, and the fertilized egg is then implanted in the woman's uterus.	$8,000 to $10,000 per attempt	31%
Intracyto-Plasmic Sperm Injection (ICSI)	A single sperm is injected into an egg, and the resulting zygote is transferred to the uterus. Technically speaking, ICSI is a form of IVF.	$10,500 to $12,500 per attempt	28.6%
Gamete Intrafallopian Transfer (GIFT)	Eggs and sperm are inserted directly into the fallopian tube via a laparoscope.	$8,000 to $13,000 per attempt	24.5%
Zygote Intrafallopian Transfer (ZIFT)	Eggs are fertilized in the lab, and those eggs that are successfully fertilized (zygotes) are transferred to the fallopian tube.	$10,000 to $13,000 per attempt	29.2%
Frozen Embryo Transfer (FET)	Surplus embryos from an IVF cycle are frozen and stored for future implantation in the uterus.	$500 to $1,500 per cycle	20.3%

Donor Eggs	Eggs from a donor female are fertilized with the male partner's sperm and then transferred to the infertile woman's uterus.	$9,000 per cycle	43.3% per retrieval
Intrauterine Insemination (IUI)	Fresh or frozen sperm is injected into the uterus via a catheter.	$250 to $350 per procedure	5-20%

Note: The Centers for Disease Control and Prevention define assistive reproductive technologies as "all fertility treatments in which both egg and sperm are handled." Consequently, high-tech procedures in which only sperm are handled (i.e., intrauterine or artificial insemination) or procedures in which a woman takes drugs to stimulate egg production without having any eggs removed for fertilization outside her body do not meet the CDC's official definition of assisted reproductive technologies.

Sources: 2000 Assisted Reproductive Technology Success Rates: National Summary and Fertility Clinic Reports. Atlanta: Centers for Disease Control and Prevention, 2000; "Infertility: *USA Today* Looks at Mandatory Coverage." *American Health Line*, December 19, 2001.

Why couples turn to ART

Wondering what types of fertility problems cause couples to seek out ART? According to the Centers for Disease Control and Prevention, the primary causes of infertility in couples using ART procedures in 2000 were

- **Male factor fertility problems** (defined as a low sperm count or problems with sperm function that make it difficult for a sperm to fertilize an egg under normal conditions) (18.9 percent)

- **Multiple factors — female and male** (when one or more female and male casues of infertility has been diagnosed) (17.6 percent)

- **Tubal factors** (blockages or damage to the fallopian tubes that makes it difficult for the egg to be fertilized or for an embryo to travel to the uterus) (16.1 percent)

- **Multiple factors — female** (when more than one female causes of infertility has been diagnosed) (12.5 percent)

- **Unexplained causes** (when no clear explanation for infertility has been found in either the male or female partner) (10.5 percent)

- **Endometriosis** (when tissue similar to the uterine lining grows in abnormal locations, interfering with the fertilization of the egg and/or embryo implantation) (7.8 percent)

- **Other factors** (other causes of infertility, such as immunological problems, chromosomal abnormalities, cancer chemotherapy, and serious illnesses) (5.7 percent).

- **Ovulatory dysfunction** (when the ovaries are not producing eggs normally) (5.4 percent)

- **Diminished ovarian reserve** (when the ovaries' ability to produce eggs is reduced for congenital, medical, surgical, or age-related reasons) (4.5 percent)

- **Uterine factor** (when a structural or functional disorder of the uterus interferes with fertility) (1.0 percent)

Choosing an ART program

Thinking of going the high-tech fertility route? The American Society for Reproductive Medicine recommends that couples consider such factors as cost and convenience; the quality of care; and the program's track record for success when they are evaluating an ART program.

Here are some questions you might want to ask the program director:

- What is the cost of the entire procedure, including drugs per treatment schedule and the costs of freezing, storing, and transferring embryos, and so on?

- What are the costs of cancelling a particular cycle at various stages of the process (such as before egg recovery or before embryo transfer)?

- How much time will my partner and I miss from work?

- Does the program meet the standards of the American Society for Reproductive Medicine (www.asrm.org)?

- Is the lab suitably accredited (by the College of American Pathologists, the Commission on Laboratory Accreditation, and the American Society for Reproductive Medicine)?

- How many physicians will be involved in my care, and what are their qualifications?

- Which of the following types of specialists does your clinic employ: a reproductive endocrinologist; a reproductive immunologist; an embryologist; a reproductive urologist; an andrologist; a geneticist; a genetic counselor; a social

 Watch Out!

There aren't any federal laws in place to regulate the safety or quality of donor sperm, nor are there any national standards for screening egg donors. Make sure that the clinic you deal with has appropriate health safety measures in place, and that they use best practices in collecting and handling both eggs and sperm.

worker; one or more surgeons with experience in infertility surgery, including laparoscopy, and the use of the ultrasound; an ultrasound technician or obstetrician/gynecologist with specialized training in interpreting ultrasounds; a program director (preferably a medical doctor)?

- What types of counseling and support services are provided?

- Who is available after hours to take my phone call?

- Are there any limitations concerning eligibility for your program (age, reproductive health, and so on)?

- Do you have access to donor eggs or donor sperm?

- Do you freeze embryos?

- How long has the clinic been in operation?

- How many IVF, GIFT, ZIFT, ICSI, and IUI procedures have you performed? How many live births have resulted?

- What is your rate of multiple births for the procedure I am considering?

The emotional aspects of ART

Success rates and costs aren't the only issues that couples contemplating ART have to consider. Here are some other matters you and your partner will want to discuss before choosing ART.

Fetal reduction

Because ART doesn't come cheap — according to some experts, it's not unusual for couples to spend upwards of $50,000 in their quest for a baby — some clinics make a point of introducing a large number of embryos into a woman's body in order to increase the odds of at least one of them implanting. If the clinic you choose makes a practice of doing this and a large number of those embryos implant, you and your partner could find yourselves faced with a very difficult choice: to selectively reduce (that is, abort) some of those embryos in order to sidestep the risks of a high-risk pregnancy and possibly increase your odds of walking out with a healthy baby or to continue carrying a larger number of embryos, something that increases your odds of losing some or perhaps all of your babies.

What to tell family and friends

Then there's the issue of deciding what to tell family and friends. Should you make it general knowledge that you're using ART in your quest for a baby? Or would you and your partner prefer to keep this information to yourselves? What will you tell your child as he gets older? These are all issues you need to think about now.

> 66 We discussed the many ways we could go about having a child: finding a friend, having a one-night stand, or using a sperm bank. We decided that the sperm-bank option was in the best interests of everyone. 99
>
> — Robin, 32, a lesbian whose partner is currently trying to conceive

Coping with financial worries

With certain high-tech methods of reproduction ringing in a hefty $10,000 or more per cycle, money worries can also become a major concern for couples who are pursuing other types of fertility treatment. Here are some pointers on minimizing your out-of-pocket expenses when it comes to fertility treatments:

- Find out whether insurance companies in your state are mandated to provide infertility insurance coverage. (In certain states, the legislation also extends to health insurance.) Because the laws are constantly changing — and because we don't want to be accused of practicing law without a degree! — we suggest that you do some digging on your own. You can get the latest news on state infertility insurance laws by calling your state's Insurance Commissioner's office. (Note: You may also want to touch base with your state representative to find out what fertility-related legislation may be pending in your state.)

▪ Shop around for the best-possible policy. Some policies cover a greater range of infertility-related treatments than others. If possible, ask your doctor or a friend who has been through fertility treatments to recommend a health insurance plan.

▪ Once you've settled on a policy, know your policy inside out. Find out which procedures are covered — and which ones aren't. (See Checklist 4.2 at the end of this list for some tips on what you'll want to find out.) You might start by writing to your insurance company to inquire about what types of treatments are covered, whether there's a cap on the amount of money that can be paid on an individual claim or a limit to the number of cycles of assisted reproduction you can attempt, and so on. Note: To avoid any nasty surprises down the road, be sure to submit this predetermination-of-benefits letter before you start treatment. It's the only way to know for sure what will and will not be covered.

▪ If you find yourself stuck with a lot of drug expenses, you might want to ask your doctor whether you can switch to a less-pricey generic brand of prescription drug or see if he has any pharmaceutical company samples he would be willing to pass your way; see if your company benefits package allows you to purchase drugs at a discount; or use the services of a discount pharmacy.

▪ Keep in mind that your financial worries won't necessarily end once you conceive. An article in the *New England Journal of Medicine* revealed that whereas the hospital charges for a single birth in 1991 were approximately $9,845, they were $37,947 for twins, and $109,765 for triplets. The authors of the article concluded that more attention needs to be paid to approaches to infertility that reduce the likelihood of multiple gestations.

Bright Idea

If your insurance company fails to underwrite the costs of your fertility-related treatments, ask the company to respond in writing with details explaining why your claim for coverage was denied. You may wish to use this information when registering a complaint with your state insurance commission.

Checklist 4.2. Finding Out What Your Health Insurance Plan Covers

You'll want to be clear about your health insurance coverage right from the start so that you can avoid any nasty — and costly — surprises once you've embarked on your treatment program. Going for fertility treatment is stressful enough as it is. You don't want to have to deal with financial curveballs, too. Here's what you need to find out:

_____ Whether or not your existing plan actually covers fertility treatments (Note: If your plan doesn't cover fertility treatments at all, find out whether there's another, more comprehensive plan that you could "upgrade" to and, if so, what the cost of changing plans would be.)

_____ What types of referral(s) you need from your doctor in order to guarantee that the insurance company will cover the cost of diagnosis and/or treatment

_____ Whether there's a waiting period before you can commence treatment for any preexisting infertility conditions (something that's particularly important to find out if you're thinking of switching plans)

_____ If there's an age limit for fertility treatments (and, if so, what that limit is)

_____ Whether or not a predetermination of benefits is required and how long your predetermination (or precertification) is valid

_____ What your plan does and doesn't cover (diagnostic procedures, treatment procedures, and/or drug therapy)

_____ Whether you are required to do business with specific pharmacies or whether you're free to do business with the pharmacy of your choice

(continued)

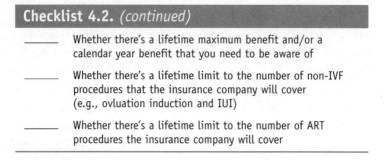

Checklist 4.2. *(continued)*

_____   Whether there's a lifetime maximum benefit and/or a calendar year benefit that you need to be aware of

_____   Whether there's a lifetime limit to the number of non-IVF procedures that the insurance company will cover (e.g., ovluation induction and IUI)

_____   Whether there's a lifetime limit to the number of ART procedures the insurance company will cover

What to do if you don't conceive

It's critical that you and your partner agree in advance about the number of cycles you're willing to try and what types of high-tech procedures you are and aren't willing to consider. Once you get involved in treatment, you can become obsessed with the idea of continuing with treatment until you end up with a baby — no matter what the physical, emotional, or financial costs may be.

Here's what writer Sharon Begley had to say about this phenomenon in an article in *Newsweek*: "Some [couples] seem trapped in their own private Vietnams: having spent $10,000 and with nary a swollen abdomen to show for it, they can't quit until they have a victory — a baby."

The problem becomes immeasurably more complex if one partner wants to continue and the other feels that it's time to call it quits. In an article in *Psychology Today* magazine, psychologist Susan McDaniel told writer Virginia Rutter why men and women often feel differently about this issue: "As much as men are invested in having children, they don't have to think about it, or perhaps be as conscious of it — because women are so focused on the problem. It makes sense, then, that . . . men will often be the ones to put on the brakes. . . . So what happens — largely because of sex roles — is [that] women become advocates of the process, and men, who may be more ambivalent, question it and wonder if it's time to stop."

Assuming that you do decide to call it quits, you'll have to grapple with another complex issue: what to do with the sperm, eggs, and embryos you and your partner have stored. Depending on the laws in your state, you might choose to donate them to another couple, have them destroyed, or continue to store them in case you have a change of heart.

If, on the other hand, the stress of infertility has taken its toll on your relationship and you and your partner decide to go your separate ways, the situation becomes even more complex. In a high-profile case that made headlines cross the country, the New York Court of Appeals ruled that five frozen embryos belonging to a divorced couple must be donated to research despite the female partner's desire to use them to have children. The reason? The man involved in the case did not wish to father any children with his former partner.

What to do if you do manage to conceive

Other emotional issues are involved, even if you do manage to conceive. Some couples using donor eggs or donor sperm have to struggle to come to terms with the fact that they weren't able to conceive naturally. Sometimes the infertile partner can have a particularly difficult time accepting the fact that someone else's egg or sperm was used to conceive his or her child.

Of course, not all couples struggle with this issue, however. Here's what Lorna, 33, has to say about her experiences with donor insemination: "We wanted a child and this was the best option for us. My husband and I chose the donor and went to all the appointments together. The clinic we chose was wonderful — very helpful and supportive. As far as we're concerned, this baby is 'all ours.' We just needed a little help with the biology!"

Some couples find that it is possible to reduce some of the stress of trying to conceive artificially if they make an effort to humanize the process as much as possible.

Couples who are attempting artificial insemination by donor sperm can often choose to do the insemination themselves at home, rather than under the bright lights of an examining table. Victoria and Dawn, a lesbian couple who are expecting their first child, decided to go this route: "We did it when we had a lot of time and weren't rushed. After the insemination, we cuddled and talked." Lorna and her husband had the procedure done at the doctor's office but managed to humanize it nonetheless: "While they did the procedure, my husband sat beside me and held my hand. He continued to do so during the resting period which followed."

Is ART the right choice for you?

Your doctor may be able to advise you about what ART may or may not be able to do for you from a medical standpoint, but you're only one who can decide whether it's the best choice for you and your partner from an emotional standpoint. Here are some questions the two of you should probably discuss *before* pursuing these types of high-tech fertility treatments:

- If you decided to proceed with a technique that uses donor sperm or eggs, would you or your partner be upset by the fact that the child is not genetically your own?

- Would you or your partner feel jealous or inadequate if a donor was able to conceive a child with one of you but the other partner wasn't?

- Would you and your partner tell your child the truth about how she was conceived, or would you try to keep it a secret?

- Would you and your partner tell friends and family the truth? What about casual acquaintances or people at work?

 Bright Idea

If your doctor prescribes fertility drugs that must be injected, ask him to train your partner to administer the shots for you. This will help cut down on the number of trips you have to make to the doctor's office.

- How many attempts would you and your partner be pre- pared to make? What would you do if one partner wanted to continue trying but the other did not?

- What would you and your partner do with any frozen sperm, eggs, or embryos you did not end up using? Donate them to another couple? Allow them to be used for genetic research? What would happen to the frozen sperm, eggs, or embryos if you and your partner separated?

- What percentage of the costs of fertility treatments, if any, would your insurance company cover? How much money would you and your partner be prepared to spend out of your own pockets?

- Are you and your partner prepared to assume the risk of having twins or other multiples? How would you cope if one or more of the babies died?

As you can see, there are a lot of complex issues to weigh before you decide to go this route. If you're having difficulty resolving these issues on your own, you might want to seek some help from a therapist who specializes in working with couples who are struggling with infertility. Your doctor may know of a therapist in your community who has developed such a spe- cialty. If not, you might want to ask other couples you know who have experienced infertility if there's someone they would recommend.

The stress of infertility

Although couples who go through ART have a lot of complex issues to deal with, they aren't the only ones who experience the stress of infertility.

Regardless of the type of fertility treatment you and your partner are receiving, you may find yourself on a roller-coaster ride that follows the pattern of your menstrual cycle: During the first part of the cycle, you are fueled by hope that this could be the cycle in which you conceive. As ovulation approaches, you may become obsessed with timing intercourse to maximize your chances of getting pregnant. Once ovulation occurs, you're left in a two-week-long holding pattern that could try the patience of a saint. You wonder if the symptoms you're experiencing are caused by PMS, whether they're due to the hormonal treatments or fertility drugs you're taking, or whether in fact you're pregnant. If your period shows up again, you may feel hopeless and depressed, wondering if you'll ever be able to conceive (or, in the case, of secondary infertility, if you'll ever conceive again).

> ❝We went to a therapist because it was so stressful. Going through fertility treatments, artificial insemination, and other procedures, we lost touch with each other.❞
>
> — Amie, 38, mother of two

Part of the stress of infertility stems from the fact that it's one area of your life over which you have little or no control. As much as you'd like to, you can't just block off some time to conceive in your PDA. (Well, actually, you can; there's just no guarantee that it will actually happen!)

Not surprisingly, those of us with Type A tendencies tend to find it particularly difficult to relinquish control over the whole business of baby-making, and may become quite depressed or discouraged as the months drag on and on.

Here are some tips on coping with the stress of infertility:

- Don't let your fertility treatments take over your entire life. Try not to lose sight of all the good things that may be happening at home and at work.

- Keep yourself healthy. Feelings of stress can be worsened if you're not sleeping well, eating properly, or exercising enough.

- Consider taking a yoga class or learning other methods of managing stress. It won't just help you relax: depending on the nature of your fertility problems, it might actually help you conceive. A study conducted at Harvard Medical

School found that women who used mind-body techniques to manage stress were more likely to become pregnant than women who did not practice such techniques: 55 percent of women practicing such techniques managed to conceive within a six-month period as opposed to just 20 percent of other women.

- Reach out for support. Consider joining a support group for couples struggling with infertility. Or find a circle of friends who will help you to weather the highs and lows of the roller-coaster ride that is infertility.

- Watch your intake of alcohol. It's not just bad for the baby you're hoping to conceive; it's also bad for you. Because alcohol is a depressant, it will only add to your feelings of depression.

- Talk about your feelings with your partner, and accept the fact that you may not always be on the same wavelength. Although you both need to have the opportunity to express all of the powerful emotions you may be feeling — hope, disappointment, excitement, frustration, guilt, and so on — it's important to realize that you may experience conflicting emotions from time to time. If this becomes a problem for you and your partner, the two of you may wish to seek the services of a therapist who can help you work through your feelings about one another and the baby you hope to conceive.

- Try to keep your sex life separate from your reproductive life. If you're finding that there's no joy left in sex, you might want to think about taking a break from trying to conceive for a cycle or two. Although it may delay your plans to have a baby, a brief time-out could help keep your relationship with your partner on track. Odd as it may sound, some infertile couples who decide to go this route make a point of using birth control during their nontrying cycles so that they don't spend the entire second half of the cycle trying to guess whether this was their lucky month.

- Try to maintain a healthy sense of optimism. A study reported in the October 2001 issue of the medical journal *Fertility and Sterility* concluded that success rates for ART procedures such as IVF or GIFT may be tied in part to levels of psychological stress. The study found that women who expressed the greatest optimism about their odds of conceiving were more likely to become pregnant.

The facts about surrogacy and adoption

Up until now, we've been focusing on the biological route to parenthood. Now we're going to zero in on two alternatives: gestational surrogacy and adoption.

Gestational surrogacy

Although most people think of the Baby M case when they think about surrogacy, the heart-wrenching custody battle fought and lost by surrogate mother Mary Beth Whitehead is far from the norm today.

Whereas the first generation of gestational surrogates were genetically related to the babies they carried — a situation that led to more than a few cases of the Baby M variety — more often than not, today's surrogates are more like human incubators than parents to the babies they carry. The reason is obvious. Advances in assisted reproduction techniques have made it possible for the so-called "gestational surrogate" or "carrier" to carry someone else's sperm and egg — either the intended couple's sperm and eggs, or a combination of donor egg and donor sperm — rather than conceiving a child with the male partner and then relinquishing parental rights to him and his partner. According to psychologist Andrea Braverman, chief psychologist at Pennsylvania Reproductive Associates, these changes to the nature of surrogacy have led to much happier outcomes for all concerned: "It is a very different psychological hurdle to navigate if you are genetically related to the child you're carrying," she told MSNBC. Because they have no genetic link to the child they are carrying, today's surrogates can tell themselves, "Hey, it's her egg and his sperm."

This is not to say that surrogacy has become a run-of-the-mill process complete with guaranteed happy endings, however. Would-be parents who choose surrogacy as their route to parenthood are still forced to confront some mind-bogglingly complex legal, financial, and psychological hurdles.

Just a couple of quick footnotes before we plunge into our discussion of these important issues related to surrogacy:

- The terms "full surrogate" and "traditional surrogate" are used interchangeably to describe situations in which the surrogate conceives and carries the child of an infertile woman's partner. This form of insemination can be either direct (that is, through intercourse) or indirect (using ART).

- The terms "partial surrogate," "gestational surrogate," and "carrier" are used to describe situations in which an egg from a woman who is unable to conceive is fertilized with her partner's sperm, and the resulting embryo is implanted into the surrogate mother's uterus.

Although we're fairly consistent with our terminology — we tend to use "traditional surrogate" and "gestational surrogate" — you're likely to find a mix of terms in other sources.

Legal hurdles

The legal status of surrogacy varies from state to state. But regardless of what state you're in, you'll need to formalize your arrangement with your surrogate by having your attorney draft a surrogacy contract which specifies

- the purpose and intent of the arrangement (that is, that you and your partner will be considered to be the child's parents at the end of the period of surrogacy);

- some guidelines regarding the selection of physicians and a counselor/mediator to resolve any disputes that may arise between you and the surrogate;

- what fees you are responsible for paying to the surrogate;

- what medical tests the surrogate must take (for example, a full prenatal blood workup, ultrasounds as required, amniocentesis if the intended parents wish to go that route, testing for HIV, and so on) and what lifestyle restrictions she must follow (for example, she will be expected to go on bed rest if her physician recommends it, and she will be expected to refrain from smoking, drinking, and taking drugs of any kind, except those specifically prescribed by her physician);

- what specific rights and responsibilities each party has under the law;

- the intended parents' and the surrogate's expectations of one another (for example, how regularly they will be in contact with one another both prior to and after the birth);

- under what terms the agreement may be terminated (for example, if the surrogate does not become pregnant within a specific period of time);

- under what terms the pregnancy may be terminated (for example, if the surrogate's life is at risk due to complications of pregnancy or if it is necessary in a multiple pregnancy);

- where and how the birth will take place (for example, what role you and your partner will play at the birth; what rights you will have in ordering medical care for the child after the birth; and so on);

- how many counseling sessions the surrogate will be required to participate in over the course of her pregnancy;

- to what extent the agreement is considered to be confidential (for example, is the surrogate free to tell other people whose child she is carrying);

- what life insurance the intended parents and the surrogate are carrying, and what would happen to the child if either or both of the intended parents were to die prior to the birth of the child.

Note: You can find a sample surrogacy agreement in "Important Documents" (www.wiley.com/go/anndouglas).

Financial hurdles

Hiring a surrogate to carry your child is quite an expensive proposition. You can expect to be approximately $70,000 poorer by the time you walk out of the hospital with a baby in your arms — assuming, of course, that you're fortunate enough to have that ultimate of happy outcomes.

Obviously, your chances of success will be determined in part by which route to surrogacy you choose — high-tech fertility methods will result in rates of success similar to those shown in Table 4.3, whereas traditional methods of conceiving will give you success rates similar to those experienced by fertile couples.

Here's a breakdown of costs, based on cost estimates posted at the Center for Surrogate Parenting and Egg Donation Inc. Website: www.creatingfamilies.com.

Table 4.3. Surrogacy: What It Costs

Legal and agency fees	
Fees to agency	$18,000
Fees paid to parents' attorney	$3,500
Fees paid to surrogate's attorney	$750

Fees paid to surrogate plus related expenses	
Surrogacy fee	$18,000
Out-of-pocket expenses	$3,000
Maternity clothes	$500
Medical expenses (initial medical and psychological screening, prenatal care, one IVF cycle)	$10,500
Medical insurance for surrogate ($200 a month for preconception period, pregnancy, and one month after birth — minimum 12 months of coverage)	$2,400

(continued)

Table 4.3 *(continued)*

Fees paid to surrogate plus related expenses

Medical co-pay and deductible	$2,500
Life insurance annual premium	$300
Lost wages for surrogate and surrogate's spouse (if surrogate is working outside the home)	$3,000
Counseling fees for surrogate	$4,850
Total	$67,300

Note: If the surrogate conceives twins, the parents can expect to pay an additional $8,000 in surrogacy fees. And if more than one IVF cycle is required to achieve a pregnancy, additional medical expenses will be incurred.

Although these costs are daunting enough in and of themselves, they often follow closely on the heels of pricey fertility treatments. That's why surrogacy continues to be an option that is open primarily to America's wealthiest families. No one else can afford it.

Emotional hurdles

Most couples find the emotional hurdles of surrogacy to be far more difficult than the legal and financial obstacles. There's the stress of finding a surrogate. (It's illegal to use an agency in some states, so would-be parents have to be extremely creative — and careful.) There's the worry that something will go wrong with the pregnancy. And then there's the biggest fear of all: that she won't be willing to give up the baby in the end.

According to the Organization of Parenting Through Surrogacy (OPTS), the last possibility is extremely unlikely: less than 1 percent of recorded surrogacy births have resulted in a custody battle. Still, it's the stuff of which nine-month-long nightmares are made, and an issue that would-be parents ignore at their own peril.

As if these issues weren't difficult enough to contend with, parents who use surrogates must also accept the fact that they may experience interpersonal conflicts with the surrogate or grow very attached to her over the course of the pregnancy. Either scenario can add to the stress of an already emotionally draining time.

Last but not least, there's the matter of bonding with a baby who's been gestating in someone else's womb — and figuring out what to tell family members, friends, and the child himself about his unconventional conception.

As you can see, surrogacy isn't an arrangement to be entered into on a whim. It's an option that needs to be researched fully. We've given you the basic facts, but you need to decide whether it's the right option for you. We've included some suggested resources for more information in the "Resource Directory" (www.wiley.com/go/anndouglas).

The facts about adoption

Adoption is an option that approximately 11 percent of infertile couples choose to pursue, but before you pick up the phone to call the domestic or international adoption agency of your choice, give some serious thought to whether adoption is right for you.

Christine Adamec, author of *Is Adoption for You?* (John Wiley & Sons, 1998), agrees that couples need to decide for themselves whether adoption is, in fact, the right choice: "Here's [a] tough issue that most people don't like to think about. Is adoption good enough for you? You may have wanted a biological child but

 Watch Out!

Make sure that you understand the difference between an open adoption (when the birth mother chooses the adoptive family) and a closed adoption (when the adoptive and birth parents never meet, and all records are sealed after the adoption is finalized). An open adoption typically allows for some contact between the child and the birth mother as the child grows up — something you may or may not be comfortable with.

couldn't have one, so you decide to adopt. . . . If you feel that what is most important is to have a child who resembles you or carries forth your genes, then adoption wouldn't be right for you. If you feel that the primary reason to adopt is to become a parent, a role you strongly want, then adoption might be right for you."

Here are some basic facts on adoption you will also want to consider as you make this important decision:

- In 1992, there were a total of 51,157 domestic adoptions of nonrelatives, according to the National Council on Adoption. Approximately half of the children involved were infants. Thirty-nine percent of these adoptions were handled by public agencies, 29 percent by private agencies, and 31 percent by private individuals. (Note: 1992 is the most recent year for which compehensive national adoption statistics are available.)

- Eligibility requirements for adoption are becoming much less rigid, even for couples who wish to adopt infants. However, you'll still be required to go through a home study (a tool that the child welfare authorities use to assess the suitability of prospective parents). You can get a sense of what adoption agencies are looking for these days by reading Checklist 4.3 at the end of this list.

- Contrary to popular belief — to say nothing of media hype — the majority of adoption stories have happy endings. Approximately 80 percent of adoptions are completed successfully. This means that such factors as birth

Moneysaver

They don't call him "Uncle" Sam for nothing! Although the costs of adopting a child can be more than a little daunting, there is some good news, courtesy of none other than Uncle Sam. If your modified adjusted gross income is less than $75,000, you are eligible for a $10,000 federal tax credit per child for certain types of adoption-related expenses: court costs, adoption fees, legal fees, traveling expenses, and so on.

mother change of heart, birth father intervention, and breakdown of communication and trust between birth parents and adopting parents become an issue only in approximately one out of every five adoptions.

▪ Foreign adoption is becoming an increasingly popular option for American couples, mainly because the waiting lists for foreign-born children are considerably shorter than those for American children. As a rule of thumb, prospective adoptive parents who are accepted into foreign adoption programs can expect to have a child within a year to 18 months, whereas those who choose to participate in domestic adoption programs can expect a wait of approximately 2½ years.

▪ According to the National Adoption Information Clearinghouse, domestic adoptions typically cost between 8,000 and $30,000 but they may, in fact, be free if you're adopting a child who is in the care of the state. (Of course, they can also run to considerably more than $30,000, as Table 4.4 at the end of this list illustrates. There's no such things as a "typical" adoption, after all.)

▪ Foreign adoptions tend to be more expensive than domestic adoptions, but intercountry adoption costs vary according to the specific laws of the foreign country from which you are adopting. According to the National Adoption Information Clearinghouse, factors that determine how much your foreign adoption ultimately costs include whether the adoption agencies in the foreign country you are considering are government agencies, government subsidized orphanages, charitable foundations, attorneys, facilitators, or any combination of these; whether the foreign country requires translation and/or authentication of the dossier documents; whether the U.S. agency requires a "donation" to the foreign orphanage or agency; and whether the foreign country requires one or both adoptive parents to make one or more trips to the country for interviews and court hearings. (Obviously, these international travel expenses can quickly add up, so you'll want to talk to other parents who've gone the international adoption route so that you'll have a clear indication of what you're getting yourself into financially before you sign on the dotted line.)

Checklist 4.3. What Adoption Agencies Are Looking for in Prospective Parents

You increase your odds of being approved by an adoption agency if

_____ you are married rather than single, and have been with your partner for a minimum of three years,

_____ you are no more than 40 years older than the child you wish to adopt,

_____ you are in good health,

_____ you are infertile,

_____ you have fewer than two children of your own,

_____ you or your partner is able to be at home with the child you adopt for a minimum of six months,

_____ you are financially stable and capable of paying the agency's fee,

_____ your home is safe, clean, and child friendly,

_____ your background check doesn't turn up any disturbing information about you,

_____ your home study goes well.

Table 4.4. What You Can Expect to Pay for a Domestic Adoption

Agency fees

Application fee	$100 to $500
Home study and preparation services	$700 to $2,500
Post-placement supervision	$200 to $1,500

Agency fees

Parent physical (per parent)	$35 to $150
Psychiatric evaluation (per parent; if required)	$250 to $400

Attorney fees

Document preparation	$500 to $2,000
Petition and court representation to finalize placement	$2,500 to $12,000
Advertising	$500 to $5,000
Attorney fees paid on behalf of the birth parent	$500 to $1,500

Birth parent expenses

Medical expenses (pregnancy/birth/postpartum)	$0 to $20,000
Living expenses (rent, food, clothing, transportation)	$500 to $12,000
Counseling	$500 to $2,000

Total: $6,285 to $59,550

Notes:

1.) There is a considerable variation when it comes to the cost of a domestic adoption. The cost may vary according to the type of adoption, the area of the United States where the adoption occurs, whether or not the agency charges a sliding-scale fee based on family income, the country of origin of a foreign-born child, the amount of state or federal subsidy available for a child with special needs, the amount of federal or state tax credits available for the reimbursement of adoption expenses, whether or not there are any employer adoption benefits available, and whether the state reimburses parents for nonrecurring expenses related to the adoption of a child with special needs.

2.) The types of expenses that can be paid on behalf of the birth parent are typically restricted by state law and subject to review by the court.

Source: National Adoption Information Clearinghouse

Note: If you are hoping to adopt a child but don't have sufficient funds sitting in the bank, you might want to turn to one or more of the following sources of financial assistance: family and friends, bank loans, employee benefit packages, home-equity loans, retirement funds, and/or life insurance policies.

Adoption is a complex issue, so you'll want to do some additional research to determine if it's the right choice for your family. You'll find a number of very useful resources in the "Resource Directory" (www.wiley.com/go/anndouglas).

Just the facts

- If you and your partner have been having unprotected intercourse for more than a year and still haven't managed to conceive, it's possible that you have a fertility problem.

- When you're shopping around for a specialist, look for a doctor who devotes a significant percentage of her medical practice to the treatment of infertility.

- Make sure that you are clear about both the costs of treatment and your odds of having a healthy baby before you agree to any type of fertility treatment.

- Your fertility workup will consist of a medical history, a physical examination, and possibly some additional tests. As a rule of thumb, the male partner should be tested first because tests of the male reproductive system are considerably less invasive than those of the female reproductive system.

- A range of fertility treatments are available, including hormone therapy, drug therapy, and surgery.

- There are also a number of high-tech methods of conceiving, including IVF, GIFT, ZIFT, IUI, and ICSI, and the use of donor sperm and donor eggs.

- Infertility can be extremely stressful for couples who are affected by it. You may want to consider going for therapy or taking a break from the Baby Olympics for a while.

- If you're considering either gestational surrogacy or adoption, be sure to research each options thoroughly so that you can be sure that the option you're considering is right for you.

**Your First Trimester
Week-by-Week**

PART II

GET THE SCOOP ON. . .
What's going on with your body • What's going
on with your head • Thinking pregnant — even
before you are • How pregnancies are dated •
Pregnancy symptoms • How you and your partner
may feel about being pregnant • Home
pregnancy test tips

The First Month: Great Expectations

The first month of pregnancy is a month like no other. While you're likely to have baby-making on the brain, you'll spend most of this month playing the role of the Lady in Waiting: waiting for ovulation to occur and then waiting to do a home pregnancy test. Even if your gut instinct is telling you that this was your lucky month, you won't know for certain whether or not you've managed to hit the reproductive jackpot until the end of the month, so you're pretty much destined to spend the entire month in pregnancy purgatory!

In this chapter, we tell you what to expect on a week-by-week basis during each of the first four weeks of pregnancy. You'll get the inside scoop on what's going on with your body, what's going on with your head, and — after conception has occurred — what's going on with your baby.

Each week-by-week section also includes answers to the most-asked questions for each week of pregnancy — our so-called "Hot List." This month, we'll be tackling everything from how pregnancies are dated to pregnancy testing do's and don'ts to early pregnancy symptoms.

We'll be sticking with this format in Chapters 6 through 13, too, so that you can quickly zero in on the real need-to-know information for each of the remaining months and weeks of pregnancy. (Pregnancy can be stressful enough without your pregnancy book driving you crazy, too.)

Week 1

The first week is all about putting in time, waiting for your period to end and the baby-making season to begin.

If this is your first month of trying, you may be eagerly loading up on ovulation predictor kits and rereading the armloads of "how to get pregnant books" that you loaded up on at the library. (Come on, 'fess up. You didn't leave any books for anyone else to check out, now did you?)

If you're a veteran of the trying-to-conceive scene, you may be feeling a little less enthused — or possibly even downright discouraged by now. (The trying-to-conceive roller-coaster ride can get pretty tiresome pretty quickly.)

What's going on with your body

Because pregnancy is dated based on the first day of the woman's last menstrual period, the first day of your pregnancy is actually the first day of your last period. So this month starts out with your menstrual cycle.

Assuming you manage to conceive this month, your uterus will begin to undergo a rather remarkable metamorphosis that will see it increasing in capacity by up to 1,000 times over the course of your pregnancy. Its weight will increase dramatically at the same time: while your prepregnant uterus weighs approximately 2.5 ounces (70 grams), by the time you're ready to give birth, your uterus will be a much heftier 2½ pounds (1,100 grams).

What's going on with your head

Assuming your pregnancy is planned, you're probably already thinking like a pregnant woman and considering the effects of your actions on the long-term health and well-being of your baby-to-be. You've probably got a million-and-one questions on the "is this safe?" theme, in fact — questions we'll attempt to answer both in this chapter and in the remainder of this book.

The Hot List: This week's must-ask pregnancy questions

Here are the answers to some of the more pressing questions that are likely to be running through your head this week.

Should I give up my morning coffee now that I'm trying to conceive?

While the medical profession has done a fair bit of flip-flopping about the caffeine issue over the years, most experts today agree that excessive quantities of caffeine can be harmful to the developing baby. Some recent studies have linked caffeine to decreased fertility, an increased risk of miscarriage (in women who consume more than five cups per day), stillbirth, premature labor, lower birthweight, and Sudden Infant Death Syndrome (SIDS).

Where things get tricky, of course, is in trying to get the experts to agree on what constitutes a "safe" amount of caffeine consumption during pregnancy — whether that means cutting out caffeine entirely or keeping your caffeine consumption in the moderate range (something in the neighborhood of 100 milligrams of caffeine per day), in which case you'd still be okay having your morning coffee. (A single, 5-ounce cup of coffee, mind you — not an entire pot!)

Watch Out!

If you're in the habit of consuming large amounts of caffeine, you might want to wean yourself off caffeine or reduce your caffeine consumption gradually. Giving up caffeine "cold turkey" can trigger headaches and flulike symptoms.

Of course, you may want to limit your consumption of caffeine during pregnancy for some entirely different reasons:

- Caffeine tends to act as a diuretic, drawing both fluid and calcium from the body.
- Caffeine can interfere with the absorption of iron.
- Caffeine can heighten mood swings.
- Caffeine can heighten the breast tenderness that many women experience during early pregnancy.
- Caffeine can cause insomnia — something that tends to be a problem for pregnant women anyway.

Caffeine is found in more foods than you may realize. If you want to cut back your consumption of caffeine, it's important to know which foods to avoid or to limit (see Table 5.1). Note: The amount of caffeine found in a typical serving of food can vary considerably, which is why we have chosen to provide a range for each of the foods and beverages listed in Table 5.1.

Table 5.1. The Caffeine Content of Food and Beverages

Item	Milligrams of Caffeine	Average Range
Coffee (8 oz. cup)		
Brewed, drip method	184	96–288
Brewed, percolator	128	64–272
Instant	104	48–192
Decaffeinated, brewed	4	3–6
Decaffeinated, instant	2	1–5

Item	Milligrams of Caffeine	Average Range
Tea (8 oz. cup)		
Brewed, major U.S. brands	64	33–144
Brewed, imported brands	96	40–176
Instant	48	40–80
Iced (12 oz. glass)	70	67–76
Some soft drinks (12 oz.)	36	30–60
Cocoa beverages	4	2–20
Chocolate milk beverages (8 oz.)	5	2–7
Milk chocolate (1 oz.)	6	1–15
Dark chocolate, semi-sweet (1 oz.)	20	5–35
Baker's chocolate (1 oz.)	26	26
Chocolate-flavored syrup (1 oz.)	4	4

Source: U.S. Food and Drug Administration and National Soft Drink Association

It's also important to remember that caffeine can be found in certain over-the-counter drug products, too, including certain brands of headache tablets, cold remedies, and wakeup pills. (Of course, you'll want to steer clear of all but the most essential medications while you're trying to conceive in order to avoid exposing your baby to anything potentially harmful.)

 Watch Out!

While beverages such as decaffeinated coffees, teas, and soft drinks can stand in for some of the caffeinated beverages that may have served as mainstays in your prepregnancy diet, you'll want to avoid overrelying on them. Not only are these beverages lacking in the important nutrients that can be found in other beverages such as milk and juice; if consumed in large-enough quantities, certain elements in decaffeinated coffees and teas may deplete your body of iron and calcium.

Is it okay to have the occasional serving of alcohol while I'm trying to get pregnant?

While candlelight and champagne may help set the stage for romance, this is one time in your life when you'll want to stick with the nonalcoholic bubbly. The reason is simple: alcohol can be extremely damaging to the developing baby. According to the March of Dimes, more than 40,000 babies are born with some degree of alcohol-related damage each year.

Babies born to mothers who drink heavily during pregnancy are often born with Fetal Alcohol Syndrome (FAS) — the leading known cause of preventable mental retardation. Approximately 30 percent to 40 percent of babies born to women who consume more than two drinks per day during the first trimester will suffer from fetal alcohol syndrome at birth. Babies with FAS are abnormally small at birth and don't catch up with other babies the same age after birth. They are also born with facial malformations, central nervous system dysfunction, and varying degrees of major organ system malfunction — a pretty rough start in life for any baby — and things don't get better as they grow older. Studies have shown that adolescents and adults with FAS experience psychological and behavioral problems that make it difficult for them to hold down a job and live on their own.

A related syndrome — Fetal Alcohol Effect (FAE) or Fetal Alcohol Spectrum Disorder (FASD) — is a milder version of FAS. Approximately 10 times as many babies are born with FAE as with FAS.

But, wait: there's more bad news. Consuming alcohol during pregnancy also increases the risk that a woman will experience a

 Watch Out!

Women who consume an average of one alcoholic beverage per week during pregnancy are three times as likely to end up with children with serious behavior problems at age six or seven.

miscarriage or give birth to a low-birthweight baby or a baby with learning disabilities, behavioral problems, and/or a lower IQ.

Because alcohol can have such a devastating effect on the developing baby, we recommend that you avoid alcohol entirely while you are trying to conceive and during the entire time that you are pregnant. Drinking at any stage of pregnancy can affect your baby's brain. It's simply not worth gambling with your baby's health. Besides, if you do manage to hit the reproductive jackpot this month, you'll spend the next nine months worrying about the potentially harmful effects of that single glass of champagne on your baby-to-be.

And, of course, smoking and the use of recreational drugs are definitely to be avoided during pregnancy, too. See Chapter 2 for more on why you may want to kick these two particular lifestyle habits before you continue with your baby-making plans.

Do I need to avoid taking headache tablets and other over-the-counter medications while I'm trying to conceive? What about my prescription medications?

Nearly 2,500 years ago, the Greek physician Hippocrates warned that for the safety of the developing baby, drugs should be administered to pregnant women only from the fourth to the seventh month. Three millennia later, we're continuing to heed his warnings about the dangers of using medications during pregnancy — although we now realize that the period of greatest risk is during the earliest weeks of pregnancy.

The period of greatest vulnerability for the developing baby is approximately 4 to 10 weeks from the first day of your last

 Watch Out!

The best time to talk about the risks of taking certain medications during pregnancy is before you start trying to conceive. If you become pregnant unexpectedly, contact your doctor's office as soon as you find out that you are pregnant so that you can talk about which medications you can continue to take safely and which you should avoid.

menstrual period — the period during which the baby's major organs are being formed. Exposure to a harmful substance during this period can result in either birth defects or miscarriages.

If the fetus is exposed to a harmful substance prior to this — that is, during the first two weeks after conception — either it will be unaffected by the exposure or the cells will die and the pregnancy will not continue.

A drug taken during the second and third trimesters may alter the growth and physiological and biochemical functioning of the developing baby.

Depending on the fetal age, drug potency, and dosage taken, a medication may

- be toxic to the developing baby;

- cause a variety of birth defects;

- interfere with placental functioning, thereby affecting the flow of oxygen and nutrients from the mother to the baby;

- alter the mother's biochemistry, something that indirectly affects the baby as well.

There are three basic categories of drugs you need to be concerned about during pregnancy: lifestyle drugs, over-the-counter products, and prescription medications. We talked about the harmful effects of lifestyle drugs in Chapters 2 and 3, so we won't repeat that discussion again, but we're going to devote the next few pages to talking about the care you need to exercise when using over-the-counter products and prescription medications during pregnancy.

Over-the-counter products

The fact that a particular drug is available over-the-counter (or that it's sitting in your own medicine cabinet) is no guarantee that it's safe during pregnancy. As Table 5.2 shows, even a seemingly harmless product such as aspirin poses particular risks during pregnancy. You'll note that each of the drugs in this table has been assigned a particular risk factor using a rating system designed by the FDA to classify drugs for use during pregnancy.

Table 5.2. Active Ingredients in Common Over-the-Counter Medications

FDA Risk Factor A: These drugs have been demonstrated not to pose any risks to human fetuses.

FDA Risk Factor B: These drugs are believed not to pose any significant risk to human fetuses, based on what has been learned from animal or human studies.

FDA Risk Factor C: These drugs may or may not be harmful to human fetuses. The data is inconclusive, either because no studies have been done or because any adverse effects that have been demonstrated have shown up in animal rather than human studies.

FDA Risk Factor D: These drugs are known to pose a threat to human fetuses, but they may be commonly found in cases where the benefits of using the drug outweigh these risks.

FDA Risk Factor X: These drugs have been proven to cause fetal abnormalities in humans and should not be used by under any circumstances during pregnancy. (In other words, Category X drugs are FDA-approved, but they are not to be used by pregnant women.)

Active Ingredient	FDA Risk Factor	Where You Can Find It	Possible Problems During Pregnancy
Acetaminophen	B	Commonly found in aspirin substitutes such as Actifed Cold and Sinus; Alka-Seltzer Plus; Comtrex; Contac Cold and Flu; Coricidin; Drixoral Cold and Flu; Excedrin; Maximum Strength Midol; Robitussin Cold; Sinutab; Sudafed Cold; Sudafed Sinus; TheraFlu; TYLENOL; Triaminic Cough; Vicks Nyquil	Doesn't appear to be linked to birth defects.
Aluminum hydroxide	Not rated (NR)	Commonly found in antacids such as Gaviscon, Maalox	Doesn't appear to be linked to birth defects. Chronic or excessive use may be associated with neonatal calcium or magnesium imbalance.
Aspirin (acetylsalicylic acid)	C; but D (if full dosage is used in third trimester)	Commonly found in aspirin compounds such as Alka-Seltzer, Ascriptin, Genuine Bayer, Ecotrin, Excedrin, St. Joseph, Vanquish	No apparent link to birth defects, though some studies disagree. In large doses close to term, causes clotting disorders with possible fetal and maternal hemorrhage. Other possible effects are low birth-weight, prolonged gestation and labor, and neonatal cardiac problems.

(continued)

Table 5.2. (continued)

Active Ingredient	FDA Risk Factor	Where You Can Find It	Possible Problems During Pregnancy
Bacitracin Zinc	C	Commonly found in antibiotic ointments such as Betadine Brand First Aid Antibiotics, Neosporin, and Polysporin	Doesn't appear to be linked to birth defects.
Benzocaine	NR	Commonly found in topical anesthetics such as Anbesol, Dermoplast, Hurricaine	Reports of use during pregnancy are not available.
Bisacodyl	NR	Commonly found in laxatives such as Correctol, Dulcolax	Reports of use during pregnancy are not available.
Bismuth Subsalicylate	C	Commonly found in products for upset stomach, indigestion, and so on, such as Pepto-Bismol	Because of aspirinlike effect with salicylates, use in pregnancy should be restricted to the first five months in amounts that do not exceed the recommended dosages.
Black Cohosh	NR	Found in health food stores and in products such as Awareness Female Balance, Remifemin	Products nonstandardized. Avoid during pregnancy.
Blue Cohosh	C	Blue Cohosh Root Liquid. Also known as Beechdrops, Blueberry Root, Blue Ginseng, Papoose Root, Squawroot, Yellow Ginseng.	Can stimulate uterine contractions and cause birth defects and other toxicity in some animals. Avoid in pregnancy, especially first trimester. Products nonstandardized.
Brompheniramine Maleate	C	Commonly found in antihistamines such as Dimetapp, Robitussin Allergy & Cough	May be associated with birth defects. Use of antihistamines in last two weeks of pregnancy increases the risk of a neonatal eye problem known as retro-lental fibroplasia.
Caffeine	B	Commonly found in Excedrin, Maximum Strength Midol, Vanquish, Vivarin	Doesn't appear to be linked to birth defects. High doses may be associated with miscarriage and infertility.

Drug	Category	Commonly found in	Effects
Calcium Carbonate	NR	Commonly found in calcium supplements and antacids such as Caltrate, Gas-X with Maalox Extra Strength, Rolaids, Tums	No adverse effects proven with usual dosages.
Camphor	C	Commonly found in antiitch and local anesthetic products and nasal inhalers such as Anbesol Cold Sore Ointment, Triaminic Vapor, Vicks VapoRub	No adverse effects from topical use.
Chlorpheniramine Maleate	B	Commonly found in antihistamines such as Actifed Cold & Sinus, Alka-Seltzer Plus, Chlor-Trimeton Allergy, Comtrex Maximum Strength, Contac, Coricidin, PediaCare, Sinutab, TheraFlu, Triaminic, Maximum Strength TYLENOL Allergy, Vicks 44m Cough & Cold	Doesn't appear to be linked to birth defects. See brompheniramine.
Cimetidine	B	Found in antacids such as Tagamet HB	Doesn't appear to be linked to birth defects. Animal research has suggested possibility of impaired sexual development of male fetuses. Use other antacids in pregnancy.
Clemastine	B	Antihistamine found in products such as Tavist	Doesn't appear to be linked to birth defects. See brompheniramine.
Clotrimazole	B	Commonly found in antifungal/yeast infection products such as Gyne-Lotrimin 3, Lotrimin AF	Doesn't appear to be linked to birth defects.
Dexbrompheniramine	C	Commonly found in antihistamines defects. See brompheniramine.	Doesn't appear to be linked to birth such as Drixoral
Dextromethorphan	C	Commonly found in cough suppressants such as Alka-Seltzer Plus Cold and Cough, Benylin Cough, Comtrex, Contac Severe Cold, Coricidin HBP, Dimetapp DM Cold, Robitussin, Sudafed Cold and Cough, TheraFlu, Triaminic, TYLENOL Cold, Vicks 44	Link to birth defects has not been completely ruled out. Use as directed by your physician and avoid alcohol-containing preparations.
Dimenhydrinate	B	Commonly found in antinausea products such as Dramamine	May be responsible for cardiovascular defects and hernias in the fetus, but research inconclusive. See brompheniramine.

(continued)

Table 5.2. *(continued)*

Active Ingredient	FDA Risk Factor	Where You Can Find It	Possible Problems During Pregnancy
Diphenhydramine	B	Commonly found in antihistamines such as Benadryl, Excedrin PM, Nytol, Sominex Original, TYLENOL Severe Allergy, Unisom Sleepgels	May be responsible for cleft palate and other birth defects, but research inconclusive. See brompheniramine.
Docusate	C	Commonly found in laxatives such as Phillips' Liqui-Gels, Senokot-S, Surfak	Chronic use may cause fetal magnesium imbalance.
Doxylamine	A	Used as a sleep aid in products such as Alka Seltzer Plus Night-Time Cold, Unisom SleepTabs, Vicks NyQuil	Safe in pregnancy. May be used as a treatment for morning sickness in combination with vitamin B6.
Echinacea	C	Herbal product also known as American Cone Flower, Black Susans, Hedgehog, Indian Head, Kansas Snakeroot, Scurvy Root	No reports of use in pregnancy available. Products nonstandardized. Avoid in pregnancy.
Ephedrine	C	Commonly found in decongestants such as Primatene Tablets and Mist	May be responsible for heart-rate disturbances, minor birth defects, hernias, and clubfoot, but research inconclusive.
Famotidine	B	Found in antacids such as Pepcid	Doesn't appear to be linked to birth defects.
Garlic	C	Herbal product/Nutritional supplement.	Appears to be safe as a food flavoring. Products non-standardized. Avoid high-doses in pregnancy.
Ginger	C	Herbal product. Sometimes used for nausea and vomiting.	Doesn't appear to be linked to birth defects. Products nonstandardized.

Ginkgo Biloba	C	Herbal product found in BioGinkgo 27/7, BioLean Free, Centrum Performance, Ginkai, Ginkgo 5, Ginkgold, One-A-Day Memory & Concentration, Phyto-Vite, Quanterra Mental Sharpness	No reports of use in pregnancy available. Products nonstandardized. Probably best to avoid in pregnancy.
Guaifenesin	C	Commonly found in expectorants such as Benylin, Primatene Tablets, Robitussin, Sudafed Cold, Vicks 44E	Doesn't appear to be linked to birth defects.
Hydrocortisone (topical)	C	Commonly found in topical and hemorrhoid sprays and ointments such as Anusol HC-1 Cortaid, Cortizone, Preparation H Hydrocortisone Cream	No reports of use in pregnancy available.
Ibuprofen	B	D (if in third trimester)	Commonly found in aspirin substitutes such as Advil, Motrin IB. No apparent link to birth defects, but third-trimester use can cause fetal cardiac malfunction. Avoid while trying to conceive.
Lactase	NR	Commonly found in products for lactose intolerance such as Lactaid	No report of use in pregnancy available.
Loperamide	B	Found in antidiarrheals such as Immodium	Doesn't appear to be linked to birth defects.
Magnesium Carbonate, Magnesium Hydroxide, Magnesium Trisilacate		Commonly found in antacids such as Gaviscon, Maalox, Phillips' Milk of Magnesia, Rolaids	No adverse effects proven with usual dosages. Chronic or excessive use may be associated with neonatal calcium or magnesium imbalance.
Meclizine	B	Commonly found in antinausea products such as Bonine, Dramamine	Causes birth defects in some animals, but no apparent link to birth defects in humans. See Brompheneramine.
Melatonin	C	Also known as MEL, a nutritional supplement.	No reports of use in pregnancy available. May inhibit ovulation in high daily doses. Avoid in pregnancy.

(continued)

Table 5.2. (continued)

Active Ingredient	FDA Risk Factor	Where You Can Find It	Possible Problems During Pregnancy
Menthol	NR	Commonly found in cough and sore throat preparations and in soothing ointments such as BenGay, Hall's Cough Drops, Listerine, Robitussin Cough Drops, Vicks Cough Drops	No reports of use in pregnancy available.
Miconazole	C	Commonly found in products used to treat yeast/fungal infections such as Desenex, Lotrimin, Monistat	Doesn't appear to be linked to birth defects.
Oxymetazoline	C	Commonly found in nasal decongestant sprays such as Afrin, Neo-Synephrine, Vicks Sinex	No apparent link to birth defects, but excessive use could impair uterine blood flow.
Passion Flower	C	Also known as Apricot Vine, Corona De Cristo, Fleur De La Passion, Maypop, Passiflora, Passion Vine, Water Lemon	No reports of use in pregnancy available. Products nonstandardized. Avoid in pregnancy.
Permethrin	B	Found in antiscabies preparations such as Acticin, Elmite, and Nix	Considered the treatment of choice for pubic and head lice, and scabies.
Phenylephrine	C	Commonly found in nasal decongestant sprays and hemorrhoid creams such as Alka-Seltzer Plus, Neo-Synephrine, Preparation H, Vicks Sinex	Causes birth defects in animals. May be responsible for minor birth defects: hernia and clubfoot. (These studies do not apply to topical creams.) Excessive use could impair uterine blood flow.
Pseudoephedrine	C	Commonly found in decongestants such as Actifed, Advil Cold and Sinus, Aleve Sinus & Headache, Alka-Seltzer Plus, Benadryl Allergy & Sinus, Chlor-Trimeton Allergy/Decongestant, Comtrex, Contac, Dimetapp, Drixoral, PediaCare, Robitussin Cold, Sinutab, Sudafed, TheraFlu, Triaminic, TYLENOL Allergy, TYLENOL Cold, Vicks 44D, Vicks DayQuil, Vicks NyQuil	May be responsible for heart rate disturbances, minor birth defects, hernias, and clubfoot, but research inconclusive.

Drug	Rating	Common use	Comments
Psyllium (a natural fiber that promotes normal bowel movements)	NR	Commonly found in laxatives such as Metamucil	No reports of use in pregnancy available. Since it is not absorbed into the bloodstream, it is felt to be safe to use.
Pyrethrins with piperonyl butoxide	C	Commonly found in antilice lotions and shampoos such as Rid	Along with permethrin, preferred drug for lice infestations in pregnancy.
Ranitidine	B	Found in Zantac 75	Doesn't appear to be linked to birth defects.
St. John's Wort (hypericum perforatum)	C	Herbal products containing Hypericum extract, Klamath weed, John's wort, amber touch-and-heat, goat-weed, rosin rose, millepertuis	Rare reports of use in pregnancy available. Products nonstandardized. Possible contamination with other substances.
Simethicone	C	Commonly found in antiflatulents such as Gax-X, Maalox, Phazyme	May be associated with cardiovascular birth defects, but cause and effect not likely.
Sodium Bicarbonate	NR	Commonly found in antacids such as Alka-Seltzer	No adverse effects with usual dosages.
Sodium Chloride (table salt)	NR	Commonly found in nasal sprays such as Ocean Nasal Mist	Safe for use during pregnancy.
Valerian	B	Herbal products containing Valerian root, radix, valerianae, Indian valerian, red valerian	Possible adverse fetal and maternal effects. Should be avoided in pregnancy.

Note: Some drugs have more than one rating. This is because they may be more dangerous at certain parts of the pregnancy, in certain dosages, or in combination with other drugs. Consult your physician for details.

Original material based on the latest data available as of June 2003. Reference material includes *The Unofficial Guide to Having A Baby* by Ann Douglas and John R. Sussman, M.D. New York: John Wiley and Sons, 1999. *Before You Conceive* by John R. Sussman, M.D., and B. Blake Levitt. New York: Bantam Doubleday Dell Books, 1989. *Drugs in Pregnancy and Lactation* (fifth edition, 1998) by Gerald G. Briggs, Roger K. Freeman, and Sumner J. Taffe. Baltimore: Williams and Wilkins, 1998. (Plus updates Volume 11 Number 2, June 1998 through Volume 16 Number 2, June 2003). *Physician's Desk Reference.* Oradell, NJ: Medical Economics Publishers, 2002. *Drugs and Pregnancy* by Larry C. Gilstrap III and Bertis B. Little. New York: Elsevier Science Publishing Co., Inc., 1992.

As helpful as these ratings can be to caregivers and pregnant women, they tend to oversimplify the highly complex issues involved. That's why it's so important for caregivers to review the sources of information available to them when recommending or prescribing medications. They should consult such reliable sources such as *Drugs in Pregnancy and Lactation,* make use of teratogen/pregnancy risk-lines (a.k.a. hotlines), tap into the *Physician's Desk Reference* or *PDR* (the so-called "bible" of FDA-approved information about prescription and nonprescription drugs that also includes a compendium of the package inserts that manufacturers are required to package with their products), and so on.

Decisions about the use of medications during pregnancy must take many factors into account, including the specific individual circumstances that necessitate the use of a medication, the dose and method of administration, the timing and duration of exposure in the pregnancy, and the simultaneous use of other drugs. All factors being equal, it is generally best to use drugs that have been available longer and therefore have more of a track record in pregnancy. No pregnant woman wants to be a guinea pig, if she can avoid it.

Prescription drugs

Over-the-counter drugs aren't the only drugs that can be harmful to the developing baby. Some of the most harmful drugs are those used to treat such serious medical conditions as epilepsy, heart disease, and cancer.

Bright Idea

You can find out more about the safety of particular types of medications by contacting the March of Dimes at the address below:

March of Dimes Birth Defects Foundation
National Office
1275 Mamaroneck Avenue
White Plains, NY 10605
1-888-MODIMES
www.modimes.org

If you take prescription drugs regularly, it's important to find out whether it's safe to continue taking these medications during your pregnancy. In some cases, your doctor will advise you to stop taking the drug because the risks to the fetus are greater than the benefits the drug provides. In other situations, she may advise you to continue taking the drug because the developing baby is more likely to be harmed by the condition the drug is treating (for example, epileptic seizures) than the medication itself.

Although there is still a great deal we don't know about the effects of drug use during pregnancy, the Food and Drug Administration (FDA) rates drugs on the basis of their safety during pregnancy. Prescription drugs are assigned to one of the previous five categories, based on their relative safety during pregnancy, as previously discussed earlier in this chapter.

As you can see from Table 5.3, only a handful of prescription drugs are considered absolutely safe to take during pregnancy.

Table 5.3. FDA Ratings for Prescription Drug Use During Pregnancy

FDA Risk Factor A: These drugs have been demonstrated not to pose any risks to human fetuses.

FDA Risk Factor B: These drugs are believed not to pose any significant risk to human fetuses, based on what has been learned from animal or human studies.

FDA Risk Factor C: These drugs may or may not be harmful to human fetuses. The data is inconclusive, either because no studies have been done or because any adverse effects that have been demonstrated have shown up in animal rather than human studies.

FDA Risk Factor D: These drugs are known to pose a threat to human fetuses, but they may be commonly found in cases where the benefits of using the drug outweigh these risks.

FDA Risk Factor X: These drugs have been proven to cause fetal abnormalities in humans and should not be used by under any circumstances during pregnancy. (In other words, Category X drugs are FDA-approved, but they are not to be used by pregnant women.)

Name of Drug	FDA Risk Factor	Possible Problems	What You Need to Know
A. Antihistamines			
Allegra (fexofenadine)	C	Reports of use during pregnancy are not available.	Product too new to evaluate. Use over-the-counter product like chlorpheniramine if treatment necessary.
Claritin (loratidine), Zyrtec (cefrizine)	B	Limited reports of use during pregnancy are available.	Product too new to evaluate. Use over-the-counter product like chlorpheniramine if treatment necessary. Cetrizine is a reasonable alternative (especially after the first trimester) if chlorpheniramine is not effective.
Hismanal (astemizole)	C	Limited reports of use in pregnancy available.	Product too new to evaluate. Use over-the-counter product like chlorpheniramine if treatment necessary.

B. Antibiotics/Anti-infectives

1. Antifungals

Terrazol (terconazole)	C	No known link to birth defects.	Use as directed by your physician for vulvo-vaginal yeast infections.
Diflucan (fluconazole)	C	Possible birth defects with continuous use at higher doses.	Should be avoided in pregnancy, if possible.
Fulvicin (griseofulvin)	C	May be associated with conjoined twins.	Avoid.
Mycostatin (nystatin) oral or cream	B	Doesn't appear to be linked to birth defects.	A possible alternative to terconazole.

2. Antimalarials

Aralen (chloroquine)	C	May be responsible for various birth defects. Research inconclusive.	A safer alternative than quinine.
Paludrine (proguanil)	B	Doesn't appear to be linked to birth defects.	May be best choice for malaria prophylaxis in pregnancy.
Quinine	D	Possible birth defects.	Use alternatives if possible.

3. Antituberculosis

Isoniazid (INH)	C	Toxic in animal embryos; may cause neuro-logical abnormalities.	Use only as directed by your physician.
Myambutol (ethambutol)	B	Doesn't appear to be linked to birth defects.	Use only as directed by your physician.
Rifampin (antituberculosis)	C	Possible increase in fetal anomalies.	Use only as directed by your physician.

(continued)

Table 5.3. *(continued)*

Name of Drug	FDA Risk Factor	Possible Problems	What You Need to Know
4. Antivirals			
Famvir (famciclovir)	B	Reports of use during pregnancy are not available.	For treatment of genital herpes. Avoid use during pregnancy, if possible.
Retrovir (zidovudine-AZT)	C	Doesn't appear to be linked to birth defects.	Effective in preventing maternal-fetal transmission of HIV.
Valtrex (valcyclovir)	B	Reports of use during pregnancy are not available.	For treatment of genital herpes. Avoid use during pregnancy, if possible.
Zovirax (acyclovir)	B	Reports of use during pregnancy are not available.	For treatment of genital herpes. Avoid use during pregnancy, if possible. Recent evidence suggests it may be warranted in certain situations.
5. Cephalosporins			
Keflex (cephalexin), Ceclor (cefaclor), Duricef (cefadroxil), Suprax (cefixime)	B	Doesn't appear to be linked to birth defects.	Use only as directed by your physician.
6. Quinolones			
Cipro (ciprofloxacin), Floxin (ofloxacin)	C	Doesn't appear to be linked to birth defects.	Should be avoided in pregnancy unless no safer alternatives exist.

NegGram (nalidixic acid)	C	Causes birth defects in animals.	Should be avoided in pregnancy unless no safer alternatives exist.
Noroxin (norfloxacin)	C	May be associated with birth defects.	Should be avoided in pregnancy unless no safer alternatives exist.
7. Penicillins			
Amoxicillin, ampicillin, cloxacillin, dicloxacillin, penicillin	B		Use only as directed by your physician.
8. Sulfonamides (Sulfa Drugs)			
Bactrim, Septra (sulfamethoxazole)	B	May be associated with birth defects. Not confirmed. If administered near term, may cause neonatal jaundice.	Use only as directed by your physician.
9. Antitrichomonas			
Flagyl, Protostat (metronidazole)	B	Controversy regarding safety during pregnancy.	Should be avoided in first trimester and used only if absolutely necessary in second and third trimesters.
10. Urinary Antibiotics			
Macrodantin/Macrobid (nitrofurantoin)	B	Doesn't appear to be linked to birth defects.	Avoid using near term or with suspected G6PD deficiency (a genetic disorder that weakens red blood cells).
Monurol (fosfomycin)	B	Reports of use during pregnancy are not available.	Taken as a single dose.

(continued)

Table 5.3. (continued)

Name of Drug	FDA Risk Factor	Possible Problems	What You Need to Know
11. Scabicides/Pediculocides (Anti-lice and Scabies)			
Kwell (lindane shampoo)	B	May be associated with nerve damage and anemia.	Use permethrin or pyrethrins with piperonyl butoxide for lice infestations in pregnancy. See Table 5.2.
12. Other			
Augmentin (clavulonate/amoxicillin)	B	May be associated with spina bifida. Not confirmed.	Use only as directed by your physician.
Betadine (povidone–iodine)	D	Prolonged use or use near term may cause fetal thyroid disorder.	Use only as directed by your physician.
Betasept, Hibiclens (chlorhexidine gluconate)	B	Doesn't appear to be linked to birth defects.	Used as a presurgical skin cleanser.
Biaxin (clarithromycin)	B	Doesn't appear to be linked to birth defects.	Related to erythromycin, but newer.
Cleocin (clindamycin)	B	Doesn't appear to be linked to birth defects.	Use only as directed by your physician.
Erythromycin	B	Doesn't appear to be linked to birth defects. Possible maternal liver toxicity with certain forms (estolate or ethylsuccinate esters).	Preferred drug in pregnancy for chlamydia.
pHisoHex (hexachlorophene)	C	Causes birth defects in animals in high doses.	Avoid in pregnancy, especially on mucous membranes or injured skin.

Drug	Category		
Vibramycin, Doryx (doxycycline), Minocin (minocycline), tetracycline	D	May cause various birth defects, tooth discoloration, and possible bone damage.	Avoid during pregnancy.
Zithromax (azithromycin)	B	Doesn't appear to be linked to birth defects.	Related to erythromycin, but newer.
C. Antilipemics (Cholesterol-Lowering Drugs)			
Lipitor (atorvastatin), Mevacor (lovastatin), Lescol (fluvastatin), Pravachol (pravastatin), Zocor (simvastatin)	X	Theoretically toxic to fetal development.	Do not use during or prior to pregnancy.
Lopid (gemfibrozil)	C	May be associated with birth defects.	Rarely necessary during pregnancy.
Questran (cholestyramine), Colestid (colestipol)	B	Doesn't appear to be linked to birth defects.	Has limited use during pregnancy.
D. Cancer Drugs			
Adriamycin (doxorubicin), fluorouracil, methotrexate, Cytoxan (cyclophosphamide), Idamycin (idarubicin), Novantrone (mitoxantrone), Oncovin (vincristine), Platinol (cisplatin), Vesanoid (tretinoin Oral)	D	Highly toxic. Multiple birth defects, neonatal bone-marrow suppression, and intrauterine growth restriction.	Benefits must clearly outweigh the risks. Occupational exposure to these agents by pregnant women is potentially toxic in the first trimester.
Novadex (tamoxifen)	D	Toxic in animal studies. Possibly carcinogenic as well.	Avoid in pregnancy and for at least two months before conceiving.

(continued)

Table 5.3. (continued)

Name of Drug	FDA Risk Factor	Possible Problems	What You Need to Know
E. Muscle Relaxants			
Flexeril (cyclobenzaprine)	B		Use only as directed by your physician.
Parafon Forte (chlorzoxazone), Robaxin (methocarbamol), Norflex (orphenadrine).	C	Doesn't appear to be linked to birth defects.	Avoid during pregnancy.
F. Cardiovascular Drugs			
1. Angiotensin-Converting Enzyme Inhibitors (ACE Inhibitors)			
Capoten (captopril), Vasotec (enalopril), Zestril (lisinopril)	D	Toxic to fetus. Causes birth defects even in second and third trimesters.	Avoid during pregnancy.
2. Antihypertensives (Blood Pressure Medications)			
Aldomet (methyldopa)	C	Doesn't appear to be linked to birth defects.	Discuss switching from your current antihypertensive to methyldopa or labetalol with your caregiver.
Inderal (propranolol)	C	Decreased heart rate, low blood sugar, possible growth restriction.	Consider switching to methyldopa or labetalol.
Lopressor (metoprolol)	C	First-trimester reports lacking; mild neonatal hypotension and decreased heart rate a possibility.	Consider switching to methyldopa or labetalol.

Normodyne (labetalol)	C	First-trimester reports lacking; mild neonatal hypotension and decreased heart rate a possibility.	Preferred to methyldopa by some maternal-fetal medicine specialists.
Tenormin (atenolol)	D	May be associated with low birth weight and intrauterine growth restriction (IUGR). Otherwise similar to labetalol.	Consider switching to methyldopa or labetalol.
3. Calcium Channel Blockers			
Calan (verapaml), Norvasc (amlopidine), Procardia (nifedipine)	C	Not proven to be safe during pregnancy. Possible temporary fetal/neonatal cardiovascular functional abnormalities.	Consult your cardiologist.
4. Cardiac Drugs			
Lanoxin (digoxin)	C	Maternal overdose may be toxic to developing baby.	Consult your cardiologist.
5. Vasodilators			
Nitroglycerin	B	Doesn't appear to be linked to birth defects.	Also used for treatment of excessive uterine contractions/premature labor.
G. Central Nervous System (CNS) Drugs			
1. Analgesics (Pain Relievers)			
Darvon, Darvocet (propoxyphene)	C/D	May be associated with multiple birth defects. Not confirmed. Neonatal withdrawal symptoms if used for prolonged periods.	Narcotic analgesics are generally preferred for occasional use in pregnancy when acetominophen is not effective.

(continued)

Table 5.3. (continued)

2. Anticonvulsants (Epilepsy Drugs)

Name of Drug	FDA Risk Factor	Possible Problems	What You Need to Know
Depakene (valproic acid), Depakote (sodium valproate)	D	High incidence of cranial, facial, and limb defects, including cleft lip and palate, and underdeveloped fingers. Impaired physical and mental development, congenital heart defects.	Untreated epilepsy poses a greater risk than valproic acid. The minimum effective dosage should be used.
Dilantin (phenytoin, diphenylhydantoin)	D	Fetal Dilantin syndrome. (High incidence (2%–26%) of cranial, facial, and limb defects, including cleft lip and palate, and underdeveloped fingers. Impaired physical and mental development, congen-ital heart defects.	Untreated epilepsy poses a greater risk than phenytoin. The minimum effective dosage should be used.
Mysoline (primodone)	D	High association with birth defects.	Untreated epilepsy poses a greater risk than primidone. The minimum effective dosage should be used.
Phenobarbital	D	Barbiturates cross the placenta and are stored in higher concentrations in the fetus than in the mother. Possible effects include fetal addiction, fetal bleeding and coagulation defects, and possible malformations.	Avoid except in cases in which seizure disorders can't be treated with safer medications.
Tegretol (carbamazepine)	C	Possible birth defects.	Preferred drug for grand mal seizures. Discuss medica-tion strategy with your neurologist.
Zarontin (ethosuximide)	C	Possible birth defects.	Preferred drug for petit mal epilepsy, especially during first trimester.

3. Antidepressants

Celexa (citalopram)	C	Limited reports of use during pregnancy available.	A selective seritonin re-uptake inhibitor (SSRI). See Prozac.
Effexor (venlafaxine)	C	Limited reports of use during pregnancy available.	Unrelated to other antidepressants.
Luvox (fluvoxamine)	C	Reports of use during pregnancy are not available.	An SSRI used to treat obsessive-compulsive disorder (OCD).
Paxil (paroxetine)	B	Limited reports of use during pregnancy available.	An SSRI. See Prozac.
Prozac (fluoxetine)	B	Limited reports of use during pregnancy available.	Because there is longer follow-up data for this drug than for newer SSRIs, this is probably the best choice of antidepressant for use during pregnancy.
Remeron (mirtazapine)	C	Reports of use during pregnancy are not available.	A tetracyclic antidepressant chemically unrelated to tricyclics, SSRIs, and monamine oxidase (MAO) inhibitors.
Serzone (nefazodone)	C	Reports of use during pregnancy are not available.	An SSRI. See Prozac.
Sinequan (doxepin)	C	May be associated with birth defects.	When antidepressants are needed in pregnancy, the SSRI drugs appear to be the safest.
Tricyclics including Elavil (amitriptyline), Surmontil (trimipramine), Tofranil (imipramine)	D	Possible facial, head, limb and central nervous system defects; possible neonatal withdrawal symptoms.	Avoid in pregnancy if possible.

(continued)

Table 5.3. (continued)

Name of Drug	FDA Risk Factor	Possible Problems	What You Need to Know
Wellbutrin (bupropion)	B	Reports of use during pregnancy are not available.	Mechanism of action unrelated to other antidepressants.
Zoloft (sertraline)	B	Limited reports of use during pregnancy are available.	An SSRI. See Prozac.
4. Narcotic Analgesics			
Codeine	C/D	May be associated with multiple birth defects. Not confirmed. If used for prolonged periods or in high doses at term.	Use only as directed by your physician.
Dilaudid (hydromorphone), OxyContin, Percodan, Tylox, (oxycodone), Synalgos-DC (dihydrocodeine), Vicodin, Lortab (hydrocodone)	B/D	Reports of use during pregnancy are not available. Falls into Risk Factor D if used for prolonged periods or in high doses at term.	Use only as directed by your physician.
Demerol (meperidine)	B/D	May be associated with hernias. If used for prolonged periods or in high doses near term, baby may experience withdrawal, respiratory depression, growth restriction, and neonatal death.	Use only as directed by your physician.
Heroin (diacetylmorphine)	B/D	Possible chromosome damage. If used for prolonged periods or in high doses near term, baby may experience withdrawal, respiratory depression, growth restriction, lagging intellectual development, and neonatal death.	Do not use during pregnancy.

Methadone	B/D	Risk Factor D if used for prolonged periods or in high doses near term, baby may experience withdrawal, respiratory depression, growth restriction, and neonatal death.	Use only as directed for treatment of narcotic addiction.
Morphine	B/D	May be associated with hernias. If used for prolonged periods or in high doses near term, baby may experience withdrawal, respiratory depression, growth restriction, and neonatal death.	Use only as directed by your physician.
Talwin (pentazocine)	B/D	Risk Factor D if used for prolonged periods or in high doses near term, baby may experience withdrawal, respiratory depression, growth restriction, and neonatal death.	Use only as directed by your physician.
Ultram (tramadol)	C	Possibly toxic in animals at high doses—related to codeine but not addictive.	Too new to recommend over traditional narcotic pain-relievers.

5. Nonsteroidal Anti-inflammatory Drugs (NSAIDs)

| Anaprox (naproxen), Ansaid (flurbiprofen), Clinoril (sulindac), Motrin (ibuprofen), Ponstel (mefenamic acid), Voltaren (diclofenac) | B/D | Doesn't appear to be linked to birth defects. Risk Factor D if used in the third trimester or near delivery, this drug can cause neonatal pulmonary hypertension. | Should not be used by women trying to conceive. May impair implantation. |
| Celebrex (celecoxib), Daypro (oxaprozin), Relafen (nabumetone), Vioxx (rofecoxib) | C/D | Doesn't appear to be linked to birth defects. Risk Factor D if used in the third trimester or near delivery, this drug can cause neonatal pulmonary hypertension. | Should not be used by women trying to conceive. May impair implantation. |

(continued)

Table 5.3. (continued)

Name of Drug	FDA Risk Factor	Possible Problems	What You Need to Know
6. Sedatives and Hypnotics			
Ambien (zolpidem)	B	Reports of use during pregnancy are not available.	Relatively new, so if sleeping pill is absolutely needed, most doctors will prescribe a barbiturate, narcotic, or antihistamine for occasional use only.
Benzodiazepines such as Valium (diazepam), Xanax (alprazolam), Klonipin (clonazepam), Ativan (lorazepam)	D	Possible birth defects, neonatal depression, "floppy baby" syndrome, neonatal withdrawal.	Avoid, especially in first trimester. Severe panic disorders may need to be treated in the second and third trimesters.
7. Stimulants/Appetite Suppressants			
Fastin, Adipex-P (phentermine)	C	May be associated with stillbirth.	Avoid during pregnancy and preconceptionally.
Meridia (sibutramine)	C	Causes birth defects in animals at higher doses.	Avoid during pregnancy.
8. Tranquilizers			
Lithium	D	Possible changes in newborn heart rhythms and thyroid function; possible goiter, jaundice, electrolyte imbalance. Possible birth defects, especially of the heart.	Avoid during pregnancy.

Drug	Category	Effects	Recommendations
Phenothiazines such as Trilafon (per-phenazine), Compazine (prochlorperazine), Fluphenazine	C	Research regarding birth defects is inconclusive. Possible neurological effects on fetus when taken close to term.	Avoid using these drugs near term. It may be safe to use some of these drugs for the treatment of severe nausea and vomiting in the first trimester.

H. Anticoagulants (Blood Thinners)

Drug	Category	Effects	Recommendations
Coumadin (warfarin)	D	High incidence of birth defects (for example, "Fetal warfarin syndrome"); may lead to fetal hemorrhage or death.	Do not use these drugs during pregnancy. Heparin is the drug of choice when anticoagulation is necessary.
Heparin	C	Fetal and maternal complications possible with prolonged use.	Generally preferable to Coumadin (warfarin) when anticoagulation is needed in pregnancy.
Plavix	B	No birth defects in two animal studies. Used in one successful human pregnancy	If medically warranted, should continue through pregnancy.

I. Diuretics

Drug	Category	Effects	Recommendations
Lasix (furosemide)	C	Possible electrolyte imbalance, increased fetal urine output.	Should be used only in cases of severe hypertension and other cardiovascular disorders.
Thiazides such as Dyazide, Maxzide, Aldactazide (hydrochlorthiazide), Diuril (chlorothiazide)	D	Bone-marrow depression, possible birth defects, decreased platelet count (poor blood clotting), electrolyte imbalance.	Should be used only in cases of severe hypertension and other cardiovascular disorders.

J. Gastrointestinal Drugs

1. Antidiarrheal

Drug	Category	Effects	Recommendations
Lomotil (diphenoxylate)	C	Doesn't appear to be linked to birth defects.	Related to narcotic meperidine. (Demerol).

(continued)

Table 5.3. (continued)

Name of Drug	FDA Risk Factor	Possible Problems	What You Need to Know
2. Antiemetics (Antinausea)			
Phenergan (promethazine), Tigan (trimethobenzamide), Compazine (prochlorperazine)	C	Doesn't appear to be linked to birth defects. Frequent use in later part of pregnancy may be associated with neonatal jaundice, depression, and withdrawal symptoms.	An option for severe morning sickness (hyperemesis gravidarum).
Reglan (metoclopramide)	B	Doesn't appear to be linked to birth defects.	Also used when needed to stimulate breast milk production in nursing mothers.
3. Antisecretory Drugs			
Cytotec (misoprostil)	X	Causes miscarriage and birth defects.	Do not use during pregnancy.
Pepcid (famotidine)	B	Reports of use during pregnancy are not available.	Use only as directed by your physician.
Prilosec (omeprazole)	C	No birth defects in animals, but effects unclear in humans.	Avoid during pregnancy, especially prior to week 20.
Prevacid (lansoprazole)	B	Reports of use during pregnancy are not available.	Structurally similar to omeprazole. Avoid during pregnancy, especially prior to week 20.
Zantac (ranitidine)	B	Doesn't appear to be linked to birth defects.	Use only as directed by your physician.

K. Hormones

1. Adrenal

Cortisone, Hydrocortisone (forms other than topical)	D	Possible birth defects. Possible neonatal adrenal suppression and electrolyte imbalance.	Switch to prednisone if necessary.
Dexamethasone	C	Birth defects in animals; no observed birth defects in humans. Possible neonatal adrenal suppression and electrolyte imbalance.	Switch to prednisone if necessary.
Prednisone	B	Doesn't appear to be linked to birth defects. Possible neonatal adrenal suppression and electrolyte imbalance.	Preferred adrenal steroid during pregnancy. Should be used instead of other corticosteroids whenever possible.

2. Antidiabetic Drugs

Diabinase (chlorpropamide)	D	Suspected birth defects, low blood sugar, fetal death.	Change to insulin if your diabetes cannot be controlled by diet alone.
Glucophage (metformin)	B	Appears to be the safest of the oral diabetes drugs. Used frequently as a treatment for ovulation problems associated with polycystic ovarian syndrome (PCOS).	Though insulin is the drug of choice for the treatment of diabetes during pregnancy, this drug may be preferred for women of childbearing age who are not planning a pregnancy.
Glucotrol (glipizide)	C	Doesn't appear to be linked to birth defects.	Change to insulin if your diabetes cannot be controlled by diet alone.
Glynase (glyburide)	D	Possible birth defects with first trimester use.	Change to insulin if your diabetes cannot be controlled by diet alone.

(continued)

Table 5.3. (continued)

Name of Drug	FDA Risk Factor	Possible Problems	What You Need to Know
Insulin	B	Low blood sugar. Maternal insulin shock can result in fetal death.	Your dose may have to be adjusted during pregnancy. Consult your physician.
Orinase (tolbutamide)	D	Possible birth defects, low fetal platelet count, low blood sugar, fetal death.	Change to insulin if your diabetes cannot be controlled by diet alone.
3. Antiprogesterone Drugs			
RU486 (mifepristone)	X	Causes abortion.	Do not use during pregnancy.
4. Antithyroid			
Propylthiouracil (PTU), Tapazole (methimazole)	D	May cause various birth defects and fetal/neonatal hypothyroidism.	PTU is the drug of choice for treatment of hyperthyroidism during pregnancy.
Radioactive Iodine	X	Causes birth defects.	Do not use during pregnancy.
5. Estrogens			
Clomid, Serophene (clomiphene)	X	Though rated X by manufacturer, no birth defects are proven.	A fertility drug. Should be used only after possibility of pregnancy has been ruled out.
DES (diethylstilbestrol)	X	Reproductive organ defects and future reproductive problems.	Should not be used during pregnancy.
Oral contraceptives including the morning-after pill (contain estrogen and/or progestogen)	X	Possible genital anomalies like with DES. Possible advanced neonatal bone age with resulting short stature.	Stop taking your oral contraceptives as soon as pregnancy is confirmed. (You should take a pregnancy test as soon as possible if you suspect that you may be pregnant.)

6. Progestogens

Crinone	Not rated.	Doesn't appear to be linked to birth defects.	Used for the treatment of infertility, luteal phase deficiency, and assisted reproductive technologies in first 10 weeks of pregnancy.
Prometrium, Micronized progesterone (progesterone)	B	Doesn't appear to be linked to birth defects.	Used for the treatment of infertility, luteal phase deficiency, and assisted reproductive technologies in first 10 weeks of pregnancy.
Provera (medroxyprogesterone)	D	Possible birth defects.	When used to treat abnormalities or absence of menstruation, pregnancy must be ruled out first.

7. Thyroid

Synthroid (levothyroxine), Armour thyroid (thyroid hormones)	A	No adverse effects with appropriate doses.	Use only as directed by your physician. Dose may need to be adjusted during pregnancy.

L. Asthma Drugs-Bronchodilators

1. Sympathomimetics

Alupent (metaproterenol), Max air (pirbuterol), Ventolin, Proventil (albuterol), Serevent (salmeterol)	C	No apparent link to birth defects in normal inhaled doses.	Generally available as inhalers. Use as directed by your physician in minimum effective doses.

2. Antispasmodics

Aminophyllin, TheoDur (theophyllin)	C	May be associated with birth defects.	One of a number of acceptable treatments for chronic asthma during pregnancy.

(continued)

Table 5.3. *(continued)*

Name of Drug	FDA Risk Factor	Possible Problems	What You Need to Know
3. Other Asthma			
Singulair (montelukast)	B	Animal studies reassuring. No reports of use in pregnancy available. Doesn't appear to be linked to birth defects.	Use as directed by your physician in minimum effective doses.
M. Other			
1. Acne			
Accutane (isotretinoin)	X	Increased risk of miscarriage and birth defects.	Stop using the drug at least one month prior to attempting pregnancy.
Retin-A (tretinoin)	C	No proven adverse effects when used topically.	Not to be confused with Accutane (above) or cancer drug Vesanoid (tretinoin oral). However, because of its similarity to Accutane, should avoid in pregnancy, especially first trimester.
2. Antimigraine			
Amerge (naratriptan)	C	Possibly toxic in animals at higher doses.	Limited reports in human pregnancy—avoid in pregnancy.
Imitrex (sumatriptan)	C	No apparent link to birth defects, but data lacking. Possible increase in risk of miscarriage.	Avoid in pregnancy.
Midrin (isometheptene)	C	Reports of use during pregnancy are not available.	Use only as directed by your physician.

3. Urinary Tract Antispasmodics

Drug	Rating	Notes	Recommendation
Cystospaz (flavoxate)	B	Reports of use during pregnancy are not available.	Avoid in pregnancy.
Detrol (tolterodine tartrate)	C	Possibly toxic in animal pregnancies at high doses.	Avoid in pregnancy.
Ditropan (oxybutynin)	B	Reports of use during pregnancy are not available.	Avoid in pregnancy.
Urospaz (l-hyoscyamine)	C	May be associated with birth defects.	Avoid in pregnancy.

4. Weight Loss/Fat Blocking

Drug	Rating	Notes	Recommendation
Xenical (orlistat)	B	Reports of use during pregnancy are not available.	Avoid in pregnancy.

5. Immunologic

Drug	Rating	Notes	Recommendation
Copaxone (glatiramer)	B	Used to treat multiple sclerosis (MS). Animal studies reassuring. No reports of use in pregnancy available.	Benefits appear to outweigh risks. Start in the second trimester, if possible.

Note: Some drugs have more than one rating. This is because they may be more dangerous at certain parts of the pregnancy, in certain dosages, or in combination with other drugs. Consult your physician for details.

Original material based on the latest data available as of June 2003. Reference material includes *The Unofficial Guide to Having A Baby* by Ann Douglas and John R. Sussman, M.D. New York: John Wiley and Sons, 1999. *Before You Conceive* by John R. Sussman, M.D., and B. Blake Levitt. New York: Bantam Doubleday Dell Books, 1989. *Drugs in Pregnancy and Lactation* (fifth edition, 1998) by Gerald G. Briggs, Roger K. Freeman, and Sumner J. Taffe. Baltimore: Williams and Wilkins, 1998. (Plus updates Volume 11 Number 2, June 1998 through Volume 16 Number 2, June 2003). *Physician's Desk Reference.* Oradell, NJ: Medical Economics Publishers, 2002. *Drugs and Pregnancy* by Larry C. Gilstrap III and Bertis B. Little. New York: Elsevier Science Publishing Co., Inc., 1992.

Before we wrap up this discussion, we want to say a quick word about antidepressants.

There's been a lot of misinformation in the media in recent years about the supposedly harmful effects of antidepressants on the developing baby. We want to counter some of that misinformation by presenting the facts. A study conducted at the University of California in Los Angeles concluded that there is no increased risk of birth defects or neonatal complications associated with the use of three selective serotonin reuptake inhibitors (SSRIs) — specifically, fluoxetine, paroxetine, and sertraline — during pregnancy. So that's one worry you can scratch off your list if your doctor has prescribed antidepressant medications for you.

Which herbal products are safe to use during pregnancy?

As you've no doubt gathered by now, there's no easy answer to this question. Because herbal products are treated as dietary supplements rather than as drugs by the Food and Drug Administration, herbal product manufacturers don't have to jump through the same product approval hoops as their pharmaceutical industry counterparts. Consequently, there isn't as much data available about the safety and effectiveness of herbal products.

But that's not even the worst of the problem. More troubling still is the lack of product standardization in the herbal products manufacturing sector. According to Donald L. Sullivan, R. Ph., Ph.D., author of *The Expectant Mother's Guide to Prescription and Nonprescription Drugs, Vitamins, Home Remedies, and Herbal Products,* the quality and strength of a particular herb may vary from brand to brand and even from manufacturing batch to manufacturing batch. As a result, it's hard to be sure about exactly what you're getting.

Because there's so little hard data to work with when it comes to evaluating the safety of herbal products, some health-care professionals advise moms-to-be to steer clear of all herbal products

Watch Out!

Don't fall into the trap of assuming that herbal products are safe because they're natural. Natural or not, many herbal products contain highly protent ingredients that may be harmful to you and your baby. In fact, it has been estimated that approximately one quarter of the world's prescription drugs are derived from plants.

during pregnancy. That may be a case of overkill, but in the absence of much hard, scientific data about the safety of herbal product use during pregnancy, we can understand why a lot of healthcare professionals choose to err on the side of caution.

If you do decide to use herbal products during pregnancy, you'll want to keep the following guidelines in mind:

- Talk to your doctor or midwife about the types of herbal products you've been using before you start trying to conceive. That way, she can let you know which products should be avoided during pregnancy. At a minimum, your healthcare provider needs to know which types of products you've been using, how much you've been taking, and in what form (i.e., tea, infusion, tincture, salve, or capsule).

- Try to avoid using any herbal products during the first trimester. This is the key period of organ and tissue formation, so exposure to potentially dangerous herbal products can be particularly damaging to the developing baby.

- If you're planning to use any herbal products that are known for their ability to stimulate the uterus, proceed with extreme caution.

- Make sure that you're clear about which product you're using. Some products have similar names but may pose varying degrees of risk to you and your baby (e.g., blue cohosh versus black cohosh).

- Avoid products that contain more than one type of herb. It can be difficult to figure out how much of each herb you are getting and to pinpoint any the source of any reactions that occur.

- If you are trusting the recommendations of a third-party (in other words, someone other that your healthcare provider), make sure that this person has the training and experience necessary to be recommending herbal products to pregnant women and that she's basing her recommendations on the most respected herbal product information available — for example, the recommendations of Commission E in Germany, which reviews and evaluates the scientific evidence regarding herbal therapies and makes recommendations regarding their safety.

- Don't exceed the recommended doses for herbal products. Whenever you exceed the recommended dosage, you put your own health as well as the health of your baby at risk.

- Be aware of the potential for dangerous drug interactions. Certain types of herbal products are known to interact with medications and anesthetics while others have been found to interfere with blood clotting. If you were to require medication during labor or your baby had to be delivered via cesarean section, you could run into trouble if you had been taking the wrong type of herbal product — particularly if your healthcare provider was unaware of the types of products you had been using or unaware of the side effects associated with using those particular herbal products.

- Treat herbal products with the respect they deserve. Mother Nature can pack a pretty powerful pharmacological punch. It's better to be safe than sorry when there's so much on the line — namely the health of you and your baby.

Week 2

You're still not officially pregnant — but you're working on it. The countdown to Ovulation Day is officially on and you're determined to do your part to arrange for a midfallopian rendezvous between sperm and egg.

What's going on with your body

Now that your period has ended, the lining of your uterus begins to build up so that it will be able to provide the most hospitable implantation environment possible in the event that you manage to conceive during this cycle.

If you had some sort of high-tech spy camera that allowed you to get a sneak peak at all the action going on inside your body right now, you'd see that your ovaries are pretty much action central.

You see, each month your body has a bit of a contest, with about 15 to 20 eggs vying for Egg of the Month rights. During most months, only one of the eggs ripens and is released but, in certain cycles, you release more than one egg. (This is, of course, one of the ways you end up with twins. See Chapter 15 for more about twins and other multiples.)

If this seems a bit wasteful on Mother Nature's part (throwing away 95 percent of the eggs she starts to "hatch" each month), you ain't seen nothing yet! Of the 6 to 7 million eggs that you were born with, all but 40,000 were destroyed naturally by the time you reached puberty; and, of these, only about 400 will be released through ovulation during your childbearing years.

And when you consider how much waste is built into the male reproductive system, Mother Nature suddenly seems downright stingy with those eggs. A typical man will produce 12 trillion sperm over his lifetime — approximately 1,000 sperm per second. And yet it only takes one sperm to fertilize an egg.

So why the reproductive overkill?

Well, for starters, only 1 percent of sperm manage to complete the journey from the upper part of the vagina into the uterus. Then they have to make it into the fallopian tube that has an egg (50 percent of sperm take a wrong turn at this point, ending up in the wrong fallopian tube).

Then those sperm that made it into the right tube (you know, the ones that actually read the road map!) have to make their way past some rather formidable obstacles like the muscle contractions and hairlike fibers that are designed to propel the egg forward but that also end up forcing some sperm backward at the same time. The net result? Fewer than 200 sperm ultimately find their way to the egg.

At that point, the competition gets particularly fierce. There can only be one winner (unless, of course, we're talking about a multiple birth). Once a sperm manages to penetrate the egg successfully, the egg locks out all competing sperm. Finally, a single sperm has emerged victorious on this episode of *Sperm Survivor!*

You're likely to notice some other changes to your body this week as well, by the way, the most noteworthy preovulatory symptom being a change to the quantity and quality of your cervical mucus. Not only is it becoming more abundant: it's also taking on a slippery, "egg white" consistency. (See Chapter 3 for more about these and other fertility signals.)

What's going on with your head

If this is your first month of trying, you're probably still having fun with the Bedroom Olympics part of the operation. (And, chances are, your partner is pretty enthused about the proceedings, too!)

If, however, you've been at this for a while, you may be feeling more like a lab rat than a seductress. (If that's the case, you may want to flip back to the section on keeping the sizzle in your sex life in Chapter 3. You don't want baby-making to turn into a chore.)

The Hot List: This week's must-ask pregnancy questions

Here are the answers to some of the pregnancy questions that are likely to be running through your head this week.

Note: You're likely to have a lot of "how do I get pregnant?" questions, too. (And why not? You've got baby-making on the brain!) You'll find the answers to those kinds of questions in Chapter 3.

What can I do to increase my odds of conceiving a baby of a particular sex?

In a word, nothing.

While you've no doubt heard about the Shettles method and other low-tech methods of timing intercourse to increase your odds of conceiving a baby of a particular sex, a 1995 study conducted by the National Institute of Environmental Health Sciences concluded that there's no hard evidence to prove that any of these low-tech gender selection methods actually work. (This shouldn't be any huge surprise since even state-of-the-art high-tech sex-selection methods aren't able to offer couples much better than 75 percent odds of getting a baby of the desired sex — which is, incidentally, the very same success rate that is often attributed to the Shettles method.) So while it's okay to have fun with these methods, you shouldn't take them too seriously or — worse — paint the nursery on the basis of the gender of the baby you *think* you're getting!

And here's something else to consider: if you limit the number of times you have intercourse in the hope of conceiving a baby of a particular sex (the Shettles method, for example, suggests that you try to time intercourse as close to ovulation as possible if you hope to conceive a boy and that you abstain during the days leading up to your one shot at glory), you simultaneously decrease your odds of conceiving, period. So if you want to experiment with the Shettles method and other low-tech methods of sex selection, you'll have to wait a little longer, on average, to hit the reproductive jackpot.

What do the terms gestational age and fetal age mean?

The terms *gestational age* and *fetal age* are used to date your pregnancy.

The term *gestational age* refers to the length of time since the first day of your last menstrual period. If your gestational age is four weeks, this means that it has been four weeks since the first day of your last period. (This is because, thanks to this particular method of dating a pregnancy, you're technically two weeks pregnant the moment you conceive!) Note: Sometimes your doctor or midwife will say that you are four weeks LMP (last menstrual period). It all means the same thing.

The term *fetal age,* on the other hand, refers to the age of your developing baby, counting from the estimated date of conception. The fetal age is typically two weeks less than the gestational age although if your menstrual cycle is markedly shorter or longer, your dates are likely to be off. This is one of the reasons why your doctor or midwife will pay particular attention to the date calculations on any ultrasounds you may have as well as the fundal measurements (measurements of the height of your uterus) that are done at your regular prenatal checkups. It's all a way of cross-checking the accuracy of your due date and ensuring that your baby's development is pretty much on track.

As you've no doubt noticed by now, we chose to organize this book according to gestational age rather than fetal age. In other words, the first week of pregnancy in this book is the week of your last menstrual period. This is because most women are used to using this method of tracking their stage of pregnancy and find it annoying to have to subtract two weeks if the pregnancy book they are reading happens to be structured on the basis of fetal age.

But just to eliminate any possible confusion, we'll make a point of mentioning your baby's fetal age from time to time, too. (Never let it be said that we don't try to give our readers the best of both worlds!)

What workplace hazards do my partner and I need to be aware of now that we're trying to conceive?

While a number of reproductive hazards in the workplace have been identified in recent years, according to the National

Institute for Occupational Safety and Health (NIOSH), there is still much that we do not know about the effects of various types of workplace environments on human reproduction. This is because, most workplace chemicals have not been tested on humans, and, in many cases, there is limited animal data as well.

Here's a quick summary of the little we *do* know about the reproductive fallout of certain types of workplace hazards on both female and male workers.

Reproductive hazards for the female worker

When the workplace environment has an effect on the reproductive system of a female worker, it tends to affect her in one of the following ways:

- by throwing her menstrual cycle out of whack;

- by affecting her fertility;

- by increasing the likelihood that she will experience a miscarriage or stillbirth;

- by increasing her odds of giving birth prematurely or of giving birth to a low birthweight baby or a baby with a birth defect or a developmental disorder,

- by increasing the risk that her baby will go on to develop-some sort of childhood cancer.

Such exposure can happen by breathing in harmful substances, ingesting harmful substances, or by having harmful substances come into contact with the skin.

To minimize the risk to yourself and your baby, you should

- wash your hands whenever you come into contact with hazardous substances and again before eating or drinking;

- avoid any direct skin contact with chemicals;

- review all material safety data sheets (MSDSs) at your workplace so that you will know exactly what types of reproductive hazards you may face on the job (see Tables 5.4 and 5.5 for a summary of the key reproductive hazards women face on the job);

- participate in all safety and health education, training, and monitoring programs offered by your employer;

- use personal protective eqiupment (gloves, respirators, and personal protective clothing) and follow safe work practices and procedures to reduce your exposure to workplace hazards.

For more information about reproductive safety and health, contact the National Institute for Occupational Safety and Health at 1-800-35-NIOSH or www.cdc.gov/niosh.

Table 5.4. The Key Chemical and Physical Agents that Pose a Reproductive Hazard to Female Workers

Type of Workplace Hazard	Potentially Exposed Workers	Potential Effects
Cancer treatment drugs (e.g. methotrexate)	Healthcare workers, pharmacists	Infertility, miscarriage, birth defects, low birthweight
Carbon disulfide (CS_2)	Viscose rayon workers	Menstrual cycle changes
Ethylene glycol ethers such as 2-ethoxyethanol (2EE) and 2-methoxyethanol (2ME)	Electronic and semiconductor workers	Miscarriages
Ionizing radiation (X-rays and gamma rays)	Healthcare workers, dental personnel, atomic workers	Infertility, miscarriage, birth defects, low birthweight, developmental disorders, childhood cancers
Lead	Battery makers, solderers, welders, radiator repairers, bridge repainters, firing range workers, home remodelers	Infertility, miscarriage, low birthweight, developmental disorders

Type of Workplace Hazard	Potentially Exposed Workers	Potential Effects
Physical labor, strenuous (e.g., prolonged standing or heavy lifting)	Workers in many occupational groups	Miscarriages later in pregnancy, premature delivery

Source: National Institute for Occupational Safety and Health

Table 5.5. Disease-Causing Agents That Pose a Reproductive Hazard to Female Workers

Agent	Potentially Exposed Workers	Potential Effects	Preventive Measures (where applicable)
Cytomegalovirus (CMV)	Healthcare workers, workers in contact with infants and children (e.g., daycare workers)	Birth defects, low birthweight, developmental disorders	Good hygenic practices such as handwashing
Hepatitis B virus	Healthcare workers	Low birthweight	Vaccination
Human immunodeficiency virus (HIV)	Healthcare workers	Low birth-, weight childhood cancers	Universal precautions
Human parvovirus B19 (fifth disease)	Healthcare workers, workers in contact with infants and children (e.g., daycare workers)	Miscarriage	Good hygenic practices such as handwashing
Rubella (German measles)	Healthcare workers, workers in contact with infants and children	Birth defects, low birthweight	Vaccination prior to pregnancy if no preexisting immunity

(continued)

Table 5.5. *(continued)*

Agent	Potentially Exposed Workers	Potential Effects	Preventive Measures (where applicable)
Toxoplasmosis	Animal-care workers, veterinarians	Miscarriage, birth defects, developmental disorders	Good hygiene practices such as handwashing
Varicella zoster virus (chickenpox)	Healthcare workers, workers in contact with infants and children (e.g., daycare workers)	Birth defects, low birthweight	Vaccination prior to pregnancy if no preexisting immunity

Source: National Institute for Occupational Safety and Health

Reproductive hazards for the male worker

Female workers aren't the only workers affected by workplace reproductive hazards, of course. Male workers can also be affected. When such exposure occurs, the male workers reproductive health is typically affected in one of the following ways:

- **Reduction in the number of sperm:** Some reproductive hazards can slow or even stop the production of sperm, something that can result in reduced fertility or even sterility.

- **Change in the shape of the sperm:** If the shape of the sperm is affected by hazards in the workplace, the sperm may have difficulty swimming to or fertilizing the egg.

- **Sperm transfer problems:** If hazardous chemicals collect in the epididymis, seminal vesicles, or prostate, the chemicals may kill the sperm, change the way the sperm swim, or attach to the sperm and be carried to the egg.

- **Sexual performance:** Hormonal changes and severe stress can interfere with male sexual performance, something that can have an indirect effect on fertility.

- **Sperm chromosomes:** Reproductive hazards can affect the chromosomes found in sperm. If the sperm's DNA is damaged, it may not be capable of fertilizing an egg; or it may result in an unhealthy conception if fertilization does occur.

Workplace substances that are harmful to male workers can also be indirectly harmful to their families. Certain substances that are unintentionally brought home from the workplace may affect his partner's reproductive system and/or the health of his unborn child.

See Table 5.6 for list of some of the better-documented male reproductive hazards in the workplace.

Table 5.6. Male Reproductive Hazards in the Workplace: Type of Exposure and Observed Effects

Type of Exposure	Lowered Number of Sperm	Abnormal Shape of Sperm	Altered Sperm Transfer	Altered Hormones/ Sexual Performance
Lead	X	X	X	X
Dibromo-chloropropane	X			
Carbaryl (Sevin)		X		
Toluenediamine and Dinitrotoluene	X			
Ethylene dibromide	X	X	X	
Plastic production (styrene and acetone)		X		
Ethylene glycol monoethyl ether	X			
Welding		X	X	
Perchloroethylene			X	

(continued)

Table 5.6. *(continued)*

Type of Exposure	Lowered Number of Sperm	Abnormal Shape of Sperm	Altered Sperm Transfer	Altered Hormones/ Sexual Performance
Mercury vapor				X
Heat	X		X	
Military radar	X			
Kepone			X	
Bromine vapor	X	X	X	
Radiation	X	X	X	X
Carbon disulfide				X
2,4-Dichlorophenoxy acetic acid (2, 4-D)		X	X	

Source: National Institute for Occupational Safety and Health

Studies to date indicate that some men experience the health effects listed here from workplace exposures. The amount of time a worker is exposed, the amount of the hazard to which the worker was exposed, and other personal factors may all help to determine whether or not an individual is affected.

Note: The data listed for kepone, bromine vapor, and radiation exposure reflects situations in which workers were exposed to high levels as a result of a workplace accident.

 Watch Out!

Video display terminals (VDTs) have been linked to a smorgasbord of health complaints, including eye strain and neck, back, hand, shoulder, and wrist pain. In fact, 25 percent of pregnant VDT workers develop carpal tunnel syndrome — a condition in which pressure on a nerve passing through the wrist to the hand causes numbness, pain, tingling, and, in some cases, mild weakness of the hand and fingers. Fortunately, exercise breaks of about 15 minutes every 2 hours and ergonomically correct equipment can help to prevent many of these problems.

Week 3

If you haven't ovulated already, you should be ovulating at any moment now (unless, of course, your cycles are highly irregular, in which case all bets are off!) But assuming you were blessed with a textbook 28-day cycle, ovulation typically occurs on day 14 of your menstrual cycle — in other words, yesterday.

Assuming your partner has done his reproductive duty, there should be ample quantities of sperm camped out inside your fallopian tubes, waiting for that newly released egg to saunter by. The moment of truth has finally arrived.

What's going on with your baby

If Lady Luck is on your side (remember, the odds of conception happening during your first cycle of trying are *not* in your favor), the sperm and egg will manage to hook up as planned. Here's a blow-by-blow description of what may happen in the deepest, darkest recesses of your fallopian tubes and your uterus while you're simply going about your daily business.

- The sperm and the egg unite, joining 23 maternal chromosomes to 23 paternal chromosomes and beginning the miraculous process that — should all go according to plan — will eventually lead to the birth of a healthy newborn.

- The fertilized egg (now known as a zygote) embarks on a three-day journey from the fallopian tube to the uterus. It then undergoes another two to three days of development in the uterus before implanting in the uterine wall.

- The uterine wall is soft and porous thanks to the hormonal changes associated with the first half of the menstrual cycle. By this point in the cycle, the uterine lining is between $\frac{1}{6}$ and $\frac{1}{3}$ of an inch thick — ideal (im)planting conditions!

- A small amount of spotting (implantation bleeding) may occur approximately 10 days following conception. You may initially mistake this spotting as the start of a menstrual period that never actually shows up.

What's going on with your body

If you and your partner have been trying to conceive for some time, you may strongly suspect that you are pregnant even before the pregnancy test actually comes back positive.

Part of this, of course, may be wishful thinking: you're hoping like crazy that this is the cycle when you've actually managed to conceive. But at least a part of this feeling may be based in biological fact. Studies have shown that some women are able to detect hormonal changes, however slight, from the time that the body begins to produce human chorionic gonadotropin (hCG) — about seven days after conception.

But if you don't notice anything particularly out of the ordinary until you've missed your first period, you're certainly in good company. Most women don't experience any of the classic symptoms of early pregnancy — morning sickness, fatigue, and tender breasts — until after their first missed period.

If, on the other hand, you aren't consciously planning a pregnancy, it may take you even longer to consider the possibility that you might be pregnant. After all, if you aren't specifically on the lookout for possible symptoms of early pregnancy, the milder symptoms may go unnoticed or be confused with premenstrual symptoms. You may explain away your feelings of fatigue by thinking about how hard you've been working lately and wonder if the touch of nausea you experienced when you woke up this morning was caused by something you ate for dinner last night — and you may give premenstrual hormonal changes credit for your tender breasts. Because these symptoms can be mild or even nonexistent, you could be well into your third month of pregnancy before you decide that it's time to dash down to the drugstore to purchase a home pregnancy test.

What's going on with your head

This week can feel a lot like reproductive purgatory. After all the excitement of the midcycle Bedroom Olympics, it can be a bit of a letdown to have to wait a good 10 to 12 days (12 days if you want a fairly accurate home pregnancy test result, 10 days if you're a bit of a gambler!) to find out whether or not all your baby-making efforts have paid off.

Of course, if you're not consciously planning a pregnancy, it's pretty much business as usual — except, of course, for that nagging worry about the condom that broke, those couple of missed birth control pills, or whatever reproductive curveball you may be dealing with this month.

The Hot List: This week's must-ask pregnancy questions

You're probably starting to think — okay, make that obsess — about the possibility that you could be pregnant, which is why a lot of the questions that are running through your head this week have to do with whether or not you're actually pregnant and how and when to do a pregnancy tests.

And, of course, if your gut instinct is telling you that you might be pregnant, a second category of pregnancy questions will start to drive you crazy in the middle of the night — questions of the "Is it safe to do this if I'm pregnant" variety!

What are the most common early pregnancy symptoms?

Find yourself running to the bathroom every couple of minutes to check for any signs of your period? You're certainly in good company. Most would-be expectant mamas tend to get a wee bit obsessed with the whole "am I pregnant?" question at this stage of the game.

You may find the list of early pregnancy symptoms in Table 5.7 helpful when you're trying to decide whether or not to take the pregnancy test when it's finally time to test.

But first a small caveat. It's possible to have some of the pregnancy symptoms listed in Table 5.7 and yet not be pregnant at all — just as it's possible to not have any of these symptoms at all and yet be 100 percent certifiably pregnant. (It's pretty rare to get off entirely scot-free in the pregnancy symptom department, but, hey, it can happen!)

Table 5.7. Early Pregnancy Symptoms

Symptom	When It Occurs	What Causes It to Occur During Pregnancy	Other Possible Causes
Menstrual changes			
A missed period	Around the time that your period is due — typically four weeks after the first day of your last menstrual cycle, but a little sooner or a little later depending on your typical cycle length.	Rising levels of progesterone fully suppress your menstrual period.	Jet lag, extreme weight loss or gain, a change in climate, a chronic disease such as diabetes or tuberculosis, severe illness, surgery, shock, bereavement, or other sources of stress. Note: Taking birth control pills can also cause you to miss a period.
A lighter-than-average period	Around the time that your period is due.	Your progesterone levels are rising, but they are still not high enough to fully suppress your menstrual period — something that can make it extra tricky for your doctor or midwife to pin down your due date.	May also be experienced by birth control pill users.
A small amount of spotting	Approximately 1 week after conception.	This type of spotting may occur when the fertilized egg implants in the uterine wall about a week after conception has occurred. Note: Only a small percentage of women experience implantation bleeding, so don't panic if you don't.	May be experienced by users of birth control pills and women with fibroids or infections. Some women routinely experience midcycle spotting. Spotting may also be one of the earliest signs of an impending miscarriage. (See Chapter 17.)
Abdominal cramping			
Abdominal cramping (periodlike cramping in the lower abdomen and pelvis and/or bloating and gassiness)	Around the time that your period is due.	Abdominal cramping may be triggered by the hormonal changes of early pregnancy. Some women describe this cramping as a feeling like their period is about to start.	PMS, constipation, irritable bowel syndrome.

Breast changes

Breast tenderness and enlargement	Breast tenderness can set in as early as a few days after conception. It doesn't typically last beyond the first trimester. The other breast changes occur as the first trimester progresses and continue throughout your pregnancy.	Breast tenderness (e.g., tender, tingly, swollen breasts) and enlargement are caused by the hormonal changes of early pregnancy. You may also notice some changes to the appearance of your breasts: the areola (the flat area around the nipple) may begin to darken and the tiny glands on the areola may begin to enlarge.	Premenstrual syndrome (PMS), excessive caffeine intake, or fibrocystic breast disease.

Nausea, food aversions and cravings, heightened sense of smell

Morning sickness (a catchall term that is used to describe everything from mild nausea to severe vomiting that can lead to dehydration)	2 to 8 weeks after conception.	Scientists believe that morning sickness is somehow linked to high levels of progesterone and human chorionic gonadotropin (hCG), but they aren't sure of the particular mechanisms involved. Note: Morning sickness tends to be worse during the morning, when your blood sugar is at its lowest, but it can make life miserable at any time of day.	Flu, food poisoning, or other illnesses.
Food aversions and cravings (e.g., a metallic taste in the mouth and/or a craving for certain types of foods)	2 to 8 weeks after conception.	Food aversions and cravings are triggered by the hormonal changes of early pregnancy.	Poor diet, stress, or PMS.
Heightened sense of smell	2 to 8 weeks after conception.	The heightened sense of smell that many pregnant women experience is the result of the hormonal changes of early pregnancy.	Illness.

(continued)

Table 5.7. (continued)

Symptom	When It Occurs	What Causes It to Occur During Pregnancy	Other Possible Causes
Increased need to urinate and/or constipation			
Increased need to urinate	As early as 2 to 3 weeks after conception.	The increased need to urinate is triggered by increased blood flow intake.	A urinary tract infection, uterine fibroids, or excessive caffeine to the pelvic region and by the production of human chorionic gonadotropin (hCG) during early pregnancy.
Constipation	As early as 2 to 3 weeks after conception.	Progesterone relaxes the intestinal muscles, resulting in varying degrees of constipation.	Inadequate intake of high-fiber foods or inadequate consumption of fluids.
Decreased energy level			
Fatigue	Anytime during the first trimester.	Fatigue is caused by increased levels of progesterone (which acts as a sedative) and an increase in your metabolic rate (your body's way of ensuring that it will be able to support the needs of you and your developing baby).	Not getting enough sleep, not eating properly, flu, illness, or some other medical condition.
Changes to the reproductive organs			
Changes to the cervix and the uterus (the cervix takes on a slightly purplish hue, and both the cervix and uterus begin to soften)	About 6 weeks.	These changes are caused by the hormonal changes of early pregnancy. Note: These changes can often be detected by your doctor or midwife during a pelvic examination.	A delayed menstrual period.

Adapted from *The Mother of All Pregnancy Books* by Ann Douglas (John Wiley and Sons, 2002). See www.themotherofallbooks.com.

What household toxins should I be avoiding at this stage of the game?

According to the March of Dimes, it's best to steer clear of cleaning products like oven cleaners, which contain highly toxic ingredients. More run-of-the-mill household cleaners that contain ammonia or chlorine are unlikely to be harmful to the developing baby (unless, of course, you mix these two products, in which case you'll create toxic fumes that are dangerous to everyone!), but it's still best to err on the side of caution by wearing rubber gloves and using the products in a ventilated area. If you can swing it, you might want to hand over the really heavy-duty cleaning jobs to someone else while you are pregnant — or at least during the first trimester when using strong-smelling cleaning products will tend to trigger nausea.

You'll also want to avoid these environmental toxins, as they may also pose a risk to the developing baby:

- **Lead:** Lead can be found in lead-based paint (found in 80 percent of homes built before 1978); lead-crystal glassware and certain types of ceramic dishes; the wicks of certain types of scented candles (lead particles are then released into the air when the candles are burned); and certain types of arts and crafts materials (for example, oil paints, ceramic glazes, and stained glass materials). Lead can occasionally show up in drinking water if a home has lead pipes, lead solder on copper pipes, or brass faucets. (Your state health department can tell you how to get your pipes tested for lead.) You'll reduce the amount of lead that shows up in your drinking water by running the tap for

Bright Idea

Looking for some less-toxic alternatives to your usual household cleaner? Check out the tip sheet entitled "Safe Substitutes at Home: Non-Toxic Cleaning Products," available on the Environmental Protection Agency Web site at es.epa.gov/techinfo/facts/safe-fs.html.

30 seconds before using it for drinking or cooking and by only using water from the cold tap for these purposes.

- **Organic solvents:** A Canadian study found that first-trimester exposure to such organic solvents as alcohols, degreasers, paint thinners, and varnish removers increased the risk of giving birth to a baby with a major birth defect by about 13 times. Other studies have demonstrated an increased risk of miscarriage. So it's probably best to avoid using these products during pregnancy, and during the first trimester in particular.

- **Pesticides:** Pesticides contain poisons that can, in large quantities, be harmful to the developing baby. (Some studies have indicated that high levels of exposures may contribute to miscarriage, preterm delivery, and birth defects.) If you're reluctant to sublet your digs to assorted creepy crawlies for the next nine months, you may decide to go with a less-toxic alternative like boric acid (available in hardware stores). If you can't avoid using a pesticide, you'll want to have someone else apply the chemicals and vacate the premises for the amount of time recommended on the product instructions; remove food, dishes, and utensils from the area where the pesticide is being used; turn off the air conditioning and close all windows to avoid unnecessary air circulation; and have someone else ventilate the room and wipe down all surfaces where food will be prepared before you arrive back on the scene.

- **Insect repellents:** The safety of insect repellents during pregnancy has not been fully demonstrated, so you'll want to avoid using these products or — if their use is absolutely unavoidable — you'll want to apply these products to your clothing rather than to your skin. (Use gloves or an applicator to avoid getting the insect repellent on your hands.) Note: If you live in an area where West Nile Virus is a concern, you'll want to talk to your healthcare

Watch Out!

Your baby's immature liver and kidneys can't process and eliminate toxins as quickly as your organs can. That's why substances that are hazardous to you are many times more hazardous to your developing baby. Consequently, it's a good idea to avoid exposing yourself to cleaning products with powerful odors (such as chlorine and ammonia-based products), paints, solvents, lawn-care products, and other powerful chemicals.

provider about the risks and benefits of using insect repellents as a means of preventing West Nile Virus during pregnancy. See Chapter 7 for more on this issue.

How can I be sure that my drinking water is safe?

The only way to be sure is to have your water tested. After all, that crystal-clear glass of water may contain a lot more than you bargain for. In recent years, some studies have indicated that drinking water that is high in certain chlorine byproducts may pose an increased risk of miscarriage and poor fetal growth.

If you're concerned about the quality of your drinking water, you can arrange to have it tested to ensure that it meets health and safety standards. (Note: You may also wish to go this route if you are concerned that your drinking water may have become contaminated with pesticides, lead, or other environmental toxins.) If that sounds too complicated, you may simply want to switch to bottled water once you start trying to conceive.

Should I pack away my electric blanket?

While the jury is still out on the issue of whether or not it's safe to use electric blankets during pregnancy, you may want to find other ways of staying warm. (Assuming you even have to worry about staying warm, that is! Increased levels of progesterone, usually take care of the problem for you.) Some preliminary studies have linked electric blanket use during pregnancy to an increased risk of miscarriage and an increased incidence of childhood brain cancers. Of course, the same studies found that sewing machine use in pregnancy was associated with a decreased occurrence of childhood leukemia, which only goes to show how important it is to take the results of these studies with a grain of salt. If you look hard enough, you can find a study for or against pretty much anything!

A friend told me I shouldn't be changing the kitty litter anymore. What's she talking about?

Your friend is trying to help you to avoid contracting toxoplasmosis — a disease that can be spread through uncooked meat or via cat feces and that can be extremely harmful or even fatal to the developing baby. Toxoplasmosis can lead to miscarriage, stillbirth, or a variety of problems, including vision problems, hearing loss, and learning disabilities.

Damage to an otherwise healthy newborn can be prevented if the toxoplasmosis is detected promptly and treated with antibiotics, which is why two states — Massachusetts and New Hampshire — have started routinely screening infants for toxoplasmosis. Screening makes sense in this situation because a mother can pass toxoplasmosis on to her baby without exhibiting any symptoms herself. Likewise the baby may be symptom-free until an eye infection or other problem develops months or even years after birth, at which point some damage has been done.

Unless you're sure you've developed immunity to toxoplasmosis (an $80 blood test can tell you for sure), you'll want to have someone else change the kitty litter for you or — the very least — wear gloves and wash your hands thoroughly once you've done the deed. A pregnant woman who becomes infected with toxoplasmosis for the first time in her life has about a 40 percent chance of passing the infection on to her baby, and the earlier in pregnancy the infection occurs, the greater the cause for concern.

You'll also want to wear gardening gloves when you're working in your garden, by the way, because there's always the chance that you'll uncover some buried treasure from a neighborhood cat. (Note: Even if you happen to live in a 100 percent cat-free neighborhood, you should plan to wear gloves to protect yourself from pesticide exposure.) And, of course, you'll want to thoroughly wash the soil off any vegetables you bring in from the garden, just in case the soil has been contaminated with cat feces.

Here are some other tips on avoiding toxoplasmosis during pregnancy:

- Cook all meats thoroughly, especially pork and lamb. Meats should be cooked to an internal temperature of 160°F throughout and should be pink or brown, not red.

- Wash your hands thoroughly each time you handle raw meat. To minimize the risk of infection, avoid touching your eyes, nose, or mouth while your hands are contaminated with raw meat juices.

- Disinfect cutting boards, utensils, and all other items used in food preparation when you are working with raw meat.

- Thoroughly wash and/or peel raw fruits and vegetables before serving.

- Don't allow other foods to come into contact with raw meat or unwashed fruits and vegetables.

- Avoid children's sandboxes as they are often used as litter boxes by cats.

- Keep your cat indoors to prevent it from hunting birds or rodents and avoid feeding your cat raw or undercooked meats.

 Watch Out!

If you've been test-driving your maternal instincts on a pet mouse or a pet hamster, you'll want to be careful about handling your pet and cleaning its cage while you're pregnant. Mice and hamsters can carry lymphocytic choriomeningitis virus (LCMV) — something that can lead to mental retardation, blindness, and seizures in a baby born to a woman who contracts this virus during pregnancy. This virus tends to be particularly nasty because you only have to breathe in dust from the feces of affected animals to pick up the virus, so you'll either want to wear gloves and a protective mask while you're cleaning your pet's cage or, better yet, you might want to send your pet on an extended vacation to visit a friend or relative who feels up to playing surrogate parent to a rodent.

Note: You can stroke your cat. You just want to make sure you wash your hands well afterwards.

Week 4

This is the week when you finally find out whether or not all your baby-making efforts have paid off. By the middle to end of this week, you should be able to get a reasonably accurate result from a home pregnancy test. (Of course, this assumes that you've been blessed with one of those textbook 28-day cycles and that you ovulated on schedule. If it hasn't been at least 10 to 12 days since conception occurred, you won't get a positive pregnancy test result even if you are pregnant.)

What's going on with your baby

By the time the pregnancy test comes back positive, your baby will have completed the first two weeks of his or her gestational development. And what an eventful two weeks it's been! Your baby has been doubling in size every 24 hours. As Alexander Tsiaras and Barry Werth note in their book *From Conception to Birth: A Life Unfolds* (Doubleday, 2002), if your baby's growth were to continue at that pace for the remainder of your pregnancy, your baby would be larger than the sun by delivery day.

Of course, your baby is anything but mammoth at this stage of the game — between 0.36 and 1 millimeter in length. But don't be fooled by your baby's microscopic size: the groundwork for its various body systems is being put into place even though your baby looks anything but human right now. The ectoderm layer of cells will evolve into your baby's nervous system (including the brain); the endoderm layer will become your baby's gastrointestinal tract, liver, pancreas, and thyroid; and the mesoderm will become your body's skeleton, connective tissues, blood system, urogenital system, and most of your baby's muscles.

Then, on the 13th day after conception, your baby's umbilical cord is formed. It will serve as a combination food pantry, oxygen tank, and waste-disposal system in the months leading to birth, delivering oxygen and nutrients to your developing baby and helping to get rid of waste products.

What's going on with your body

The biggest thing you're likely to notice about your body this week is the fact that you've missed a period. (Of course, if your cycles tend to be erratic at the best of times, the fact that your period hasn't arrived may be a distinct nonevent as far as you're concerned.)

Some women end up experiencing some light spotting around the time that their period was due. You may notice some light spotting about 10 days after the fertilized egg implants in the uterine wall. Of course, if the spotting occurs any later on in pregnancy and/or is accompanied by any of the symptoms of an ectopic pregnancy or a miscarriage (see Chapters 7 and 17), you'll definitely want to get in touch with your doctor or midwife right away.

What's going on with your head

You may find yourself second-guessing the pregnancy test results and calling all the pregnancy test kit help lines to ask for help in confirming that your positive really is a positive. (Hey, you want to be *positively* positive, right?) If you're like most newly pregnant women, you may still be finding it a little hard to believe that all the baby-making theory you've been reading up on for the past few months actually works when you put it into practice.

> 66 Our second pregnancy was the closest thing we had to having an unplanned pregnancy. It wasn't really, as we weren't taking precautions, but it did happen a little sooner than I expected. I struggled with coming to terms with being pregnant for the first few months. 99
>
> — Jacqueline, 34, pregnant with her second child

How you may be feeling

Now that this pregnancy thing is a done deal, you may find yourself experiencing a mix of emotions — everything from shock to panic to euphoria. After all, it's one thing to *think* about having a baby: it's quite another to find out you have one on order!

Some women find that they need a little time to wrap their heads around the fact that they are pregnant, even if they were consciously planning a pregnancy. "Even though I very much wanted to get pregnant, it was still difficult to accept the reality, when I did conceive, that I would be host to a fetus for nine months, and then have to give birth to it!" recalls Tracy, a 31-year-old mother of one.

> 66 We weren't planning this one. It just happened. We had previously discussed waiting until we were in a house and financially sound. It was stressful when we discovered we were pregnant. 99
>
> — Andrea, 34, mother of one

Of course, the adjustment tends to be a little greater if the pregnancy was completely unplanned, as was the case for 25-year-old Erika, who is currently expecting her third child. "I conceived while using an IUD," she explains. "I took the pregnancy test because I was four days late, and just wanted to rule out the possibility of pregnancy so that I could relax. Well, the test came back positive and I was in shock. This may sound horrible, but I bawled for almost an hour afterwards."

Jennifer, a 27-year-old mother of one, also hit the panic button initially when her pregnancy test came back positive: "Our pregnancy was unplanned — the result of failed contraception," she explains. "It was a surprise and initially not a welcome one. We had been married 2½ years, but had recently moved to New York City and were living in a tiny studio apartment. On top of that, I was five months into a new job. We were panicked and afraid at first, and briefly and irrationally considered not going forward with the pregnancy. After a couple of days, we came to terms with the fact that we were going to be parents many years earlier than expected or planned. Now was as good a time as any, and fate brought us here."

Of course, some women are positively over-the-moon with excitement when they find out that there's a baby on the way. Amie, a 38-year-old mother of two, remembers what a thrill it was to get the happy news: "I was so excited I could barely contain myself. Finding out on Christmas Eve was so wonderful. I remember that night every year: the feelings I had inside — scared, excited, nervous. I was in heaven!"

Kim, a 35-year-old mother of one, also felt tremendous joy when she finally managed to conceive after three years of trying: "It was a magical time, one that I had waited for so long. I will never forget how wonderful I felt finally being pregnant."

> 66 Since I had just suffered a miscarriage and my period hadn't resumed, neither my husband nor I thought I was pregnant. I was over nine weeks pregnant when I finally took a blood test. The pregnancy didn't seem real until we saw our baby move her tiny arms and legs on ultrasound. Seeing a living, moving baby filled us both with incredible joy and awe and brought tears to our eyes. 99
>
> — Dawnette, 28, mother of one

How your partner may be feeling

You've no doubt seen the commercials on TV: a pregnant woman shows her partner the positive home pregnancy test result, and the two of them dance around the room.

Although scenes like this do get played out in some bedrooms across the country, in at least as many homes the scene is less than a scriptwriter's dream: for one reason or another, the partner is less than euphoric when presented with the news that there's a baby on the way.

There may be a lot of conflicting emotions going on inside his head.

He may have developed a full-fledged case of Breadwinner Syndrome — a deathly fear that he won't be able to adequately provide for the little bambino the two of you have just managed to conceive. "I think the biggest concern thing for me was the overwhelming sense of responsibility — knowing that a completely helpless life was now absolutely dependent on us for every-thing," recalls Bob, a 36-year-old father of three. "Now, every decision we made could have repercus-sions for this other life."

Your partner may also be grappling with a question that has troubled genera-tions of expectant fathers before him: Is it really okay to be having sex with *some-one's mother*? (See Chapter 7 for more on how pregnancy affects your sex life, for better and for worse.)

> 66 I was late, but I also had a pretty irregular cycle, so when I saw two lines on the little stick, one of which was pretty pale, I wasn't sure I really was pregnant. I showed my husband and he said, 'You're definitely preg-nant.' I think we were both pretty shocked and amazed for the next couple of hours. 99
>
> — Jennie, 30, pregnant with her first child

Your partner may express his feelings of uncertainty by second-guessing the pregnancy test result — a reaction that isn't likely to score very many points with you, of course. "After I showed him the faint line, I had to convince him that it was positive," recalls Melissa, 24, who is pregnant with her first child. "Then he asked to see the instructions to make sure I did it right! He was a lot more convinced two days later when he watched me take a test first thing in the morning and it showed a definite positive. He was very enthusiastic and has been ever since."

Tracy, 31, mother of one, had a similar experience with her partner: "My husband was home, eating breakfast and reading the newspaper the morning I took the pregnancy test," she recalls. "I tried to show him the stick, and he said, 'You peed on that, and I'm eating so keep it away.' He didn't even get up to hug me until I asked him to. He kept telling me not to get my hopes up, that it might be a false positive. He didn't see any reason to get excited or happy until the pregnancy was confirmed with a blood test."

In most case, guys who react like this are demonstrating healthy skepticism — not deliberately attempting to drive their partners crazy (although it may seem that way to you). Your partner may simply want to play it cool until he's sure the pregnant test result can be trusted. "My husband was very hesitant to believe the news, based on a home pregnancy test, which was disappointing to me because at that point I was sure," recalls Wendy, 30, who is pregnant with her first child. "However, when the doctor told us that they take positive home pregnancy tests as a 'yes,' he finally jumped for joy."

Of course, not all guys go into panic and/or denial mode when they're hit with the big news. Some are positively thrilled right from the start. "I told my husband when we went out to dinner," recalls Colleen, a 29-year-old mother of three. "I had a pair of knit booties wrapped up in a small gift box, hoping he would understand without me having to say anything. I was so nervous. He opened the box, looked at it, and started to cry. Then he smiled."

> ❝He was out of town and I called him at 6:00 a.m. to tell him. He was very sleepy and kept saying, 'Are you sure? Maybe it's wrong.' I was very frustrated because I wanted him to be excited and he didn't believe it was real. He finally believed the test from the doctor's office, which was done about three days later.❞
>
> — Laura, 31, mother of one

> 66 All in all, I'd have to say that my husband was much more excited than I. Our doctor had indicated that it would probably take about three months to get pregnant, and I was counting on that time to adjust to the idea of being a mom. 99
>
> — Susan, 29, pregnant with her first child

Michelle, a 28-year-old mother-to-be, has equally tender memories of watching the pregnancy test go positive with her partner (another woman). "Finding out we were pregnant was not unlike the typical TV commercial. My partner went and bought the pregnancy test. After being fully educated on all the different types of tests by the pharmacist, my partner chose one and we took our first test. It went according to script from there as we watched a pink line appear after two minutes. We were both ecstatic, with it being our first time with artificial insemination and our first child."

The Hot List: This week's must-ask pregnancy questions

At this point in your pregnancy, you're likely to have pregnancy tests on the brain, which is why this week's Hot List focuses on what's involved in getting your pregnancy confirmed.

How soon can I do a home pregnancy test?

If you suspect that you're pregnant, you should arrange to take a pregnancy test as soon as possible. That way, you can ensure that both you and your baby receive the best possible care during the months ahead.

You have two basic choices when it comes to confirming pregnancy: using an over-the-counter home pregnancy test or making an appointment to have your pregnancy confirmed by your doctor or midwife.

Home pregnancy tests

Home pregnancy tests are designed to detect the presence of hCG, the hormone manufactured by the blatocyst (the name

Moneysaver

You can save yourself the cost of a home pregnancy test if you're tracking your basal body temperature. If your period is late, you simply need to note whether your luteal phase — the number of days since you ovulated — is longer than normal. If you have 18 consecutive elevated temperatures or your temperature remains elevated for at least three days longer than your longest luteal phase to date, you're probably pregnant.

for the hollow clump of cells resulting from the meeting of sperm and egg) following implantation. Enough hCG is present in the urine to allow a pregnancy to be confirmed as soon as 9 to 12 days after conception, although it takes some pregnant women a little longer to test positive.

It may not be in your best interest to jump the gun on testing, however. A study reported in the October 2001 edition of the *Journal of the American Medical Association* concluded that the best time to do a home pregnancy test is a week to seven days *after* your period is due. While most women would argue that you would have to have the patience of a saint to wait that long, there's a case to made for waiting: if you get a false negative because you've tested too early — in other words, the test says you're not pregnant, when, in fact, you are — you might not be quite as careful about avoiding alcohol and other potentially harmful substances as you would if you believed that you were pregnant. The researchers involved in this study concluded that approximately 10 percent of pregnancies are missed when home pregnancy tests are performed on the day that a woman's period is due.

If you do decide to test early and you get a negative result, you'll want to take that negative test result as a "probably not pregnant" rather than a "definitely not pregnant" and either do another home pregnancy test in another couple of days if your period still hasn't started or get in touch with your doctor to see if she can order a more sensitive pregnancy blood test.

And until you know otherwise, you should continue to play the part of the mama-to-be by avoiding anything that could be potentially harmful to a developing baby.

Having your doctor or midwife confirm your pregnancy

If you decide to have your doctor or midwife confirm your pregnancy, she will order either a urine test or blood test.

The urine test you take at the lab is virtually identical to the urine test you can find in any home pregnancy test kit. You either urinate directly on the test stick or dip the test stick into a sample of urine. If your doctor wants you to bring in a sample of first morning urine, remember to keep it at room temperature.

The blood test you take to confirm pregnancy can be either qualitative (that is, a test that gives you a "yes/no" answer as to whether you are pregnant) or quantitative (it gives a rough idea of how pregnant you are providing your health-care practitioner with a reading of the level of hCG in your blood).

Your health-care practitioner is more likely to order a quantitative blood test if she has reason to believe that your pregnancy may be in jeopardy, if you've experienced a series of first-trimester miscarriages in the past, if ectopic pregnancy is a concern, or if she intends to start you on progesterone in an effort to prevent you from miscarrying (see Chapter 17). Quantitative blood tests are sometimes referred to as beta hCG tests, quantitative beta hCG tests, quantitative serum beta-hCG tests, human chorionic gonadotropin-quantitative, and beta-hCG-quantitative.

You may be asked to take a series of these tests to determine that the hCG levels are rising appropriately (doubling every 48 hours) and that your pregnancy is a viable, intrauterine pregnancy. The series of tests is known as serial beta-hCG tests or repeat quantitative hCG tests.

hCG can be detected in the blood of approximately 5 percent of pregnant women eight days after conception and in the blood of 98 percent of pregnant women by day 11.

Is there anything I can do to reduce my chances of getting a false test result?

Although home pregnancy tests are proven to be about 97 percent accurate, false positives and false negatives can occur. To ensure that you obtain the most accurate results possible, you should

- check that the test has not yet passed its expiration date;

- follow the test instructions to the letter, paying particular attention to the amount of time you have to wait before you read the results of the test and at which point the test results lose their validity (for example, a pregnancy test can change from negative to positive if you leave it sitting around long enough, so the reading it displays the next day if you happen to fish it out of the garbage can is totally irrelevant);

- make sure that you use your first morning urine (it has a higher concentration of hCG than the urine you pass later in the day);

- use a clean, soap-free container if your test requires that you collect a sample rather than test your urine while you urinate.

Note: Contrary to popular belief, taking contraceptive pills, antibiotics, and analgesics such as acetaminophen should not affect the results of your pregnancy test.

 WATCH OUT!

Although the current generation of home pregnancy tests is highly accurate, it's still possible to get a false positive or negative. Your test results may be inaccurate if, 1) the urine has been improperly collected or stored, 2) the urine and the test kit are not at room temperature at the time you conduct the test, 3) there is blood or protein in your urine, 4) you have a urinary tract infection, or 5) you're approaching menopause.

Here are some important points to keep in mind when you're interpreting your test results:

- If you get a positive test result, you're probably pregnant. When errors occur during testing, they are most likely to result in false negatives.

- If your test comes back negative but your period still hasn't arrived a week later, test again. It's possible that you ovulated a few days later than usual during this particular cycle.

- If your test shows only a very faint positive, test again a few days later to see if your hormone levels have begun to increase.

- If your test is initially positive but a subsequent pregnancy test comes back negative, it's possible that you have experienced an early miscarriage. (See Chapter 17.)

By the way, don't make the mistake of assuming that there's no need to see your doctor or midwife now that you've managed to confirm your pregnancy via a home test. It's a good idea to start your prenatal care as soon as possible for the health of yourself and your baby. Besides, your healthcare provider may still want to confirm your pregnancy through a physical exam by checking for some of the physical signs of pregnancy (for example, a softening of the uterus and a change in the texture of the cervix) or perform a quantitative hCG blood test.

By the time this all happens, you'll have at least the first four weeks of pregnancy under your belt and you'll be ready to head into month two. The motherhood marathon has officially begun.

Just the facts

- It's a good idea to limit your intake of caffeine and to stop drinking alcohol entirely once you start trying to conceive. You'll also want to talk with your doctor or midwife about the advisability of taking any over-the-counter or prescription medications and herbal products during pregnancy. (Remember, herbal products may be natural, but they can pack a powerful pharmacological punch.)

■ There is little hard evidence to prove that timing intercourse a particular way increases your odds of conceiving a baby of a particular gender. It's okay to have fun with these so-called gender selection methods, but it's best not to take them too seriously.

■ Be aware of any workplace hazards that may pose a threat to the baby you hope to conceive.

■ While it's important to familiarize yourself with the symptoms of early pregnancy, you'll want to bear in mind that there's no such thing as a typical pregnancy, and that some women experience few, if any, symptoms.

■ Resist the temptation to use a home pregnancy test too soon or you will simply be wasting your money. Your hCG levels need time to rise in order for the pregnancy test to come back positive.

GET THE SCOOP ON. . .
What's going on with your baby ▪ What's going
on with your body ▪ What's going on with your
head ▪ Sharing your news with other people ▪
Choosing a doctor or midwife ▪ Nutrition ▪
Weight gain ▪ Prenatal fitness ▪ First trimester
aches and pains

The Second Month: Newly Pregnant

If you aren't experiencing a lot of symptoms at this stage of the game, you may find it difficult to believe that this pregnancy thing is for real. You may even feel like a bit of an imposter — someone who's merely playing the part of the mother-to-be.

It may not happen overnight, but eventually your pregnancy will start to feel a bit more real. You'll wake up one morning and realize that the last thing you want to face is a cup of coffee (this from someone who was a card-carrying member of the International Order of Caffeine Addicts until, what, just last month?) Or you'll go to do up the zipper on one of your more form-fitting skirts and realize that your belly actually *is* changing shape after all.

In this chapter, we tell you what to expect on a week-by-week basis during the fifth to eighth weeks of pregnancy. You'll get the inside scoop on what's going on with your body, what's going on with your head, and what's going on with your baby each week.

And, along the way, you'll also find answers to some of the most-asked month two pregnancy questions.

Week 5

Week 5 is all about settling into pregnancy — getting used to the idea that there really *is* a tiny human being growing inside your body and adjusting to any pregnancy-related symptoms that begin to crop up around this time.

What's going on with your baby

Your baby is now 1.25 millimeters in length — roughly the size of an apple seed. Your baby may be miniscule, but his or her body is surprisingly complex: by the end of this week, the beginnings of all of your baby's major organ systems will be in place.

What's going on with your body

You may be starting to experience a few of the symptoms of early pregnancy — queasiness, breast tenderness, and a need to urinate more frequently. (See Chapter 5 for a full list of the earliest signs of pregnancy and when they are likely to kick in.)

But don't panic if you're not feeling pregnant yet. Not everyone experiences pregnancy symptoms this early on. It's perfectly normal to feel, well, *perfectly normal.*

What's going on with your head

Other people's reactions to the news of your pregnancy can really mess with your head. If you're expecting each and every person you share your news with to yelp with joy, you're bound to be disappointed.

While a lot of people will be genuinely thrilled for you, others may question the timing of your pregnancy ("But you just got that great promotion at work!") or have their own reasons for not being overly excited about your news. (Maybe they were hoping you'd fly across the country to serve as their matron of honor at their as-yet-unannounced wedding that same month.)

And, of course, you boss's reaction can be a total wild card. She may be happy for you, but completely panicked about what your pregnancy may mean for the company and for her.

So try not to take other people's reactions too personally. Realize that your news may come as a shock to them if they had no idea that a baby was in your plans and that they may need a bit of time to wrap their head around the whole idea of the new maternal you. (Fortunately, they've got the next nine months to adjust to the idea, thanks to some rather sensible planning on Mother Nature's part. Clearly, they don't call her *Mother* Nature for nothing!)

The Hot List: This week's must-ask pregnancy questions

This week you're probably wondering when your due date is likely to be and when you should start sharing your news with the world.

How do I go about calculating my due date?

To calculate your due date (a.k.a. your estimated date of confinement), you simply need to add 266 days or 38 weeks to the date when you conceived or, assuming that your menstrual cycles are 28 days in length, add 280 days or 40 weeks to the first day of your last menstrual period. (Note: Figure 6.1 will do the math for you if you have classic 28-day cycles.)

If your cycles are slightly longer or shorter than average, your doctor or midwife may decide to adjust your due date slightly. Likewise, if your cycles are highly irregular — or if you conceived before having your first post-Pill period — your due date may be adjusted as your pregnancy progresses and your doctor or midwife is better able to judge your stage of pregnancy by tracking your baby's development in the weeks ahead. (Because fetal development occurs in a predictable and orderly fashion, an ultrasound can be very helpful in dating a pregnancy.)

Your Estimated Date Of Delivery

Month	1	2	3	4	5	6	7	8	9	10	11	12	13	14	15	16	17	18	19	20	21	22	23	24	25	26	27	28	29	30	31
January / *October*	8	9	10	11	12	13	14	15	16	17	18	19	20	21	22	23	24	25	26	27	28	29	30	31	1	2	3	4	5	6	7
February / *November*	8	9	10	11	12	13	14	15	16	17	18	19	20	21	22	23	24	25	26	27	28	29	30	1	2	3	4	5			
March / *December*	6	7	8	9	10	11	12	13	14	15	16	17	18	19	20	21	22	23	24	25	26	27	28	29	30	31	1	2	3	4	5
April / *January*	6	7	8	9	10	11	12	13	14	15	16	17	18	19	20	21	22	23	24	25	26	27	28	29	30	31	1	2	3	4	
May / *February*	5	6	7	8	9	10	11	12	13	14	15	16	17	18	19	20	21	22	23	24	25	26	27	28	1	2	3	4	5	6	7
June / *March*	8	9	10	11	12	13	14	15	16	17	18	19	20	21	22	23	24	25	26	27	28	29	30	31	1	2	3	4	5	6	
July / *April*	7	8	9	10	11	12	13	14	15	16	17	18	19	20	21	22	23	24	25	26	27	28	29	30	1	2	3	4	5	6	7
August / *May*	8	9	10	11	12	13	14	15	16	17	18	19	20	21	22	23	24	25	26	27	28	29	30	31	1	2	3	4	5	6	7
September / *June*	8	9	10	11	12	13	14	15	16	17	18	19	20	21	22	23	24	25	26	27	28	29	30	1	2	3	4	5	6	7	
October / *July*	8	9	10	11	12	13	14	15	16	17	18	19	20	21	22	23	24	25	26	27	28	29	30	31	1	2	3	4	5	6	7
November / *August*	8	9	10	11	12	13	14	15	16	17	18	19	20	21	22	23	24	25	26	27	28	29	30	31	1	2	3	4	5	6	
December / *September*	7	8	9	10	11	12	13	14	15	16	17	18	19	20	21	22	23	24	25	26	27	28	29	30	1	2	3	4	5	6	7

(Handwritten annotation near the May row: the values "24", "25" and "31", "6 7" are boxed/circled, with the note "6th or 13th".)

Figure 6.1. The first row of numbers refers to the date of the first day of your last menstrual period (LMP). The second row of numbers refers to your baby's estimated date of delivery (a.k.a. your due date). If, for example, your last menstrual period started on January 1, you could expect to give birth on or around October 8, assuming that your menstrual cycles are typically 28 days in length.

Bright Idea

Any information you may have about the timing of conception can be extremely valuable to your doctor or midwife. Be sure to share anything that might prove useful to your healthcare provider in estimating your due date: ovulation predictor kit results, basal body temperature charts, records of the dates on which you had intercourse, and so on. (You should, of course, make a point of recording the dates of the first day of your menstrual periods whenever you're trying to conceive.)

Don't forget that your due date is only an estimate. A healthy pregnancy can last anywhere from 38 to 42 weeks. Although it's impossible to exactly pinpoint your baby's due date, you can feel relatively confident about the timing of his or her arrival. Even though your chances of delivering on your due date are pretty small — 5 percent — your chances of giving birth during the week prior to or following your due date are considerably higher: approximately 85 percent.

How long should my partner and I wait before we start sharing our news with other people?

While doctors used to advise patients to keep their pregnancy news to themselves until they had passed the peak risk period for miscarriage, most couples today choose to share the news a little sooner that that — sometimes as soon as the pregnancy test comes back positive. "The pregnancies were so much on my mind that it felt weird to be talking to a good friend or my sister and not tell her the most important thing that was happening in my life," explains Johnna, a 33-year-old mother of three.

Like Johnna, Jennie, a 30-year-old first-time mother, also made the decision to share her news sooner rather than later. "At first I was paranoid about telling before three months," she recalls. "But the best advice came from my midwife. She said that women who tell people they're pregnant and then miscarry feel terrible because people say insensitive things. And people who don't tell, and then lose the baby, feel terrible because they don't have anyone to mourn with. Either way, losing a baby is a terrible thing."

Of course, sharing the news right away doesn't work well for everyone. Debbie, a 38-year-old mother of six, regretted sharing her news with a lot of people when she experienced some complications during one of her pregnancies. "The problems of bleeding and threatened miscarriage were made worse by all the phone calls of concern," she recalls. "Of course, if anything tragic had happened, we would have needed their support, but the added stress of them worrying, too, made it harder on me."

> 66 The first time around, I told everyone right away. I figured if anything went wrong, I'd want their support. When I had a miscarriage during my second pregnancy, I was glad of their kind words when things ended. When I got pregnant the third time, I told all my close friends right away but held off on telling casual acquaintances, whom it would be more awkward to 'untell.' 99
>
> —Sarah, 31, mother of two

One thing's for certain, however, once you tell one family member, you had better plan to hang up and hit speed-dial for the next person on your list. News of pregnancies spreads like wildfire in most families, and you don't want the grandparents-to-be (particularly first-time grandparents-to-be!) to hear the news from anyone but you.

Note: You'll find some tips on announcing your pregnancy at work in Chapter 7.

Week 6

Now that some of the novelty and/or shock of being pregnant has started to wear off, it's time to get busy making decisions about your pregnancy — like deciding who will care for you and your baby from now through delivery day.

What's going on with your baby

This week marks the beginning of the embryonic period — the period that spans from the 6th to 10th weeks of pregnancy or the 4th to 8th weeks of fetal development.

This is a critical period for your baby's organ development. By the end of this week of pregnancy, it may be possible to see your baby's heartbeat on an ultrasound screen. Picking up the heartbeat is nothing short of a technological miracle: your baby's heart is no larger than a poppy seed at this stage of pregnancy.

Your baby's lungs have started to form and your baby's brain has started to develop. Over the next five months, more than 100 billion neurons will be formed in your baby's brain, laying the necessary groundwork for a lifetime of learning.

By the end of this week, your baby will be approximately 4 millimeters in length.

What's going on with your body

The needle on the bathroom scale may be starting to move around. If your appetite has increased, you may have gained a pound or two. If you've been feeling queasy, you may have lost weight. But even if the number on the scale has stayed the same, your clothes may be starting to fit you differently. The mama-to-be metamorphosis has begun!

What's going on with your head

You may find yourself spending a lot of time thinking about how your life will change now that you're pregnant: e.g. "I'll be five months pregnant by the time we take our summer holidays" or "I'll be eight months pregnant when the family gets together at Thanksgiving." You may even find that you end up with vivid pictures in your head of a very pregnant you sporting a maternity bathing suit, passing platters of turkey over your mega-pregnant belly, and so on. It's all part of the process of conceiving of life with a baby.

The Hot List: This week's must-ask pregnancy questions

Of course, you can't daydream your entire pregnancy away, even if you're tempted. (Being preoccupied is a big part of being pregnant, however, as you're about to discover.) You've also got some important decisions to make, like choosing a doctor or midwife to care for you and your baby during your pregnancy and scheduling your first prenatal checkup. Here are answers to some of the most-asked questions about prenatal care.

What is the best way to go about choosing a doctor or midwife to provide prenatal care to me and my baby?

You have three basic options when it comes to choosing a healthcare practitioner to care for you during your pregnancy:

- an obstetrician (a general obstetrician or one who has specialized training in high-risk pregnancy)

- a family physician (a medical doctor who has had several years of specialized training in primary care, including obstetrics) or

- a midwife (a certified nurse-midwife — a registered nurse who has been specially trained to care for women with low-risk pregnancies; a certified midwife — someone with a background in a health-related field other than nursing who has received specialized training through a midwifery education program accredited by the American College of Nurse-Midwives' Division of Accreditation; or a lay midwife — a midwife who has apprenticed with other midwives). Note: Midwifery laws vary from state to state, so, depending on where you live, you may not be able to access the services of a certified midwife or lay midwife (sometimes known as an independent midwife or direct-entry midwife).

Watch Out!

If you are considering a midwife, be sure to ask her if she has physician backup. If not, and your pregnancy turns high-risk, you could end up having to deal with a physician you've never met in the event that you are transferred to a hospital.

Before you make your final decision, you should set up an appointment to meet with the doctor or midwife that you're considering so that you can determine whether or not the caregiver's birthing philosophy and approach to care are compatible with your own. See Checklist 6.1 for a list of suggested questions.

Checklist 6.1. What to Ask a Doctor or Midwife

About the practice

____ How long have you been in practice? How many babies have you delivered?

____ Are you certified by the American Board of Obstetrics and Gynecology, the American Board of Family Practice, or the American College of Nurse-Midwives?

Do you have

____ a solo medical practice (a single doctor or midwife plus her support staff);

____ a partnership or group practice (two or more doctors or midwives who share patients, costs, and space);

____ a combination practice (one or more obstetricians and one or more midwives and other specialists work cooperatively);

____ a maternity or birth-center practice (a practice in which certified nurse-midwives provide the majority of care, but physicians are available if they are needed); or

____ an independent certified nurse-midwife practice (midwives work on their own but have a physician backup available for consultation and emergency care)?

(continued)

Checklist 6.1. *(continued)*

About the practice

_____ Who other than you might be present at the birth? Will I have the opportunity to meet the backup caregiver before I go into labor?

_____ How would I get in touch with you in the event of an emergency? Are there times when you are unavailable? If so, whom would I call in that situation?

_____ Will you be available to take my nonemergency phone calls during working hours? If you are not available, who will be able to answer my questions or address my concerns?

_____ What is your call schedule? Will you be available around the time I am due to deliver my baby?

_____ What percentage of your patients' babies do you deliver yourself?

_____ Do you use residents or interns as part of your practice?

_____ What hospital(s) and/or birth center(s) are you affiliated with?

_____ Do you attend home births?

_____ What proportion of your fees are likely to be covered by my insurance company or HMO?

Approaches to pregnancy

_____ What is your recommended schedule of prenatal visits? How long do you set aside for each appointment?

_____ What tests will you order during my pregnancy (ultrasound, amniocentesis, genetic screening, and so on)? What if I have a concern about a certain test?

_____ Under what circumstances, if any, would you need to transfer me into the care of another healthcare practitioner? (That is, if you develop certain types of complications, will the caregiver be able to manage these complications, or will you be transferred to someone else?)

_____ Under what circumstances do you induce labor?

Approaches to birth

_____ How do you feel about the fact that we intend to prepare a birth plan? Will you set aside time to review our birth plan with us before the onset of labor?

_____ How much time will you spend with me when I'm in labor?

_____ Do the majority of women in your practice have medicated or nonmedicated births? What percentage have epidurals?

_____ What are your thoughts on natural childbirth?

_____ How would you feel if I wanted to use the services of a doula or other support person?

_____ In what positions do most of the women in your practice labor and give birth?

_____ What percentage of women are induced?

_____ Do you routinely use electronic fetal monitoring during labor?

_____ What percentage of women in your practice have episiotomies?

_____ What percentage of women in your practice have cesareans?

_____ What percentage of women attempting a VBAC (vaginal birth after cesarean) manage to deliver vaginally?

_____ Do you allow labor support people other than the father to be present at the birth?

_____ Will my baby and I be separated after the birth?

_____ Do you provide breastfeeding support and/or postpartum care?

How soon should I schedule my first appointment?

Up until quite recently, pregnant women were not seen by their healthcare providers until the end of the first trimester (approximately 12 weeks after the start of their last menstrual period). It was argued that there was no point in scheduling that initial visit until the risk of miscarriage had passed.

> 66 We were one of the first—if not the first—lesbian couple our obstetrician/gynecologist had ever worked with. We like to think we blazed a trail through his office, but we can't take that credit. He went to bat for us on more than one occasion and prepared the hospital staff before we delivered. He warned everyone on staff that if they had any problems with our situation, they were to stay away from our room. He didn't want them assisting him or taking care of Beth. It helped tremendously, and we were treated no differently than a heterosexual couple. 99
>
> —Michele, 31, a first-time parent

These days we know differently. Study after study has demonstrated the benefits of first-trimester prenatal care. That's why most doctors and midwives recommend that pregnant women be seen as soon as they realize that they are pregnant — typically 6 to 10 weeks after the start of the last menstrual period. This is particularly important if you haven't been in to see your doctor or midwife for a prepregnancy consultation.

If your doctor or midwife isn't willing to see you this early in your pregnancy, you might want to reconsider your choice of caregiver. Clearly, this person is a little behind the times when it comes to understanding best practices in prenatal care.

What should I expect from my first prenatal checkup?

During your initial prenatal checkup, you can expect your doctor or midwife to

- confirm your pregnancy with a urine test, blood test, and/or physical examination;
- estimate your due date by considering such factors as the types of pregnancy symptoms you are experiencing and when they first occurred, the date of your last normal menstrual period, the results of ovulation predictor tests

you used or any temperature charts you kept, and changes to the cervix and uterus;

- take a general medical history or review the findings from your preconception checkup (see Chapter 2);

- take an obstetrical history (assuming, of course, that you have had other pregnancies);

- conduct a general physical exam (heart, lungs, breasts, abdomen, and so on);

- conduct a pelvic exam (a visual examination of your vagina and cervix, as well as a bimanual exam of your pelvic organs);

- do a blood test to check for anemia, hepatitis B, HIV, syphilis, and antibodies to rubella, as well as certain genetic diseases (for example, sickle-cell anemia or Tay-Sachs disease), if your history warrants it;

- take a vaginal culture to check for the presence of infection, if warranted;

- do a Pap smear to check for cervical cancer or potential precancer;

- check your urine for infection, sugar, and protein;

- weigh you to establish a baseline weight;

- take your blood pressure;

- provide you with advice on nutrition and lifestyle issues;

- answer any questions you may have;

- talk to you about how you are feeling about being pregnant.

You can expect to see your doctor or midwife again in about a month's time. You'll continue to see her at monthly intervals until you reach week 28, at which point you'll start coming for checkups every two to three weeks. Once you reach week 36, you will generally be seen weekly.

Watch Out!

Your weight can fluctuate significantly if you wear different amounts and types of clothing to subsequent prenatal checkups. Try as much as possible to wear the same type of clothing to each appointment. Sudden weight gain can indicate that you are retaining fluid and possibly developing a condition called preeclampsia.

What kind of information does a doctor or midwife record on the prenatal record?

Doctors and midwives are required by law to keep detailed records for their maternity patients. Each time you go for a prenatal visit, your doctor or midwife records the pertinent facts about your pregnancy on your prenatal record. You can find a list of the key terms and abbreviations that are likely to turn up on your prenatal record in Table 6.1.

Table 6.1. Decoding Your Prenatal Record

Your obstetrical history

Para 1011: This is your doctor's or midwife's way of summarizing your obstetrical history. The first digit (in this case "1") represents the total number of full-term births. The second digit ("0") indicates the number of preterm births. The third digit ("1") represents the total number of miscarriages, abortions, and ectopic pregnancies. The fourth digit ("1") indicates the total number of living children. Therefore, a woman who is para 1011 has had one full-term birth; has had one miscarriage, abortion, or ectopic pregnancy; and has one living child.

Gravida 31011: This is another method of summarizing your reproductive history. In this case, the first digit ("3") represents your total number of pregnancies, including the present one; the second digit ("1") represents the total number of full-term births; the third digit ("0") represents the number of preterm births; the fourth digit ("1") represents the total number of miscarriages, abortions, and ectopic pregnancies; and the fifth digit ("1") represents the total number of living children. Therefore, a woman who is gravida 31011 is in her third pregnancy and has had one full-term birth; has had one miscarriage, abortion, or ectopic pregnancy; and has one living child.

Primigravida: You are pregnant for the first time.

Your obstetrical history *(cont.)*

Primipara: You are giving birth for the first time.

Multigravida: You are pregnant for the second or subsequent time.

Multipara: You've given birth one or more times.

The dating of your pregnancy

LMP: The first day of your last menstrual period.

EDC/EDD: Estimated date of confinement, or estimated date of delivery (that is, your due date).

Prenatal tests

AFP: Alpha-fetoprotein test (also a component of what is called triple or quadruple screen or maternal serum screening). An AFP test is designed to tell you whether you are at increased risk of giving birth to a child with either Down syndrome or a neural tube defect such as spina bifida. (See Chapter 14.)

BP: Blood pressure. There are two readings: the systolic pressure (the upper figure) and the diastolic pressure (the lower figure). You are generally considered to have high blood pressure if the reading exceeds 140/90.

Hb/Hgb: Level of hemoglobin, an oxygen-carrying substance present in red blood cells; anything less than 10.5 percent or so indicates that you are anemic.

Blood group: Your blood type and whether you are Rh positive or Rh negative.

Rh antibodies: Indicates whether you have any anti-Rh antibodies, which are capable of crossing the placenta and destroying the baby's red blood cells.

VDRL test: Test for syphilis (also referred to as RPR).

HIV test: Test for the presence of the AIDS virus.

HCG: Refers to the blood level reading of human chorionic gonadotropin (hCG).

CBC: Complete blood count: hemoglobin, red and white cells (RBCs and WBCs respectively), and blood platelets.

(continued)

Table 6.1. *(continued)*

Your physical health

Edema: Swelling or the retention of water.

Fe: Iron. Indicates that you have been prescribed iron.

Your baby's well-being and position

FH or FHR: Fetal heart or fetal heart rate.

FM: Fetal movement.

Eng/E: Engaged. The baby's head has dropped into the bony pelvis.

Floating: The baby's head is not yet engaged.

Presenting part: The part of the baby's body that is likely to come through the cervix first.

0, -1, -2, -3, +1, +2, +3: The baby's station (an indicator of how high or low in the pelvis the presenting part is). Generally, negative numbers mean the presenting part is unengaged, and positive numbers mean it is engaged.

Vertex: Baby is head-down.

Breech: Baby is bottom-down.

LOA, LOP, ROA, ROP: Left occipito-anterior, left occipito-posterior, right occipito-anterior, right occipito-posterior. These terms refer to the position of the crown of the baby's head (that is, occiput) in relation to your body (right or left), and anterior (toward your front) or posterior (toward your back).

Fundal height: The measurement of fundal height (distance in centimeters from the upper edge of the pubic bone to the top of the uterus) is used to give a rough idea of the growth of the fetus and the amount of amniotic fluid at any given point in pregnancy after about 20 weeks. On average, the measurement is equal to the number of weeks of pregnancy, but it may vary by as many as 3 to 4 centimeters or more, depending on the person's height, weight, and body shape; the position of the baby; and, of course, the size of the baby and the amount of amniotic fluid. The measurement technique is subjective to some degree, and different caregivers can get different measurements on the same day.

Typically, over time, the fundal height increases about one centimeter per week from about 20 to 36 weeks, but this is also variable, especially in the short run (that is, from week to week) and near term.

Watch Out!

If you are a plus-sized woman, make sure that your caregiver notes in your prenatal record that all blood pressure readings have been taken with the large-sized blood pressure cuff. This is because there may be a discrepancy in readings if someone subsequently checks your blood pressure with the regular-sized cuff since a blood pressure cuff that is too small will give falsely elevated readings.

My prenatal blood work revealed that I'm anemic. What causes iron-deficiency anemia and what can I do to boost my iron levels during pregnancy?

It's not at all uncommon for pregnant women to be deficient in iron. You may be low in this important nutrient if

- you're are in the habit of drinking tea or coffee close to mealtime (something that makes it difficult for your body to absorb iron from food sources);

- you have a history of heavy menstrual bleeding;

- you give blood three or more times each year;

- your diet is low in meat, fish, poultry, and/or vitamin C (vitamin C plays a key role in iron absorption);

- you have had two or more pregnancies spaced closely together.

Your doctor may recommend an iron supplement to try to boost your iron levels, particularly if you're carrying more than one baby. (Note: A mother carrying multiples faces a greater risk of becoming anemic as her pregnancy progresses as compared to a mother carrying a single baby.). If your doctor prescribes such a supplement for you, it's best to take your iron supplement with a glass of orange juice in between meals, if your stomach will let you. (Some women find that taking any supplement — iron, calcium, or a prenatal vitamin — on an empty stomach triggers morning sickness.)

If you find that the iron supplement that your doctor prescribed causes you to become constipated, see if you can switch to a liquid iron supplement instead. Some women find them to be less constipating.

If you're not able to tolerate any sort of iron supplement, you'll have to make a concerted effort to obtain your iron through food sources. The best food sources of iron (food sources that deliver 3.5 milligrams/serving or more) include cooked beans, white beans, soybeans, lentils, and chick peas; clams and oysters; pumpkin, sesame, and squash seeds; and iron-enriched breakfast seeds. Note: We talk more about food sources of iron in the prenatal nutrition section of Week 7.

Week 7

Your baby is growing — and so are you. And chances are you're experiencing at least the odd symptom of early pregnancy, whether it's morning sickness, frequent urination, tender breasts, food cravings, or (lucky you!) all of the above.

What's going on with your baby

If you could get a sneak peak at your baby at this stage of his or her development, you'd swear you had a budding genius on your hands. Your baby's head is the largest part of his or her body by far — indicative of the rapid brain growth that has been occurring.

Your baby is also a marvel of engineering. All four chambers of the baby's heart are now in place — this despite the fact that your baby is just 4.5 millimeters in length.

Your baby's intestines are developing, but they are not yet encased inside your baby's body. Instead, they bulge out into the umbilical cord.

What's going on with your body

You may experience some mild cramping or pain as your uterus starts to expand. (Some women describe it as an abdominal tightening that is not unlike a labor contraction.)

Still, despite all the action going on inside your body, your belly is not yet big enough for anyone to guess your secret yet.

(Assuming, of course, it's still a secret. You may have shared your news with the entire world by now!)

What's going on with your head

Find yourself being hit with a bad case of nutrition guilt every time something other than organic lettuce passes through your lips? You may have set the bar a little high for yourself on the nutrition front.

Although it's important to understand some basic facts about prenatal nutrition — what nutrients your baby needs and why — no one expects you to analyze every bite you eat to determine its nutritional composition. Nor are you expected to swear off junk food for the next nine months, simply because you're having a baby.

What's more, it's perfectly okay to "fall off the wagon" from time to time. In fact, we'd prefer it if you didn't feel as if there was a wagon to fall off in the first place! If you feel as though you're on some sort of diet — that you're depriving yourself of the foods you enjoy for the good of your baby — you're probably attempting to change your eating habits too quickly, something that in all likelihood will lead you to more than one secret rendezvous with a few Twinkies at some point during your pregnancy.

And if you're trying to reform your eating habits, don't go "cold turkey" overnight. Make gradual changes to your eating habits — ones you can sustain during your pregnancy and beyond.

And whatever you do, don't diet during pregnancy. Diets and babies don't mix, period.

The Hot List: This week's must-ask pregnancy questions

Questions about prenatal nutrition, weight gain, and prenatal fitness are likely to be providing you with plenty of food for thought these days. Here are answers to some of the questions that are likely to be on your mind this week.

Do I need to totally change my eating habits now that I am pregnant?

It all depends what your eating habits were like before you became pregnant. If you were already in the habit of eating in accordance with the Food Pyramid — the U.S. Department of Agriculture's guidelines for healthful eating (see Figure 6.2) — you aren't going to need to embark on a major nutrition makeover. All you'll need to do is gradually increase the amount of food that you consume each day — you need an extra 100 calories per day during the first trimester and an extra 300 calories per day during the second and third trimesters — and to try to zero in on those foods that will give you the most bang for your nutritional buck.

Note: If you follow the *Food Pyramid* guidelines, approximately 50 percent to 60 percent of your diet will come from carbohydrates, 20 percent to 30 percent from fats, and 15 percent to 20 percent from proteins.

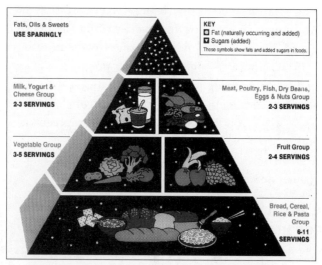

Figure 6.2. The Food Pyramid shows which foods you should be emphasizing in your diet and which types of foods you should be eating more sparingly.

Wondering what this means in terms of the number of servings you should be consuming from the various food groups? The American College of Obstetrics and Gynecologists (ACOG) recommends that pregnant women consume the following foods each day:

- nine servings from the bread, cereal, rice, and pasta group;
- four servings from the vegetable group;
- three servings from the fruit group;
- three to four servings from the milk, yogurt, and cheese group;
- two to three servings from the meat, poultry, fish, dry beans, eggs, and nuts group;
- fats, oils, and sweets in moderation.

   Servings are defined in the following ways:

- **Bread, cereal, rice, or pasta:** one slice of bread; 1 cup of ready-to-eat cereal; ½ cup of cooked cereal, rice, or pasta; or five or six small crackers
- **Vegetables:** 1 cup raw, leafy vegetables; ½ cup of cooked or chopped raw vegetables; or ¾ cup of vegetable juice
- **Fruit:** one medium apple, banana, or orange; ½ cup of chopped, cooked, or canned fruit, or 1 cup of berries; or ½ to ¾ cup of fruit juice
- **Milk, yogurt, and cheese:** 1 cup of milk or yogurt, 1.5 ounces of natural cheese, or 2 ounces of processed cheese
- **Meat, poultry, fish, dry beans, eggs, and nuts:** 2 to 3 ounces of cooked lean meat, poultry, or fish (this portion is about the size of your palm or a deck of cards); ½ cup of cooked dry beans; one egg; 2 tablespoons of peanut butter; or ⅓ cup of nuts.

Watch Out!

Make sure your fluid intake is adequate. You can tell if you're drinking enough by noting the color of your urine. If your urine is light yellow or clear, you're drinking enough; if it's dark yellow, it's too concentrated and you need to increase your fluid intake.

Is it possible to follow a vegetarian diet during pregnancy?

Whether you are a vegan (a vegetarian who doesn't consume any animal products), a lacto-vegetarian (a vegetarian who consumes dairy products), a lacto-ovo vegetarian (a vegetarian who eats dairy and eggs), or a semi-vegetarian (a vegetarian who consumes dairy products, eggs, fish, and chicken), you will need to pay careful attention to your diet to ensure that you're getting adequate levels of nutrients. Specifically, you will want to maximize your iron absorption by combining iron-rich foods with foods that help with the absorption of iron (that is, those that are rich in vitamin C) and ensure that you are obtaining an adequate number of complete protein exchanges — either from legumes and grains or from legumes, grains, and dairy foods.

Vegetarians are also at risk of developing deficiencies in vitamins B12, B2, and D, and in calcium, iron, and zinc.

Make sure that your doctor or midwife is aware that you are following a vegetarian diet. She may want to check your hemoglobin regularly during your pregnancy and recommend a vitamin B12 supplement.

 Watch Out!

Milk, tea, coffee, and antacids inhibit the absorption of iron. Try to avoid ingesting them at the same time as iron-rich foods.

I am lactose intolerant. What can I do to ensure that I'm getting enough calcium in my diet?

If you are someone who is lactose intolerant (that is, someone who has difficulty digesting the sugar in milk), you may have difficulty getting enough calcium in your diet. Here are some tips on maximizing your intake of calcium-rich foods:

- Get your calcium from other sources, such as tofu (specifically, calcium-fortified soy milk), calcium-fortified bread or juice, dark-green leafy vegetables, sardines, and salmon.

- Drink milk at mealtimes rather than on its own.

- Try lactose-reduced cottage cheese and yogurt.

- Experiment with smaller portion sizes (such as one-half cup of milk rather than a full glass).

- Choose low-fat cheeses (because a large percentage of the lactose is removed during processing) and hard cheeses such as Swiss and cheddar (because they are naturally lower in lactose).

- Eat yogurt that contains acidophilus or active cultures (because these active cultures can actually help you to digest lactose).

- Drink lactose-reduced milk or add over-the-counter enzyme drops (for example, Lactaid) to your milk to help break down the lactose. You may also opt to take a Lactaid pill with dairy foods.

 Watch Out!

If your intake of calcium is inadequate, your baby may draw calcium from your bones, something that can put you at increased risk for osteoporosis later in life. If you are concerned that you are not getting enough calcium in your diet, talk to your caregiver about the possibility of taking a calcium supplement. If you are taking prenatal vitamins, make sure that they contain calcium.

I had an eating disorder when I was younger. Should I tell my healthcare provider?

Definitely. Not only are you likely to need some extra support in coping with the bodily changes that occur during pregnancy: there are also some solid medical reasons for letting your doctor or midwife know about your eating disorder. A study conducted at Harvard Medical School found that women with eating disorders face a higher-than-average risk of developing pregnancy-related complications, giving birth to a baby with a congenital problem, or experiencing postpartum depression. If your midwife is aware of the problem, she can ensure that you get any additional help you need to manage your eating disorder during pregnancy.

> **❝** If you have an eating disorder like I have, ignore all that sanctimonious preaching in certain pregnancy books about how if you eat a donut you're a bad pregnant lady. Getting stressed out about food is bad anytime, and it's worse when you are pregnant. **❞**
>
> —Laura, 31, mother of one

I have been having difficulty keeping anything other than soda crackers down. I'm worried that my morning sickness may be depriving my baby of important nutrients.

This is one worry you can strike off your worry list. Unless you are experiencing a severe form of morning sickness known as *hyperemesis gravidarum* — a condition that is characterized by dehydration, weight loss, acid-base imbalance, and electrolyte deficiencies, and that generally requires hospitalization — you can feel confident that your baby is not being unduly harmed by your inability to stomach anything other than soda crackers. Note: We offer some tips on managing morning sickness in Week 8.

How important is it that I take a prenatal vitamin supplement?

Although the American College of Obstetricians and Gynecologists (ACOG) does not formally endorse the routine use of prenatal multivitamins during pregnancy, ACOG does advise daily supplementation with 0.4 milligram of folic acid both before and during pregnancy to reduce the risk of neural tube defects such as spina bifida. Most doctors and midwives however, recommend that pregnant women do take some sort of multivitamin supplement. The reason is simple. It's almost impossible for pregnant women to meet their bodies' demands for iron and folic acid during pregnancy through diet alone (this despite the fact that your body is able to absorb twice as much iron from foods when you're pregnant as it can when you're not!). As Table 6.2 illustrates, your body's demand for these and other nutrients increases dramatically once you become pregnant.

The challenge in choosing a prenatal vitamin is that it can be difficult to know what you're getting. Because neither the Food and Drug Administration nor the American College of Obstetricians and Gynecologists has established any clear standards for prenatal vitamins, you could find yourself paying top dollar for a so-called "prenatal" vitamin that is virtually identical to your standard run-of-the-mill multivitamin.

 Moneysaver

Ask your doctor if he has any pharmaceutical-company samples you can try before you go out and buy a super-sized bottle of prenatal vitamins that your stomach may or may not be able to keep down.

Table 6.2. Nutrients, Vitamins, and Minerals: What Your Body Needs Each Day

Nutrient	What It Does	Where to Find It (Major Sources)	Pre-Pregnancy Requirements	First Trimester Requirements	Second Trimester Requirements	Third Trimester Requirements	Requirements During Breastfeeding
Calories Note: Your caloric requirements will be greater if you are carrying more than one baby. See Chapter 15. Your caloric requirements may also vary depending on your prepregnancy weight, your nutritional status, and your activity level.	Provides the energy your body needs to meet the increased metabolic demands of pregnancy.	Carbohydrates, fats, proteins	2,200 calories	2,300 calories	2,500 calories	2,500 calories	2,700 calories

	Function	Food Sources					
Water and other fluids	Provides the fluid required for increased blood, tissue, and amniotic fluid volume; carries nutrients to cells; flushes waste products away; aids in digestion and helps to prevent constipation; helps to regulate body temperature.	Water, juice, milk, other caffeine-free beverages (Note: Caffeine acts as a diuretic, flushing water from your system.)	4 cups or more	8 cups or more	8 cups or more	8 cups or more	8 cups or more
Protein	Builds and repairs tissues; helps build blood, amniotic fluid, and the placenta; and assists in the creation of antibodies.	Meat, fish, poultry, eggs, milk, cheese, dried beans and peas, peanut butter, nuts, whole grains, cereals	45 to 50 grams	60 grams	60 grams	60 grams	65 grams

(continued)

Table 6.2. (continued)

Nutrient	What It Does	Where to Find It (Major Sources)	Pre-Pregnancy Requirements	First Trimester Requirements	Second Trimester Requirements	Third Trimester Requirements	Requirements During Breastfeeding
Key vitamins and minerals from A to Z							
Vitamin A (retinol and carotene) Note: Large quantities of vitamin A (more than 4,000 mcg per day) can be toxic to the fetus.	Maintains skin, body tissues, and vision; helps your body to fight infection. Necessary for the growth of fetal tissue as well as bone formation and growth.	Liver, fortified milk, carrots, cantaloupe, whole milk, butter, cheese, egg yolk, cod, and other fatty fish	700 mcg	750 to 770 mcg	750 to 770 mcg	750 to 770 mcg	1,200 to 1,300 mcg
Vitamin B1 (thiamine)	Helps your body to convert food (particularly carbohydrates) into energy. Needed for normal functioning of the nervous system.	Whole grains, enriched grins, legumes, nuts, beans, organ meats, pork, brewer's yeast, wheat germ	1.0 to 1.1 mg	1.4 mg	1.4 mg	1.4 mg	1.4 mg

| Vitamin B2 (riboflavin) | Promotes tissue growth and regeneration and enables your body to use carbohydrates, fat, and protein. | Brewer's yeast, wheat germ, whole grains, green leafy vegetables, milk, cheese, other milk products, eggs | 1.0 to 1.1 mg | 1.4 mg | 1.4 mg | 1.4 mg | 1.6 mg |
| Vitamin B3 (niacin) | Helps to release energy from food. Needed for protein metabolism. Aids in the production of lipids, hormones, and red blood cells and plays a role in DNA synthesis and the maintenance of healthy skin, nerves, and digestive system. | Whole grains, wheat germ, organ meats, green vegetables, cereals, dried beans and peas | 14 mg | 18 mg | 18 mg | 18 mg | 17 mg |

(continued)

Table 6.2. (continued)

Nutrient	What It Does	Where to Find It (Major Sources)	Pre-Pregnancy Requirements	First Trimester Requirements	Second Trimester Requirements	Third Trimester Requirements	Requirements During Breastfeeding
Vitamin B5 (pantothenic acid)	Aids in the metabolism of food, especially proteins. Assists in the production of lipids, hormones, and neurotransmitters.	Meats, whole grains, legumes	5 mg	6 mg	6 mg	6 mg	7mg
Vitamin B6 (pyridoxine)	Enables your body to make use of protein. Required for fetal growth.	Chicken, fish, organ meats, pork, eggs, unprocesssed cereals, oats, soybeans, brown rice, nuts, seeds, legumes	1.2 to 1.5 mg	1.9 mg	1.9 mg	1.9 mg	2.0 mg

Vitamin B12 (cobalamin)	Used to form hemoglobin and the baby's central nervous system. Helps your body to make use of protein, folic acid, and fatty acids. Also plays a role in maintaining nerve fibers.	Organ meats, milk, clams, oysters, eggs	2.4 mcg	2.6 mcg	2.6 mcg	2.6 mcg	2.8 mcg
Vitamin C	Helps with the formation of connective tissue and the absorption of iron.	Citrus fruits, strawberries, dark-green leafy vegetables, tomatoes, potatoes, fortified cereals	65 to 75 mg	80 to 85 mg	80 to 85 mg	80 to 85 mg	115 to 120 mg

(continued)

Table 6.2. (continued)

Nutrient	What It Does	Where to Find It (Major Sources)	Pre-Pregnancy Requirements	First Trimester Requirements	Second Trimester Requirements	Third Trimester Requirements	Requirements During Breastfeeding
Vitamin D Note: Large quantities of Vitamin D can be toxic to the fetus.	Aids in the absorption of calcium. Necessary for the formation of bones and teeth.	Fortified milk, fish liver oils, fatty fish, egg yolks. Vitamin D can also be absorbed through the skin through direct sunlight.	5 mcg	5 mcg	5 mcg	5 mcg	5 mcg
Vitamin E	A potent antioxidant. Protects cells from damage and degeneration. Necessary for the growth of fetal tissue.	Wheat germ, egg yolks, cereals, meats, peanuts, seeds, vegetable oils	15 mg	15 mg	15 mg	15 mg	19 mg

	Function	Sources					
Vitamin K	Aids in blood coagulation. Necessary for the growth of fetal tissue.	Leafy green vegetables	75 to 90 mcg	75 to 90 mcg	75 to 90 mcg	75 to 90 mcg	75 to 90 mcg
Biotin	Assist with energy metabolism. Aids with the synthesis and breaking down of fatty acids.	Egg yolks, soybeans, yeast	25 to 30 mcg	30 mcg	30 mcg	30 mcg	35 mcg
Calcium	Strengthens bones and teeth, promotes blood clotting, and regulates nerve and muscle function.	Milk, cheese, sardines, salmon, oysters, shrimp, tofu, kale, and broccoli	1,000 to 1,300 mg	1,000 to 1,300 mg	1,000 to 1,300 mg	1,000 to 1,300 mg	1,000 to 1,300 mg

(continued)

Table 6.2. *(continued)*

Nutrient	What It Does	Where to Find It (Major Sources)	Pre-Pregnancy Requirements	First Trimester Requirements	Second Trimester Requirements	Third Trimester Requirements	Requirements During Breastfeeding
Folic acid	Assists with cell division and the development of the baby's central nervous system.	Raw leafy vegetables, enriched flour, grains, cereals, soy flour, oranges, bananas, walnuts, brewer's yeast, legumes	400 mcg	600 mcg	600 mcg	600 mcg	500 mcg
Iodine	Iodine plays a key role in the functioning of the metabolism. It is a necessary nutrient for the production of thyroid hormones and normal thyroid function.	Iodized table salt, shellfish, seaweed	150 mcg	220 mcg	220 mcg	220 mcg	290 mcg

Iron	Combines with protein to form hemoglobin. Necessary for the formation of red blood cells, which carry oxygen to your tissues and the baby. Also provides iron for fetal storage.	Kidneys, fish, egg yolks, red meat, cereal, molasses, apricots, shellfish, dried fruits.	15 to 18 mg	27 mg	27 mg	27 mg	9 to 10 mg
Magnesium	Aids in muscle contraction and relaxation. Plays a role in tissue growth and energy metabolism. Also functions as an enzyme activator.	Nuts, green vegetables, whole grains, dried beans and peas.	310 to 360 mg	350 to 400 mg	350 to 400 mg	350 to 400 mg	320 to 360 mg

(continued)

Table 6.2. (continued)

Nutrient	What It Does	Where to Find It (Major Sources)	Pre-Pregnancy Requirements	First Trimester Requirements	Second Trimester Requirements	Third Trimester Requirements	Requirements During Breastfeeding
Phosphorus	Needed for fetal skeletal and tooth formation.\n\nNote: Calcium and phosphorus need to exist in balance. Having too much phosphorus will prevent your body from being able to make proper use of calcium.	Milk and milk products, meat, poultry, fish, whole-grain cereals, legumes.	700 to 1,250 mg	700 to 1,250 mg	700 to 1,250 mg	700 to 1,250 mg	700 to 1,250 mg

| Zinc | Strengthens the enzymes that drive the metabolic system. May play a role in strengthening the baby's immune system. Required to produce insulin. | Wheat bran, eggs, nuts, onions, shellfish, sunflower seeds, wheat germ, whole wheat, lean meat, turkey, dried beans and peas | 8 mg | 11 to 13 mg | 11 to 13 mg | 11 to 13 mg | 12 to 14 mg |

Sources: Food and Nutrition Board Institute of Medicine. *Dietary Reference Intakes for Thiamin, Riboflavin, Niacin, Vitamin B6, Folate, Vitamin B12, Pantothenic Acid, Biotin, and Choline.* Washington, D.C.: National Academy Press, 1998; Food and Nutrition Board Institute for Medicine. *Dietary Reference Intakes for Calcium, Phosphorus, Magnesium, Vitamin D, and Fluoride.* Washington, D.C.: National Academy Press, 1998; Simkin, Penny, Janet Whalley, and Ann Keppler. *Pregnancy, Childbirth, and the Newborn: The Complete Guide.* New York: Meadowbrook Press, 2001; and an earlier version of this chart that appeared in the first edition of this book.

And here's some more vitamin-related info for you to chew on. Despite the pretty packages, there is no evidence that pre-natal supplements (both over-the-counter and prescription) have anything more to offer the majority of pregnant women than a standard multivitamin formulation containing at least 0.4 milligrams of folic acid.

If you were in the habit of eating well before you become pregnant, you probably don't need to worry about taking a pre-natal vitamin other than the recommended 0.6 milligrams of folic acid. Chances are your diet will give you all of the nutrients you and your baby need — if not more. The secret is to let your hunger be your guide and to reach for nutritious foods most of the time. (You'll note that we said "most of the time." Although some pregnancy books will leave you feeling like an unfit mother if you occasionally indulge your junk food habit, we'd rather see you treat yourself occasionally than turn your pregnancy into a nine-month-long exercise in junk-food deprivation.)

Although there is no proof that vitamin supplementation is necessary in pregnancy (other than to ensure an adequate amount of folic acid), many women take supplements to cover any possible deficiencies in their diets, recognizing that in real life it is difficult, at best, to eat the recommended foods in the recommended amounts.

But remember: although prenatal supplements can play an important role during pregnancy, they are no substitute for healthful eating.

 Moneysaver

The top four vitamin money-wasters according to *Good Housekeeping* maga-zine: "Natural" formulations that are chemically identical to their synthetic counterparts; multivitamins that are supposedly designed to meet the unique nutritional needs of women, but that are no different than any other multivi-tamin; brand-name vitamins that are chemically identical to generic brands; and "high potency" multivitamins that give you higher doses of nutrients you don't need.

Do I need to swear off salt for the next nine months?

While your mother and grandmother were no doubt told that salt was a no-no for pregnant women, the medical establishment's take on this issue has changed considerably over the years. While it was once believed that restricting salt intake would help to reduce water retention during pregnancy, we now know that doing so can actually make water retention worse.

Of course, some women still need to reduce their salt intake during pregnancy. If you have high blood pressure, you've developed edema (water retention), or you suffer from certain types of kidney diseases, your doctor or midwife may advise you to avoid highly salted foods and to avoid adding additional salt to your foods for the duration of your pregnancy.

Is is safe to consume artificial sweeteners during pregnancy?

Three artificial sweeteners have been approved for use in foods and as sugar replacements in the United States: aspartame, saccharin, and acesulfame K. All three are considered to be safe for pregnant women — with one exception. Pregnant women who have phenylketonuria — PKU — and must restrict their intake of phenylalanine, an amino acid, will need to avoid products containing aspartame.

Because artificial sweeteners can't deliver the smorgasbord of nutrients your body needs to grow a healthy baby, it's best to limit their use during pregnancy.

Is it safe to consume Olestra?

Olestra — a synthetic mixture of sugar and vegetable oil that is designed to pass through the body undigested — is a fat substitute that has been approved for use in low-fat snack foods.

While there's no hard evidence that Olestra is likely to be harmful to your baby, you may want to limit its use during pregnancy. Here's why:

- It can deplete the body of the fat-soluble vitamins (vitamins A, D, E, and K) and interfere with the absorption of carotenoids such as the beta carotene that is found in carrots.

- It can lead to a range of unpleasant gastrointestinal symptoms (diarrhea, greasy stools, and all-round discomfort) at a time when you may already be dealing with constipation, nausea, and other unpleasant pregnancy symptoms.

As you can see, Olestra is not exactly your best bet during pregnancy, so you'll probably want to limit its use for now.

Is it true that it's unsafe to eat feta cheese when you're pregnant?

Unfortunately, yes. You'll have to hold off on having that feta-laden Greek salad until after you deliver — or find a way to make it with another type of cheese in the meantime. Certain types of foods, including soft cheese, can carry the listeria monocyotogenes bacterium — a bacterium that can cause a serious infection known as listeriosis in humans. If you happen to develop this infection while you're pregnant, you could end up experiencing a range of very serious complications, including miscarriage, stillbirth, and premature labor. Or your baby could be born with pneumonia, septicemia, or meningitis.

Here's a list of foods that you'll need to avoid until after your baby arrives:

- Hot dogs and luncheon meats (unless they have been reheated until they are steaming hot)

- Soft cheese such as feta, brie, Camembert, blue-veined cheeses, and Mexican-style cheeses such as queso blanco fresco (Hard cheeses, semi-soft cheese such as mozzarella, pasteurized cheeses such as cheese slices and spreads, cream cheese, and cottage cheese are all perfectly safe to eat during pregnancy, by the way.)

- Smoked seafood (unless it is served as part of a cooked entrée)

- Unpasteurized milk and foods that contain unpasteurized milk.

I've heard that it's dangerous to eat fish during pregnancy. What's that all about?

You don't have to steer clear of all types of fish during pregnancy. The only ones you have to avoid outright are shark, swordfish, king mackerel, and tilefish. These fish are on the Food and Drug Administration's hit list because they contain high levels of a type of mercury called methylmercury that is known to be harmful the nervous system of the developing baby.

Because smaller amounts of mercury can be found in other types of fish, the FDA recommends that pregnant women limit their weekly intake of fish to 12 ounces and that they choose from a wide variety of types of fish (as opposed to just eating tuna or salmon exclusively, for example).

Note: You can find out more about food safety during pregnancy by visiting the FDA's Food Safety Web site www.cfsan.fda.gov.

 Watch Out!

While you might be tempted to eliminate fish from your diet entirely in order to avoid exposing your baby to methylmercury, you could be missing out on a major means of protecting yourself against prenatal and postpartum depression. A British study found that the more seafood a woman consumed during the third trimester of pregnancy, the less likely she was to show signs of a major depression for up to eight months after the birth.

How much weight should I gain during my pregnancy?

Just as there's no such thing as one-size-fits-all maternity wear, there's no such thing as a one-size-fits-all pregnancy weight gain recommendation. Your doctor or midwife will take a number of different factors into account when helping you to come up with a pregnancy "gain plan." Here are the key issues that she will consider when she talks to you about how much weight you should aim to gain over the course of your pregnancy:

- **Your prepregnancy weight:** If you start your pregnancy at a healthy weight (see Table 6.3 for some guidelines on what constitutes a healthy weight), your doctor or midwife will likely encourage you to gain between 25 and 35 pounds during pregnancy — a figure recommended by the National Academy of Sciences/Institute of Medicine (NAS/IOM). If you are underweight, you'll be encouraged to gain a little more — 28 to 40 pounds — and if you are overweight, you'll be encouraged to gain a little less — 15 to 25 pounds.

- **Your age:** Because their own bodies are still developing, adolescent women are encouraged to gain more weight than women in their 20s, 30s, and 40s — typically something in the range of 28 to 40 pounds.

- **Your height:** Short women are often encouraged to gain slightly less than their taller counterparts — typically 18 to 30 pounds.

- **The number of babies you are carrying:** If you are carrying twins, you will need to gain between 35 and 45 pounds during your pregnancy. If you are carrying triplets or other high-order multiples, you will need to gain even more.

Table 6.3. Are You At a Healthy Weight?

BMI	19	20	21	22	23	24	25	26	27	28	29	30	31	32	33	34	35
		Ideal Weight (20-25)						Overweight (26-29)				Obese (30-35)					
Height in Inches							**Body Weight (pounds)**										
58	91	96	100	105	110	115	119	124	129	134	138	143	148	153	158	162	167
59	94	99	104	109	114	119	124	128	133	138	143	148	153	158	163	168	173
60	97	102	107	112	118	123	128	133	138	143	148	153	158	163	168	174	179
61	100	106	111	116	122	127	132	137	143	148	153	158	164	169	174	180	185
62	104	109	115	120	126	131	136	142	147	153	158	164	169	175	180	186	191
63	107	113	118	124	130	135	141	146	152	158	163	169	175	180	186	191	197
64	110	116	122	128	134	140	145	151	157	163	169	174	180	186	192	197	204
65	114	120	126	132	138	144	150	156	162	168	174	180	186	192	198	204	210
66	118	124	130	136	142	148	155	161	167	173	179	186	192	198	204	210	216

(continued)

Table 6.3. *(continued)*

BMI	19	20	21	22	23	24	25	26	27	28	29	30	31	32	33	34	35
		Ideal Weight (20–25)						Overweight (26–29)					Obese (30–35)				
Height in Inches								Body Weight (pounds)									
67	121	127	134	140	146	153	159	166	172	178	185	191	198	204	211	217	223
68	125	131	138	144	151	158	164	171	177	184	190	197	203	210	216	223	230
69	128	135	142	149	155	162	169	176	182	189	196	203	211	216	223	230	236
70	132	139	146	153	160	167	174	181	188	195	202	209	216	222	229	236	243
71	136	143	150	157	165	172	179	186	193	200	208	215	222	229	236	243	250
72	140	147	154	162	169	177	184	191	199	206	213	221	228	235	242	250	258
73	144	151	159	166	174	182	189	197	204	212	219	227	235	242	250	257	265
74	148	155	163	171	179	186	194	202	210	218	225	233	241	249	256	264	272
75	152	160	168	176	184	192	200	208	216	224	232	240	248	256	264	272	279
76	156	164	172	180	189	197	205	213	221	230	238	246	254	263	271	279	287

	36	37	38	39	40	41	42	43	44	45	46	47	48	49	50	51	52
					Obese												
						Body Weight (pounds)											
58	172	177	181	186	191	196	201	205	210	215	220	224	229	234	239	244	248
59	178	183	188	193	198	203	208	212	217	222	227	232	237	242	247	252	257
60	184	189	194	199	204	209	215	220	225	230	235	240	245	250	255	261	266
61	190	195	201	206	211	217	222	227	232	238	243	248	254	259	264	269	275
62	196	202	207	213	218	224	229	235	240	246	251	256	262	267	273	278	284
63	203	208	214	220	225	231	237	242	248	254	259	265	270	278	282	287	293
64	209	215	221	227	232	238	244	250	256	262	267	273	279	285	291	296	302
65	216	222	228	234	240	246	252	258	264	270	276	282	288	294	300	306	312
66	223	229	235	241	247	253	260	266	272	278	284	291	297	303	309	315	322
67	230	236	242	249	255	261	268	274	280	287	293	299	306	312	319	325	331

(continued)

Table 6.3. *(continued)*

Obese

Body Weight (pounds)

	36	37	38	39	40	41	42	43	44	45	46	47	48	49	50	51	52
68	236	243	249	256	262	269	276	282	289	295	302	308	315	322	328	335	341
69	243	250	257	263	270	277	284	291	297	304	311	318	324	331	338	345	351
70	250	257	264	271	278	285	292	299	306	313	320	327	334	341	348	355	362
71	257	265	272	279	286	293	301	308	315	322	329	338	343	351	358	365	372
72	265	272	279	287	294	302	309	316	324	331	338	346	353	361	368	375	383
73	272	280	288	295	302	310	318	325	333	340	348	355	363	371	378	386	393
74	280	287	295	303	311	319	326	334	342	350	358	365	373	381	389	396	404
75	287	295	303	311	319	327	335	343	351	359	367	375	383	391	399	407	415
76	295	304	312	320	328	336	344	353	361	369	377	385	394	402	410	418	426

Adapted from a similar chart at the National Heart, Lung, and Blood Institute Web site: http://www.nhlbi.nih.gov/guidelines/obesity/bmi_tbl.htm

Bright Idea

If you're concerned that you are gaining weight too quickly, measure the circumference of your upper thighs weekly. If the weight you're gaining is within the normal range, the measurement should stay about the same.

Regardless of your actual weight gain target, you should aim for slow, gradual weight gain during pregnancy. Although you may not gain any weight during the first trimester (and, in fact, you may actually lose a few pounds if you're having particular difficulty with morning sickness), you should aim to gain one pound a week during your second and third trimesters — slightly less if you're overweight, and slightly more if you're underweight. You may not gain any weight during the last four weeks of pregnancy. In fact, you may even lose a pound or two.

This means that you can expect to gain approximately 25 percent of your weight between weeks 12 and 20, another 50 percent between weeks 20 and 30, and the remaining 25 percent between weeks 30 and 36.

By the time you deliver, you will have consumed an extra 80,000 calories — the amount of energy it takes to "grow" a baby.

Why is it necessary to gain so much weight?

Some women find it hard to believe how much weight gain is required to support a healthy pregnancy. After all, if the baby weighs in at 7 ½ pounds, where does the other 22 ½ pounds of a 30-pound weight gain end up?

As you can see from Table 6.4, you gain far more weight during pregnancy than your baby does. If you keep your weight gain within the recommended range, you can expect to lose most of this weight within the first few months after birth. So even though you may worry that all 30 pounds are going to end up on your hips or thighs, you could be pleasantly surprised by how easy it can be to lose this "baby fat" after the delivery.

Table 6.4. Weight Gain: Where the Pounds Go	
Maternal stores of fat, protein, and other nutrients (for both pregnancy and lactation)	7 lbs.
Increased body fluid	4 lbs.
Increased blood	4 lbs.
Breast growth	2 lbs.
Enlarged uterus	2 lbs.
Amniotic fluid	2 lbs.
Placenta	1½ lbs.
Baby	7½ lbs.
Total	30 lbs.

How much weight do you need to gain if you're carrying twins?

The American College of Obstetricians and Gynecologists recommends that mothers who are carrying twins gain 35 to 45 pounds during their pregnancies. Some experts in twin pregnancies recommend a slightly higher weight gain, however — something in the 40- to 50-pound range.

You'll need to gain even more than this if you're carrying triplets or other higher-order multiples. A weight gain of 50 to 60 pounds when you're carrying triplets and 65 to 80 pounds when you're carrying quadruplets is not at all unusual. But more important than the actual number of the scale is the amount of nutrient-rich food you're consuming. When you're carrying that many babies, you need to ensure sure that every bite counts.

Watch Out!

It's important not to gain too little or too much weight during pregnancy. Gaining too little weight can put you at risk of giving birth to a low-birth-weight baby (that is, a baby who is 5.5 pounds or less at birth), who may experience developmental delays, and increases your chances of experiencing stillbirth or neonatal death. And gaining too much weight during pregnancy increases your chances of experiencing back strain, high blood pressure and preeclampsia, gestational diabetes, macrosomia (an excessively large baby), weight problems after your baby is born, of requiring a cesarean section, and of experiencing the death of a baby through stillbirth or neonatal death.

How important is it to remain physically active during pregnancy?

The benefits of exercise during pregnancy are enough to make even a card-carrying coach potato head for the gym. Prenatal exercise can

- boost your energy;
- help you to keep your weight gain within the target range;
- contribute to an overall sense of well-being;
- help to regulate your blood glucose levels, something that may help to reduce your chances of developing gestational diabetes;
- help to lower your blood pressure, which can reduce your risk of developing pregnancy-induced hypertension;
- prevent or relieve backache, hip soreness, leg cramps, and constipation;
- help you to get the sleep your body needs;
- help your body to prepare for childbirth (studies have shown that women who are physically fit experience faster labors and are less likely to require inductions, forceps deliveries, and cesarean deliveries than their less fit counterparts); and
- reduce the amount of time it takes you to recover from the birth.

Watch Out!

Excessive exercise during pregnancy can increase your risk of giving birth to a low-birthweight baby. One study found that moms-to-be who engage in strenuous exercise five or more times each week during the last trimester are four times as likely to give birth to a low-birthweight baby as pregnant women who follow more moderate exercise regimes.

Of course, prenatal exercise isn't for everyone. Your doctor or midwife will likely advise against a prenatal fitness program if

- you are experiencing pregnancy-induced high blood pressure;

- you are having problems with persistent bleeding in the second or third trimester;

- you have had preterm rupture of the membranes (PROM) or preterm labor in either your current pregnancy or a previous pregnancy;

- your baby is experiencing intrauterine growth restriction;

- you have been diagnosed with a condition known as incompetent cervix, in which the cervix dilates prematurely;

- you have been diagnosed with placenta previa;

- you have a history of second-trimester miscarriage;

- you are carrying more than one baby;

- you have a serious medical condition such as chronic hypertension; an overactive thyroid; or cardiac, vascular, or pulmonary disease;

- you are significantly underweight;

- you have become anemic over the course of your pregnancy; and/or

- you are experiencing significant pubic or lower back pain.

Which types of fitness activities are — and aren't — recommended during pregnancy?

When it comes to prenatal fitness, all activities are not created equal. Some types of exercise may do you and your baby more harm than good.

The following types of exercise are generally considered to be good choices for pregnant women:

- walking;
- swimming;
- riding a stationary bicycle;
- participating in a prenatal fitness class that emphasizes stretching and low-impact aerobics. (See Checklist 6.2 for tips on finding the class that's right for you.)

> **66** Swimming is great. Don't worry about how you look in a bathing suit. You get bathing suit amnesty when you're obviously pregnant! **99**
>
> —Laura, 31, mother of one

Checklist 6.2. What to Look for in a Prenatal Fitness Class

_____ Is the class held at a convenient location?

_____ Is the class held at a convenient time?

_____ Is it affordable?

_____ Is the class leader a certified fitness instructor?

_____ Does she have any specialized training in prenatal fitness?

_____ How long has the instructor been teaching prenatal fitness classes?

_____ Does the instructor encourage each participant to modify the workout to suit her own fitness level and stage of pregnancy?

_____ Is there a warmup period at the beginning of the class?

_____ Is the workout designed to be low-impact?

_____ Is there a cool-down period at the end of the class?

(continued)

Checklist 6.2. *(continued)*

____ Are pillows or mats available for extra cushioning?

____ Is the exercise room kept at a comfortable temperature?

____ Are there showers available?

On the other hand, the following types of exercises are generally not recommended for pregnant women — especially in the later stages:

- floor exercises that could leave you vulnerable to injury (e.g., deep knee bends, full sit-ups, double-leg raises and straight-leg raises);

- contact sports such as football, basketball, and volleyball

- adventure sports such as parachuting, mountain climbing, and scuba diving;

- sports with a high risk of trauma, such as skiing, horseback riding, surfing, and ice skating;

- high-impact, weight-bearing sports such as running or jogging.

  Note: It's particularly important to avoid weight-bearing exercises such as running or high-impact aerobics if you are having problems with sciatica (pain in the sacroiliac joints). You may further stress the joints and add to the amount of pain that you are experiencing.

 Bright Idea

Find out ahead of time if you are required to produce a certificate from your doctor or midwife to prove that it is safe for you to exercise during pregnancy. That way, you can arrange to have this certificate ready in time to bring to your first prenatal fitness class.

Watch Out!

If you plan to continue with your strength training program during pregnancy, be sure to avoid the tilted supine (semireclined) and full supine (fully reclined) positions—positions that reduce the amount of oxygen available to the fetus.

And now that you have an idea of what types of activities are — and aren't — recommended, here are some tips on getting started on a prenatal fitness program:

- Always consult your doctor or midwife before starting a prenatal fitness program. (If you're already active, you should also ask your doctor or midwife if you should modify your existing fitness program.)

- Be conscious of the fact that the bodily changes of pregnancy may leave you more susceptible to injury. (See Table 6.5 for a list of some of the key ways that the physiological changes of pregnancy can impact on your workout.)

- Start slowly and pay attention to your body's signals. If you're huffing and puffing, you're working too hard. Rather than making exercise an unpleasant experience (and one you're unlikely to stick with), gradually increase the length and intensity of your workouts as your strength and endurance increase.

- Aim to exercise for 20 to 30 minutes at least three times per week. (Note: If you're experiencing a lot of morning sickness in the first trimester, you may not feel up to working out much, if at all. Rather than beating yourself up about it, simply wait until you start feeling better before you launch your prenatal fitness program.)

- Drink plenty of water while you are exercising to prevent overheating and dehydration. As a rule of thumb, you should limit strenuous exercise to 30 minutes (or less in humid weather) and then skip the postexercise hot tub or sauna (to avoid potential damage to the fetus).

- Ensure that your workout includes both a warm-up and a cool-down.

- Wear a bra that provides adequate support. Your breasts are larger and heavier than they were in your prepregnancy days, and the ligaments that support breast tissue can be permanently damaged if they become overstretched.

- Use an abdominal support for more strenuous exercise.

- If you find that exercising on your back makes you feel lightheaded or nauseated, then avoid this position. (When you are lying on your back, the weight of your pregnant uterus is placed on the inferior vena cava — the vein responsible for returning blood from the lower body to the heart. This can cause dizziness.)

- Avoid deep knee bends, full sit-ups, double-leg raises, and straight-leg toe touches.

- Make sure that your workout includes the four most important prenatal exercises: squatting, pelvic tilting or rocking, abdominal curl-ups, and pelvic floor exercises (also called Kegels). (See Table 6.6.)

- Remember that pregnancy alters your center of gravity, so it may be easier for you to lose your balance.

- Never exercise to the point of exhaustion.

 Bright Idea

A study at the University of Michigan confirmed that performing Kegel exercises both during and after pregnancy reduces your chances of experiencing incontinence both in late pregnancy and after birth. Pregnant women should practice their Kegels by starting and stopping the flow of urine. (Once you have the hang of things, though, you can do your Kegels anywhere—in your car or sitting at your desk at work. Starting and stopping the flow of urine may have harmful effects, so don't do your Kegels while you're urinating.)

- Stop exercising immediately if you experience vaginal bleeding or uterine contractions, or if your membranes rupture.

- Avoid increasing the intensity, duration, or frequency of your workouts at any point after the 28th week of pregnancy. Fetal demands for oxygen and nutrition are at their greatest during the last trimester, so it's better to just coast a bit on the fitness front.

Table 6.5. How the Physiological Changes of Pregnancy Affect Your Workout

Although it is generally safe to exercise during pregnancy, it's important to be aware of the ways in which the bodily changes that occur during pregnancy may impact on your workout. Here's what you need to know.

Your respiratory rate increases. Your respiratory rate increases during pregnancy. This is your body's way of ensuring that the baby receives adequate amounts of oxygen. This tends to reduce the amount of oxygen available for exercise, however, and can result in both breathlessness and decreased endurance.

Your center of gravity changes. Your growing uterus causes your center of gravity to change, which can cause you to lose your balance more easily and put strain on your lower back muscles.

Your joints loosen. During pregnancy, your body releases a hormone called relaxin. Its function is to relax your joints and ligaments to make it easier for your body to give birth. Because relaxin loosens up all of the joints in your body—not just those in the pelvic region—you are more susceptible to spraining or straining your muscles and joints.

Your metabolism increases. Your metabolism speeds up during pregnancy. Because exercise also increases your metabolism, it's possible to experience low blood sugar during exercise.

Your heart rate increases. To speed up the delivery of oxygen to your baby, your blood volume increases by approximately 40 percent during pregnancy, and your heart rate increases by approximately 15 beats per minute. This can result in occasional lightheadedness—particularly if you're anemic.

(continued)

Table 6.5. (continued)

Your uterus contracts. When you exercise, your body releases a neuro-transmitter called norepinephrine. It increases smooth muscle contractions, including painless uterine contractions.

Your core body temperature increases. Because an elevated core body temperature can be harmful to the fetus, it's important to consume adequate quantities of fluids when you are exercising—particularly if you're exercising in very hot weather.

Table 6.6. The Big Four: Preparing Your Body for Labor

The Exercise	The Benefits	How to Do It
Squatting	Stretches the legs and opens the pelvis; a useful position for laboring, provided you have the leg strength and balance down pat.	Stand straight. Place your feet a shoulder's width apart and hold on to the back of a chair or your partner for balance. Bend your knees and lower your body as far as is comfortable while keeping your heels firmly on the floor. Hold this position for a few seconds, and then gradually rise to a standing position.
Pelvic tilting and rocking	Strengthens the muscles in your abdomen and back; helps to prevent or relieve backache while improving your overall posture.	Stand with your legs a comfortable distance apart. Breathe out and tilt your pelvis forward and upward by simultaneously pulling in your abdominal muscles and bringing your buttocks forward. Hold this position for a few seconds and then release while breathing in.

The Exercise	The Benefits	How to Do It
Abdominal curl up	Strengthens the abdominal muscles that support the uterus.	Lie on your back and bend your knees. Raise your head and shoulders until your neck is about 8 inches from the floor. Cross your hands over your abdominal area and gently pull yourself upward. Breathe in and lower your body gently.
Pelvic floor exercises (Kegels)	Strengthens the muscles that support the abdominal organs. Can help prevent pregnancy incontinence and make birth easier.	Exercise these muscles by tightening them the way you would if you were trying to stop yourself from urinating. Hold for three seconds and then release gradually.

Are hot tubs, saunas, and steam rooms really off limits during pregnancy?

Anything that raises your body's core temperature over 102°F can be dangerous to the developing baby, particularly if that temperature increase occurs during the all-important first trimester. So, yes, it's best to skip the postworkout trip to the hot tub, sauna, or steam room. Treat yourself to a relaxing soak in a warm (not hot) bath instead.

Week 8

While you may still feel like a total newbie when it comes to this whole pregnancy thing, you're already 20 percent of the way to delivery day.

At this point in pregnancy, you're probably wondering about the various aches and pains you're starting to experience and trying to figure out when there is — and isn't — cause for concern.

What's going on with your baby

Mother Nature has been hard at work fine-tuning your baby's body systems. At about 36 days of development, your baby's ears begin to assume a more human shape and your baby's nasal pit grows deeper and assumes a position closer to the eye. The baby is starting to look more like a newborn.

A number of other noteworthy events occur this week, too: the precursors of the teeth and the facial muscles begin to develop, the eyes begin to develop color, the eye muscles begin to form, the eyelids start to develop, and the nerve fibers that connect the nose to the brain begin to form.

By the end of this week, your baby will be approximately 11 millimeters long — just under half an inch.

What's going on with your body

Your clothes may feel a bit tighter around the waist — hardly surprising given that your uterus is now the size of an apple.

Your uterus isn't the only part of your body that has been growing. Your breasts have been getting larger, too. In fact, you may notice that your regular bras have become uncomfortably snug. Maybe it's time to make a pit stop in the lingerie department of your favorite maternity store.

What's going on with your head

As you've no doubt discovered by now, there's no such thing as a one-size-fits-all pregnancy experience. You may be experiencing every early pregnancy symptom in the book — or you may be feeling so "normal" that you can practically convince yourself that something has gone wrong with your pregnancy.

There's no right or wrong way to be feeling at this stage of the game, so rather than worrying if you're feeling the way you "should" be feeling, why not plan to send your inner control freak on an extended vacation and simply take things as they come?

The Hot List: This week's must-ask pregnancy questions

At this stage of pregnancy, you're likely to be highly tuned into all the changes that are going on inside your body, so a lot of this week's questions are of the "is this normal" variety.

What kind of symptoms can I expect to experience at this stage of pregnancy?

Perhaps you have known a Ms. Perfect Pregnancy — a friend or coworker who felt so well during her pregnancy that she never missed a single aerobics class, got grumpy with her partner, or bolted out of an important meeting because she couldn't stomach the smell of coffee.

Although women like these do exist — and heaven knows they make their presence known to the rest of us — most pregnant women feel somewhat less than euphoric about the mind- and body-morphing that occurs during the first few weeks of pregnancy.

As you've no doubt discovered by now, pregnancy is one of life's greatest levelers. No matter how fit you are, how painstakingly you planned your pregnancy, or how much you want to be a mother, you could very well find yourself being sideswiped by the powerful hormonal cocktail your body needs in order to grow a baby.

Although the symptoms of early pregnancy vary tremendously from woman to woman — and even from pregnancy to pregnancy — most women can expect to experience one or more of the early pregnancy symptoms listed in the following table.

> 66 People ask me how it's been to be pregnant, and I have to say I've enjoyed it. Even with the stress, sickness, aches, and pains, it's all part of the pregnancy experience, in my opinion. 99
>
> —Marie, 28, pregnant with her first child

Note: It's possible that you may be experiencing some aches and pains that are normally associated with the second or third trimester. If you've got a particular complaint that isn't listed here, you'll likely find it discussed in Chapter 8 or 11. Table 6.7 provides a rough snapshot of what types of pregnancy-related aches and pains are likely to kick in when.

Table 6.7. Your Pregnancy Symptoms Month-by-Month

Symptom	Month of Pregnancy When It's Most Likely to Be a Problem								
	1	2	3	4	5	6	7	8	9
Abdominal muscle separation				X	X	X	X	X	X
Backache							X	X	X
Belly button soreness					X				
Bleeding gums (pregnancy gingivitis)	X	X	X	X	X	X	X	X	X
Bleeding or spotting	X	X	X						
Braxton Hicks contractions						X	X	X	X
Breast enlargement	X	X	X	X	X	X	X	X	X
Breast tenderness	X	X	X						
Breathlessness	X	X	X	X	X	X	X	X	X
Carpal tunnel syndrome				X	X	X	X	X	X
Constipation	X	X	X	X	X	X	X	X	X

Symptom	Month of Pregnancy When It's Most Likely to Be a Problem								
	1	2	3	4	5	6	7	8	9
Cramping (abdominal)	X								
Cravings	X	X	X						
Edema (fluid retention) and swelling							X	X	X
Eye changes (dryness and vision changes)	X	X	X	X	X	X	X	X	X
Faintness and dizziness	X	X	X	X	X	X	X	X	X
Fatigue	X	X	X				X	X	X
Food aversions	X	X	X	X	X	X	X	X	X
Gas and bloating	X	X	X	X	X	X	X	X	X
Headaches	X	X	X	X	X	X	X	X	X
Heartburn							X	X	X
Hemorrhoids				X	X	X	X	X	X
Hip soreness				X	X	X	X	X	X
Insomnia	X	X	X	X	X	X	X	X	X
Itchiness		X					X	X	X
Leg cramps							X	X	X
Linea nigra (vertical line down center of abdomen)				X	X	X	X	X	X

(continued)

Table 6.7. (continued)

Symptom	Month of Pregnancy When It's Most Likely to Be a Problem								
	1	2	3	4	5	6	7	8	9
Mask of pregnancy (chloasma)				X	X	X	X	X	X
Morning sickness	X	X	X						
Nasal congestion (rhinitis)	X	X	X	X	X	X	X	X	X
Nosebleeds	X	X	X	X	X	X	X	X	X
Perineal aching									X
Pubic bone pain				X	X	X	X	X	X
Rashes							X	X	X
Round ligament pain				X	X				
Sciatica							X	X	X
Skin changes	X	X	X	X	X	X	X	X	X
Smell, heightened sense of	X	X	X						
Stretch marks							X	X	X
Sweating, increased				X	X	X	X	X	X
Swelling and edema (fluid retention)							X	X	X
Thirstiness	X	X	X	X	X	X	X	X	X

| | Month of Pregnancy When It's Most Likely to Be a Problem | | | | | | | | |
Symptom	1	2	3	4	5	6	7	8	9
Urinary incontinence (leaking of urine)							X	X	X
Urination, increased frequency of	X	X	X				X	X	X
Vaginal discharge, increased	X	X	X	X	X	X	X	X	X
Varicose veins							X	X	X
Weepiness	X	X	X	X	X	X	X	X	X
Yeast infections	X	X	X	X	X	X	X	X	X

Adapted from a similar chart in *The Mother of All Pregnancy Books* by Ann Douglas (John Wiley and Sons, 2002). See www.themotherofallbooks.com

Abdominal cramping or a bloated, heavy feeling

Many women report that in the first few weeks of pregnancy, they have a bloated, heavy feeling that is not unlike what they experience around the time that their periods are due. Headaches and irritability may accompany these PMSlike symptoms, as can some minor cramping.

Note: Sharp, one-sided pain is not normal and should be reported to your caregiver immediately. Such pain may indicate that your pregnancy is ectopic (see Chapter 17 for details).

Bleeding gums

The hormonal changes of pregnancy can cause your gums to bleed a little more easily than usual. To minimize this condition — known as pregnancy gingivitis — you will want to brush and floss regularly, rinse your mouth with antiseptic mouthwash

> 66 All of the pregnancy books I read described the early signs of pregnancy as being much more prominent than mine were. I searched book after book to find one that said, 'Some people don't have any early symptoms.' As a result, I didn't really believe I was pregnant until I saw the first ultrasound of my baby. 99
>
> —Susan, 29, pregnant with her first child

several times a day, and choose foods that are rich in gum-friendly vitamin C. You'll also want to see your dentist at least once during your pregnancy so that your dentist can scrape off some of the plaque that builds up on your teeth. This will help to minimize the severity of any pregnancy gingivitis you are experiencing.

Note: If you're experiencing bleeding from tiny nodules on your gums, you have likely developed *pyogenic granulomas* — harmless, noncancerous growths that sometimes occur during pregnancy. They typically disappear on their own after you give birth, but, if they're causing you a lot of grief in the meantime, you can have your dentist remove them for you.

Breast changes

Some of the most dramatic changes in early pregnancy are the changes that occur to the breasts. Many women go up a bra size or two overnight — a situation that can be either disconcerting or delightful, depending on how you feel about your breasts.

The hormones at work behind this sudden increase in breast size are also responsible for other changes in the appearance of your breasts. Your nipples sometimes become enlarged and erect, the areola broadens and becomes darker, and the increased blood flow through your body causes the veins in your breasts to become more visible.

Many women also experience a certain amount of breast discomfort during this stage of pregnancy. The swelling, tingling, throbbing, and aching that you may be feeling are indications that your body is getting ready to go into the milk-production business a few months down the road.

Breathlessness

This particular pregnancy symptom is one of the medical world's greatest mysteries. Your uterus and your baby haven't grown enough to start compressing your lungs — something you can look forward to a little further down the road — but you're likely to find yourself huffing and puffing at the top of each flight of stairs.

Some doctors believe that dyspnea (the medical term for shortness of breath) is caused by increased levels of progesterone. It's not likely to be a cause for concern for you unless you're asthmatic, in which case you may need to have your medications adjusted.

Constipation

Many pregnant women experience problems with constipation — and for good reason. Increased levels of progesterone can make the muscles of the small and large intestines rather sluggish.

Although laxatives are not believed to be harmful during pregnancy, it's best to find natural ways of improving your bowel function, such as exercising regularly; adding more fruits, vegetables, grains, and fluids to your diet; and reducing your consumption of dairy products, fatty foods, and processed sugar. You could also try the tried-and-true method that probably worked for your grandmother: 2 tablespoons of unsulphured blackstrap molasses dissolved in a glass of warm water.

Cravings

The jury is still out on whether there's a biological basis to cravings or not, but we're not about to argue with any pregnant woman who claims to have a hankering for pickles and ice cream. (After all, if a woman can develop a craving for inedible substances like road salt or laundry starch — a bizarre phenomenon known as *pica* — who's to say she can't develop cravings for plain old food? Not us!) All we're going to say on the subject is that using cravings as an excuse for nine months worth of overindulgence can be a recipe for disaster — literally. So proceed with caution if the chip wagon starts calling your name.

Eye changes

This may sound too outlandish to be true, but we swear it's for real: the fluid retention that occurs during pregnancy can actually affect the shape of your eyeballs. This causes some pregnant women to experience problems with nearsightedness and others to develop a condition called dry eye, which is characterized by dryness and burning, blurred vision, and increased sensitivity to light. (Using an artificial tears product to restore moisture to the eyes and wearing protective eyewear when you're out in the sunlight will usually take care of your dry eye woes, by the way.)

Faintness and dizziness

In the days before home pregnancy tests, a sudden episode of fainting was a sure-fire indication of pregnancy.

As is the case with many other pregnancy-related complaints, progesterone is to blame. It dilates the smooth muscle of the blood vessels and causes a pooling of blood in the legs.

Most pregnant women can minimize their dizziness problems by shifting their weight from foot to foot. Those who experience faintness due to hypoglycemia (low blood sugar) simply need to eat better-quality foods at more regular intervals. Here are some other ways to cope with the faintness you may be experiencing:

- Drink more fluids.

- Rise more slowly after sitting or lying down.

- Avoid hypoglycemia and its resulting dizziness by minimizing your intake of sweets and not going more than two hours without eating something.

Watch Out!

It's important not to play do-it-yourself-doctor where eye changes during pregnancy are concerned because vision problems can be a warning sign of diabetes. So be sure to report any eye changes you notice to your doctor or midwife promptly.

Fatigue

Most women start feeling extremely tired shortly after their first missed period, and their energy levels don't return to normal until well into the second trimester (weeks 14 to 20 on average). Although it's hard to get enough rest when you're working full-time, at least you can try to

- take a power nap at your desk during your lunch hour or during your morning and afternoon breaks;

- flop out on the couch as soon as you get home from work;

- head to bed earlier than usual so that you can get the 10 hours of sleep per night that is recommended during pregnancy.

Eating as well as possible and getting some form of regular exercise will also help you to ward off fatigue.

Gas

Gas is a common complaint throughout pregnancy, but it can be particularly problematic during the first trimester, when there is a tendency to swallow a lot of air in an effort to relieve feelings of nausea. Gas then has to make the 22-foot trip through the intestines — no small feat, given that the high progesterone levels of pregnancy and the expanding uterus make it difficult for the intestines to do their job.

You can minimize your problems with gas by steering clear of gassy foods such as beans and cabbage, avoiding carbonated beverages, and not sipping at hot drinks and soup or talking while you are chewing (both can cause you to swallow air).

Bright Idea

Apply an ice pack to your forehead, or to the source of the pain, as soon as a tension headache sets in. The ice will cause your blood vessels to contract, eliminating the cause of your headache. You should feel better within 20 minutes—roughly the amount of time it takes for a painkiller to work.

Headaches

Headaches are another pregnancy rite of passage for many women. If you're reluctant to take acetaminophen (for example, Tylenol), which, by the way, is generally considered to be perfectly safe to take during pregnancy, you might want to try a few other techniques for getting rid of a headache:

- Lie down with a cool cloth on your head.

- Eat more frequently to keep your blood sugar on an even kilter.

- Ask your partner to massage your feet. (The big toe is the acupuncture point for the head.)

Insomnia

If you haven't already kicked the caffeine habit, now's the time to do it. Many women experience insomnia at various points in their pregnancies, and caffeine will only add to the problem. If you find yourself wide awake in the middle of the night — even though your body is begging for sleep — a cup of warm milk or chamomile tea may help you get the rest that you and your baby need.

Morning sickness

Morning sickness is a catchall term used to describe everything from a hypersensitivity to odors or an aversion to certain foods to severe vomiting. And despite what the name implies, it can cause misery at any time of day — not just in the morning.

Bright Idea

Can't stomach your prenatal vitamins? To increase the odds that you'll be able to keep your vitamin down, try taking it in the middle of a meal rather than on an empty stomach, switching to a less troublesome brand, using liquid vitamins instead of a tablet, or just taking folic acid until the nausea subsides.

Morning sickness is thought to be caused by the hormonal, metabolic, and chemical changes of early pregnancy. Kicking in around six weeks after the first day of your last menstrual cycle, and lasting until well into the second trimester, nausea can strike at any time of day or night and affects between 60 percent and 80 percent of pregnant women. It is more likely to be a problem for women who are carrying twins or other multiples or who are feeling somewhat run down.

Although you may be feeling anything but grateful about experiencing this classic symptom of pregnancy, scientists feel that there's something good to be said about morning sickness. Studies have shown that women with little or no nausea or vomiting are two to three times more likely to miscarry because their levels of pregnancy-related hormones may not be sufficiently high to support a pregnancy. (So there you go — some good news to take to the bathroom with you.)

Note: Some scientists speculate that morning sickness may serve as a defense mechanism, encouraging pregnant women to avoid alcohol, tobacco, coffee, and other substances that could be harmful to their developing babies. There's just one small problem with this theory: human genetic evolution has occurred over a period of many thousands of years, but most of the substances that make pregnant women feel queasy have been around for only the past few hundred years. After all, the caveman lifestyle didn't exactly lend itself to leisurely after-dinner cigars!

Bright Idea

If you're worried about missing time from work due to morning sickness, ask your boss if you can either telecommute or shift your working hours to a time of day when nausea is less of a problem for you.

You can minimize nausea at home and at work by

- eating something before you get out of bed in the morning;

- keeping crackers in your desk so that you can eat before you get really hungry;

- eating only those foods that genuinely appeal to you rather than limiting yourself to vegetables and other nutrient-rich foods that may not necessarily sit well with you right now;

- avoiding foods that are likely to trigger nausea (fried foods, greasy foods, high-fat foods, sausages, fried eggs, spicy foods, foods containing monosodium glutamate [MSG], onions, sauerkraut, cabbage, cauliflower, and beverages that contain caffeine);

- seeking out foods that are less likely to cause your stomach to do flip-flops (potatoes, soda crackers, applesauce, yogurt, and so on);

- chewing gum or sucking on mints or hard candy;

- sniffing slices of lemon or inhaling the scent of mint or grated ginger root;

- eating neither too much nor too little food at a time (either can make you feel rather queasy);

- drinking plenty of water and fruit juices if you can't stomach milk;

- taking a vitamin B6 supplement if you're experiencing particularly severe symptoms of nausea;

- avoiding cigarette smoke and other strong odors;

- wearing loose-fitting garments and avoiding pants that are too tight and belts that dig into your waist; and

- getting as much rest as possible.

About 1 out of every 300 pregnant women develops a severe form of morning sickness known as *hyperemesis gravidarum* (Latin for "excessive vomiting in pregnancy"). This condition occurs when the body is unable to compensate for the relentless vomiting and loses valuable body salts (electrolytes) and body fluids. The disorder is thought to be linked to higher-than-usual levels of the hormones hCG and estrogen, and it is more common in first pregnancies, young women, and women carrying multiples.

If you are experiencing the following symptoms, you may be developing hyperemesis gravidarum:

- excessive vomiting (you haven't been able to keep any food or drink down for 24 hours);

- reduced frequency of urination (particularly if your urine appears darker in color and consequently is becoming more concentrated);

- dryness of the mouth, eyes, and skin;

- extreme fatigue, weakness, or faintness;

- confusion.

If you develop hyperemesis gravidarum, you will probably be hooked up to an IV (either in a hospital or at home) and given the salts and fluids necessary to rehydrate your body. Your doctor may also decide to prescribe an antinausea medication.

 Bright Idea

Some women find that antinausea wristbands provide some relief from morning sickness. These wristbands are designed to apply constant pressure to the acupressure points on the wrists that control nausea and vomiting. They're inexpensive—you can pick up a pair for roughly $10—so you might want to try a pair if morning sickness has you feeling particularly miserable.

Nasal congestion (rhinitis)

A stuffy nose is a common complaint during pregnancy. Congestion in the nasal passages is caused by the increased blood supply to the mucus membrane. The condition does not require any treatment and will disappear automatically after your baby is born.

Nosebleeds

Bleeding from the veins in your nose may be an indicator of high blood pressure (hypertension), but more often than not it's simply caused by the very same increase in blood flow that is responsible for so many other pregnancy-related symptoms. If you have recurrent nosebleeds, however, you should mention this problem to your healthcare provider so that he can rule out the possibility of hypertension.

Skin changes

Skin changes during pregnancy vary from woman to woman. Some take on that much-talked-about maternal glow; others break out in acne. If you tend to break out in pimples right before your period, you're likely to be a candidate for complexion problems during pregnancy. Note: We talk about other pregnancy-related skin changes in Chapters 8 and 11.

Smell, heightened sense of

A heightened sense of smell is a common first-trimester pregnancy complaint. Suddenly, you can barely tolerate the smell of a coworker's perfume or (gag) the burnt sludge at the bottom of the office coffee pot.

Fortunately, this too shall pass — and sooner than you might think. You'll likely find that you're less bothered by odors once the peak period of morning sickness passes (around the end of the first trimester, for most women).

In the meantime, you can always fall back on a trick that worked for your great-granny — carrying around a handkerchief dipped in lemon juice and applying it to your nose whenever you're accosted by an overpowering odor that might otherwise cause you to lose your lunch (or your breakfast or your dinner).

Thirstiness

Your body needs extra fluids during pregnancy, so it's hardly surprising that you're extra thirsty. In fact, you should plan to drink at least eight glasses a day of water or other decaffeinated beverages to keep up with your body's increased need for fluid.

Urinary tract infections

If you experience burning while you urinate or feel a constant urge to urinate (even if you've just gone to the bathroom), you could be suffering from a urinary tract infection.

If it turns out that you do, in fact, have a urinary tract infection, your doctor will treat the infection with an antibiotic such as ampicillin, amoxicillin, or sulfamethoxazole/trimepthoprim, all of which are thought to be safe during pregnancy. Because UTIs tend to recur, you'll need to have your urine checked at regular intervals throughout the remainder of your pregnancy.

You may be able to keep urinary tract infections at bay by consuming one to two cups of cranberry juice each day. Studies have shown that cranberry juice helps reduce the number of bacteria in urine and may actually prevent the bacteria from sticking to cells in the bladder.

Urination, increased frequency of

Another classic symptom of early pregnancy is the need to run to the bathroom at frequent intervals throughout the day and night. The cause of increased frequency of urination is obvious: as your uterus expands, it begins to put pressure on your

 Watch Out!

Not all urinary tract infections are symptomatic. That's why it's important to ensure that your healthcare provider tests your urine at each prenatal visit. Untreated urinary tract infections have been proven to cause premature labor.

bladder. The hormonal changes of early pregnancy are also thought to play a role.

Vaginal discharge, increased

An increase in the amount of leukorrhea (the odorless white mucosy discharge that your body produces throughout your childbearing years) is triggered by hormonal changes and is perfectly normal during pregnancy. If, however, you experience a vaginal discharge that is greenish-yellow, foul-smelling, or watery, you should contact your healthcare provider immediately.

Weepiness

If you find yourself becoming downright weepy each time a baby powder commercial flickers across the TV screen, don't assume that you've lost your marbles: just blame it on the hormonal changes of pregnancy. It's completely normal to feel totally emotional about things that wouldn't have even shown up on your radar screen a few weeks ago!

Yeast infections

Severe itching or burning and a curdlike or cottage cheeselike discharge from the vagina are classic symptoms of a vaginal yeast infection. Other symptoms include painful urination (due to irritation to the urethra); painful intercourse; and swelling, redness, and irritation of the outer and inner lips of the vagina.

Yeast infections are usually caused by candida albicans, a type of fungus that tends to run rampant during pregnancy for three key reasons: hormonal changes make your vaginal environment less acidic; increased amounts of sugar are stored in the cell walls of the vagina; and your immune system is less effective during pregnancy, making you more susceptible to infection.

Yeast infections tend to be a particular problem for women who require antibiotics to treat UTIs or other bacterial infections during their pregnancies. Although there are numerous over-the-counter medical and herbal remedies for yeast infections, you should not use any of these products until your

Moneysaver

Increased vaginal secretions combined with your growing belly can wreak havoc on your designer panties. Invest in cheap cotton undies instead. Not only will you be less concerned about ruining your favourite lingerie: the breathable cotton fabric will leave you less prone to yeast infections.

healthcare provider both confirms that you do, in fact, have a yeast infection and recommends an appropriate treatment.

This is definitely one of those situations in which an ounce of prevention is worth a pound of cure. You can help prevent yeast infections by

- avoiding tight clothing around your vaginal area;
- choosing clothing made from natural rather than synthetic fibers;
- wiping from front to back when you go to the bathroom;
- making sure that your vagina is well-lubricated before intercourse; and
- reducing the amount of time you spend sitting on vinyl seats in your home, car, or office.

Note: While there is a popular belief that eating yogurt with acidophilus (live cultures) is an effective method of preventing yeast infections, this particular claim has yet to be proven. However, when more purified forms of the same bacteria have been taken orally or administered vaginally, some promising results have been seen. So stay tuned. Maybe we'll have something more to report in the next edition of this book!

I find find myself worrying about every little ache and twinge. How can I tell what's normal and what I really need to worry about?

As you've no doubt noticed by now, worrying kind of goes along with the whole pregnancy turf — Mother Nature's way of preparing you for the lifetime of worry that goes along with being a mother.

Still, it's easy to go overboard in the Worrying Department, obsessing about anything and everything. Hopefully, the previous section of this chapter that talked about all the various first trimester aches and pains will help to reassure you that a lot of what you're experiencing is perfectly normal. And, strangely enough, you may also find that you're less likely to worry if you familiarize yourself with the list of situations when there definitely *is* cause for concern (the theory being that if the symptom you're experiencing isn't on the reasons to worry list, you can probably hold off on hitting the panic button for now). See Table 6.8 for a list of the top 12 warning signs that every pregnant woman definitely needs to know about.

Table 6.8. The Top 12 Warning Signs that Every Pregnant Woman Needs to Know About

You should call your doctor immediately if you experience any of the following symptoms:

1. **Heavy vaginal bleeding or clotting.** (If it happens in the first trimester, it could be an indication that you are having a miscarriage; if it happens in the second or third trimester, it could be an indication of some sort of problem with the placenta.)

2. **Lighter bleeding that lasts for more than one day.** (If it happens in the first trimester, it could be an indication that you are going to have a miscarriage; if it happens in the second or third trimester, it could be an indication of some sort of problem with the placenta.)

3. **The passage of greyish or pinkish tissue or any amount of bleeding that is accompanied by cramps, fever, chills, or dizziness.** (This could be a sign that you may be having a miscarriage.)

4. **Severe pain in abdomen or in your shoulder area.** (This is a symptom of an ectopic pregnancy.)

5. **A severe or persistent headache, particularly one that is accompanied by dizziness, faintness, or blurry vision.** (This is a possible symptom of high blood pressure or preeclampsia—a serious medical condition that is characterized by high blood pressure.)

You should call your doctor immediately if you experience any of the following symptoms:

---

6. **Dehydration** (e.g., dry mouth, thirst, reduced urine output, low-grade fever). This can be a sign of illness or something as simple as an indication that you haven't been consuming enough liquids on a hot day.

7. **A fever of more than 101°F.** (This is a possible symptom of an infection that may require treatment.) Note: Even if you don't have an active infection, your doctor will want to bring your temperature down because, depending on your stage of pregnancy, an elevated core body temperature can be harmful to the developing baby and may trigger premature labor.

8. **Painful urination.** (This is a possible symptom of a urinary tract infection—something that can trigger premature labor and/or lead to a kidney infection.)

9. **A watery discharge from the vagina.** (This is a sign that your membranes may have ruptured.)

10. **A sudden swelling of the face, hands, or feet.** (This is a sign that you may be developing preeclampsia.)

11. **Uterine contractions, vaginal bleeding or discharge, vaginal pressure in the pelvic area, menstrual-like cramping, a dull backache, stomach or intestinal cramping and gas pains, and a general feeling of unwellness.** (These are symptoms of premature labor.)

12. **A significant decrease in the amount of fetal movement after the 24th week of pregnancy.** (This is a possible sign that your baby may be running into difficulty.)

Just the facts

- To calculate your due date, simply add 266 days or 38 weeks to the date when you conceived or, assuming that your menstrual cycles are 28 days in length, you add 280 days or 40 weeks to the first day of your last menstrual period.

- You have three basic options when it comes to prenatal care: an obstetrician, a family physician, or a midwife. Regardless of which type of health care provider you choose, you should try to schedule your first prenatal appointment as soon as early as possible during your first trimester — ideally 6 to 10 weeks after the first day of your last menstrual cycle.

- You may be eating for two, but that doesn't mean you need twice as much food when you're pregnant. All that most women require to support a pregnancy is an extra 100 calories per day during the first trimester and an extra 300 calories per day during the second and third trimesters.

- Most women can count on gaining between 25 and 35 pounds during pregnancy. Underweight women may be advised to gain a little more while overweight women may be advised to gain a little less.

- When it comes to prenatal fitness, your best bets are walking, swimming, riding a stationary bicycle, and participating in a prenatal fitness class that emphasizes stretching and low-impact aerobics.

- Hormonal changes are responsible for a number of early-pregnancy symptoms, including headaches, constipation, breast tenderness, skin changes, and morning sickness.

GET THE SCOOP ON. . .

What's going on with your baby ▪ What's going on with your body ▪ What's going on with your head ▪ Miscarriage worries ▪ Sex during pregnancy ▪ Stress worries ▪ Health concerns ▪ Working during pregnancy

The Third Month: Anxiety Alley

If Mother Nature intended pregnancy to be a nine-month-long apprenticeship in the art of worrying, the third month tends to be when the training program really gets off the ground. Worrying seems to be pretty much *de rigueur* at this stage of pregnancy, whether you're experiencing a whole smorgasbord of pregnancy symptoms or practically none at all.

If you're being sideswiped by symptoms at every turn (in other words, you feel like you've signed up for the Symptom of the Day Club!), you may slowly but surely be wearing out the pages in each of your pregnancy books in your ongoing effort to confirm that what you're experiencing is "normal" as opposed to something truly panic-worthy.

And if you're pretty much breezing through pregnancy (in other words, you've yet to experience as much as a single bout of morning sickness or a single run-in with any other "classic" pregnancy symptom), you may be becoming seriously panicked

Chapter 7

about the fact that you're feeling so well. (Psst. . . . If you happen to be one of those lucky gals who manage to breeze through the first trimester, try not to obsess too much about your lack of symptoms: some women simply get off a little easier than others in the symptoms department. Besides, it's still early days. Odds are you'll have at least a few aches and pains to complain about between now and delivery day. We can practically guarantee it.)

You see, you really can't win when it comes to this worrying thing: it's going to get you one way or another. That's why this chapter is packed with information on the areas of greatest concern to moms-to-be at this stage of the game: miscarriage, stress, sex, illness, and being pregnant on the job.

We also give you an idea of what to expect on a week-by-week basis during the 9th to 13th weeks of pregnancy. You'll get the inside scoop on what's going on with your body, what's going on with your head, and what's going on with your baby each week, along with answers to some of the most-asked pregnancy questions for each week of pregnancy.

Week 9

If the majority of your friends seem to be in baby-making mode these days, chances are you know at least a few women who have experienced the heartbreak of miscarriage — something that may leave you wondering — and worrying — if this could happen to you.

Miscarriage is most likely to be on your mind at this stage of pregnancy. Once you're into the second trimester, the peak risk period for miscarriage will be behind you, and you will likely find it a little easier to relax. (Or at least that's the theory!) But, for now, you may find yourself doing the famous toilet paper test every time you step foot in the bathroom to pee — obsessively checking for any signs of spotting and then heaving a huge sigh of relief when the toilet paper comes back spot-free. (It's pretty much a standard rite of passage for most pregnant women, whether they're prepared to admit it or not. So don't think you're completely crazy or obsessed. Sounds like you're pretty normal to us!)

What's going on with your baby

Your baby is now a little more than an inch long — roughly the size of a large grape. Your baby's head is more erect and his or her neck is more developed than in previous weeks, and your baby's eyelids have started to close up and his or her external ear has started to form.

Your baby has also sprouted the beginning of what will eventually develop into hands and feet. Your baby's hands and fingers develop a few days ahead of his or her feet and toes.

The penis begins to form in the male, and milk lines — which will eventually become mammary glands — are already present in babies of both sexes.

The first of three successive kidney systems that your baby will rely upon before birth is now fully functional — allowing your baby to produce urine at regular intervals.

What's going on with your body

Your uterus is expanding along with your knowledge of everything pregnancy-related. Your uterus is now a little bit bigger than an apple.

Your breasts may be noticeably larger and may be starting to feel slightly lumpy as the ducts inside the breasts start to grow and develop. You may also notice a "roadmap" of bluish blood vessels appearing beneath the skin in your breasts — the result of the increased blood supply to your breasts.

You can expect your breasts to gain a fair bit of weight over the course of your pregnancy, by the way. While a typical non-pregnant breast weighs about 7 ounces, by the end of pregnancy, you can expect your breasts to be tipping the scales at between 14 and 28 ounces each.

What's going on with your head

You may find yourself experiencing a powerful (some might even say obsessive!) urge to learn everything you can about pregnancy, birth, and babies. And why not? It's only natural to want to understand how your life is likely to change during the exciting months ahead.

> 66 The moment I discovered I was pregnant, I began a nine-month-long research project. I read everything I could get my hands on regarding pregnancy, labor and delivery, and raising babies and children. 99
>
> —Jennifer, 21, mother of one

Besides, knowledge can be empowering. The more you know about pregnancy, the less likely you are to feel panicked by every bizarre sensation or mysterious twinge you experience. Who knows? That towering stack of pregnancy books on your night table may be the very thing that makes it possible for you to get a good night's sleep on nights when your worry-o-meter is working overtime!

The Hot List: This week's must-ask pregnancy questions

At this point in your pregnancy, you may find yourself wondering about this month's prenatal checkup and worrying about your odds of having a miscarriage.

What should I expect from this month's prenatal checkup?

This month's prenatal checkup won't be quite as involved as your initial prenatal checkup, but your doctor or midwife still has a lot of important ground to cover. The purpose of this visit, like all subsequent visits, is to monitor the health of you and your baby and to ensure that your pregnancy is continuing to progress normally.

You can expect your doctor or midwife to check

- the size of your uterus (your healthcare provider will palpate your uterus to verify that your uterus is roughly the size that it should be for this stage of pregnancy);

- the fundal height (your healthcare provider will measure the distance between your pubic bone and the top of your uterus — the fundus, starting after week 12);

- your weight (to see if you are continuing to gain weight slowly);

- your blood pressure (to spot any signs of chronic hypertension) (Note: as your pregnancy progresses, your caregiver will be watching for early warning signs of pregnancy-related hypertension or preeclampsia, too.);

- your urine (to ensure that your sugar and protein levels are within the normal range as they, too, can provide early warning of any emerging problems);

- the fetal heartbeat (your healthcare provider will use a Doppler or hand-held ultrasound unit to try to pick up a fetal heartbeat — an effort that's more likely to be successful if this month's prenatal appointment falls during or after Week 12, when your baby is a little bit bigger).

How accurate is ultrasound in dating a pregnancy?

Ultrasound is extremely accurate when it is used during the first trimester. Measuring the baby's crown to rump length at this stage of pregnancy can pinpoint a baby's gestational age within three to five days. (Similar measurements of fetal development taken during the second and third trimesters of pregnancy are accurate within 7 to 11 days and 14 to 21 days respectively, so you can see why the first trimester is the preferred time to date a pregnancy.)

What are the other main reasons for performing a first-trimester ultrasound?

Your doctor might also decide to order a first-trimester ultrasound in order to

- pinpoint the location of the gestational sac (the fluid-filled structure containing the developing fetus), something that can be helpful in diagnosing an ectopic pregnancy (a pregnancy that occurs outside the uterus, usually in the fallopian tube);
- look for evidence of an embryo;
- check for a fetal heartbeat;
- find out if you are carrying more than one baby;
- examine the uterus for structural abnormalities or other problems that could pose problems during your pregnancy.

How safe is ultrasound during pregnancy?

Ultrasound has been used in obstetrics for more than 30 years and is not known to pose any harm to a pregnant woman or her baby. That said, the American College of Obstetricians and Gynecologists does not recommend its routine use during pregnancy. In other words, if your doctor or midwife orders an ultrasound, he or she should have a specific medical reason for doing so.

Note: You will find a more detailed discussion of the use of ultrasound during pregnancy in Chapter 14.

I'm starting to get a little nervous about my ultrasound appointment. Is it normal to feel this way?

It's not at all unusual to experience a mix of anxiety and excitement before your ultrasound appointment — excitement about finally getting a chance to catch a glimpse of your baby-to-be on the ultrasound screen, but also a bit of anxiety in case the ultrasound brings less-than-happy news.

While the odds of receiving positive news about your pregnancy are decidedly in your favor, it's always best to hedge your bets by ensuring that your partner or some other support person is able to accompany you to your ultrasound appointment. That way, if the news is less than happy, you won't have to face it on your own. And if you have experienced a miscarriage or stillbirth in the past, you will particularly appreciate having this support person along to help ease your anxiety level a little.

> 66 The biggest emotional challenge of the first trimester for a mom who has lost a baby through miscarriage is worry. Pregnancy is no longer a simple, natural process. It's as if someone has stolen your naivete'. Along with the massive hormonal changes of early pregnancy, you're faced with a nagging doubt that something will go wrong this time, too. You don't want to tell anyone you're pregnant, and every little twinge is a reason to panic. 99
>
> —Julie, 45, mother of six

What are my odds of experiencing a miscarriage?

Approximately 15 percent of confirmed pregnancies end in miscarriage (the spontaneous death of a baby prior to the 20th week of pregnancy). While it's easy to get freaked out by that statistic, we'd like to encourage you to turn that number on its head and remind yourself that you have an 85 percent chance of *not* miscarrying.

What are the warning signs of miscarriage?

You should at least consider the possibility that you may be experiencing a miscarriage, if you experience one or more of the following symptoms:

- Spotting or light bleeding that may or may not be accompanied by menstrual-like cramping;

- Heavy or persistent bleeding (with or without clots) that is accompanied by abdominal pain, cramping, or pain in the lower back;

- A gush of fluid from the vagina (an indication that your membranes may have ruptured);

- The sudden disappearance of all pregnancy symptoms.

Note: It's normal for such first-trimester pregnancy symptoms as morning sickness and breast tenderness to disappear around the end of the first trimester, so you'll want to consider the timing of this particular sign. If it happens midway through your first trimester, there may be cause for concern. If it happens at the end of the first trimester, your pregnancy is likely progressing perfectly normally.

What else could be responsible for spotting during pregnancy?

Spotting is quite common after an internal exam — a reason why some healthcare practitioners are reluctant to perform internal examinations during the early weeks of pregnancy when the cervix is most prone to bleeding. It can also occur after sex if the penis happens to bump against the cervix during intercourse, causing the tender cervix to bleed slightly.

This type of cervical bleeding is absolutely harmless. Therefore, your caregiver shouldn't hesitate to do an exam if the information obtained from that

> 66 During the first trimester, I had some bleeding on and off for about two weeks. I was terrified that I was going to lose the baby. I remember walking into our bedroom once and my husband asked me what was wrong, and all I said was, 'I'm bleeding' and I just cried all night long. I was put on a few days of bedrest and had a couple of ultrasounds and, in the end, everything was okay. 99
>
> —Jennifer, 21, mother of one

exam will make a difference in her ability to provide you with good health care. Similarly, if you want to have sex and your caregiver has determined that any bleeding you are experiencing is cervical in nature, then you should be reassured that there is no increased risk of miscarriage. If, however, you can't stop obsessing about the bleeding, despite your caregiver's reassurances, you might want to postpone the bedroom gymnastics for now. Note: We talk more about sex during pregnancy later on in this chapter.

Is it possible to experience a miscarriage without knowing that you've miscarried?

While most women who are experiencing a miscarriage experience bleeding or other symptoms, it is possible to experience a "missed abortion" (the medical profession's rather insensitive term for a miscarriage that occurs without any accompanying symptoms — in other words, a miscarriage in which neither the baby nor the placenta are expelled from the uterus). In this case, the first indication that something that has gone wrong may be the doctor or midwife's inability to detect a fetal heartbeat during a late first-trimester checkup — something that can result in a pretty shocking turn of events for a previously happy mom-to-be.

Note: See Chapter 17 for more about miscarriage.

Week 10

While you may still feel like a total newbie when it comes to being pregnant, you've already made it through the first quarter of your pregnancy. And things are going to get a whole lot more eventful from this point forward. By the time you've made it to the halfway mark in another 10 weeks' time, you'll be boasting a decidedly maternal profile and you may even be feeling some baby kicks and flutters. This pregnancy thing is getting serious, you know!

Bright Idea

If you haven't taken any photos of yourself since the pregnancy test came back positive, grab your camera right now. If you make a habit of taking a side profile shot of yourself wearing the same outfit each month from now until delivery day, you'll end up with a highly visual record of your incredible growing belly! (Obviously, you'll want to pick a loose-fitting garment or to dip into your maternity wardrobe when you're picking out your outfit. That tight-fitting pair of jeans will soon be history, assuming, of course, it isn't already!)

What's going on with your baby

The tubes in your baby's lungs are fully formed and his intestines have migrated from the umbilical cord (their first home) into the abdominal cavity. Around the same time, your baby's taste buds start to develop and — if your baby is a girl — her ovaries start to descend into the pelvis.

Your baby's still quite the featherweight, however: he or she measures about 1 ½ to 1 ¾ inches in length and weighs just ⅓₀th of an ounce.

What's going on with your body

You're likely to notice subtle changes in your body shape from one week to the next. A pair of pants that zipped up last week may not longer zip up this week. And a blouse that has always fit you to a T may suddenly feel too tight across the bustline.

Other people are unlikely to notice these changes yet, however, so if you're still trying to keep your pregnancy under wraps, odds are your secret is still safe (for now).

In terms of complaints at this stage of pregnancy, you may be experiencing some of these "classic" first trimester pregnancy complaints — or you may be feeling remarkably unpregnant. (Don't worry, you don't have to experience a lot of symptoms in order to have a healthy pregnancy.)

- Fatigue;
- Nausea and/or vomiting (a.k.a. morning sickness);

- Occasional faintness or dizziness, particularly if you're standing in one position;

- Increased bulkiness around your waist and bust;

- Breast changes (increased fullness and heaviness; tenderness and tinging; and/or physical changes such as a darkening of the areola, the sweat glands in the areola becoming more prominent and goosebump-like, and a "roampap" of pale blue lines that appears under the skin of your breasts);

- Food aversions and/or food cravings and an increased appetite;

- Increased need to urinate;

- Constipation, flatulence, and bloating;

- Heartburn and indigestion;

- Increased vaginal discharge;

- Occasional headaches.

(See Chapter 6 for more about these common first trimester pregnancy complaints.)

What's going on with your head

You may find that you have sex on the brain — but not for the usual reason. If your libido is currently missing in action (either because morning sickness is making you feel queasy rather than passionate or because you're secretly worried that sex may somehow be harmful to your baby), you may be seriously worried about how your sudden lack of desire is likely to affect your relationship with your partner during the weeks and months ahead.

And if your partner's the one who keeps rolling over and going to sleep with little more than a bedtime kiss, you may be worried that your changing body shape is responsible for The Big Chill in the bedroom.

While it's tempting to blame yourself, odds are there's something else to blame. Your partner may simply need a bit of time to work through some pregnancy-related hang-ups of his own. Some men worry that having sex will hurt the baby (even if they know in their heads that there's nothing to be concerned about), or they may feel that it's somehow not right to have sex with someone's mother (that would be you!) or to make love while the baby is "watching."

> 66 I have a wonderful husband, and as my body grew—I gained 60 pounds in total—he continually told me how beautiful I was and tried to make me feel as though all the added weight was a good thing and not to feel ugly because of it. This helped with sex because it made me feel a little less self-conscious about my body and about being naked in front of him. 99
>
> —Mother of one, 25

In most cases, these issues tend to resolve themselves over time, particularly if you're able to talk to your partner about what you're feeling, so try not to get too obsessed about what is — or isn't — happening in the bedroom. Odds are your born-again virgin status will be relatively short-lived.

The Hot List: This week's must-ask pregnancy questions

Still obsessing about sex? The answers to this week's set of questions should help to set your mind at ease about pregnancy and sex.

Is it safe to have sex during pregnancy?

In most cases, yes. Your doctor will only advise you to douse the flames of passion if you're experiencing complications in your current pregnancy or if you have a history of complications in previous pregnancies and your doctor feels that having it would be risky for you to have intercourse or achieve orgasm. (It's not that he's a spoil-sport who wants you to miss out on all the fun, by the way. Orgasms can trigger uterine contractions that can be bad news for women experiencing high-risk pregnancies. You can find out more about sex restrictions in high-risk pregnancies in Chapter 16.)

What about oral sex? I heard it's not recommended during pregnancy.

Oral sex is considered safe during pregnancy provided that your partner avoids blowing air into your vagina — a practice that could allow an air bubble to find its way into your bloodstream and result in a potentially fatal air embolism.

And while we're talking about oral sex, here's something else you need to know: the hormonal changes of pregnancy can change the taste and odor of your vaginal secretions — something that could cramp your sexual style if your partner finds your new taste and odor off-putting.

 Watch Out!

Not everyone is a good candidate for sex during pregnancy. Your doctor or midwife is likely to advise you to forgo intercourse or orgasm, or both, for at least part of your pregnancy if

- you have a recurrent history of first-trimester miscarriage;
- you have been diagnosed with placenta previa (when the placenta blocks all or part of the cervix);
- you have been diagnosed with a placental abruption (when the placenta begins separating from the uterine wall prematurely);
- you are carrying more than one baby;
- you have a history of premature labor or are showing signs that you may be about to go into premature labor;
- you or your partner has an untreated sexually transmitted disease;
- your membranes have ruptured.

Is it normal to experience cramping after having sex?

Yes, that's your body's response to the oxytocin that is released during orgasm. (As you'll find out later on in this book, oxytocin is the hormone responsible for triggering labor transactions, so it's hardly surprising that sex can leave you feeling a little crampy.)

There's no need to worry about sex putting you into labor prematurely, by the way, unless, of course, you're already at risk of premature labor: the contractions that occur during sex aren't powerful enough to send most women experiencing low-risk pregnancies into bona fide labor.

And as for the old wives' tale about late-pregnancy sex helping to bring on labor, it appears that the old wives got that one wrong: a study reported in *Obstetrics and Gynecology* found that intercourse and orgasm during late pregnancy actually *reduce* the risk of preterm delivery in low-risk patients.

Is it safe to use sex toys when you're pregnant?

According to Anne Semans and Cathy Winks, authors of *The Mother's Guide to Sex,* if you and your partner were in the habit of using sex toys in your prepregnancy days, there's no need to pack them away just because you're having a baby. Just make sure you keep your toys clean and well lubricated and be sure to adjust the angle and depth of insertion to avoid bumping your cervix — something that can led to spotting, which, although harmless to your baby, can be very worrying for you.

Is it normal to lose all interest in sex when you're pregnant?

There's no such thing as "normal" when it comes to pregnancy and sex. Pretty much anything goes. Pregnancy may change your feelings about sex totally — or it may have no effect on your sex life at all. Whereas some couples find that their sex lives improve tremendously during pregnancy (some women who've never had an orgasm in their lives report having them for the first time during pregnancy), others find that the flames of passion all but fizzle out.

Some women find that their interest in sex diminishes during the first weeks of pregnancy, when fatigue, morning sickness, and tender breasts can make sex sound considerably less than appealing. "My interest in sex decreased. I didn't even want my husband touching me. I was just too uncomfortable," admits one first-time mother.

Others find that their interest in sex goes through the roof, even during the first trimester. "My interest in sex really increased at the beginning of this pregnancy, my third. I felt very sexy and always in the mood, even before I knew that I was pregnant. I think we had sex more often during the first trimester than at any time other than our newlywed stage," says one woman who is currently pregnant with her third child.

"My appetite for sex was voracious the whole nine months," admits one first-time mother. "So was my husband's. He thought my pregnant body was very sexy, although he did laugh at some of my attempts to be the pregnant sex kitten."

Sometimes it's your partner's feelings about sex that puts your sex life on ice: "My husband wanted nothing to do with me sexually. After he saw the ultrasound picture, he thought that sex with a pregnant woman was disgusting," laments one mother of one.

If there's been a history of miscarriage, both partners may be afraid about having sex — even though sex is considered to be perfectly safe for women with low-risk pregnancies: "The interest in sex was certainly there, but we were both overcome with fear," recalls one first-time mother. "We had a miscarriage with our previous pregnancy, which had us too scared to have sex for the entire subsequent pregnancy!"

Many women find that their interest in sex picks up once morning sickness begins to wane and fatigue begins to lift. "During the second trimester of each pregnancy, my sex drive definitely increased," recalls one third-time mother. "I felt very sexy, even as my tummy expanded. Actually, it was wonderful to have an excuse for my tummy to stick out, and for the first time in my life, I was totally unselfconscious about my husband stroking it," admits one first-time mother.

Although many couples find that their interest in sex begins to taper off as the birth of their baby approaches — one study found that one-third of couples were abstaining by the time the ninth month rolled around — others manage to enjoy moments of sexual intimacy right up until the very end — blossoming belly and all. "You just have to get creative with positioning," confides one first-time mother.

Some women report that sex is more pleasurable than ever during pregnancy as rising estrogen levels cause the vagina and labia to become slightly swollen and increasingly sensitive. Others find this increased sensitivity to be uncomfortable or irritating. "I don't have a problem achieving orgasm, except during pregnancy," complains one third-time mother.

What positions work best during pregnancy?

Most couples find that they start experimenting with different positions early on in pregnancy, long before there's a blossoming belly to work around. The reason is simple: positions that may have been comfortable during your prepregnancy days may not work for you as well now that you're having a baby.

During the early weeks of pregnancy, you'll want to avoid any position that puts weight on your oh-so-tender breasts or that worsens any morning sickness you may be experiencing.

In the second and third trimesters, you're likely to have other concerns — for example, the need to avoid lying flat on your back after the fifth month (a position that can cause you to feel faint and that may interfere with the flow of oxygen to your baby) and the need to avoid putting a lot of pressure on your belly (baby is well protected, but having your partner lean on your belly may be very uncomfortable for you).

So, without any further ado, here's our very concise version of the Pregnant Kama Sutra — our top three picks for sex positions during pregnancy:

- Woman on top ("female superior"): This position allows you to control the depth and angle of penetration and avoids the need to lie on your back.

- Side-by-side ("spoons"): This position gets your tummy out front and out of the way and allows for lots of foreplay and cuddling.

- Rear entry ("doggy style"): This position gets your tummy out of the way, but allows for greater ease of movement than is possible with the side-by-side position.

I experienced a bit of spotting after having sex the other night. Does this mean that having sex hurt the baby?

Try not to panic if you experience a small amount of spotting after intercourse. A small amount of spotting can occur if your cervix gets bumped with your partner's penis during intercourse. Because it's difficult to differentiate between harmless bleeding and bleeding that may indicate a problem with your pregnancy, some caregivers will suggest that you hold off on intercourse until your cervix becomes a little less prone to this type of bleeding — typically after the first trimester.

Of course, if it can be determined that the pregnancy is not threatened and the bleeding is simply coming from these small cervical blood vessels, then intercourse is harmless. If, on the other hand, you think that you will be excessively worried about the bleeding, should it occur (or recur), then abstinence during this time frame may make sense for you.

Week 11

You're starting to develop a bit of a pot belly — proof positive that this pregnancy thing is for real! At times you may feel completely on top of the world about being pregnant; at other

340 PART II ■ YOUR FIRST TRIMESTER WEEK-BY-WEEK

times, you may be surprised by how moody and emotional you are. The pregnancy roller-coaster ride has begun!

What's going on with your baby

Your baby is approximately 1 ¾ inches in length and weighs approximately ⅓ of an ounce. Your baby's head makes up nearly half of its length.

Your baby's external genitalia are beginning to show more distinguishing features, and within another three weeks, the sex differentiation process will be complete.

What's going on with your body

Your uterus is now the size of a grapefruit — almost big enough to fill your pelvis. If you put your hand across your lower abdomen, you may feel your uterus rising above the middle of your pubic bone.

What's going on with your head

You may be surprised by how emotional you're feeling — and how rapidly your emotions can change. One moment, you're totally euphoric about being pregnant. The next, you're feeling weepy, irritable, or anxious. You're not going crazy, although you may find that difficult to believe if you just burst into tears while watching a long-distance telephone commercial. Your body is simply doing its best to adjust to the most radical bio-chemical changes you'll experience during your lifetime.

"My frustration tolerance was very low," recalls Jennie, 30, who recently gave birth to her first child. "I'd cry if the mailman was mean to me or if someone told me I couldn't park my car where I wanted to park it. One of the hardest things about being pregnant is the feeling of being out of control."

And if you wanted desperately to become pregnant, you may be surprised to find yourself feeling less than elated — perhaps even a little letdown — now that you've actually managed to conceive. That letdown feeling is perfectly understandable. After all, you're no longer fantasizing about being pregnant;

you're now coping with the less-than-delightful realities of morning sickness, constipation, and overwhelming fatigue. ("I had this feeling, like I'd gotten on a roller coaster but couldn't get off," confides Laura, a 31-year-old mother of one.)

The first-trimester reality check can also be a difficult one for partners, says Troy, 30, a first-time father. "During the first trimester, Yvonne was extremely ill with morning sickness. In fact, it was so bad that she was off work for almost two months. I ended up having to do everything around the house — after working for about nine hours in front of a computer. It wasn't too bad at first, but after a while it started to really wear on me. All our friends would ask, 'How's Yvonne?' but no one would ask, 'How are you?' The truth was I was very tired and feeling alone, neglected, and somewhat dumped on."

It's important to remember that this challenging stage will pass and that your spirits (and your partner's spirits) are likely to pick up as you settle into your pregnancy. If you're still feeling down in the dumps in a couple of weeks' time, however, you'll want to talk to your doctor or midwife about how you are feeling. It's possible you're suffering from prenatal depression — a subject we discuss at length in Chapter 10.

The Hot List: This week's must-ask pregnancy questions

Find yourself feeling stressed about, well, feeling stressed? You're not the only pregnant woman to worry about the possible effects of stress on her developing baby. This week's set of questions focus on stress, relaxation, and that interesting emotional baggage that you may be bringing along for the pregnancy ride.

I'm dealing with a lot of stress right now, both at work and at home. I can't help but worry that my stress level is hurting my baby.

In a perfect world, pregnant women would automatically be granted a nine-month-long exemption from stress. We wouldn't have to deal with job frustrations, financial worries, marital conflicts, and other sources of day-to-day anxiety. But because we live in a decidedly imperfect world, most of us find ourselves doing battle with these "real world" stresses on top of the stress of being pregnant. (Yes, being pregnant can be stressful in and of itself, particularly if you're feeling particularly miserable — think morning sickness! — embarking on a high-risk pregnancy, or if you're pregnant again after a previous miscarriage or stillbirth.)

You're wise to want to keep your stress level under control, by the way. A 1999 study conducted at the University of California Los Angeles School of Medicine found that women who reported that they were under a great deal of stress were more likely to have high levels of corticotropin-releasing hormone (CRH) in their blood — a stress hormone that prompts the body to release prostaglandins (chemicals that trigger uterine contractions and that has been linked to preterm labor and the birth of low-birthweight babies). And other studies have shown that even babies born at term to women who experienced high levels of stress during their pregnancies were more likely to be low birthweight than babies born to less-stressed moms. (Scientists believe that stress-related hormones such as norepinephrine, which constrict blood flow to the placenta, may prevent the baby from receiving the nutrients and oxygen it needs for optimal growth.)

Fortunately, Mother Nature seems to provide a measure of stress protection as pregnancy progresses: a study at the University of California at Irvine concluded that women become less sensitive to stress as pregnancy progresses, something that may help to protect the baby from some of the more severe effects of stress.

Of course, you'll also want to lend Mother Nature a helping hand by applying some of the following stress-management techniques:

- Practice your relaxation breathing. It's a skill that will serve you well during labor and beyond, so you might as well master the art of relaxation breathing now. (Hint: Taking a couple of deep breaths and heading for the nearest bathtub with bubble bath in hand, has helped more than a few mothers weather their kids' toddler and teen years!) What you want to do is breathe deeply enough that your belly rises and falls — but not so deeply that you hyperventilate and pass out! You may have to experiment a little before you learn what pace and intensity of relaxation breathing works best for you.

- Pay attention to your physical health. This one is a bit of a no-brainer, but it bears a mention because we sometimes overlook the fact that there's a clear link between our physical health and our psychological well-being. Exercising regularly (as long as you have your doctor's or midwife's go ahead to be physically active during pregnancy), eating ample quantities of healthy food, and ensuring that you're getting the rest you need can help to bring your stress level down tremendously.

- Kick your caffeine habit, if you haven't already. If you're already feeling edgy, caffeine will only serve to heighten your stress level.

- Line up some support. Talk to your partner or a trusted friend about how you are feeling or join an e-mail list for moms-to-be so that you can vent your emotions in relative anonymity. If you feel like you need some professional help in managing your stress level, try to find a counselor who has some experience in helping women to navigate the sometimes-tumultuous waters of pregnancy.

Watch Out!

Resist the temptation to turn to alcohol, drugs, or cigarettes as a means of coping with your stress. These products pose serious risks to the health of your developing baby and should be avoided at all costs during pregnancy.

Is it safe to have a massage during pregnancy?

If you decide to go for a massage during the first trimester (some doctors and midwives say it's fine to have a first trimester massage, others suggest that you hold off until the second trimester), it's important to make sure that the massage thera-pist you see has received specialized training in working with pregnant women. Deep massage work — particularly on the legs — is a definite no-no during pregnancy. Pregnant women are highly prone to varicose veins and vigorous leg massage could cause a blood clot in the leg to become dislodged, caus-ing disability or even death.

A less-vigorous massage, however, has plenty to offer: pregnancy massage can ease such pregnancy-related complaints such as leg cramps, headaches, fluid retention, or swollen ankles.

Of course, you will need to vary your massage position while you are pregnant. During the early weeks of pregnancy, you'll want to avoid any position that puts a lot of weight on your breasts, which tend to be extremely tender at this stage of the game. Then, as your pregnancy progresses, you'll need to work around your rapidly growing belly. And after the fifth month, you'll need to avoid lying flat on your back because this position can lead to extreme dizziness, even fainting.

While the side-lying position is a perennial favorite with moms-to-be, it's not the only position that works. You and your massage therapist may want to experiment with different posi-tions until the two of you stumble across the one that works best for you. (Hint: Those little wedge-shaped massage table pillows can be a pregnant woman's best friend!)

What other spa treatments are considered suitable for pregnant women?

Let's start out by talking about the types of spa treatments that you'll definitely want to steer clear of while you're pregnant. As a rule of thumb, you should plan to avoid any treatments that involve high temperatures (whirlpools, saunas, steam rooms, heat wraps, etc.) or the use of any herbal or botanical products that could be potentially harmful to your developing baby.

It's also a good idea to steer clear of the tanning bed. Not only is the heat potentially harmful to your developing baby: the tan that you acquire will only serve to make the mask of pregnancy (a.k.a. chloasma — the butterfly-shaped area of pigmentation that can occur on the cheeks and forehead) more prominent.

Wondering what that leaves you? There are still quite a few delectable choices on the spa treatment menu that you can enjoy, including the following:

- **A facial.** Facial treatments designed to unplug oily pores can help to minimize the severity of the hormonally driven acne outbreaks that many women experience during pregnancy.

- **A pedicure.** A foot massage and pedicure can be sheer heaven for a pregnant woman. Not only does it feel great to have someone massage your feet (particularly if your feet start to feel really tired and swollen towards the end of your pregnancy): by the time you're into your ninth month, painting your own toenails may be a near impossibility, so it only makes sense to subcontract this job to someone else.

- **A body scrub:** A moisturizing body scrub will help you to get rid of the buildup of dead skin cells that can otherwise lead to an itchy belly. It can also help to replenish some of the moisture that your body may be losing as a result of hormone-induced skin dehydration.

Bright Idea

Be sure to let the spa staff know about your pregnancy at the time you book your appointment. That way, they'll be able to help you to steer clear of any treatments that aren't suitable for pregnant women.

Is it normal for pregnancy to bring up a lot of heavy-duty emotional stuff?

What you're experiencing is very common. Just don't expect your other pregnancy books to have much to say on the topic.

As you've no doubt noticed, there's a bit of a conspiracy taking place at your local bookstore. Most of the pregnancy books seem to be intended for some mythical pregnant woman who actually lives the twenty-first century version of the American dream: she has a fabulous career, a wonderfully supportive husband, and no complicated health problems or messy psychological baggage.

If you don't happen to fit that dubious profile, it's easy to fall through the cracks, which is why we've chosen to include a brief mention of a few not-so-unusual circumstances that can affect your pregnancy experience, such as

- pregnancy after infertility;
- pregnancy after miscarriage;
- pregnancy after abortion or adoption;
- pregnancy after sexual abuse;
- being pregnant when you're in an abusive relationship; and
- coping with grief during pregnancy.

Pregnancy after infertility

If you've struggled with infertility, you may find it hard to believe your good fortune when the pregnancy test finally comes back positive. In fact, you may rush out to buy another test or two before you allow yourself to believe that the good news could actually be true. (Hey, it's no wonder those pregnancy test companies keep posting record profits!)

Once you accept the fact that you are really and truly pregnant, you may find yourself dealing with a whole list of pregnancy-related worries: Does the spotting you're experiencing mean that you're having a miscarriage? Does the disappearance of your nausea mean that you've experienced a missed abortion? Does the fact that your baby isn't moving around as much as usual mean that there's some kind of serious problem?

Such anxiety is natural and understandable, given what you've been through to get across the starting line in the Baby Olympics. Here are some tips on coping with it:

- Find a doctor you respect and trust. "You have enough worries when you're pregnant," says Molly, 29, a first-time mother and former infertility patient. "You don't need to be worrying about the competency of your doctor."

- Don't be afraid to turn to your caregiver for reassurance and information whenever the need arises, adds Heather, 31, who also experienced infertility prior to the birth of her first child. "You will enjoy this pregnancy more than you imagined, but you will also be very worried about everything. That is very normal. You can never ask too many questions during your prenatal visits."

- If you find yourself rushing to the bathroom every five minutes to check for signs of bleeding, try to focus on something other than the possibility of miscarriage. Remind yourself that you have an 80 percent or greater chance of carrying your baby to term.

- Hook up with other mothers who are experiencing pregnancy after infertility. If you can't find such a group in your community, seek support online. You can find leads on some helpful Web sites in the "Resource Directory" (www.wiley.com/go/anndouglas).

Pregnancy after miscarriage, stillbirth, or infant death

Whether you decide to become pregnant as soon as possible after the loss of your baby or to postpone your next pregnancy for a while, it's never easy to go through another pregnancy. Your joy at being pregnant may be overshadowed by fears about what might happen to this baby, grief about the baby who died, and guilt about "being disloyal" to that baby because you are going ahead with another pregnancy.

It's important to choose a caregiver who will help you cope with your many conflicting emotions and who will understand your need for ongoing support. "My obstetrician was extra sensitive to my need for reassurance that things were going well with my pregnancy," recalls Cindy, 34, who experienced three consecutive miscarriages prior to the birth of her first child. "She did ultrasounds for me when there wasn't any other medical reason except to reassure me."

During your initial prenatal visit, you should have a frank discussion about what — if anything — can be done to maximize your chances of experiencing a happy outcome this time around. For example, are there any tests that can be done to improve your outcome or reduce your anxiety? Would your doctor or midwife be prepared to teach you how to use a fetoscope or Doppler so that you could monitor your baby's well-being at home in between appointments, if you wished to do so?

> **❝** Don't feel as if you are being unfaithful to the baby you lost if you are happy about the new pregnancy. **❞**
>
> —Dawnette, 28, mother of one who had a miscarriage prior to the birth of her first child

You may find it helpful to connect with other women who are pregnant after a loss — either by seeking this type of support group in your own community or by joining an online support group for parents who have experienced the death of a baby either prior to or after birth.

Bright Idea

If you are planning to deliver in the same hospital or birthing center where your previous baby died, you may find it helpful to plan a return visit to the facility before you arrive there in labor. While you're there, give some thought to whether you'd like to deliver your new baby in the same—or another—birthing suite as you had the last time around, assuming that you have that choice.

(See the "Resource Directory" (www.wiley.com/go/anndouglas) for leads on online support groups that may be helpful to you.)

Note: You can find a detailed discussion of the joys and challenges of pregnancy after miscarriage, stillbirth, or infant death in our book *Trying Again: A Guide to Pregnancy After Miscarriage, Stillbirth, and Infant Loss* (Taylor Publishing).

Pregnancy after abortion or adoption

Sometimes a pregnancy brings painful memories to the surface — such as your decision to have an abortion or to give up a child for adoption earlier on in life. If you have not yet come to terms with the choice you made, you may find it helpful to seek the services of a therapist who can help you to work through your feelings. But even if you have come to terms with your choice, you should anticipate the occasional difficult moment during your pregnancy.

Kate, 33, who gave up her first child for adoption when she was a teenager, explains: "Almost 16 years ago, I became pregnant and chose to have the baby," she explains. "After a lot of soul-searching, I gave her up for adoption. Not everyone knows this piece of my history, but my doctor needed to know, so I told him."

Although Kate believes that being open with her doctor about her situation was the best way to go, she did run into some awkward moments during her pregnancy: "The codes the doctor used on my chart were pretty universal, so most of the healthcare professionals I saw knew that I'd had a previous pregnancy. There were an awful lot of embarrassing silences after people asked me, 'So what do you have at home?'"

If there's something from your reproductive past that you'd prefer not to have broadcast to the four corners of the earth, ask your doctor if it would be possible to omit some of this information from the medical record that will be used at your delivery. Here's what one prominent obstetrician has to say about the issue: "I think that doctors often don't need to know everything their patients think they need to know, especially about previous abortions that were uncomplicated. Even if they do know, they're not obligated to put the information onto forms that are circulated to other healthcare personnel, who may not have been briefed on the patient's need for discretion."

> ❝I got a lot of comments from well-meaning individuals about this being my first child. I got around the question, 'Is this your first?' with 'Yes, this is our first,' meaning my husband's and my first baby.❞
>
> —Kate, 33, who gave up her first child for adoption 16 years ago

Pregnancy after sexual abuse

Survivors of sexual abuse often find that pregnancy or childbirth can be difficult because of what they have been through in the past.

"Pregnancy whacks your hormones and opens up all sorts of hidden things," explains Heather, 32, a mother of one and sexual-abuse survivor. "Memories may come up, or old feelings of body-shame and fear may come back full force. You'll need help dealing with these."

Here are some tips on coping with pregnancy if you have a history of sexual abuse:

- Bring up your history with your caregiver. If you don't feel comfortable enough to share this information with your current doctor or midwife, change caregivers.

- Write a birth plan that includes a stress reaction list so that the members of your labor support team and the hospital staff will know how you may react to the pain of labor and what you would like them to do to help you work through it. You should be aware that it's not uncommon for a sexual-abuse survivor to experience abuse flashbacks or to begin to disassociate (that is, psychologically withdraw) during labor.

- Make sure that your caregiver is aware of potential triggers that may cause anxiety or body memories of childhood sexual abuse to surface during labor.

- Decide whom you do — and don't — want to have present at the birth. Many abuse survivors bring in close friends or hire doulas so that there will be plenty of people to provide support and encouragement when the going gets tough.

- Have confidence in your body's ability to give birth and your own personal strength. "If you survived the abuse, you can survive anything," Heather stresses. "Remember that you are strong, able, and creative. You managed to get through something very nasty, and pregnancy and childbirth isn't nasty — just difficult — so you can do this too. Put your faith in yourself and allow yourself to be astonished, amazed, and awestruck at your own strength."

- Above all, stay focused on the positive, most-important outcome of labor — your baby!

Being pregnant and in an abusive relationship

According to a study reported in *Obstetrics and Gynecology,* one in five pregnant teens and one in six pregnant women can expect to experience physical or sexual abuse during her pregnancy — abuse that puts her at increased risk of experiencing miscarriage or giving birth to a low-birthweight baby.

Some pregnant women report an escalation of abuse during pregnancy, whereas others indicate that they only feel safe while they are carrying a child because they feel confident that their partner wouldn't do anything to hurt the baby — something that can lead to repeated pregnancies as a way of escaping abuse.

Many women who have been putting up with abuse decide to make the break during pregnancy or shortly after the birth, fearing that the abuser may harm the baby. (Their concern about their baby's well-being is justified, by the way: studies have shown that more than 50 percent of men who abuse their female partners also abuse their children and many others threaten to abuse their children.)

"It took me nine months after my son was born to finally leave an abusive relationship," says Janna, a 35-year-old mother of two. "When I realized that my partner would be abusing my son, I realized I'd had enough."

If you are in an abusive relationship and have made the decision to leave, here are some steps that can help you and your children get out as safely as possible:

- Pack a suitcase and leave it in the care of a trusted friend or neighbor. Include clothing for yourself and your children, prescription medicines, toiletries, and an extra set of car keys.

- Set up your own bank account and leave the passbook in the care of a friend.

- Make sure that all of the important records you might need are in a place where you can find them quickly. These include birth certificates, Social Security cards, your voter registration card, your driver's license, medical records, financial records, and documents proving ownership of the house and car.

- Know exactly where you're going and how to get there. If you will be staying with a friend or family member, make sure that person is prepared for the fact that you could show up at their doorstep at any time.

- Call the police if you need help leaving or if you wish to press charges against your partner.

- Arrange for counseling for yourself and any children you may already have. You may need some support in breaking free of the cycle of abuse and preparing for a happier future with your new baby.

Coping with grief during pregnancy

Pregnancy is an emotional time, so it's hardly surprising that it can trigger painful feelings of grief about the deaths of loved ones. If, for example, you recently lost a parent or a grandparent, or your partner died during your pregnancy, you may regret the fact that this special person in your life didn't live long enough to meet your new baby. And, of course, the breakup of a marriage can trigger waves of grief that are not unlike the grief that many people experience following the death of a loved one. So if you find yourself unexpectedly single midway through your pregnancy, you may find yourself grieving the loss of your marriage and your hopes and dreams of co-parenting along with your ex.

A loved one's death doesn't have to be recent to trigger waves of emotion, incidentally. Some women who lost their mothers during childhood or their early teens find that they experience a period of "regrieving" when they find themselves motherless during pregnancy. "I found myself with so many questions that a woman would normally ask her mother," says Kelly, a 35-year-old mother of one. "It was the loneliest feeling in the world to realize that I didn't have a mother to share my own journey to motherhood with."

If you find that grief is affecting your ability to enjoy your pregnancy, you may want to talk to a friend who has been through a similar loss, find out if there is a grief support group operating in your community, or set up an appointment with a grief counselor who has experience with your particular type of loss.

Regardless of what type of support you line up for yourself, it's important to find a healthy way to vent your feelings of loss so that you can break free from the tidal wave of grief that may threaten to drag you down and give yourself permission to look forward to the wonderful future that awaits you and your new baby.

Week 12

You're into the homestretch of the first trimester now. If you've been battling morning sickness for the past few weeks, you can expect a reprieve soon. (Assuming, of course, that you're one of the lucky majority who gets to kiss their morning sickness symptoms goodbye at the end of the first trimester. An unfortunate few end up experiencing morning sickness right up until delivery day.)

What's going on with your baby

Your baby is now approximately 2 inches long and weighs approximately ¼ of an ounce. Small amounts of hair are beginning to appear on your baby's body, your baby's fingernails and toenails are beginning to grow, and your baby's first permanent tooth buds have started to form. The thyroid gland that regulates your baby's metabolism has started to function and the fetal nervous system is beginning to mature. Your baby is quite literally changing day by day.

The amniotic sac that your baby is housed in now contains approximately 1 ½ ounces of amniotic fluid. By the time you give birth, the amniotic sac will contain between three and four cups of amniotic fluid.

Your doctor or midwife should be able to detect your baby's heartbeat anytime now by using a hand-held Doppler — a truly magical sound to hear.

What's going on with your body

Your uterus is now too large to be hidden away in your pelvis. (See Figure 7.1.) You may still be able to squeeze into your regular clothes, if this is your first pregnancy, but if you've had other pregnancies, you are likely to be into your maternity wardrobe by now.

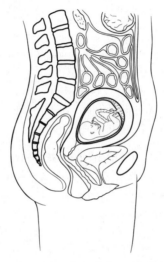

Figure 7.1. The approximate size of your baby and belly at 12 weeks of pregnancy.

What's going on with your head

You may find yourself more conscious of danger than usual. For example, you decide to avoid walking across an icy parking lot because you're worried about the impact of a possible fall on your baby-to-be. And you opt to steer clear of the "mystery leftovers" in the refrigerator for the very same reason.

While it's wise to be prudent, you don't want to allow yourself to become totally paranoid. Otherwise, you'll have difficulty enjoying your pregnancy. So take the necessary precautions, yes, but don't allow yourself to become totally paralyzed with anxiety. That's not healthy for you or your baby.

The Hot List: This week's must-ask pregnancy questions

Even if you've never been much inclined to worry about your health, you may find yourself playing the role of the hypochondriac now that you're pregnant, obsessing about every cold or sniffle that comes your way. (And why not? You're not just responsible for your own health anymore, after all: you're watching out for the health of your baby-to-be, too.)

The best way to deal with your newfound health worries is to arm yourself with the facts so that you'll know when there is — and isn't — cause for concern.

To help you get your fact-minding mission off to a roaring start, here are answers to some of the most-asked questions about illness during pregnancy.

Are colds and flus harmful to the developing baby?

Garden-variety colds and flus won't do your baby any harm (although they're likely to leave *you* feeling quite miserable). Where there might be cause for concern is if you were to develop a high fever. High fevers (particularly during the first trimester) can result in birth defects, including heart defects. (A study reported in the medical journal *Epidemiology* found that nearly twice as many new mothers who gave birth to babies with heart defects reported having had a fever in the three months prior to conception or during the first three months of pregnancy than new mothers who did not give birth to babies with heart defects.)

If you get hit by the cold or flu while you're pregnant, you'll want to drink lots of liquids (any viral illness will tend to dehydrate you, and pregnancy only makes the problem worse); take acetaminophen to bring down your fever, should you develop a fever; and get plenty of rest.

If your cold is severe, you may want to talk to your doctor about the advisability of using a decongestant nasal spray or taking certain types of oral decongestants to relieve some of your misery.

Watch Out!

If your fever won't go away, if you develop a cough with greenish or yellow-ish phlegm, or if you experience difficulty breathing, get in touch with your doctor right away. You may be developing pneumonia.

I had a really nasty bout of the stomach flu last week. Could this have been harmful to my baby?

The key risk that stomach flu poses is dehydration. If you become seriously dehydrated as a result of vomiting and diar-rhea, you may start to experience premature contractions. If you get hit with the stomach flu again and you're having a hard time keeping things down, try sipping on chicken soup, ginger ale, tea, or water. It doesn't matter what kind of healthy bever-age you consume as long as you're getting something into your system.

And don't worry about the few pounds you might have dropped while you were feeling so ghastly. Babies don't suffer unduly just because their moms end up missing a few meals. Remember, they're built for survival.

I tend to get hit with seasonal allergies at the end of each summer. What can I do to manage my allergies during my pregnancy?

You may end up getting off lucky in the allergy department this year. Some pregnant women find that their allergy symptoms are much less severe when they are pregnant.

If, however, you do end up experiencing some fairly severe symptoms, you will want to talk to your doctor about the pros and cons of taking various types of allergy medications during pregnancy (see Chapter 5 for more about the effects of various types of medications on the developing baby). Your doctor will need to balance the risks posed by medication exposure against the known risks of severe allergy symptoms such as poorly controlled asthma. (Poorly controlled asthma can result in preterm birth and low-birthweight babies.)

Note: Most asthma inhalers are safe and can be used as required during pregnancy — something that should allow you to breathe easy on this particular front.

I tend to be susceptible to urinary tract infections. Could these infections be harmful to my baby?

You'll definitely want to seek treatment for any urinary tract infections that occur during pregnancy. If left untreated, they can potentially lead to premature labor.

Note: You can find out more about urinary tract infections in Chapter 9.

What types of common childhood illnesses do daycare center workers like me need to worry about most during pregnancy?

There are four basic illnesses that you need to be concerned about if you're working in a daycare setting: chickenpox (varicella), fifth disease (human parvovirus B19), rubella (German measles), and cytomegalovirus (CMV). Here's what you need to know about each.

Chickenpox

Most adults are immune to chickenpox, either because they're had it in the past or because they have been immunized against the disease. If you're not sure if you're immune, it's best to avoid coming into contact with anyone you know who either has been exposed to the chickenpox or who has developed the illness because chickenpox can be harmful to you as well as your developing baby. You may develop flulike symptoms, and possibly even pneumonia, as well as the chickenpox skin rash. And your baby is at risk of developing congenital varicella syndrome — a rare condition in which the baby may be born with abnormal limbs, chickenpox scarring, and may experience growth and development delays.

Bright Idea

If you're unsure whether or not you're immune to chickenpox, ask your doctor to perform a varicella immunity blood test. The test will tell you whether you are immune or not. Note: Many doctors routinely test for varicella immunity when you have blood work done at your preconception or pregnancy confirmation checkup, so he may already know whether you're immune.

The worst time to contract chickenpox is during the five days before or after you give birth. If exposure occurs during this time, you may have time to pass the chickenpox on to your baby, but not the antibodies that could help your baby to fight the illness, something that could lead to your baby developing a severe case of the chickenpox.

If you are exposed to the chickenpox during pregnancy and you don't think you're immune to the disease, your doctor may decide to give you a drug called varicella-zoster immune globulin (VZIG), which can help to minimize the severity of your outbreak. VZIG has to be administered within three days of your chickenpox exposure, so it's important to get in touch with your doctor right away if you think you have been exposed.

Fifth disease

Fifth disease is a viral infection that is caused by human parvovirus B19. About 50 percent of adults are immune to the disease, likely as the result of previous infection. Your doctor can order a test to see if you are immune to fifth disease — something which you may wish to consider, especially if you work with children.

Fifth disease is spread through exposure to airborne droplets from the nose and throat of infected individuals. The illness is most contagious during the week before the appearance of the rash.

Symptoms (which may include coldlike symptoms such as a low-grade fever, a "slapped cheek" rash, a lacey rash on the trunk,

Watch Out!

Measles can lead to fetal loss and prematurity. Fortunately, because most pregnant women have been immunized against the disease, it is extremely rare for a pregnant woman to contract the disease.

legs, and arms, and — in some adults — sore or swollen joints) typically appear 4 to 14 days after exposure, but sometimes take as long as 20 days to appear. Approximately 20 percent of people who contract fifth disease are totally symptom-free. (If you suspect that you may have fifth disease, but you're not exhibiting any symptoms, your doctor can order a blood test that will determine whether or not you've been infected.)

Not every woman who becomes infected with fifth disease during pregnancy will experience problems. (In fact, only 10 percent will.) But those who do become infected face an increased risk of miscarriage or stillbirth — which is why it's best, whenever possible, to avoid exposing yourself to anyone you know who has fifth disease while you're pregnant. And, if you happen to work with young children, it only makes sense to try to avoid getting coughed and sneezed upon by the children in your care, both to minimize your odds of contracting fifth disease and to reduce your chances of picking up any other illness that is transmitted via airborne droplets from the nose and throat.

Rubella (German measles)

Most adults are immune to rubella because they have either had the disease or have received the measles, mumps, and rubella vaccine. (If you went for a preconception checkup to discuss your baby-making plans, odds are your doctor likely checked your rubella immunity and recommended a booster shot if you weren't immune.)

The effects of rubella on a developing baby can be nothing short of devastating: if a pregnant woman contracts rubella

Watch Out!

Mumps can be hazardous to a developing baby. One study showed that babies who are exposed to mumps are 15 times as likely to suffer from adult onset diabetes as babies who were not exposed to the mumps in utero. Fortunately, most adults have been immunized against the mumps, so this particular childhood illness poses much less of a threat to the current generation of babies than it did to babies in generations past.

during her pregnancy, her baby may be born deaf or with heart defects, be born prematurely, or be miscarried or stillborn. Approximately half of babies whose mothers contract rubella during the first month of pregnancy experience serious problems. The risk to the baby is less, however, if rubella is contracted later in pregnancy.

The symptoms of rubella include a nonitchy rash, a fever, swollen lymph glands, and joint pain and swelling. The symptoms typically appear two to three weeks after exposure to someone with rubella. (Rubella is contagious from 10 days before until 10 days after the first symptoms appear.)

Cytomegalovirus (CMV)

Cytomegalovirus is the most common cause of congenital viral infections in the United States, with approximately 0.2 percent to 2.2 percent of liveborn infants acquiring the virus perinatally. Ninety percent of infected newborns do not show symptoms of the virus at birth, but many subsequently demonstrate some form of impairment (progressive hearing impairment, mental retardation, developmental abnormalities, or delayed psychomotor development). CMV exposure also increases the odds that you will experience a miscarriage and that your baby will experience intrauterine growth restriction in the womb.

Your baby is less likely to have serious problems if the CMV exposure occurs after the second trimester and the infection is a secondary infection (in other words, you've experienced a CMV infection in the past).

Watch Out!

Studies have shown that it's possible for a pregnant woman to pass West Nile virus on to her baby. If you live in an area where the virus is active, you should limit the amount of time you spend outdoors at dawn and dusk when the risk of mosquito bites is greatest; wear light-colored long-sleeved shirts, long pants, and a hat when you are outdoors in an area where mosquitos are present; and use inspect repellents that contain DEET or other ingredients that have been proven to repel mosquitoes. (Note: There's no evidence to prove that DEET is harmful to pregnant women or their babies, but you may wish to err on the side of caution by using nonchemical methods to minimize the chance of getting bitten or apply the spray to your clothing rather than directly onto your skin.)

You may or may not have any symptoms of CMV, should you become infected. And if you do get some symptoms, they are likely to be flulike in nature, making them difficult to distinguish from a garden-variety flu bug.

Because preschool children often carry the virus, if you work with young children, you should make a point of minimizing your contact with the urine and saliva of the children in your care and of adhering to handwashing guidelines and other hygiene practices designed to minimize the spread of disease.

I read somewhere that gum disease can increase your chances of going into labor prematurely. Is this true?

Yes, if your gum disease is severe enough, you could face an increased risk of preterm labor. According to the American Academy of Peridontology, pregnant women who have periodontal disease — gum disease — are seven times more likely to deliver prematurely than women who do not have periodontal disease, although this doesn't prove any direct cause-and-effect.

It's important, however, to distinguish between gum disease and pregnancy gingivitis — a swelling, bleeding, redness, or tenderness in the gums that is triggered by the hormonal changes of pregnancy. Pregnancy gingivitis tends to show up around the second or third month of pregnancy and tends to increase in intensity until around the eighth month. Note: You may want to switch to a softer toothbrush to minimize the amount of bleeding you experience.

I have noticed some strange lumps on my gums. Should I be concerned?

Chances are what you've noticed on your gums are pregnancy tumors — noncancerous and generally pain-free growths that some women develop on their gums during pregnancy. These tumors tend to occur when gums that are already swollen by pregnancy gingivitis react strongly to irritants and form large lumps.

Pregnancy tumors usually disappear on their own after you give birth, but in some cases they may need to be removed by a dentist.

Is it safe to have dental X-rays during pregnancy?

It's always best to avoid any kind of X-rays during pregnancy, but if one is required because you are in pain or you have an infection, you can rest assured that the lead X-ray apron that the dentist covers your abdomen with ensures that there is virtually no radiation getting through to your baby. Local anesthetics and most pain medications and antibiotics are similarly safe, but you'll want to make sure that your dentist knows that you are pregnant and ensure that she sticks with medications and antibiotics that are known to be safe for use during pregnancy. Note: If you need dental work during your pregnancy, try to schedule it during the second trimester.

What types of diagnostic-imaging procedures can be safely performed during pregnancy?

Here's what you need to know about the use of X-rays, CAT scans, and MRIs during pregnancy:

- Diagnostic X-rays to areas other than the abdomen pose little threat to the developing baby, provided that appropriate radiation shields are used.

- Abdominal CAT scans (CT scans) are not recommended during pregnancy, due to the increased risk that the baby will end up with developmental malformations and/or childhood cancers.

- MRIs are a relatively new technology, so doctors tend to limit their use during pregnancy to situations where critical medical information needs to be obtained and cannot be obtained in any other manner, or the only available procedure — surgery, for example — poses major risks to the mother and the baby.

Note: Radioactive dyes containing iodine should not be used at all during diagnostic-imaging procedures performed during pregnancy because of the risk of damage to the fetal thyroid.

Week 13

You're on the verge of moving into the second trimester — a time when women traditionally announce their pregnancies at work. (Of course, you may have spilled the beans long ago if you've been battling a severe case of morning sickness or if you had to request job modifications for the health of your baby-to-be. Some women don't have the luxury of keeping their pregnancies under wraps for very long at all!)

What's going on with your baby

Your baby's face is starting to look more human, mainly because his or her eyes have moved to the front from the side of the face. Your baby's vocal cords have begun to form. (Of course, it'll be another six months before they get their first workout.)

Your baby's hand is structurally complete. It consists of 27 bones that are held together by a complex network of ligaments. Your baby's foot is also architecturally complete: the toes, heel, and bones are all in place.

What's going on with your body

If you lie down on your back and gently massage your uterus, you should be able to find the fundus — the hard ridge at the top of your uterus. At this point in pregnancy, it's located about 4 inches (10 cm) below your belly button.) By the time you give birth, the top of your uterus will be sandwiched right under your breasts — something that will leave you quite breathless (literally!). (See Figure 7.2.)

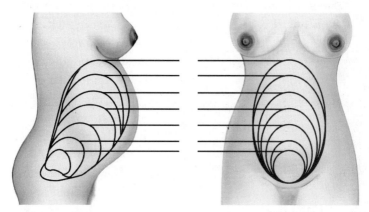

Figure 7.2. Your uterus grows at a steady rate over the course of your pregnancy. It will be many times its prepregnancy size by the time you give birth.

What's going on with your head

If you haven't already shared the news of your pregnancy at work, you may be feeling a little bit stressed about how to break the news to your boss. Like it or not, you're going to have to take care of that bit of business sooner rather than later. You can't keep that growing belly a secret forever, after all!

Bright Idea

Meet with your supervisor or the manager of human resources to find out what pregnancy-related benefits are provided by your company. You may find that the company designates certain plum parking spots for women in their third trimester of pregnancy or that the group health insurance plan covers the services of a doula (a professional labor-support person).

Although there's no "perfect time" to share your news at work, you increase your chances of meeting with a positive response if you plan your announcement carefully. Here are some tips on deciding when — and how — to announce your pregnancy:

- Share your news with your boss before she hears it from someone else. That doesn't mean that you can't tell anyone else first: you just have to be discreet. In fact, you may want to make a point of getting the lowdown from co-workers who have had babies recently before you go public with your news. They should be able to tell you how well or how poorly your boss is likely to react and provide you with tips on breaking the news to her. They should also be able to give you the inside scoop on what concessions, if any, they were able to negotiate with the company (for example, a partially paid maternity leave or the ability to work part-time hours upon their return).

> ❝I had just accepted a job offer the week before I found out I was pregnant. I kept the news to myself for about two months, until it started becoming obvious. I felt uneasy at first because I was pregnant when I was hired, even though I did not know it at the time. My employer took it well, but I had worked very hard for those two months to prove myself.❞
>
> —Jennifer, 28, mother of one

- If you think your boss will react negatively to your news, you might want to wait until you have passed the highest-risk period for miscarriage before announcing your pregnancy. That way, you won't end up causing waves at the office only to discover that you aren't going to need a maternity leave after all. ("I told my assistant and close friend at work right away, but waited until I was three months along before I told my boss," says Kim, a 35-year-old mother of one. "I just wanted to make sure that everything was okay before I let the cat out of the bag.") Of course, if you are suffering from severe morning sickness or other pregnancy-related complications, you may have to spill the beans a little sooner that you had hoped in order to explain why you are late coming in each morning or why you have been taking so much time off for medical appointments.

> ❝I knew I would have to tell my staff as soon as I felt that the pregnancy was safe because they were beginning to pick up on some of my symptoms and were wondering why I was going to the doctor so often. I wanted to tell my boss before I told them, so I broke the news to him on a Monday and asked him to keep my secret until the following Friday so no one would have to find out through the grapevine. After telling my staff, I shared the news with my co-workers. ❞
>
> —Susan, 29, pregnant with her first child

■ If you are expecting a performance or salary review in the near future, you may want to keep your news to yourself until it has been completed. That way, if the results of your review are less than what you'd hoped for, you won't have to wonder whether you're the victim of a subtle form of pregnancy discrimination.

■ Time your announcement to coincide with a major achievement at work (such as the completion of a major project). That way, you can show your boss through actions rather than words that you are as productive and committed to your job as ever — thereby addressing a perennial fear of many employers that you'll be a less valuable worker now that you've got a baby on board.

- Don't be afraid to postpone your announcement if your boss is having a bad day. If she is in a particularly foul mood or is scrambling to meet an important deadline, hold off on sharing your news until she's in a more receptive frame of mind.

- Be prepared for a lukewarm reaction. Although your boss may be genuinely happy for you, she may be concerned about what your pregnancy may mean to the company. If yours is the first pregnancy she has had to deal with on the job, she's likely to be particularly apprehensive.

- Be ready to talk about what work modifications, if any, may be required during your pregnancy. If you work in a hazardous environment — for example, an X-ray laboratory or a chemical manufacturing plant — you may need to ask to be reassigned to a different type of work for the duration of your pregnancy.

- Don't make promises you can't keep — such as when you plan to take your maternity leave and how quickly you will return to work. Instead, simply agree to discuss these plans when your pregnancy is a little further along.

Of course, if you are self-employed, it's your clients rather than your boss that you have to share your news with — something that can be scary, to say the least. Here's some advice from Suzi, 27, a self-employed mother of two:

> **❝**I had to tell people at work as soon as I knew in order to avoid doing any X-rays.**❞**
>
> —Karen, 34, mother of three

"With my first baby, I told my clients right away. My thought was that if they had a problem with the fact that I was expecting, then I didn't need to be working with them. I also thought that in this day and age people wouldn't have a problem with a career woman having a baby. Unfortunately, I experienced a lot of problems by being so open about it with my professional contacts. I found that if clients

knew, they thought that I was falling off the planet or something. They worried about their accounts, and if I was unavailable for a meeting or something fell through the cracks, they
blamed it on the pregnancy — even though that was never a
problem for me.

"With my second baby, I didn't tell a soul. Some of my clients
to this day don't know that I had a baby last November! After
the resistance I experienced with this first baby, I decided to
keep my personal and professional lives completely separate."

The Hot List: This week's must-ask pregnancy questions

Now that you've spilled the beans at work, you no doubt have a
lot of questions about working during pregnancy: what rights
you have as a pregnant employee and how you can stay safe and
comfortable on the job for the duration of your pregnancy.

Here are the answers to some of the questions that are likely
to be running through your head right about now.

Can my employer fire me because I'm pregnant?

Your employer is unlikely to fire you outright (it's against the
law, after all), but you could face subtler forms of discrimination
in the workplace. You might, for example, be passed over for a
promotion because someone in management thinks that you
are unlikely to return to your job after your maternity leave.
That's why you owe it to yourself to understand your rights
under the law. That means familiarizing yourself with the provisions of the Pregnancy Discrimination Act and the Family and
Medical Leave Act.

 Bright Idea

Get the scoop on working during pregnancy from women who've been there.
Call the free job problems hotline operated by 9 to 5, the National Association
for Working Women, at 800-522-0925. Or write to 9 to 5, the National
Association for Working Women, 231 West Wisconsin, Suite 900, Milwaukee,
WI. 53203.

The Pregnancy Discrimination Act

The federal Pregnancy Discrimination Act of 1978 (an amendment to the Civil Rights Act of 1964) prohibits any type of discrimination on the basis of pregnancy in companies that have 15 or more employees. (Don't panic if you work for a two-person shop. In most cases, state legislation kicks in to provide similar protection to employees of smaller companies.)

Here's a brief summary of what the Pregnancy Discrimination Act means to you:

- **Hiring:** An employer cannot refuse to hire a woman solely because she is pregnant, provided that she is capable of fulfilling the major requirements of the job.

- **Pregnancy and Maternity Leave:** An employer may not introduce special procedures that in any way single out pregnant women. If, for example, a pregnant woman is temporarily unable to fulfill the requirements of her job due to her pregnancy, the employer must treat her in the same manner as any other temporarily disabled employee (provide modified tasks, alternative assignments, disability leave, or leave without pay — whatever the case may be). Pregnant women are also entitled to continue working as long as they are able to perform their jobs. And if you take sick leave for a period of time during your pregnancy, but your medical condition subsequently resolves itself, making it possible for you to return to work, your employer must allow you to go back to your job. It's illegal for employers to force pregnant employees who are capable of working to remain on leave until after they give birth.

- **Health Insurance:** Any health insurance provided by an employer must treat expenses for pregnancy-related conditions in the same manner as costs for other medical conditions. In other words, pregnancy-related expenses should be reimbursed using the same formula used to calculate reimbursement for other types of medical expenses. (The employer's health insurance plan can't introduce a larger deductible or any additional deductibles on pregancy-related expenses.) What's more, employers must provide the same level of health coverage for spouses of male employees as they do for spouses of female employees.

- **Fringe Benefits:** Pregnancy-related benefits cannot be limited to married employees. What's more, any benefits provided to employees with other types of medical conditions must be extended to women with pregnancy-related conditions. Employees who are off work because of pregnancy-related disabilities must be treated in the same fashion as other temporarily disabled employees when it comes to such matters as the accrual and crediting of seniority, vacation calculations, pay increases, and temporary disability benefits.

If you think that you are being discriminated against because of your pregnancy, you should

- keep detailed notes on everything that happens, and keep copies of any e-mail messages or other correspondence that might support your claim;

- ask to review the contents of your personnel file, and make copies of anything that might help you make your case (for example, copies of particularly glowing performance appraisals);

- follow appropriate channels as much as possible, but be prepared to go to your company's human resources department or the U.S. Equal Employment Opportunity Commission (800-669-4000; www.eeoc.gov) if that's what it takes to ensure that your complaint is handled appropriately.

 Watch Out!

If your employer's health insurance plan does not cover any preexisting medical conditions, you could be denied benefits for any medical costs arising from a pregnancy that occurred before the policy went into effect.

The Family and Medical Leave Act

The Family and Medical Leave Act (FMLA) of 1993 requires employers covered by the legislation to provide up to 12 weeks of unpaid, job-protected leave to employees for certain family and medical reasons.

The FMLA applies to all

- public agencies (including state, local, and federal employers, and schools); and

- private-sector employers who have (or had) 50 or more employees for 20 or more workweeks in either the current or the preceding calendar year and who are engaged in commerce or any industry or activity affecting commerce.

To be eligible for benefits under the Act, you must

- work for an employer who is covered by the Act;

- have been employed by this employer for a total of at least 12 months;

- have worked at least 1,250 hours over the previous 12 months;

- have worked at a location that is either inside the United States itself or any of its territories or possessions, and where at least 50 employees are employed within a 75-mile area.

Eligible reasons for leave include

- giving birth to a baby;

- adopting a child;

- providing foster care to a child;

- caring for an immediate family member (your spouse, child, or parent) who has a serious health condition (that is, one requiring hospitalization or bedrest at home), or

- having a serious health condition (for example, complications of pregnancy).

Bright Idea

Find out how flexible your employer is when it comes to allowing employees to take their FMLA leave in bits and pieces. Some employers allow new parents to take their FMLA intermittently (for example, a few weeks now and a few weeks later) or use their FMLA entitlement to cut back on their usual daily or weekly working hours—something that can work particularly well if you intend to breastfeed.

In order to take the leave, you must

- provide your employer with 30 days' notice of your intention to take FMLA leave (assuming that it is possible to provide such notice);

- supply a medical certificate supporting the reason for your leave (if your employer requests it);

- obtain second and third medical opinions (if your employer requests it);

- have your doctor or midwife periodically report to your employer about your ability and intention to return to work (if your employer requests it).

Here's some additional fine print you need to know about:

- If you and your partner share the same employer, you are entitled to a combined total of 12 workweeks of family leave for the birth and care of a newborn child, to welcome an adopted or foster child, or to care for a parent who has a serious health condition.

- You must take your leave within 12 months of the birth, adoption, or foster-care placement of your child.

- During your leave, your employer is required to maintain your group health insurance coverage on the same terms as when you were at work. If you were required to pay for a portion of your insurance costs prior to your leave, you may still be expected to cover those costs while you are on leave. This could mean that you might be expected to fork over some hefty premiums during a period of time when you're not actually receiving a paycheck. What's more, if you decide not to return to work following FMLA leave, your employer could decide to recover the cost of any healthcare premiums it paid while you were on leave.

▪ In most situations, when you return from leave, your employer must give you back your original job or an equivalent job with equivalent pay, benefits, and other terms and conditions of employment. What's more, you can't lose any employment benefits that you were entitled to prior to leave, nor can the time you took be counted against you under the provisions of the company's attendance policy.

▪ If you are deemed to be a "key" employee (that is, a highly paid employee whose reinstatement at the company following a period of leave may cause "substantial and grievous economic injury to its operations"), your employer may not be required to hire you back following your leave. If this provision applies to you, your employer must notify you in advance of your status as a "key" employee; inform you that it will not restore you to your original position, should you decide to take FMLA leave; explain the reasons for its decision; offer you a reasonable period of time in which to return to work (assuming that you're already on leave at the time the company designates you as a "key" employee); and make a final decision about whether you will get your old job back if you request such reinstatement in writing.

Under what circumstances is it dangerous to work during pregnancy?

Women of your grandmother's generation were expected to resign from their jobs the moment the pregnancy test came back positive, but today's pregnant working women are every bit

Watch Out!

You are at greatest risk of injuring yourself through lifting during the third trimester. The reason? Your larger stomach size requires that you hold objects further away from your body when you are lifting things—something that puts a greater load on your back. A nonpregnant woman who lifts a 10-pound object puts about 65 pounds' worth of pressure on her lower back. When a woman in her third trimester of pregnancy lifts that same 10-pound object, she ends up puttings a full 150 pounds' worth of stress on her back. Ouch!

as much a part of the modern office as the computer and the fax machine. Most women experiencing low-risk pregnancies are able to work throughout their entire pregnancies.

There are, of course, some situations in which you may want to consider leaving work early or requesting some modifications to your working environment. You might choose to go this route if

- you are exposed to infectious diseases, heavy metals, toxic chemicals, oil-based paints, radiation, anesthetic gases, or other hazardous substances, including tobacco smoke, at work;

- your job requires that you stand for more than three hours per day;

- your work is highly strenuous or physically demanding;

- your job involves a lot of repetitive work that could increase your chances of developing carpal tunnel syndrome (repetitive stress syndrome);

- your job involves a lot of bending, stooping, stair- or ladder-climbing, or heavy lifting;

- you work in an extremely hot, cold, or noisy environment;

- you work long hours or rotating shifts.

When you are requesting workplace modifications from your employer, try to be as specific as possible about the type of modification you are requesting, when you will require the

Watch Out!

Try not to let job stress get to you while you're pregnant. Studies have shown that women with highly stressful jobs may be at increased risk of experiencing miscarriages or developing preeclampsia (a pregnancy-related disorder that is characterized by high blood pressure).

modification, and how making that job modification will help to promote the health of you and your baby. You may also want to provide your employer with some additional information or documentation in support of your request (for example, a doctor's note stating that it's important that you limit the amount of time you spend standing on the job) to help you make your case.

Any tips on staying comfortable on the job?

Your biggest challenge during your nine months on the job will be staying comfortable as you find yourself battling morning sickness, fatigue, and/or an ever-changing lineup of pregnancy-related aches and pains. Here are some tips on maximizing comfort at the office:

- Put your feet up on a stool or an open desk drawer to relieve pressure on your lower back. Your boss may not approve, but your chiropractor will.

- Take regular breaks from your computer. Although there's no hard evidence that working in front of a computer screen is harmful to your baby, working at a computer all day can be hard on your body. Pregnant women are at increased risk of suffering from carpal tunnel syndrome — a painful condition that can affect the wrist and lower arms if you spend a lot of time typing.

- Keep a glass of cold water on your desk so that you'll remember to drink frequently, and do not — we repeat, do not — skip meals, no matter how hectic things may be at the office.

Watch Out!

Prolonged standing and shift work increase the risk of premature birth. And physically demanding work is linked to high blood pressure during pregnancy.

- Take 5- or 10-minute catnaps on your break or over your lunch hour. You can either hit the couch in the company nurse's office or put your head on your desk for a couple of minutes.

- Keep stress to a minimum and accept any and all offers of help. People love to help pregnant women. You'll never have it this good again!

Just the facts

- Approximately 15 percent of confirmed pregnancies end in miscarriage (the spontaneous death of a baby prior to the 20th week of pregnancy).

- While sex is generally considered safe for most couples experiencing low-risk pregnancies, some women find that their interest in sex diminishes during the first weeks of pregnancy, when fatigue, morning sickness, and tender breasts can make sex sound considerably less than appealing.

- High levels of stress during pregnancy have been linked to premature birth and the birth of low-birthweight babies.

- Most garden-variety illnesses like colds and flus are not harmful to you or your developing baby. There may, however, be cause for concern if you contract chickenpox, fifth disease, rubella, or cytomegalovirus during pregnancy.

- Bring yourself up to speed about your rights as a pregnant employee by familiarizing yourself with the provisions of both the Pregnancy Discrimination Act and the Family and Medical Leave Act.

Your Second Trimester Week-by-Week

PART III

The Fourth Month: Settling In

Chapter 8

The second trimester is truly the Golden Age of Pregnancy — a time to relax and enjoy your pregnancy. With any luck, the nausea and extreme fatigue of the first trimester have begun to subside, and it will likely be a few more weeks before the third-trimester aches and pains begin to kick in.

And here's something else that's likely to ease your mind: the risk of miscarriage declines significantly at this point in your pregnancy, so if you spent the first trimester running to the bathroom every 10 minutes, looking for any tell-tale signs of bleeding, you may find it a huge relief to be into your second trimester. (Okay, maybe *you* were able to play the role of the calm, cool, and collected mama-to-be right from day one, but we know some women who practically drove themselves to the point of distraction with all those first-trimester bathroom checks.)

Week 14

Now that you're starting to feel more settled into your pregnancy and you've mastered the pregnancy lifestyle — the steepest learning curve associated with the first trimester, for most women! — you will probably find that you start focusing more on the your baby's birth. And, of course, one of the key decisions you'll have to make is where you'd like to give birth — a topic we'll be discussing at length in this week's "Hot List" section.

> **"** The second trimester is the time to conquer Mount Everest because by the time the third trimester rolls around, you won't have the energy. **"**
>
> — Jacqueline, 34, mother of two

What's going on with your baby

While fetal development during the first trimester focused on architecture — creating the various body systems that your baby will require after birth — from this point in pregnancy onward, the emphasis will be on fetal growth. Your baby will start growing at a rapid rate. In fact, this month alone, your baby will almost double in length and quadruple in weight.

What's going on with your body

Now that your baby is embarking on a period of rapid growth, your pregnancy is going to become increasingly obvious to those around you, so don't be caught off guard if total strangers start guessing your "secret." (It may not be a secret any longer.)

What's going on with your head

If you spent most of the first trimester feeling wiped out and queasy, odds are you've just been through a bit of a sexual drought. You may find that once you start feeling better and your energy level begins to pick up, you begin to experience a bit of a sexual renaissance. As Anne Semans and Cathy Winks note in their book *The Mother's Guide to Sex: Enjoying Your Sexuality Through All Stages of Motherhood* (Three Rivers Press, 2001), "Many women find that their sexual interest during pregnancy follows a bell curve, with desire decreasing during the first trimester, rebounding during the second trimester, and decreasing again for the final trimester."

> **❝** I am enjoying this pregnancy more than my first. Instead of feeling out of control, I feel more like I am in partnership with my baby. **❞**
>
> — Marie, 40, pregnant with her second child

Of course, not every pregnant woman experiences this so-called classic pattern, so don't assume there's something wrong with you if your desire for sleep continues to override your desire for sex — or if you simply don't have any interest in sex at this stage of your life. What's important is that you talk to your partner about how you're feeling and that the two of you negotiate some sort of sexual truce for the months ahead so that no one ends up feeling hurt or angry. Communication is key.

The Hot List: This week's must-ask pregnancy questions

Here are the answers to some of the questions that may be going through your head this week.

What should I expect from this month's prenatal checkup?

At this month's prenatal visit, you can expect your doctor or midwife to check

- **the size of your uterus** (to verify that your uterus is roughly the size that it should be for this stage of pregnancy);

- **your weight** (to see if you are continuing to gain weight slowly);

- **your blood pressure** (to spot any signs of pregnancy-related hypertension or preeclampsia);

- **your urine** (to ensure that your sugar and protein levels are within the normal range as they, too, can provide early warning of any emerging problems);

- **the fetal heart rate** (to keep tabs on your baby's general health and well-being). Note: Your baby's heart beats much more rapidly than your own — at a rate of 120 to 160 beats per minute on average. So don't be concerned that there may be something wrong with your baby if the fetal heart rate seems alarmingly high. It's normal for a baby's heart to beat much more rapidly than an adult's.

- **a discussion of prenatal testing options** (Your doctor or midwife will talk to you about the pros and cons of having the quadruple screen blood test and/or amniocentesis performed during pregnancy. See Chapter 14 for a detailed explanation of what each of these tests involves. Because these tests have to be performed at specific points in your pregnancy, you may have to make up your mind relatively quickly about what to do about these tests if you intend to have them done.)

What factors do I need to keep in mind when choosing a place to give birth?

You have three basic choices when it comes to choosing a place to give birth: a hospital, a birth center, and your own home.

 Watch Out!

If you have your heart set on giving birth in a particular setting — that is, in a birth center, at a specific hospital, or at home — you will need to decide on the birthing environment before you finalize your choice of a caregiver. This is because most caregivers have privileges only at a particular hospital or birth center, and the majority are unwilling to attend home births at all. See Chapter 6 for a detailed discussion on choosing a doctor or midwife.

Bright Idea

Want to find out if the hospital or birth center you're considering is forward-thinking in its practices? Find out if it has been designated "mother-friendly" by the Coalition for Improving Maternity Services (CIMS). According to its Web site, CIMS is endorsed by a number of organizations including the American College of Nurse-Midwives (though not by the American College of Obstetricians and Gynecologists). It designates hospitals as mother-friendly if they treat birth as a natural, healthy process; empower the birthing woman by providing her and her family with supportive, sensitive, and respectful care; enable her to make decisions based on accurate information and provide access to the full range of options for care; avoid the routine use of tests, procedures, drugs, and restrictions; and emphasize evidence-based care that focuses exclusively on the needs and interests of mothers and infants. You can find out more about the mother-friendly model of maternity care by visiting the CIMS Web site at www.motherfriendly.org or by contacting the organization at 888-282-2467.

Here's the lowdown on the pros and cons of each of these options.

Hospital

Not all hospitals are created equal. Some are extremely family-friendly; others are anything but. Some boast state-of-the-art obstetrical facilities; others do not. There's no such thing as a "typical" hospital. That said, it's important to consider the basic pros and cons of giving birth in a hospital when you are weighing your various birthing options.

Pros:

- If you give birth in a hospital, all the high-tech bells and whistles are there if you or your baby needs them, and you can be prepped for an emergency c-section in a matter of minutes. Most doctors and midwives agree that a hospital is the safest place to give birth if your pregnancy is considered high-risk because of a preexisting medical condition, complications of pregnancy, or previous birth-related complications. Where they sometimes disagree is on the matter

Watch Out!

Don't get misled by the jargon. Some hospitals refer to alternative birth centers (ABC) as family birth centers (FBC) or 24-hour suites. In other hospitals, the term *alternative birth center* is used to refer to either birthing rooms or a hospital-owned childbearing center. Sometimes, these terms are misused entirely (for example, when a hospital launches an aggressive marketing campaign designed to convince consumers that its facilities are considerably more family-friendly than they actually are).

of low-risk deliveries. While home births may be as safe as hospital births much of the time, there's one important caveat that often gets left out of this debate: complications can develop without warning — sometimes within a matter of minutes. When one of these unanticipated emergencies arises, the best place to be is in a hospital. That's why most doctors argue that the safest place to give birth is in a hospital, period, whether a woman is low risk or not. Obviously, you'll have to decide which setting is right for you. What's important is that you make an informed choice.

- You have more options for pain relief if you give birth in a hospital setting than you do if you give birth in a birth center or at home.

- A growing number of hospitals are introducing family-friendly birthing facilities that allow women to labor, deliver, and receive postpartum care in the same room (as opposed to laboring in one room, delivering in another, recovering in a third, and then moving to the postpartum floor for the duration of your stay — the norm in days gone by). Some hospitals have even introduced alternative birth centers (also called family birth centers or 24-hour suites). These consist of a group of rooms for the family's use during labor: living room, small kitchen, private bath, birthing room.

Cons:

- Despite efforts to create a warmer, more intimate setting, many labor and delivery wards continue to have a sterile, clinical atmosphere.

- Rigid or archaic hospital policies may leave you and your partner feeling as though you have little or no control over the process of giving birth.

- If the technology is there, it may be used, whether you need it or not. Studies have shown that women giving birth in a hospital can be subjected needlessly to such interventions as artificial rupture of membranes (AROM), fetal monitoring, augmentation of labor, and cesarean sections.

- A hospital delivery is more expensive than a birth-center delivery or home birth. You pay for all that high-tech equipment even if you have a low-tech delivery.

If you think you would like to give birth in a particular hospital, arrange to take a tour before you make up your mind. Sometimes hospitals that claim to be family-friendly are anything but. Checklist 8.1 will give you an idea of what to look for — and what to ask — while you take your tour. (Note: You may not need to ask all the questions on the checklist. You'll probably just want to zero in on the areas of particular concern to you and

> ❝I got a detailed list of my in-hospital charges after my first delivery and was shocked to see that a pad cost $10 and Tylenol was $3 per dose! With my second baby, I packed my own pads, Tylenol, and diapers for the baby.❞
>
> — Suzi, 27, mother of two

your partner. But ask as few or as many questions as you need — and don't be afraid to follow up with a phone call after your visit if you wish to clarify some points with hospital staff.)

Checklist 8.1. What to Look for in a Hospital

Location

_____   Is the hospital located relatively close to your home?

_____   How long would it take you to get there during rush-hour traffic?

_____   Is the parking lot designed to allow laboring women and their partners easy access to the building?

Costs

_____   What percentage of costs are covered by your health insurance company?

_____   What are the payment terms for your portion of the costs?

_____   Does the hospital have a written description of its services and fees?

_____   Are staff members available to help you obtain financial assistance if you need it?

Expertise/accreditation

_____   Is it a level I facility or primary-care center (a hospital that provides services to low-risk clients);

_____   Is it a level II or secondary-care center (a hospital that is able to provide care to both low-risk clients and clients with about 90 percent of maternal or neonatal complications); or

_____   Is it a level III facility or tertiary-care center (a hospital that provides care to high-risk clients who require highly sophisticated types of medical and technical interventions)?

_____   Do the services and specialties of the hospital meet your specific medical needs? (In other words, if yours is a high-risk pregnancy, are the staff up to the challenge of meeting your needs and/or your baby's needs?)

_____   Is the hospital accredited by a nationally recognized accrediting body such as the Joint Commission on Accreditation of Healthcare Organizations (630-792-5800; www.jcaho.org)?

Hospital staff

_____ Are the staff on the labor and delivery floor friendly and willing to answer your questions?

_____ Do they seem to be genuinely interested in helping you, to the extent that it is possible, to have the type of birth experience you are hoping for, as specified in your birth plan?

_____ How receptive are they to any special requests you may have (bringing a doula or other support person with you to the birth, for example)? Can they recommend a qualified doula?

_____ Are they comfortable dealing with any special circumstances related to your situation (if you're young, disabled, a single mother or part of a nontraditional family, for example)?

_____ Is the labor and delivery floor adequately staffed? How many laboring women does each nurse care for?

_____ Is there an anesthetist at the hospital 24 hours a day, or does someone have to be called if an emergency occurs in the middle of the night?

_____ Are midwives available?

_____ What is the hospital's cesarean rate? (Note: This may not be relevant if you are under the care of a physician whose own cesarean rate varies significantly from the hospital average. And while the cesarean rate of the attending obstetrician is more important than the hospital's cesarean rate, even that stat isn't as clear-cut as you might think. An obstetrician's cesarean rate is as much determined by the nature of his practice — that is, the number of high-risk patients that he takes on — as by his individual tendency to resort to cesareans.)

_____ What hospital policies are in place to encourage hospital staff to keep mother and baby together after the birth as much as possible?

_____ Is an anesthesiologist available around the clock in case you need an emergency cesarean section?

(continued)

Checklist 8.1. *(continued)*

Labor policies and procedures

_____ Does the hospital offer its own childbirth preparation classes to parents who will be delivering at the hospital in order to familiarize them with hospital policies and procedures?

_____ Does the hospital invite you to prepare an individualized birthing plan that specifies your hopes and desires for the birth and your thoughts on such issues as medication, epidurals, and episiotomy? (You can find the template for a birth plan in "Important Documents," www.wiley.com/go/ anndouglas)

_____ Does the hospital offer facilities for water birth?

_____ Are there limits on the number of labor support people who are allowed to be present at the birth?

_____ Are children permitted to be present at the birth? If so, does the hospital offer any special sibling preparation classes?

_____ Can photos and videos be taken during the birth?

_____ Are women in labor encouraged to walk around or to try other labor positions in an effort to help nature along?

_____ Are you allowed to eat or drink once you are in labor?

_____ Under what circumstances might your labor support person be required to leave the room (if fetal distress necessitates an emergency cesarean, for example)?

_____ Are labor support people allowed to be with you in the operating room and the recovery room if you have a cesarean?

_____ What are the hospital's (or caregiver's) policies regarding the active management of labor (for example, interventions in the event that labor doesn't progress at a prescribed rate)?

What procedures are performed routinely during labor?

_____ Enemas?

_____ IVs?

_____ Pubic shaving?

_____ External and/or internal fetal monitoring?

_____ Artificial rupture of membranes (AROM)?

Labor policies and procedures *(cont.)*

_____ What are the hospital's policies regarding the use of intravenous lines? Can the IV unit be converted to a heparin lock (a device that allows you to be temporarily disconnected from the IV unit to allow you more freedom to move around)?

_____ What are the hospital's policies regarding the use of epidurals and pain medications during labor?

_____ Does the hospital offer so-called "walking epidurals" (that is, the use of narcotic pain medication through the epidural catheter as opposed to anesthetic, so as not to cause numbness or weakness in the legs)?

_____ Does the hospital offer patient-controlled epidurals that allow a woman to push a button when she needs additional pain relief?

_____ What is the hospital's cesarean rate? How does this compare to the national average of 25 percent to 30 percent? Under what circumstances are cesarean sections performed at this hospital?

_____ Under what circumstances might you be required to be moved from a labor room to a delivery room? Does the hospital require that all women move from labor rooms to delivery rooms as their labor progresses, or does the hospital use birthing rooms (that is, rooms that are designed to be used for both labor and delivery)?

_____ Will your baby be handed to you immediately after the birth (assuming, of course, that the baby doesn't require any special care)?

Who is responsible for examining the newborn upon delivery?

_____ The midwife or doctor delivering the baby?

_____ The pediatrician of your choosing?

_____ The pediatrician who happens to be on call at the time?

What procedures are performed on the baby shortly after birth?

_____ Apgar testing?

_____ Vitamin K injections?

_____ Placing antibacterial drops into the baby's eyes?

_____ Suctioning of the baby's nose and throat?

(continued)

Checklist 8.1. *(continued)*

Labor policies and procedures *(cont.)*

What procedures are performed on the baby later?

_____   HIV testing?

_____   Hepatitis B vaccination?

_____   Testing for hypothyroidism, phenylketonuria (PKU) and other genetic disorders?

_____   Which of these procedures are required by the state or province in which you are giving birth?

_____   What are the hospital's policies in the event that you and your partner decide to decline procedures, such as vitamin K injections or antibacterial drops in the baby's eyes or HIV testing and Hepatitis B vaccination?

_____   Can the newborn examination be conducted in the birthing room while the baby is resting on his mother's breast, or does the baby have to be taken somewhere else? If the baby needs to be moved, can one or both of the parents accompany the baby?

_____   Can any of these procedures be delayed until after you have had some time to bond with your new baby?

_____   If you are choosing to breastfeed, will you be encouraged to breastfeed your baby as soon as possible following the birth?

Birthing facilities

_____   Does the hospital have birthing rooms or labor, delivery, recovery rooms (LDR, a room where the mother labors, gives birth, and recovers for an hour so after the delivery)? (The two terms are often used interchangeably.)

_____   Does the hospital have labor, delivery, recovery, postpartum (LDRP) rooms (that is, a room in which the mother labors, gives birth, recovers, and then remains throughout her hospital stay)?

_____   Does the hospital have an alternative birth center (ABC) (that is, a homelike suite of rooms for the use of the woman and her family)?

Birthing facilities *(cont.)*

_____ Are the birthing rooms fully equipped to handle any emergencies that may arise?

_____ Are the birthing rooms designed to give you and your partner as much privacy as possible? Is there more than one bed in each room? Is it possible that you will have to share your room with another laboring woman? Is there a place where your partner can rest (a bed or pull-out cot)?

_____ Will you have your own bathroom, or will you have to share one with another laboring woman?

_____ Are the birthing rooms attractive and homelike, or clinical and sterile? Do they look like a place where you would want to give birth?

_____ Are the rooms large enough for you to be able to move around while you're in labor?

_____ Do the birthing rooms have any amenities, such as birthing stools, squatting bars, showers, oversized bathtubs, or Jacuzzis you can use while you are in labor?

_____ Are all birthing rooms in the unit equally well equipped, or are there a few older rooms that lack some of these amenities?

_____ Is there a phone you can use to call family and friends during labor or after the birth?

Nursery facilities

_____ How extensive are the hospital's intensive care facilities?

_____ If your baby was born with a serious birth defect or develops respiratory or other problems after delivery, would he have to be transported elsewhere to receive specialized care?

_____ What safety procedures does the hospital have in place to ensure that your baby is released only to you and your partner?

(continued)

Checklist 8.1. *(continued)*

Postpartum floor

_____   How many private rooms are available?

_____   What are the costs of private, semiprivate, and ward rooms?

_____   Is rooming-in available (that is, the baby stays with the mother)?

_____   Can your partner stay at the hospital overnight if the two of you want to spend some time together with your new baby?

_____   Is there a shower in each room, or do you need to use shared shower facilities down the hall? Who will watch your baby while you're in the shower?

_____   What are the hospital's policies regarding visiting hours? Are there different hours for members of your immediate family as opposed to other relatives and friends?

Postpartum care

_____   What will the hospital do to support your decision to breast-feed your baby? Do they follow "baby-friendly" hospital practices? (See www.unicef.org/programme/breastfeeding/baby.htm for information on the United Nations Children's Fund (UNICEF)'s baby-friendly hospital initiative — an effort to promote hospital policies that support breastfeeding.)

_____   Are lactation experts available to help troubleshoot any breastfeeding problems?

_____   If you choose to bottle-feed, will this choice be respected as well?

_____   How much instruction on newborn care is provided to new moms? Are you able to phone the postpartum floor after discharge to ask any questions that might occur to you once you're home?

Birth center

Birth centers (also called childbearing centers, birthing centers, or alternative birth centers) are homelike facilities that provide

Watch Out!

The most progressive hospital policies in the world mean nothing if your care-giver doesn't choose to follow them. Make sure you and your caregiver are on the same wavelength when it comes to issues such as having other people present at the birth and your desire to remain mobile during labor.

care during pregnancy, labor, birth, and the first few hours postpartum. The birth-center movement started in the 1970s, when women began to demand more control over the process of giving birth. They are now a well-established birthing alternative for women who are looking to give birth somewhere other than at home, but yet do not feel that a hospital is the right choice for them and their families. Unfortunately, rising liability insurance costs have caused some highly respected birth centers to close their doors in recent years — a very worrying development for those who support the birth center movement.

Pros:

- Birth centers provide a relaxed, family-friendly setting. You can wear your own clothing, eat and drink when you're hungry, have a shower or bath if you'd like, and have friends and family present for the birth if that is your choice.

- Many birth centers offer such amenities as whirlpool baths and special birthing chairs.

- You're less likely to end up with a c-section if you deliver in a birth center. According to the National Birth Center Study, the cesarean rate for mothers using birth centers is 4.4 percent as opposed to the national average of 25 percent. Although most of the low rate can be explained by the fact that women with high-risk pregnancies are not permitted to use birth centers, it's an impressive statistic nonetheless.

Cons:

- Birth centers aren't available in all communities, so you might not even have the option of using one.

- If you run into an unexpected emergency during your delivery (something that happens to approximately 2 percent of women, according to the National Association of Childbearing Centers), you will need to be transported to a nearby hospital. The time you lose in transit could adversely affect the well-being of you or your baby, which explains why many caregivers believe that birth centers don't provide as safe an option as hospitals. (Note: Approximately 12 percent of women who labor in birth centers end up being transported to a hospital, but only 2 percent of these situations can be classified as true emergencies. The other 10 percent of cases are less-urgent situations where the woman needs medical assistance that cannot be provided in the birth center environment.)

- Birth centers are not equipped to care for women with high-risk pregnancies. The definition of high risk is often very broad and may prevent you from delivering in a birth center, even if you and your baby are perfectly healthy. If you pass the center's initial screening process but pregnancy complications do arise, you may be required to give birth somewhere other than at the center.

- Most birth centers are unable to offer their clients any type of pharmacological pain relief. Analgesics are a rare commodity, and epidurals are nonexistent. However, the staff will focus on a variety of other noninterventive methods of pain relief.

- You will be expected to leave the birth center shortly after you give birth. Birth-center clients are expected to do their recuperating at home.

- Some insurance companies and HMOs refuse to cover the costs of birth-center deliveries. This means that you could be out of pocket $3,000 or more.

Assuming that you're fortunate enough to have the option of giving birth in a birth center, you will want to conduct a tour of the facility before settling on this particular birthing environment. You can find some suggested questions in Checklist 8.2.

Checklist 8.2. Birth Center

If you ask the birth center to mail you information before you go on your tour, you may be able to answer many of these questions for yourself — something that will allow you to zero in on the remaining questions.

Practical concerns and administrative issues

_____ How close to your home is the birth center?

_____ How long would it take you to get there during rush-hour traffic?

_____ Is the parking lot designed to allow laboring women and their partners easy access to the building?

_____ In the event that you required an emergency cesarean section or you or your baby required other emergency care, how long would it take for you to be transported by ambulance to the closest hospital? What might the risks be to you and your baby?

_____ What is the birth center's rate for transfer of care? (A rating of 5 percent or higher may suggest that the center isn't screening its clients carefully enough.)

_____ What percentage of costs is covered by your insurance company or HMO? What are the payment terms for your portion of the costs?

Birth-center credentials

_____ Is the birth center licensed by the state or province? (Check with your state department of health, or your provincial health ministry if you're in Canada.)

_____ Is the center a member of the National Association of Childbearing Centers (215-234-8068)? Has it been accredited by the Commission for the Accreditation of Birth Centers (an independent accrediting authority established by NACC)?

(continued)

Checklist 8.2. *(continued)*

Birth-center credentials *(cont.)*

_____   Is the center affiliated with any hospitals? If so, which ones?

Birth-center staff

_____   What are the professional credentials of the birth-center staff? Who will actually deliver your baby?

_____   Are the birth-center staff friendly and willing to answer your questions?

_____   Are they genuinely interested in helping you have the type of birth experience you want, as specified in your birth plan?

_____   How receptive are they to any special requests you may have (bringing a doula or other support person with you to the birth, for example)? Can they recommend a qualified doula?

_____   Are they comfortable dealing with any special circumstances related to your situation (if you're young, disabled, a single mother or part of a nontraditional family, for example)?

_____   Is the birth center adequately staffed?

Birthing policies and procedures

_____   What policies are in place to ensure that you're a good candidate for a birth-center delivery rather than a hospital delivery?

_____   Does the birth center offer its own childbirth preparation classes to familiarize parents who will be delivering there with birth-center policies and procedures?

_____   Are there limits on the number of labor support people who are allowed to be present at the birth?

_____   Are children permitted to be present at the birth? If so, does the birth center offer any special sibling preparation classes?

_____   Can photos and videos be taken during the birth?

_____   Does the birth center have facilities for water births?

Birthing policies and procedures *(cont.)*

_____ Under what circumstances would you and/or your baby be transported to a nearby hospital?

_____ What types of procedures are performed routinely during labor?

_____ What diagnostic equipment is available?

_____ Are any pain medications available to laboring women? What about anesthesia?

_____ Will the baby be given to you immediately after birth (assuming, of course, that the baby doesn't require any special care)?

_____ Who is responsible for examining the newborn upon delivery?

What procedures are performed on the baby shortly after birth?

_____ Apgar testing?

_____ Vitamin K injections?

_____ Placing antibacterial drops into the baby's eyes?

_____ Suctioning of the baby's nose and throat?

What procedures are performed on the baby later?

_____ HIV testing?

_____ Hepatitis B vaccination?

_____ Testing for hypothyroidism, phenylketonuria (PKU) and other genetic disorders?

_____ Which of these procedures are required by the state or province where you will be giving birth?

_____ Can the newborn examination be conducted in the birthing room while the baby is resting on her mother's breast, or does the baby have to be taken somewhere else? If the baby needs to be moved, can one or both of the parents accompany the baby?

_____ Will you be encouraged to breastfeed your baby as soon as possible following the birth?

_____ How soon after the delivery will you be encouraged to go home? What is the maximum period of time you will be allowed to stay at the birth center?

(continued)

Checklist 8.2. *(continued)*

Birthing rooms

_____   Are the birthing rooms fully equipped to handle any emergencies that may arise?

_____   Are the birthing rooms designed to give you and your partner as much privacy as possible? Is there more than one bed in each room?

_____   Are the birthing rooms attractive and homelike, or clinical and sterile? Do they look like a place where you would want to give birth?

_____   Are the rooms large enough for you to be able to move around while you're in labor?

_____   Will you have your own bathroom, or will you have to share one with another laboring woman?

_____   Do the birthing rooms have any amenities, such as birthing stools, squatting bars, and Jacuzzis, you can use while you are in labor?

_____   Is there a phone you can use to call family and friends during labor or after the birth?

Home birth

There's no denying it: women have been giving birth at home for thousands of years, and the majority of babies born in the world today are born at home. If you are in the care of a qualified doctor or midwife and you are able to get to a hospital quickly, a home birth is no more dangerous than a birth-center delivery, but it isn't as safe as a hospital delivery, given the fact that unexpected complications can and do arise, and you don't have the same access to medical care if you are giving birth somewhere other than a hospital setting.

Although some women choose to have their babies at home, home birth isn't the best option for everyone. You should consider a home birth only if

Watch Out!

The fact that previous pregnancies have been problem free is no guarantee that subsequent pregnancies will be risk free. There is always an element of risk with any delivery, regardless of the setting in which you choose to give birth.

- you are in good overall health;

- your pregnancy can be characterized as low risk (that is, your baby is neither premature nor postmature; you haven't developed any complications of pregnancy, such as preeclampsia or gestational diabetes; your baby is in a head-down position; and you are giving birth to one baby rather than multiples);

- there are no red flags in your obstetrical history (for example, you don't have a history of difficult delivery of the baby's shoulders or one that required the use of forceps or vacuum extraction; or a history of cesarean section, maternal hemorrhage, or stillbirth);

- you are willing to take the responsibility for the full range of home birth preparations, from buying all the supplies needed for labor and delivery to preparing yourself physically and mentally for the birth itself;

- you have a doctor or certified nurse-midwife who is willing to attend a home birth and who has access to the appropriate emergency medical supplies (oxygen, resuscitation equipment, and so on);

- your home is reasonably close to a hospital, given road and weather conditions at the time of year when you are due to deliver (ideally, you want to be within 10 minutes of a hospital in case an emergency situation arises and you and your baby need to be transported to hospital in a hurry);

Moneysaver

Health insurance companies do not generally cover the costs of home births. Make sure that you understand in advance what type of fee you will be required to pay your birth attendants. It could be as much as $2,000 — possibly even more.

- you are prepared to head to the hospital immediately if any sort of complication arises;

- your partner and/or children are comfortable with the idea of a birth at home;

- you have support people available to help before, during, and after the birth.

Even if you're an ideal candidate for a home birth, unexpected complications can and do arise. Here are some situations that might necessitate a trip to the hospital:

- a prolapsed cord (an emergency situation in which the umbilical cord precedes the baby's head in the birth canal, potentially leading to severe brain damage or death);

- undetected placenta previa (when the placenta blocks all or a portion of the cervix, preventing the baby from exiting) or a placental abruption (when the placenta detaches from the uterine wall prematurely, potentially causing fetal death or maternal hemorrhage);

- poor fetal heart rate (when the baby's heart rate is too slow — under 100 beats per minute — or too fast — over 180, something that may indicate fetal distress);

- your amniotic fluid is greenish or brownish when your membranes rupture — a sign that your baby has passed her first stool (meconium) and could be in distress;

- you are experiencing a prolonged labor that doesn't appear to be going anywhere or it's been more than 18 hours since your membranes ruptured;

- your baby has moved into a breech position (bottom first) or transverse position (across your middle) and will need to be either turned or delivered by cesarean section;

- your newborn is blue, limp, and not breathing, and requires specialized medical attention in a neonatal intensive care unit after being revived at home by the attending doctor or midwife;

- the placenta has not been delivered within an hour of the birth of the baby, or your body has retained pieces of the placenta;

- you have received some tears to the perineum, vagina, or cervix that cannot be repaired at home;

- you experience a maternal hemorrhage after birth (either a great gush or a continuous flow of blood).

Now that we've considered who's a good candidate for home birth, and who's not, let's quickly run through the pros and cons of giving birth at home:

Pros:

- A home birth tends to be a more intimate experience than a hospital birth. You give birth in the privacy of your own home surrounded only by those people you invite to the birth.

- There's no need to drive to a hospital or birthing center while you're in labor.

- You're in control of your birth experience. You can move around and labor in any position that feels comfortable, and you can follow your body's own schedule when it comes to eating and sleeping.

- Because you are likely to be more relaxed laboring in your own home than in a hospital or birth center, you may be able to work with your body, thereby enabling your labor to progress more efficiently and with less pain, even

Bright Idea

Don't assume that you have to give birth at home in order to be in control of your birth experience. Many birth centers and even hospital birthing units today can offer this kind of freedom and flexibility.

though you don't actually have access to medical pain relief.

- You avoid the possibility of being infected by the types of highly resistant germs that live in hospitals and other healthcare facilities.

- You are less likely to be subjected to unwanted interventions such as intravenous feeding, electronic fetal monitoring, and hormonal augmentation of labor if you don't give birth within a certain time frame.

Cons:

- If a critical emergency arises during the delivery, you or your baby could be at risk. It may not be possible to transport the two of you to the hospital in time, even if the hospital is just minutes away.

- Home birth is meant for women with low-risk pregnancies, and it's impossible to guarantee in advance that a particular pregnancy and delivery will remain low risk. If you develop pregnancy- or birth-related complications, you may have to abandon your plans for a home birth — possibly at the 11th hour.

- You need to equip your home with the necessary supplies to give birth — something that a hospital or birthing center will do for you. Although you're likely to have many of these supplies in your home anyway, you will have to spend a bit of money on a few odds and ends. (See Checklist 8.3.)

Watch Out!

An unplanned home birth is not a safe option. If you're planning to give birth at home, you need to hire a competent caregiver and devote the time and effort necessary to prepare for the birth. That means getting the necessary prenatal care and ensuring that you are, in fact, a good candidate for home birth.

Checklist 8.3. Home Birth Supplies

If you decide to have a home birth, you will need to have the following supplies on hand:

_____ two sets of clean sheets (one for during the birth and one for after the birth)

_____ a waterproof pad or waterproof sheet to prevent the mattress from being damaged (Note: Shower curtains or large plastic tablecloths make excellent waterproof sheets)

_____ disposable absorbent pads or large diapers to place underneath the mother

_____ clean towels and washcloths

_____ sterile gauze pads

_____ a dozen pairs of sterile disposable gloves

_____ umbilical-cord clamps

_____ a 3-ounce bulb syringe for suctioning mucus from the baby's mouth and nose

_____ a large bowl to catch the placenta

_____ receiving blankets for the newborn baby

_____ sanitary napkins

If you are planning a water birth at home (see Chapter 18), you will also need:

_____ a suitable birthing tub (a hot tub, Jacuzzi, bathtub, or portable tub)

_____ an accurate water thermometer (to ensure that the temperature stays between 99°F and 101°F)

(continued)

Checklist 8.3. *(continued)*	

_____ an underwater flashlight to allow the caregiver to view the birth

_____ an inflatable plastic pillow so that you can stay comfortable

_____ a fish net to catch any remnants from the birth or other debris

_____ clean towels

Note: The American College of Obstetricians and Gynecologists' Committee on Obstetric Practice recently concluded that there is insufficient data, particularly concerning rates of infection, to state definitively that laboring in water and "water birth" are safe for pregnant women and their babies; and that these procedures should only take place in facilities that conform with best practices regarding infection control. So if you are planning a water birth at home, you need to be aware of the potential risks.

Week 15

Now that this pregnancy thing is starting to get serious and you're actually starting to look the part of the mama-to-be, you may find yourself wondering how things are going to play out on the physical front. "In the beginning of my pregnancy, I was fearful of the changes my body was going to have to go through," recalls Tracy, a 31-year-old mother of one. "My body was no longer familiar to me. It was no longer my own." In this section of the chapter, we talk a bit about how pregnancy can affect your body image, for better and for worse.

What's going on with your baby

Your baby is about 4 ½ inches long and weighs just under 2 ounces. Your baby's skin is translucent and covered with thin, downy hair known as lanugo.

While your baby is moving around a great deal, you're not able to feel any movement yet. You'll have to wait until your baby gets a bit bigger.

What's going on with your body

Week 15 can be a bit of a "no man's land" (or "no woman's land") when it comes to pregnancy-related aches and pains. You're likely to be rid of the morning sickness and extreme fatigue that may have made the early weeks of your pregnancy a bit rough, and yet you're not likely to be feeling a lot of fetal movement quite yet.

If you're the kind of person who tends to worry about things a lot, this lack of pregnancy symptoms can send your imagination into overdrive. You may be wondering if it's okay to be feeling this good. Try to relax (although we know that's easier said than done!) and do your best to enjoy this part of your pregnancy. It won't be long before your baby is using your bladder as a trampoline and kicking you in the ribs on a regular basis, so you may as well make the most of this momentary reprieve from pregnancy symptoms!

What's going on with your head

Worried that you look fat rather than pregnant? This is a common concern for moms-to-be during the early second trimester.

After all, at this stage of the game, you're likely to be too big for regular clothes — particularly the more tailored garments — but too small for tent-style maternity fashions. (Of course, if this is your second or subse-

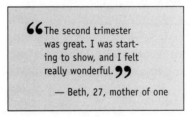

6 6 The second trimester was great. I was starting to show, and I felt really wonderful. 9 9
— Beth, 27, mother of one

quent pregnancy, you may have been wearing your maternity clothes for a while by now since you seem to show sooner if you have been pregnant before.)

If looking fat is at the top of your list of concerns, take heart. By the end of this trimester, there will be no question about the fact that you're pregnant. During weeks 12 to 27, your uterus will quadruple in height and rise out of your pelvis, causing your body to take on those classic curves of pregnancy. You'll be a walking, talking maternity billboard, and no one will be mistaking your baby belly for a beer belly any longer.

The Hot List: This week's must-ask pregnancy questions

While pregnant women have always struggled with body image concerns, in recent years, Demi Moore and other celebrity mamas have certainly raised the bar on what it means to look good during pregnancy — something that can leave non-celebrity mamas questioning their physical attractiveness in a major way. Here are answers to some of the most-asked questions bout pregnancy and body image.

I tend to struggle with my body image at the best of times. Am I likely to have a particularly rough time with my body image during pregnancy?

It depends. Some women find that they're able to call a truce with their bodies during pregnancy because they know that there's a reason for the weight gain that they are experiencing — to help grow a healthy baby. On the other hand, other women really struggle with the physical changes of pregnancy.

If you find that your self-esteem is starting to nose-dive — rather than feeling radiant and glowing you feel frumpy and fat — you may want to share your body image concerns with other mothers or talk to a counselor who specializes in pregnancy and body image. It's particularly important to seek out such support if you've struggled with an eating disorder such as anorexia or bulimia in the past. You don't want your concern about your pregnancy weight gain to cause you to go back to severe dieting or purging, both of which can be extremely harmful to you and your baby.

Is there any thing that can be done to prevent stretch marks?

Stretch marks — bright red marks that generally fade to silver over time — may appear on the abdomen, breasts, hips, or buttocks during pregnancy. They occur when the skin is over-stretched. While you can reduce your chances of developing stretch marks by keeping your weight gain within the healthy range, there's no guaranteed way to avoid them.

If you do end up accumulating a few stretch marks during your pregnancy and they don't fade as much as you'd like after the birth, you might want to set up an appointment with a dermatologist to talk about ways of getting rid of them (e.g,. laser treatment or the application of a prescription cream that can help to improve the appearance of stretch marks). Of course, some women have a totally different attitudes toward these pregnancy "souvenirs," viewing them more as ribbons of valor earned in the front lines of motherhood than as anything unattractive or to be ashamed of. (Hey, why not!)

Is it true that your breasts get bigger during pregnancy or is that a myth?

It's true. Most women find that their breasts grow by one full cup size by the end of the first trimester and by another full cup size by the time that they give birth. Some women welcome these changes, while others are less than thrilled to see their bra size inching upward. It's a very individual thing.

What tips can you offer on being plus-sized and pregnant?

Approximately 40 percent of American women wear size 14 or larger. If, like many moms-to-be, you fall into the plus-sized category, here are some tips on managing your pregnancy:

- Choose a doctor or midwife who will treat you with respect rather than fixating on your weight, and who will provide you with useful information on nutrition and exercise during pregnancy. While there are some added risks to being overweight during pregnancy (risks we discussed back in Chapter 2), your healthcare provider doesn't need to make you feel that your weight is the sole focus of each prenatal visit.

■ Prepare yourself for the possibility that complete strangers may make rude comments about your weight. Although all pregnant women tend to run into this situation, the comments can be particularly hurtful if you're already sensitive about your weight.

■ Try to find ways to exercise without feeling uncomfortable. "Consider swimming — even if you hate the way you look in a bathing suit," suggests Heather, 32, a plus-sized mother of one. "Swimming — or even just floating in the pool — helps take the weight off your back and reduces sciatica."

■ Accept the fact that finding attractive, affordable, plus-sized maternity wear may be a bit of an uphill battle. For whatever reason, a large portion of the fashion world has yet to catch on to the fact that large women actually have sex, and consequently can get pregnant. And those maternity stores that do carry plus-sized maternity clothes tend to charge top dollar for them, which is why Debbie, a 31-year-old mother of three, suggests that you bypass these stores entirely: "Just say no to maternity stores. You can save large amounts of money by avoiding the word 'maternity' altogether."

■ Pull together a maternity wardrobe of your own: buy leggings that are two sizes larger than what you usually wear, and top them off with oversized T-shirts or baggy sweaters. Dress up the look with an oversized men's blazer — something you can usually pick up secondhand for just a few dollars.

■ If you're planning to give birth somewhere other than at home, be sure to bring a couple of old pairs of underwear with you to the hospital or birthing center; the bizarre mesh underwear some of these places give you after the delivery is at best one-size-fits-some.

■ Don't be afraid to insist that your weight be kept private if that's important to you. One plus-sized mom in labor didn't want to tell the nurse her weight while her partner was in earshot, so she wrote down the figure on a piece of paper.

> 66 Many of the newer-style empire-waist dresses work great as maternity wear, and you can wear them after your pregnancy. 99
>
> — Heather, 32, plus-sized mother of one

■ Compare notes with other plus-sized moms you know who've given birth recently. They may be able to pass along some valuable tips on everything from finding a size-friendly healthcare provider to locating a maternity store that carries pregnancy fashions in a variety of sizes.

Week 16

At this point in your pregnancy, you're likely to be focusing on distinguishing between baby movements and gas bubbles and getting serious about shopping for maternity clothes. (Hint: You can't afford to wait too much longer unless you're into the whole pregnancy nudist scene.)

What's going on with your baby

Your baby is swimming inside a tiny sea of amniotic fluid. (Very tiny, of course. At this stage of pregnancy, there's just a single cup of amniotic fluid inside your uterus.) But even though the quantities are small at this point, this fluid plays an important role in the development of your baby's pulmonary system. The amniotic fluid allows your baby to "breathe" in utero, moving amniotic fluid in and out of his or her lungs.

The amniotic fluid also contains antibiotic agents that help to inhibit the growth of bacteria that could be harmful to your baby, providing your baby with some important protection prior to birth.

What's going on with your body

You may be feeling some initial flutters (very light fetal movements). At this stage of pregnancy, it can be extremely difficult to differentiate between bona fide baby movements and gastrointestinal sensations, but, as your baby's movements become stronger, you'll gradually become more certain that what you're feeling is, in fact, little kicks and flutters from your baby as opposed to a less-than-enthralling gas bubble.

What's going on with your head

You're likely to be thinking about the quadruple screen test and wondering whether you made the right decision about whether to have (or not to have) the test done. (See Chapter 14 for more about the pros and cons of this and other prenatal tests.)

The Hot List: This week's must-ask pregnancy questions

Wondering about some of the skin and hair changes you can expect to experience over the course of your pregnancy? Here are some of the most commonly asked questions.

What kind of skin changes can I expect to experience during pregnancy?

Some women find that their skin improves during pregnancy and they acquire that much-lauded maternal glow. Others experience a number of skin-related problems. Here's what you need to know about the more common pregnancy skin complaints:

- **Mask of pregnancy (chloasma):** Some women experience a darkening of the skin on their face because increased levels of estrogen and progesterone stimulate production of melanin (skin pigment). The so-called "mask of pregnancy" is a butterfly-shaped darkened area that extends around the eyes and across the nose and cheeks. Because chloasma is made worse by exposure to sunlight or other sources of ultraviolet light, be sure to use a sunblock with an SPF of at least 15 when you are outdoors.

■ **Increased pigmentation:** Ninety percent of pregnant women experience some sort of increased pigmentation. This skin darkening occurs on the nipples or areola (the area around the nipples), on the perineum, and on the line that runs from the navel to the pubic bone (the linea nigra).

■ **Changes to moles:** Some women find that their moles become darker and larger during pregnancy. Note: Because these types of changes can also be a sign of cancer, it's important to report these changes to your doctor.

■ **Red and itchy palms and soles:** Some women find that the palms of their hands and the soles of their feet become extremely itchy during pregnancy. These symptoms can usually be relieved by applying a moisturizing cream.

■ **Skin tags:** Some pregnant women develop skin tags — small, loose growths of skin under the arms or breasts. These are painless and usually disappear after your baby is born. If they persist, however, you can arrange to have them removed through minor surgery.

■ **Rashes:** Some pregnant women develop a heat rash during pregnancy. The best way to cope with this particular problem is to sprinkle cornstarch (rather than scented baby powders) on the affected areas after bathing and to keep the skin cool and dry.

■ **Acne:** Some women find that their skin breaks out during pregnancy. Here's what Jennifer, 25, had to say about the breakouts she experienced during pregnancy: "The absolutely worst aspect of my entire pregnancy was how terrible my skin broke out. I had no idea this would happen. I assumed pregnant women got wonderful skin — you know, 'the glow.' By my fifth month, I was so broken out on my back, chest, shoulders, and all over the sides of my face, forehead, and chin that there wasn't a spot you could touch without pimples."

I've heard that you don't lose any hair during pregnancy. Is this true?

Well, it's partially true. Pregnancy hormones reduce the rate at which hair falls out, something that can leave you with a thick head of hair until at least a few months after the delivery. At that point, Mother Nature goes into housekeeping mode and gets rid of all the extra hair that you accumulated over the course of your pregnancy, something that can have you going from lush to limp overnight.

Is it safe to get your hair dyed during pregnancy?

While there aren't any studies on record to prove any increased incidence of birth defects in mothers who used hair dye during pregnancy, if you do decide to get your hair dyed at some point during the next few months, you'll want to make sure that the dye is applied in a well-ventilated area so that you're not breathing in all kinds of strong fumes. (Not only are those fumes potentially unhealthy: they're likely to leave you feeling a little queasy.)

Of course, if you're the kind of person who tends to worry a great deal about everything, you may want to hold off on getting those roots colored until after your baby is born. That way, you won't be dooming yourself to spending the remainder of your pregnancy second-guessing your decision to expose your baby to hair dye. You'll have to decide which approach will work best for you.

What advice can you offer on shopping for maternity clothing?

First of all, count your lucky stars that you're pregnant today and not in your mother's day. Maternity clothing has come a long way since it hit its ugly peak during the 1960s and 1970s.

Gone are the days when being pregnant meant wearing dresses that looked like oversized versions of what you might find in the toddler fashions section at JCPenney.

The only downside to today's maternity fashions is their price. Although you will find a few bargains out there, far too many maternity clothing manufacturers take advantage of the fact that pregnant women need to wear something. (Think captive market.)

Here are some tips on shopping for maternity wear:

- Purchase just a few items at a time. It's hard to predict how your belly will grow during the months ahead. Besides, it's nice to have something new to wear during the never-ending third trimester.

- Think comfort. You've got the rest of your life to be a fashion queen. Look for fabrics that breathe rather than fabrics that are high on glitz — and leave your high heels in the back of the closet for now. Remember, your metabolic rate increases by about 20 percent when you're pregnant, and your feet may grow as much as a full size!

- Avoid anything that cuts or binds. Although Victorian women were encouraged to wear corsets throughout much of their pregnancies, you're free to wear whatever you want. Pass on tight belts, girdles, and waistbands.

- If you make a habit of wearing bikini underwear, you'll be able to continue to wear them through most — if not all — of your pregnancy. If, however, you wear hip or waist-height underwear, you're going to have to search out some oversized briefs. If you're not already in the habit of wearing cotton underwear, switch now. Pregnant women are more susceptible to yeast infections, so spending nine months in polyester underpants is pretty much asking for trouble.

- Pick up a pair of maternity support hose. They may not be the sexiest piece of lingerie you'll ever own, but they can help prevent or minimize varicose veins.

■ You can't scrimp on bras during your pregnancy or you'll be downright uncomfortable. As a rule of thumb, you will need two bras in each size as your bustline expands — and expand it may: some women increase by three cup sizes during pregnancy. You'll be more comfortable with cotton, but make sure that whatever type of bra you purchase provides adequate support. Note: You can save yourself a bit of cash by making your last set of bras nursing bras since you'll still be able to wear them after baby arrives.

■ Don't make this mistake when it comes to the rest of your wardrobe, however: You're not likely to want to wear anything from your maternity wardrobe while you're nursing. In fact, most women avoid their maternity clothing like the plague once the baby has arrived, both because they're sick of wearing the same old thing and because they don't want anyone to think that they're still pregnant. (Perish the thought!) Note: You can pick up some tips on putting together a postpartum wardrobe at www.themotherofallbooks.com/parenting_tips.htm.

■ Go for the layered look. Rather than buying long-sleeved dresses, pair up a short-sleeved top with a cardigan. That way, you can peel off the cardigan if you start to feel too hot.

■ Casual maternity clothing doesn't have to come from a maternity store. Shop in the plus-size section of your local department store or hit a plus-size retailer, and you'll find leggings, shirts, jackets, empire-style dresses, and other oversized garments galore. (These stores are also a great source of comfortable, oversized cotton underwear, by the way.) You might also try raiding your husband's side of the closet — assuming, of course, that he's larger than you — or hitting a quality secondhand boutique.

■ If you have to look professional at the office, you'll probably have to break down and purchase at least two or three

maternity suits. Instead of spending $200 or more to pur-
chase each outfit new, see if there's a secondhand clothing
store in your community that specializes in maternity wear.
You could save yourself a bundle.

■ If you need a dress for a highly formal occasion, see if you
can rent it rather than buying it. Maternity-clothing rental
boutiques are springing up in many large U.S. cities.
(Note: Some of these boutiques also specialize in career
wear. Check your local Yellow Pages.)

Week 17

Now that you're heading into the middle of the second
trimester, you're likely to find yourself dealing with some new
pregnancy-related aches and pains, including bellybutton soreness and middle-of-the-night leg cramps. (There's always something new to look forward to when you're pregnant!) We'll be
discussing some of these complaints *du jour* in this next section
of the chapter.

What's going on with your baby

A baby girl's fallopian tubes are formed during the early part
of the second trimester. They are fashioned out of the now-
redundant first set of kidneys that the fetus relied on earlier on
in pregnancy — an impressive bit of intrauterine recycling on
the part of Mother Nature, don't you think?

What's going on with your body

You've probably gained between 5 and 10 pounds by this point
in your pregnancy, so your belly is definitely starting to take on
a new, more rounded look.

Of course, your growing uterus is also responsible for your
changing body shape. The top of your uterus is now just a couple of finger-widths below your bellybutton. Note: You may
experience some bellybutton tenderness over the next few
weeks as your uterus rises up and starts pressing directly against

the inside of your bellybutton. It will begin to subside once your uterus is above bellybutton level, but while it lasts, it can be surprisingly painful.

What's going on with your head

You've no doubt heard plenty of talk about "pregnancy brain": how being pregnant can supposedly leave you feeling unusually preoccupied and absentminded. Well, according to a recent study, you might not want to read too much into this much-talked about phenomenon. A study conducted at Britain's University of Sunderland concluded that pregnancy doesn't actually impair women's critical thinking and concentration abilities, but that when pregnant women *do* forget something or make a mistake, they immediately blame their pregnancies for the error because they've been culturally conditioned to believe that the hormonal changes of pregnancy are responsible.

The Hot List: This week's must-ask pregnancy questions

As wonderful as the second trimester may be, it isn't entirely blissful. Aches and pains are, after all, part of the pregnancy turf. Although you are likely to have ditched some of the more distressing first-trimester symptoms by now (think morning sickness and head-to-toe exhaustion!), your constipation and breathlessness are likely to hang around and to be joined by a few new complaints. This week's set of question's focus on the second trimester aches and pains.

Just a reminder: if you can't find the particular pregnancy complaint you're looking for in this chapter, we've probably covered it elsewhere in this book — most likely in Chapter 6 or Chapter 11 (Complaint Central, it would seem!).

I'm barely into my second trimester and already starting to experience some back pain. What's going on?

Look at any cartoon of a pregnant woman and you'll see someone with two hands on her back, leaning into the classic swayback position. You don't have to be pregnant for very long to figure out why pregnant women do this. They're supporting their aching backs!

Back pain during pregnancy occurs for a number of reasons. First of all, progesterone (the hormone responsible for so many of your other pregnancy aches and pains) causes the ligaments and connective tissue holding the bones in the pelvic region together to soften so that they can open up during the birth, something that frequently causes pain around the pubic bone as well. Second, the heavier uterus throws off a pregnant woman's center of gravity, something that can lead to a change of postures that can cause back pain. Third, the rectus abdominis muscles — the muscles that run along the front of the abdomen from the rib cage to the pubic bone — can separate during pregnancy, a condition that tends to worsen back pain.

> 66 The extra weight really makes whatever side you are lying on ache. Really ache. I would flip to the other side, but eventually that side would hurt too. 99
>
> — Molly, 29, mother of one

Although it's useful to know what causes back pain, it's more important to know how to prevent or manage it. Here are a few tips:

- Wear low-heeled (but not flat) shoes with good arch support.

- Ask for help when you are lifting heavy objects, and lift by bending your knees rather than your waist. (This is no time to play the martyr. Let people help you, for once!)

- To reduce your chances of injury, make gentle rather than jerky motions when you are reaching or stretching.

- Sit in chairs that provide adequate back support or place a small pillow between the chair and your lower back.

- Pay attention to your posture. Keep your pelvis tucked in and your shoulders back when you are sitting or standing.

- Place one foot on a step stool if you're going to be sitting or standing for long periods of time.

- Get up and walk around every half-hour if your job requires that you sit for long periods of time.

- Take the pressure off your lower back when you are sleeping on your side by placing one pillow under your abdomen and another between your knees. (Yes, a couple of strategically-positioned pillows can work wonders when it comes to managing back pain!)

My hips are so sore that they wake me up at night. What can I do to deal with this particular problem?

One of the most aggravating pregnancy complaints for many women is hip pain and stiffness. Unfortunately, it's hard to avoid when your growing belly pretty much limits you to sleeping on one side or the other.

Some women find that putting a pillow between their knees and tucking another pillow under their abdomen provides at least a measure of relief.

Fortunately, hip pain quickly disappears after the baby is born, so you aren't doomed to toss and turn forever. It just feels that way.

Sometimes when I roll over, I feel this awful, ripping sensation in my abdomen. It really freaks me out. Is this normal?

It sounds like you're describing round ligament pain — the shooting pain in the lower abdomen that many women experience when they change position suddenly. It is caused by the sudden stretching of the ligaments and muscles that support the expanding uterus. It tends to be at its worst between weeks 14 and 20, when the uterus is big enough to exert its pressure on the ligaments, yet not big enough to rest some of its weight

Watch Out!

Besides being caused by round ligament pain, abdominal pain can also be caused by appendicitis, a gall bladder attack, the stretching of adhesions from previous abdominal surgery, an ectopic pregnancy, or preterm labor. If the pain you are experiencing is particularly severe or lasts for an extended period of time, call your doctor or midwife immediately.

on the pelvic bones. In the meantime, you can minimize the amount of round ligament pain you experience by moving slowly and supporting your belly when you're changing positions. And if you are left with some tenderness after moving too quickly one day, warm baths can also help to ease some of the discomfort. Round ligament pain can be incredibly painful, but this too shall pass. (Sorry if we're beginning to sound like a broken record.)

Almost every night, I get hit by painful leg cramps while I'm sleeping. What causes this and what can I do to avoid it?

It's not unusual to experience painful leg cramps during the second and third trimesters. These cramps — which occur most often while you are sleeping — are believed to be caused by the pressure of the uterus on the nerves in the legs or by a calcium deficiency.

Here are some tips on preventing and managing leg cramps in your calf muscles:

- Stretch your calf muscles before you head to bed. Point your toes up toward your knees while pushing your heel away from you. You should repeat this exercise at least

> **❝**I didn't realize that two pregnancies could be so different. I was so worried with my second because I felt more kicking, more heartburn, more sickness. **❞**
> — Jackie, 34, mother of two

10 times for each leg in order to really stretch the muscles out.

- Ask your partner to massage your calf muscles.

- As soon as a cramp starts, aim your toes upward toward your knees. Whatever you do, don't point your toes. The pain will only intensify.

- If you're not already taking a calcium supplement, ask your caregiver to recommend one. Getting adequate amounts of calcium in your diet can help to prevent leg cramps.

Heartburn is becoming a huge problem for me. What can I do to prevent it?

Heartburn — a burning sensation in the middle of your chest or upper digestive tract — is another common complaint during pregnancy. It occurs because progesterone (1) relaxes the muscle that is responsible for controlling the opening at the top of the stomach and (2) causes the stomach to empty more slowly so that as many nutrients as possible can be absorbed from the food you eat.

Here are some tips on preventing heartburn:

- Avoid fatty and greasy foods, carbonated drinks, processed meats, and junk food.

- Eat slowly. The more slowly you eat, the more time the enzymes in your saliva have to break down the food before it reaches your stomach.

> **❝**I had terrible heartburn during all three of my pregnancies. It started at about five months with my second and third children. I tried papaya enzyme, which tasted great but didn't do much. Then my midwife recommended Gaviscon tablets. They foam in your mouth like a butterscotch-flavored fire extinguisher, but they really work. The only good thing about heartburn is that within minutes of giving birth, you realize you don't have it anymore.**❞**
>
> — Karen, 34, mother of three

- Eat less. Heartburn is more likely to flare up if you overfill your stomach, particularly if you're eating a lot of carbohydrates.

- Don't eat too close to bedtime.

- Avoid lying flat on your back when you are resting or sleeping because this will only intensify your heartburn. Try propping yourself up with pillows instead.

- If you're feeling particularly miserable, ask your caregiver if would be a good idea for you to take an antacid.

I have been experienceing a lot of dizziness lately. Is this a normal part of pregnancy?

Many women experience low blood pressure during pregnancy. This can lead to dizziness and feelings of faintness — particularly if you're standing in one spot for a prolonged period of time (for example, when you're waiting in line at the grocery store or the bank). If you find yourself in this situation and you feel as though you're going to faint, you should

- shift your weight from foot to foot, or

- sit with your head between your knees.

Don't worry about looking silly if you have to sit down on the floor in the middle of the grocery store or bank. Anyone who has been pregnant before will understand what you're going through. As for anyone who hasn't been pregnant before — who really cares what they think anyway?!!

I think I may be developing carpal tunnel syndrome. What are the symptoms?

Carpal tunnel syndrome is another common pregnancy complaint — particularly for moms-to-be who work on computers all day or do work that involves repetitive hand and wrist motions. It is caused when the nerves in the wrist become compressed by fluids being retained by the surrounding tissues.

The symptoms of carpal tunnel syndrome include numbness, tingling, or shooting or burning pain in the middle and

Bright Idea

Bothered by a sore wrist? Use a bag of frozen vegetables or a bag of chilled, uncooked rice to ease the pain of carpal tunnel syndrome.

index fingers and thumb; cramping or stiffness of the hands; weakness in the thumb; and a tendency to drop objects. Some pregnant women report numbness as far up their arm as their elbow.

If you develop carpal tunnel syndrome, your caregiver will likely recommend that you wear a splint at night to reduce your discomfort and pain. In some situations, a steroid injection may be recommended, but this is unusual. Although the condition usually corrects itself spontaneously after delivery, minor surgery may be required if it persists.

I'm noticing some swelling in my hands and feet. What causes this and what can I do to minimize it?

Edema occurs during a normal pregnancy for two reasons: the growing uterus places pressure on the veins carrying blood back from the lower extremities, forcing water into the tissues around your feet and ankles; and the increased levels of progesterone in your body encourage fluid retention.

You will know if you are retaining extra fluids if your feet feel swollen and uncomfortable or your fingers start to feel puffy.

Here are some tips on coping with edema:

- Lying on your side helps reduce fluid retention by allowing gravity to pull fluid from your tissues back into your bloodstream so that it can be passed out of your body through your kidneys. If you can't lie down, sit and put your feet up.

- Warm — not hot — baths can help to reduce swelling.

- Avoid diuretics ("water pills"). Not only are they ineffective, but they affect your body's fluid balance and can be dangerous during pregnancy.

- Increase your fluid intake. Believe it or not, this can have a diuretic effect and help reduce water retention and swelling.

- Watch your salt intake but don't eliminate salt from your diet entirely. You need salt to maintain your normal fluid balance.

- Remove your rings before they start getting tight so that you won't have to have them cut off.

Just the facts

- You'll need to make up your mind about a place to give birth early on in your pregnancy so that you can be sure that your caregiver is willing and able to attend births in your chosen location — at home, in a birth center, and/or in a hospital.

- Some women find it difficult to come to terms with the physical changes of pregnancy. If you're struggling with your body image, try talking to other moms or setting up an appointment with a counselor who specializes in body image concerns.

- Don't buy all your maternity clothes at one time. Not only is it hard to predict exactly what size you'll need during your final weeks of pregnancy, it's nice to be able to treat yourself to a late third trimester wardrobe edition.

- Bellybutton soreness, hip pain, and dizziness are a few of the pregnancy complaints that you may start to experience during the second trimester.

GET THE SCOOP ON. . .
What's going on with your baby ▪ What's going
on with your body ▪ What's going on with your
head ▪ Vaginal discharges and yeast infections ▪
What a childbirth education class can do for
you — and what it can't ▪ Traveling during
pregnancy ▪ Keeping baby safe

The Fifth Month: The Halfway Mark

Depending on how your pregnancy has been going so far, you may be amazed that you're fast approaching the halfway mark of your pregnancy — or you may be seriously questioning whether you've got the patience and stamina required to weather the emotional highs and lows of the next 20 weeks!

In this chapter, we zero in on the issues that are likely to be on your mind as you head into month five: vaginal discharges and vaginal infections, urinary tract infections, childbirth education classes, traveling during pregnancy, and so on. And, as in chapters past, we give you an idea of what to expect on a week-by-week basis — this time for weeks 18 through 22. You'll get the inside scoop on what's going on with your body, what's going on with your head, and what's going on with your baby each week, as well as answers to some of the most-asked pregnancy questions for each week of pregnancy.

Week 18

If you've got an ultrasound scheduled for around this point in your pregnancy (as many women do), you may be looking forward to this on-screen rendezvous with your baby. Never mind the fact that your tiny offspring is likely to look more like E.T. than the Gerber baby when viewed on the ultrasound screen: you're still likely to consider your baby to be beautiful beyond measure.

By the way, if you're half-dreading your second trimester ultrasound because you have heard that you need an overly full bladder during your ultrasound, we've got good news for you: at this stage of pregnancy, it's not necessary to have an overly full bladder in order for the ultrasound to be able to pick up an image. So you can expect to feel a whole lot more comfortable this time around.

What's going on with your baby

Your baby now measures about 5 ½ inches from crown to rump and weighs about 5 ounces. The hair on your baby's body is becoming coarser, the eyelashes are beginning to appear on your baby's eyelids, your baby's lips have formed, tastebuds have started to develop on the tongue, and regardless of your baby's sex, nipples are starting to develop on top of the mammary glands.

The placenta — your baby's life support system before birth — is approximately half an inch thick and three inches across. By the time you give birth, it will be 1 ½ inches thick and measure approximately 10 to 12 inches across.

What's going on with your body

You're at the point in pregnancy when you're likely to gain the majority of your pregnancy weight, so you're likely to find yourself feeling extra hungry. In fact, you may find you actually start to feel kind of sick if you don't eat meals and snacks on a regular basis. So make sure you keep your body — and your baby — well nourished by eating at regular intervals: ideally every two to three hours.

Bright Idea

Want to get the lowdown on other common myths about predicting the sex of your baby? Read "Pink or Blue: Myths About Predicting the Sex of Your Baby" at www.themotherofallbooks.com/parenting_tips.htm.

What's going on with your head

Even if you're not generally a superstitious person, you may find yourself buying into a lot of pregnancy-related old wives' tales these days — particularly those about predicting the sex of your baby. You may have heard the old wives' tale about boys being carried lower than girls (because they're supposedly more independent and therefore don't have to be held as close to their mother's heart!) or you may have even snuck off to the bathroom to try the infamous Drano sex prediction urine test. (The test — which is completely unscientific, of course — involves mixing urine with drain cleaner in order to supposedly predict your baby's sex. Ask around and you'll be shocked to discover just how many women you know have actually done this test — assuming, of course, that they'll actually admit it to you.)

The Hot List: This week's must-ask pregnancy questions

Here are the answers to the questions that are likely to be on your mind at this point in your pregnancy.

What should I expect from this month's prenatal checkup?

At this month's prenatal visit, you can expect your doctor or midwife to check

- **The fundal height** (your healthcare provider will measure the distance between your pubic bone and the top of your uterus — the fundus);
- **Your weight** (to see if you are continuing to gain weight slowly);

Watch Out!

If you experience edema and high blood pressure, and your caregiver detects protein in your urine, you could be developing preeclampsia — a serious pregnancy-related condition.

- **Your blood pressure** (to spot any early warning signs of pregnancy-related hypertension or preeclampsia);

- **Your urine** (to ensure that your sugar and protein levels are within the normal range as they, too, can provide early warning of any emerging problems);

- **The fetal heart rate** (to keep tabs on your baby's general health and well-being). Remember: Your baby's heart beats much more rapidly than your own — at a rate of 120 to 160 beats per minute on average. So don't be concerned that there may be something wrong with your baby if the fetal heart rate seems alarmingly high. It's normal for a baby's heart to beat much more rapidly than an adult's.

What if I'm measuring a bit large for my dates?

The fact that your doctor didn't see a need to order an ultrasound right away probably means that you're only measuring a little bit large for your dates (in other words, your fundal height is more than the 18 centimeters plus or minus 2 centimeters that would be expected at this point of pregnancy) and he simply wants to keep an eye on the situation. If you're still measuring large at your next appointment, he may decide to do an ultrasound to see if you're carrying twins, if your baby is extra large, if you have one or more large uterine fibroids (noncancerous growths), or if you have an excessive amount of amniotic fluid. Some women measure a little large throughout their entire pregnancies, while others go through a bit of a temporary growth spurt (they measure large at one appointment, but their growth is back on target by the following prenatal checkup).

It's also worth pointing out that there's more art than science to measuring the fundal height. While you'll get relatively consistent readings if you have the same doctor or midwife measuring your belly at each and every prenatal visit, each caregiver can get a slightly different measurement on the same day. If a different doctor or midwife took your measurements this time around and your measurement is way out of whack, it's possible that their method of measuring may be at least partially responsible for your "growth spurt."

What if I'm measuring small for my dates?

If you're measuring small for dates (e.g., your fundal height is less than the 18 centimeters — plus or minus two centimeters — that would be expected for someone who is 18 weeks along), your doctor or midwife will likely want to do an ultrasound — or possibly a series of ultrasounds — to find out why you're measuring small.

It could be that your baby is temporarily lagging behind and will go through a growth spurt shortly, that you tend to be quite slight and may measure smaller than average for that reason, or that you are a little low in amniotic fluid (something that's only cause for concern if your amniotic fluid is abnormally low), but your doctor will want to rule out the possibility that your baby could be experiencing some sort of growth-restriction problem, such as a problem with the placenta.

Week 19

At this point in your pregnancy, you may find that you constantly misjudge your growing girth: you may catch yourself bumping into doorframes or countertops because you forget just how far your stomach is sticking out now. Over time, you'll get used to your new, more maternal proportions, but you may end up with a few minor bumps and bruises before you learn how to navigate your belly. (Don't worry about hurting your baby, by the way. As you'll learn in Chapter 10, your baby is well protected against these types of bumps and bruises.)

What's going on with your baby

Your baby now measures about 6 inches from crown to rump and weighs approximately 7 ounces. At this stage of pregnancy, the sebaceous glands (the same glands that produce the natural oils that keep your skin supple during childhood and adulthood) are busy producing the greasy white protective covering known as vernix, which covers your baby's body before birth. (Vernix and amniotic fluid are what's responsible for that positively intoxicating newborn baby smell, by the way.)

What's going on with your body

Your heart is working twice as hard as it did during your pre-pregnancy days, due to your vital organs' increased needs for blood during pregnancy. Your uterus and skin need twice as much blood as they did before you became pregnant while your kidneys need 25 percent more.

What's going on with your head

If you haven't had complete strangers comment on your size yet, odds are you'll be in for that particular experience sometime soon. Most women learn early on in their pregnancies to either tune these comments out completely or to nod politely and pretend they're listening. These comments can get pretty annoying at times, what with one person telling you you're "carrying high" and the next insisting you're "carrying low" and still others offering completely contrary opinions as to whether or not you look further long than you really are. It kind of makes you wonder what these folks did with all their spare time until you and your belly arrived on the scene, now doesn't it?

The Hot List: This week's must-ask pregnancy questions

Find yourself with a lot of questions about what's normal and what's not when it comes to vaginal discharges during pregnancy? Here's what you need to know.

What's responsible for the increase in vaginal discharge during pregnancy?

The hormonal changes of pregnancy combined with increased blood flow to the vaginal region result in an increased vaginal discharge during pregnancy. You'll find that your secretions become increasingly more abundant right up until the time you give birth.

To keep yourself clean and comfortable despite the added wetness, wear cotton underwear (or at least cotton crotch underwear); avoid tight-fitting pants; and steer clear of perfumes and deodorant soaps.

If the discharge is particularly abundant, you may want to use a sanitary napkin to absorb some of the added moisture. Note: Tampons should not be used during pregnancy due to the possibility of toxic shock syndrome.

How can I tell if I've developed some sort of vaginal infection?

You should suspect that you've developed a vaginal infection if your vaginal discharge becomes foul-smelling, thick, yellow, or greenish or if your vaginal discharge causes itching or burning. You'll want to seek treatment promptly, both because certain types of vaginal infections (most notably, bacterial vaginosis) increase your changes of experiencing a premature birth and because you don't want to risk passing along a vaginal infection such as a yeast infection to your baby during birth.

What is bacterial vaginosis?

Bacterial vaginosis (BV) is a very common type of vaginal infection. In fact, it's the most prevalent infection among women of

 Watch Out!

Douching is not recommended during pregnancy. Douching during pregnancy can introduce air into your circulatory system via the vagina, something that could result in a potentially fatal air embolism.

Watch Out!

It's important to seek treatment for BV, if you suspect you're infected. BV has been linked to both an increased risk of miscarriage after 13 weeks as well as premature labor.

reproductive age. It is caused by an overgrowth of "bad" bacteria in the vagina. When symptoms are present, bacterial vaginosis is characterized by a fishy odor that becomes particularly strong after intercourse or during your period.

Why are yeast infections so common during pregnancy?

Yeast infections are more common during pregnancy because the conditions during pregnancy are ideal for developing a yeast infection; there is extra sugar stored in the cell walls of the vagina, the vaginal environment is less acidic, and the immune system is less rigorous. The only thing Mother Nature hasn't done is roll out the official welcome mat!

How can I tell if I have a yeast infection?

If you have developed a thick, cheese-curdlike white or yellowish vaginal discharge that is accompanied by severe itching or a very red rash that is surrounded by red spots; or if you experience vulvar pain and soreness whenever you urinate, you probably have a yeast infection. Your doctor can confirm your diagnosis by taking a vaginal swab.

What can be done to prevent yeast infections?

While there's no guaranteed way to head yeast infections off at the pass, you can make your vaginal environment less hospitable to yeast infections by

■ keeping your genital area as dry as possible (something that's admittedly easier said than done, given those more abundant vaginal secretions we were just talking about!);

- wiping from front to back when you use the washroom;
- ensuring that you're well lubricated when you have inter-course (generally not a problem during pregnancy, due to those more abundant secretions, mind you);
- avoiding overly tight jeans, synthetic underwear, panty-hose, perfumed soaps, and vaginal deodorants.

You may also want to try cutting back on the amount of sugar in your diet and keeping your overall stress level under control. Studies have shown that too much sugar and too much stress can leave you more susceptible to yeast infections.

Are yeast infections dangerous to the developing baby?

Yeast infections aren't dangerous to the developing baby, but they can interfere with breastfeeding if a baby acquires the yeast infec-tion during the birth process and develops a condition known as thrush. Thrush can make breastfeeding difficult and painful by leading to extreme nipple soreness in the mother. It can also cause a yeast-based diaper rash in the baby that can be very painful and extremely difficult to get rid of. And, of course, it's worth noting that labor isn't likely to be a picnic if your perineum is already extremely sore, thanks to a raging yeast infection.

Fortunately, there are all kinds of highly effective products available for treating yeast infections. Ask your doctor, midwife, or pharmacist to recommend such a product.

 Watch Out!

If you experience a lot of watery vaginal discharge after having amniocente-sis performed, get in touch with your doctor immediately. It's possible that you may be experiencing an amniotic fluid leak. Your doctor will likely rec-ommend that you rest for a day or two to see if the leak repairs itself. If it does, your pregnancy is then likely to progresses normally. (Note: See Chapter 14 for more about amniocentesis.)

I've heard that it's dangerous to get a urinary tract infection during pregnancy. What can I do to keep my baby safe?

The first thing you need to know is that urinary tract infections are relatively common during pregnancy. Approximately 1 in 12 pregnant women can expect to experience a UTI at some point over the course of her pregnancy. Increased bladder volume, decreased bladder tone, hormonal changes that make it more difficult for the lower urinary tract to fight off invading bacteria, and a tendency for small bits of urine to remain in the bladder longer than they should all tend to conspire against you when you're pregnant and to leave you more susceptible to urinary tract infections.

You should suspect that you're developing a urinary tract infection if you're experiencing pain during urination, excessive frequency of urination, if you've detected blood in your urine, if your urine has a very strong odor, or if you're experiencing a lot of pain in the bladder region.

However, approximately 6 percent of women with urinary tract infections don't know that are infected, which is one of the reasons why doctors and midwives routinely screen for urinary tract infections at each prenatal checkup. So even if you aren't experiencing any symptoms, if you develop a UTI, chances are your doctor or midwife will be able to diagnose it promptly and ensure that you receive appropriate treatment.

You can reduce your odds of developing a UTI by drinking plenty of fluids, urinating frequently, wiping from front to back after you use the bathroom, and urinating after having sexual intercourse.

 Watch Out!

If you are diagnosed with a urinary tract infection, the infection will need to be treated with antibiotics in order to prevent it from progressing into a full-blown kidney infection — something which increases your odds of going into labor prematurely.

Week 20

Now that it's obvious to the rest of the world that you're having a baby, you'll probably find that you attract a lot of attention from well-meaning strangers and other pregnant women. While you could probably do without the random belly pats and birth stories from people you don't even know, you may enjoy the sense of kinship that you're feeling with other moms-to-be — a feeling that you have just been initiated into the sisterhood of the big bellies by virtue of being pregnant.

And if you're enjoying this aspect of your pregnancy — this sense of being part of something much bigger than yourself — then you're a prime candidate for childbirth classes. (As you'll see when you read through this week's "Hot List," childbirth classes are as much about getting to know other expectant parents as they are about learning about the mechanics of giving birth.)

What's going on with your baby

At this stage in your pregnancy, your baby is about 6 ½ inches from crown to rump (roughly the size of your hand) and weighs about 9 ounces.

If your baby's hands happen to rub up against one another inside the womb, one hand may grasp the other. However, these are involuntary movements rather than movements that are being consciously orchestrated by the brain, so if you happen to be lucky enough to observe such a maneuver on the ultrasound screen, don't assume that your baby is necessarily a budding genius. (The jury's still out on that point.)

What's going on with your body

You may have started to develop a dark line — the so-called linea nigra — down the center of your abdomen between your belly button and your pubic area. The linea nigra generally lengthens upwards, following the fundus (the top of your uterus) as your uterus grows — a very visual way to track your growing belly. This line is caused by the hormonal changes of pregnancy and will disappear on its own after you give birth.

What's going on with your head

Now that you've reached the halfway mark in your pregnancy, you may be trying to decide whether or not to sign up for child-birth classes and, if so, which set of classes to sign up for.

You've no doubt got your own ideas about what childbirth classes are like — and whether or not you think they're for you. (There's no doubt about it: parents are passionate when it comes to the subject of childbirth classes. They either love 'em or hate 'em; there's no in-between. Some couples swear by them, insisting that they're every bit as important a part of having a baby as choosing a good caregiver and finding the right place to give birth. Others view them as a complete and utter waste of time.)

If your knowledge of childbirth classes is based on what you've seen on TV, you could be in for a pleasant surprise. Although the sitcom writers seem to take perverse delight in portraying childbirth classes as a form of boot camp for pregnant women and their partners, they can actually be fun and informative — provided, of course, that you choose the right class. The information in this week's "Hot List" should help you to do just that.

The Hot List: This week's must-ask pregnancy questions

Wondering what childbirth classes have to offer? Here's what you need to know.

What are the key advantages to signing up for childbirth classes?

You're exhausted after a day at the office, and nothing looks halfway near as appealing as your very own couch. Why on earth would you want to head out the door to spend the evening at childbirth class?

Here are six reasons why you might want to make the effort:

■ Childbirth classes can help reduce your anxiety about giving birth by giving you an idea of what to expect — whether you end up having a vaginal or cesarean delivery.

■ They educate you about various birthing options so that you have the facts you need in order to plan for the birth you want.

■ They give you the opportunity to make friends with other expectant couples — contacts that can be pure gold if you find yourself housebound with a colicky baby a few months down the road.

■ They can help you master breathing, relaxation, and coping techniques designed to reduce your perception of pain during labor.

■ They give your partner the chance to play an active role in your pregnancy while familiarizing him with his role during the delivery — that is, providing you with support and encouragement and acting as your advocate.

■ They give you the opportunity to ask questions about pregnancy, labor, childbirth, breastfeeding, and life after baby, and help draw your attention to issues that you need to be thinking about (for example, the pros and cons of episiotomy, circumcision, rooming in, "drive-through deliveries," and more).

There are so many childbirth class choices. Which type should I take?

As you've already discovered for yourself, there's no such thing as a "typical" childbirth class. Childbirth classes can be taught by highly trained instructors who provide you with an in-depth look at the wonders of birth — or by shockingly incompetent instructors who haven't had any experience with childbirth at all, firsthand or otherwise. They can be fun and informative — or deadly boring and completely useless. They can have you eagerly anticipating the birth of your baby — or leave you paralyzed with fear at the thought of the pain that will accompany that first contraction.

Here's a quick introduction to each of the major birthing philosophies:

- **Lamaze:** Lamaze childbirth classes operate on the philosophy that birth is a normal and natural process and that women's inner wisdom guides them through the process of giving birth. The Lamaze philosophy also states that women have the right to give birth free from routine medical intervention and that a woman's confidence and ability to give birth can be either enhanced or undermined by her birthing environment.

- **Bradley:** The Bradley Method (previously known as "husband-coached childbirth") was developed by Denver obstetrician Robert Bradley. Bradley classes encourage the husband to play an active role in the birth of his baby while promoting the principles of natural childbirth.

- **International Childbirth Education Association:** The International Childbirth Education Association's motto summarizes the organization's philosophy: "freedom of choice based on knowledge of alternatives." ICEA-certified childbirth educators believe that, with appropriate physical and mental preparation, parents will be fully prepared to face the challenges of giving birth and successfully make the transition to new parenthood.

- **Association of Childbirth Educators and Labor Assistants:** Classes offered by instructors who have been certified through the Association of Childbirth Educators and Labor Assistants "seek to help all women experience birth's transforming power with dignity, in safety, support, and confidence." The classes emphasize the importance

of making informed decisions as you prepare for the
birth of your baby.

- **Birth Works:** Birth Works classes teach women that their
  bodies are designed to give birth, that the knowledge
  about how to give birth already exists within each woman,
  and that because there is no one right way to give birth,
  expectant parents should play an active role in making
  decisions about their baby's birth.

- **Birthing from Within:** Birthing from Within classes operate on the assumption that women don't need to be
  taught how to give birth, but rather benefit from being
  gently mentored through the process. While Birthing from
  Within classes cover the physical aspects of giving birth,
  they also delve into personal and cultural beliefs about
  labor and labor pain.

- **Other childbirth classes:** Some of these classes serve up a
  smorgasbord of childbirth philosophies that might include
  a main course of Lamaze accompanied by a side dish of
  Bradley — or vice versa. (By the way, these "Heinz 57"
  classes are far more prevalent than any of the pure-bred
  classes we described above, so don't be surprised if your
  prenatal instructor ends up teaching you the basics about
  more than one childbirth school of thought.)

 Watch Out!

Be sure to scrutinize the credentials of a childbirth educator before you sign up
for her class. The fact that a woman has experienced childbirth herself doesn't
necessarily mean that she's qualified to teach you anything useful about giving birth. Although there's no such thing as a single Good Housekeeping Seal
of Approval when it comes to childbirth classes, some organizations do offer
the next best thing: certification programs that require childbirth instructors
to meet at least minimal standards before they are set loose on unsuspecting
parents-to-be. So be sure to inquire about the childbirth instructor's background and experience before you sign up for the class. You want to make sure
she's got the appropriate credentials to be teaching this class.

Bright Idea

Don't have time to participate in weekly childbirth classes? Consider an alternative format. Either take a weekend "crash course" that allows you to get through the entire curriculum in a single weekend; take your prenatal classes online; or think about hiring a childbirth educator to give private childbrith classes in your own home.

What should I look for when I'm sizing up my various childbirth class options?

The most important factor in the childbirth education equation is the instructor. You and your partner are going to be spending a lot of time with this person and will share details about some of the most intimate aspects of your lives with her. That's why it's important to choose this person wisely.

Basically, you should look for someone who

- has the necessary training and experience;
- has a realistic idea of what childbirth classes can and can't do for you (regardless of what some folks would have you believe, childbirth classes don't guarantee you a quick or painless labor);
- has given birth herself or, in the case of a male instructor, has played an active role in someone else's birth and therefore has firsthand knowledge of the joys and challenges of giving birth;
- is familiar with the routines at the hospital or birth center where you plan to deliver your baby or understands the steps involved in planning a home birth;
- is willing to tolerate a variety of viewpoints on such perennially hot topics as pain relief during labor, episiotomy, and circumcision.

Of course, the teacher isn't the only factor you need to consider when you're weighing the pros and cons of your various childbirth education options. You also need to consider factors such as

- the location of the classes (Are they offered in a pregnancy-friendly setting, or do you have to cram your blossoming belly into an impossibly small desk? Is the room well-ventilated and kept at a comfortable temperature, or does it bring to mind a seventeenth-century sweatshop?);

- the size of the group (no fewer than five and no more than 10 couples is ideal);

- the composition of the group (married couples versus single women, first-time mothers versus women having their second baby or subsequent babies, women in their late teens or early 20s versus women in their late 30s or early 40s, women having planned c-sections versus those planning vaginal deliveries, women who have experienced pregnancy loss versus those who haven't, women planning home versus hospital versus birth-center deliveries, and so on);

> ❝ It was good to see other soon-to-be dads who were as excited as I about being a parent. I sometimes thought I was the only goofy to-be dad in the world until I went to the class. ❞
>
> — Thomas, 31, father of one

- the cost of the classes (you can expect to pay $100 or so for a series of Lamaze or other childbirth classes, or $200 or more for Bradley classes);

- the format of the classes (Does the class seem to have the right blend of hard facts and touchy-feely stuff? Is a hospital or birthing-center tour included?);

- who is offering them (the hospital where you will be giving birth, an independent childbirth educator, and so on);

Moneysaver

Before you fork over your own cash, be sure to ask whether the cost of child-birth classes is covered by your HMO, insurance company or benefits package at work. Who knows? They might be willing to pick up the tab for you.

- whether or not there's an early-bird class (a class offered during your first or second trimester that covers important pregnancy-related lifestyle issues such as nutrition and exercise), in addition to the regular classes that are offered later in your pregnancy;

- what your caregiver thinks of these classes (assuming that he has some knowledge of the course content or the instructor's style);

- whether there is an adequate number of hours of instruction (a minimum of 10 hours of instruction, ideally spread out over a period of weeks so that you have time to absorb and practice what you've learned).

What topics should childbirth classes cover?

Make sure that the childbirth education class you sign up for covers as many of the following topics as possible:

- the physiology of pregnancy (how your body changes and why, and how you can cope with some of the common discomforts of pregnancy);

- the basic elements of prenatal care (your caregiver's role in caring for both you and your baby and the role of tests and technology during both pregnancy and labor);

- the psychological and emotional experience of giving birth;

- what's involved in delivering both vaginally and through cesarean section;

- relaxation techniques and/or breathing techniques;

- laboring positions that can reduce pain or help your labor to progress;
- the role of pain relief during labor;
- tips on getting breastfeeding off to the best possible start (assuming, of course, that you choose to breastfeed your baby);
- advice on caring for a newborn — ideally from couples who recently gave birth themselves;
- advice on choosing a pediatrician;
- the lowdown on what the postpartum period is really like;
- instruction on breastfeeding techniques;
- the pros and cons of giving birth in various childbirth settings (in a hospital, in a birth center, or at home).

The classes should also include

- the opportunity to view films or videos of actual vaginal and cesarean births so that you and your partner will be prepared for either alternative;
- the chance to tour the hospital or birth center at which you will be giving birth (assuming, of course, that you've decided to give birth in a place other than home);
- the opportunity to ask questions or express concerns you may have about pregnancy or childbirth;
- time at the end so that you can chat informally with other couples and cement friendships that could be real sanity savers during the weeks and months ahead.

 Bright Idea

Be sure to schedule your childbirth classes so that they end around your 37th week of pregnancy. If they finish much earlier than that, you might forget what you've learned when the big moment arrives. If they go much later, you could end up giving birth before you "graduate."

Watch Out!

Make sure that the childbirth philosophies of your childbirth educator mesh with those of your doctor or midwife. Otherwise, you could find yourself dealing with contradictory information and conflicting advice. The last thing you need is to have the childbirth educator undermining your confidence in your caregiver.

Other features you might want to look for include a fathers-only session (assuming your partner is into this kind of thing!) and/or a sibling preparation class (if you have other children).

Here's something else you need to know: Childbirth education classes should provide as much information and as little propaganda as possible. Rather than shoving her own views down your throat, the childbirth educator's role is to provide you with the facts and let you and your partner make your own decisions about various birthing options. Bottom line? You shouldn't be left feeling that your baby's birth was a failure because it didn't follow the childbirth educator's script to a T.

Just one more quick bit of advice before we move on: Don't decide against a particular childbirth education class simply because the instructor has chosen to de-emphasize breathing techniques. Although breathing techniques were once regarded as the key to childbirth preparation, they are now regarded as just one of many tools a pregnant woman and her partner should have in their labor bag. To a woman in labor, an understanding of relaxation techniques, the support of a caring partner, and an overall feeling of confidence in her ability to give birth are every bit as important as breathing techniques.

Are childbirth classes really worth it? My partner isn't convinced and I have my doubts, too.

For whatever reason, the average father-to-be finds childbirth classes to be about as fulfilling and exciting as a typical bridal shower. Even fathers-to-be who are totally involved in their partners' pregnancies sometime find the classes a little hard to take:

"The classes were a little too touchy-feely, and it sometimes became more of a support group than a way to gather information," admits John, 44, a second-time father.

Not all fathers feel this way, however. Some actually get more out of the classes than their partners: "We took childbirth classes once a week for six weeks. I didn't think they were worthwhile, but my partner thinks he definitely got something out of them," says Molly, 29, who recently gave birth to her first child.

And as for the advantages of taking childbirth classes, many couples have fond memories of the times they spent preparing for the birth of their baby: "My husband and I took childbirth classes together," recalls Brenda, 34, a mother of one. "Because of the classes, we had a better idea of what to expect, and my husband was able to coach me through labor with the breathing techniques we learned."

Meeting other parents is another big perk. "The best thing about Lamaze class is meeting other parents-to-be," insists Jennie, 30, who is currently pregnant with her first child. "We exchange information about pediatricians and plan to spend some park time together when our babies are born. And it's great to have others to commiserate with!"

And, of course, the classes definitely have their lighter moments, too. This is what Lisa, 27, had to say about the classes she and her husband took before their baby was born eight months ago: "At one point, the instructor asked everyone in the class to lie down on the floor with their partners, and then she turned out the lights. She played a record of what was supposed to be relaxing music with a commentator's voice explaining the breathing techniques. My husband and I could not stop laughing. We were trying so hard not to disturb the other people in the class, but we just couldn't help ourselves. Before long, we had everyone in the class cracking up."

If there's a universal benefit to attending childbirth classes, it's this, says Allison, 27, a mother of one: "Childbirth classes helped me to realize that the birth was coming soon, and that

I'd better get to planning. They helped my husband because it made it seem more 'real' to him that we were actually having a baby."

Week 21

Now that you're into the second half of your pregnancy, you may find that you get hit with a bit of wanderlust — an urge to do a bit of traveling before baby arrives. Or you may be hit with the opposite urge — a desire to switch into homebody mode and stay as close to home as possible for the duration of your pregnancy.

What's going on with your baby

Your baby is now just over 7 inches long from crown to rump and about 10 inches from crown to heel (roughly half the length he or she will be at birth). Your baby is still a relative featherweight, however; he or she still weighs just over 10 ounces. That's why, from this point onward in pregnancy, your baby will focus more on gaining weight than growing in length; she'll double her length but increase her weight by approximately 12 times.

What's going on with your body

Your waistline is but a far-distant memory and you may even be starting to notice the odd stretch mark. You're also likely to notice that you feel hot all the time — the result of the metabolic changes of pregnancy.

What's going on with your head

It's easy to go overboard in the guilt department when you're pregnant: you down a huge cup of decaf with great gusto, only to discover to your dismay after the fact that the decaf wasn't really decaf after all; or you breathe in a lungful of window cleaner or second-hand cigarette smoke, and then worry about the potentially harmful effects on your baby.

While it's noble to want to provide your baby with the ideal womb environment during the first nine months of his life, it's important to remember that you're a human being — not a petri dish — and that it's impossible to steer clear of every potential hazard. What matters is that you make the healthiest possible choices as often as you can — and then ease up on the mommy guilt. You won't be doing yourself or your baby any favors if you turn pregnancy into a nine-month-long apprenticeship in the art of feeling guilty about anything and everything.

The Hot List: This week's must-ask pregnancy questions

The second trimester is the perfect time for travel. You're likely to be free of the nausea and fatigue that may have made first-trimester travel a less-than-appealing proposition, and yet your pregnancy hasn't progressed to the point where you have to start worrying about giving birth out of town (that is, in most cases: If your pregnancy is high-risk, even second trimester travel may be ill-advised). Here's what you need to know about travel during pregnancy.

Is it safe to fly during pregnancy?

The American College of Obstetricians and Gynecologists' guidelines on travel during pregnancy state that "in the absence of medical or obstetric complications, air travel is safe up to 36 weeks." Not every mom-to-be should necessarily be planning to fly during pregnancy, however. Your doctor or midwife will

 Watch Out!

If you have heart problems that may lead to increases in heart rate and blood pressure while flying, you may need to bring a supply of supplemental oxygen along with you on the flight. Talk to your doctor about your oxygen needs while flying.

likely encourage you to rethink your plans to fly if you are at risk for preterm delivery, you have poorly controlled diabetes, or you have been diagnosed with placental abnormalities.

Note: There's no need to worry about a lack of oxygen when you're flying in a commercial aircraft. According to the American College of Obstetricians and Gynecologists, such planes are fully pressurized, which means that the air inside the cabin has more oxygen than the air outside. Many small planes aren't pressurized, however, so it's best to avoid altitudes higher of 7,000 feet if you're flying in a small plane.

Here are some important health and safety tips to keep in mind if you'll be flying during pregnancy:

- Avoid flying during the last month of pregnancy, when the risk of labor is greatest (and when many airlines may refuse to allow you to travel, with or without a doctor's certificate).

- Don't travel to areas where it may be difficult to obtain proper medical care.

- Avoid destinations that involve a significant change in altitude, or in which good, clean drinking water is in chronically short supply. If you end up traveling to a Third-World country, drink bottled water (and cook with boiled water) rather than gambling on the safety of the local water supply. You should even use bottled water to brush your teeth.

 Bright Idea

If you will be traveling out of town during your pregnancy, ask your doctor or midwife if you can take a copy of your prenatal record along. That way, if you run into complications, the attending physician will have some idea of how your pregnancy has been progressing to date. And be sure to keep your doctor's name and telephone number handy, in case you need this information while you're traveling.

Bright Idea

Traveling abroad? Call the Centers for Disease Control and Prevention's International Traveler's Hotline (1-404-332-4559) for up-to-date safety tips and vaccination information for various countries. You may also want to read the CDC's Pregnancy, Breastfeeding, and Travel bulletin, available online at www.cdc.gov/travel/pregnant.htm.

- Ensure that your immunizations are up-to-date — or talk to your doctor about what you should do if they're not.

- Keep your options open. Problems can arise at any point during pregnancy (although, fortunately, most women experience relatively low-risk pregnancies), so you'll want to make sure that you take out cancellation insurance on any airplane tickets, just in case you're unable to make the trip.

- Cancel your trip if you are experiencing cramping or bleeding, unless your caregiver is aware of your symptoms and has given you the go-ahead to travel anyway.

- Carry a copy of your medical records with you, and keep your doctor's name and telephone number handy.

- To avoid any potentially costly surprises, make sure that your health insurance will be valid while you're traveling and that it will cover your baby, should you give birth unexpectedly.

- Ask your doctor or your health insurance company to pass along the name and phone number of a doctor that you can get in touch with if you need medical care during your trip.

- Wear support stockings to prevent any fluid from accumulating in your legs and make a point of getting up and moving around to help decrease the amount of swelling in your ankles and your feet. Moving around will also help to prevent blood clots. (Note: This latter bit of advice is given to all airline passengers these days, not just to pregnant women, so don't feel unduly panicked by this particular recommendation.)

■ Get up and move around at least once an hour, if flying conditions allow for it. Not only will this help to lessen the odds that you will develop a blood clot, but moving around at regular intervals will help to decrease the amount of swelling in your ankles and feet.

Are airport security checks safe?

That's one travel-related worry you can strike off your worry list right away: the metal detectors at the airport won't pose any risk to you or your baby.

What are the keys to staying comfortable when you're flying during pregnancy?

There's no doubt about it: it can be quite a challenge to try to stay comfortable if you find yourself packed into an airline seat like a pregnant sardine. Here are some tips on coping with airline travel during pregnancy:

■ Try to book an aisle seat so that you can stretch your legs and make those inevitable treks to the washroom as easily as possible.

■ Try to snap up a seat near the front of the plane, where the ride tends to be little smoother.

■ Drink plenty of fluids to avoid dehydration.

■ Carry a healthy snack with you so you won't have to go hungry — or rely on airline pretzels for nourishment — if your flight is unexpectedly delayed.

Are seat belts recommended when you're traveling by car during pregnancy?

Seat belts provide important protection to you and your baby. It's not enough to rely on an airbag for protection. Airbags are designed to work with seat belts, not replace them, and — in the event of an accident — a pregnant woman who is not wearing a seatbelt could be thrown into a rapidly opening air bag, something that could be harmful or even fatal to her and her baby.

Here are some tips on buckling up safely during pregnancy:

- Make sure that the shoulder belt is positioned between your breasts and away from your neck. Don't place the shoulder belt behind your back or under your arm.

- Make sure that the lap belt is positioned snugly across your hips and pelvis and below your belly. If the belt is too loose or too high, it could result in broken ribs or injuries to your belly. Just don't assume that means you'd be better off without the seat belt. If you can sustain those kinds of injuries with a seat belt on, just imagine how hard you and your baby would hit the dashboard or the steering wheel if you weren't wearing that seat belt.

- Try to keep your seat at least 10 inches back from the dashboard.

 Watch Out!

Don't turn your airbags off just because you're pregnant. Research has shown that the benefits of airbags outweigh the risks. And if you *do* happen to get involved in a car accident — even a seemingly minor fender-bender — get in touch with your doctor or midwife right away. She'll want to give you and your baby a quick checkup.

Watch Out!

If you're traveling by bus or train, hold on to railings or seat backs while you're making your way to and from the washroom while the bus or train is moving. Your balance is already a little off when you're pregnant, so you'll need to take extra care to avoid taking a tumble.

Week 22

As your baby and your belly continue to grow, you may find yourself worrying about taking a tumble and wondering if it's okay to give into any pregnancy cravings you may be experiencing.

What's going on with your baby

The amniotic fluid that your baby is floating in is replenished on a regular basis. In fact, approximately one-third of the amniotic fluid volume is exchanged every hour. Here's how it works: Your baby swallows amniotic fluid and some of this fluid is absorbed back into your body via the umbilical cord and placenta. The rest is simply urinated back into the amniotic fluid. (Yes, your baby is in the habit of drinking his or her own "bathwater"!)

Note: While your baby receives some nutrients via this amniotic fluid "cocktail," the placenta meets the bulk of her nutritional needs before birth.

What's going on with your body

You may find that lying on your back causes you to become extremely lightheaded. This is because this position places the entire weight of your uterus on the aorta (the artery that carries blood from the heart to the rest of your body) and the inferior vena cava (the vein that carries blood from the lower body back to the heart), something that can cause low blood pressure.

To avoid this problem, you'll want to start sleeping on your side (sleeping on your belly is out of the question, after all!) and to use a semireclined or side-lying position when you're doing floor exercises. (See Chapter 6 for more on prenatal fitness.)

What's going on with your head

While you may have been thrilled initially by all the attention that your pregnancy attracted, by this stage of the game, the novelty of being the center of attention may be starting to wear off. And if there's one thing that is likely to be driving you completely up the wall, it's random belly pats from complete strangers. People who would never dare to grab any other part of your body without your permission may tend to view your growing belly as public property and feel well within their rights to offer unsolicited belly pats.

The best way to cope with this particular invasion of your privacy (to say nothing of your personal space!) is to stare down the belly-patter and to firmly remove her hand. If you're reluctant to take a stand for fear of offending the offender, simply remind yourself that she didn't stop to consider whether or not she might end up offending you and that you will be doing the other mamas-to-be of the world a major favor if you can stop at least one belly-patter in her tracks.

The Hot List: This week's must-ask pregnancy questions

It's only natural to want to protect your baby against any sort of accident — major or minor. This week's Hot List tackles your worries related to car accidents and falls. And because your growing appetite may be causing you to want to eat everything but the kitchen sink, we're going to talk about the ins and outs of managing food cravings, too.

What are the risks to my baby if — heaven forbid — I were involved in a car crash?

Your baby is well protected in the event of all but the most serious of car accidents. Generally, there is only cause for concern if the steering wheel or airbag hits your belly; if the impact is severe (in which case there's a risk of a placental abruption); or if you are seriously injured in the accident.

While the majority of moms and babies walk away from minor car accidents completely unscathed, it's always best to err on the side of caution by getting in touch with your doctor or midwife. Your healthcare provider may want to arrange to give you and your baby a quick checkup to confirm that all is well.

> 66 When I was pregnant with my daughter, I was in a car accident. Every part of my body was bruised and cut and battered except my tummy where the baby was. I had an ultrasound to make sure everything was okay. It was. I saw two arms, two legs, and a heartbeat. I didn't know who she was yet, but it was a great relief to see that she was fine. 99
>
> — Nancy, 31, mother of three

How much protection does my uterus provide my baby if I should trip and fall?

Fortunately, quite a lot. Not only do the bones of your pelvis provide a measure of protection, the muscles that line the wall of your uterus help to keep your baby safe, as does the "cushion" of amniotic fluid that Mother Nature saw fit to provide. There's generally only reason to worry if you experience severe abdominal pain, contractions, bleeding, or a leakage of some amniotic fluid, or if you notice a decrease in fetal movement after your fall. In such a situation, you would want to get in touch with your doctor or midwife immediately to arrange for a thorough checkup.

I've been craving fudge brownie sundaes. What's the deal with this?

There's considerable debate about whether there's a biological basis to food cravings or whether they're more likely to be triggered by the same sort of psychological factors that can trigger emotional eating in nonpregnant women, but regardless of what causes them, it's important to know how to manage them. After all, if you treat yourself to a fudge brownie sundae per day, you could be left with a lot of extra weight to lose after your give birth. That's not to say that you can't treat yourself occasionally, but what you want to avoid is using pregnancy as a 40-week license to overindulge.

Here are some tips on handling cravings:

▪ Ask yourself if food is what you're really craving. Are you really hungry or are you craving something else — like sleep or water. Studies have shown that food is often used as a substitute for sleep and that sometimes when we think we're hungry, we're actually thirsty. (For some reason, when our bodies are slightly dehydrated, we can get our signals crossed and think we need food when what our bodies really need is water.)

▪ Ask yourself if something healthier than a fudge brownie sundae will do as a substitute. If an oatmeal cookie and a glass of milk sounds like it would fit the bill, then have that instead. But if nothing on the planet but a fudge brownie sundae is going to satisfy this particular craving, consider treating yourself to the fudge brownie sundae today — and then declaring a fudge brownie sundae moratorium for the next week (of whatever you think you can reasonably live with).

▪ Don't make it too easy for yourself to give into your cravings. If you keep ice cream, brownies, and fudge sauce in your house, your fudge brownie sundae habit can easily become a nightly indulgence. But if you have to drive

across town to the local ice cream shop to get your fix, you
may be less inclined to overindulge your fudge brownie
sundae cravings. (Well, at least in theory. . . .)

Just the facts

- Try not to be unduly alarmed if your caregiver tells you
  that you are measuring large or measuring small for your
  dates. Not every baby follows the fetal growth curve to a T.

- Untreated bacterial vaginosis and untreated urinary
  tract infections increase your odds of going into labor
  prematurely.

- Look for childbirth classes that are low on propaganda
  and high on content.

- While most women can travel safely during pregnancy,
  there are a few exceptions. Ask your doctor or midwife
  if you're a good candidate for travel during pregnancy,
  or if you'd be better off staying a little closer to home.

- Don't hit the panic button if you accidentally take a
  tumble. Your body is designed to provide your baby with
  plenty of protection against minor mishaps.

GET THE SCOOP ON. . .

What's going on with your baby ▪ What's going on with your body ▪ What's going on with your head ▪ Fetal movement ▪ Gestational diabetes ▪ Preterm labor ▪ Prenatal depression ▪ Maternity leave ▪ Hiring a doula ▪ Choosing your baby's doctor

The Sixth Month: The Waiting Game

Chapter 10

The late second trimester tends to be a time of quiet introspection: a chance to take stock of all the remarkable physical and emotional changes that you have experienced to date and to get psyched for the roller-coaster ride of late pregnancy, birth, and early motherhood.

In this chapter, we zero in on the issues that are most likely to be on your mind as the second trimester draws to a close, including keeping track of your baby's movements, screening for gestational diabetes and preterm labor, spotting the warning signs of prenatal depression, and choosing your baby's doctor.

And, as in chapters past, we also give you an idea of what to expect on a week-by-week basis — this time for weeks 23 through 27. You'll get the inside scoop on what's going on with your body, what's going on with your head, and what's going on with your baby each week, as well as answers to some of the most-asked pregnancy questions for each week of pregnancy.

Week 23

Your baby's movements are likely to be a lot more noticeable than they were a few weeks ago, when you first felt those initial butterflylike flutters. You may find yourself becoming increasingly preoccupied with your pregnancy — tuning out in the middle of a meeting with your boss because your baby suddenly decided to do a flip-flop, or forgetting what it was you went to the grocery store to pick up because you're just so happy to be pregnant. (It sounds kind of sickening, but it's true. This is the point in pregnancy when that whole blissful mama-to-be thing really kicks in.)

What's going on with your baby

If you could see inside your uterus right now, you'd notice that your baby's eyes are very large and bulbous at this stage of fetal development. This is because your baby's face is still quite skinny. Once your baby starts gaining some weight in her face, she won't look quite so "bug-eyed." (Despite the fact that your pregnancy is more than halfway finished, your baby still only weighs about a pound.)

What's going on with your body

You may find yourself experiencing some sharp pains down the sides of your abdomen as your uterine muscles stretch. These pains — which may remind you of the pains you used to get after running around the track in high school gym class! — can totally freak you out if you don't know that they are perfectly normal at this stage of pregnancy.

What's going on with your head

You may feel like you belong to an international sisterhood of pregnant women — something that may cause you to smile and nod at every mama-to-be that you pass on the street. After all, whether or not you've actually spent any time with any of these women, you share a powerful bond — the fact that you're each expecting a baby.

You will likely find that this bond intensifies after you give birth — that whenever you lock eyes with another new mom in the doctor's office or the grocery store, you can't help but exchange knowing looks (and perhaps birth stories and phone numbers, too). Motherhood makes for pretty powerful relationship glue, after all. Many a friendship has been forged during heartfelt discussions over breastfeeding challenges or colic!

The Hot List: This week's must-ask pregnancy questions

As you head into month six, you may be wondering about fetal movement counts and what to expect from this month's prenatal checkup.

What should I expect from this month's prenatal checkup?

At this month's prenatal visit, you can expect your doctor or midwife to check

- **the fundal height** (your healthcare provider will measure the distance between your pubic bone and the top of your uterus — the fundus)

- **your weight** (to see if you are continuing to gain weight slowly)

- **your blood pressure** (to spot any early warning signs of pregnancy-related hypertension or preeclampsia)

- **your urine** (to ensure that your sugar and protein levels are within the normal range as they, too, can provide early warning of any emerging problems)

- **the fetal heart rate** (to keep tabs on your baby's general health and well-being). Note: Your baby's heart beats much more rapidly than your own — at a rate of 120 to

160 beats per minute on average. So don't be concerned that there may be something wrong with your baby if the fetal heart rate seems alarmingly high. It's normal for a baby's heart to beat much more rapidly than an adult's.

- **iron level** (to check for signs of anemia). It is fairly common practice to test for iron deficiency at this stage of pregnancy. Although you might have entered pregnancy with healthy hemoglobin (the substance that carries oxygen in the blood) and hematocrit readings (the concentration of red blood cells in the blood), you could be anemic by now. This is because anemia can be caused by either (1) the dilutional effect of the expanded blood volume that can outpace the growth of red blood cells in a pregnant woman's body, or (2) an inadequate intake of iron.

- Rh antibody screen (for Rh-negative women with Rh-positive partners — See Chapter 17 for a detailed discussion on Rhesus disease)

- HIV screen (some states recommend a third-trimester HIV screen in addition to a first-trimester HIV screen).

Note: Your doctor or midwife may also decide to screen you for gestational diabetes or risk factors for preterm labor (see the discussions under Week 24) at this stage of pregnancy.

When is fetal movement counting (e.g., keeping a kick chart) recommended?

You've no doubt heard a lot of talk about the value of fetal movement counting in assessing fetal well-being. Unfortunately, it isn't quite as simple as some people would have you believe. Here are the three key problems:

- Some pregnant women don't experience fetal movement as consistently as other women (or even as they themselves experience on other occasions), either because the baby's movements aren't consistent or because their perceptions of those movements aren't consistent. (It tends to be an inexact science at the best of times.)

- The quality and strength of fetal movements vary as pregnancy progresses and as the relative ratios of amniotic fluid to baby size change.

- Studies using ultrasound to observe the movements of fetuses have shown that women typically feel fewer than half of fetal movements, even when they are consciously trying to feel them and the baby is awake and actively moving.

- The third-trimester sleep-wake cycle of the fetus (30 minutes awake and 30 minutes asleep) makes it easy for an expectant mother to miss her baby's active time. If she is working, if she is busy with other children, or if her attention is otherwise diverted during her baby's active period, she may fail to perceive any movement. Likewise, if she does her fetal movement counting when the baby is sleeping, she won't detect any movement.

Despite these limitations, fetal movement counting does have a role to play in prenatal care. In some cases, it can serve as an early warning signal that the baby may be encountering problems inside the womb.

If you are concerned that you are not feeling enough fetal movement, you might want to practice fetal movement counting at the start of the day (see Figure 10.1).

To use this chart, you simply count fetal movements from the time you wake up in the morning until you have experienced 10 movements. Then, record the time at which the 10th movement is felt each day on the chart. This will help you to determine what pattern is normal for your baby and to notice if there is a significant deviation from that pattern — in which case, you would want to notify your caregiver that there could be a possible problem.

Day of the Week	Start Time	1	2	3	4	5	6	7	8	9	10	Finish
Monday													
Tuesday													
Wednesday													
Thursday													
Friday													
Saturday													
Sunday													

Figure 10-1. Fetal Movement Counting Chart.

Even if you don't want to practice fetal movement counting on a daily basis (if, for example, you're concerned that a daily routine of fetal movement counting might make you overly anxious), you can still use fetal movement counting as a tool to detect potential problems. Here's how: If you happen to notice that you've felt less than two fetal movements over the course of an hour, spend the next hour lying on your side or sitting in a recliner with a glass of fruit juice and focusing on your baby's movements. If there are still fewer than two movements in the subsequent hour, then your caregiver should be notified. Odds are your baby will be fine — just sleepy — but it's always best to check these things out.

Sometimes I feel these sudden jerky movements. Is there something wrong with my baby?

It sounds like your baby may be prone to the hiccups, as many babies are before birth. Scientists have observed babies hiccuping in the womb, starting as early as two months postconception. You may be surprised by the strength of your baby's hiccups and by how long some of these episodes can last. While most episodes of hiccuping only last for a couple of minutes, some episodes can last for 30 minutes or longer.

> **❝** I heard my baby's heartbeat during the second trimester, and things really hit home that I was having a baby. **❞**
>
> —Jennifer, a 28-year-old mother of one

While there's still considerable debate about the evolutionary purpose of these hiccups, a group of scientists in Paris believes that hiccuping may help to develop some of the motor patterns a baby will need for nursing and swallowing after birth.

Week 24

You're likely to be continuing to feel well at this stage of pregnancy — marveling at your increasingly maternal curves and reflecting on the tiny miracle that's unfolding inside the womb.

What's going on with your baby

That's one smart and "well-connected" baby you're carrying. Researchers at the University of Chicago have discovered that there are 124 million neural connections in each pinhead-sized piece of brain tissue inside the brain of a 24-week-old fetus.

What's going on with your body

Your heart is working a whole lot harder than it did before you became pregnant. (This only makes sense. After all, your heart is now pumping for two!) Your resting heart rate increases by about 10 beats per minute during pregnancy, so don't be alarmed if you notice that your doctor or midwife has recorded a higher-than-normal resting heart rate for you on your prenatal health record.

What's going on with your head

You may find yourself worrying about your baby's well-being — possibly even having nightmares that there could be something terribly wrong with your baby. If you have one of these dreams (which, by the way, can be extremely frightening and upsetting), don't interpret your dream as some sort of super-spooky premonition. These types of dreams are very common during pregnancy — your unconscious mind's attempt to work through some of your fears and anxieties surrounding your pregnancy and the upcoming birth. In the vast majority of cases, women who experience these disturbing types of dreams end up giving birth to perfectly healthy babies.

The Hot List: This week's must-ask pregnancy questions

Has your doctor or midwife recommended that you be screened for gestational diabetes? Here are answers to some of the most frequently asked questions about the gestational diabetes screening process.

My doctor is screening me for gestational diabetes, but other pregnant women I know are not being asked to go for the screening test. What's up with that?

Gestational diabetes — also known as gestational glucose intolerance — is caused by the hormonal and metabolic changes of pregnancy. It occurs in 2 percent to 10 percent of pregnant women and needs to be managed carefully in order to ensure the continued good health of both mother and baby.

Some doctors and midwives make a point of routinely screening all pregnant women for gestational diabetes. They do so because the screening test is readily available and the disease can be difficult to diagnose without the test (half of pregnant women with gestational diabetes don't exhibit any of the classic risk factors). Other doctors and midwives choose to screen only those women who have one or more of the following risk factors:

- age 25 or older
- member of an ethnic group with a high prevalence of diabetes (Hispanic, African, Native American, South or East Asian, or Pacific Islands ancestry)
- gestational diabetes in a previous pregnancy
- obesity
- family history of diabetes
- having previously given birth to a very large baby (over 9 pounds) or a baby who was stillborn

So whether or not you get the test is sometimes a simple matter of your choice of caregiver and whether or not he or she routinely screens pregnant women for gestational diabetes; and other times it can be a more specific indication of your individual health risk factors.

How does the gestational diabetes screening test work?

The glucose screening test — which is usually performed between 24 and 28 weeks of pregnancy — involves drinking a glucose solution (a super-sugary drink that tastes like an overly sweet bottle of orange soda or cola). With this test, there is no need to fast overnight or to skip or delay a meal. After an hour, a blood sample is taken and your glucose level is measured. The results of the test indicate whether you face an above-average risk of having gestational diabetes.

What's the difference between the glucose screening test and the glucose tolerance test?

A glucose screening test is designed to let you know if you face a higher-than-average risk of having gestational diabetes while the glucose tolerance test is designed to provide a definitive diagnosis — in other words, to tell you whether or not you have gestational diabetes. Approximately 15 percent of pregnant women who take the glucose screening test obtain an abnormal result on the test, but only about 15 percent of women who receive an abnormal result on the glucose screening test and who go on to take the glucose tolerance test are actually found to have gestational diabetes. (Note: You may want to flip ahead and read our discussion of the difference between screening tests and diagnostic tests in Chapter 14.)

What does the glucose tolerance test involve?

If your doctor or midwife orders a glucose tolerance test for you, you will be asked to fast the night before the test (that is, to not eat or drink anything for at least eight hours prior to the test). Then, after a blood test has been taken to measure your fasting level of blood sugar, you'll be asked to drink a beverage with an extremely high concentration of glucose. Once you've swallowed the beverage, the clock starts ticking. A series of blood tests are taken over a three-hour period to measure your blood sugar levels. Generally, if the fasting blood sugar level is high or two out of three of the post-glucose-drink blood sugars are high, the test result is considered abnormal.

A fair number of pregnant women report that drinking such a sugary beverage on an empty stomach leaves them feeling somewhat queasy. A handful of pregnant women are unable to stomach the beverage at all. There are alternatives to drinking the beverage (e.g., eating servings of food sources of sugar, for example), so if you find that the test makes you ill, your doctor or midwife will find a way to work around the problem.

How is gestational diabetes managed during pregnancy?

If you are diagnosed with gestational diabetes, you will need to follow a special diet (typically 2,200 to 2,400 calories per day, made up of 45 percent carbohydrates, 25 percent protein, and 30 percent fat) and you may need to have frequent blood tests to monitor your blood sugar levels. A small percentage of women will require insulin to control their blood sugar level. Your doctor may also decide to perform nonstress tests (tests that are designed to monitor your baby's well-being) during your last few weeks of pregnancy to monitor your baby's health in the womb and one or more ultrasound tests to assess fetal growth, although the value of these procedures in women with well-controlled gestational diabetes has not been proven. Note: You can find out more about gestational diabetes by reading Chapter 16.

Week 25

You may find that your pregnancy complaints change from week to week as certain problems that were bothersome at one stage of pregnancy fall off the aches-and-pains radar screen only to be replaced by some new pregnancy complaint. (Hey, if there's one thing you can say about being pregnant, it's this: You rarely have a chance to get bored!)

What's going on with your baby

Your baby is busy working on mastering the art of breathing — rhythmically inhaling and exhaling amniotic fluid to give her breathing muscles an important prebirth workout.

Oddly enough, your baby doesn't do her breathing exercises while she's wide awake. She does her workout in her sleep — literally. Studies have shown that the only time that the fetus breathes amniotic fluid in and out is during REM sleep.

Your baby now weighs in at about 1.5 pounds and measures about 9 inches from crown to rump.

What's going on with your body

Feel like you're walking on pins and needles — literally? That numb sensation in your hands and feet may be caused by the added fluid in your body pressing on nerve endings.

While it can be disconcerting and annoying to have your hands and feet taking impromptu naps on you, there's no need to become concerned that you've developed some sort of serious circulation problem. This is simply one of those strange pregnancy complaints that can arise during pregnancy. The problem will go away on its own after you give birth and your fluid levels return to normal.

What's going on with your head

You may be wondering about your odds of going into labor prematurely and of giving birth to a preterm baby. This particular worry is most likely to show up on your worry list if you have a friend or family member who has given birth prematurely in the past or if you are believed to be at risk of a preterm birth (e.g., you are carrying multiples), but it's not unusual for women who are considered at low risk of giving birth prematurely to worry about this, too.

The best way to cope with this particular worry is to arm yourself with the facts. Talk to your doctor or midwife about your specific risk factors and find out if there's anything out of the ordinary you should be doing to reduce your risk of a preterm birth. If your healthcare provider doesn't feel that you're at any particular risk, simply focus on leading a baby-friendly lifestyle and knock this particular worry down to the bottom of your worry list until you have reason to give it star billing. It may not even be an issue for you.

> 66 For me, the first trimester was a total breeze—a fact that I wasn't expecting because everyone told me it's one of the most difficult. So when I was barely into the second trimester, I wasn't expecting to suddenly be hit with such a big physical change. I kept trying to do everything like I always had, assuming I had the energy reserves I've always had, and that I could handle the massive stress of work, get seven hours of sleep, keep my house clean during the week, and still be a nice spouse (oh yeah, and keep up a regular exercise schedule). I pretty much worked myself up into a state of panic before my doctor told me to get more sleep and lay off the exercise for a few weeks. 99
>
> —Wendy, 30, mother of one

The Hot List: This week's must-ask pregnancy questions

Depending on your reproductive history, your doctor or midwife may decide to screen you for preterm labor. Here are the answers to some of the most frequently asked questions about screening for preterm labor.

Who should be screened for preterm labor?

Preterm birth — the birth of a baby before the start of the 37th week of pregnancy — occurs in approximately 10 percent of all pregnancies and accounts for 60 percent to 75 percent of all infant health problems and deaths. Studies have shown that 50 percent of cases of preterm birth are caused by premature rupture of the membranes and 20 percent by other maternal fetal complications.

If you've previously given birth to a premature baby, your doctor or midwife is likely to recommend that you be screened for preterm labor this time around. This is because women who have given birth prematurely are three times as likely to give birth to another premature baby as other mothers-to-be (15 percent risk versus 5 percent risk). The risk increases with the number of consecutive preterm births: a woman who has experienced two premature births in a row has a 32-percent chance of giving birth prematurely during her next pregnancy.

What types of tests are used to predict a woman's risk of giving birth prematurely?

Four types of tests are used to predict which pregnant women are at increased risk of going into labor prematurely:

- checking cervical length (women with shorter than average cervixes are at increased risk of experiencing premature labor);

- screening for bacterial vaginosis and treating affected women with oral antibiotics (women who have bacterial vaginosis — an abundance of a variety of vaginal bacteria that is often, but not always, associated with a thin, milky discharge and fishy odor — are at increased risk of experiencing preterm labor);

- premature rupture of membranes, and/or preterm birth;

- or administering the fetal fibronectin (fFN) test or the salivary estriol test (see the following for information on these two tests).

What is the fetal fibronectin test?

The fetal fibronectin test (fFN) is a diagnostic test used to predict a woman's risk of experiencing preterm labor. Similar to a Pap smear, the test is performed when a woman is 24 to 34 weeks pregnant and experiencing some of the symptoms of preterm labor. The test can be performed if a woman's membranes are still intact and cervical dilation is minimal (that is, less than 3 centimeters). Because the test is relatively expensive ($200), it is not routinely offered to every pregnant woman. Note: You can learn more about this test at the March of Dimes Web site: www.marchofdimes.com/professionals/681_1149.asp.

What is the salivary estriol test?

The salivary estriol test — its brand name is SalEst — is a saliva test that is performed between 22 and 36 weeks of pregnancy. It is primarily used to rule out the likelihood of premature labor in women who would otherwise be considered high risk. It is considered to be 98 percent accurate in identifying those who are not at high risk for delivering prematurely but only 9 percent to 20 percent accurate in pinpointing those who are. The test costs less than $100.

Week 26

You may be doing some serious navel-gazing at this stage of pregnancy — and wondering whether your "popped" belly button means that your baby's nearly cooked. (Sorry, your belly button doesn't work like a turkey tester. Chances are you've still got another three months to go.)

What's going on with your baby

At this stage of pregnancy, your baby acquires a special layer of fat that is designed to help keep her warm during the early weeks after the birth. This fat — known as "brown fat" because of its brownish color — is laid down at the nape of the neck, around the kidneys, and behind the breastbone. It's a special kind of fat that produces heat and acts as an insulator and that can be found in both newborn babies and hibernating animals.

What's going on with your body

Your belly button may "pop" — if it hasn't already — around this point in your pregnancy, something that may leave you wondering if you're doomed to sport an "outie" for the rest of your life. As you might expect, pressure from your expanding uterus is to blame for these belly button changes.

> 66 During the second trimester, the hormone attacks began to hit. The slightest thing would set me off. When it did, I'd bawl for hours, often uncontrollably for no reason at all. 99
>
> —Christy, 25, mother of one

After you give birth and your uterus shrinks back to its prepregnancy size, your belly button will revert back to its usual position, but — after all the stretching your belly button experienced during the nine months of pregnancy — you may find that it's slightly stretched and a little less taut than it was in your pre-baby days. (Depending on how much weight you gain and how diligent you are about hitting the gym again after the birth, other parts of your body may suffer the same fate, but in a less dramatic way. For whatever reason, many women find that the belly button seems to bear the brunt of the bodily changes. Ah, motherhood!)

What's going on with your head

While most women find that the wild mood swings that tend to make the first trimester such a challenge are less of an issue during the second trimester, this isn't necessarily the case for every mama-to-be. Depending on what else is going on in your life, you could be feeling euphoric one moment and downright weepy the next.

While mood swings tend to be part of the pregnancy experience for most pregnant women, there may be cause for concern if your mood swings are extreme or if they are interfering with your enjoyment of your pregnancy and your life.

The "Hot List" section which follows should help you to differentiate between garden variety prenatal moodiness and bona fide prenatal depression.

The Hot List: This week's must-ask pregnancy questions

Wondering where mood swings end and prenatal depression begins? Here are answers to some of the most frequently asked questions about depression during pregnancy.

How common is prenatal depression?

Much more common than most people believe. A group of researchers at Bristol University in England recently concluded that depression during pregnancy may occur even more frequently than postpartum depression, even though postpartum depression is much more talked about. The researchers found that while 9.1 percent of the 9,000 women involved in the study met the criteria for depression eight weeks after delivery, 13.5 percent met the criteria for depression at 32 weeks of pregnancy.

A second study at the University of Michigan concluded that approximately one in five pregnant women is depressed, but that only 13.8 percent of these women were receiving counseling, drugs, or other treatments. The researchers concluded that pregnant women may resist seeking treatment for depression during pregnancy because they may incorrectly conclude that

 Watch Out!

A recent study conducted at the University of California's Neuropsychiatric Institute and Hospital found that infants of mothers who were depressed for more than two months tended to gain weight much more slowly during the first six weeks after birth than other infants. The researchers suspect that severe depression may affect the feeding behaviors of mothers and that maternal depression may influence "biological variables" in breastmilk, both of which could interfere with infant weight gain.

there aren't any antidepressants that can be safely taken by an expectant mother. There are, in fact, a growing number of medications that are believed to pose little, if any risk, to the developing baby, so it's worth discussing this issue with your doctor if you think you may be experiencing some symptoms of depression (e.g., a loss in appetite, a loss of interest in activities you usually enjoy, extreme fatigue, feelings of guilt and inadequacy, or sleep disturbances). If you wish to avoid drug treatment, interpersonal therapy may be a valid option. A recent study at Columbia University in New York found that 60 percent of severely depressed women participating in a treatment program consisting of 16 weeks of psychotherapy combined with a parent-education program experienced a significant improvement in symptoms. So don't be afraid to seek out treatment just because you think that medication will be your only option. There may be alternatives.

It's important to seek treatment for the sake of both yourself and your baby if you're suffering from prenatal depression. Some studies have indicated that depression and anxiety during pregnancy may be linked to low birthweight, premature birth, reduced uterine blood flow, and stress-related changes to the fetal heart rate, and that women who become depressed during pregnancy may face an increased risk of postpartum depression. (See Chapter 19 for more on postpartum depression.)

Can dads get depressed, too?

A recent study in Australia documented what doctors and midwives have long observed in a less formal way — some dads exhibit symptoms of depression during their partners' pregnancies. Researchers at the Adelaide-based Finders Medical Centre found that anxiety about impending fatherhood combined with decreased action in the bedroom may cause 5.2 percent of men to become depressed and anxious. The researchers found that the men involved in the study tended to respond to their increased stress levels by gaining weight (3.5 pounds for an average dad!) and increasing their alcohol consumption.

Week 27

As you head into the final week of the second trimester, you may be starting to think ahead to trimester three and wondering about what lies beyond — the birth and your maternity leave.

What's going on with your baby

A 27-week-old fetus is capable of differentiating between light and dark. Scientists have observed babies in utero turning their heads the other way when a bright light is shone on their mother's belly.

What's going on with your body

You may experience some pain in your rib cage area as your ribs rise up and your lower ribs begin to spread outward to make more room for your expanding uterus and your growing baby — yet another strange-but-true, late-second-trimester pregnancy complaint.

What's going on with your head

Starting to think about your maternity leave? Your timing is bang on. The second trimester is the ideal time to plan your maternity leave. Your pregnancy is now well established, but your due date is still several months away.

When you start planning for your maternity leave, you will want to have two alternative scenarios in your head: what you will do if everything goes according to plan, and what you will do if complications arise and it is necessary for you to leave your job sooner than originally planned.

Even if you're used to being a bit of a loner, you should make an effort to keep colleagues apprised of your progress on various projects. That way, if your baby decides to make its grand entrance before opening night, you won't be caught off guard.

And here's something else you'll want to consider when you're making your maternity leave plans: just how close to delivery day you want to remain on the job. Although the conventional wisdom says that you should work right up until the moment the

> **❝**I wish someone had told me how unrealistic it was to work up until the baby was born. My thinking was that as long as I felt good, I should keep working so that I could spend my maternity leave with the baby. I worked up until the day I gave birth, went home from work, stopped at the store, and my water broke. So it was off to the hospital. I wish I had taken a week off to rest.**❞**
>
> —Kim, 35, mother of one

contractions start in order to maximize the amount of time you can spend with your baby after the birth, there's something to be said about taking some time off before your baby arrives. Consider these words of wisdom from Debby, a 37-year-old first-time mother: "I had planned to work until a week or two before my due date. On the advice of a friend, however, I stopped working almost two months before I delivered. It was a very good decision. I enjoyed the summer, took long walks, read a lot, and prepared myself emotionally for having the baby. I was very rested by the time I delivered. It was tempting to keep working to get ahead financially, but I'm very happy I made the decision to stop working early."

If you don't want to stop working very far in advance of your due date, you might consider asking your boss if you can arrange to work part time during your final weeks on the job. You might, for example, choose to arrange to put in a solid morning's work and then hit the couch in the afternoon when the urge to nap is at its strongest. Whatever work schedule you ultimately decide to propose to your boss, you should try to come up with a schedule that will allow you to be well rested when those first labor contractions begin to kick in. (Trust us, labor is tiring enough. You don't want to be totally exhausted right from the get go!)

The Hot List: This week's must-ask pregnancy questions

The late second trimester is also the ideal time to decide whether or not you'd like to hire a doula to provide labor support to you and your partner during the birth, and to start looking for a doctor to care for your baby after the birth. Here are answers to some of the questions you may have about each of these issues.

What is a doula?

You've no doubt heard a lot of talk about doulas, but you may not be totally clear about exactly doulas do. There are actually two types of doulas: birth doulas (who help couples to write a birth plan and then provide support during labor and the first few hours after the birth) and postpartum doulas (who dish up a reassuring mix of motherly advice, breastfeeding assistance, and hands-on help with household chores like cooking and cleaning during the days and weeks after baby's arrival).

Some doulas offer both types of services to their clients while others specialize in providing one or the other type of service.

What are the benefits of hiring a birth doula?

Virtually unheard of in North America until the late 1980s, doulas are now well-established players in the birthing arena — and for good reason. Research has shown that women who use the services of a doula are less likely to require pain medication during labor, a forceps delivery, a cesarean section, or to experience a prolonged labor, and they are more likely to be satisfied with their birth experience and to be nurturing toward their newborns than women who opt for doula-free deliveries.

What does it cost to have a doula attend your baby's birth and what does that fee cover?

A doula's services — which typically run between $300 and $600 — usually include

- holding one or more meetings with you and your partner to talk about your plans for the birth;
- helping you to draft your birth plan;
- making herself available by telephone to address any concerns about the birth;

- providing continuous support during labor (for example, suggesting different positions and breathing techniques that may help ease the pain of childbirth);

- providing support during the first hours or days postpartum and offering assistance with breastfeeding, if required.

Note: Doulas do not perform clinical tasks such as monitoring blood pressure, conducting fetal heart checks, and so on; and they are not trained to serve as professional birth attendants in either a home or a hospital setting.

How do I go about finding a doula and what types of questions should I ask a prospective doula?

You can locate a birth doula who is in practice in your area by getting in touch with Doulas of North America (www.dona.org; 888-788-DONA). Some hospitals are affiliated with one or more doulas or can provide a referral. Here are some of the questions you'll want to ask a prospective doula:

- Are you accredited through Doulas of North America (DONA)?

- How many births have you attended?

- What is your philosophy about chilbirth?

- What role do you see yourself playing at your baby's birth?

- Do you work with a backup doula? If so, could we meet her ahead of time?

- What services do you provide?

- Can you provide us with references?

- What are your fees?

Note: A growing number of HMOs are starting to insure doula services, and some hospitals now provide the services of a doula free of charge upon request.

How should I go about choosing a doctor for my baby?

Although you may find it a little odd to be interviewing doctors for your baby before she even arrives on the scene, this is one task that needs to be handled before the birth. After all, you need to know ahead of time who will be responsible for performing the newborn examination and the healthy-baby checkups during your child's first few weeks of life. Besides, if a medical complication arises that needs immediate attention, you will want to have had the opportunity to begin to establish some rapport with the person who will be caring for your baby.

Here are some tips on choosing a doctor or other healthcare professional to care for your baby:

- Decide whether you would like to have your baby cared for by a doctor with training in pediatrics or family medicine or by a pediatric nurse practitioner (an RN who has specialized training in caring for children and who often practices alongside a physician).

- Ask your health insurance company for a list of doctors who are covered by the plan.

- Ask other parents with young children to pass along the names of doctors whom they and their children like.

- If you're in the market for an M.D., look for a doctor who has been board-certified and who has received at least three years of specialized training in pediatrics or family medicine. (You can get this information from the receptionist at the doctor's office or by calling your state medical society.)

- Set up an initial interview with at least one doctor so that you can find out about her child-rearing and healthcare philosophies and decide whether this is the right caregiver for your child.

- Look for a doctor with a waiting room that is clean, bright, pleasant, and safe for crawling babies.

- Note how friendly and helpful the office staff appears to be. It doesn't matter how wonderful the doctor may be if the Receptionist from Hell won't put your call through.

- Find out how difficult it is to get an appointment. If you call first thing in the morning, how likely is it that the

Bright Idea

Ask if the doctor has a separate waiting area for children who have infectious diseases (for example, chickenpox) or who are seriously ill. There's nothing worse than bringing your baby in for a well-baby checkup when the waiting room is full of sick kids.

doctor will be able to see your child the same day? Does the doctor or one of his associates have any evening or weekend office hours?

- Find out how much time the doctor sets aside for each appointment. If it's less than 15 minutes, you and your child may not get the attention you both need and deserve.

- Find out how quickly the doctor is able to return phone calls both during and after office hours, and who will care for your child when she is not on call. And make sure that you understand whether there is a charge for telephone consultations so that there won't be any surprises down the road.

Just the facts

- Fetal movement counting can be a useful tool for monitoring your baby's well-being while in utero.

- A glucose screening test is designed to let you know if you face a higher-than-average risk of having gestational diabetes while the glucose tolerance test is designed to provide a definitive diagnosis — in other words, to tell you whether or not you have gestational diabetes.

- Prenatal depression is even more common than postnatal depression.

- The late second trimester is the ideal time to plan your maternity leave, decide whether or not to hire a doula, and start looking for a doctor to care for your baby after the birth.

Your Third Trimester Week-by-Week

PART IV

GET THE SCOOP ON . . .

What's going on with your baby ▪ What's going on with your body ▪ What's going on with your head ▪ Common third-trimester pregnancy complaints ▪ Shopping for baby ▪ Insomnia and breathlessness

The Seventh Month: Seriously Pregnant

By the time you reach the third trimester, the novelty of being pregnant may be starting to wear off. You may be getting tired of your maternity wardrobe, and you may be secretly wishing that friends and strangers alike would keep their comments on your size and shape to themselves! (Of course, if you haven't been troubled by many of the infamous third-trimester aches and pains or subjected to an abundance of annoying comments from well-meaning and not-so-well-meaning strangers, you may still be enjoying pregnancy as much as you did during the second trimester. In fact, you may be cherishing this very special time with your baby.)

In this chapter, we zero in on the issues that are likely to be on your mind as you head into month seven: shopping for baby, staying connected to your partner, and getting the sleep you so desperately crave. And, as was the case in chapters past, we give you an idea of what to expect on a week-by-week basis — this time for weeks 27 through 31. You'll get

Chapter 11

the inside scoop on what's going on with your body, what's going on with your head, and what's going on with your baby each week, as well as answers to some of the most-asked pregnancy questions for each week of pregnancy.

Week 28

Your baby is growing by leaps and bounds, and you are, too. Not surprisingly, you're likely to be starting to experience some of the smorgasbord of pregnancy complaints for which the third trimester is famous. (Or infamous.)

What's going on with your baby

Your baby's lungs have now started to manufacture surfactant — the detergentlike substance that prevents the lungs from sticking together and that allows them to expand and take in air — something that dramatically increases a baby's odds for survival if born prematurely. (Note: While some babies born weeks earlier survive — or even thrive — the odds of doing well outside the womb increase with each additional week of gestation.)

Your baby is now approximately 14 to 16 inches long and weighs approximately 2 ½ to 3 pounds.

What's going on with your body

By the start of the third trimester, your uterus is large and hard, your baby's movements are visible, and you may be experiencing Braxton Hicks contractions (the so-called practice contractions that prepare your body for labor).

You may continue to experience some of the aches and pains that you experienced during the first and second trimesters, but you will likely experience a few other complaints as well, including increased heartburn and indigestion — the result of your digestive organs having to share space with your increasingly large uterus and your growing baby.

What's going on with your head

You may find yourself with a million-and-one questions that fall under the "is this normal?" umbrella. You may wonder if each new pregnancy ache and pain that you experience is something that generations of pregnant women before you have experienced or if you're experiencing something that your doctor or midwife has never seen before.

The best way to reassure yourself that what you're experiencing is normal is to learn as much as you can about pregnancy by reading books like this and by visiting credible health Web sites (see "Resource Directory" — www.wiley.com/go/anndouglas — for some of our picks). And, of course, there's nothing wrong with putting in a quick call to your doctor or midwife's office to seek some much-needed reassurance. That's what your healthcare provider is there for, after all.

The Hot List: This week's must-ask pregnancy questions

This week's questions focus on this month's prenatal checkup plus some of the pregnancy-related aches and pains you can expect to experience now that you're heading into the third trimester.

What should I expect from this month's prenatal checkup?

At this month's prenatal visit, you can expect your doctor or midwife to check

- **the fundal height** (your healthcare provider will measure the distance between your pubic bone and the top of your uterus — the fundus)

- **size and position of the baby** (your doctor or midwife will assess this by placing her hands on your abdomen and feeling for the baby)

- **your weight** (to see if you are continuing to gain weight slowly)

- **your blood pressure** (to spot any early warning signs of pregnancy-related hypertension or preeclampsia)

- **your urine** (to ensure that your sugar and protein levels are within the normal range as they, too, can provide early warning of any emerging problems)

- **the fetal heart rate** (to keep tabs on your baby's general health and well-being). Reminder: Your baby's heart beats much more rapidly than your own — at a rate of 120 to 160 beats per minute on average. So don't be concerned that there may be something wrong with your baby if the fetal heart rate seems alarmingly high. It's normal for a baby's heart to beat much more rapidly than an adult's.

Your doctor or midwife will also monitor you for signs of edema (swelling) and check your legs for any signs of protruding varicose veins. Note: While varicose veins are rarely cause for concern, if you have a tender, reddened area on the surface of a varicose vein combined with fever and/or soreness in your leg, call your doctor. It's possible that you could be experiencing thrombophlebitis, a blood clot in the veins of your leg. If this is untreated, it could lead to a pulmonary embolism (a dangerous medical condition that occurs when a blood clot travels to the lungs). Note: Please see the discussion on varicose veins under Week 29's "Hot List."

My caregiver was in an accident and won't be back for the rest of my pregnancy. What should I do?

If you have to change caregivers during pregnancy, arrange to have your prenatal records forwarded to the new caregiver prior to your next appointment. Better yet, offer to hand-deliver them to the new caregiver yourself.

Week 29

You're almost three-quarters of the way through your pregnancy now. Assuming you give birth right on target, you've got just 11 weeks to go until you finally get to meet your baby.

What's going on with your baby

Your baby's hearing is keenly developed by this point in your pregnancy. She may be startled by loud noises (although there is likely to be a bit of a lag between the loud noise and her reaction).

Your baby is exposed to a symphony of sound while in the womb, including the pounding of your heart, the churning of your digestive system, and the rushing of blood through the umbilical cord. Scientists who have studied these sounds have described them as being dishwasherlike, which is why newborns can sometimes be lulled back to sleep by exposing them to dishwasher sounds and other similar types of "white noise" that may be reminiscent of womb sounds.

Your baby can also hear your voice clearly, and he's starting to recognize the voices of other family members, too.

What's going on with your body

As your skin stretches to accommodate your growing uterus, you may find that it becomes dry and itchy. Although it's difficult to get rid of your itchy belly entirely until after the birth, a good-quality moisturizing cream can provide a certain degree of comfort, so slather on the most luxurious cream you own. Your belly will thank you for this bit of pampering.

What's going on with your head

Finding it hard to sort through all the conflicting information on the pregnancy hot topic du jour? You're not alone. Information overload is a common complaint amongst pregnant women, and the problem is made all the more frustrating when your various sources of information rarely agree about anything.

If you're unsure who or what to believe or how to sort through all the pregnancy propaganda, cross-check your facts by consulting a credible source like your doctor or midwife or consulting "Resource Directory" (www.wiley.com/go/anndouglas) for leads on other helpful pregnancy sources.

The Hot List: This week's must-ask pregnancy questions

At this point in your pregnancy, you may be wondering about varicose veins, vascular spiders, skin rashes, and hemorrhoids. Here's what you need to know.

What causes varicose veins?

Varicose veins are the fine bluish, reddish, or purplish lines that show up under the skin (most often on the legs, ankles, and vulva). They are caused by a weakness in the small veins that carry blood back to the heart.

You are more likely to develop varicose veins if

- you have gained a lot of weight during your pregnancy,
- you have a family history of varicose veins,
- this is your second or subsequent pregnancy. (Note: Varicose veins tend to become worse with each pregnancy.)

Varicose veins tend to be a particular problem during pregnancy because the weight of the growing uterus places pressure on the veins passing through the pelvic region and the legs. This, combined with the fact that progesterone causes the walls of the blood vessels to relax, spells trouble for any pregnant woman with a predisposition to varicose veins.

You can prevent or ease the discomfort of varicose veins by

- not standing for prolonged periods of time;
- not sitting with your legs crossed;

- elevating your legs whenever you can;

- avoiding underwear with tight elastic around the legs or abdomen, because this may interfere with blood flow and contribute to varicose veins;

- exercising regularly to improve your overall circulation;

- wearing support stockings to help to improve the circulation in your legs. (Support stockings are designed to be tight at the ankle. They prevent the blood from pooling in your ankles and lower calves and lend support to the veins in these areas.)

In most cases, varicose veins improve after delivery when the uterus returns to its normal size, the progesterone level is no longer high, and the weight you've been carrying is reduced. If they don't improve to your satisfaction, minor surgery or light treatments will correct them.

What causes vascular spiders?

Vascular spiders — also known as spider veins — are tiny red raised lines that branch out from a particular spot on the skin in a spiderlike fashion. Appearing most often on the upper body, face, and neck, they are caused by the effects of hormones on the circulatory system. They don't cause any pain or discomfort, and they usually disappear after delivery.

My doctor just diagnosed me with pruritic urticarial papules and plaques of pregnancy (PUPP). What can you tell me about this condition?

Pruritic urticarial papules and plaques of pregnancy is a condition characterized by itchy, reddish, raised bumps or patches on the skin. Occurring in approximately 1 in every 150 pregnancies, the condition tends to run in families and usually occurs in first pregnancies. It can be treated with oral medications, anti-itching creams, and oatmeal or baking-soda baths.

I have itchy, inflammed patches of skin underneath my breasts and abdomen. Can something be done to treat this condition?

It sounds as if you are suffering from intertrigo — a red, irritating skin rash caused by a fungal infection that occurs when folds of skin are in close contact, preventing the normal evaporation of sweat. It is more common in women who are overweight, and it tends to be localized to the area under the breasts and the groin area. It is treated with antifungal cream.

You can prevent intertrigo from becoming a problem in the first place by washing the above areas frequently and powdering them with talcum powder or cornstarch. If significant itching occurs, it can be controlled with either calamine lotion or hydrocortisone ointment, in addition to the antifungal cream.

> ❝ The worst ache I've been dealing with — besides my back, of course! — is my pubic bone. My doctors say it is normal and it has to do with both my weight and the stretching of ligaments, but it was scary at first. None of the books I read mentioned this ache, and I thought something was wrong. ❞
>
> — Barbara, 26, pregnant with her first child

Is there anything that can be done to prevent hemorrhoids during pregnancy?

Hemorrhoids — firm, swollen pouches that are formed underneath the mucus membranes both inside and outside of the rectum — are experienced by half of pregnant women. They are actually varicose veins of the anus. Some suffer from them throughout their pregnancies; others develop them only during the pushing stage of labor.

Hemorrhoids are caused by

- straining to empty the bowel — something that can be caused by either constipation or uncontrolled diarrhea;
- the effects of the high levels of progesterone in your body on the veins in the anal canal;
- the pressure of the baby's head in the pelvis during late pregnancy, which can interfere with the flow of blood to and from the pelvic organs.

You can lessen the likelihood that you will develop hemorrhoids by

- preventing constipation: ensure that your fluid intake is adequate,
- eating plenty of high-fiber foods to keep your stools soft,
- exercising regularly,
- not straining during bowel movements.

If you do develop hemorrhoids, you can ease your pain and itching by

- keeping the area around the anus clean by gently washing it after each bowel movement using either soft, undyed, unscented toilet paper or hygienic witch hazel pads);
- soaking in a sitz bath (a shallow basin that fits over the toilet);
- soaking in a bathtub containing oatmeal bath formula or baking soda;
- not sitting for long periods of time, particularly on hard surfaces.

Although most hemorrhoids go away on their own, some become filled with blood clots and require minor surgery.

Note: Consult your doctor before using any over-the-counter treatments for hemorrhoids. Not every product is recommended for use during pregnancy.

Week 30

At this point in pregnancy, you may be starting to think about shopping for baby — something that can lead to major worries on the money front.

What's going on with your baby

Your baby's eyebrows and eyelashes are now visible and your baby's eyelids are now open.

Your baby now weighs about 3 pounds and is about 17 inches long.

What's going on with your body

Your breasts now contain colostrum — the sweet, yellowish, nutrient- and antibody-rich fluid, which will serve as your baby's first food. Because there's a slight lag before your body starts producing breast milk, colostrum plays an important role in keeping your baby nourished while your body is switching into breast-milk production mode. (Your body stops producing colostrum and starts producing breast milk about three to five days after the birth.)

What's going on with your head

You may find that your partner gets hit with a heavy-duty case of the financial heebie-jeebies around now — a phenomenon that Armin A. Brott and Jennifer Ash describe in their book *The Expectant Father: Facts, Tips, and Advice for Dads-to-Be:* (Abbeville Press, Inc. 2001). "American society values men's financial contributions to their families much more than it does their emotional contribution. And expressing strong feelings, anxiety, or even fear is not what men are expected to do when their wives are pregnant. So, as the pregnancy progresses, most expectant fathers fall back on the more traditionally masculine way of expressing their concern for the well-being of their wives and little fetuses: they worry about money."

Make sure you give your partner plenty of opportunity to talk about his feelings about the pregnancy and the birth of your baby. It's easy to get so wrapped up in your own feelings and emotions that you lose sight of the fact that he's part of Operation Baby, too!

The Hot List: This week's must-ask pregnancy questions

Looking for some advice on shopping for baby? This week's "Hot List" offers all that and more.

How can you differentiate between the frills and the necessities when it comes to shopping for baby gear?

The U.S. juvenile products business manages to rack up billions of dollars in sales each year — and for good reason. Their marketing messages are everywhere. You'll find baby-product catalogs tucked in the prenatal magazines you pick up in your doctor's office, and you'll probably leave the hospital or birthing center with even more slick marketing materials designed to put a dent in your dwin-

> 66 Don't go overboard. It is so easy to overbuy. Purchase essentials as you need them. Borrow from friends. 99
>
> — Serene, 31, mother of two

dling baby-equipment budget. But no matter how lean-and-mean your budget may be, there are four pieces of baby equipment that most parents consider to be essential: a safe place for baby to sleep, a car seat, a stroller, and a baby carrier.

Here's what you need to know about shopping for each of these items.

A safe place for baby to sleep

Some parents use a crib right from the beginning, others opt for a cradle or bassinet until the baby gets a little older, and still others choose to take their babies into their own beds.

If you're shopping for a crib, look for one that

- conforms to current government safety standards (you can find out if a particular juvenile product is affected by a recall by phoning the U.S. Consumer Product Safety Commission at 800-638-2772; by writing to the U.S. Consumer Products Safety Commission, Washington, D.C. 20207; or by visiting the commission's Web site at www.cpsc.gov);

- has been certified by the Juvenile Products Manufacturers Association (call 856-638-0420; write to JPMA, 17000 Commerce Parkway, Suite C, Mount Laurel, NJ 08054; or visit the organization's Web site at www.jpma.org);

- has a tight-fitting mattress (that is, there is no more than two fingers' width of space between the edge of the mattress and the side of the crib);

- has slats that are no more than 2 ⅜ inches apart;

- is height adjustable (so that you can lower the mattress as your baby learns to stand and climb);

- is painted with nontoxic paint;

- has a teething rail (to prevent your baby from chewing the finish off the crib rails);

- has a railing that can be dropped or raised using one hand and that doesn't make a loud noise that could wake a sleeping baby;

- has a firm mattress (because soft mattresses are dangerous for babies);

- has metal rather than plastic casters (they wear better).

 Watch Out!

Never purchase a crib that has corner posts that are more than one-sixteenth of an inch above the end panels. Babies can strangle themselves if their clothing gets caught on a corner post.

Here are few money-saving tips on shopping for a crib:

- You can save about $50 by purchasing a crib with a single-drop railing rather than double-drop railings.

- Cribs that convert to toddler beds (also called junior beds) are no bargain. You often pay more for this feature than you would pay for a crib and a single bed combined. What's more, if you have your next child before the first child is finished with the bed, you'll need to purchase another crib anyway.

Here are some pointers on shopping for a cradle or bassinet:

- Make sure that the mattress is firm and fits the bassinet snugly so that your baby can't get caught between the mattress and the sides.

- Make sure that the cradle or bassinet is sturdy and stable — particularly if there are other children in your home.

- Follow the manufacturer's guidelines for weight and size. Most babies outgrow cradles and bassinets by the time they are three to four months of age.

> 66 Although change tables are great for holding supplies, they're completely unnecessary. I change my babies on the floor or on the bed and rarely use the change table. 99
>
> — Suzi, 27, mother of two

- You can get more mileage out of a portable playpen with a built-in bassinet than a standard bassinet or cradle. Whereas the bassinet or cradle will be gathering dust in the basement within a matter of weeks, you can get two or more years' worth of use out of a portable playpen. Just one quick word of caution: Not all portable playpens are designed to be used for sleeping. Check with the manufacturer.

A car seat

A car seat is one product you should plan to purchase new. Otherwise, you're taking a chance that the seat may have been in a car accident — something that can damage the seat and make it unsafe to use.

There are three basic choices when it comes to a car seat:

- an infant seat (designed for infants up to 20 to 22 pounds, depending on the make and model)
- a toddler seat (designed for children over 20 pounds)
- a convertible seat (designed to be used in the rear-facing position by babies who weigh less than 20 pounds and in the front-facing position by babies who weigh more than 20 pounds)

Although some parents choose to purchase the convertible seat because it eliminates the need to buy an infant seat, which is used only for about six to nine months, there are some disadvantages to going this route. First of all, you could find yourself shopping for a second car seat if you space your children closely together — something that eliminates the advantages of purchasing a convertible seat. Second, it's virtually impossible to remove a sleeping baby from a convertible seat without waking him or her up. Most parents feel that this is enough justification for going with an infant seat that can be carried into the house, baby and all.

Here are some tips on shopping for a car seat:

- Before you reach for your wallet, make sure that you actually need to buy a car seat. Certain health insurance providers provide free car seats to their clients.
- Assuming that you do need to purchase a car seat, look for a model that has a handle that makes the seat easy to carry and that can be folded back to make it easier to get your baby in and out of the seat; a seat-belt system that can be adjusted easily as your baby grows; and a car-seat cover that can be removed easily and that is fully washable.

Watch Out!

Convertible car seats are not recommended for premature or very small babies who may slump over and possibly suffocate. The American Academy of Pediatrics recommends that infant seats be used instead — and that they be used in the reclined position. See www.aap.org/family/carseatguide.htm for more about the AAP's policies on car seat use.

- Numerous car seats have been recalled in recent years. You can get the scoop on the problems with various makes and models by contacting the National Highway Traffic Safety Administration (NHTSA) at 1-888-DASH-2-DOT or or by downloading the information yourself from the NHTSA Web site at www-odi.nhtsa.dot.gov/cars/problems/recalls/childseat.cfm.

- NHTSA can also tell you whether a particular car seat will fit into your make and model of vehicle. (This can be more of a problem than you might think.)

A stroller

Shopping for a stroller is not unlike shopping for a car at a dealership: you have an enormous range of makes and models to choose from. Here's what you can expect to see on the showroom floor:

- **Umbrella strollers:** As the name implies, umbrella strollers fold up like an umbrella. They're lightweight and inexpensive ($30 to $40), but they don't last very long and don't provide much back support for your baby.

- **Carriages:** Carriages (also called prams) look like bassinets on wheels. They are the aristocratic-looking contraptions pushed by the Mary Poppinses of the world. The only disadvantage to one of these is the price: $500 to $1,500 for a piece of equipment your baby will outgrow in a matter of months.

- **Carriage/strollers:** As the name implies, carriage/strollers are hybrids. They can function either as a carriage (when the seat is fully reclined) or as a stroller (when the seat is partially or fully lifted). Typically, they can be had for $150 to $450, although some name brands will set you back more than that.

- **Jogging strollers:** Jogging strollers have big wheels and lightweight frames that make it easy for a new mother or father to take baby along for a run. They tend to come in at about $200 to $300.

- **All-terrain strollers:** All-terrain strollers are sturdy contraptions designed for off-road strollering — the baby world's equivalent of the ATV. They have oversized tires and better undercarriage clearance than other models, and they typically ring in at about $100.

- **Lightweight strollers:** Lightweight strollers are souped-up versions of your basic umbrella stroller. Their frames are a bit sturdier, but they're nowhere near as heavy to lug around as full-blown carriage/strollers. They ring in at about $200 to $300.

- **Car seat/strollers:** Combination car seat/strollers are a perfect example of what happens when an idea that looks good on paper gets tested in the real world. Most of these units are more expensive than the two separate components (that is, a stroller and a car seat), and they tend to be quite cumbersome to use. You can expect to pay well over $200 for a name-brand combination car seat/stroller.

Here's what to look for in a stroller:

- a strong but lightweight frame (aluminum)

- a stable design (that is, securely balanced and not prone to tipping)

- a handle that is reversible (that flips from one side of the stroller to the other so that you can keep the sun and wind out of baby's face, regardless of what direction it's coming from)
- a handle that is the right height for you (tall people can find it particularly difficult to find a stroller that is comfortable to push)
- a fully reclining seat so that baby can nap on the run
- fabric that is stain resistant
- a pad that can be removed for washing
- a broad base, for added stability
- secure and easy-to-use restraining straps
- sun and rain shields
- a model that can be folded with one hand while you're holding a baby
- a lightweight construction
- storage space underneath so that you won't be tempted to hang grocery bags from the handle of the stroller
- an adjustable footrest
- a removable front bar (to make it easier for your child to get in and out of the stroller when he reaches toddlerhood)
- lockable wheels (to make it easier to travel in a straight line) and locking wheels (to prevent the stroller from rolling away when it's on a slope).

 Bright Idea

Check out the cost and availability of replacement parts for your stroller before you decide which brand to purchase. Some brands are extremely expensive to repair — assuming that parts are even available.

A baby carrier

There are two basic types of baby carriers: ones that are worn on the front of your body (suitable for younger babies) and ones that are worn on your back (suitable for older babies). Whatever type you decide to choose, make sure that it

> **66** One of the most important pieces of gear we bought was the sling. I have used it every day since my daughter was born, and she's almost 10 months old. **99**
>
> — Leila, 34, mother of one

- is constructed from a sturdy; washable fabric;
- has some type of support for baby's back and neck;
- has leg holes that are small enough to prevent the baby from slipping through, yet not so small that they are tight and uncomfortable.

Backpack carriers typically incorporate some type of aluminum frame. A backpack carrier should be

- stable enough to stand up on its own so that you can put the baby in and take her out without needing help from another adult;
- sufficiently padded to ensure that both you and the baby are comfortable;
- made of stain-resistant fabric.

Are there any other items I should consider purchasing?

Now that we've discussed the must-haves, let's talk about some items that, though hardly essentials, can certainly make a new parent's job a whole lot easier.

A baby swing

You've been pacing the floor with an unhappy baby for the past eight hours, and you're about to collapse from exhaustion.

What would you be willing to pay to have the baby lulled to sleep by someone — or something — else?

As much as $100, if the marketing gurus at the brand-name baby equipment manufacturers have it right. That's about what you can expect to pay for a top-quality battery-operated baby swing. It's a small price to pay for peace of mind and a break from a fussy baby — or at least that's how some parents feel.

"After her early morning feeding, Chelsea went in the swing and I went to sleep on the couch, sometimes for as long as three or four hours," recalls Ellen, 29, a mother of one. "I owe almost all the sleep I got during her early infancy to that beautiful swing."

If you decide to purchase a baby swing, be sure to look for a battery-operated model. The wind-up swings tend to make enough noise to wake a sleeping baby — something that defeats the whole purpose of owning a baby swing (and which explains why the wind-up models have pretty much gone the way of the dodo bird). Here are some other features to look for:

- multiple speeds (slower for young babies and faster for bigger babies);
- seat adjustability (the seat moves from upright to reclining to suit your baby's developmental stage);
- a model without an overhead bar (so that you don't have to worry about banging your baby's head as you take him in and out of the swing);
- thick padding for comfort;
- washable fabric.

 Moneysaver

Form a purchasing co-op with other members of your childbirth class, and negotiate the best possible deal on cribs, car seats, and so on.

A playpen (or playyard)

Although a playpen was considered to be a necessary piece of equipment for parents a generation ago, most parents today choose to baby-proof the environment rather than to confine baby to a playpen. Here's what Stephanie, a 25-year-old first-time mother, had to say about the playpen she purchased for her baby: "For me, the playpen was a complete waste of money. Isabel won't sit in it. She likes to be seen and held and does not want to be confined to a playpen. It has just become a very large toy-storage container in the living room."

Playpens still have their place, however, particularly if you're traveling. That's why a growing number of parents are choosing portable playpens (that is, playpens that collapse into a carry bag that is roughly the size of a gym bag and that function as cribs-away-from-home).

When you're shopping for a portable playpen, look for a model with

- mesh sides (fine enough to prevent baby's fingers and toes from getting trapped),
- walls that are at least 19 inches tall,
- a sun canopy (if you intend to use it outside).

Although all portable playpens claim to be easy to fold, some require a postgraduate degree in mechanical engineering. Test-drive this feature of the playpen before you agree to purchase it.

Note: If you intend to use your portable playpen as a crib for your baby to sleep in, make sure that it's designed for this use. Some are and some aren't.

A baby monitor

Many parents rate baby monitors as nothing short of essential — even those who initially saw no use for them.

"I highly recommend a baby monitor," says Tracy, 31, mother of one. "I didn't think I'd need one, but whenever I put Ben down for a nap, I'd be terrified to go too far from his room for

Watch Out!

Don't have a heated discussion with your partner when the baby monitor is turned on. You could be broadcasting your dirty laundry to the entire neighborhood.

fear that I wouldn't hear him when he woke up. We got a monitor when he was three months old, and I suddenly felt so free!"

Here are some features to look for in a baby monitor:

▪ a model that provides for maximum flexibility by allowing you to use a battery or an AC adapter at both the sending and the receiving ends;

▪ a monitor with a sturdy AC adapter that looks as though it will withstand a fair amount of wear and tear;

▪ a monitor that has more than one channel (so that you can switch channels if you're picking up the sounds of your neighbor's baby rather than your own).

The only downside to baby monitors is that they have an annoying habit of interfering with cordless phones — and vice versa. Be sure to keep your receipt until you're sure that all systems are go on the baby-monitor front. While today's generation of baby monitors and cordless phones are less likely to interfere with one another than their predecessors, you can still run into some unexpected glitches.

How much should I expect to spend on baby clothes?

Your baby clothing expenditures will be determined by your budget and your eagerness to avoid doing laundry every day. "If you don't mind doing laundry every day, you can get by with half a dozen outfits," says Dawnette, 28, mother of one.

Although it's impossible to predict how much laundry a particular baby will generate — some babies have leaky diapers a couple of times per day; and some babies spit up so much that they have to be changed after every feeding — you should expect to change your baby's clothes approximately three to six times each day.

Here are some tips on picking out baby clothes:

- Don't buy too many clothes in the newborn size. Some babies are born too large to wear them or can wear them only for a couple of weeks. Although some books advise you to bypass the newborn size entirely, we don't go quite that far. Because there's no way of telling in advance whether you're going to be having a 7- or 10-pound baby, you should plan to have at least one outfit in the newborn size on hand. Then, if you need more, you can send a friend or relative out to load up on a few extra outfits.

- Keep your baby's initial wardrobe as simple as possible. You might be tempted to buy all kinds of cute frilly dresses or adorable sailor suits, but keep in mind that these types of outfits can be a royal pain to get on and off your baby.

- Keep your baby's comfort in mind at all times. Believe it or not, many baby clothes are designed for fashion rather than comfort. Outfits with poorly positioned buttons or zippers can be uncomfortable for baby to sleep in, and frilly dresses are about as much fun to sleep in as a wedding dress.

- Don't even think about buying a sleeper that doesn't have crotch snaps. These poorly designed items are such a pain to use that you simply won't be bothered and the item will languish unworn in the bottom of the pile of baby outfits.

- Look for clothing that's designed to grow with your baby (for example, sleepers with adjustable foot cuffs). You'll get more mileage out of these garments and therefore save more money.

- Baby booties are almost impossible to keep on tiny little feet. Look for miniature stretch socks instead.

- Stick to unisex colors as much as possible. That way, you don't have to go out and buy a second wardrobe if your next baby happens to be of the opposite sex.

- Buy clothing only as your baby needs it. That way, you can factor in what other people lend or give you and avoid overbuying.

- Don't buy too far ahead. Although it's tempting to pick up next year's snowsuit during this year's winter sales, it's hard to predict what size your baby will be wearing a year from now. That $30 bargain could end up being a $30 waste of money.

Is it a good idea to purchase baby items secondhand?

Although you will probably want to purchase certain items new — a car seat and crib, for example — you can stretch your dollars a lot further if you pick up other baby items secondhand. You'll probably be able to borrow a lot of secondhand baby equipment from family members and friends, but you may still find it necessary to purchase some of the items you'll need.

You can find secondhand baby equipment

- by shopping at consignment stores (particularly those that specialize in children's clothing and baby equipment);

- by visiting secondhand clothing stores operated by charitable organizations;

- by hitting garage sales;

- by reading the classified ads;

- by checking out bulletin boards at the grocery store or community center or by hanging up a "baby equipment wanted" ad of your own;

- by contacting the local twins club and finding out when its annual garage sale will be held.

Although you can save a lot of money by shopping secondhand, you also run certain risks. Some of the most unsafe juvenile products ever made — baby walkers, for example — regularly crop up at garage sales.

Here are some questions to ask when you're shopping secondhand:

- Who manufactured this product and when was it made?

- What is the model number?

- Where is the instruction manual?

- How many families have used it?

- Has it ever been repaired?

- Are any of the parts missing? (If the missing parts are essential to the functioning of the product, call the manufacturer to confirm that parts are still available before you buy the product.)

- Does the product conform to current safety standards? (The vendor may or may not be able to answer this question accurately, so you'll have to do some research yourself. See "Resource Directory" (www.wiley.com/go/anndouglas) for leads on organizations that can provide you with information on safety standards.)

Week 31

Finding a comfortable sleeping position is no easy task — not with your watermelon-sized belly to work around! You may be seriously wondering if the Sandman will ever come, or if you're doomed to have to wait until Junior makes his grand entrance before you start getting some decent shut-eye. (Like you'll be getting a lot of sleep around then. . . .)

What's going on with your baby

Believe it or not, you only have about half as much amniotic fluid as you did at the start of this month. Scientists believe that some of the fluid has to be eliminated at this point in pregnancy in order to make more room for the growing baby.

Because there's less fluid to cushion your baby's movements, you are likely to feel your baby's kicks and wriggles more. At the same time, his movements are likely to be less dramatic from this point forward. This is the last month when he'll be capable of doing a full somersault!

What's going on with your body

You may find it increasingly difficult to find a comfortable sleeping position at night and once you do fall asleep, you're likely to wake up at least a few times in the night, either because you have to go to the bathroom or because your hips are sore that and you need to change position (something that's much easier said than done at this stage of the game).

What's going on with your head

There may be days when you feel like someone's stuck an "I'm pregnant! Give me advice!" sign on your back without telling you. After all, what else could possibly explain why complete strangers feel compelled to stop you on the street to offer their best (or worst) advice on coping with everything from morning sickness to labor pains to unruly toddlers and teens. (It would be nice if they at least let you get through labor before they started scaring you with the toddler and teen tales, now wouldn't it?)

The best way to cope with the onslaught of unwanted advice is to smile sweetly and tune out everything that's of no use to you (approximately 99 percent of what people tell you). You can then tuck away the other 1 percent of genuinely good advice for future reference in that rapidly expanding part of your brain that's devoted to all things parental.

The Hot List: This week's must-ask pregnancy questions

Wondering what's standing behind you and between a good night's sleep or why you constantly seem to be out of breath? Here's what you need to know.

I am exhausted, but I can't seem to get a good night's sleep no matter what I do. Any tips?

Just when you'd do just about anything for a good night's sleep, the Sandman is strangely elusive. Mechanics have a lot to do with your sleeping problems, of course, because it isn't easy to get comfortable when you've got a uterus the size of a water-melon. Then there are the metabolic changes that can have you burning up in bed when your partner is huddled under a down comforter. Those midnight treks to the washroom don't help either, nor does your growing preoccupation with what lies ahead — labor, delivery, and life after baby.

Here are some tips on coping with sleep problems during pregnancy:

- Surround yourself with pillows. You can either load up on everyday pillows or purchase one of those oversized body pillows that are specially designed for sleeping during pregnancy. You'll probably be able to find one at your local home-healthcare products store or maternity boutique.

- Keep your bedroom a comfortable temperature. If you're too warm (a common complaint for most pregnant women), you'll find it difficult to get the rest you need.

- Sleep on your side with your legs and knees bent. Tuck one pillow under your abdomen and put another pillow between your knees. If you're experiencing a lot of achiness in your hip, tuck a pillow underneath the side you're sleeping on to take some of the pressure off your hip.

- Don't exercise too close to your bedtime. Although exercise will ultimately help you get a better night's sleep, a late-evening walk may actually keep you awake.

- Don't eat a heavy meal within two to three hours of going to bed. Your metabolism will go into overdrive, something that can keep you awake.

- Pass on the midnight snack if heartburn and indigestion are causing you grief. Otherwise, you could be up a good part of the night dealing with these particular discomforts.

- Stretch your calves before you go to bed if leg cramps are waking you up in the middle of the night.

- Make yourself a batch of bedtime tea by enjoying a sooth-ing cup of herbal tea. Note: Be sure to choose a type of tea that is considered safe for use during pregnancy.

- Drink a cup of warm milk. If it tastes too bland on its own, add a small amount of cinnamon and honey or sugar.

- Have a warm (not hot) bath. The heat and the feeling of being sur-rounded by water will help to relax you.

> 66 My husband had to endure our air-condi-tioning going full blast all the time during heat waves. We even had to install ceiling fans in the hallway and our bedroom because I was just too hot. 99
>
> — Jacqueline, 34, mother of two

- Practice relaxation breathing in bed. Not only is it a great opportunity to do your homework from your childbirth class, but it also may help put you to sleep.

- Get up and do something rather than tossing and turning in bed. Then, hit the sack again once you start feeling sleepy.

I am normally a very fit person, but I can't even climb a set of stairs without feeling out of breath. Is this normal?

The breathlessness you're experiencing is a common third-trimester complaint. It's caused by pressure from your growing uterus. During the third trimester, the diaphragm — the broad, flat muscle that lies underneath your lungs — is pushed out of its place by a good 1 ½ inches, decreasing your lung capacity. You'd be feeling even more breathless if it weren't for the fact that the high levels of progesterone in your body trigger the res-piratory center in your brain, causing you to breathe more deeply. This helps to ensure that your baby receives plenty of oxygen, despite your diminished lung capacity.

Watch Out!

Severe shortness of breath, chest pain, rapid breathing, or pain when taking a deep breath are not normal third-trimester complaints. If you experience any of these symptoms, call your caregiver or head for the emergency room immediately.

Although there's no cure for breathlessness other than giving birth, you can do a few things to minimize your discomfort in the meantime. Make a habit of sitting and standing with your back straight and your shoulders back. And to ensure that you can breathe comfortably when you are lying down, either prop yourself up with a pile of pillows or lie on your side so that some of the pressure will be taken off your diaphragm. But as for those stairs — there's not much we can suggest at this point to eliminate the huffing and puffing.

Just the facts

- Resist the temptation to overshop for baby by learning to differentiate between the necessities and the frills.

- Don't feel that you have to buy everything your baby might need during his first year of life before he's even born. You can pick up some of this stuff later on.

- Make a point of purchasing your baby's car seat brand new. That way, you won't have to worry about whether or not it's been involved in a car accident. (Car seats that have been involved in car accidents — even minor fender-benders — need to be taken out of commission.)

- Don't be surprised if you start to have difficulty with insomnia and breathlessness — two common third-trimester pregnancy complaints.

GET THE SCOOP ON. . .
What's going on with your baby ▪ What's going
on with your body ▪ What's going on with your
head ▪ Writing a birth plan ▪ Perineal massage ▪
Cord blood banking ▪ Breastfeeding ▪
Circumcision ▪ Group B strep

The Eighth Month: Getting Psyched

Chapter 12

As you head into your eighth month, you may be totally convinced that you're going to have your baby early. After all, your belly is huge, you're already having trouble sleeping and breathing — surely Mother Nature can't intend for you to go on like this for another *eight weeks!*

Well, as hard as you may find it to believe right now, chances are you and baby still have a few more weeks of growing ahead of you. And while you may be secretly wishing that you could go into labor sooner rather than later, if only so that you can start feeling a little more comfortable, it's healthier for your baby if she has the chance to "cook" for a few more weeks. (Of course, it's one thing to understand that fact intellectually; it's quite another to try to be patient 24 hours a day while some tiny little person is doing headstands on your bladder and kicking you in the ribs!)

In this chapter, we zero in on some of your key month eight pregnancy concerns: writing a birth plan, practicing perineal massage, making up your mind about cord blood banking, and getting generally psyched for the remaining weeks of pregnancy. And, as in chapters past, we'll give you an idea of what to expect on a week-by-week basis — this time for weeks 32 through 35. You'll get the inside scoop on what's going on with your body, what's going on with your head, and what's going on with your baby each week, plus you'll find answers to some of the most-asked pregnancy questions for each week of pregnancy.

Week 32

This week, you may be wondering about your baby's sleeping and waking patterns, Braxton Hicks contractions, and whether or not you're doing this pregnancy thing "right."

What's going on with your baby

Your baby will develop more clearly distinct patterns of sleeping and waking this month, but because your baby is likely to be highly active during the period of light sleep preceding REM sleep (rapid-eye-movement sleep), you may have a hard time trying to figure out whether your ultra-wiggly baby is actually wide awake or doing those moves in her sleep.

What's going on with your body

You may be starting to experience some Braxton Hicks contractions — the so-called "practice contractions" that ready your uterus for the hard work of giving birth. These contractions — which typically last for about 30 seconds at a time — may not be noticeable initially, but by late pregnancy they can start to become quite uncomfortable, and even mildly painful. You're most likely to notice them when you're walking or engaging in other forms of exercise. You may notice that your uterus tightens considerably, almost as if someone had put a blood pressure cuff around your belly and pumped it full of air. See Chapter 18 for more about Braxton Hicks contractions.

What's going on with your head

Feel like you're being asked to measure up to some superhuman standard of what it means to be the perfect mother-to-be? That you're somehow letting your baby down if you purchase the regular lettuce rather than the organic lettuce, or if you opt out of supposedly *de rigueur* pregnancy experiences, like playing prenatal music to your baby while you soak in the tub, reading your prenatal meditation book?

We just want to remind you that while it's always best to do whatever you can to lead a baby-friendly lifestyle (e.g., steering clear of alcohol and cigarettes, providing your body with a steady stream of healthy food, and generally taking good care of yourself and your baby during pregnancy), you don't have to carry things to extremes.

If pregnancy perfectionism (the desire to do everything perfectly and make all the right decisions for the entire 40 weeks of pregnancy) is causing your stress-o-meter to go off the scale, you might want to talk to your doctor or midwife about which lifestyle habits are most important so that you can focus your energies in those areas.

Bottom line? You don't want to drive yourself totally crazy trying to play the role of supermom-to-be and miss out on all the joy that goes along with being pregnant. For most of us, pregnancy is a once or twice in a lifetime experience. Don't miss out on what's really important by sweating the stuff that really doesn't matter at all.

The Hot List: This week's must-ask pregnancy questions

Prenatal checkups and the ins and outs of writing a birth plan are likely to be on your mind at this point in your pregnancy.

What should I expect from this month's prenatal checkups?

Yes, we said *checkups*. That's because you're going to be trudging off to the doctor's or midwife's office a bit more often from this point onward. You'll likely be going for prenatal checkups every two weeks this month and then weekly during month nine.

At each of this month's prenatal visits, you can expect your doctor or midwife to check

- **the fundal height** (your healthcare provider will measure the distance between your pubic bone and the top of your uterus — the fundus)

- **size and position of the baby** (your doctor or midwife will assess this by placing her hands on your abdomen and feeling for the baby)

- **your weight** (to see if you are continuing to gain weight slowly)

- **your blood pressure** (to spot any early warning signs of pregnancy-related hypertension or preeclampsia)

- **your urine** (to ensure that your sugar and protein levels are within the normal range as they, too, can provide early warning of any emerging problems)

- **the fetal heart rate** (to keep tabs on your baby's general health and well-being). Reminder: Your baby's heart beats much more rapidly than your own — at a rate of 120 to 160 beats per minute on average.

Your doctor or midwife will also monitor you for signs of edema (swelling) and check your legs for any signs of protruding varicose veins.

What are the key advantages of writing a birth plan?

The key advantage of writing a birth plan is that it encourages you to think about your various birthing options and to discuss them with your caregiver.

Despite what you might have heard from other people, writing a birth plan doesn't have to be a difficult or time-consuming process. You don't need a formal document — just a simple letter from you to your caregiver that spells out your hopes and dreams for the birth of your baby.

Depending on what is important to you and your partner, you may wish to include in your birth plan a discussion of such issues as

- where you would like to give birth (in a hospital, in a birthing center, or at home);

- your feelings about the use of medications during labor;

- whom you would like to have present at the birth, and what each person's role will be;

- what clothing you would like to wear while you're in labor (your own street clothes versus a hospital nightie);

- the atmosphere you would like to have while you are in labor (for example, dim lights and quiet music);

- where you would like to labor (for example, in the Jacuzzi or the shower) and in what positions (sitting, standing, squatting, or leaning against your partner);

- under what circumstances, if any, you would agree to such procedures as episiotomies, inductions, and internal examinations;

- whether you are willing to permit medical students or residents to be present during the birth;

- what birthing equipment you would like to use (for example, a birthing stool, a birthing bed, a beanbag chair, a squatting bar, or a birthing tub);

- whether you would like the newborn examination to be performed in your presence to avoid separation from your baby.

Note: See "Important Documents" (www.wiley.com/go/ann douglas) for a sample birth plan.

It's important to keep reminding yourself that your birth plan is not a blueprint for labor. Neither you nor your caregiver can predict in advance whether it will be possible to follow your birth plan to the letter. That's why it's important to be flexible and to understand that you and your caregiver may have to scrap the birth plan entirely if a medical emergency arises. "Our birth plan was very simple," says Jacqueline, 34, who recently gave birth to her second child. "Deliver a healthy baby from a healthy mom. It didn't matter to us how we got there."

On the other hand, you don't want to make the mistake of leaving everything to chance — for example, assuming that you don't need a birth plan if you've given birth before. That's a lesson that Anne, 39, a third-time mother, learned the hard way. "I wish we had written a birth plan. The nurses were about to change shift at the hospital and took sort of a kamikaze approach to the birth — fast and furious. In retrospect, I wish we had more control and had taken a bit more time with the birth plan. They were so anxious to get the baby out. If we had a birth plan, my partner (a first-time father) would have felt more confident stepping in and taking charge."

Likewise, don't assume that you don't need a birth plan if you're having a planned cesarean. If you feel strongly about how you would like the birth to be handled, spell that out in black and white. Here's what Heidi, a 27-year-old mother of three, had to say about her and her partner's decision to write a birth plan for their planned c-section: "I never thought you could have a birth plan with a planned c-section, but my midwife set me straight. It was wonderful having things written down: that is, the fact that I wanted my husband to be in the operating room when they gave me the spinal. I did not have to fight with anyone about what I wanted because it was all there in writing. Once you've finished writing your birth plan, review it with your

> 66 I wrote a birth plan. It was valuable, mostly because it made me decide what I wanted and forced me to research issues. It was also valuable because the hospital staff knew that I had prepared and made plans. I actually deviated from my birth plan, but it was okay because I knew what those changes were and why we were making them. 99
>
> — Dawnette, 28, mother of one

caregiver, revise it as mutually agreed, and then make several copies. Keep one at work and one at home, and give two copies to your caregiver. (Your caregiver should keep one copy with your prenatal records and forward the second copy to the hospital or birthing center where you plan to deliver.)

You probably won't need to use your birth plan for at least another few weeks, but it will be one less thing for you to think about as you enter those exciting but exhausting final weeks of pregnancy.

Week 33

Some of the issues that may be on your mind this week include your baby's physiological responses to sex, your feelings about being the center of attention wherever you go (hey, it's hard to be inconspicuous when you're sporting a belly like that!), and whether or not perineal massage and cord blood banking are for you.

What's going on with your baby

Your baby weighs roughly 4 ½ pounds and measures about 19 inches in length. Dimples have appeared on your baby's cheeks and creases have formed around your baby's neck. Mother Nature's busy applying the finishing touches to her work of art!

What's going on with your body

You may notice that your baby becomes less active — or more active — after you have sex. Some babies seem to be lulled to sleep by the uterine contractions that accompany orgasm while others find them invigorating. Both reactions are perfectly normal, so try not to be freaked out or alarmed by your baby's tendency to either roll over and go to sleep or be hit with a burst of energy after you and your partner are finished doing the deed.

What's going on with your head

Now that you're megapregnant, you'll probably find that you're the center of attention wherever you go. You may be tempted to wear a sign around your neck that states (1) your due date, (2) whether or not this is your first child, and (3) whether or not you know if you're having a boy or a girl — the three questions you're likely to be asked 1,001 times per day!

> ❝I wish someone had told me how pregnant women become public property. I can't believe how everyone presumes to tell me how to eat, sleep, work, work out, and how they just reach out and touch me.❞
>
> — Kathi, 31, pregnant with her first child

While some women find these questions annoying, others very much enjoy playing the role of the Pregnant Princess, being fussed over by friends, relatives, and even complete strangers. After all, the attention tends to be relatively fleeting. It's only a matter of time before you'll be upstaged by an even more attention-grabbing understudy: your baby!

The Hot List: This week's must-ask pregnancy questions

Wondering whether perineal massage or cord blood banking are right for you? Here's what you need to know about these two third-trimester hot topics.

Is it true that practicing perineal massage in the weeks leading up to the birth can reduce your chances of requiring an episiotomy?

Yes — but only if you're a first-time mom. A 1999 study in Quebec, Canada, found that perineal massage (massaging the tissues surrounding the opening of the vagina that need to stretch during childbirth) can be effective in helping first-time moms to avoid an episiotomy, but that perineal massage doesn't deliver quite the same benefits to women who have previously given birth vaginally.

And, of course, there are no guarantees that practicing perineal massage will guarantee that you avoid an episiotomy. In certain situations, an episiotomy may be unavoidable: if, for example, your baby is in a breech position, in distress, if your baby's shoulders are too wide to be delivered without an episiotomy (shoulder dystocia), or if a forceps delivery is required.

What's involved in practicing perineal massage?

If you decide to try practicing perineal massage, you'll want to set aside 10 minutes once or twice a day, starting at around the 34th week of pregnancy.

To get started, wash your hands and apply a bit of lubricant such as KY jelly, cocoa butter, olive oil, vitamin E oil, or pure vegetable oil to your thumbs and around your perineum (the tissues surrouding the opening to your vagina). (Or, if you prefer, hop in a warm tub and do your perineal massage in the tub instead, either as a solo act or with a little help from your partner.) Then place your thumbs about 1 to 1.5 inches inside your vagina and apply pressure downwards and to the sides at the same time. Continue to stretch until you feel a slight burning sensation. Hold this position for about two minutes, and then slowly and gently massage the lower half of your vagina, using the same pulling and stretching technique. If you pull gently outward while keeping your thumbs tucked inside, you'll be emulating the stretching sensations that you'll experience when your baby's head starts crowning during the birth process.

After about a week of practicing perineal massage, you'll start to notice your perineal tissues becoming more flexible — proof positive that all that stretching is starting to pay off.

Is cord blood banking a good idea?

It depends whether you're talking about public cord blood banking (e.g., donating the blood within your baby's umbilical cord and placenta to a public cord blood bank so that valuable stem cells can be harvested from your baby's cord blood and made available to those who would benefit from treatment for malignant, benign, and inherited disorders) or private cord blood banking (e.g., paying a private cord blood bank a fee to collect, process, freeze, and store your baby's cord blood for the exclusive use of members of your own immediate family).

While some families would be wise to consider private cord blood banking (they already have a family member with a medical condition that requires treatment with stem cells, for example, or there's a strong family history of these types of medical conditions), neither the American College of Obstetricians and Gynecologists nor the American Academy of Pediatrics is in favor of routine private cord blood banking. The AAP's policy states that private cord blood banking should be considered if a family member is facing an emergency situation where stem cells are currently required or are likely to be required in the immediate future, but that it's not something that every expectant parent needs to routinely consider.

Without those specific risk factors, you're looking at paying some pretty high fees ($300 to $1,500 initially plus $50 to $100 in annual storage fees) to collect, process, freeze, and store a cord blood sample that your family has a very remote chance of actually needing (1 out of 1,400 odds, according to the experts). Obstetrician/gynecologist John R. Sussman, M.D. (one of the authors of this book) explains it to his patients this way: "Consider private cord blood banking a form of insurance that you and your loved ones will probably never need. Now look at your needs for all types of insurance. If you have all the life, health, disability, property, and liability insurance you and your family need, and you still have $1,000 or so left over in your insurance budget, then consider cord blood banking. Otherwise, get more coverage where it's more likely to do you good."

Of course, there's an alternative to going the private cord blood bank route. You may want to consider donating your baby's cord blood to a public cord blood bank that makes stem cells available to people with specific medical conditions.

Bright Idea

If you're thinking of using the services of a private cord blood bank, make sure that you find out about the number of successful transplants they've performed to date. That will give you clear indication of how effective the bank's collection, processing, freezing, and storage techniques have proven to be. If they haven't performed any successful transplants to date, you have no way of knowing whether your cord blood sample will even be usable, should you ever need it.

Unfortunately, public cord banks are in fairly short supply, so you'll want to check with your doctor or midwife ahead of time to find out if this is even an option for you. If you're thinking of going this route, you should plan to have this discussion as soon as possible. Some public cord blood banks are only able to accept donations if collection arrangements are made prior to the 35th week of pregnancy.

We'd like to give the final word on the highly controversial issue of cord blood banking to Charles J. Lockwood, M.D., Chair of the Department of Obstetrics and Gynecology at Yale University School of Medicine in New Haven, Connecticut, who made the case for greater government investment in public cord blood banks in a recent editorial in the medical journal *Contemporary Ob/Gyn:* "The weight of current evidence . . . suggests that government-funded public umbilical blood banking is an idea whose time has come. From a cost-benefit and ethical perspective, it is hard, at present, to justify the value of private umbilical cord blood banking."

Week 34

At this stage in your pregnancy, you may be trying to make up your mind about breastfeeding and circumcision and wondering what you can do about the small amounts of urine leakage you may be experiencing under certain circumstances — a sensation that many pregnant women find highly disconcerting, to say the least.

What's going on with your baby

Now that there is a layer of white fat underneath your baby's skin, her skin has a pinkish glow to it. (Up until now, her skin has been very reddish because she lacked this layer of fat.)

Your baby's fingernails are quite long — they reach the ends of her fingers — but her toenails have not grown in fully yet.

What's going on with your body

You may find yourself leaking small amounts of urine when you laugh, cough, sneeze or are involved in strenuous activity. This condition — known as stress incontinence — is caused by growing pressure by the uterus on your bladder. You can minimize urinary stress incontinence by emptying your bladder more frequently (i.e., even before you have an urge), avoiding caffeinated beverages, citrus fruits and juices, tomatoes, spicy foods, and carbonated beverages, all of which have a tendency to irritate the bladder; doing your Kegels to help strengthen your pelvic floor muscles; and keeping your weight gain in the moderate region (to minimize the amount of pressure on your bladder). And to prevent any embarrassing leaks when you're out and about, simply get in the habit of wearing a panty liner. That should take care of the problem.

What's going on with your head

Unsure whether you want friends and family members to throw your baby shower before your baby is born, out of fear that doing so may somehow "jinx" your pregnancy? You're not alone. In some cultures, it's believed to be extremely bad luck to buy certain items or to set up the nursery before the baby has arrived on the scene.

In North America, most baby showers (particularly baby showers that take place in the workplace) tend to take place during the weeks leading up to the birth of a new baby. If you have strong feelings about this issue, you'll want to be upfront with friends and family members about your desire to hold off

Watch Out!

While you might be tempted to cut back on your fluid intake in an effort to minimize the amount of urine leakage you're experiencing, your plan may lead to other, more serious problems, including urinary tract infections or dehydration.

on having your baby shower until after your baby arrives. You may find that it works well to sell them on the benefits of waiting until after the birth before they throw you a baby shower (e.g., they'll get a chance to check out the new arrival).

Of course, there's no reason to buy into these pregnancy superstitions. They're just that — superstitions. So if you think you can toss your superstitions aside and enjoy a bit of prebaby fun, why not go with the flow and see if you can get yourself into the party spirit? If you're still worried about tempting fate, you can always leave your baby gifts in the packages until Junior arrives safely. Or you can ask a friend or family member to store them for you. Whatever works for you.

The Hot List: This week's must-ask pregnancy questions

Having a hard time making up your mind about breastfeeding versus bottle-feeding? Unsure whether or not you want to have your baby circumcised (assuming, of course, that you are giving birth to a boy)? This week's "Hot List" should arm you with the facts you need to make up your mind on these two important issues.

I'm having a hard time deciding whether to breastfeed or bottle-feed my baby. Any advice?

A generation ago, only one-third of American women chose to breastfeed their babies. Today, that figure has more than doubled. According to the U.S. Centers for Disease Control and Prevention, in 2000, 69 percent of American babies were breastfed during the early weeks of their lives. (However, the breastfeeding rate dropped off quite rapidly. By age three months, only 26 percent of American babies were still being breastfed exclusively.)

If you're having a hard time making up your mind, it's generally best to give breastfeeding a chance. You can always change your mind and stop breastfeeding if things don't work out for you and your baby. It's a lot more difficult to switch from bottle-feeding to breastfeeding if you decide after the fact that breastfeeding would have been a better option.

What are the health benefits of breastfeeding?

Breastfeeding offers a number of significant health benefits to both mother and baby, which is why the American Academy of Pediatrics recommends that women breastfeed their babies exclusively for at least the first six months of a baby's life, and that they continue to breastfeed throughout the first year — longer if mother and baby are willing.

In terms of the health benefits to the baby, there are 400 substances in breast milk (including hormones, antibodies, and growth factors) that are missing in formula. These "secret ingredients" deliver a lot of benefits, including added protection against Sudden Infant Death Syndrome, gastrointestinal infections, urinary tract infections, respiratory infections, middle ear infections, food allergies, eczema, tooth decay, pneumonia, and meningitis. Breastfeeding also helps to promote normal development of the muscles in the jaw and face — something that can help to eliminate the need for costly orthodontic work down the road.

Breastfeeding is also good for mothers. The activity triggers the release of oxytocin, the hormone that helps the uterus to contract to its prepregnancy size and can give you a natural high. (Don't believe us? Watch how many breastfeeding mothers drift off to sleep while nursing their babies.) And because it requires 500 or more calories a day to breastfeed even the youngest of babies, breastfeeding can also help promote weight loss. (Remember: One of the reasons your body packed on some extra pounds during pregnancy was so that it would have some food stores to draw upon during lactation.) Studies have even shown that women who breastfeed for at least three months may be less likely to develop premenopausal breast cancer, ovarian cancer, or osteoporosis so breastfeeding can have long-lasting and far-reaching benefits for new moms.

Here are some other points that may convince you to give breastfeeding a chance.

- **Breastfeeding is convenient.** There are no bottles to prepare and no nipples to sterilize, and you can feed your baby at 3:00 a.m. without having to fully wake up. What's more, you can feed your baby anywhere, anytime.

- **Breastfeeding is inexpensive.** In fact, it's practically free. Other than having to consume a few extra calories each day and possibly purchase some breast pads or a breast pump, there's nothing else to buy.

- **Breast milk is designed for babies.** It contains the right balance of nutrients such as proteins, fats, and carbohydrates. Both the composition and the quantity of breast milk changes as the baby matures. It's the perfect supply-and-demand production system.

- **Breastfeeding promotes closeness and intimacy with your baby.** This isn't to say that you can't feel close to your baby when you're bottle-feeding. (Of course you can!) It's just that there's something particularly warm and intimate about having your baby's cheek tucked up against your breast.

 Bright Idea

Take a breastfeeding class or sit in on a La Leche League meeting before your baby arrives. There's no better way to learn the art of breastfeeding than by picking up tips from experienced breastfeeding moms.

Of course, breastfeeding isn't necessarily the right choice for every mother and baby, and you shouldn't allow anyone to make you feel like a second-class mother if you choose to bottle-feed your baby. That's simply not the case.

Finally, here's something else to consider before we wrap up our breastfeeding discussion: breastfeeding doesn't have to be an all-or-nothing proposition. A message that often gets lost in the breastfeeding-versus-bottle-feeding debate is the fact that you can, in fact, do both. If you would like to breastfeed but are unwilling or unable to do so on a full-time basis, you may choose to combine bottle-feeding and breastfeeding. Although there are risks involved in going this route — your baby may decide to go with the bottle exclusively because it's less work! — if you were going to bottle-feed anyway, you've got nothing to lose by giving breastfeeding a shot. Bottom line? Any amount of breast milk is better than none.

Do I have to do anything special to prepare my breasts for breastfeeding?

Despite what you might have heard, there's no need to toughen up your nipples to prepare them for breastfeeding. (Some books will tell you to rub them with a washcloth daily during pregnancy. Strange but true.) Although there is a certain amount of wear and tear on the nipples during the first few days of breastfeeding, most pain and discomfort can be eliminated through proper positioning, so this is one less thing you need to worry about while you're pregnant.

The only women who need to prepare for breastfeeding are those who are likely to experience nipple problems. If, for example, your nipples are flat or inverted (that is, the nipple is depressed inward), you may need to massage your nipples regularly to encourage the nipple to protrude or consider wearing breast shields (flexible, dome-shaped devices with a small hole in the center that is used to pull retracted nipples outward). Your healthcare provider can give you some advice on this issue.

Bright Idea

Some women with protruding nipples can experience breastfeeding difficulties if their nipple has a tendency to invert when the baby latches on. You can tell if this is likely to be a problem for you and your baby by trying this simple test. Place your thumb and forefinger above and below the nipple on the areola — the pigmented skin surrounding the nipple — and squeeze gently. The nipple should move outward. If it goes inward, you may need to wear breast shields or to manually extract the nipple regularly in order to prepare for breastfeeding.

My partner is for circumcision; I'm against it. What are the experts recomending these days?

Another hot topic — particularly with fathers-to-be — is the whole issue of circumcision. This surgical procedure, which involves removing the foreskin, the sheath of tissue covering the head of the penis, is performed on approximately 65 percent of U.S. boys, making it the most commonly performed surgical procedure on males.

While the American Academy of Pediatrics has spoken out against routine circumcision, it acknowledges that parents have to make up their own minds about the issue by considering personal, religious, and/or cultural factors. (You can read more about the AAP's stand on the issue by visiting the organization's web site at www.aap.org, by the way.)

Here are the pros and cons of circumcision from a medical standpoint.

Pros:

- Males who are circumcised are only one-tenth as likely to experience urinary tract infections as their noncircumcised counterparts.

- Circumcised men are less likely to pick up sexually transmitted diseases such as syphilis, genital herpes, genital warts, and AIDS.

- Males who are circumcised as newborns almost never develop cancer of the penis and are unlikely to experience problems with phimosis (the inability to retract the foreskin by approximately five years of age).

- Circumcision prevents paraphimosis — an emergency situation that occurs if the foreskin gets stuck when it is first retracted.

- Circumcision reduces the incidence of balanoposthitis (inflammation of the skin of the penis caused by either trauma or poor hygiene).

- It is easier to practice good hygiene on a circumcised rather than uncircumcised penis.

- Circumcision during the newborn period is far less risky and expensive than circumcision later in life.

Cons:

- Circumcision is painful. Studies have shown that circumcision is a stressful event for the newborn — one that affects the baby's behavior both during and for as long as 24 hours after the procedure. A study reported in the British medical journal *The Lancet* even found that infants who had been circumcised without pain relief appeared to experience greater pain during childhood vaccinations at age four to six months than uncircumcised babies or babies who had received pain relief during circumcision. (See our note on pain relief options below.)

- Complications — primarily bleeding problems — occur in approximately 1 in 1,000 procedures. In very rare circumstances, severe penile damage can occur. Circumcision is not recommended for a baby who is sick, who is premature, or who has any sort of penile abnormality.

- Circumcision may not be necessary. Proper penile hygiene and safe sexual practices can prevent phimosis, paraphimosis, balanoposthitis, penile cancer, sexually transmitted diseases, and many other health problems associated with the uncircumcised penis.

■ Some anticircumcision advocates believe that circumcision results in decreased sexual pleasure for the male partner and argue that the procedure basically amounts to genital mutilation.

Note: If you do decide to opt for circumcision, be sure to talk to your doctor about what pain relief options are available. He will probably recommend either a dorsal nerve block or a ring block (injections of anesthetic at the base of the penis that numb the pain impulses that travel to the brain), a topical anesthetic (a cream or gel that is applied to the foreskin before the procedure to numb the area), or both (a topical anesthetic followed by a injected anesthetic). Note: Topical anesthetics alone are less effective than local (injected) anesthetics.

Week 35

This week, you may be busy playing the baby name game and pondering the facts about Group B strep.

What's going on with your baby

Your baby weighs about 5 ½ pounds and measures just over 20 inches in length. You may enjoy watching your baby move from side to side when you're lying in the tub. You can tell which side your baby is lying on by comparing the two sides of your belly!

What's going on with your body

You may notice a small amount of swelling in your feet and ankles at the end of the day. While extreme swelling can be a warning sign of preeclampsia, small amounts of swelling are relatively common during pregnancy — the result of the added fluid volume. (By the time you give birth, you'll be carrying around 26 more cups of liquid than you were before you became pregnant.)

What's going on with your head

Some couples have their babies' names picked out long before they ever hit the reproductive jackpot; others are still debating the merits of "Morgan" versus "Madison" after their baby has made her grand debut.

If you're still trying to decide on the perfect name for your baby-to-be, here are a few tips that may help you to reduce the number of names on your short list.

- Think long-term. Resist the temptation to go with a trendy name that will sound dated even before your baby cuts her first tooth.

- Steer clear of names that sound too babyish. You want to choose a name that will work for your baby throughout her entire life.

- Test-drive the prospective name by pairing it with your last-name and by checking out the initials you'd be saddling your kid with. (Hint: If the initials spell "BAD," you could be borrowing trouble.)

- Keep the spelling simple. Your child's future teachers and employers will thank you for it.

- Only consider naming your baby after a friend or relative if you feel confident that that person is going to be part of your life for a very long time — and that they're going to keep their nose clean. Otherwise, you'll have a explain to your child why he was named in honor of the family jailbird!

The Hot List: This week's must-ask pregnancy questions

Your doctor or midwife is likely to screen you for Group B strep at some point during the next few weeks. Here are the answers to some of the most frequently asked questions about the Group B strep test.

What is Group B strep and who should be tested for it?

Group B streptococcus (GBS) is a type of bacteria that causes particular problems for pregnant women and newborn babies. It is carried by 10 percent to 30 percent of pregnant women. It is found most often in the vagina and the rectum, though it sometimes is detected in the initial urine culture performed at the first prenatal visit.

The American Academy of Pediatrics recommends that all pregnant women be screened for Group B strep bacteria between 35 and 37 weeks of pregnancy, and that all women who have risk factors prior to being screened for Group B strep (for example, women who have preterm labor beginning before 37 completed weeks' gestation) be treated with IV antibiotics during their labors or after their membranes have ruptured until it is determined whether they are group B carriers. This is because a baby who becomes infected with Group B strep can become seriously ill. A baby who is infected with Group B strep may end up with blood, lung, brain, and spinal-cord infections. Five percent of babies who are infected with Group B strep die.

How is Group B strep transmitted to the baby?

A pregnant woman can pass Group B strep on to her baby during pregnancy, during delivery, or after the birth. This happens in approximately 1 to 2 of every 100 babies born to women who are Group B strep carriers. A baby may also be infected through contact with other people who are Group B strep carriers.

 Watch Out!

A pregnant woman with Group B strep may either experience no complications at all or develop bladder infections, amnionitis (an infection of the amniotic fluid and membranes), or endometritis (an infection of the uterus that generally occurs postpartum).

When is the Group B strep test typically performed and what does it involve?

The Group B strep test is typically performed at 35 to 37 weeks of pregnancy — although there is some controversy concerning the timing of the test. A woman who tests negative at week 37 (meaning that she doesn't have Group B strep) may, in fact, be Group B strep positive by the time she goes into labor. This is why some caregivers choose to forgo the screening and decide instead to treat any pregnant woman who has the following risk factors with antibiotics during labor:

- preterm labor (labor before 37 postmenstrual weeks),
- preterm rupture of membranes (membranes rupture before 37 weeks LMP),
- prolonged rupture of membranes (membranes have been ruptured for more than 18 hours before the baby is born),
- has previously given birth to a baby with GBS infection,
- has a fever during labor,
- has previously tested positive for GBS in a prenatal urine culture taken earlier in this pregnancy . Note: A woman who has tested positive for Group B strep and who is having a cesarean delivery does not need to be treated with intravenous antibiotics during labor if her delivery occurs before the onset of labor and the rupture of membranes.

What does the test involve?

The Group B strep test involves taking a culture from the vagina, perineum, and rectum during pregnancy. The results of the culture are available within two days. If your test comes back positive (meaning that you are carrying Group B strep), you should strongly consider taking antibiotics during your labor to minimize the risk of passing on Group B strep to your baby. Only a very small percentage of babies whose mothers take antibiotics during labor end up being infected with Group B strep.

Watch Out!

A 2001 study indicated that women who have tested positive for Group B strep face an increased risk of giving birth prematurely.

What will happen if I test positive for Group B strep?

Your doctor or midwife will arrange for you to receive antibiotics during labor. According to the Centers for Disease Control, if all pregnant women were screened for Group B strep at 35 to 37 weeks' gestation and all women who tested positive were treated with antibiotics during labor, 75 percent of cases of Group B strep that appear during the first week of life could be prevented.

Just the facts

- Your birth plan is not a blueprint for labor. Neither you nor your caregiver can predict in advance whether it will be possible to follow your birth plan to the letter.

- If you're giving birth for the first time, practicing perineal massage during the last six weeks of pregnancy may reduce the odds that you will require an episiotomy.

- Neither the American College of Obstetricians nor the American Academy of Pediatrics routinely recommend private cord blood banking to parents-to-be, but the AAP notes that cord blood banking may be a sensible option for families facing specific medical risks.

- Breastfeeding delivers a number of significant health benefits to mother and baby. Any amount of breastfeeding is good for babies: it doesn't have to be an all-or-nothing proposition.

- The American Academy of Pediatrics is opposed to routine circumcision, but acknowledges that parents have to make up their own minds about the issue by weighing the personal, religious, and/or cultural factors involved.

- Group B strep is a bacteria that can be harmful — even fatal — to newborn babies. Your caregiver may recommend that you be screened for it during your last few weeks of pregnancy. If you test positive for it, you'll be treated with antibiotics during your labor.

GET THE SCOOP ON. . .
What's going on with your baby ▪ What's going
on with your body ▪ What's going on with your
head ▪ Your partner's role during labor ▪ Late
pregnancy aches and pains ▪ Late pregnancy
worries ▪ Going overdue

The Ninth Month: Nine Months and Counting

Chapter 13

As you head into the homestretch of pregnancy, you may feel as though you've been pregnant forever. It may seem like a lifetime ago since you were able to touch your toes, sleep on your stomach, or run up a flight of stairs without huffing and puffing.

At the same time, you may find that you're extremely absentminded and preoccupied. You may be spending a lot of time and energy wondering about what lies ahead — when you will go into labor, how the birth will go, and how your life will change once your baby arrives on the scene. (Of course, some expectant parents are so focused on giving birth that they fail to give much thought to what life will be like in their postbaby universe — something that can lead to a bit of culture shock down the road!)

In this chapter, we discuss the issues that are likely to be on your mind as you head into the final leg of the pregnancy marathon: late pregnancy aches and pains, late pregnancy worries, and your partner's role during the birth. And, as in chapters past, we'll give you an idea of what to expect on a week-by-week basis — this time for weeks 36 through 40. You'll get the inside scoop on what's going on with your body, what's going on with your head, and what's going on with your baby each week, plus you'll find answers to some of the most-asked pregnancy questions for each week of pregnancy.

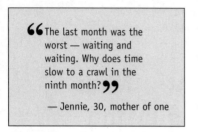

❝The last month was the worst — waiting and waiting. Why does time slow to a crawl in the ninth month?**❞**

— Jennie, 30, mother of one

Week 36

Now that the birth of your baby is, at most, a few weeks away, you may be wondering what your baby's doing to get ready for the birth and what you yourself should be doing in terms of preparations.

What's going on with your baby

Space is getting cramped (as if you hadn't noticed!), so it only makes sense that your baby's rate of growth starts to slow down at this stage of the game. Unlike some months of pregnancy when he managed to double his weight in a single month, this month, he'll only increase his weight by about 25 percent. He'll start the month weighing about 6 pounds and measuring close to 21 inches and — by the time you give birth — he'll weigh about 7.5 pounds and measure about 21 ½ inches long.

Of course, we're talking about an average-sized baby here. Some babies are considerably smaller, while others are much heftier — something you'll discover for yourself when you meet your classmates' babies at your childbirth class reunion!

What's going on with your body

You may find it hard to eat normal-sized meals, due to the increased pressure of the uterus on your stomach. You'll likely find that it works best to eat a series of healthy snacks and mini-meals throughout the day rather than trying to eat a lot of food in a single sitting.

Here are a few suggestions of healthy meals and snacks that are easy to prepare and that pack a lot of nutritional punch. (You don't want to head into labor powered by little more than a Twinkie, after all!)

- Yogurt mixed with cereal and diced fruit;
- Fruit and yogurt smoothies;
- Hard-boiled eggs;
- Low-fat cheese (just be sure to avoid soft and semi-soft cheeses — see Chapter 6 for more on prenatal nutrition);
- Cooked meats (be sure to stick to products that are safe for use during pregnancy) ;
- Hummus and bean dips ;
- English muffins, breads, and pitas;
- Bran muffins;
- Whole grain crackers;
- Dried fruits and nuts;
- Fresh fruits; and,
- Fresh vegetables.

By the way, a lot of these foods make for great meals and snacks after your baby arrives, so be sure to keep the refrigerator and pantry well stocked. It can be hard to predict when you'll have time to go grocery shopping again!

What's going on with your head

Many women worry about labor from the moment they find out that they are pregnant. Others don't start worrying until their pregnancies are considerably further along (obviously the Scarlett O'Haras in the bunch, who prefer to "think about it tomorrow").

Tracy, 31, remembers being frightened throughout her entire pregnancy about the prospect of giving birth: "One of the first thoughts that went through my head when I read that positive on the pregnancy test was, 'Oh no. Now I have to give birth!' My fear of giving birth was pretty steady throughout the pregnancy. Whenever I'd read birth stories or the chapters on birth in my pregnancy books, or watch a birth video, my hands would shake and I'd feel myself turn hot and cold. I was afraid that I wouldn't be able to handle it; that I'd fall apart, that I'd panic."

Johnna, 33, also spent a great deal of time worrying about the delivery during her first pregnancy. "My biggest concern during the pregnancy was labor. It was such a big unknown and you hear so many scary stories from other moms. The books make it sound like if you just breathe right, it will be manageable, but you know from talking to others that is sometimes really difficult. It was hard to sit and wonder what it would be like."

Fear of labor can also be a big issue for dads-to-be, as first-time father Troy, 30, explains: "One of my concerns was what would labor be like and whether I would be up to the challenge. All the pregnancies I'd ever seen were on TV shows. You know — first the mother's water breaks and then within about 3 minutes she goes into extreme contractions, but of course it's all over in 10 minutes! Lastly — and this is selfish — I was hoping her water would not break while riding in our new car. I just kept thinking about all this amniotic fluid running over my leather seats. Yuck!"

Note: You can find a detailed discussion of many common labor-related fears in Chapter 18.

The Hot List: This week's must-ask pregnancy questions

You may be wondering about sciatica, restless legs syndrome, and how your prenatal checkups are likely to play out during the final weeks of pregnancy.

What should I expect from my weekly prenatal checkups?

You will be seeing your doctor or midwife on a weekly basis this month. During these weekly checkups, you can expect your doctor or midwife to check

- **the fundal height** (your healthcare provider will measure the distance between your pubic bone and the top of your uterus — the fundus);

- **size and position of the baby** (your doctor or midwife will assess this by placing her hands on your abdomen and feeling for the baby and may be able to tell you your baby's approximate size, his presentation — e.g., head first or buttocks first — and how far your baby has descended into the pelvis);

- **your weight** (don't be surprised if it stays the same or if you've actually dropped a pound or two; your caregiver is only likely to become concerned if your weight shoots up quite dramatically — a possible indication of preeclampsia);

- **your blood pressure** (to look for any signs of pregnancy-related hypertension or preeclampsia);

- **your urine** (to ensure that your sugar and protein levels are within the normal range as abnormal values can indicate potential problems);

- **the fetal heart rate** (to keep tabs on your baby's general health and well-being). Reminder: Your baby's heart beats much more rapidly than your own — at a rate of 120 to 160 beats per minute on average.

- **your cervix** (to see if your cervix has begun to thin out or to dilate in anticipation of labor).

Watch Out!

Applying hot or cold compresses or rub-in lotions to the affected area can help manage the pain, but check with your doctor or midwife first before you start administering these types of treatments. You don't want to risk making the problem worse by going with the wrong type of treatment or using a product or treatment technique that may not be recommended during pregnancy.

My doctor just diagnosed the hip pain that I've been experiencing as sciatica. What is sciatica and what causes it?

Sciatica is the name given to pain, tingling, or numbness that runs down the buttock, hip, and thigh. It is typically caused by the pressure of the pregnant uterus on the sciatic nerve. (You have two sciatic nerves, which run from your lower back down your legs to your feet.)

Sciatic pain can be excruciatingly painful — even immobilizing. But as painful as it may be to move around, it's important to get up and walk around at least every half hour during the day or the sciatica will worsen. Some pregnant women report that floating in a swimming pool provides tremendous relief. Mmmm . . . heaven!

Sometimes, in the middle of the night, it feels like bugs are crawling all over my legs. Is there anything I can do to stop this feeling?

It sounds like you may be experiencing restless legs syndrome (RLS) — an aptly named disorder that affects 15 percent of Americans but that tends to be more common during pregnancy. It consists of unpleasant sensations in the limbs — creeping, crawling, tingling, burning, or aching in the calves, thighs, feet, or upper portions of the legs.

It is more likely to occur when you are resting and it is typically relieved if you get up and walk around.

RLS symptoms tend to be particularly troublesome at night, so the syndrome is often accompanied by insomnia. It is also sometimes associated with nighttime leg twitching — a condition that is formally known as periodic limb movements of sleep.

If you suffer from RLS, you can minimize your symptoms by

- taking a warm bath;
- massaging your legs;
- exercising regularly (but not too late at night);
- avoiding alcohol and caffeine, which tend to make the condition worse. (Obviously, you should be avoiding alcohol and limiting your caffeine use anyway.)

You may require some form of pain relief if your RLS symptoms are particularly severe. Talk to your doctor or midwife if your symptoms are making it difficult for you to get a good night's sleep.

Week 37

You may be wondering about the immunities against disease that you're able to pass along to your baby prior to giving birth, why you seem to be becoming klutzier by the day, and whether or not you've really and truly got what it takes to be a good parent.

What's going on with your baby

Your baby is acquiring important antibodies from you that will provide potentially life-saving protection against diseases and illnesses that would otherwise be deadly to a vulnerable newborn baby. And, if you choose to breastfeed, you'll also be topping off these immunities after the birth. This natural form of "immunization" provides a baby with about six months of protection after the birth, which is why your baby's doctor will likely advise that you have him immunized starting at age two months.

What's going on with your body

You may find that you have a tendency to bump into things, either because you misjudge your ever-changing body proportions or because your altered center of gravity has thrown off your sense of balance.

Don't assume that you've permanently morphed into a klutz extraordinaire. You'll regain your old sense of balance and coordination in a few weeks' time after your baby has been born.

What's going on with your head

Now that the countdown to the birth is officially on, you may find yourself wondering if you've got what it takes to be a good parent. "Having a child is so irreversible," explains Tracy, a 31-year-old mother of one. "Any other decision you make in life can be changed. You can quit a job, grow out a bad haircut, drop out of school, or get a divorce, but nothing stops you from being a parent. I often felt like I was trapped on a speeding train, destination unknown, and I just hoped I'd like where I was when the train finally stopped."

"The hardest part for me was the overwhelming sense of responsibility," adds Heather, a 32-year-old first-time mother. "Suddenly, I was carrying another life — one that had no say in what happened. If I made a mistake and crashed my car, I could live with me paying for it with injuries, and so on, but I couldn't imagine the guilt of having injured my child."

If you're being hit with a last-minute case of parenting cold feet, don't take this as proof positive that you've made a huge mistake in deciding to start a family. It's normal to have these doubts during the weeks leading up to the birth (and for the subsequent 18 years, too, in fact!). The simple fact that you're putting this much thought and energy into parenting matters before your baby has even arrived on the scene means that you're likely to be an exceptionally committed parent. So try to cut yourself a bit of slack.

The Hot List: This week's must-ask pregnancy questions

Feel like an imposter who has been sent in to care for some poor, unsuspecting baby who has no idea just how inexperienced his parents truly are? The answers to the following health and safety questions should help to reassure you that you've actually got what it takes to take great care of your baby.

How will I know when my baby is sick?

A lot of first-time parents worry that they will fail to pick up on the warning signs that their baby is seriously ill. Fortunately, most quickly discover that their "parent radar" is more finely tuned than they thought and that they are able to zero in on the following symptoms of illness with relatively little difficulty:

- Runny nose (usually caused by a viral infection such as the common cold, but can also be triggered by allergies or chemical sensitivities);

- Coughing (can be caused by the common cold, allergies, exposure to cigarette smoke and other irritants, or chronic lung diseases);

- Wheezing (caused by the narrowing of the air passages in the lungs and the presence of excess mucus in the major airways);

- Croup (a noisy, seal-like bark that is caused by an inflammation of the windpipe below the vocal cords);

- Diarrhea and/or abdominal cramps (can be riggered by a gastrointestinal problem, a food sensitivity, or other illnesses);

- Vomiting (caused by a related illness and generally only cause for concern if your child is becoming dehydrated);

- Changes to your baby's skin color (e.g., extreme paleness or extreme flushedness; can be the result of a systemic or localized infection);

- Rashes (caused by a viral or bacterial infection or an allergic reaction to a food, medication, or other substances);

- Behavioral changes such as extreme fussiness or lethargy (caused by an illness or infection);

- Fever (caused by an infection, a reaction to an immunization, or overdressing your baby).

Watch Out!

Dehydration can occur quite rapidly in young infants. You should seek medical treatment for your baby immediately if he has a dry mouth, if he isn't drinking as much as usual, if he is crying less often than usual, if he isn't shedding any tears when he cries, if he is having less than six wet diapers per day, and/or if he is experiencing some vomiting and/or diarrhea.

Will I be able to protect my baby from harm?

The world can suddenly feel like a very scary place when you're entrusted with the task of caring for a newborn. Fortunately, newborn babies aren't nearly as fragile as they look, and common sense and parental instinct enable most parents to keep their babies safe from harm.

You may feel a little less out of your element if you do some reading on baby care and sign up for an infant and toddler first aid course before your baby arrives. That may help to bring your anxiety level down a notch.

> 66 Newborns aren't as fragile as I was led to believe. I bumped my baby's head by accident when she was about two weeks old, and just as she was about to cry, I pulled her close. Then I cried and she just looked at me, puzzled. 99
>
> — Andrea, 27, mother of one

Week 38

At this point in your pregnancy, you may be wondering if your baby is in the best position for labor and how your partner is likely to fare during the birth.

What's going on with your baby

Your baby may have assumed the head-down position by now (the position that the majority of babies are in when their mothers go into labor) but, if he hasn't, he still has a week or two yet to change positions.

Of course, some babies remain in a breech (bottom down) or transverse (sideways) position right up until their moms go into labor. (See Chapter 18 for more about the baby's position during birth.)

What's going on with your body

If you notice that a decrease in the pressure on your diaphragm and an increase in the pressure in your pelvis, chances are your baby has "dropped." This process — called "lightening" can occur a couple of weeks ahead of the onset of labor or just as labor begins, so while it can't be taken as a sign that your baby's birth is imminent, it's a sign that labor is at most a couple of weeks away.

What's going on with your head

Wondering how having a baby will affect your relationship with your partner? If the bond between the two of you is strong enough, you can expect to weather this particular relationship storm without too much difficulty. A study at the University of Washington revealed that couples who are good friends before they start their families are better able to adjust to the stresses of new parenthood than couples who are less satisfied with their relationships.

Of course, you won't be able to keep your relationship on track purely by accident. You need to make spending time with your partner a priority, even if that means keeping your eyes open for an extra hour after the baby goes to bed or asking a friend or relative to stay with the baby for an hour or two so that you and your partner can have dinner out at a favorite restaurant.

If you can't bear the thought of being away from your baby for even that short a period of time — a not-uncommon reaction amongst new mothers, by the way — you might decide to have "date night" at home. (Just one word of warning: you have to be prepared to roll with the punches. It's impossible to predict ahead of time whether the first hot-and-heavy kiss you've enjoyed in weeks will be interrupted by the cries of a hungry baby!)

It's also important to spend time talking with your partner about how he's finding the adjustment to parenthood — to check in with him regularly to find out how he's coping with the sleep deprivation, less-frequent sex, and other challenges associated with being a new dad.

Dads sometimes feel that they get overlooked entirely because everyone is so interested in what's going on with Mom and the new baby. So try to find little ways to let your partner know that he's still as important to you as ever, whether it's something as corny as drawing a toothpaste heart on the bathroom mirror or as simple as sending him a quick "I love you" e-mail at work. These little things can serve as powerful relationship glue during an otherwise very challenging period in your life and may help the two of you to navigate the sometimes stormy seas of new parenthood as a couple.

The Hot List: This week's must-ask pregnancy questions

Dads-to-be often have a lot of questions about pregnancy and birth — more specifically what will be asked of them when the moment of truth arrives. Here are answers to some of the questions that may be running through your partner's head right about now.

How will I know what to do during labor? What if I do the wrong thing?

Follow your partner's lead and rest assured that she'll let you know in no uncertain terms if you're doing something that's driving her completely and utterly around the bend. (If, for example, she grabs your watch and chucks it across the room, you could take that as a sign that she's less than thrilled with your plan to time her contractions using the electronic beeper on your watch!) You know your partner better than most other people on the planet, so you'll be able to sense if she's worried, tired, frustrated, or in need of some added reassurance and to respond accordingly. Remember, the doctor or midwife is responsible for meeting her healthcare needs; your role is to provide her with emotional support — something you already do on a daily basis. Chances are you'll do just fine.

Is it okay for the labor coach to take a short dinner break?

No one expects you to survive indefinitely on the meager snacks that you squirreled away in your partner's labor bag. You're allowed to leave the labor room and go and grab a sandwich every now and again. But you'll want to time your breaks for points in labor when your partner seems to be coping particularly well, as opposed to heading for the hospital cafeteria at a point in your partner's labor when the contractions are coming particularly fast and furious.

If you think you'd like to have a backup person on hand to step in as labor coach at times like this, you and your partner might consider inviting a third person to be part of your baby's birth — perhaps a friend or relative or a professional labor support person such as a doula (see Chapter 12). While some dads don't like having anyone else around, others welcome an extra set of hands. Only you and your partner can decide what will work best for you.

Week 39

You may find it hard to get motivated to do anything — or you may find yourself being hit with a powerful nesting instinct that sees you rearranging the baby's room a dozen times a day. To each her own. . . .

What's going on with your baby

Your baby's intestines are filled with meconium — a sticky greeny-black substance that is made up of alimentary gland secretions, lanugo, pigment, and cells from the wall of your bowel. Your baby will pass this meconium during his bowel movement after the birth.

Watch Out!

Some babies pass meconium before or during labor. This can be a sign of fetal distress, so if your membranes rupture and you notice that your amniotic fluid contains meconium, you should get in touch with your doctor or midwife right away. She will want to monitor you and your baby quite closely and — depending on how your baby is doing — she may want to induce your labor right away.

What's going on with your body

You may experience a prebirth burst of energy — the much-talked-about "nesting instinct." While the jury is still out on whether this occurs for biological or psychological reasons — because of biochemical changes or because you realize that you're about to have a baby and there's still a lot to be done — it seems to be quite common.

But even if you *are* hit with an urge to reorganize the nursery a dozen times, try to conserve some of that energy for the birth. You don't want to be exhausted from an all-night wallpapering marathon by the time the first labor contraction kicks in. Remember, a well-rested mama beats a coordinating nursery hands down any day of the week.

What's going on with your head

If you have other children at home, you may be secretly worried whether you have enough love to share with another baby. "I loved my first child so intensely that I couldn't imagine loving another baby that much again," admits Marie, 34, a mother of four. "Of course, I've since learned that I have more than enough love for four kids — and possibly even a few more!"

And, of course, you may be quietly wondering if you're about to ruin your other child's life by throwing a sibling into the mix. "During my second pregnancy, I worried how the new baby would affect my firstborn," admits Debbie, a 39-year-old mother of two. "I mean, he was still a baby himself."

You may find it helpful to compare notes with other parents you know who've recently added a new baby to their families and do some reading on sibling issues. You'll quickly discover that you're not the only parent to grapple with these issues. They're pretty much par for the course for parents with more than one child.

The Hot List: This week's must-ask pregnancy questions

You've no doubt heard all kinds of folk remedies for bringing on labor — remedies that can range from completely ineffective to downright dangerous. Here's what you need to know about attempting to jump-start labor on your own.

A friend told me that I can get labor started by taking castor oil. Is this true?

While a study at Winthrop University Hospital in Mineola, New York, indicated that taking castor oil may increase the likelihood that you will go into labor within the next 24 hours, this method isn't recommended because it can also trigger some powerful bowel cramps that will only add your misery during labor. (Some women who've tried this method swear that had they known what they were in for, they would have gladly chosen to remain pregnant forever!)

I've heard that having sex will help to bring on labor. Is this true?

Everyone knows someone who swears this worked for them, but, there's no hard science behind this particular bit of folk wisdom. While there are prostaglandins in semen and prostaglandins can be used to induce labor, there isn't enough prostanglandin in semen to move things along in a major way. So if your best friend went into labor right after enjoying a late-pregnancy romp in the hay, perhaps she was due to go into labor anyway.

Bright Idea

Find yourself with a lot of questions about labor? Chapter 18 addresses all the most common labor-related worries: when to call your doctor or midwife, how to differentiate between true and false labor, and what labor is *really* like. So you might want to flip ahead and read that chapter sooner rather than later.

Of course, there are worse things you could be doing to help while away the time while you're waiting for labor to start, so if having sex is going to help make the time pass a little more quickly (and hopefully a little more pleasurably), then you may want to have a bit of fun with this particular labor induction "method."

Is it safe to use herbal products to induce labor?

To put it bluntly, no. It's not a good idea to use herbal products to induce labor. The reason is simple: herbal products have not been sufficiently standardized in terms of dosage and potency for you to have an accurate sense of how much of a particular substance you're taking. Consequently, you risk triggering labor contractions that are dangerously strong — so strong, in fact, that they could potentially cause the placenta to separate prematurely from the uterine wall, causing a medical emergency for you and your baby.

Trust us, you don't want to go there.

What about spicy foods, long walks, and drives on bumpy roads?

While these techniques can all help to pass the time, they aren't going to do much to bring on labor. Sorry.

Week 40

As you head into week 40, you may be wondering when you're finally going to have the chance to meet your baby. While we can't guarantee it will happen this week, we can promise you it will happen soon. You don't have to worry about being pregnant forever. Honest!

What's going on with your baby

Your baby plays a key role in deciding when he's ready to be born. Scientists believe that once the baby has reached a certain stage of maturity, he sends out a series of biochemical and hormonal signals that indicate that the moment of truth has arrived. These signals, in turn, cause the mother's body to trigger a series of biochemical and hormonal changes which ultimately culminate in labor.

What's going on with your body

Prior to pregnancy, your uterus weighed 2 ounces and was capable of holding half an ounce of liquid. By the time you deliver, it will weigh over 2 pounds and hold a quart of amniotic fluid.

Your baby has also undergone a remarkable process of growth and development. An 8-pound baby weighs approximately 2 billion times more than the fertilized egg that initiated the journey to birth.

Much of your baby's weight gain has occurred during the last few months. Most babies double their weight during the last 2 ½ months of pregnancy.

What's going on with your head

If your due date comes and goes, you could find yourself going a little stir crazy, wondering how much longer you're going to have to play the labor waiting game. You may even find that you start becoming anxious and depressed as you wait for labor to get underway. After all, you signed up for 40 weeks of pregnancy — not 40-plus!

Debbie, 31, a mother of three, remembers how frustrated she became when her due date for her third baby came and went without as much as a single uterine twinge. "My youngest daughter was two weeks overdue, something that was especially torturous because my other two children were two and three weeks early. I cried everyday, was a real jerk to be around, and tried every old wives' tale to bring on labor. None of them worked. I became depressed, withdrawn, and obsessed with the calendar. I would wake up every morning disappointed again."

Carrie, a 31-year-old first-time mother, experienced similar emotions: "My baby arrived 10 days late. What made it really bad was the fact that the doctor told me I would probably go into labor early, so I was expecting that and she ended up being 10 days late. I tried to stay sane, but it was really hard. I worked all the way up until I had her, and the worst part was walking into work everyday and having everyone say, 'You haven't had that baby yet? When is that baby coming?' I was ready to strangle someone. I felt like making an announcement over the intercom each morning that I was still here and had not had the baby yet."

> 66 One thing nobody talks about is the depression that can go along with being overdue. 99
>
> — Melissa, 24, mother of two

Danielle, a 27-year-old mother of three, recalls how impatient she was to get labor underway: "I did aerobics, I jogged up and down my street, I massaged buckets of essential oils into my tummy, and I even did the castor-oil and juice thing — the worst idea in the world. None of these tactics worked. I still had to be induced."

One first-time mom — 32-year-old Heather — took things a step further: "I drove over a bumpy road (my mom drove), I ate a spicy Mexican meal, I drank a glass of red wine (okay, it was actually ruby port because I didn't want to open a whole bottle!), and I spent three hours belly-dancing. This didn't start things right away, but by the middle of the night I was in early labor."

Of course, not every mom-to-be necessarily considers these bonus weeks of pregnancy to be a bad thing. Mary, a 27-year-old first-time mother, didn't mind having her pregnancy go on a little longer than anticipated: "My son was due on Labor Day, but arrived seven days late. Frankly, I was glad for each extra day I had to get used to the idea of having a baby."

If, however, like the majority of pregnant women, you're feeling less than grateful about having your pregnancy drag on, here are some tips on staying sane:

- Keep yourself busy. It's easy to get hit with a heavy-duty case of cabin fever if you're home alone day after day. (Hint: Don't be afraid to make plans because you might have to cancel them. Going into labor is the ultimate excuse for getting out of *anything!)*

- Pamper yourself. Enjoy all those special indulgences that you'll find it hard to fit in after your baby arrives. Soak in a bubble bath, spend an afternoon reading magazines, or meet one of your girlfriends for lunch.

- Let your answering machine screen your calls. Better yet, let it run interference for you. Here's what Jennie, a 30-year-old first-time mother, did: "In response to all the phone messages that said, 'Oh, you're not home. You must be out having your baby,' we finally changed our answering machine message to say, 'We're just out, we're not having our baby.' (Of course, we had to change the message when my water broke and we really were out having our baby!)"

- Realize that your caregiver doesn't have a crystal ball and can't pinpoint the day and hour of your delivery. "The doctors have no idea exactly what day the baby is coming," confirms Jackie, 34. "With my first, I went for my 38-week checkup and was told, 'See you next week,' but ended up seeing my doctor in the delivery room the very next day."

The Hot List: This week's must-ask pregnancy questions

If your due date comes and goes and there's still no baby, you are likely to find yourself with a lot of questions about going overdue. Here's what you need to know.

Is it possible for your doctor or midwife to predict ahead of time if your baby is likely to be overdue?

Not really. While you may have heard a common pregnancy myth, which states that you're more likely to experience a post-date pregnancy if you're having your first baby, despite what other pregnancy books may tell you, the studies in the medical literature on this subject are contradictory, at best.

The only situation in which your doctor or midwife is likely to be able to look inside her gestational crystal ball and tell you if you're likely to go overdue is if you have a repeated history of postdate pregnancy. In this case, it's quite likely that your current pregnancy may extend past your due date — but, of course, there are no guarantees. Your baby can always surprise you.

What's the difference between being overdue and being postdate?

There's overdue, and then there's *really* overdue. Ten percent of all babies don't arrive until at least two weeks past their due date, at which point they're described as being postdate or post-term.

At what point does being postdate start posing a risk to the developing baby?

Although some babies benefit from a little extra time in the womb, there is cause for concern if a pregnancy continues for too long. Postdate babies are at increased risk of becoming too large for a safe delivery or of experiencing fetal postmaturity syndrome (which occurs if the deteriorating placenta is no longer functioning as well as it did earlier in the pregnancy). At 43 weeks, it is five times riskier for a baby to remain inside the womb than to be born. At 44 weeks, this figure rises to seven times.

 Watch Out!

If you notice a significant decrease in fetal movement, contact your caregiver promptly. Although usually a false alarm, it could indicate that your baby is in some degree of distress.

Of course, some babies who are classified as post-term are, in fact, right on schedule; it's the due date that's out of whack. These types of due-date miscalculations are more common in women who have irregular menstrual cycles or who were using oral contraceptives prior to the pregnancy. Before your doctor or midwife makes a decision to induce you, your caregiver will review your prenatal record in an attempt to verify whether or not your due date is likely to be accurate. She will begin to suspect that it's inaccurate if

- your baby's heartbeat wasn't heard as early as usual (10 to 12 weeks with a Doppler device or 18 to 20 weeks with a fetoscope);

- the measurements taken during any ultrasounds (especially those taken before 20 weeks) seem to call your due date into question.

If your pregnancy goes beyond 41 to 42 weeks but your baby appears to be doing well, your caregiver may decide to give you the choice of either waiting it out for a little while longer or being induced, but chances are she won't want you to remain pregnant for much longer: studies have suggested that routine induction of labor at 41 weeks may result in healthier babies and fewer cesareans, so most doctors and midwives are reluctant to let pregnancy drag on for weeks beyond that point.

If you decide to let nature take its course, your healthcare practitioner will want to monitor your baby closely to ensure her continued well-being by performing one or more of the following types of tests — although some doctors and midwives advise beginning testing at 41 weeks just in case the due date is off by a week and you're actually further along than your doctor or midwife thought):

- **a nonstress test** (NST) (the baby's heart rate is monitored via external monitoring equipment for up to 40 minutes to look for the reassuring accelerations that occur in reaction to fetal movements);

- **an amniotic fluid index** (AFI) ultrasound is used to assess the quantity of amniotic fluid);

- **a biophysical profile** (an NST plus a detailed ultrasound that assesses the baby's breathing movements, his body or limb movements, his fetal tone, and the quantity of amniotic fluid);

- **a contraction stress test** (the baby's response to uterine contractions is monitored, looking for potentially worrisome decelerations in the heart rate).

Based on what the tests reveal, you and your caregiver may decide to continue to play the waiting game or to opt for induction. (See Chapter 18 for information on what's involved in an induction.) Either way, you can feel confident that your baby's birthday is fast approaching. It's only a matter of time before the 9 ½ months of waiting will be behind you and you will finally get to meet your baby.

Just the facts

- By the time you give birth, your baby will weigh about 7.5 pounds and measure about 21 ½ inches long.

- If you notice a decrease in the pressure on your diaphragm and an increase in the pressure in your pelvis, chances are your baby has "dropped."

- If your membranes rupture and you notice that your amniotic fluid contains meconium, you should get in touch with your doctor or midwife right away.

- Ten percent of babies don't arrive until at least two weeks past their due date, at which point they're described as being postdate or post-term.

What Other Pregnancy Books Won't Tell You

PART V

Chapter 14

To Test or Not to Test?

To our mothers' and grandmothers' generations, modern prenatal tests must sound like the stuff of which science fiction novels are made. Miniature cameras inserted right into the uterus allow doctors to assess the well-being of the developing baby. Samples of amniotic fluid, umbilical cord blood, and fetal tissue provide expectant parents with a genetic and chromosomal fingerprint of their unborn child. And a simple blood test can be used to predict the probability that a particular woman will give birth to a child with either a neural tube defect or Down syndrome.

Although prenatal tests have proven beneficial to large numbers of pregnant women, the information they provide doesn't come without a price. Prenatal tests can cause unnecessary stress to couples who might otherwise be enjoying problem-free pregnancies and, in a small percentage of cases, can lead to complications that may result in the loss of an otherwise healthy baby.

In this chapter, we provide you with the facts you need in order to make informed choices about prenatal testing. We discuss the pros and cons of prenatal testing, the risks and benefits of the various types of tests, and the options you have in the event that the test brings bad news rather than good.

Tests, tests, and more tests

Prenatal tests fall into one of two basic categories: screening tests and diagnostic tests.

Prenatal screening tests are designed to do what their name implies — to screen a large number of women in order to identify those who have a higher-than-average risk of giving birth to a child with a serious or life-threatening health problem (in the case of the maternal serum alpha-fetoprotein test, which is wrapped into the quadruple screen test) or of developing gestational diabetes (in the case of the glucose tolerance test — a test we discussed back in Chapter 10). Screening tests are not designed to state definitively that there *is* a problem. Their job is simply to alert a pregnant woman and her caregiver to the possibility that there *could be* a problem.

Diagnostic tests, on the other hand, pick up where screening tests leave off. They are used to determine whether there is, in fact, something wrong with the baby. Diagnostic tests that are commonly used in pregnancy include amniocentesis, chorionic villus sampling, level 2 or targeted ultrasound, and the three-hour glucose tolerance test.

Unfortunately, screening tests tend to get an undeservedly bad rap because pregnant women or their caregivers sometimes expect them to do more than what they're designed to do.

This is where all the controversy about the high level of false positives fits in. In order to ensure that as many problems are detected as possible, screening tests inevitably end up generating a certain percentage of so-called false positives (that is, cases in which a pregnant woman is identified as being at risk of having a particular problem when, in fact, she and her baby are perfectly healthy).

Moneysaver

Although most insurance companies and HMOs will cover the cost of prenatal testing that is medically necessary, there are exceptions. That's why it's a good idea to find out up front which tests you may be required to pay for out of your own pocket.

As you can see, there's an art to designing a good screening test. You need to strike a balance between maximizing the rate of detection and minimizing the rate of false positives. Here's the difficulty: the only way to eliminate all false positives is to make the testing criteria so rigid that the test ignores any results that are less than clear-cut (that is, situations in which there may or may not be a problem, but it isn't obvious which is the case). This results in an increased number of false negatives — situations in which problems are missed.

Let's take a moment to consider where the most maligned screening test of them all — the AFP test, also known as the triple or quadruple screen — fits into the picture. If the AFP screening test were designed to be a diagnostic test, its track record would be horrendous: 95 percent of women who receive a positive result on the test are, in fact, carrying perfectly healthy babies. But since it's designed to be a screening test, it makes sense to assess its effectiveness on that basis (that is, how good it is at identifying women who are at risk of giving birth to a baby with a serious birth defect).

Consider the numbers for yourself. Quadruple screening testing results from the University of Connecticut show, for example, that the test has a respectably high detection rate: approximately 81 percent of cases of neural tube defects and 71 percent of cases of Down syndrome in women under age 35 are picked up by the test.

There's just one other point we want to make before we get down off the screening-test soap box — something that makes perfect sense but that isn't intuitively obvious. Screening tests such as the AFP have a very important role to play in prenatal testing because they alert pregnant women who, for age or other reasons, might not otherwise have considered diagnostic testing for the possibility that there could be problems in their pregnancies.

> 66 I wanted to know if my child was going to be healthy and to be able to prepare myself if my baby was going to be less than healthy. 99
>
> —Helena, 42, mother of one

Fortunately, the reverse is also true. The quadruple screen is also capable of providing women in so-called high-risk categories (for example, women in their 40s) with sufficient reassurance to enable them to decline more invasive procedures such as amniocentesis or chorionic villus sampling if their quadruple screen results indicate a low risk of Downs.

The prenatal testing merry-go-round: Do you really want to get on?

The sheer number of prenatal tests is enough to make any expectant parent feel uneasy. After all, the fact that these tests even exist is proof positive that some babies are born with serious — even fatal — birth defects, something that most pregnant women don't even want to think about. Although the odds of having a healthy baby are extremely high — even for women in their 40s — a growing number of expectant couples are choosing to undergo prenatal testing.

Here are the pros and cons of deciding to go that route.

Pros

Prenatal testing allows you to find out if there's a problem with your baby before you give birth. This may allow you to

- treat your baby's condition during pregnancy (for example, provide blood transfusions to a baby with Rh incompatibility problems);

- make appropriate
  choices for the delivery
  (for example, schedul-
  ing a cesarean delivery
  to minimize birth-
  related injuries to a
  baby with spina bifida
  or avoiding an emer-
  gency cesarean for
  fetal distress if it's
  known in advance that
  your baby will be born
  with a fatal birth
  defect);

- prepare to give birth
  to a baby who has spe-
  cial needs (for exam-
  ple, ensure that you give birth in a hospital with top-notch
  neonatal care facilities or have time to prepare emotionally for a mentally retarded child) or a baby who may be
  stillborn;

- choose to terminate the pregnancy.

> **❝** We decided to pro-
> ceed with amniocente-
> sis because of my age
> and because my brother
> had a child born with
> Down syndrome. My
> partner and I decided
> that if there was a
> problem with the baby-
> to-be, we would con-
> sider abortion because
> neither of us wanted to
> care for a child with
> such special needs. It
> sounds selfish, but we
> both had careers and
> other children to think
> about. **❞**
>
> —Anne, 39, mother of three

Cons

Prenatal testing also has its downside. Here are some points you
need to consider:

- Prenatal tests can't detect all problems. They're able to
  test for only a limited number of conditions. No prenatal
  test can guarantee that you're going to give birth to a perfectly healthy baby. There are simply too many unknowns.

- Prenatal tests often can't tell you how severe your child's
  disability may be — something that can make it difficult
  for you to determine what kind of quality of life your child
  can expect to enjoy.

- Once you get on the prenatal testing merry-go-round, it can be hard to get off. A positive test result on an AFP test, for example (a test result that indicates that you are at increased risk of having a baby with either an open neural tube defect or Down syndrome), can lead to a follow-up AFP test, an ultrasound, an amniocentesis, and possibly even riskier and more invasive procedures. If you take the AFP without giving much thought to the consequences of a positive test result, you could end up subjecting yourself to a series of follow-up tests and invasive procedures that might ultimately serve only to prove that the baby is perfectly healthy. That's why you need to understand the reasons for agreeing to a particular test, the possible outcomes, what course of action would be advised in the event that the test came back positive (and the risks of those next steps), and so on. Bottom line? Never consent to a prenatal test just because your doctor or midwife routinely orders one for every pregnant woman.

Why the age argument doesn't hold water

Typically, the medical profession routinely recommends that women over 35 be tested for chromosomal anomalies such as Down syndrome by using diagnostic procedures such as amniocentesis or chorionic villus sampling. However, many caregivers question this inflexible approach, preferring instead to counsel their patients about the pros and cons of the tests and then reach a decision together with their patients that takes into account the patient's values about things such as abortion, her tolerance for risks of various types, and even her intuition about her body and her pregnancy.

Although the all-too-common obsession with a pregnant woman's age might lead you to conclude that the risk of giving birth to a baby with a chromosomal anomaly increases dramatically at a certain age, this is simply not the case. As Table 14.1 demonstrates, your risk of giving birth to a baby with a chromosomal anomaly does increase as you age, but the increase is gradual rather than sudden.

What's behind this move to routine diagnostic tests for pregnant women over age 35 is what can at best be described as flawed logic. You've no doubt heard someone argue the case that diagnostic procedures such as amniocentesis and chorionic villus sampling are justified only when the risk of miscarriage (as a result of the test) is less than the risk of giving birth to a child with a birth defect — something that typically happens, statistically speaking, at around age 35.

Unfortunately, this argument fails to take into account that three distinctly different issues are involved: (1) a woman's odds of giving birth to a child with a chromosomal anomaly (for example, Down syndrome); (2) her desire to know for certain whether her baby has a chromosomal anomaly; and (3) her willingness to accept the risks involved with the tests that will give her that answer.

A 25-year-old woman might decide, for example, that she wants to know for certain whether she is carrying a child with a particular birth defect — even though the risks involved in obtaining that information (she has a 1 in 250 chance of miscarriage if she chooses to undergo amniocentesis) may be significantly higher than her actual risk of having a baby with such defects (1 in 476 — see Table 14.1). Of course, if she's had the AFP test, she should have a clearer idea of her risks, but even that may not be enough information to satisfy her need to know. She may decide that she is willing to pay any price — including inadvertently miscarrying a healthy baby — in order to avoid giving birth to a child with a chromosomal anomaly. She may argue that whereas a miscarried pregnancy can be replaced (in most cases, at least), a child with a severe disability may require a greater commitment that she and her partner are prepared to make.

A 40-year-old woman who has had a great deal of difficulty becoming pregnant may be unwilling to risk miscarrying her baby (once again, a 1 in 250 chance) even though the odds of having a baby with a chromosomal anomaly are considerably higher (1 in 66 — see Table 14.1) — even if forgoing that test means that she may end up giving birth to a child with a chromosomal anomaly.

> **❝** I didn't have any genetic testing done since there is no family history of disease and I didn't think I could handle the stress of waiting for the results. **❞**
>
> —Laura, 21, pregnant with her first child

This is why any "across-the-board" policy about prenatal testing is a bad idea. It fails to take into account the varying circumstances of people in a particular age category. You don't listen to the same music or read the same books as everyone else your age; why, then, should medical science assume that you'll make the same choices as your peers when it comes to an issue as deeply personal as prenatal testing?

There's one other important fact about chromosomal disorders and aging that seems to get lost in all the media hype about older women having babies. Even if you give birth at age 45, you still have an excellent chance of having a healthy baby. In 31 cases out of 32, for example, you will *not* give birth to a child who has Down syndrome. That puts the odds decidedly in your favor, at about 97 percent.

Table 14.1. Risk of Having a Liveborn Child with Down Syndrome or Another Chromosomal Anomaly

Maternal Age	Risk of Down Syndrome	Total Risk for Chromosome Abnormalities
20	1/1,667	1/526
21	1/1,667	1/526

Maternal Age	Risk of Down Syndrome	Total Risk for Chromosome Abnormalities
22	1/1,429	1/500
23	1/1,429	1/500
24	1/1,250	1/476
25	1/1,250	1/476
26	1/1,176	1/455
27	1/1,111	1/455
28	1/1,053	1/435
29	1/1,000	1/417
30	1/952	1/384
31	1/909	1/384
32	1/769	1/323
33	1/625	1/286
34	1/500	1/238
35	1/385	1/192
36	1/294	1/156
37	1/227	1/127
38	1/175	1/102
39	1/137	1/83
40	1/106	1/66
41	1/82	1/53
42	1/64	1/42
43	1/50	1/33

(continued)

Maternal Age	Risk of Down Syndrome	Total Risk for Chromosome Abnormalities
44	1/38	1/26
45	1/30	1/21
46	1/23	1/16
47	1/18	1/13
48	1/14	1/10
49	1/11	1/8

Table 14.1. *(continued)*

Source: The Merck Manual, 16th edition.

Who's a good candidate for prenatal testing . . .

Although the decision to proceed with prenatal testing is a highly personal one, you may want to consider prenatal testing if

- you have a family history of genetic disease or you know that you are a carrier of a particular disease;
- you have been exposed to a serious infection during pregnancy (for example, rubella or toxoplasmosis);
- you have been exposed to a harmful substance that could cause a birth defect;
- you have had one or more unsuccessful pregnancies or have previously given birth to baby with a birth defect;
- you feel a need to know with certainty whether your baby has a detectable abnormality, even though you are not considered at particularly high risk.

. . . and who's not . . .

You might choose against prenatal testing if

- you have concerns about the accuracy of certain tests;

- taking the test would increase your anxiety rather than alleviate it;

- you are opposed to abortion and wouldn't consider terminating the pregnancy even if the news was bad;

- you don't want to take the risk of inadvertently harming a perfectly healthy baby — something that can be a concern with certain types of prenatal tests.

What to do before you sign the consent form

Before you agree to take any type of prenatal test, you should make sure that you have a clear understanding of both the risks and the benefits of having the test performed. Our prenatal testing checklist (see Checklist 14.1) may help you to formulate some of the questions you may want to ask your doctor or midwife.

Checklist 14.1. Prenatal Testing Checklist	
_____	What are the benefits of taking this test?
_____	What does the test involve?
_____	Will it be painful?
_____	What risks, if any, does the test pose to me or my baby?
_____	Where will the test be performed? How experienced is that person/facility in performing this particular test?
_____	How accurate is this test? Is it meant to be a screening test or a diagnostic test? What is the rate of false positives or false negatives?
_____	How quickly will I receive the test results? Who will be available to help interpret the test results for me?

(continued)

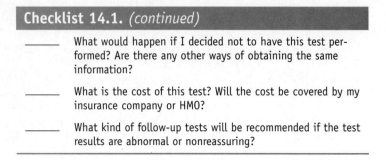

Checklist 14.1. *(continued)*

_____   What would happen if I decided not to have this test performed? Are there any other ways of obtaining the same
information?

_____   What is the cost of this test? Will the cost be covered by my
insurance company or HMO?

_____   What kind of follow-up tests will be recommended if the test
results are abnormal or nonreassuring?

The last question on our checklist is particularly important.
You need to know what other testing options will be available to
you, should you choose to proceed with the test. This may help
you to make up your mind about stepping on board the prenatal testing merry-go-round — or deciding to sit out the ride.

Now that we've talked about the factors that should be taken
into account when weighing the pros and cons of taking a particular test, let's consider the various types of tests that are available to you and your baby. The first four tests we'll discuss —
alpha-fetoprotein, amniocentesis, chorionic villus sampling,
and ultrasound — are widely used. The remaining tests —
Doppler blood flow studies, magnetic resonance imaging, percutaneous umbilical blood sampling (PUBS) (or cordocentesis)
and fetoscopy — are used far less frequently, either because the
technology is less widely available or because the tests pose
greater risks to the developing baby.

Alpha-fetoprotein

The alpha-fetoprotein test (also known as the triple or quadruple screen) is a blood test that is used to assess the likelihood
that a pregnant woman is carrying a child with an open neural
tube defect or Down syndrome (also called Trisomy 21). It can
also pick up evidence of other problems, including Trisomy 18
and a variety of other birth defects including omphalocele and

absence of the kidneys. A high level of alpha-fetoprotein (a substance produced in the fetal liver and abbreviated AFP) may indicate that a woman is carrying a child with a neural tube defect such as spina bifida or anencephaly, whereas a low level may indicate a higher than expected chance that she is carrying a child with Down syndrome. (Note: You will screen positive for an open neural tube defect if your AFP level is twice the mean level for all women who are the same number of weeks pregnant. If you are known to be carrying multiples, your test results will be interpreted accordingly.)

> **66** My doctor gave me the option of having the AFP, but we declined. We knew that no matter what, we would not terminate the pregnancy, so we didn't want to have to go through any unnecessary stress, thinking that something might be wrong when it really wasn't. **99**
>
> —Beth, 27, mother of one

The results of the test are plugged into a formula that takes into account such factors as gestational age at the time of the test, and maternal age, to produce a probability that the fetus being carried is affected by Down syndrome.

Note: The AFP test is often combined with tests of human chorionic gonadotropin (hCG) and unconjugated estriol, in which case it is called the triple screen test, or referred to simply as Maternal Serum Screening (MSS). If it's combined with a fourth measurement — inhibin-A, a chemical produced by the ovaries and the placenta — it is known as the quadruple or quad-screen test. Note: We will use these terms interchangeably in this chapter.

The AFP test is usually done between the 15th and 18th weeks of pregnancy, and it takes anywhere from a couple of days to a week to get the results.

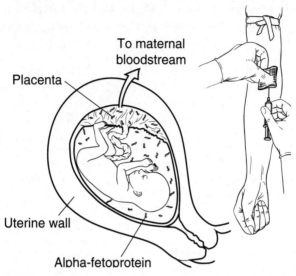

Figure 14.1. The maternal serum alpha-fetoprotein test. *Figure created by Articulate Graphics.*

The benefits

The AFP test can be used to identify women who are at risk of giving birth to children with so-called open neural tube defects, severe kidney or liver disease, esophageal or intestinal blockages, Down syndrome and another chromosomal anomaly known as trisomy 18, urinary obstructions, and osteogenesis imperfecta (that is, fragile bones). Women who have elevated levels of AFP not associated with any identifiable birth defect are at increased risk for preterm labor, intrauterine growth restriction, and still-birth and therefore are watched particularly closely for problems in their third trimester. Note: The AFP test was initially designed to screen for open neural tube defects. It was only after scientists began analyzing the data that they discovered its capability to screen for Down syndrome as well.

As a rule of thumb, screening for chromosomal anomalies is of greatest value to younger women who might not otherwise consider diagnostic testing such as amniocentesis and chorionic villus sampling.

The risks

Although the AFP test itself doesn't pose any real risks to the mother or fetus, a false positive result may lead a woman to subject herself and her baby to other riskier prenatal tests such as amniocentesis. Consequently, the key problem with this test is the high number of false positives. For example, 49 out of every 1,000 women under age 35 who take this test will be told that their readings have come back as higher risk for Down syndrome, but only one will actually be carrying a child with this condition. Twenty-five out of 1,000 women will be told they are at risk for having a baby with an open neural tube defect, but, in the end, only one of their babies will actually have an open neural tube defect. (As you will recall from our earlier discussions, this high rate of false positives helps to ensure that fewer false negatives occur.)

Who's a good candidate for this test?

The test is increasingly becoming a routine part of prenatal care across the United States, although it's technically optional in the majority of states. Doctors and midwives in some states are, however, legally required to offer AFP testing to pregnant women.

The fine print

The quadruple screen test can't tell you whether you are carrying a child with a birth defect; it can only give you a risk assessment. It's considered to be equally accurate in assessing your risk of giving birth to a child with a neural tube defect or Down syndrome (81 percent of each condition detected).

 Watch Out!

Current studies now show that the quadruple screen can give a reliable estimate of the risk of Down syndrome to all women (excluding those carrying multiples), regardless of age. However, a reassuring result for Down syndrome doesn't eliminate the possibility that an older woman may be carrying a baby with another chromosomal abnormality, so amniocentesis may still be an option even if the Down syndrome risk is found to be low.

Bright Idea

Arrange to have your quadruple screen test done as early as possible (that is, at 15 weeks, 0 days if possible). This will ensure that you receive the results early and have the maximum amount of time to consider your options and pursue whatever course of action you ultimately choose.

A false positive can be caused by either a miscalculation in the dating of your pregnancy or the presence of twins, so an ultrasound is typically the next step if your initial AFP (and a follow-up AFP test if you and your caregiver choose to do one) indicates that there could be a problem. If an earlier ultrasound has been done, or if your caregiver feels there is adequate evidence of good pregnancy dating and the lack of twins, this extra step can be omitted.

If your AFP test indicates a risk of Down syndrome, your caregiver may suggest an aneuploidy screen (an ultrasound procedure designed to detect particular abnormalities common in babies with Down syndrome). If none of the markers (abnormal features) for Down syndrome is detected during the aneuploidy screen, it is less likely that you are carrying a baby with Down syndrome. Many high-risk specialists feel comfortable reducing a woman's quadruple screen risk for Down by anywhere from 50 percent to 85 percent if the aneuploidy screen is negative. However, if you absolutely want to know for certain whether your child has Down syndrome, you may choose to proceed with amniocentesis and forgo ultrasound testing.

If your AFP test suggests a risk of having a baby with an open neural tube defect, you will also be given the option of having a level II or targeted ultrasound. If your level II ultrasound doesn't reveal anything unusual, you can feel about 90 percent certain that you are not carrying a child with a neural tube defect. If, however, you want to know for certain, you will need to proceed with amniocentesis.

Early serum screening and ultrasound

What was only recently considered experimental may soon become an established part of prenatal care. Those women who would like information about their Down syndrome risk earlier in their pregnancies than 15 to 18 weeks (the earliest in pregnancy it has been possible to make such an assessment up until quite recently) can now ask their caregivers to do a blood test and perform an ultrasound at 11 to 14 weeks to assess their Down syndrome risk.

The blood tests measure two substances, PAPP-A and free beta-hCG, while the ultrasound assesses an area of the fetal neck for what is known as nuchal translucency (swelling under the skin at the back of the fetal neck). This measurement is considered to be significant because babies with a lot of swelling in this area are frequently born with Down syndrome or a major heart defect or both.

These ultrasounds are not yet widely available but, in expert hands, the detection rate for Down syndrome is similar to that of the quadruple screen, and with similar false positive rates. Those women with a positive screen on this early screening test would then be offered CVS or amniocentesis depending on their how far along in their pregnancy they are — something that would ultimately allow them to have a definitive answer about their baby's health several weeks earlier than what would be previously have been possible with conventional quadruple screening.

The downside of going this route as opposed to sticking with traditional quadruple screening at 15 to 18 weeks is that a woman may undergo this screening, only to miscarry a short time later anyway. Approximately 20 percent of Down syndrome fetuses are spontaneously miscarried between 12 and 17 weeks.

Amniocentesis

Amniocentesis involves inserting a fine needle through a pregnant woman's abdomen and into the amniotic sac and withdrawing less than an ounce of amniotic fluid for analysis.

(See the following figure.) Ultrasound is used to locate the pocket of fluid and to minimize the risk to the fetus and the placenta. Although local anesthetic is frequently used to numb the area in which the needle is inserted and the majority of women find the procedure to be at most mildly uncomfortable, some women do find amniocentesis to be painful. (Note: Some doctors will encourage you to skip the anesthetic, arguing that the needle prick required to numb the area is every bit as painful as the needle prick required to do the amnio. If you have strong feelings about this either way, make your feelings known. This particular issue should be open to negotiation.)

Amniocentesis is typically done at 15 weeks of pregnancy, although some healthcare practitioners perform it at 12 to 14 weeks (early amnio). This practice, though initially promising an alternative to the extra heartache and complications associated with the mid- to late-second-trimester results from standard amniocentesis, has already been abandoned by many reputable academic centers because of unacceptably high miscarriage rates.

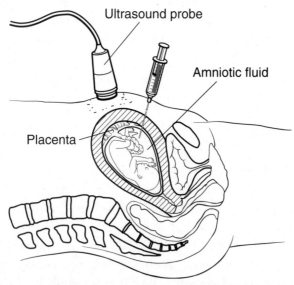

Figure 14.2. Amniocentesis. *Figure created by Articulate Graphics.*

It takes approximately 10 to 14 days to get the test results. If the test is done prior to 20 weeks or so, the woman can get the results back in time to terminate her pregnancy, if she chooses. Note: In some states, it is legal to terminate a pregnancy at any gestational age, if certain conditions are met. Your doctor or midwife should be able to advise you on the laws in your state if you are considering terminating your pregnancy or refer you to resources that can inform you of options in other states.

The benefits

Amniocentesis is used to detect

- chromosomal defects (for example, Down syndrome or Turner's syndrome);
- neural tube defects (for example, spina bifida);
- genetic diseases (for example, cystic fibrosis);
- skeletal diseases (for example, achondroplasia);
- fetal infections (for example, herpes or rubella);
- central-nervous-system disease (for example, Huntington's disease);
- blood diseases (for example, sickle-cell anemia);
- chemical problems or deficiencies (for example, Tay-Sachs disease).

It can also be used to

- determine the sex of the baby (important in the case of sex-linked diseases such as hemophilia);
- assess the lung maturity of the baby closer to term (important when premature labor is threatened or a decision has to be made about inducing labor in a high-risk pregnancy);
- measure the bilirubin count of the amniotic fluid (an indicator that a baby with Rh disease may need a blood transfusion) during the second half of pregnancy.

Watch Out!

Contact your caregiver immediately if you experience any bleeding or watery discharge following either amniocentesis or chorionic villus sampling. There is a small risk of miscarriage with each procedure.

The risks

In a very small percentage of cases, amniocentesis results in injury to the fetus, placenta, or umbilical cord. Approximately 1 out of every 200 women who have amniocentesis will miscarry or go into premature labor as a result of the procedure. Those who undergo early amniocentesis (that is, during the late first trimester) are at a greater risk of experiencing a miscarriage than women who have the procedure during their second trimester.

Most women do not have amniocentesis performed until well into the second trimester. Given the length of time it can take to receive the test results, a pregnant woman who receives abnormal results from amniocentesis may decide to terminate her pregnancy in the middle of her second trimester, an experience that can be both physically difficult and emotionally traumatic.

The fine print

Amniocentesis is recommended for couples with a history of certain genetic diseases and birth defects affecting themselves, their prior offspring, or members of their families; or who have been shown to be high risk for chromosomal anomalies based on a woman's age or on her quadruple screen test.

Chorionic villus sampling

Chorionic villus sampling involves passing a catheter through the cervix (see the first of the following two figures) or a needle through the abdomen (see the second of the following two figures) to obtain a sample of chorionic villus tissue (the tissue that will eventually become the placenta). Because this tissue comes from the baby, it is capable of providing information about the baby's genetic makeup.

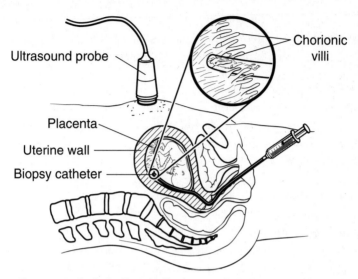

Figure 14.3. Chorionic villus sampling—transcervical. *Figure created by Articulate Graphics.*

Some women find the procedure painful, but most describe it as merely uncomfortable.

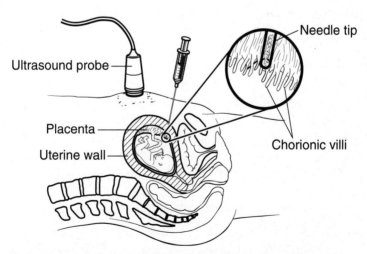

Figure 14.4. Chorionic villus sampling—transabdominal. *Figure created by Articulate Graphics.*

Chorionic villus sampling is typically done at 10 to 12 weeks. It can take anywhere from a few days to a few weeks to get the results, depending on the extent of the testing performed.

The benefits

Chorionic villus sampling is safer than early amniocentesis and can be done sooner than conventional amniocentesis, a key consideration in the event that the decision is made to terminate a pregnancy.

The risks

Chorionic villus sampling is less accurate, because of the possibility of contamination with maternal cells and certain placental cells that can confuse the picture by giving mixed results and is riskier than amniocentesis performed at 16 to 18 weeks. The rate of miscarriage following the procedure is approximately 1 percent, and approximately 30 percent of women report some type of bleeding.

Note: Early concerns about limb reduction abnormalities in babies whose mothers underwent chorionic villus sampling during pregnancy have not been borne out by the evidence, so this is one less thing to worry about.

The fine print

Chorionic villus sampling is often recommended to women who are at risk of giving birth to a baby with Down syndrome; those with sickle-cell disease or thalassemia; those who are at risk of giving birth to a baby with cystic fibrosis, hemophilia, Huntington's disease, or muscular dystrophy; and those who prefer to get an answer by the end of the first trimester.

 Watch Out!

CVS is a tricky procedure that should be performed by a skilled practitioner. Don't just settle for a referral to a particular facility—ask to be referred to a specific person who has a proven track record with CVS (that is, someone with acceptably low miscarriage rates when performing the procedure).

Unlike amniocentesis, chorionic villus sampling can't be used to detect neural tube defects.

Ultrasounds (sonograms)

Although the American medical establishment has yet to prove that routine ultrasounds result in better outcomes for mothers and babies, the majority of pregnant women continue to receive at least one ultrasound during their pregnancies. This is one testing procedure that most pregnant women enjoy, because it gives them the opportunity to "meet" their babies — if only on-screen (see Figure 14.5).

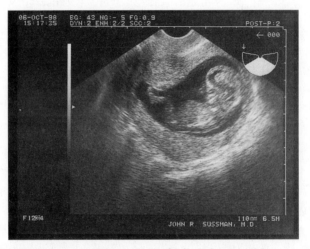

Figure 14.5. Sonogram. Image courtesy of John R. Sussman, M.D.

An ultrasound involves bouncing high-frequency sound waves off the fetus to create a corresponding image on a computer screen. It can be done either by rubbing a transducer on a pregnant woman's abdomen or by inserting an ultrasonic probe in her vagina.

If you're having a transabdominal ultrasound, you may be required to have a full bladder. This is because a full bladder helps to push the uterus out of the pelvic cavity and into full view of the ultrasound equipment. You will be asked to consume

32 ounces of liquid before the test. You can best accomplish this by drinking 32 ounces of liquid an hour before your test. You'll find it easier to get the liquids down if you consume a variety of beverages: herbal tea, fruit juice, clear soup, club soda, and so on. Just be sure to avoid beverages that are overly filling (for example, milkshakes) or you'll never manage to get 32 ounces of liquid down.

Before you start downing a tray full of drinks, call your doctor's office to make sure that everything is proceeding on schedule. You may want to delay your intake of fluids by a quarter-hour or so if the doctor is falling behind schedule.

If, on the other hand, you're having a transvaginal ultrasound, you will need to have an empty bladder. Be sure to allow enough time to go to the bathroom right before you have your ultrasound.

> **❝**I did not have any early ultrasounds done. My midwife's attitude was that unless there was a problem, a routine ultrasound wasn't necessary, and David and I agreed.**❞**
>
> —Leila, 33, mother of one

Ultrasounds can be performed at any stage of pregnancy. Some women will have a series of ultrasounds during their pregnancies; others will have one or none. The results will be conveyed either immediately (if the ultrasound is being conducted by your doctor) or later (if the ultrasound is being performed by someone other than your doctor).

You can find some detailed information about ultrasound, including some actual ultrasound images, at the Obstetric Ultrasound Web site: www.ob-ultrasound.net.

The benefits

Ultrasound can be used to

- confirm your due date by measuring the size of the fetus at 16 to 20 weeks' gestation or earlier (a measurement that is accurate within plus or minus 5 to 10 days at that stage of pregnancy and even more accurate when done at 6 to 12 weeks);

- verify the presence of a fetal heartbeat before it can be heard with a doptone device;

- check for multiples;

- monitor the baby's growth and assess her well-being;

- detect certain fetal abnormalities;

- locate the fetus, the umbilical cord, and the placenta during amniocentesis and chorionic villus sampling;

- measure the amount of amniotic fluid;

- determine the cause of any abnormal bleeding;

- assess the condition of the placenta if it appears that the baby is developing slowly or is in distress;

- determine the condition of the cervix (for example, whether it has begun to open prematurely);

- check for miscarriage, an ectopic pregnancy, a hydatidiform mole (that is, "molar pregnancy"), or fetal demise (a concern if no fetal movement has been detected by week 22 or if movements appear to cease at any time thereafter);

- determine the baby's sex (the accuracy of which depends both on the baby's position and the skill of the person conducting the ultrasound);

- decide which delivery method to use (vaginal versus cesarean) based on the baby's size and position, the position of the placenta, and other factors;

 Bright Idea

If you have an ultrasound—particularly a screening ultrasound at 18 to 20 weeks—find out if you can have it done at a facility that allows you to take home a video of your baby. While most facilities will give patients still pictures of their babies, many are now equipped to make a video as well—a wonderful keepsake for our high-tech times.

Watch Out!

Some insurance companies and HMOs do not cover the cost of routine ultrasound or only cover a limited number of ultrasounds. Others require that pregnant women be preapproved for the procedure. Make sure that you know who's picking up the tab before you consent to the procedure.

- reassure the mother that the pregnancy is proceeding well (a valid use of ultrasound in cases in which the mother has a history of pregnancy loss or appears to need reassurance).

The risks

Although there are no known risks to ultrasound, it is still a relatively new technology. That's why the American College of Obstetricians and Gynecologists does not recommend its routine use during pregnancy. If your caregiver recommends that you have an ultrasound, make sure that you find out whether he routinely sends all of his patients for ultrasounds or whether an ultrasound is warranted in your case.

The fine print

Some doctors and ultrasound technicians will allow you to tape your ultrasound — and others won't. Some will provide you with one or more still photos of your baby, either free or for a nominal charge.

Although partners and support people are welcome to be present at most ultrasounds, the situation varies from facility to facility. Make sure that you understand the policies at a particular facility up front and plan accordingly.

Doppler blood flow studies

Doppler blood flow studies are sometimes conducted to monitor fetal circulation and/or the condition of the baby or the placenta. Basically, a doppler ultrasound unit is positioned over your abdomen and the rate of blood flow through the umbilical artery, the fetal blood cells, and/or the uterine artery are recorded. The differences in blood flow during and between heart beats is then analyzed to look for any indications of possible problems.

The benefits

A Doppler blood flow study is a relatively noninvasive way of gathering information about your baby's well-being.

The risks

Although there are no known risks to Doppler blood flow studies, like all forms of ultrasound, Doppler blood flow studies are a relatively new form of technology and should not be used indiscriminately.

The fine print

Doppler blood flow studies are neither widely used, nor are they widely available, and their ability to accurately predict maternal fetal outcomes is still in question.

Magnetic resonance imaging (MRI)

Magnetic resonance imaging involves using a highly powerful magnet to gather a series of images that are then projected on to a video screen. These images allow the health care provider to examine the various layers of the baby's organ systems.

The benefits

An MRI can be very useful in helping to estimate the size, volume, and maturity of fetal organs and for studying maternal and fetal anatomical structures.

An MRI is a noninvasive type of technology in that no dyes or ionizing radiation is used.

 Watch Out!

X-rays are rarely performed on pregnant women today and, when they are, they are generally only performed after the second trimester. Early prenatal exposure to radiation has been linked to leukemia and genetic mutations.

The risks

There are no known risks to the use of MRI during pregnancy.

The fine print

MRIs are not widely available and, when they are available, they are costly to perform. Your doctor will only order an MRI is there is a specific medical reason for doing so.

The FDA recommends against performing MRIs during the first trimester of pregnancy.

Percutaneous umbilical blood sampling (PUBS) (cordocentesis)

Percutaneous umbilical blood sampling, also called cordocentesis, involves taking a sample of fetal blood from the umbilical cord by using an amniocentesislike needle inserted through the maternal abdominal wall into the baby's umbilical cord near the cord's junction with the placenta, using ultrasound for visual guidance. The sample is then analyzed for blood disorders and infections (see Figure 14.6).

The procedure is generally performed after 16 weeks' gestation and is typically offered at larger medical centers that have staff with specialized expertise in PUBS. It is rarely necessary to perform except in cases in which additional fetal cells are necessary to clarify genetic results from CVS or amniocentesis or when needed to assess for fetal anemia in conditions in which the baby is at high risk.

The benefits

Percutaneous umbilical blood sampling can be used to detect

- Rh incompatibility problems (to see if a fetal blood transfusion is warranted);
- blood disorders;
- infections (for example, rubella, toxoplasmosis, and herpes);
- chromosomal problems.

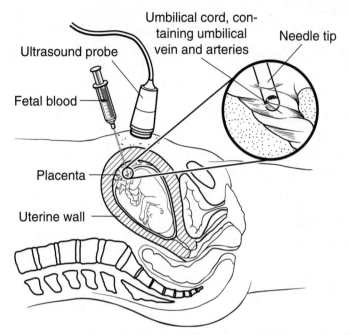

Figure 14.6. Percutaneous Umbilical Blood Sampling. *Figure created by Articulate Graphics.*

The risks

PUBS is a riskier procedure than amniocentesis: between 1/50 and 1/100 babies die as a result of complications resulting from the procedure.

The fine print

PUBS is typically reserved for cases in which the test results are needed right away (that is, if you are considering the possibility of terminating the pregnancy, and time is running out) or if there is no other method of obtaining the same information.

Transabdominal embryo fetoscopy

A transabdominal embryo fetoscopy is a rarely performed procedure that involves passing an ultrafine scope into the uterus via a tiny needle inserted through the pregnant woman's abdomen. It can be used to diagnose a potentially lethal skin disorder, multiple Ptyerigium syndrome, and another called Epidermolysis Bullosum by skin biopsy. It is typically performed after 10 weeks' gestation.

The benefits

A transabdominal embryo fetosocopy allows the doctor to observe the fetus, placenta, and amniotic fluid. The procedure can also be used to take blood samples from the junction of the umbilical cord and placenta and to remove small amounts of fetal or placental tissue.

The risks

Transabdominal embryo fetoscopy has a miscarriage rate of 3 percent to 5 percent.

The fine print

Transabdominal embryo fetoscopy is recommended for couples who have previously given birth to a child with a condition that cannot be detected by using any other prenatal diagnostic technique.

The future of prenatal testing

So what lies ahead in the Brave New World of prenatal testing? Plenty, it would appear.

There are a few developments that appear to have particular promise: A combination approach using early screening at 11 to 14 weeks and a quadruple screen at 15 weeks may raise the Down syndrome detection rate to 90 percent while reducing the false positive rate to 1 percent to 1.5 percent. Also on the horizon is a way of gathering fetal cells from the maternal blood, allowing for fetal diagnostic tests of a wide variety to be done with a sample of the pregnant mother's blood.

There are also, of course, a growing number of genetic tests available to couples who wish to obtain detailed information on their risks of giving birth to a child with a birth defect prior to planning a pregnancy. (As you may recall, we discussed this issue back in Chapter 2.)

What to do if the test brings bad news

Although the odds of receiving good news from any of the prenatal tests that we have just discussed are decidedly in your favor, sometimes the news you receive is nothing short of devastating. If you find out that you are carrying a child with a severe — even fatal — condition, you will be forced to make some very difficult decisions concerning your pregnancy.

You may decide to carry your pregnancy to term if

▪ you are prepared to raise a child with a severe disability or give birth to a baby who either is stillborn or dies shortly after birth;

▪ you are morally opposed to abortion under any circumstances;

▪ you feel more comfortable carrying your baby to term and then letting nature take its course;

▪ you want to cherish the remaining time with your baby, even if much or all of the time you are able to spend together takes place during your pregnancy rather than after the birth.

On the other hand, you may decide to terminate your pregnancy as soon as possible if

▪ you are not prepared emotionally or financially to raise a child with a severe disability;

▪ you are not willing to carry a child to term, only to watch him or her die during or shortly after birth;

▪ you are not morally opposed to abortion;

▪ you are concerned that your baby is suffering and do not wish to prolong his suffering any longer than necessary;

▪ you are concerned that your baby will be subjected to painful and costly interventions if he is born alive and

that you will not be legally permitted to refuse those
interventions;

■ you wish to put this painful experience behind you as soon
as possible.

Some parents choose to proceed with their pregnancies,
even if that means facing life with a severely disabled child, giving birth to a stillborn child, or giving birth to a child who may
live for only a few hours or days. Others choose to terminate
their pregnancies.

Here are some factors you may wish to weigh as you go about
making this incredibly difficult decision:

■ What chance does the baby have of being born alive? Of
leading a "normal" life?

■ How much would the baby suffer physically and
emotionally?

■ Would the baby be able to live at home? If so, who would
be prepared to care for her? You? Your partner?

■ Is your marriage strong enough to survive the strain of caring for a severely disabled child? How might it affect your
relationships with your other children?

■ Are the baby's disabilities treatable? If so, how many and
what types of surgeries would be required?

■ What are the odds that these treatments would be successful? What quality of life could your baby expect to enjoy
after these treatments?

■ Would you be able to find the funds to pay for these
treatments?

■ What are your feelings about abortion?

As you can see, there are no easy answers to these questions.
Deciding whether to proceed with your pregnancy or terminate
it at this stage is probably one of the most difficult choices you will
ever have to make. You and your partner may find it helpful to

sit down with a therapist who has experience in helping families to work through these issues. If you don't know whom to turn to for support, ask your doctor to recommend someone who will treat you with sensitivity and compassion regardless of what option you ultimately choose.

Because you may have to come to a decision fairly quickly, you may find that you have a tendency to second-guess your decision after the fact. This reaction is perfectly normal, according to Deborah L. Davis, Ph.D, author of *Empty Cradle, Broken Heart,* who offers these words of wisdom: "It is important to remember that whether you had two minutes or two years, emotional turmoil would accompany whatever decision you made. After all, you had to make an impossible choice between 'terrible' and 'horrible.'"

Preparing for the birth of a child with a severe disability

If you will be giving birth to a child who will be severely disabled, you need to find out as much as you can about the challenges of raising a child with this particular disability and then spend some time planning for your child's birth. It's important to find out from your caregiver what medical interventions may be necessary following the birth and what role you can expect to play during your baby's first few hours of life. You might find it helpful to write a birth plan that specifies which interventions you would like your child to receive — and which ones you would prefer to decline (assuming, of course, that you have that choice).

Just the facts

- Although prenatal tests can be a source of valuable information about the health of the baby, they are not the best choice for everyone.

- Alpha-fetoprotein (quadruple screen) is used to screen for neural tube defects, trisomy 18, and Down syndrome.

- Amniocentesis is used to diagnose chromosomal defects, neural tube defects, genetic defects, and other problems. The miscarriage rate following the procedure is approximately 1 in 200 or less.

- Chorionic villus sampling (CVS) can be used to detect a number of disorders, but not neural tube defects. It is riskier than amniocentesis: the miscarriage rate is approximately 1 in 100.

- Ultrasound is one of the most common types of prenatal tests. It is widely believed to be safe during pregnancy, but the American College of Obstetricians and Gynecologists argues against its routine use at the present time.

- Percutaneous umbilical blood sampling (PUBS) involves taking a sample of fetal blood from the umbilical cord. The sample is then analyzed for blood disorders, infections, and a range of other problems. It has a miscarriage rate of 1 percent to 2 percent.

- Transabdominal embryo fetoscopy is used to observe the fetus, placenta, and amniotic fluid in utero or to take blood or tissue samples. It has a miscarriage rate of 3 percent to 5 percent.

- A combination of serum screening and ultrasound at 11 to 14 weeks and quadruple screen at 15 weeks shows promise for the earlier detection of Down syndrome.

- If prenatal testing reveals that you are likely to give birth to a baby with a severe — or even fatal — disability, you may decide to terminate the pregnancy.

GET THE SCOOP ON. . .

What causes a multiple birth ▪ What it's like to be pregnant with multiples ▪ What you can do now to prepare for your babies' arrival ▪ How to shop for your babies without going broke ▪ Possible complications ▪ Selective reduction

Carrying Multiples

I f you've just discovered that you're carrying multiples, you are probably experiencing a mix of emotions. On the one hand, you may feel really lucky to be carrying two or more babies — particularly if you had a great deal of difficulty conceiving. On the other hand, you may feel concerned about what this pregnancy may mean to the health of you and your babies, and worried about what giving birth to more than one baby may mean to your finances and your relationship with your partner or other children.

Once you and your partner have had a chance to absorb the news, you will probably find that you have a million questions about being pregnant and giving birth to multiples. You may be wondering what causes a multiple pregnancy, how a multiple pregnancy differs from a singleton pregnancy, what you should do to prepare for your babies' arrival, and what possible complications can develop during a multiple pregnancy. These are the key issues we address in this chapter.

Chapter 15

595

Why the number of multiple births is on the rise

According to a recent article in the medical journal *Obstetrics and Gynecology*, the number of multiple births increased by 59 percent (from 19.3 to 30.7 multiple births per 1,000 live births) between 1980 and 1999. And while the birth rate for twins increased by 53 percent during this period, the birth rate for higher-order multiples increased by an astounding 423 percent.

> 66 Our first reaction was, 'Wow, isn't that neat?' Our second reaction was, 'Oh my God, what have we done?' 99
>
> — Anita, 35, mother of twins

All told, multiples now account for approximately 3 percent of births in America. Not surprisingly, the vast majority of multiple births result in twins. In 2000, for example, there were 118,916 twin births, while there were 6,742 triplet births, 506 quadruplet births, and 77 births of quintuplets and other higher-order multiples.

Two key factors are responsible for the increasing numbers of multiples, according to the National Center for Health Statistics: the fact that an increasing number of women in their late 30s are giving birth and the growing popularity of fertility treatments such as ovulation-inducing drugs and in vitro fertilization.

Older moms

How can giving birth later in life increase your odds of having more than one baby? Scientists believe that women between the ages of 35 and 39 are more likely to give birth to multiples than women in other age groups because the body begins to produce higher levels of gonadotropin hormones, which cause more eggs to mature and be released from the ovaries. The National Center for Health Statistics attributes one-third of the rise in multiple births to this age factor.

Fertility treatments

The second factor — the growing popularity of fertility treatments — is credited with the other two-thirds of the increase in multiple births. About 20 percent of women undergoing fertility treatments have multiple births, as opposed to approximately 1.5 percent of all women giving birth in the United States.

Fertility drugs used to induce ovulation frequently cause more than one egg to be released. The rate of multiple pregnancy among women using Clomid is less than 5 percent, whereas the rate for women using gonadotropins is between 10 percent and 20 percent.

Assisted reproductive technologies (ART) are also responsible for many multiple births. Because in vitro fertilization techniques are so costly — $20,000 a cycle for some types of treatments — and only a fraction of implanted embryos survive, many fertility specialists try to tip the odds in their patients' favor by implanting a large number of embryos at a time (for example, four). If an unusually high number of these embryos manage to "take," the couple can end up being pregnant with a large number of babies.

Can you have too much of a good thing? Some people think so. In fact, many in the medical community feel that reproductive medicine needs to find ways of reducing the odds that a woman undergoing fertility treatments will end up with triplets or quadruplets — or even more babies. Multiple pregnancies are, after all, far riskier than pregnancies that involve single babies, and they can be financially ruinous to families that lack the funds to foot the necessary bills for three, four, or five babies. The burden may spill over into the healthcare system as well, becoming a nightmare for healthcare providers and health insurance carriers alike.

Unfortunately, because these fertility treatments often represent the only shot at parenthood for couples desperate to have a baby, there are no easy answers. Just a whole lot of questions.

What causes a multiple birth

Twin pregnancies result from either the fertilization of two separate eggs by two separate sperm (a process that results in dizygotic, or fraternal, twins) or the separation of a single fertilized egg into two fetuses (a process that results in monozygotic, or identical, twins). Higher-order multiple pregnancies involve fraternal twins, identical twins, or a combination of both types of twins.

Here are some basic facts about multiples:

- Twins occur naturally in 1 out of every 90 births; triplets in 1 out of every 10,000 births; and quadruplets in 1 out of every 650,000 births.

- Fraternal twins occur more often in certain families and in certain ethnic groups (the rates are 1 in 70 in African Americans and 1 in 300 for women of Chinese descent with whites falling in between). The incidence of fraternal twins also increases with maternal age, weight, height, and parity (that is, the number of pregnancies a woman has had).

- Identical twins occur in approximately 4 out of every 1,000 births and are unrelated to maternal age, race, or parity.

- Fraternal twins typically look no more alike than any other pair of siblings. They can be either of the same sex or one of each sex.

- Identical twins have identical features: hair, eye color, blood type, and so on. If, however, one twin developed more rapidly in utero than the other one, they may not look identical at birth.

 Watch Out!

If your first pregnancy resulted in a twin birth, you are five times more likely to have a twin or multiple birth occur with your next pregnancy than a woman who hasn't previously given birth to multiples.

Bright Idea

Find out if special prenatal classes are offered in your community to couples who are expecting multiples. If you can't find specialized classes in your community, you might consider hiring a childbirth educator or a doula with expertise in multiple birth to conduct private classes in your home.

- Identical twins have similar handprints and footprints, but they do not share the same fingerprints. (This was good news to one family of identical twins who had to rush their babies off to FBI headquarters to get them refingerprinted so that they could figure out who was who!)

- Some identical twins are known as "mirror twins" because one is virtually a mirror image of the other (for example, a birthmark that appears on the left arm of one appears on the right arm of the other, one is left-handed and the other is right-handed, and so on).

- Identical triplets can also occur, but they are extremely rare.

- It is possible for fraternal twins to be conceived by two different fathers, a process known as superfecundation.

- Scientists believe that approximately one in eight natural pregnancies starts out as a twin pregnancy — even though only 1 out of every 90 births results in the birth of twins. This is one reason why many caregivers routinely do ultrasounds to confirm that there are no other viable fetuses left in the uterus when they suspect that a patient is miscarrying.

- It is possible to miscarry one multiple and go on to carry the others to term. It is also possible to have a combination ectopic and uterine pregnancy (that is, one or more babies implant in the fallopian tubes and the others in the uterus). Fortunately, this is rare.

- Although most twins are born within minutes of one another, sometimes days — even months — can elapse between the births of twins.

- Often, it isn't immediately obvious at birth whether same-sex twins are identical or fraternal. If the parents want to know for medical reasons, blood from the umbilical cord is drawn and analyzed for type, Rh factor, and so on. If the results are still inconclusive, parents can choose to opt for DNA testing — a little pricey at $600 or more, but highly accurate.

How a multiple pregnancy is diagnosed

The increased use of ultrasound has made it possible for the vast majority of parents to find out in advance whether there's more than one baby on the way. This wasn't the case a decade or two ago, when it wasn't unusual for as many as 40 percent of multiple pregnancies to be undiagnosed prior to labor and delivery.

Even if you haven't had an ultrasound, certain red flags may alert you and your caregiver to the possibility that you may be carrying twins. These are the warning signals:

- Fraternal twins tend to run in your family.

- You have been taking fertility drugs.

- You experienced excessive nausea and vomiting during the first trimester.

- Your uterus is growing more quickly or is larger than what would be expected at a particular point in your pregnancy.

- You notice more fetal movement in this pregnancy than in previous pregnancies (assuming, of course, that this is your second or subsequent pregnancy).

- More than one fetal heartbeat is heard.

If your caregiver suspects that you may be carrying multiples, he will likely send you for an ultrasound. Early ultrasound can detect more than 95 percent of multiple pregnancies.

What it's like to be pregnant with multiples

There are significant differences between pregnancies that involve one baby and those that involve two or more babies. If you are carrying multiples, you may experience

- heightened symptoms of early pregnancy (for example, morning sickness, breast enlargement, fatigue) due to the high level of pregnancy hormones in your body;

- a range of discomforts caused by the pressure of your heavy, stretched uterus on surrounding organs (for example, shortness of breath, heartburn, constipation, pelvic discomfort, urinary leakage, back pain, and hemorrhoids);

- a range of other discomforts that are often associated with multiple pregnancies (for example, insomnia, water retention, difficulty walking, abdominal itching, and anemia);

- increased fetal movement;

- substantial weight gain (according to Barbara Luke and Tamara Eberlein, authors of *When You're Expecting Wins, Triplets, or Quads,* you should aim for a weight gain of 40 to 50 pounds if you're carrying twins; 50 to 60 pounds if you're carrying triplets; and 65 to 80 pounds if you're carrying quadruplets);

> ❝ Because I was carrying twins, I was ordered to leave work at 28 weeks. I felt like a real fraud for the first two weeks because I felt great. Then suddenly, at 30 weeks, I felt like someone had thrown a huge wet blanket over me, and all my energy went. ❞
>
> — Nicola, 35, mother of four (including a set of twins)

- a shorter pregnancy than what you would expect if you were carrying a single baby (40 weeks). The mean pregnancy length is 37 to 38 weeks for twins and 34 weeks for triplets.

You may also need to abstain from sex or vigorous exercise during your pregnancy; leave work weeks or months earlier than originally planned, if you develop any serious complications; or have a planned or emergency cesarean section, depending on how your pregnancy progresses.

Prenatal care

A woman who is carrying multiples needs to be monitored more closely than a woman who is carrying a single baby. This is because more things can go wrong in this situation than during a single pregnancy.

As a result, your caregiver will probably want to see you every two weeks (rather than once a month) until week 28, and then weekly thereafter. During that time, you will probably receive one or more of the following tests:

- **Ultrasound:** Ultrasound is used to check on fetal growth, to detect abnormalities, and to determine what position the babies are in before you go into labor. It can also be used to measure blood flow through the umbilical cord, something that can be useful in evaluating growth disorders.

- **A nonstress test (NST):** A nonstress test involves strapping fetal monitors — one for each baby — to your abdomen and then monitoring your babies' heartbeats to determine whether they are reactive (which indicates that the baby is doing well) or nonreactive (which indicates that there could be a problem such as cord entanglement, oxygen deprivation, pregnancy-induced hypertension, and intrauterine growth restriction).

- **A biophysical profile (BPP):** The biophysical profile is a detailed ultrasound used to assess your babies' overall well-being by looking at such factors as heart-rate activity, body movements, muscle tone, and amniotic-fluid volume.

If complications arise during your pregnancy, your caregiver may suggest bed rest (to improve uterine blood flow) or prescribe contraction-stopping drugs (tocolytics). She may also suggest home monitoring (hooking yourself to an electronic monitoring device for an hour or more per day to record uterine activity and hopefully detect premature-labor contractions before you go into active labor).

Note: Although the jury is still out on the effectiveness of bed rest in preventing preterm labor, most doctors agree that bed rest combined with tocolytics is effective in reducing or stopping contractions. You can get some practical tips on coping with bed rest in Chapter 16.

> **66** Plan for bed rest — even if you never get any! Buy whatever supplies you will need for anything you can do lying down. I worked on the computer, folded laundry, reorganized my address book, and did other lying-down projects. **99**
>
> — Marcie, 29, mother of 11-month-old twins

What you can do now to prepare for your babies' arrival

There's no way around it: giving birth to more than one baby is going to throw your life into upheaval for at least the foreseeable future. That's why it's a good idea to do as much as you can ahead of time to prepare for Life After Babies.

Prepare to pamper thyself

By the time you walk out of the hospital with your babies, you will have been through a lot. Even if your pregnancy was relatively straightforward, you've been carrying around a heavy load

 Bright Idea

Dress each twin in his or her own color if you have difficulty telling them apart. If you're worried that the color-coding system might fall apart in your sleep-deprived state, paint their toenails instead. (It sounds crazy, but some moms of multiples swear by this technique.)

for many months and subletting your uterus to some very demanding tenants. If it was complicated, you may have spent months on bed rest — which, ironically, tends to be anything but restful — or had a cesarean delivery. Add that to the fact that you're not likely to get a whole lot of sleep for at least the foreseeable future, and you can see why it pays to pamper thyself during the postpartum period.

To help make things as stress-free as possible after the births of your babies, consider doing a few of the following things before they arrive:

- Make extra batches of soup, casseroles, stews, meatballs, and other entrees that freeze well (just remember to go lightly on the spices; some babies don't appreciate garlic-flavored breastmilk).

- Pay as many of your bills ahead of time as possible so that you don't forget to make the car payment or pay credit card bills as a result of the postpartum chaos.

- Address your birth announcements before the babies arrive.

- Join a club or online newsgroup for parents of multiples, and ask experienced mothers of multiples for tips on surviving the postpartum period.

- If you have older children, prepare them for the disruption that is likely to accompany the babies' arrival (for example, arrange for them to take a hospital tour or to participate in a sibling-preparation class — ideally one that is targeted at siblings of multiples).

 Bright Idea

Looking for some more advice on weathering the highs and lows of the postpartum period? You'll find tip sheets on this and other pregnancy and parenting-related topics at having-a-baby.com — the official Web site for pregnancy book author Ann Douglas (one of the authors of this book).

■ Spend some quality time with your spouse and talk about ways you can try to stay connected during the crazy weeks and months ahead.

Ask not what you can do for your community . . .

There are times in your life when you have to be prepared to wave the white flag — and the day when you arrive home from the hospital with a baby in each arm (or perhaps with more babies than arms) definitely qualifies as one of those times. That's why experienced parents of multiples suggest that couples who are expecting multiples spend some time before the birth lining up help for after their babies arrive.

Here are some tips on rallying the troops:

■ Let everyone in your circle of friends know that help is welcome, and encourage them to spread the word. (Who knows? Maybe one of them belongs to a church or youth group that would be happy to take your family on as a special project!)

■ Make a list of jobs you wouldn't mind delegating to someone else (making a salad, picking up a package at the post office, and so on), and ask one of your volunteers to serve as a volunteer coordinator. (Having a volunteer coordinator was a lifesaver for one family when their quadruplets arrived. At one point they had 32 volunteers working around the clock caring for the new arrivals.)

 Bright Idea

You can track down the contact information for a twins club or other multiple-birth association in your area by contacting the National Organization of Mothers of Twins Clubs at 877-540-2200 or by visiting the organization's Web site at www.nomotc.org. Canadian parents should call the Multiple Births Canada at 866-228-8824 or visit the organization's Web site at www.multiple birthscanada.org.

■ Invite a much-loved family member to move in for a couple of weeks to help with meals, laundry, housework, and child care. (Just make sure the family member in question is of the low-maintenance variety. You don't need any prima donnas underfoot at a time like this.)

■ If you can't line up enough volunteers, resort to paying someone to help you. Neighborhood teenagers can be had for a fairly decent hourly rate — particularly if you hire them on a regular basis (such as two or three days a week after school). Ditto for retired people who may be looking for an interesting part-time job. Note: You can find some practical tips on lining up occasional and part-time child-care in *Choosing Childcare for Dummies* (Wiley Publishing, Inc., 2003) by Ann Douglas, one of the authors of this book.

How to shop for your babies without going broke

Equipping a nursery for one baby is expensive enough. Equipping one for two or more babies can be enough to bankrupt a family — or so you might think. "A lot of parents have to get past the idea that everything has to be new for the babies," says childbirth educator and mother of twins Joyce MacKenzie. "It's safety and practicality you're after, not the most beautiful crib in the store window."

Although there's a real temptation to run out and buy your babies matching brand-name gear, there are cheaper ways to acquire what your babies need. Here are some tips from parents who've been there:

■ **Borrow as much baby gear as you can.** Just make sure that whatever you borrow meets current safety standards.

■ **Shop secondhand.** You can find nearly new brand-name baby products at most consignment stores for half their original price or less. Although the better secondhand stores go out of their way to avoid carrying cribs or car seats that don't comply with current safety standards, mistakes can and do happen. Therefore, the onus is still on you to make sure that the items you're purchasing are up to snuff.

■ **Don't scrimp on the double (or triple or quadruple) stroller.** It's the one thing that will keep you mobile. Note to parents expecting quadruplets: You might want to consider purchasing two doubles rather than one quadruple stroller if someone else will always be with you when you're out with the babies. They're easier to maneuver and easier to pick up secondhand.

■ **Get by with a little help from your friends.** If your friends are planning to have a baby shower for you and they ask what you want, suggest a car seat or other big-ticket item. Your friends can pool their funds and buy you something you really need, rather than a lot of cutesy frilly dresses or sailor suits!

■ **Go bargain hunting.** See if a local baby store or department store would be willing to give you a break if you bought all of your baby gear through them. If you're purchasing two or more cribs, car seats, high chairs, and so on, you represent a lot of purchasing power. Don't be afraid to bargain a little.

■ **See if you can solicit some outright donations.** One family was able to convince the owner of a local pharmacy to let them have every seventh bag of diapers free.

 Moneysaver

Some companies provide free coupons or samples to parents who have multiples. You can get the scoop on the latest offers by joining your local parents of multiples association or by doing a Web search to see what types of offers you can track down. Some Web sites for parents of multiples keep updated lists of freebies.

- **Eliminate the frills.** Save money on baby wipes either by making your own (fill a squirt bottle with a mixture of liquid baby soap and plain water, and then buy some inexpensive washcloths) or by making a box of wipes go further by cutting the wipes in half (one family swears that an electric knife works like magic).

- **Cut corners where you can.** You can save on disposable diapers by using high-quality brand names during the night (when you really want the babies to stay dry!) and lower-quality generic brands during the day. Another good strategy is to start buying diapers when you're pregnant: one couple expecting triplets had 1,600 diapers stockpiled by the time their babies came home.

- **Don't look a gift horse in the mouth.** Save items such as used baby bottles, nipples, caps, lids, and acetaminophen samples from the hospital if your children spend some time in the NICU (neonatal intensive care unit). Otherwise, these items are thrown away by hospital staff.

- **Don't overspend in the clothing department.** As a rule of thumb, twins need 1 ½ times rather than 2 times as much clothing as a single baby.

- **Ask your baby's doctor for a deal.** See if your children's pediatrician will reduce the copay per visit given that you're buying his services in bulk! Also, don't be embarrassed to ask for any free coupons and baby-product samples that he may be able to pass your way.

 Bright Idea

Eager to pick up some real from-the-trenches advice on what it takes to get through those challenging first months with your new babies? Subscribe to one of the many online discussion groups for parents of multiples. Most of the major parenting Web sites feature such groups, but if you're looking for some leads on specific groups, check out bellysurf.com — the pregnancy search engine.

- **Keep the taxman at bay.** Give your weekly cash flow a boost by changing the federal withholding rate on your Form W-4 to reflect the fact that you will receive additional personal exemptions and credits in the year your babies are born. Visit the IRS Web site for details: www.irs.gov.

- **See if Uncle Sam will buy you lunch.** Find out if you qualify for the Women, Infants, and Children (WIC) program, which provides nutritional assistance during pregnancy and lactation and during infancy and early childhood. Because family size is factored into the program eligibility criteria, many families of multiples qualify for assistance. You can find the phone number of your local WIC office in your phone book.

You'll find plenty of other money-saving ideas in Chapter 11.

Problems that can arise in a multiple pregnancy

There's no doubt about it: your risk of experiencing pregnancy-related complications increases with the number of babies you are carrying.

- According to the National Center for Health Statistics, the rate of complications for a woman who is pregnant with twins is eight times that of a woman who is carrying a single baby.

- Whereas just 6 percent of single births result in low-birth-weight babies (that is, babies who weigh less than 5.5 pounds), 53 percent of twins and 93 percent of triplets are classified as low birthweight.

- Fifty-three percent of twins and 92 percent of triplets are born prematurely, as compared to 8 percent of single babies.

In this next section of the chapter, we talk about some of the complications that can arise during a multiple pregnancy. If you're the kind of person who gets totally freaked about this type of information, you might want to skip this section unless you need it. But if you're the type of woman who feels more in control of her pregnancy if she has all the facts, then this section is for you.

Just one final point before we set you loose to read (or not read!) this section: we just want to stress that while complications are more common in multiple pregnancy, you shouldn't necessarily assume that you're doomed to run into trouble. That's simply not the case.

Decided to continue reading?

The following are some of the pregnancy complications that can occur during a multiple pregnancy.

Anemia

The increased blood volume during pregnancy puts any pregnant woman at risk of anemia, but women carrying multiples are particularly susceptible to this problem. In fact, one study showed that women who are pregnant with twins are 2.4 times as likely to develop anemia as women who are carrying singletons. If blood tests indicate that you are becoming anemic, your caregiver will likely prescribe an iron supplement.

Miscarriage and stillbirth

Women who are pregnant with multiples are at increased risk of experiencing the miscarriage or stillbirth of one or both of their babies. Although most pregnancy losses occur in the first trimester, they can also occur in the second or third trimesters as a result of such factors as placental abruptions, cord accidents, toxemia, and twin-to-twin transfusion syndrome.

When a baby dies before the 20th week of pregnancy, the baby's death is classified as a miscarriage; when it occurs after the 20th week of pregnancy, the baby's death is classified as a stillbirth. Twins are four times as likely to be stillborn as singletons, and triplets are four to six times as likely to be stillborn as singletons. The rates of stillbirth in higher-order multiples are even higher. (See Chapter 17 for more about miscarriage and stillbirth.)

Pregnancy-induced hypertension

Pregnancy-induced hypertension (high blood pressure) is approximately 2 ½ times more likely to occur when a woman is carrying multiples as when she is carrying a single baby.

Women with mild pregnancy-induced hypertension before 36 weeks are usually placed on bed rest and monitored closely. If both the mother and the babies appear to be doing well, delivery may be delayed until fetal lung maturity is achieved. If the situation worsens, however, it may be necessary to deliver the babies as soon as possible. Amniocentesis can be performed to assess lung maturity if the fetal age is in question. (See Chapter 14 for more about amniocentesis.)

Preeclampsia

Women carrying multiples are twice as likely as women carrying single babies to develop preeclampsia (or toxemia) — a condition characterized by a rise in blood pressure, fluid retention, and the leakage of protein into the urine. When severe, preeclampsia can be life-threatening to mother and baby. If you experience the following symptoms of preeclampsia, be sure to report them to your doctor or midwife immediately:

- sudden weight gain;
- swelling of your hands, face, or feet;
- headaches;
- dizziness;
- seeing spots before your eyes;
- nausea, vomiting, and abdominal pain (particularly severe pain in the upper abdomen) during your second or third trimester of pregnancy.

Problems with the placenta

Three major types of problems with the placenta can occur during a multiple pregnancy:

- a placental abruption, when the placenta partially or fully detaches itself from the uterine wall, causing bleeding and endangering the lives of the pregnant woman and her babies;

- placenta previa, when the cervix partially or fully blocks the cervical opening, something that can lead to bleeding during pregnancy or necessitate a cesarean delivery;

- intrauterine growth restriction, caused by the inadequate flow of nutrients through the placenta to the babies.

Polyhydramnios

Polyhydramnios occurs when there is an excessive amount of amniotic fluid. It is sometimes associated with fetal problems (for example, congenital abnormalities) or maternal problems (for example, gestational diabetes), but in many cases it occurs for no apparent reason.

Polyhydramnios can cause extreme discomfort and, in some cases, premature labor. In certain circumstances, the condition is treated by removal of excess fluid through amniocentesis. (See Chapter 14 for more on amniocentesis.)

Growth discordance

Growth discordance occurs when one of the babies grows more slowly or more quickly than the others. Growth discordance can be caused by either placental problems (such as twin-to-twin transfusion syndrome) or crowded conditions in the uterus.

Intrauterine growth restriction

Intrauterine growth restriction occurs in 12 percent to 47 percent of multiple pregnancies, as opposed to 5 percent to 7 percent of singleton pregnancies. It is widely believed that intrauterine growth restriction in a multiple pregnancy is

Watch Out!

Nearly half of multiple pregnancies are complicated by preterm birth. If you experience any of the following symptoms, you could be experiencing premature labor: a watery, mucusy, or bloody discharge; pressure in the pelvic area or lower abdomen; a low, dull backache; abdominal cramps with or without diarrhea; or regular contractions or uterine tightening, whether painful or not.

caused by fetal competition for the available nutrients — just one more reason to make sure that you're eating ample quantities of nutritious foods.

Preterm birth

Preterm birth is the leading cause of neonatal death in multiples. Although the mere fact that you are carrying multiples puts you at increased risk of experiencing a preterm birth, there are other factors that add to your risk. You're at increased risk if

- you have had abdominal surgery during the current pregnancy (for example, an appendectomy);
- you have an abnormal uterine structure;
- you have fibroids (benign uterine tumors);
- you are experiencing emotional or physical stress;
- you have high blood pressure;
- you develop a high fever during pregnancy;
- you have a kidney infection;
- you are outside of the optimal age range (that is, if you are under 16 or over 35);
- you are a DES daughter (your mother took diethylstilbestrol — DES — when she was pregnant with you);
- you have been diagnosed with placenta previa;
- you have been diagnosed with polyhydramnios;
- you haven't gained enough weight;

- you have previously experienced premature labor or delivery;

- you have been experiencing unexplained vaginal bleeding;

- you are a smoker.

Although cerclage (a surgical procedure in which the cervix is stitched shut to prevent it from dilating prematurely) was once considered to be an effective means of preventing premature labor, most doctors no longer agree with its routine use in women carrying multiples. These days, cerclage is performed only on women with weak cervixes — a condition that the medical profession charmingly refers to as cervical incompetence. (As you probably realize, this is just a less-than-diplomatic way of saying that the cervix is unable to withstand the weight of the developing fetus, or fetuses, and opens prematurely.)

Birth defects and complications

Multiples are twice as likely to be born with birth defects as singletons. What's more, there is a higher percentage of malformations in identical twins than in fraternal twins.

Consider these facts:

- Although most malformations occur early in pregnancy, some — such as twin-to-twin transfusion syndrome or problems resulting from compression of the fetuses — can occur later in the pregnancy.

- Heart anomalies occur in approximately 1 of every 50 twin pregnancies. Either one or both twins may be affected.

- Acardia — absence of the fetal heart — occurs in 1 percent of identical-twin pregnancies.

- Conjoined twins (that is, Siamese twins) occur approximately once in every 100,000 births.

You may want to consider prenatal testing to determine whether your baby has a serious genetic or chromosomal birth defect. If conditions such as conjoined twins or fetal acardia (the absence of a fetal heart) are detected, you will need to come to a decision about whether or not you wish to terminate the pregnancy.

If you wish to have chorionic villus sampling performed during a multiple pregnancy, your doctor will advise you whether or not the procedure can be performed. If the placentas are positioned in such a way that CVS is a technical impossibility, you will be offered the option of having amniocentesis performed further on in your pregnancy.

If you choose to have amniocentesis performed during a multiple pregnancy, a sample of amniotic fluid needs to be taken from the sac of each fetus. To avoid sampling the same sac twice, the doctor performing the amniocentesis leaves the needle in place after removing the first sample and then injects blue dye into that baby's amniotic sac. Then, when the doctor takes a second sample, if the sample comes out clear (as opposed to baby blue!) he'll know that the second sample came from the other baby's sac. If there is a triplet in there, too, dye gets added to the second baby's sac and the procedure gets repeated again.

The issues of prenatal testing and pregnancy termination are discussed in greater detail in Chapter 14.

Complications in identical twins

Women carrying identical twins are two to three times as likely to experience problems as women carrying fraternal twins. The types of problems that can occur when a woman is carrying identical twins include

- miscarriage, since identical twins are miscarried more often than fraternal twins;

- twin-to-twin transfusion syndrome, a disorder in which there is an unequal sharing of nutrients from the shared placenta between identical twins. The blood-deprived "donor" twin may become anemic and be smaller than the "recipient" twin, who may experience jaundice, respiratory problems, or heart failure due to excessive blood flow;

- complications that can arise when two babies share the same amniotic sac (that is, monamnionic twins). There is a 50-percent mortality rate in such cases because of the high risk of problems with cord entanglement and the possibility that the two babies will be conjoined. Fortunately, monamnionic twins occur in only 1 percent to 2 percent of identical twins, but that's small consolation if your babies happens to die as a result of this particular pregnancy complication.

Presentation problems

Another possible complication in a multiple pregnancy concerns the position the babies assume at the time of birth. Here are some points worth noting:

- In 43 percent of cases, both twins are vertex (head down). A vaginal delivery is considered to be a good option in 70 percent to 80 percent of so-called vertex-vertex cases. In most cases, the second twin is born shortly after the first. The second twin is carefully monitored during this period before its birth as complications can arise during this time that can put the second twin at risk. A recent study reported in the *British Medical Journal* indicated, in fact, that planned cesarean births may be a safer bet for women giving birth to twins. A group of Scottish researchers found that the majority of deaths occuring during the vaginal delivery of twins occurred when the second twin was deprived of oxygen as a result of complications following the delivery of the first twin. While this particular complication is rare — it only occurred in 7 of the 3,874 vaginal twin deliveries they studied — the reseachers recommended that pregnant women at least be counseled about the possible benefits of cesarean: "We propose that women with twins should be counseled about the risk to the second twin and the theoretical possibility of a protective effect of planned cesarean section when considering mode of delivery at term."

- In 38 percent of cases, the first twin is in a vertex position and the other twin is in a breech (foot or bottom down) or transverse (sideways) position. Though cesarean section is usually preferred in such cases, if a vaginal delivery is planned, external version (a procedure in which the doctor or midwife places her hands on the pregnant woman's abdomen and gently turns the baby) may be attempted. There is a success rate of 70 percent for external version. If the procedure is unsuccessful, the baby is usually delivered by cesarean section, although some doctors feel comfortable delivering the second baby as a breech vaginally.

- In 19 percent of cases, the first twin is in a breech or transverse position and the second twin is in a vertex position. A cesarean delivery is the best option in this situation.

Low birthweight

Approximately half of twins are classified as low birthweight (that is, they weigh less than 5.5 pounds at birth). Even those multiples who are carried to term may have low birthweights because of both crowded conditions in the uterus and the need to share nutrients with one or more babies. Fraternal twins tend to weigh more than identical twins.

Postpartum hemorrhage

Women who give birth to multiples are at increased risk of experiencing a postpartum hemorrhage (that is, loss of a significant amount of blood following the delivery). This is because the uterus has been severely stretched and may have difficulty contracting after the babies are born.

Perinatal mortality

Twins are three to five times more likely to die within the first 28 days of life as singletons. The most common cause of death among twins born before 36 weeks is respiratory failure, whereas the most common cause of death in twins born after 36 weeks involves problems with the placenta.

Sudden infant death syndrome (SIDS)

Sudden infant death syndrome (SIDS) is believed to be twice as common in twins as in singletons — not surprising given that SIDS is more likely to occur in babies with low birthweight than babies of average weight.

If one twin dies, the second twin is closely monitored during the month following the loss because statistically the other twin is at greater risk.

The facts about selective reduction

Selective reduction involves selectively aborting one or more fetuses. It is typically performed when a couple wishes to terminate the pregnancy of a fetus that has birth defects or to reduce the total number of fetuses being carried.

During the first trimester, the fetus that has been terminated can be removed through the cervix. During the second and third trimesters, the fetus that has been terminated is carried along with the live one.

There is an element of risk involved in selective reduction. The procedure can result in the inadvertent loss of the remaining baby or babies due to miscarriage, infection, premature labor and birth, or the need to terminate the entire pregnancy because of complications that arise as a result of the procedure.

Couples who decide to reduce the total number of fetuses in order to increase their odds of ending up with at least one healthy baby often find it extremely difficult to abort other healthy fetuses. They may experience the same type of grief as other parents experience upon the loss of a pregnancy. See Chapter 17 for more about grief following the death of a baby.

Just the facts

- The number of multiple births increased by 59 percent between 1980 and 1999.

- Twin pregnancies result from either the fertilization of two separate eggs by two separate sperm (a process that results in dizygotic, or fraternal, twins) or the separation of a single fertilized egg into two fetuses (a process that results in monozygotic, or identical, twins). Higher-order multiple pregnancies involve fraternal twins, identical twins, or a combination of both types of twins.

- You will likely experience increased pregnancy symptoms (such as nausea, fatigue, and morning sickness) due to the high level of pregnancy hormones in your body. You are also likely to experience a range of discomforts caused by the pressure of your heavy, stretched uterus on surrounding organs (shortness of breath, heartburn, constipation, pelvic discomfort, urinary leakage, back pain, and hemorrhoids).

- You should be prepared for the possibility of a preterm birth. The average length of pregnancy for a woman carrying twins is 37 to 38 weeks; for triplets, 34 weeks.

- Your caregiver may monitor the well-being of your babies through ultrasound, a nonstress test (NST), and a biophysical profile (BPP).

- Accept any and all offers of help. If you don't get enough offers, ask people to help.

- Negotiate bargains and freebies whenever you can to reduce the cost of parenting multiples.

- You and your babies are at increased risk of experiencing complications during pregnancy. According to the National Center for Health Statistics, a woman carrying multiples is eight times as likely to experience complications as a woman who is carrying a single baby.

- Some pregnant women choose to undergo selective reduction to either terminate a fetus with severe anomalies or reduce the total number of babies in order to lower the risk of losing all of the babies to pregnancy-related complications.

GET THE SCOOP ON. . .
What being "high risk" means to you and your
baby ▪ Chronic conditions that can place a pregnancy at risk ▪ Conditions that can develop during pregnancy ▪ Coping with your anxiety ▪
Staying sane while you're on bed rest

Coping with a High-Risk Pregnancy

There's nothing warm and fuzzy about the term "high-risk pregnancy." In fact, it can be downright scary. What many people don't realize, however, is that the term "high-risk pregnancy" is a catchall term that's used to describe women who are on the risk continuum at any point during their pregnancy: women who are at a slightly higher-than-average risk of experiencing complications during pregnancy or birth, or giving birth to a baby with a minor birth defect; and those who have the odds of a happy outcome firmly stacked against them, but who are willing nonetheless to take their chances at starting a family.

If you are at the low end of the risk continuum, your pregnancy may be, for all intents and purposes, perfectly normal. If, on the other hand, you're at high risk of experiencing complications, your pregnancy will be a major commitment — one that will change virtually every aspect of your life during the months ahead. "Your perfect pregnancy — the one we're brought up to believe every woman gets to experience — has now become that other thing you read about in magazines," writes Laurie A. Rich in *When Pregnancy Isn't Perfect: A Layperson's Guide to Complications in Pregnancy* (Plume, reprint ed., 1993). "You are now in the high-risk category. Everyone, from your obstetrician to your own mother, is behaving differently toward you."

In this chapter, we talk about what being high risk is likely to mean to you and your baby. Then we discuss both chronic conditions that require special management during pregnancy and conditions that can arise during pregnancy and plunge a low-risk pregnancy into the high-risk category in the blink of an eye. We wrap up the chapter by discussing what it feels like to experience a high-risk pregnancy and offering some practical tips on staying sane during bed rest — one of the biggest challenges many women face during a high-risk pregnancy.

What being high risk means to you and your baby

The term *high risk* is used to describe pregnancies in which the mother, the baby, or both are at higher-than-average risk of experiencing complications. You are likely to be classified as high risk if you have

- a chronic medical condition that may affect your pregnancy;

- a history of previous pregnancy-related complications or pregnancy-related complications during your current pregnancy;

- a recurrent history of miscarriage or stillbirth.

Note: We discuss chronic medical conditions and pregnancy-related complications in this chapter, and miscarriage and stillbirth in Chapter 17.

As you can see from the following checklist, there are a number of reasons why your pregnancy may be classified as high risk.

Checklist 16.1. Is Your Pregnancy High Risk?

Your pregnancy may be treated as high risk if

_____ you are over 35 years old and are therefore at increased risk of giving birth to a child with a chromosomal anomaly;

_____ you are under 17 and are therefore at increased risk of experiencing intrauterine growth restriction;

_____ you are carrying more than one baby and are therefore at risk of experiencing a number of pregnancy-related complications, including preterm labor;

_____ you have a chronic health condition such as diabetes, heart problems, or a blood-clotting disorder that has the potential to affect your pregnancy;

_____ you have a history of gynecological problems such as pelvic inflammatory disease (PID), endometriosis, or large symptomatic fibroids;

_____ you have a history of miscarriage, ectopic pregnancy, stillbirth or premature birth;

_____ you have an STD, including HIV, that could be transmitted to your baby during pregnancy or at the time of birth;

_____ you are pregnant as a result of assisted reproductive technologies (something that may put you at increased risk of having a multiple pregnancy);

_____ you have had two or more second-trimester abortions (which may increase your chances of having problems with an incompetent cervix);

_____ your mother took DES during her pregnancy (which may increase your odds of having difficulty carrying a pregnancy to term);

_____ you conceived while using an IUD (something that increases your chances of experiencing a miscarriage);

_____ you have a child with a genetic disorder or are a carrier for a genetic disorder (something that may increase your risk of giving birth to a child with that particular genetic disorder).

Watch Out!

Any pregnancy can become high risk. Although the occurrence of any of the following symptoms may not necessarily indicate a problem, you should call your caregiver immediately if you experience
- vaginal bleeding or spotting
- swelling in the face or fingers
- a leakage of fluid or increased vaginal discharge
- severe or persistent headaches
- pain in the abdomen or shoulder
- persistent vomiting that is not related to morning sickness
- chills or a fever
- a noticeable change in the frequency or strength of your baby's movements
- painful or urgent urination
- dizziness or faintness

If your doctor or midwife lacks the specialized expertise to deal with someone with your particular risk factors, you may need to switch to a high-risk-pregnancy specialist. You may find this upsetting if you've established a good rapport with your current caregiver, but switching caregivers is probably the best option for you and your baby. As Candace Hurley, the founder of Sidelines (www.sidelines.org; a national support group for moms on bed rest) put it in an interview with the *Los Angeles Times:* "You're not a Ford anymore, you're a Ferrari. You need a mechanic who works on Ferraris."

Regardless of who your caregiver is, however, your pregnancy will be more closely monitored than it would be if your pregnancy were classified as low-risk. Consequently, you may be required to make more frequent visits to the doctor, and your doctor may recommend additional tests. If complications do arise — or seem likely to arise — your doctor may prescribe certain types of medications or bed rest.

Bright Idea

If you are at risk of experiencing blood-pressure problems during pregnancy, purchase a blood-pressure machine at your local drugstore or medical supply store so that you can keep track of your blood pressure between prenatal checkups.

Chronic conditions that place a pregnancy at risk

Advances in obstetrical medicine have made motherhood a possibility for large numbers of women who might have been discouraged from starting a family a generation ago. Not everyone, however, is able to have a baby. Some chronic conditions place such a tremendous burden on the body that pregnancy is unlikely to occur in the first place, or if it does, the odds of miscarriage, stillbirth, or neonatal loss are extremely high. In certain situations, a woman with a serious medical condition who manages to beat the odds and become pregnant will be encouraged to terminate her pregnancy because the risks to herself or her baby, or both, are simply far too high.

If you are dealing with such a condition, the time to weigh the risks and benefits of a pregnancy is before you become pregnant. Set up an appointment with your doctor to discuss how your pregnancy may affect your condition, how your condition may affect your pregnancy, how past treatments (chemotherapy, radiation therapy, surgery, and so on) for your condition may affect your pregnancy and delivery, what warning signs you need to be aware of, what prenatal tests you may wish to consider, and what — if anything — can be done to minimize the risks to you and your baby.

High blood pressure

There's high blood pressure — and then there's *really* high blood pressure.

If you have mild hypertension (that is, your blood pressure is from 140/90 to 179/109) and it is not complicated by other factors such as kidney disease or heart disease, your odds of developing preeclampsia are just 10 percent, and your chances of having a healthy baby are excellent.

If, however, you suffer from severe chronic hypertension (that is, your blood pressure is over 180/110 or your condition is complicated by either kidney disease or heart disease), having a baby will be a fairly risky venture for you. You have a 50-percent chance of developing preeclampsia and a 10-percent chance of experiencing a placental abruption, and you are at increased risk of intrauterine growth restriction, premature delivery, and maternal complications such as stroke and cardio-vascular problems.

You are at highest risk of experiencing blood-pressure-related problems during your pregnancy if

- you are over 40;
- you have a lengthy history of hypertension (you've had problems with your blood pressure for more than 15 years);
- your blood pressure is higher than 160/110 early on in your pregnancy;
- you have diabetes, cardiomyopathy (a disease of the heart muscle caused by either hypertension or other problems), kidney disease, or connective tissue disease (for example, lupus);
- you have previously experienced blood-clot complications;
- you developed severe preeclampsia early on in a previous pregnancy;
- you experienced a placental abruption in a previous pregnancy.

Women with extremely complicated cases of hypertension typically spend 15 days in the hospital during their pregnancies. What's more, they have a 50-percent chance of requiring a cesarean section, a 50-percent chance of experiencing major complications such as deteriorating kidney function, and a 50-percent chance of developing preeclampsia — with a 25-percent chance that the baby will die.

Heart disease

The increased blood volume during pregnancy means that your heart already has to work 50 percent harder than usual. That's why women with pre-existing heart problems can run into serious difficulty during pregnancy. Heart disease is, in fact, the third-leading cause of maternal death during pregnancy, exceeded only by hemorrhage and infection.

Fortunately, not every woman with a heart condition needs to be totally panicked about the possible life-threatening consequences of embarking on a pregnancy. Some women with less-serious heart conditions have far less to worry about. Here are the facts on how pregnancy typically affects some of the most common types of heart disease:

> 66 Because of my heart murmur, I need to take antibiotics before any procedure in which I will bleed. I was striving for a natural delivery, so I wasn't thrilled at the prospect of having to be attached to an IV pole, but as it turned out, the IV pole was not a hindrance at all. I was able to walk around, change positions, even get in the shower. 99
>
> — Tracy, 30, mother of one

- **Rheumatic heart disease:** Rheumatic heart disease is caused by rheumatic fever — an autoimmune response to an infection (typically, untreated strep throat). If it results in mitral stenosis — a particular form of heart-valve damage — the rate of maternal mortality during pregnancy is high. Women affected by this condition require intensive monitoring and multiple cardiac drugs during labor.

- **Congenital heart diseases:** Although the majority of congenital heart defects are mild or repair themselves spontaneously during childhood, some more serious types of congenital heart diseases can endanger a pregnant woman and her baby. Some of these diseases have maternal mortality rates of 50 percent and fetal mortality rates of 25 percent to 50 percent. What's more, babies who survive are also at increased risk of developing congenital heart defects themselves. Women with Eisenmenger's syndrome and primary pulmonary hypertension are advised to avoid pregnancy because of the high rates of maternal mortality associated with these problems. Women with mitral valve prolapse (a disorder in which the heart valve clicks and murmurs) don't face any significant risk during pregnancy, although some caregivers will prescribe antibiotics during labor to prevent potential complications.

Lung disorders

Like the heart, the lungs have to work harder during pregnancy. Although most preexisting lung diseases (for example, tuberculosis and sarcoidosis) don't cause problems during pregnancy, asthma warrants special monitoring and care.

According to the U.S. Department of Health and Human Services, approximately 1 percent of pregnant women have chronic asthma, and another 1 percent will develop the disease as a complication of pregnancy.

Some women with asthma will experience an improvement (25 percent), others will experience a deterioration (25 percent), and others will find that their condition remains stable (50 percent). Unfortunately, there's no way to predict in advance what will happen to any particular woman.

Watch Out!

Don't stop taking your medications without talking to your doctor first. Although certain medications (for example, epilepsy drugs) may be harmful to your baby, the risks of not taking your medications may be even higher. Only your doctor can help you decide whether it's safe to discontinue your medications during pregnancy and, if so, how you can safely wean yourself off them.

If you are asthmatic and become pregnant, you should

- avoid substances that tend to trigger asthma attacks;
- minimize your exposure to colds, flus, and respiratory infections;
- consider having a flu shot (particularly if you will be pregnant during flu season);
- continue to take your allergy shots (with your doctor's approval);
- continue to use your asthma medications (with your doctor's approval);
- treat asthma attacks immediately to avoid depriving your baby of oxygen.

Kidney disease

The kidneys — which are responsible for filtering the blood — are also required to work harder during pregnancy because they must contend with the waste products that the baby releases into the mother's bloodstream, as well as the increased volume of blood.

Here are the facts on kidney disease and pregnancy:

- Women with mild kidney disease experience very few problems during pregnancy, but those who have more severe forms of the disease are at risk of developing pyelonephritis (an acute kidney infection that can cause permanent damage), experiencing a premature delivery, or having a baby with intrauterine growth restriction.

Watch Out!

An untreated urinary tract infection can spread to the kidneys, causing kidney damage or premature delivery.

- Women who have both chronic kidney disease and high blood pressure have a 50-percent chance of developing severe hypertension during pregnancy.

- Women who are on dialysis prior to pregnancy will require dialysis treatments more frequently during pregnancy.

- Women who are pregnant after a kidney transplant will continue to require medications to prevent rejection of the kidney. They have a 33-percent chance of developing preeclampsia, a 50-percent chance of experiencing a premature delivery, an increased risk of having a baby with intrauterine growth restriction, and a higher risk of cesarean due to pelvic bone disease or narrowing of the birth canal.

Note: To maximize their chances of giving birth to a healthy baby, women who have had a kidney transplant should wait two to five years before attempting a pregnancy. Women who have minimal protein in their urine, normal blood pressure, and no evidence of kidney rejection are considered to be the best candidates for a pregnancy.

Liver disorders

The liver plays a role in a number of important bodily functions. It produces substances the body needs in order to metabolize fats, vitamins, minerals, proteins, and carbohydrates; it controls blood sugar level and lipids; it stores essential vitamins, minerals, and glucose; and it detoxifies substances such as drugs, alcohol, and chemicals.

Although most forms of hepatitis do not appear to worsen during pregnancy and therefore don't appear to pose a significantly increased risk to the mother, certain liver disorders can endanger the fetus (for example, it's possible that a woman with hepatitis B or C could transmit the disease to her baby).

Some women develop a particular form of jaundice during pregnancy (intrahepatic cholestasis). It tends to develop during the third trimester, and it results in severe itching and mild jaundice. It disappears spontaneously within two days of delivery. Note: Some studies have shown that women who experience jaundice during pregnancy may be at increased risk of experiencing a premature delivery or a stillbirth.

> **❝** If you have previously given birth to a premature baby, make sure you see a high-risk-pregnancy specialist during your next pregnancy. Ask for every test available, particularly if they don't know the cause of your first premature labor. **❞**
>
> — Susan, 33, mother of two boys who were each premature

Diabetes mellitus

Pregnancy can be risky for a woman with diabetes. Hormonal changes cause an increase in insulin requirements that a diabetic woman's body can't meet. If a pregnant woman does not manage to keep her blood sugars under control, she is at increased risk of experiencing miscarriage, stillbirth, or fetal death, or of giving birth to a baby with heart, kidney, or spinal defects. She is also more likely to give birth to an extremely large baby — something that can lead to problems during the delivery or necessitate a cesarean section.

And some new research indicates that women with type 1 diabetes (preexisting diabetes) are at increased risk of developing pregnancy gingivitis — a condition that itself increases the risk of preterm birth.

A diabetic woman is likely to experience the best possible outcome if she manages to tightly control her blood sugars

Watch Out!

A family history of diabetes is one of the factors that increases your risk of developing gestational diabetes during your pregnancy.

during the two months prior to becoming pregnant, as well as throughout her pregnancy. Blood sugar levels of 70 to 140 milligrams/deciliter in the months prior to pregnancy and an average of 80 to 87 milligrams/deciliter during pregnancy are associated with positive pregnancy outcomes. A diabetic woman can find out how well her blood sugars are under control by taking a glycosylated hemoglobin (hemoglobin Alc) test at two to three months of pregnancy. A favorable result on the test indicates that she is at no greater risk of giving birth to a baby with birth defects than any other pregnant woman.

Most of the damage that causes birth defects occurs during the first trimester. Some of the problems that can result are minor and correctable; others can be fatal to the developing baby. That's why it's important for a diabetic pregnant woman to check her blood levels up to six or seven times daily using a home glucose monitor and to report any problems in controlling her blood sugar levels to her caregiver. (Note: Women with preexisting diabetes — as opposed to gestational diabetes — always need insulin.)

A diabetic woman may require additional tests during pregnancy to check on the status of her eyes, her kidneys, the placenta, and the baby. What's more, her baby may need to be checked over in the neonatal intensive care unit after delivery to be observed for both respiratory problems and hypoglycemia.

Thyroid disorders

The thyroid is responsible for regulating the body's metabolic processes.

If it is overactive — a condition known as hyperthyroidism — the metabolism speeds up; the heart rate increases; and such symptoms as muscle weakness, nervousness, anxiety, heat sensitivity, flushed skin, bulging eyes, weight loss, and goiter are experienced. Pregnant women with hyperthyroidism can develop thyroid storm — a severe form of the disorder — during pregnancy. Thyroid storm is associated with an increased risk of premature delivery and low birthweight.

If the thyroid is underactive — a condition known as hypothyroidism — the metabolism slows down, causing lethargy, aching muscles, intolerance to cold, constipation, weight gain, voice deepening, facial puffiness, and dry skin.

Thyroid function needs to be monitored closely in pregnant women with either type of disorder, and where appropriate, medication should be prescribed or adjusted.

Pituitary disorders

The pituitary gland is responsible for regulating the flow of hormones in the body. A couple of pituitary-related disorders can cause problems during pregnancy:

- **Pituitary tumors:** Some women have undetected pituitary tumors. Pregnancy hormones can cause these tumors to grow, causing severe headaches and visual-field disturbances (that is, spots before the eyes or obstructions to vision). If this occurs, the pregnant woman will need to be monitored by a team of specialists, including an obstetrician, an endocrinologist, and an opthamologist.

- **Diabetes inspidus:** Diabetes inspidus is a rare condition caused by a deficiency in an antidiuretic hormone manufactured by the pituitary gland. This disorder causes increased thirst and a correspondingly increased output of urine. The condition tends to get worse during pregnancy but can be controlled through medication.

- **Pituitary insufficiency:** Pituitary insufficiency — a deficiency in overall pituitary function — can be caused by damage from a tumor, surgery, radiation, or complications from a previous pregnancy. If the condition is not corrected during pregnancy, a woman has only a 54-per-cent chance of having a healthy baby. Women who have had previous surgery or radiation in the pituitary region or who have experienced a severe hemorrhage during a previous pregnancy — particularly if the hemorrhage was followed by an inability to lactate — should be tested for pituitary insufficiency.

Adrenal gland disorders

The adrenal glands are responsible for maintaining the correct levels of salt in the body, for producing sex steroids (hormones), and for manufacturing other hormones known as glucocorticoids. Two types of adrenal gland disorders tend to cause problems during pregnancy:

- *Cushing's syndrome* — the result of too much cortisone — is associated with a high rate of premature delivery and stillbirth. The syndrome is characterized by muscle weakness and wasting; thinning and reddening of the skin; an accumulation of excess fat on the face, neck, and torso; and excessive hair growth. Later stages of the syndrome may also result in high blood pressure, diabetes mellitus, and an increased susceptibility to various infections. This syndrome is difficult to diagnose during pregnancy because many of the symptoms are also associated with pregnancy: weakness, weight gain, edema, stretch marks, high blood pressure, and diabetic tendencies.

- *Addison's disease* — the result of inadequate adrenal production — can result in life-threatening infections. It is characterized by fatigue, loss of appetite, nausea, dizziness, fainting, skin darkening, and abdominal pain.

Blood disorders

The following five blood disorders can cause problems during pregnancy:

- **Anemia:** Anemia — a blood disorder that is caused by deficiencies in iron, vitamin B12, or folic acid — can result in fatigue; weakness; shortness of breath; dizziness; tingling in the hands and feet; a lack of balance and coordination; irritability; depression; heart palpitations; a loss of color in the skin, gums, and fingernails; jaundice of the skin and eyes; and — in particularly serious cases — heart failure. Because many women become anemic during pregnancy, you're at increased risk of experiencing these types of difficulties if you are anemic prior to pregnancy.

- **Sickle-cell anemia:** Sickle-cell anemia is a hereditary blood disease. Women with sickle-cell anemia who become pregnant have a 25-percent chance of miscarriage, an 8- to 10-percent chance of stillbirth, and a 15-percent chance of neonatal death. They have a 33-percent chance of developing high blood pressure and toxemia and also tend to have problems with urinary tract infections, pneumonia, and lung tissue damage. Sickle-cell crises — painful episodes that can lead to organ damage due to the lack of proper blood flow into the fine capillaries — are more likely to occur during pregnancy. As if that weren't enough, a pregnant woman runs the risk of passing along sickle-cell anemia to her baby if her partner also happens to carry the gene for the disease.

- **Thalassemia:** Thalassemia is another hereditary blood disease. Although most people with Cooley's anemia (alpha-thalassemia) die before they reach childbearing age, the handful of women who do live long enough to become pregnant often suffer severe anemia and congestive heart failure requiring blood transfusions. Those pregnant women who have the less-severe form of thalassemia (beta-thalassemia) may require blood transfusions during pregnancy and run the risk of giving birth to a baby with the disease if their partner is also a carrier.

- **Thrombocytopenia:** Women with thrombocytopenia — a deficiency of blood platelets — are at increased risk of requiring a cesarean section. Babies born vaginally to mothers with severe thrombocytopenia may have decreased platelet counts and problems with hemorrhaging — particularly around the brain.

- **Von Willebrand's disease:** Von Willebrand's disease is an inherited disorder that affects the blood's capability to clot. It can lead to severe blood loss during surgery, accidents, or delivery, which is why pregnant women with this disease need to be treated with intravenous clotting factors.

Autoimmune disorders

Autoimmune disorders occur when the body's immune system develops antibodies to its own body tissue, resulting in damage to its own major organs.

Here are the facts on four of the most common autoimmune disorders and pregnancy:

- **Lupus:** A generation ago, women with lupus were advised not to become pregnant because of the risks that pregnancy posed to both the mother and the baby. Today, a growing number of women with the disorder are trying to have children. This is not to say that it's an easy journey to make: according to the Lupus Foundation of America, although 50 percent of women with lupus can expect to enjoy a normal pregnancy, 25 percent will experience either stillbirth or a miscarriage, and another 25 percent will experience preterm labor. What's more, 20 percent of women with lupus develop preeclampsia, and 3 percent give birth to babies with "neonatal lupus" — a form of the disease that lasts until the baby is six months old and that may cause a permanent heart abnormality. Women with moderate-to-severe involvement of the central nervous system, lungs, heart, kidneys, or other internal organs are advised to avoid pregnancy.

- **Rheumatoid arthritis:** Rheumatoid arthritis is a common form of arthritis. Its symptoms include joint pain and swelling, and stiffness (especially in the morning). Almost all women with rheumatoid arthritis go into remission during pregnancy. Unfortunately, the disease recurs in 90 percent of women after they give birth — 25 percent within a month of the delivery.

- **Scleroderma:** Scleroderma is a progressive connective tissue disorder that can cause lung, heart, kidney, and organ damage and that is characterized by both joint inflammation and reduced mobility. In 40 percent of cases the disease worsens during pregnancy, in another 40 percent there is no change, and in the remaining 20 percent of cases the condition actually improves. Pregnant women with the disorder face an increased risk of premature delivery and stillbirth, but the majority of babies born to mothers with scleroderma are born healthy.

- **Myasthenia gravis:** Myasthenia gravis is an autoimmune disease that causes skeletal muscle weakness and easy fatigability. Thirty percent of women with the condition experience no change to their condition during pregnancy, 40 percent experience a worsening of symptoms, and 30 percent go into remission. There is a 25-percent rate of premature delivery associated with the disorder and a 10- to 20-percent chance that the baby will experience a temporary case of myasthenia gravis within two days of delivery.

Gastrointestinal disorders

Here's what you need to know about chronic gastrointestinal disorders and pregnancy:

- **Peptic ulcers:** Peptic ulcers are chronic sores that protrude through the gastrointestinal tract lining and can penetrate the muscle tissue in the duodenum, stomach, or esophagus. Forty-four percent of women with peptic ulcers experience an improvement during pregnancy because the high levels of progesterone in the body stimulate the production of mucus, which can help to provide a protective shield in the stomach lining. Another 44 percent experience no change in their condition, however, and the remaining 12 percent actually report a deterioration.

- **Ulcerative colitis:** Ulcerative colitis is an inflammatory disease of the colon and rectum. It can lead to bloody stools, diarrhea, cramping, abdominal pain, weight loss, and dehydration. It can also be linked to fever, anemia, and a high white-blood-cell count. A woman whose colitis is inactive when she becomes pregnant has a 50- to 70-percent chance of having it remain inactive during pregnancy — good news for both her and her baby. The condition tends to be a significant problem only if emergency surgery is required, because this type of surgery can cause premature labor or necessitate a cesarean delivery.

- **Crohn's disease:** Crohn's disease is similar to ulcerative colitis, but it affects the entire gastrointestinal tract (that is, from the mouth to the anus), although it tends to be focused in the intestines. If Crohn's disease is active at the time of conception, a pregnant woman faces 50 percent odds of miscarrying. If, however, she is in remission, she has an 85-percent chance of having the remission continue during her pregnancy.

Neurological disorders

Here's what you need to know about neurological disorders and pregnancy:

- **Epilepsy and seizure disorders:** Pregnancy is risky business for a woman with epilepsy. Many of the drugs used to control the disorder are linked to birth defects; facial, skull, and limb deformities; fatal hemorrhages in newborns; unusual childhood cancers; cleft palate or lip; congenital

Bright Idea

You can reduce the likelihood of experiencing problems with your epilepsy if you take your medications as prescribed. Studies have shown that women who take their epilepsy medications as directed have an 85- to 90-percent chance of giving birth to a healthy baby. If morning sickness is making it difficult for you to keep your medications down, try taking them at times when your nausea is less severe or with plain crackers and a drink of milk.

heart disease; spina bifida; intrauterine growth restriction; and fetal death. Women with epilepsy also have a 1 in 30 chance of giving birth to a child with a seizure disorder. Not everyone faces an equal risk of running into problems; however: women who experience frequent seizures prior to becoming pregnant are four times as likely to experience problems during pregnancy as women who don't. And epileptic women with a history of miscarriage are more likely to give birth to a child with epilepsy than epileptic women who have not experenced miscarriages in the past. (A study at Columbia University in New York found that 13 percent of children born to epileptic women with a history of miscarriage developed epilepsy by age 25 as compared to less than 5 percent of epileptic women with no such history of miscarriage.)

- **Migraines:** Nearly one in five pregnant women suffers from migraine headaches. Fortunately, 80 percent find that their condition improves during pregnancy, and others are able to avoid problems by avoiding such dietary triggers as MSG (often found in Asian food), sodium nitrates and nitrites (found in cured meats), and tyramine (found in strong cheese). Note: If you're prone to migraines, don't allow yourself to get too hungry. Low blood sugar can trigger migraines.

- **Multiple sclerosis:** Multiple sclerosis is a disease in which the insulating material covering the body's nerve fibers is destroyed, causing weakness in the legs, vision problems, poor coordination and balance, spasticity or trembling in one hand, loss of bladder control, and other difficulties. Women with multiple sclerosis are able to give birth to perfectly healthy babies since there is only a 1- to 5-percent chance that the baby will develop the disease. Women with a lack of sensation in their lower bodies are monitored closely during the ninth month in case they are unable to detect the onset of labor. They also may require a forceps or vacuum-assisted delivery since the disorder can affect their ability to push.

Cerebrovascular disease

Pregnancy can pose a significant risk to women with a history of strokes, hemorrhages, and blood clots.

If a pregnant woman has a known blood-vessel disorder of the brain, such as an arteriovenous malformation, she has a 33-percent chance of dying during pregnancy.

Malignant diseases

As a rule of thumb, women with cancer should delay becoming pregnant until they are reasonably sure that a recurrence won't occur during pregnancy. This is because women who are diagnosed with cancer during pregnancy are often advised to terminate their pregnancy so that they can obtain the medical treatment they need. Delaying treatment can, in many cases, reduce their odds for long-term survival.

 Bright Idea

You and your doctor can obtain the latest information on the effects of chemotherapeutic agents on pregnancy through the Registry of Pregnancies Exposed to Chemotherapeutic Agents. The database contains details on the known effects of cancer drugs during specific stages of pregnancy. Contact the Department of Human Genetics, University of Pittsburgh, A300 Crabtree Hall, GSPH, Pittsburgh, PA 15261; phone, (412) 624-3018.

Watch Out!

If you suffer from an eating disorder, you may find it difficult to allow your-self to gain weight during pregnancy. You may wish to continue with an existing treatment program or seek the services of a professional to ensure that you are able to give your baby the healthiest possible start in life.

Phenylketonuria (PKU)

Phenylketonuria is a genetically transmitted disorder that can cause severe mental retardation in the newborn if it is unde-tected within two days of birth. People with PKU are deficient in a particular liver enzyme needed to metabolize phenylalanine, an amino acid found in most foods. Pregnant women with PKU face a higher risk of miscarriage and tend to give birth to more children with microcephaly, heart defects, mental retardation, growth restriction, and low birthweight. Women with PKU must follow a special diet during pregnancy. Studies have shown, however, that women who begin following the diet prior to becoming pregnant have better outcomes, so preconception planning is highly recommended in this case.

Group B Beta-hemolytic strep

Group B Beta-hemolytic strep (the more scientific name for Group B streptococcus mentioned in Chapter 12) is a strain of bacteria that is carried by somewhere between 20 percent and 40 percent of pregnant women. Two percent of babies born to women who are infected with the bacteria develop Group B strep disease — a serious condition with a 6-percent mortality rate. Group B strep is more likely to be a problem if a baby is premature, if the membranes have been ruptured for more than 30 hours when labor commences, or if the woman had a previous baby who contracted a Group B strep infection. Most caregivers screen for Group B strep when a woman is 35 to 37 weeks pregnant and prescribe antibiotics during labor to women who are carriers or who have other risk factors. (See Chapter 12 for more about Group B strep.)

Sexually transmitted diseases

Nearly 2 million pregnant women experience STDs each year. (See Table 16.1.) If you or your partner has had unprotected sex with someone since your last STD screening, you should be retested. STDs can occur at any time — even during pregnancy — and can be harmful to the unborn baby. Fortunately, there are treatments available to minimize the risk to the baby. Consider the facts for yourself:

- Babies of HIV-positive mothers who have been treated with AZT prior to birth and who are delivered by cesarean section have, for example, a less than 1-percent chance of developing HIV, according to the National Institute for Child Health and Human Development. Babies born to women who do not receive any form of treatment, on the other hand, have a 20- to 32-percent chance of developing the disease.

- Babies whose mothers test positive for hepatitis B can usually avoid developing the disease if they are given hepatitis B vaccine and immune globulin within 12 hours of birth. These treatments are repeated one month and six months later.

Table 16.1. The Number of Pregnant Women in the U.S. with STDs Each Year

STD	Estimated Number of Pregnant Women Who Get the Disease Each Year
Bacterial vaginosis	800,000
Herpes simplex	800,000
Chlamydia	200,000
Trichomoniasis	80,000

STD	Estimated Number of Pregnant Women Who Get the Disease Each Year
Gonorrhea	40,000
Hepatitis B	40,000
HIV	8,000
Syphilis	8,000
Total	1,976,000

Source: Goldenberg et al., 1997

Psychiatric illness

Psychiatric illness is relatively common in women of reproductive age. Between 8 percent and 10 percent of women of childbearing age experience depression and approximately 1 percent are schizophrenic.

Although certain drugs used to treat psychiatric illness have been linked with birth defects, others are considered to be relatively safe for use during pregnancy (although, ideally, you will want to avoid taking any drug during your first trimester). Your obstetrician or your psychiatrist will be able to provide you with specific information on the relative risks of continuing to use your medication during pregnancy, but you can find some general information about the relative safety of various psychiatric medications by consulting the Table 5.4 in Chapter 5.

Conditions that can develop during pregnancy

As we mentioned earlier, any pregnancy can change from low risk to high risk overnight. That's why it's important to be prepared to spot the warning signals of the most common pregnancy-related complications. (See Table 16.2.)

Table 16.2. Conditions That Can Arise During Pregnancy

Condition	What Can Happen	Risk Factors and Warning Signs	Treatment
Hyperemesis gravidarum (severe morning sickness)	Can lead to malnutrition and dehydration.	Occurs in 1/200 pregnancies. More common in first-time mothers, women carrying multiples, and mothers who have experienced the disorder during a previous pregnancy.	You will usually be hospitalized so that intravenous drugs and fluids can be administered.
Chorioamnionitis (an infection of the amniotic fluid and fetal membranes)	Can lead to premature rupture of the membranes or premature labor.	Occurs in 1/100 pregnancies. Often there are no symptoms early on except a rapid heartbeat and a fever over 100.4° F.	Treatment options include antibiotics and/or prompt delivery
Gestational diabetes	Can lead to excessive fetal growth. An overly large baby may have to be delivered by cesarean section and may have difficulties at birth. The diabetes may continue after delivery or recur later in life.	Risk factors: subsequent pregnancy, family history of diabetes, have previously given birth to a baby over 9 lbs., have experienced unexplained pregnancy losses, overweight, high blood pressure, recurrent yeast infections.	You may be admitted to a hospital if your blood sugar remains high despite efforts to control your sugar levels through diet. You may require insulin injections.

| Preeclampsia (also known as toxemia) | Associated with increased risk of placental abruption and fetal distress. In severe forms, it can cause a life-threatening condition that includes blood clotting problems, liver dysfunction, stroke, and possibly even the death of the mother or baby. When seizures are present, it is known as eclampsia. The rate of deep vein thrombosis — another potentially life-threatening condition — is nearly twice as high in women with preeclampsia than other pregnant women. And there's some new research to indicate that preeclampsia may be a significant risk factor for maternal cardiovascular illness and death later in life. | Symptoms of early-stage preeclampsia include swelling of hands and feet, sudden weight gain, high blood pressure (140/90 or higher), increased protein in the urine, and headaches. Most likely to occur in: first-time mothers, women carrying multiples, women with chronic high blood pressure, diabetes, kidney disease, or a family history of preeclampsia, or women who have conceived through assisted reproductive technologies. A recent study indicated that women who conceived through ART are five times as likely to develop preeclampsia as other pregnant women. | Mild cases can be treated through bed rest. Severe cases require hospitalization for treatment with antihypertensive drugs. The condition is cured when the baby is born, although the danger period extends to approximately 24 hours after delivery. Labor may be induced or cesarean performed if the condition progresses to a certain point. *Note:* Some recent research has shown that a daily low dose of aspirin may significantly reduce the risk of preeclampsia. Researchers found that women with a history of preeclampsia in a previous pregnancy (or those with certain medical conditions such as hypertension and diabetes) who took a daily dose of baby aspirin were significantly less likely to develop preeclampsia than other women who didn't take aspirin. There was also a reduction in the rate of preterm birth and a corresponding increase in the birth weight. |

(continued)

Table 16.2. (*continued*)

Condition	What Can Happen	Risk Factors and Warning Signs	Treatment
Intrauterine growth restriction (IUGR) (also known as intrauterine growth retardation)	Can result in low-birthweight babies or infants who are less alert and responsive.	Diagnosed when the developing baby consistently measures small for dates. Most likely to occur in: women with chronic health problems or an unhealthy lifestyle, women with high blood pressure, women carrying multiples, woman having first or fifth (or later) pregnancy, a fetus with chromosomal abnormalities.	Bed rest and/or hospitalization. Labor may be induced if it is felt that the baby will do better in the relatively hostile uterine environment.
Amniotic fluid-level problems: polyhydramnios (too much fluid) or oligohydramnios (too little fluid)	Polyhydramnios may indicate Rh- incompatibility problems, diabetes, or the presence of multiple fetuses. Oligohydramnios may indicate a malfunction or absence of fetal kidneys or leakage of amniotic fluid due to premature rupture of the membranes.	Suspected when a woman measures too large or too small for dates; diagnosed via ultrasound.	Polyhydramnios: If severe and causes significant symptoms or fetal compromise, can be treated by removing excess liquid through amniocentesis. This is a serious condition that is generally treated by delivering the baby as soon as it is considered safe to do so. Oligohydramnios:

Premature labor	Health of premature newborn is determined by week of gestation, type of neonatal care available, birthweight, and general health. Babies born before 25 weeks who weigh more than two pounds have a 50-percent chance of survival if they're born in a hospital that is equipped to deal with a baby who is this premature. On the other hand, babies who weigh in at three pounds or more have a 95-percent chance of survival.	Contractions accompanied by cervical dilation, vaginal bleeding or discharge, or vaginal pressure between the 20th and 37th week of pregnancy. Other symptoms include menstrual-like cramps, with possible diarrhea, nausea, or indigestion. Risk factors include smoking, urinary tract infections, poor general health, diabetes or thyroid problems, bacterial infections or STDs, placental problems, physical trauma (car accident, spouse abuse), a history of premature labor, multiple fetuses, abdominal surgery during pregnancy, or a history of second-trimester miscarriages.	Bed rest, intravenous fluids, and/or the prescription of drugs to prevent labor. *Note:* Medications are generally effective only if your cervix is dilated less than three centimeters and is not yet effaced.
Placenta previa (placenta covering the cervical opening)	The baby cannot pass out of the mother's body without dislodging the placenta and disrupting its own blood supply. A postpartum hemorrhage may occur after the birth of the baby.	Bleeding can be triggered by coughing, straining, or sexual intercourse. More common in women who have had several children. Occurs in 1/200 pregnancies.	Bed rest, monitoring, and/or hospitalization. A cesarean section may be required. *Note:* If placenta previa is diagnosed in the second trimester, the condition may correct itself by the time you deliver.

(continued)

Table 16.2. (continued)

Condition	What Can Happen	Risk Factors and Warning Signs	Treatment
Placental abruption (placenta prematurely separates from uterus, either partially or wholly)	Can be harmful — even fatal — to mother and baby.	Warning signs include heavy vaginal bleeding, premature labor, contractions, uterine tenderness, and lower back pain. More common in women who have had two or more children, who smoke, who have high blood pressure, or who have had a previous placental abruption. Sometimes caused by the trauma of an automobile accident. Occurs in 1/150 pregnancies.	Bed rest and careful monitoring. If fetus goes into distress, an emergency cesarean section may be necessary.
Placental insufficiency	Can result in a low-birthweight baby.	Can be caused by abnormal development, restricted blood flow due to a clot, a partial abruption, a placenta that is too small or poorly developed, a pregnancy that is postdate, or maternal diabetes.	Sometimes warrants the delivery of the baby before term.

Watch Out!

Pregnant women are particularly susceptible to diabetes because the placenta produces hormones that counteract the effects of insulin. As a result, a pregnant woman's body needs to produce 30 percent more insulin than normal.

Coping with the stress of a high-risk pregnancy

Nine months can seem like an impossibly long time when you're dealing with the stress of a high-risk pregnancy. If your pregnancy has been categorized as high risk, you may be dealing with a lot of conflicting emotions. "At some point during your confinement, you can expect to feel angry at your baby (for keeping you in bed), your husband (for getting you into bed in the first place), your doctor (for not fixing the problem), and everyone else you can think of," explains Laurie A. Rich.

Here's the lowdown on some of the types of emotions you may be experiencing:

- **Guilt:** You may be wondering if you are somehow responsible for the fact that you and your baby are at risk. Did you overdo things at work? Did you fail to follow your doctor's orders to the letter? It's easy to beat yourself up after the fact even if you know in your heart you did everything within your control to take good care of your baby.

- **Anger and sadness:** If your pregnancy necessitates bed rest, you may feel angry about your lack of control over your life and sad and lonely at being cut off from the rest of the world.

- **Resentment:** You may find yourself feeling resentment toward those women who seem to sail through pregnancy with nothing more significant to worry about than whether they're getting stretch marks.

Bright Idea

If you are feeling extremely anxious, ask your doctor or a social worker at the local hospital to recommend a therapist who specializes in working with women who are experiencing high-risk pregnancies. Sometimes simply talking about your feelings can help to bring your stress level down considerably.

- **Helplessness:** If your pregnancy becomes complicated and you are put on bed rest or hospitalized, you may feel helpless because you have to rely on other people to make your meals, take care of your other children, and so on. You may find it difficult to ask friends and family members for favors, assuming that you'll never in a million years be able to repay them for all the help you need right now.

- **Fear:** You may be afraid that despite everything you're doing to increase your odds of having a healthy baby, something could still go wrong.

Because there are so many emotions to deal with in a high-risk pregnancy, many women find it helpful to find someone who will take the time to talk to them about their worries and concerns. If your caregiver doesn't have the time, training, or bedside manner necessary to talk with you about your concerns, you may wish to see a therapist — ideally one who has experience in dealing with clients experiencing high-risk pregnancies. You may also want to hook up with a local or national support group specializing in your particular type of pregnancy complications. (See "Resource Directory" — www.wiley.com/go/anndouglas.)

The facts about bed rest

Bed rest sounds like a wonderful thing until you're sentenced to it 24 hours a day. The novelty of surrounding yourself with pillows and junky novels wears thin fairly quickly for most women, who then find themselves facing weeks — if not months — of bed rest.

Watch Out!

If you suspect that you are experiencing premature labor, drink several glasses of water and lie down on your side. This will often stop the contractions.

How bed rest feels

Crazy as it sounds, bed rest can be exhausting. When you're on bed rest, you tire more easily and feel tired more often. You may feel achy and sore from spending so much time lying in the same position. You may feel stiff when you get out of bed, and you may actually find it painful to walk if you've been on bed rest for some time. (This is because lying in bed with your legs relaxed for an extended period can cause the Achilles tendon to tighten.)

You can help minimize some of the effects of bed rest by getting your doctor's go-ahead to do some exercises in bed. (Note: Not all women on bed rest are good candidates for exercise, so don't do as much as a single leg-lift without checking with your doctor first.) A well-designed exercise program can help you prevent muscle weakness, limit the loss of your range of motion, prevent lung congestion, minimize the effects of bed rest on the heart, and help you maintain sufficient muscle tone to be able to walk without assistance after delivery.

Assuming that you get the nod of approval from your caregiver, you may be able to do pelvic tilts; Kegels; gluteal sets; leg, ankle, and heel raises; knee extensions; arm raises; shoulder shrugs; wrist circles; and neck circles.

How to survive it

Here are some tips on staying sane while you're on bed rest:

- Arm yourself with the facts. Find out exactly what you can and cannot do. (See the following checklist.)

Checklist 16.2. Questions to Ask Your Doctor About Bed Rest

_____ Can you sit up in bed, or do you have to lie on your left side (the side that allows for maximum blood flow to the baby) all the time?

_____ Is it okay to get out of bed to go to the bathroom, or do you need to use a bedpan?

_____ Do you need to eat your meals lying down?

_____ Can you take a shower, or do you have to have a sponge bath?

_____ Is it okay to work while you're lying down?

_____ How long will you be on bed rest?

_____ Is exercise allowed?

_____ Is any type of sexual activity permissible?

_____ Are you allowed to sleep on the sofa, or do you have to stay in bed?

_____ Are you allowed to lift anything? If so, how heavy an object are you allowed to lift?

There are other issues to consider before you go on bed rest:

■ Give your notice at work. Because the need for bed rest can arise virtually overnight, you may not be able to give your employer much notice of your need to leave work. Try to pull your thoughts together before you call your employer. Be sure to let him know how long you're likely to be on bed rest (for example, for a week or two, or for the rest of the pregnancy); what type of work, if any, you could do

Moneysaver

Don't forget to make a call to human resources. Your company maternity-leave or disability-leave program may cover part or all of your salary while you're on bed rest.

from home; who might be able to assume responsibility for any projects that are in progress; and so on.

■ Be creative when it comes to choosing where to spend your bed rest. "If it's nice outside, have someone set up a table for you outside with your favorite books, a radio, a cooler filled with fruit, drinks, and food," suggests Stephanie, 26, mother of one and veteran bed-rester. If your doctor gives you the go-ahead to set up camp somewhere other than in your own bed, go for it. A change of scene will do you good.

■ Organize your environment so that you'll be less tempted to get out of bed and go searching for something you need. Here are some things you'll want to keep within reaching distance: a phone, a telephone book, a radio, the remote control for the radio or TV, tissues, a cooler (packed with cold beverages, healthy snacks, and your lunch), craft supplies, a laptop computer with Internet access ("I spent three hours a day on the Internet, and it literally kept me sane," says one former bed-rester), a cassette tape player and books on tape, photo albums to work on, and plenty of reading materials.

> **❝** If you end up on bed rest in the hospital, be sure to bring snacks. I got supper at 5:00 p.m. and no more food until 8:00 a.m. I was starving by then since I was used to supper at 6:00 p.m., a snack in the evening, and breakfast at 6:30 a.m. **❞**
>
> — Susan, 33, mother of two

■ Come up with a routine to prevent yourself from going stir-crazy. Pencil in the times of your favorite TV shows, arrange to meet another pregnant woman on bed rest online in one of the bed rest chat forums, plan when you're going to make phone calls to friends and family members, and so on.

- Reach out to other moms on bed rest by phone or via the Internet. You can get in touch with Sidelines (www.sidelines.org; an online and telephone support network for moms on bedrest) or ask your doctor if he knows of a local support group for moms on bed rest.

- Stay connected with people. "Have a friend come over and just talk — or make you lunch — as often as possible. It will make the whole day better," says Heather, 22, mother of one, who spent three weeks on bed rest during her pregnancy.

- Make suitable childcare arrangements for any other children. If you're a stay-at-home mother with young children, you may need full-time childcare.

- Call your insurance company or HMO to find out if it will cover the costs of a personal care attendant while you're on bed rest. Some companies do and some don't. Sometimes all it takes to sway the claims department is a phone call or letter from your doctor, so don't be afraid to ask him to intervene on your behalf if you run into difficulty.

- Reassure your children that it won't be like this forever. Your stint on bed rest will be over as soon as the baby is born — sometimes sooner.

- Spend some time alone with your partner each day, and keep the lines of communication open. This is a stressful time for both of you.

- If you can afford it, arrange for a childbirth educator or doula to give you childbirth classes at home. If possible, find someone who is familiar with the particular medical conditions or pregnancy-related complications you are dealing with and who understands how they may affect on the birth.

Just the facts

- The term "high risk" is used to describe pregnancies in which the mother, the baby, or both are at higher-than-average risk of experiencing complications.

- You are likely to be classified as high risk if you have a chronic medical condition that may affect your pregnancy, a history of pregnancy-related complications, or pregnancy loss.

- If your doctor prescribes bed rest, it's important to find out exactly what you are and aren't allowed to do.

- Connecting with other moms on bed rest can help you to stay sane. Either ask your obstetrician to recommend a local support group or get in touch with Sidelines.

GET THE SCOOP ON. . .
Miscarriage ▪ Ectopic pregnancy ▪ Molar
pregnancy ▪ Stillbirth ▪ Intrapartum death ▪
Important decisions you will have to make ▪
Grieving ▪ Trying again

What Every Pregnant Woman Needs to Know About Miscarriage, Stillbirth, and Infant Death

Chapter 17

osing a baby can be an incredibly painful experience. Regardless of when your baby dies, you lose all of the hopes and dreams you have invested in that child from the moment you first found out you were pregnant.

Although you may feel, initially, that you are the only person in the world to experience this heartbreak, you will discover — as you begin talking about your loss — that miscarriage, stillbirth, and infant death happen far more frequently than most of us are led to believe.

The problem is that there continues to be a conspiracy of silence when it comes to talking about these types of losses — a strange holdover from the Victorian era, given that we're now "out of the closet" on so many other matters. Although most childbirth classes give you some basic facts about miscarriage, they tend to ignore the possibility of stillbirth and infant death altogether. This is true of most pregnancy books, too. Is it any wonder that the majority of parents who experience the death of a baby report feeling terribly alone?

This chapter wasn't much fun for us to write, and it might not be much fun for you to read, either. Indeed, you may find it extremely difficult to even think about the possibility that something could happen to the baby you are carrying. But things can and do go wrong during pregnancy, and that's why we felt it was important to include a chapter that acknowledges the fact that some pregnancies end in something other than picture-perfect happy endings. Whether you actually choose to read this chapter or not is totally up to you. If you're the kind of person who is going to drive yourself totally crazy for the next nine months, obsessing about every possible symptom, then maybe you should skip this chapter. But if you are the kind of person who finds knowledge empowering, you may want to keep reading. There's no "right" or "wrong" way of handling this issue. You'll have to decide what works best for you: reading this chapter right away or only flipping to it if you have reason to believe that there could be a problem with your pregnancy. To each her own, we say.

> 66 I hated when people said, 'It's for the best' or 'You are still young; there is lots of time.' I desperately wanted that baby. 99
>
> — Laura, 21, pregnant after a miscarriage

The facts about miscarriage

As you no doubt realize, miscarriages are extremely common, occurring in approximately 15 percent to 20 percent of all confirmed pregnancies (that is, pregnancies that have been confirmed via a home pregnancy test or a visit to the doctor).

Although the majority of miscarriages occur during the first 8 to 10 weeks of pregnancy (with the lion's share occurring before a woman even suspects that she is pregnant), miscarriages can and do occur up to the 20th week of pregnancy. (A pregnancy loss after that point is classified as a stillbirth.)

The causes of miscarriage

Certain factors are known to cause miscarriages. These factors include

- **Chromosomal abnormalities:** Up to 60 percent of miscarriages are caused by chromosomal abnormalities — problems with the structure or number of chromosomes in the embryo or with the genes that the chromosomes carry. Many of these embryos would not have developed normally: scientists believe that the high rate of miscarriage helps to ensure that only 2 percent to 3 percent of babies are born with serious congenital anomalies rather than 12 percent, as would be the case if these miscarriages didn't occur. Most miscarriages caused by chromosomal abnormalities are random occurrences and consequently are less likely to recur during subsequent pregnancies than other causes of miscarriage. Note: Twenty percent of miscarriages are associated with gestational sacs in which there is no apparent embryo, yolk sac, or umbilical cord. This type of nonviable pregnancy is sometimes referred to as a *blighted ovum* — a term that we detest but that is still widely used in obstetrical circles.

- **Maternal disease:** Conditions such as lupus and other autoimmune disorders, congenital heart disease, severe kidney disease, uncontrolled diabetes, thyroid disease, and intrauterine infection are associated with higher-than-average miscarriage rates — just one more reason to make sure that any chronic health conditions that you have are under control before you become pregnant. (See Chapter 16 for more about high-risk pregnancy.)

- **Hormonal imbalances:** Hormone imbalances are known to cause miscarriages. If, for example, your progesterone levels are not high enough during the early weeks of pregnancy, you may experience a miscarriage. (This condition, which is known as a luteal phase defect, is thought to be responsible for as many as one-third of recurrent pregnancy losses.) Polycystic ovarian syndrome (a condition characterized by irregular menstrual periods or even the absence of menstrual periods altogether as well as excessive hair growth) has also been linked to a higher-than-average rate of miscarriage.

- **Rhesus (Rh) disease:** Rhesus disease — a blood incompability problem that occurs when the mother's blood is Rh-negative and the father's is Rh-positive — was once the leading cause of miscarriage. It can usually be prevented by ensuring that an Rh-negative woman with an Rh-positive partner receives shots of Rh Immune Globulin (e.g. Rhogam) following each delivery or miscarriage; whenever there is a sign or possibility of bleeding in the womb during pregnancy, including after amniocentesis; and during the 28th week of pregnancy. The Rhogam helps to prevent a woman from producing antibodies to Rh-positive cells, something that could cause problems during future pregnancies. Unfortunately, this treatment isn't effective for every woman and it isn't capable of destroying existing antibodies, which is why it is critical that a Rhogam shot be administered promptly in the event of miscarriage or any other episode of bleeding during pregnancy. If a woman develops Rh antibodies, her next pregnancy will have to be monitored very closely and her baby may require a blood transfusion either prior to or shortly after birth in order to prevent severe anemia. If left untreated, this condition can lead to oxygen deprivation and heart failure, or a condition called hydrops fetalis in which the baby becomes extremely swollen, all of which can lead to stillbirth or neonatal death.

■ **Immune system disorders:** Immune system disorders occur when a woman's immune system — which has been carefully programmed to fight such foreign invaders as bacteria and viruses — makes a mistake and begins attacking normal cells in her body instead. Immune disorders are thought to be resonsible for between 5 percent and 10 percent of recurrent miscarriages, with a condition known as antiphospholipid antibody syndrome (APA) being responsible for a large number of such cases. APA occurs when a woman's body mistakes phopholipids (the parts of a cell's membrane that function as nerve insulators) for foreign material and launches an antibody attack in response. The resulting antibodies are believed to cause clots in the placental blood vessels — something that disrupts the flow of nutrients between mother and baby, increasing the risk of miscarriage, fetal growth restriction, preeclampsia, and placental abruptions. A number of methods of treating this condition have been pioneered in recent years, however. Treatment methods include the use of aspirin, heparin (a blood-thinning drug that prevents clots from forming in the placental blood vessels that supply nourishment to the fetus), prednisone, and intravenous immunoglobulin (IVIg), in which the mother is injected with donor antibodies, which function as decoys. There are pros and cons to each method of treatment, of course, which your doctor will be able to discuss with you if you're a candidate for such treatment.

■ **Allogeneic factors:** Some women develop antibodies to their partner's leukocytes (white blood cells) — something that increases the chances of miscarriage. Treatment methods for this particular condition include immunizing a woman with her partner's or a third party's leukocytes in order to trick her body into not rejecting the developing baby.

- **Anatomical factors:** Anatomical problems of the uterus and cervix (for example, uterine adhesions, abnormal uterine structure, uterine fibroids, and incompetent cervix) are known to cause miscarriages. Congential uterine abnormalities alone are believed to be responsible for 10 percent of recurrent miscarriages.

- **Viral and bacterial infections:** Viral and bacterial infections are thought to play a role in miscarriage, although the cause-and-effect relationship is not 100 percent clear.

- **Recreational drug and alcohol use:** Using recreational drugs and consuming large quantities of alcohol increase your chances of experiencing a miscarriage. Cigarette smoke and heavy doses of caffeine also increase the miscarriage risk.

- **Environmental toxins:** Exposure to environmental toxins such as arsenic, lead, and formaldehyde can lead to miscarriage. You'll also want to avoid high-dose radiation.

- **Age:** Your chances of having a miscarriage increase as you age. Whereas women in their 20s have a 10-percent risk of experiencing a miscarriage during any given pregnancy, the rate for women in their 40s is 50 percent.

Note: You can find a more-detailed discussion of the causes of miscarriage in our book *Trying Again: A Guide to Pregnancy After Miscarriage, Stillbirth, and Infant Loss* (Taylor, 2000).

How to tell if you're experiencing a miscarriage

You could be having a miscarriage if you experience

- spotting or bleeding without pain;

- heavy or persistent bleeding — with or without clots — with abdominal pain or cramping;

- a gush of fluid from your vagina but no pain or bleeding — an indication that your membranes may have ruptured;

Watch Out!

Try to save any fetal or other tissue (other than blood clots) that passes out of your body when you are having a miscarriage. Your caregiver may wish to examine it in order to obtain clues about what may have caused you to miscarry.

■ a sudden disappearance of pregnancy symptoms such as morning sickness or breast enlargement (unless, of course, classic first-trimester symptoms such as morning sickness disappear at the end of the first trimester, when you would expect them to disappear).

Note: Not all first-trimester bleeding is an indication that you are having a miscarriage. See Chapter 6 for a detailed discussion of other possible causes of first-trimester bleeding.

How miscarriages are classified

Your doctor may use the following terminology when describing your miscarriage (or "spontaneous abortion" — the medical correct albeit horribly insensitive term for a miscarriage):

■ **Threatened miscarriage:** Threatened miscarriage (or threatened abortion) means that a miscarriage is possible but not inevitable. You are probably experiencing bleeding and possibly pain.

■ **Inevitable miscarriage:** Inevitable miscarriage (or inevitable abortion) means that your cervix has begun to dilate and it's only a matter of time until you miscarry.

■ **Incomplete miscarriage:** An incomplete miscarriage (or incomplete abortion) occurs when some of the products of conception (for example, gestational sac, fetus, umbilical cord, placenta) are left in the uterus after the miscarriage. A dilation and curettage (D and C) or suction curettage (a form of D and C where the contents of the uterus are removed through a tube using suction) is usually performed if an incomplete miscarriage has occurred.

- **Complete miscarriage:** A complete miscarriage (or complete abortion) occurs when all of the products of conception are expelled from the uterus during the miscarriage.

- **Missed miscarriage:** A missed miscarriage (or missed abortion) occurs when the fetus and placenta die but remain in the uterus. Even though pregnancy symptoms may disappear almost immediately, many women do not realize that they have miscarried until a few weeks later in their pregnancy — typically when a Doppler or ultrasound fails to detect a fetal heartbeat. Just remember: there's no reason to automatically go into panic mode if your pregnancy symptoms disappear overnight — something that often occurs toward the end of the first trimester in a perfectly healthy pregnancy.

- **Blighted ovum:** A blighted ovum (an old-fashioned and medically inaccurate term, by the way!) is a form of missed miscarriage that generally refers to the earliest pregnancies (that is, pregnancies in which a fetus is not yet evident at the time of diagnosis). We almost didn't include this term on our list, but because it's still used so often, we thought we'd better define it for you, even though we wish this particular term would disappear once and for all.

Recurrent miscarriage

Doctors used to wait for a woman to have three consecutive miscarriages before attempting to determine if there were any

 Bright Idea

Although it's theoretically possible to become pregnant within two weeks of experiencing an early miscarriage, most caregivers recommend that you wait until after you have had two to three normal menstrual cycles before trying to conceive. Some doctors suspect that waiting this additional time may give your uterus time to heal and your endometrial lining time to build back up to healthy levels.

Bright Idea

If you've had two or more miscarriages, you should plan to have a complete preconception workup before you try to get pregnant again. If you unexpectedly find yourself pregnant again before you have a chance to have a full medical workup, see your doctor or midwife right away so that appropriate treatments can be considered.

underlying medical problems causing her to miscarry, but the thinking in recent years is that it doesn't make any sense to wait until a woman has had a third miscarriage to determine the causes — particularly if her biological clock is ticking particularly loudly.

Unfortunately, the cause of recurrent miscarriage remains a mystery in as many as 50 percent of cases. Still, couples who experience miscarriage from unknown causes have a 52- to 61-percent chance of giving birth to a live baby in their next pregnancy — lower-than-average odds, but still significantly high enough to encourage many couples with a history of miscarriage to pursue their dream of having a baby.

Part of the difficulty in pinpointing a cause for recurrent miscarriages, of course, is the fact that a series of miscarriages may be caused by a number of different factors (for example, one may be caused by a chromosomal abnormality and a second by a viral infection).

A study reported in *Obstetrics and Gynecology* concluded that a number of different factors need to be considered when assessing a woman's chances of having a successful pregnancy after one or more miscarriages. The researchers found that a woman under the age of 25 who has no anticardiolipin antibodies (a type of antiphospholipid antibody), a regular menstrual cycle, and one previous live birth has an 88-percent chance of experiencing a live birth during her next pregnancy. On the other hand, a woman who is over the age of 30, has irregular periods, has had more than four previous miscarriages, has elevated anticardiolipin antibodies, and has had no previous live births has a 60-percent chance of having a successful outcome in her next pregnancy.

Searching for clues

If you experience three miscarriages in a row, you will be classified as a "habitual aborter" (a dreadfully insensitive term that simply means that you have a history of recurrent miscarriage), and you may be given one or more of the following tests:

- blood tests (to detect any hormonal or immune-system problems);

- genetic tests of you and your partner and/or chromosomal testing of tissue from a miscarriage (to determine if you or your partner is a carrier of a disorder that could be causing you to miscarry repeatedly — something that's a problem for approximately 2 percent to 3 percent of couples);

- genital-tract cultures (to look for the presence of infection);

- endometrial biopsy (the removal and analysis of a sample of endometrial tissue to determine if the tissue that lines the uterus is sufficiently hospitable to allow the embryo to implant and grow);

- a hysterosalpingogram (HSG) (an X-ray of the uterus and fallopian tubes that is used to look for blockages and other problems);

- a hysteroscopy (an examination of the inside of the uterus using a telescopelike instrument inserted through the vagina and cervix that is ordered if the HSG is abnormal);

- a laparoscopy (an internal examination of the pelvic organs using a slender light-transmitting instrument);

- ultrasound or sonohysterogram (to detect structural problems with the uterus, as well as fibroids or adhesions that could be causing you to miscarry).

Genetic Conditions that Can Cause Thrombosis

There are a number of genetic conditions that can increase the tendency of blood to clot within the blood vessels of your body (a phenomenon known as thrombosis). These conditions collectively are known as "thrombophilias." The most common of the inherited thrombophilias are Factor V (five) Leiden and prothrombin G20210A mutation, found in approximately 11 percent of U.S. Caucasian women. In addition to causing thrombosis, these genetic mutations are associated with an increased risk of adverse pregnancy outcomes such as fetal loss/stillbirth in the second and third trimesters, placental abruptions, severe intrauterine growth restriction, and early-onset, severe preeclampsia. Treatment involves the use of blood thinners such as heparin, throughout the pregnancy. Therefore, it is critical that you make your caregiver aware of any history of thrombosis or thromboembolic events (blood clots that travel to the lungs or other sites), or a history of severe preeclampsia, placental abruption, stillbirth or other second or third trimester fetal loss, or intrauterine growth restriction. Your caregiver will want to test for genetic causes of thrombophilia if you have a history of any of these conditions.

Treatment options

Depending on the suspected cause of your recurrent miscarriages, your doctor may recommend

- surgery to correct any uterine abnormalities (something that gives you a 70- to 85-percent chance of having a live baby in your next pregnancy) or to remove large fibroids;

- a cerclage procedure around week 14 of your next pregnancy (to stitch the cervix shut so that it won't open prematurely);

Bright Idea

If you have experienced a series of miscarriages, ask your doctor if it might be a good idea to have your partner's sperm tested. Researchers at the University of Utah School of Medicine have noted that sperm samples obtained from couples who have experienced three or more consecutive miscarriages frequently contain higher than average quantities of abnormal sperm. Poor quality or defective sperm can interfere with the development of a healthy embryo, something that can result in miscarriage or stillbirth.

- antibiotics to cure any infections;
- improved management of any chronic diseases, including Rh disease during a subsequent pregnancy;
- hormone therapy;
- treatment for immune-system problems;
- treatment for allogeneic factors.

Ectopic pregnancy

Approximately 1 percent of pregnancies are ectopic, meaning that the fertilized egg implants somewhere other than inside the uterus — most often in the fallopian tube. (In 95 percent of ectopic pregnancies, the fertilized egg implants in the fallopian tube; in the other 5 percent of pregnancies, it implants in the abdominal cavity, the ovaries, or the cervix.)

An embryo that implants in the fallopian tube cannot develop normally. It can only grow to about the size of a walnut before it causes the tube to burst, causing a medical emergency that can result in major bleeding or even death.

Ectopic pregnancies are classified as either unruptured or ruptured:

- An unruptured ectopic pregnancy is one in which the fallopian tube has not yet burst. It is characterized by pain on one side of the abdomen and in the shoulder region (as a result of blood pooling under the diaphragm), vaginal bleeding, and fainting (if the blood loss has been substantial). If an unruptured ectopic pregnancy is detected soon enough, it may respond to medication, or if surgery is needed, it is often possible to save the tube.

▪ A ruptured ectopic pregnancy is one in which the fallopian tube bursts, causing pain and shock, a weak but rapid pulse, paleness, and falling blood pressure. Treatment for a ruptured tube typically involves removal of the tube and possibly a blood transfusion.

You are at increased risk of experiencing an ectopic pregnancy if

▪ you smoke (women who smoke more than 30 cigarettes per day are five times as likely to experience an ectopic pregnancy as other women);

▪ you have previously experienced pelvic inflammatory disease (PID), STDs such as gonorrhea and chlamydia, endometriosis, or salpingitis (inflammation of fallopian tube);

▪ you have already had an ectopic pregnancy (even though you still have an 88-percent chance of not experiencing another ectopic pregnancy);

▪ you have a luteal phase defect (inadequate levels of progesterone can make it difficult for the fertilized egg to make its way through the fallopian tube by weakening the tube's propulsive force — something that can result in the egg implanting in the fallopian tube);

▪ you have been treated for infertility using ovulation-stimulating drugs, such as human menopausal gonatropin

---

 Watch Out!

Women who smoke face an increased risk of ectopic prgnancy. Scientists theorize that nicotine's effect on estrogen is responsible for the increased risk of ectopic pregnancy in women who smoke. Reduced levels of estrogen affect the fallopian tube's ability to contract and transport the embryo to the uterus.

or clomiphene citrane (these drugs also alter the body's hormonal balance);

- you have a structural abnormality of the fallopian tube that leaves you more susceptible to ectopic pregnancies;

- you have had pelvic or abdominal surgery (for example, an appendectomy) and especially if you have had tubal surgery such as a sterilization reversal;

- you were using an intrauterine device (IUD) at the time you became pregnant (approximately one in every 200 IUD users will expeirence an ectopic pregnancy);

- you are in the habit of douching (douching increases your chances of experiencing an ectopic pregnancy);

- you are unlucky enough to become pregnant after having had a tubal sterilization (approximately 7.3 out of every 1,000 women having tubal sterilizations can expect to experience an ectopic pregnancy during the subequent 10-year period, even though they thought their families were finished).

An ectopic pregnancy is typically diagnosed through a pelvic exam, blood tests, ultrasound, or a combination of these methods. In some cases, it is necessary to perform a D and C (to check for signs of an early miscarriage).

Once the diagnosis has been confirmed, your doctor will recommend either surgery (to remove the pregnancy or all or part of the fallopian tube) or drug treatment (to stop the growth of the tissue and allow it to be reabsorbed over time). Drug treatment is an option only if the pregnancy is small, the tube has not yet ruptured, and there is no internal bleeding. Although occasionally the pregnancy will die and reabsorb on its own, in all other cases, surgery is your only option.

You will need to go for a series of blood tests in the weeks following treatment. These blood tests are to check for escalations in hCG, which may indicate that some tissue was left behind and that it is continuing to grow.

Molar pregnancy

A molar pregnancy (also known as gestational trophoblastic disease, or GTD) is a rare disease of pregnancy, occurring in just one 1 of every 1,500 to 2,000 pregnancies in the United States. (Note: The incidence of molar pregnancy varies with ethnicity and is far more common in Asians.)

A molar pregnancy occurs when a pregnancy results in the growth of abnormal tissue rather than an embryo, and it typically results in miscarriage before the fourth month of pregnancy. Scientists believe that molar pregnancies are caused by some sort of genetic error that occurs at the very beginning of pregnancy.

In a *complete molar pregnancy*, there is a mass of abnormal cells that — in a normal pregnancy — would have become the placenta.

In a *partial molar pregnancy*, there is a mass of abnormal cells that would have become the placenta and an abnormal fetus as well. In very rare cases, a normal twin may be present as well, but this twin will only survive until the mother goes into very premature labor.

The symptoms of a molar pregnancy include

- vaginal bleeding during the first trimester;
- severe nausea, vomiting, and high blood pressure caused by unusually high hormone levels;
- a uterus that grows too quickly;
- enlarged ovaries (detected through ultrasound or pelvic exam);
- extremely high levels of hCG (detected through a blood test).

In most cases, women who are experiencing a molar pregnancy will miscarry spontaneously. If they don't, however, and their pregnancy is only diagnosed when they begin to experience some of the symptoms of a molar pregnancy, then it is necessary to terminate the pregnancy immediately in order to safeguard the health of the mother.

A molar pregnancy is removed by suction curettage. Follow-up is required for six months to a year to ensure that no abnormal cells have been left behind (a condition known as persistent GTD — something that happens in 10 percent of molar pregnancies). It is sometimes necessary to resort to chemotherapy to treat persistent GTD.

In 2 percent to 3 percent of cases, a cancerous form of GTD develops. This disease — known as choriocarcinoma — can spread to other parts of the body, including the lungs. That's why it's necessary for women who have had a molar pregnancy to postpone any subsequent pregnancy until such a possibility has been ruled out, since the rising hCG levels of a normal pregnancy would be difficult to distinguish from the rising levels of persistent GTD.

Women who have experienced one molar pregnancy have a 1.3- to 2.9-percent chance of experiencing another molar pregnancy. Molar pregnancies tend to run in families, which has led some scientists to conclude that there may be some sort of genetic basis to molar pregnancy.

Stillbirth

According to the Wisconsin Stillbirth Service Program at the University of Wisconsin, approximately 68 babies are stillborn each day in the United States — approximately 1 out of every 115 births.

A stillbirth is typically diagnosed when the mother reports a cessation of fetal movements or when the doctor or midwife is unable to detect a fetal heartbeat during a routine prenatal checkup.

Most parents find stillbirth to be an utterly devastating experience. "A stillbirth robs you, as a parent, of part of your future," said one mother to a reporter from Britain's *The Daily Telegraph*. "That child is so wanted and is suddenly taken away. It is so difficult leaving a child behind in the maternity ward when all the other mothers are leaving with their babies."

What makes it even more difficult is that many people — even family members and very close friends — may fail to understand what this baby meant to you. Many women find their grief after stillbirth to be a very lonely experience, a phenomenon that C. Elizabeth Carney writes about in her book *The Miscarriage Manual:* "I thought that if my baby had lived for a while, if people had gotten to know and love her, maybe then I would have been given the affirmation to grieve the way I needed to. But I was the only one with any memory of her, the only one who had the chance to love her. I had no one to share her with, not even my husband."

The causes

Although researchers have identified a number of causes of stillbirth, it is possible to come up with a firm explanation of what led to a particular baby's death only in approximately 40 percent of cases.

When a cause is identified, it is usually one of the following:

- a problem with the umbilical cord (for example, umbilical cord knots, abnormalities with the umbilical cord structure, abnormalties with the way the cord is inserted into the placenta, prolapsed cords when the umblical cord slips into the vagina ahead of the baby during labor, nuchal cords when the cord is wrapped around the baby's neck, torsion of the umbilical cord, cord strictures, and amniotic band syndrome);

- a problem with the placenta (for example, placental insufficiency, placental failure, placental abruption, or placenta previa);

- problems with the uterus (for example, incompetent cervix, uterine fibroids, or congeintal abnormalities such as a bicornate or septate uterus);

- maternal disease (for example, diabetes, epilepsy, heart disease, kidney disease, liver disease, lung disease, lupus, chronic hypertension, parathyroid disease, sickle-cell disease, preeclampsia, metabolic diseases, Rh incompatibility);

- an infection that has occurred during pregnancy (for example, cytomegalovirus, human parvovirus B19 or fifth disease, listeriosis, rubella or German measles, toxoplasmosis, and sexually transmitted diseases);

- congenital abnormality (responsible for approximately 25 percent of stillbirths);

- complications arising from a multiple pregnancy (women who are pregnant with multiples face a higher-than-average risk of experiencing the stillbirth or one or more of their babies due to placental abruptions, cord accidents, twin-to-twin transfusion syndrome, or other pregnancy complications). Studies have shown that between 0.5 percent and 1 percent of multiple pregnancies result in the death of at least one baby.

- complications at the time of delivery — a so-called intrapartum death.

Note: Some doctors attribute any unexplained stillbirth to either a cord accident or a problem with the placenta. In fact, only a relatively small number of stillbirths involve these particular problems. But in the absence of any other obvious cause of death, they have been the catchall explanation provided to grieving parents in search of answers.

You will find a detailed explanation of each of these causes of stillbirth in our book *Trying Again: A Guide to Pregnancy After Miscarriage, Stillbirth, and Infant Loss.*

Intrapartum death

The intrapartum death is used to describe a particular type of stillbirth — a stillbirth that occurs when a baby dies during labor, typically due to a lack of oxygen. Fortunately, intrapartum death is relatively rare today — small consolation, however, for the families who lose much-wanted babies due to complications during birth.

Studies have identified a number of factors associated with an increased risk of intrapartum death: preeclampsia (toxemia/pregnancy-induced hypertension), intrauterine growth restriction, prolonged pregnancy (more than two weeks beyond the due date), prolonged labor or a labor in which there are excessively frequent contractions; vaginal breech delivery; a pregnancy in which the baby is already in fragile condition (perhaps due to a congenital anomaly), previous perinatal death, and even physician (or other caregiver) inexperience.

One of the key signs that a baby may be running into trouble during the delivery is the presence of meconium in the amniotic fluid. When a baby is in distress, the baby's bowels may release meconium — the baby's first stool — into the amniotic fluid. Other signs of fetal distress include an unusually fast or slow fetal heart rate, decelerations in the heart rate during uterine contractions, or a decrease in the normal variability of the heart rate over time.

If your baby dies during labor, you will need the support of family, friends, your caregiver, and a social worker or therapist to help you work through your feelings of grief and trauma about this shocking end to your pregnancy.

Waiting to go into labor versus being induced

If you find out that your baby has died, you will have to decide whether you would prefer to go into labor naturally — something that occurs within two weeks of fetal death in 80 percent to 90 percent of cases — or be induced as soon as possible. There are risks associated with carrying a dead fetus for longer than four weeks (maternal blood coagulation problems, for example), so your doctor or midwife will encourage you to consider induction if you don't go into labor naturally within the allotted time period.

If you choose to be induced — as the majority of women who find themselves in this situation do — your doctor will use either laminaria (a seaweed product that dilates the cervix mechanically), vaginal prostaglandin supplements, or pitocin (an artificial form of oxytocin) to get labor started.

You may wish to request pain relief during labor. "I remember telling my midwife and the attending obstetrician that I didn't want to feel anything during the delivery since I didn't think I could cope with the pain of labor as well as the overwhelming feelings of grief I was experiencing," recalls Marie, a 35-year-old mother of four who also lost a baby through stillbirth. "In fact, I asked to be put under general anesthetic at one point so that I could be completely unaware of what was going on, but my midwife convinced me that it would be better for me both physically and emotionally if I chose another alternative. In the end, I opted to be awake and alert during a vaginal delivery. While I did receive pain relief throughout the delivery, it wasn't enough to eliminate all of the sensations of pain, however — just enough to make the pain bearable and to allow me to be alert enough to spend some very precious time with my daughter — the only time we would ever have together after she was born."

> 66 When you experience a loss, your naivete is gone. You are suddenly acutely aware of the fact that all kinds of things can go wrong, and that pregnancy is indeed a very fragile thing. 99
>
> — Johnna, 33, mother of three living children and a baby who was stillborn

Some women choose to give birth by cesarean section rather than vaginally, although many caregivers will discourage this choice given the increased risks involved. If you feel quite strongly that this is the route you would like to go, you will need to discuss this issue with your doctor or midwife.

Preparing for the birth of a child who will be stillborn

If you will be giving birth to a child who will be stillborn, you will need to decide whether you and your partner would like to spend some time with your baby after the birth. Although you may think that the experience of spending some time with your baby's body might be tremendously upsetting, most families who go through this experience actually find it to be incredibly comforting. "I spent a few moments with my son after delivery," recalls Johnna, 33, whose son was stillborn at 27 weeks. "It was the most precious time."

Here's another reason to spend some time with your stillborn baby, according to one obstetrician: "I've always encouraged patients to spend enough time with their stillborn baby to see how relatively normal and peaceful the baby appears, because if the mother never allows herself the chance to see her stillborn baby, her fantasies about that baby may be far more upsetting than the reality of the baby's appearance."

> 66 The fullness of motherhood was compressed into that day. A mother's deep love for her son, her tender concern, her exquisite pain of separation, her comforting touch for a lifetime's scraped knees, her worry for a lifetime's dangers, her peace in their inseparable bond, all came together in that rich moment as she gazed upon her precious little boy. 99
>
> — pediatrician Dr. Alan Greene of www.drgreene.com, recalling the experience of a patient who lost a baby to Trisomy 13 shortly after birth

Neonatal death

Although the U.S. infant mortality rate has been declining steadily throughout this century, it is still unacceptably high. Despite all the high-tech bells and whistles at our disposal, the United States ranked 28th among industrialized nations in 1998 (the last year for which the National Center for Health Statistics has such data available). By 2002, the U.S. infant mortality rate stood at 6.69 deaths per thousand live births. Note: The top 10 causes of infant mortality in 2000 (ranked in order of frequency) are shown in Table 17.1.

Table 17.1: Ten Leading Causes of Neonatal and Postneonatal Death in the United States in 2000

Neonatal Deaths (deaths during the first 28 days of life) and Cause	Number of Deaths
Disorders related to preterm/low birthweight	4,318
Congenital malformations, deformations, and chromosomal abnormalities	4,144
Problems in the newborn caused by maternal complications during pregnancy	1,394
Problems in the newborn caused by placenta, cord, and membrane problems	1,049
Respiratory distress of the newborn	929
Bacterial sepsis of the newborn	737
Intrauterine hypoxia and birth asphyxia	589
Neonatal hemorrhage	563
Atelectasis (a shrunken, airless state affecting all or part of a lung)	483
Necrotizing enterocolitis of the newborn (death of tissue in the bowel)	313
All other causes	4,257
Total	18,776

If you know (from the results of amniocentesis, for example) that you will be giving birth to a child who is likely to live for just a short time after birth, you will want so spend some time thinking about how you want to spend the time you have with your child. Here are some questions to ask yourself: Do you want to spend that time alone with your baby and your partner? Would you like your other children or your baby's grandparents to be present as well? Do you want to hold your baby as she passes away? Would you like some time alone with your baby after her death? There are no easy answers to these questions because what you really want is the one thing you can't have — a healthy baby to take home.

You will also need to consider whether you would like your baby to receive pain relief and whether you wish to donate the baby's organs to another child — a decision that allows many families to make something good come of an otherwise nightmarish experience.

Important decisions

While you are trying to come to terms with the death of your baby, you are likely to find yourself being asked to make a number of important decisions — such as whether you wish to have an autopsy performed, what you would like to do to collect some memories of your baby, and what type of funeral arrangements you would like to make.

Deciding whether to have an autopsy performed

Most parents who lose a baby have very strong feelings about having a detailed physical examination performed on their baby after the delivery. Such an examination typically involves

- an extensive physical evaluation;
- an internal postmortem examination (autopsy);
- photographing the baby's face, body, and unusual features;

- taking X-rays;

- performing genetic tests on some of the baby's tissues.

If the cause of death is not obvious and the parents hope to have other children, they may request an autopsy in the hope that they will gain some information that may be helpful to them as they plan a subsequent pregnancy. These results are usually available within a few weeks, but sometimes it can take as long as a few months to get the full autopsy report back from the pathologist.

Some parents choose not to proceed with an autopsy because they are concerned about how their baby's body will be treated during the procedure. If you are struggling with this issue, you may find it helpful to know that the majority of medical examiners treat the bodies that have been entrusted to them with the utmost respect and dignity. They understand that the baby who died was someone's child and deserves to be treated as such.

If you do decide to go ahead with an autopsy, you should be prepared for the fact that you may still be left with some unanswered questions. A recent study of 166 British mothers who had autopsies performed on their babies found that nearly half were disappointed by the amount of information the autopsy was able to uncover.

Some of these mothers did, however, take solace in the fact that their babies' autopsy results might benefit other families down the road. Approximately one-quarter said that they hoped that the results of their babies' autopsies would contribute to medical knowledge in general.

And a number of parents mentioned that the information they obtained from the autopsy process helped to alleviate some of their guilty feelings about their babies' deaths.

Only 7 percent of mothers regretted their decision to have the autopsy performed, either because the autopsy had not provided them with the information they were seeking or because it had left them with more questions than answers.

The researchers also found that those mothers who *didn't* have autopsies were similarly likely to second-guess their decisions. Some wondered after the fact if having an autopsy performed might have helped to answer some of their questions about their babies' deaths or to alleviate some of their guilty feelings.

Clearly, this is a difficult issue for many parents.

Making funeral arrangements

If your baby is born any time after 20 weeks' gestation, you may be required by law to have your baby's remains buried or cremated. (The laws are slightly different in each jurisdiction, so ask your caregiver or hospital social worker to clarify your legal and financial obligations.)

In many communities, there are one or more funeral homes that waive the majority of their fees as a service to bereaved parents. If you're not up to researching funeral homes on your own, have a trusted friend or family member make some initial phone calls for you to help narrow down your options. Then, once you've made a few phone calls of your own and you have zeroed in on a particular funeral home, you can arrange to meet with the funeral director to finalize the arrangements.

Just a word of caution to parents who will be giving birth to stillborn babies. You may be shocked to learn that your life-insurance policy won't cover the cost of burying a child who is stillborn, and that you cannot claim a stillborn child as a dependent on your tax return (something you would be permitted to do if your child was born alive and then died). Many parents of stillborn children consider these policies to be a slap in the face at a time in their lives when they are at their most vulnerable.

 Bright Idea

Although traditional Jewish law doesn't allow mourning rituals for a baby who lived less than 30 days, a growing number of Jewish families are choosing to have funerals or memorial services to mark the loss of a child in the perinatal period.

Watch Out!

Well-meaning people in your life may try to protect you by making funeral arrangements and other decisions on your behalf. Remind them that making these choices is your way of caring for and saying goodbye to your baby and that you need to make as many of these decisions as possible as part of the grieving process.

Something else that may surprise you is the fact that birth certificates are not routinely offered to parents whose babies are stillborn, although a growing number of states are now starting to offering a "Certificate of Birth Resulting in Stillbirth," thanks to the lobbying efforts of groups of bereaved parents who sought some sort of formal recognition of their baby's birth and death. Your state Office of Vital Records can advise you whether such a certificate is available in your state.

Creating memories

As you begin the grieving process, you may find yourself struggling to come to terms with the fact that you and your baby didn't have the chance to share the lifetime of memories you had dreamed about. Many parents find that it helps to ease their grief if they make a conscious effort to create memories that will allow them to remember and honor their baby.

Here are a few suggestions:

- Name your baby.
- Announce your baby's birth and death to family and friends, either by placing an advertisement in the newspaper or by sending out announcements.
- If possible, take photos of your baby and store the negatives in a safe-deposit box. (Note: Most hospitals routinely photograph babies who are stillborn or who die during labor — even if the grieving parents are certain they do not wish to have a photograph of their baby. These photographs are kept on file in case the parents change

their mind after the fact — a reaction that is not at all unusual.)

- Create a memory box and fill it with memorabilia from your pregnancy: for example, the positive home pregnancy test, photos of your blossoming belly, cards and letters you sent to friends describing your excitement at being pregnant, anything special you bought for your baby, your prenatal and birth records, and so on.

- Write about your pregnancy. Describe how you felt when the pregnancy test came back positive, how you shared your news with family and friends, how excited you were the first time you heard the baby's heartbeat or felt him move.

- Write a letter to your baby expressing your love for him and, if applicable, explaining why you made the choices you made about your pregnancy.

- Make a donation to a charity in your baby's memory.

- Set up an appointment with your caregiver so that you can discuss the circumstances surrounding your baby's birth and death.

Coping with grief

Grief is a powerful emotion, one that can rob you of your interest in life and zap you of your energy. It's no wonder therapists refer to the process of coming to terms with a death as "grief work" — it's probably the hardest thing you'll ever have to do. During the early days after the loss, you may find yourself feeling numb. Then you may start to feel a lot of physical symptoms of grief: headaches, a loss of appetite, extreme fatigue, and difficulty concentrating or sleeping. You can also expect to experience a variety of different emotions, including some or all of the following:

- Sadness and longing. You may spend a lot of time thinking about what might have been. Something as simple as packing away your maternity clothes or looking at some of the baby gifts you received may trigger painful feelings of sadness and longing.

- Anger toward your partner. You may feel angry with your partner if he doesn't appear to be grieving as deeply as you are. More often than not, the other partner is grieving, too — just in a different way. Sometimes one parent feels obligated to hold things together for the sake of the other — something that can be misinterpreted as a lack of compassion by the more outwardly grieving partner.

- Feelings of hurt or frustration at the reactions of family members and friends. If your family and friends fail to acknowledge your loss, or pressure you to "pull yourself together" while you're still grieving deeply for your baby, you may feel hurt and frustrated. Parents who experience miscarriage are particularly likely to be disappointed by the support — or lack thereof — that they receive from family members and friends. Often people who have not experienced miscarriages themselves underestimate what this kind of loss can mean to parents who were already deeply attached to their baby. As Esther B. Fein explained in an article in *The New York Times,* this attachment is happening earlier on in pregnancy than ever before: "Improvements in pregnancy tests and monitoring equipment . . . have greatly increased the identification men and women feel toward their growing fetuses. Where once many women miscarried before even knowing they were pregnant, now home-testing devices let them know they are pregnant within days of missing their periods. Then they hear heartbeats and see ultrasound images."

- A need to connect with other parents who have experienced this type of loss. Sharing your experiences with other parents who understand what you're going through can be tremendously healing. If you don't know anyone personally who has been through a loss of this kind, you might want to contact one of the many perintatal loss organizations or support groups listed in the "Resource Directory" (www.wiley.com/go/anndouglas).

- A feeling that you're never going to be happy again. In the days following the loss of your baby, you may be convinced this is so, but if you work through your grief and give yourself time to heal, you will feel happy again. That's not to say that you ever "get over" your loss, or that you will ever forget your baby (something many women agonize about as they begin to feel better). You will just find new ways of feeling happy despite the tiny piece of your heart that will always be broken.

- A strong need to become pregnant right away or a fear of never being pregnant again. Some women feel a powerful need to become pregnant right away; others feel equally strongly that they need time to come to terms with their loss before they even begin to contemplate another pregnancy. Although many caregivers will advise you to postpone your next pregnancy for six months to a year (in order to give yourself time to grieve and to avoid giving birth to another baby around the anniversary of the loss of the first), only you know for certain what's best for you.

> 66 I once read that the grief a mother feels when she has lost a baby is so intense that it would be considered psychotic at any other time. It is important to remember that you will never 'get over' this, but that you can accept it and feel more at peace about it. 99
>
> — Johnna, 33, mother of four children, including a son who was stillborn at 27 weeks

Although it's easy to get caught up in your own grief, if you have other children, it's important not to lose sight of the fact that your other children will need an opportunity to grieve the loss of their baby brother or sister. Even very young children can be encouraged to express their grief by

Bright Idea

The last thing you probably want at a time such as this is being bombarded with baby-related junk mail. Write to the Mail Preference Service, Direct Marketing Association, P.O. Box 9008, Farmington, NY 11735-9008, or the Mail Preference Service, Direct Marketing Association of Canada, 1 Concorde Gate, Suite 607, Don Mills, Ontario M3C 3N6, and indicate that you don't wish to receive any mail from its members.

- talking about how they are feeling;
- helping to pick out flowers for the baby's grave;
- drawing a picture to express how they are feeling;
- writing a letter to the baby;
- participating in a family memorial service.

There are also a number of excellent books and other resource materials designed to help parents explain death to young children. Your funeral director or the librarian in the children's department at your local library should be able to recommend some appropriate books based on the age of your child.

Pregnancy after miscarriage, stillbirth, or infant death

Whether you decide to become pregnant as soon as possible after the death of your baby or to postpone it for a while, it's never easy to go through another pregnancy. Your joy at being pregnant may be overshadowed by fears about what might happen to this baby, grief about the baby you lost, and guilt about "being disloyal" to her because you are going ahead with another pregnancy.

Parents who have been there will tell you that it's important to choose a caregiver who will help you cope with your conflicting emotions and who will understand your need for ongoing reassurance. You want to have someone like that in your court: "My obstetrician was extra sensitive to my need for reassurance that things were going well with my pregnancy," recalls Cindy,

34, who experienced three consecutive miscarriages prior to the birth of her first child. "She did ultrasounds for me when there wasn't any other medical reason except to reassure me."

During your initial prenatal visit, you should have a frank discussion about what — if anything — can be done to maximize your chances of experiencing a happy outcome this time around. For example, are there any new treatments you should know about? Are there any tests that could be done to help reduce your anxiety? Would your doctor or midwife be prepared to teach you how to use a fetoscope or Doppler so that you could monitor your baby's well-being at home in between appointments?

> 66 Don't feel as if you are being unfaithful to the baby you lost if you are happy about the new pregnancy. 99
>
> — Dawnette, 28, mother of one who had a miscarriage prior to the birth of her first child

You may find it helpful to connect with other women who are pregnant again after the death of a baby — either by looking for a support group in your own community or by joining an online support group such as Subsequent Pregnancy After Loss (SPALS) (www.spals.com).

If you are planning to deliver in the same hospital or birthing center in which you lost your previous baby, you may find it helpful to plan a return visit to the facility before you arrive there in hard labor. While you're there, give some thought to whether you'd like to deliver your new baby in the same — or another — birthing suite you had the last time around, assuming, of course, that you have that choice. Making these key decisions ahead of time may help you to feel more in control of your birth experience.

Note: You can find a more-detailed discussion of the complex issues involved in pregnancy after miscarriage, stillbirth, or infant death in our book *Trying Again: Pregnancy After Miscarriage, Stillbirth, or Infant Loss.*

Just the facts

- Miscarriage occurs in approximately 15 percent to 20 percent of pregnancies that have been confirmed through a pregnancy test.

- Most miscarriages occur during the first trimester.

- Miscarriages can be caused by chromosomal abnormalities, maternal disease, hormonal imbalances, immune-system disorders, allogeneic factors, anatomical problems of the uterus and cervix, viral and bacterial infections, recreational drug and alcohol abuse, environmental toxins, and maternal age.

- Approximately 1 percent of pregnancies are ectopic.

- A molar pregnancy occurs in 1 in 1,500 to 1 in 2,000 pregnancies.

- Stillbirth occurs in approximately 1 percent of pregnancies and the cause is only determined 40 percent of the time.

- The leading causes of neonatal death in the United States in 2000 were preterm birth and low birthweight, congenital malformations, and chromosomal abnormalities.

- You may wish to have an autopsy performed on your baby if the cause of death is not obvious.

- You may require additional reassurance if you choose to proceed with another pregnancy.

PART VI

Birth and Beyond

GET THE SCOOP ON. . .
What happens to your body before labor starts ▪
True versus false labor ▪ Pain-relief options during labor ▪ When to leave for the hospital or
birthing center ▪ What to expect during each
stage of labor ▪ Getting to know your new baby

Labor and Delivery

Despite what some pregnancy books would have you believe, there's no such thing as a textbook delivery. Birth experiences are every bit as individual as the babies they produce.

This may come as a tremendous relief to you if you've been listening to birth-related horror stories for the past nine months, or as a big shock if you've been counting on having the intense but satisfying birth experience like the woman in the labor video your Lamaze teacher showed at childbirth classes. ("I'll have what she's having," you might have piped up, in a moment reminiscent of that oh-so-famous restaurant scene in *When Harry Met Sally*.)

The best way to prepare for what lies ahead is to learn as much as you can about giving birth and to spend some time anticipating virtually every possible scenario — a long labor and a short labor; a labor that requires fetal monitoring and one that doesn't; a pushing stage that warrants an episiotomy and one that doesn't; a planned vaginal delivery, a planned cesarean delivery, and an emergency cesarean

Chapter 18

delivery; and so on. It's important to have at least some idea of how you would handle each situation if it became necessary to deviate from your birth plan, however slightly. (Forget the Boy Scouts: A mom-to-be's motto needs to be "Be Prepared.")

What happens to your body before you go into labor

Just when you think you're going to be pregnant forever, some tell-tale signs clue you to the fact that your baby's birth is fast approaching.

You may experience one or all of the following symptoms during the weeks and days leading up to your baby's birth:

- **Lightening ("dropping"):** The term "lightening" refers to a descent into the pelvis that causes the abdomen to protrude at a lower position than before, resulting in a sense of reduced pressure and crowding in the upper abdomen. What most pregnancy books fail to tell you is that it is a very subjective phenomenon (in other words, you and your best friend could have your babies shift position in exactly the same way, but only one of you might actually notice any corresponding change in physical sensations) and it is not experienced by all women, first-time mothers or otherwise, to the same degree — or even at all. Once lightening has occurred (be it a few weeks prior to the onset of labor or as labor starts), you will carry your baby differently: your breasts will probably no longer touch the top of your abdomen, and you may find it easier to breathe. On the other hand, because the baby is now being carried in a much lower position than previously, you may experience an increased urge to urinate. Note: The term "lightening" is often used interchangeably with the term "engagement" — even though the two terms mean totally different things. Engagement is a measurable and detectable event that occurs when the leading bony edge of the fetal head descends into the pelvis and reaches the level of the ischial spines (at which point the baby is said to be at zero station).

■ **Increasing pressure in the pelvis and rectum:** You may experience crampiness, groin pain, and persistent lower backache. These symptoms are likely to be more pronounced if this is your second or subsequent birth. One fourth-time mother describes the sensation as being like carrying a bowling ball around in a sling — the sling, of course, being your just-plain-weary pelvic floor muscles — the collection of muscles that support the pelvic organs.

> 66 Our Lamaze instructor . . . assured our class . . . that our cervix muscles would become 'naturally numb' as they swelled and stretched, and deep breathing would turn the final explosions of pain into 'manageable discomfort.' This description turned out to be as accurate as, say, a steward advising passengers aboard the Titanic to prepare for a brisk but bracing swim. 99
>
> —Mary Kay Blakely
> in *American Mom*

■ **Slight weight loss or reduced weight gain:** Your weight gain may taper off at the end of your pregnancy despite adequate nutrition and continuing fetal growth. (Blame it on the biochemistry of pregnancy and plain old-fashioned water retention.)

■ **Fluctuating energy levels:** Some pregnant women feel fatigued to the point of exhaustion during the last few weeks of pregnancy. Others get a sudden burst of energy (often referred to as a "nesting instinct") that makes them want to clean out closets, organize the baby's room, and generally go a little crazy preparing for baby's arrival. Just a quick word of wisdom from all the mothers who have been there: Even if it kills you, force yourself to rest and relax. You don't want to be feeling burned out and exhausted by the time the first contraction hits.

- **Passage of mucus plug:** Anytime from a few days before to
  the onset of labor, the mucus plug — the wad of thick,
  sticky, sometimes blood-tinged mucus that seals off the
  cervix during pregnancy and protects your baby from
  infection — may become dislodged as your cervix begins
  to dilate. Despite what other pregnancy books may tell
  you, the loss of your mucus plug is not helpful in predicting with any accuracy the timing of the onset of labor.

- **Pink or bloody show:** As the cervix effaces and dilates, capillaries on the surface of the cervix may rupture, causing a
  small amount of bleeding. For the majority of women, this
  is a strong indication that labor is hours — or at most a
  few days — away.

- **Increasingly painful Braxton Hicks contractions:** The so-
  called "practice contractions" of pregnancy become
  stronger and more frequent. Some women find that they
  are every bit as painful as real labor contractions.

True versus false labor

It's one of those classic nightmare scenarios that run through
your mind when you're pregnant: you'll have your doctor or
midwife racing across town at 3:00 a.m., convinced that you're
about to deliver your baby, when in fact you're not really in
labor at all.

Or, even worse, you'll ignore your labor contractions, mistaking them for a particularly persistent bout of Braxton Hicks
contractions, and then suddenly deliver your baby while you're
standing in the checkout line at the grocery store.

Although a fair number of women find it extremely difficult
to differentiate between true and false labor, only a handful actually end up delivering their babies in supermarkets. Most women
clue in pretty quickly as to whether or not they're dealing with
true labor or simply a very good impression of the real thing.

(Note: If your false labor contractions are intense enough that you have to resort to labor breathing to cope with them, you may not be 100 percent sure that you're not experiencing "the real thing" until your doctor of midwife confirms that your cervix has not yet started to dilate. Don't be embarrassed. It happens.)

In the next section of the chapter, we arm you with some important facts that may help you figure out whether the moment of truth has arrived — or whether you're dealing with a most unwelcome false alarm. But before we get to that, we want to help you scratch one other major worry off your pregnancy list — the fear that your membranes will rupture while you're in the grocery store or some other public place. This statistic should help to reassure you that it's safe to venture out in public: Only 10 percent of women experience premature rupture of membranes (PROM) — that is, having your membranes rupture before labor has actually started. Therefore, your chances of having your water break in the grocery store are decidedly slim — unless, of

> 66 During the false labor, I questioned if this was the real thing; during the real labor, there was no doubt in my mind. 99
>
> —Nicola, 35, mother of four

course, you plan to pick up a few last-minute baby items while you're in active labor! And even if your membranes do rupture in public, you're likely to feel a minor popping sensation followed by a bit of dribbling. Your baby's head will act as a cork and help to stop the flow of amniotic fluid, so you don't have to worry about leaving too big of a puddle. If you're really concerned, simply get in the habit of wearing a sanitary pad while you're out and about. (That should help to ease your mind about any unforeseen events in the produce department!)

Now let's get back to the subject at hand — true versus false labor.

Why do they call it false labor?

If false labor kept you from getting a good night's rest last night — and false labor does tend to happen more often at night — you're probably cursing the person responsible for coining the term "false labor." Although there is nothing false about the contractions, which can in fact be extremely painful, false labor is false in the sense that it does not dilate the cervix or result in the birth of a baby.

Still, some practitioners recognize that the term "false labor" can be extremely discouraging to some women, and prefer, instead, to call it "prelabor" in recognition of the fact that these contractions help prepare a woman's body for labor. You may not end up with your baby right away, but your false labor is helping you inch toward that goal.

How is false labor different from true labor?

Just as no two pregnancies are the same, no two labors are the same. No one can tell you any hard-and-fast rules that will allow you to definitely differentiate between true and false labor, but there are some general characteristics that may help you distinguish between the two.

You can be fairly confident that you are experiencing false labor as opposed to true labor if

- your contractions tend to be irregular and are not increasing in either frequency (the interval in minutes from the start of one contraction to the start of the next is decreasing) or severity (when the contractions are sufficiently

 Watch Out!

Some pregnancy books may suggest that you consume an alcoholic beverage to see if the contractions you are experiencing are real. We don't agree with this advice. Not only is alcohol known to be harmful to babies, but it's not likely to have any effect on your contractions. Back in the day when alcohol was used to stop premature labor, it was administered intravenously (although in much larger doses than what you would receive in a single drink).

Bright Idea

Make sure that your labor support person knows where you're supposed to park your car and what entrance you're supposed to use at the hospital or birth center. You don't want to be trying to figure this out when your contractions are two minutes apart.

severe that you need to use breathing techniques or other methods of relaxation to cope with them). As a rule of thumb, if your contractions are becoming difficult to cope with and they're coming at four- to five-minute intervals, you're probably in labor;

■ the contractions subside altogether if you change position or have two large glasses of any nonalcoholic beverage;

■ the pain is centered in your lower abdomen rather than your lower back;

■ your show (that is, blood-tinged mucus), if any, is brownish (most likely the result of either an internal examination or intercourse within the previous 48 hours).

On the other hand, you can be fairly confident that you are experiencing true labor as opposed to false labor if

■ your contractions tend to be falling into some type of regular pattern, and they are getting longer, stronger, more painful, and more frequent;

■ the contractions intensify with activity and are not relieved by either a change of position or two large nonalcoholic drinks;

■ the pain begins in your lower back and spreads to your lower abdomen and may also radiate to your legs. It may feel like a gastrointestinal upset, and may be accompanied by diarrhea;

■ show is present and either pinkish or blood-streaked;

■ your membranes have ruptured.

Although these characteristics may hold true for the majority of women, some women experience false labor that is virtually indistinguishable from true labor. Likewise, some women have true labors in which the contractions fail to fall into any recognizable pattern, and that may initially seem to be a bout of false labor.

If you fall into this category, the only way you'll know for sure if you're actually in labor is to have your practitioner conduct an internal exam.

Are some women more likely to experience false labor?

Although women who are expecting their first child tend to spend a great deal of time worrying about false labor, those who tend to experience it are most likely women who are expecting second or subsequent babies. This is because a uterus that has previously been through labor is more easily stimulated to contract during subsequent pregnancies.

What if I rush to the hospital, only to find out that it's false labor?

First of all, try not to be too discouraged. You aren't the first pregnant woman to make this mistake, and you certainly won't be the last. Besides, it's far wiser to check things out with your caregiver than it is to give birth in the car just because you wanted to wait "a little longer" to make sure that the labor pains you were experiencing were, in fact, "the real thing."

To try to avoid false alarms, call your practitioner before you head for the hospital. Be prepared to describe the length of the contractions and their frequency, and to comment on any other significant occurrences (for example, "Have your membranes ruptured?" "Did you have any bloody show?"). Try not to minimize your discomfort or hide how you're feeling as you talk through a contraction. Your doctor or midwife will be trying to assess whether you are in active labor. If he or she isn't sure either, you may be asked to come in for an examination. (For additional information on when to call your caregiver, see Checklist 18.1.)

Checklist 18.1. When to Call Your Doctor or Midwife

You should call your doctor or midwife if

_____ your contractions are strong and regular (5 minutes apart for most women, but 6 to 10 minutes if you have a history of rapid labors, you have a long trip into the hospital or birth center, or your doctor or midwife has indicated that she would like to have you evaluated earlier than usual during your labor, perhaps to rule out the possibility that you are having an active herpes outbreak, to treat you for Group B strep, or when a cesarean is planned);

_____ your past experience with labor tells you that this is the real thing, and your gut instinct says that it's time to call your doctor or midwife;

_____ your membranes have ruptured or you suspect that they may have ruptured.

Note: You should call your doctor or midwife immediately and/or seek emergency assistance if

_____ you experience a lot of bleeding (something that can indicate premature separation of the placenta or placenta previa, both of which require special care);

_____ you notice thick, green fluid coming from your vagina (an indication that your baby has passed meconium into the amniotic fluid and may be in distress);

_____ you see a loop of umbilical cord showing at your vaginal opening, or you think you feel something inside your vagina (an indication that the umbilical cord may have prolapsed, blocking the flow of oxygen to your baby). While you are waiting for the ambulance to arrive, lie with your head and chest on the floor and your bottom in the air. This will help prevent the weight of your baby from interrupting the flood of oxygen through the umbilical cord. (Fortunately, this type of obstetrical emergency is rare.)

 Bright Idea

Tape to your phone a list of the names and phone numbers of people who have volunteered to care for your older children while you're in labor. That way, you can find someone quickly when the contractions start coming.

Watch Out!

Keep the vaginal area as clean as possible once your membranes have ruptured. Don't take a bath, have sexual intercourse, use a tampon to absorb the
flow of amniotic fluid, or attempt to conduct an internal exam on yourself to
assess your progress.

Now let's consider a few issues you need to think about
before you find yourself in the heat of labor: namely, pain relief,
episiotomy, fetal monitoring, and the presence of other people
at the birth.

Pain relief during labor

During labor, you can expect to experience a combination of
sensations: a tightening of the uterus that feels as if someone
has put a blood pressure cuff around your abdomen and
pumped it up it too tightly, a pulling sensation as your cervix
stretches open, and a stretching and burning sensation as your
baby's head makes its way through your vagina and perineum.

Some women find the pain of labor to be bearable; others
do not. If you are finding labor difficult to cope with, you are
perfectly justified in requesting pain relief. Here's what the
American College of Obstetricians and Gynecologists has to say
about this issue: "The pain of labor varies and can be severe for
many women. . . . Maternal request is sufficient justification for
pain relief during labor. The full range of pain relief should be
available and should not be denied because of an absence of
other 'medical indications.'"

That said, it's important to understand the pros and cons of
using pharmacological pain relief during labor. Table 18.1
briefly summarizes your various options.

Table 18.1. Medicinal Forms of Pain Relief for Labor and Birth

Type of Pain Relief	How It Works	Risks to You or Your Baby	Other Considerations
Demerol and other narcotics and narcoticlike medications, such as Nubain and Stadol	Administered intravenously or via injection into a muscle. Effective within 15 minutes and lasts for two to four hours.	Can cause drowsiness, nausea, vomiting, respiratory depression, and maternal hypotension (low blood pressure). Will be present in the newborn if injected within 5 hours of delivery and can result in breathing difficulties.	The small doses that are typically given to laboring women often don't provide sufficient pain relief, particularly during advanced labor.
Epidural (lumbar epidural)	An anesthetic and/or narcotic is injected into the space between the sheath surrounding the spinal cord and the bony vertebrae of your spine. An epidural numbs you from the waist down, providing complete relief in 85% of women, partial relief in 12%, and no relief in 3%. Takes effect within 15 to 20 minutes.	Maternal hypotension (low blood pressure), difficulty in urinating, and severe postpartum headache (in 2% of cases). Not appropriate for women with certain neurological disorders. Can slow labor if given before the cervix is 5 cm dilated. May also diminish ability to push, necessitating forceps or vacuum delivery. Baby's heartbeat may also drop when an epidural is being used.	Most widely used form of regional block for pain relief during labor. A continuous low-dose epidural (the so-called "walking epidural") injects enough anesthesia into the back to block the pain sensations but doesn't immobilize your legs (a key disadvantage to a regular epidural). The lower dosage decreases the likelihood of side effects. A more recent option is patient-controlled epidural, which allows a woman to push a button that delivers small doses of analgesic on demand.

(continued)

Table 18.1. (*continued*)

Type of Pain Relief	How It Works	Risks to You or Your Baby	Other Considerations
Spinal	Injected into the spinal fluid in the lower back. Numbs you from the waist to your knees. Takes about four minutes to take effect. You may have to lie flat on your back for several hours after delivery to avoid developing a postspinal headache, though new technology in spinal needles has made this complication rare.	Can cause maternal hypotension (low blood pressure), severe postdelivery headache, temporary impairment of bladder function, nausea, and (in rare cases) convulsions or infections.	Depending on what drugs are used, can be used as anesthetic for cesarean and for labor. Can be used in labor in combination with an epidural to give a more rapid onset of pain relief. Not recommended for women with severe preeclampsia.
Paracervical block	Local anesthetic is inserted into the tissues around the cervix to numb the pain caused by cervical dilation.	Can slow baby's heartbeat. Should be avoided if caregiver feels that baby's health would be compromised.	Lasts only 45 to 60 minutes. Additional injections can be given if necessary.
Pudendal block	Anesthetic is injected into the nerves of the vaginal area and perineum. Does not reduce uterine discomfort.	Provides rapid pain relief in the perineum for the actual delivery. No ill effects on baby.	Not effective for all women. Can't be used if the baby's head is too far down the birth canal. Sometimes used when an episiotomy is being performed.

Caudal block	Anesthetic is injected into the spinal area around the sacrum, numbing the vagina and perineum.	Can inhibit labor.	Used when short-term relief is needed (for example, for a forceps delivery or vacuum extraction). A less popular option today than in the past.
Local anesthetic	Anesthetic is injected into the tissues of the perineum in preparation for episiotomy or is given prior to placing sutures after delivery.	No significant risks except rare allergic reactions and inadvertent intravascular infections.	Some believe injection may weaken perineal tissue and increase the likelihood of tearing if episiotomy is not needed.

Bright Idea

A birth ball (a large ball that looks a lot like the oversized exercise balls you've no doubt seen at the gym) can allow you to adopt a variety of different positions during labor. It can be particularly comfortable to sit on because it helps you to relax your trunk and perineum. If you need to purchase a birth ball because your hospital or birthing center doesn't have them or because you'll be birthing at home, be sure to buy the right size. As a rule of thumb, you should choose a 65-centimeter diameter ball if you're of average height, a 75-centimeter ball if you're over 5 feet 10 inches, and a 55-centimeter ball if you're under 5 feet 2 inches.

Natural pain relief

There are also all kinds of nonmedicinal forms of pain relief that are available to you. The following are a few of the more popular options, but if you talk to other women who have given birth recently, you're bound to hear some other creative ideas.

- **Laboring in water:** According to childbirth educator and author Penny Simkin, the relief that women get from laboring in warm water is second only to that provided by an epidural. Laboring in water helps counteract the effects of gravity, something that can make labor less painful. Depending what facilities are available to you at the location where you will be birthing and what appeals to you at the time, you might choose to labor in a bathtub, a Jacuzzi, a shower, or a special birthing tub designed for water births.

- **Massage and touch:** Massage can bring comfort and relief during labor, but you need to let your labor support person know what feels good and what is simply annoying. You may want firm preessure on your neck, shoulders, back, thighs, feet, and hands; light stroking on your lower abdomen; or the mere thought of someone touching you may completely break your concentration and throw you off your labor "game." So you need to be the one to set the pace and call the shots. You may find counterpressure particularly effective if you experience a lot of back pain during labor. Note: Make sure you have massage oil, cornstarch, or baby powder in your labor bag to prevent friction during massage. Otherwise, your skin may get red and sore.

- **Relaxation and positive visualization:** Women who have been trained in relaxation methods and positive visualization are able to put these techniques to work during labor. Most childbirth classes include this type of training. Such training may include practice on focusing your attention internally (within yourself) or externally (on something in the room — perhaps a picture you brought with you or your partner's face) during contractions.

- **Movement and position changes:** Changing positions frequently helps to keep labor moving by putting gravity to work for you and — as an added bonus — it can help to relieve pain. Try walking, sitting, kneeling, standing, lying down, getting on your hands and knees, rocking back and forth, swaying from side to side — whatever seems to work best for you.

> ❝The birth process is not a contest. Do what you think will make you comfortable. No one will think you're 'wimpy' or whatever.❞
>
> —Debbie, 31, mother of three

- **Applying heat and cold:** Applying heat to your lower abdomen, back, groin, or perineum can be very soothing when the contractions are coming fast and furious or you're feeling just plain crampy and miserable. Electric heating pads, hot water bottles, and warm compresses all work well, but, if you're thinking of going the electric heating pad route, you'll need to check with your caregiver ahead of time about what types of electric devices can be brought from home. (Some hospitals have strict rules about such things.) Some women prefer the opposite of heat — cold! Whether you want a cold pack on your back during labor or on your oh-so-tender perineum after you give birth, it can feel wonderful. In fact, some women head off to labor and delivery with a cooler full of ice packs, frozen washcloths, bags of frozen vegetables, hollow plastic rolling pins filled with ice, instant cold packs (the kind that drugstores sell), and frozen gel packs that are meant for wilderness excursions.

- **Hypnosis:** A woman who has been trained in self-hypnosis may be able to use self-hypnosis techniques to relax herself during labor.

- **Transcutaneous electronic nerve stimulation (TENS):** A battery-powered stimulator is connected by wires to electrodes placed on either side of your spine. You can use the accompanying handset to regulate the amount of stimulation your lower back receives to block the transmission of pain impulses to the brain.

- **Acupuncture:** With acupuncture, needles are inserted in your limbs or ears to block pain impulses.

Making up your mind

As you no doubt realize, the issue of pain relief during labor continues to be a hot topic. Some women know they want an epidural right from day one; others are determined to do everything they can to avoid it, regardless of how their labor experience plays out; and still others find themselves rethinking their ideas about pain relief as labor progresses.

"I knew before I had the baby that I was going to get an epidural," says Carrie, a 31-year-old mother of one. "I received it about two hours into labor. It was the best thing I ever did. It allowed me to rest. I will definitely have an epidural again."

"I had planned a labor with no drugs or interventions, but never imagined that labor would be so excruciatingly painful," confesses Susan, a 33-year-old first-time mother. "Labor started at 7:00 a.m. and I ended up having the first epidural at about 4:00 p.m. or so. It didn't numb me as it was supposed to, so I ended up having a second one at 11:00 p.m. I would make the same choice again because I was practically hallucinating from the pain by the time I got it — not to mention all of the throwing up I had done! They let the epidural wear off in time to push, and I would do that again too. I think it helped me have the motivation to push and to better feel when to push."

> 66 About a week before my son was born, a peace and calm came over me, and I actually looked forward to experiencing the power and beauty of giving birth. Perhaps that was my hormones kicking in, in preparation for the coming birth. And I did have a wonderful birth experience—one where I was in control and not panicky or upset. 99
>
> —Tracy, 31, mother of one

"I was really worried about my ability to cope with the pain of childbirth — I'm not a big one for pain! — but to my amazement, I managed to get through childbirth naturally four times," recalls Marie, a 35-year-old mother of four. "Yes, the contractions were painful, but they weren't unmanageably so. I just took them one at a time."

Although it helps to think through the issue of pain relief during labor in the weeks and months before the birth, it's important to keep an open mind about this issue. After making your caregiver promise that you will be able to have an epidural as early on in your labor as possible, you may decide that the contractions are far more bearable than you had anticipated, and that you don't really need one after all. Similarly, you may be opposed to any kind of medication during labor — until your labor drags on for more than 24 hours and exhaustion begins to set in.

What's important about the whole issue of pain relief is not whether you use any form of medication. It's the fact that you need to feel comfortable with those choices. It doesn't matter if your childbirth educator thinks you were crazy because you chose to have an epidural or if your mother thinks you were crazy because you didn't; ultimately, it's your call.

Labor interventions

Technology can be a wonderful thing — when it's used wisely. When it's used indiscriminately in the labor room, however, it can lead to an escalation in interventions that may result in an unnecessary cesarean or lead to other birthing complications. That's why it's important to arm yourself with the facts about these types of interventions.

In this next part of the chapter, we talk about three interventions that you may experience during labor or while giving birth: fetal monitoring during labor, an IV during labor, or an episiotomy while you are giving birth.

Fetal monitoring

Fetal monitors are used to monitor the baby's response to contractions. Although some hospitals and caregivers monitor all patients routinely, you are more likely to be monitored if your pregnancy is high risk, if your amniotic fluid was stained with meconium (a possible indication of fetal distress), if you're having an especially difficult labor, if you're hoping to deliver vaginally after a previous cesarean, or if your labor is being induced.

Fetal monitors record both the baby's heartbeat and the mother's contractions. Each of these functions can be monitored either "internally" or "externally." In other words, it's possible to obtain these two measurements by using an internal monitor, an external monitor, or one of each.

External fetal monitoring

An external fetal monitor consists of devices worn on elastic belts fastened around your abdomen (or held on by elasticized panties): an ultrasound transducer designed to pick up your baby's heartbeat, and a pressure-sensitive gauge designed to monitor your contractions (although it is not reliable for assessing their strength).

Internal fetal monitoring

An internal fetal monitor consists of devices inserted through the vagina to monitor the baby's heartbeat and the mother's contractions. The electrical impulses of your baby's heartbeats are detected by an electrode attached to your baby's scalp via the cervix. It is used when a particularly accurate reading is required. The actual pressure generated by your uterine contractions can be measured with a pressure transducer attached to the end of a fine catheter inserted through the vagina and cervix into the inside of the uterus alongside the baby. (It is sometimes necessary to know the exact strength of the contractions when the caregiver is concerned about a lack of progress during the labor or needs to make decisions about stimulating the contractions with medications.)

Though insertion of these devices can be temporarily uncomfortable or even painful, once they are placed you will not be aware of their presence. In order for an internal fetal monitor to be put into place, your membranes will have to be ruptured (if they haven't ruptured by this point), and your cervix will need to be at least 1 to 2 centimeters dilated. There is a small risk of infection associated with the use of an internal fetal monitor. On rare occasions, use of the scalp electrode may cause your baby to develop a rash, an abscess, or a permanent bald spot.

What to expect during fetal monitoring

With both internal and external monitoring, the reading is displayed or printed out, and your baby may be monitored either continuously or intermittently, depending on your situation. If your hospital has a portable fetal monitor, you will be able to remain active during your labor; if it doesn't, you may find that you are confined to the area where your monitor is plugged into the wall while you are being monitored — but you may not necessarily be confined to bed.

If you're being monitored and an alarm goes off, try not to panic. False alarms are common with fetal monitors and more often than not simply indicate an interruption in the heartbeat signal being detected by the device due to a loose connection or the fact that you're in a certain position. If, on the other hand, a true abnormal reading is obtained, you will probably be asked to change positions and/or you will be given IV fluids and oxygen.

If you change position and the reading continues to provide cause for concern, your caregiver may decide to test your amniotic fluid for the presence of meconium (a possible sign of fetal distress) by breaking your water (if your membranes are still intact), assess fetal responsiveness to sound and pressure, or take a fetal blood sample from the scalp to measure your baby's pH levels (which assesses the oxygen and carbon-dioxide content in the baby's blood). If these measures fail to produce reassuring results, you may require an emergency cesarean section, though cesareans for fetal distress are not very common.

IVs: what you need to know

Some caregivers routinely insert intravenous (IV) needles connected either to continuous IV fluids or to heparin locks into all laboring women. The heparin lock (a device that keeps the blood in the needle from clotting while fluids are not flowing) allows for instant intravenous access yet does not limit a laboring woman's mobility by tying her to an IV pole and a bag when continuous IV fluids are not needed.

Other caregivers prefer to reserve IVs for only those women who have a known increased risk of postpartum hemorrhage, fetal distress, or cesarean section, or who have a particular need for intravenous medications during labor.

Because caregiver and institutional policies about the use of IVs vary considerably, you may want to broach this subject with your caregiver ahead of time. Once you and your caregiver have come to an agreement about the use of IVs during your labor, be sure to note your preferences in your birth plan (assuming, of course, that you choose to write one).

Episiotomy

An episiotomy is a surgical incision made in the perineum to enlarge the vaginal opening before the birth of the baby's head. It is generally (but not always) needed in cases of fetal distress, shoulder dystocia (that is, when the shoulders are stuck), a vaginal breech delivery, if an especially fragile baby is being delivered, and during a forceps or vacuum delivery. It is also done as a preventive measure by many caregivers if it appears that without one a potentially serious laceration may occur. Most caregivers agree that it should be used when warranted, but not routinely.

Two types of cuts are made when an episiotomy is performed:

- **Medio-lateral** (an episiotomy that slants away from the rectum).
- **Median** (a median cut is made directly back toward the rectum).

There are both pros and cons to each type of incision. You might want to ask your doctor which type she performs and why.

Your episiotomy may be performed under local anesthetic injected into the perineum at the height of a contraction (when pressure from the baby's head is numbing the area). The incision is also timed to take advantage of this natural pain relief.

An episiotomy can occasionally lead to a lot of postpartum discomfort and possible complications such as rectal problems, so it's in your best interests to avoid one, if at all possible. You can reduce chances of tearing or needing an episiotomy if you listen to your doctor or midwife's instructions during this time because she will tell you to stop pushing when the head is almost born so that the final delivery of the head can be gently guided rather than explosive. Your caregiver can then support the perineal tissue and gently ease the baby out.

There's also some evidence to indicate that perineal massage (gently stretching the tissues at the opening of the vagina) during the weeks leading up to the birth can help to reduce the need for episiotomies in first-time mothers. (Women giving birth for the second or subsequent time don't derive quite the same benefits, unfortunately.) You can either do perineal massage in the tub, when your tissues are already wet, or you can do them on your bed, using a small amount of olive oil or natural cocoa butter for lubrication. For best results, you should spend about 10 minutes a day on perineal massage from week 34 onward, either on your own, or with a little help from your partner.

Finally, here's a bit of interesting trivia about episiotomies, just in case you are interested: The episiotomy was invented in Ireland in 1742 as a means of assisting with difficult births. It was not, however, widely performed until the mid–twentieth century. Today, 80 percent to 90 percent of first-time mothers and 50 percent of women having subsequent births can expect to have an episiotomy.

The pros and cons of inviting other people to the labor

Another issue you'll need to consider before you go into labor is whether you would like to have anyone other than your partner present at the delivery.

As we mentioned earlier, some parents-to-be choose to hire doulas to provide professional labor support. Others invite family members or friends to witness the birth.

"I think that having a couple of people with you is a good idea so that your partner can have a break and you don't have to be alone," explains Danielle, 27, a three-time mother.

Not everyone feels this way, however. Some couples feel quite strongly that they want to be alone. "We didn't invite anyone to either labor or delivery," explains Suzi, a 27-year-old mother of two. "We felt it was a private thing and wanted to use the moment to be close to one another and experience the miracle together. I'm glad we did. It was the most romantic experience of our lives to bring our children into this world together."

Some couples who wouldn't dream of having strangers present at the birth of their baby feel quite strongly, however, that their baby's siblings should be present. If you decide to have children present at the birth, you should

> 66 Remove your nail polish before you go to the hospital. I didn't know that most hospitals require that you remove nail polish before surgery, and I had just redone my nails—deep red, three coats. Needless to say, the little 1-inch-square pads of polish remover that the nurses provided were almost useless. I ended up with icky, red-stained fingers. 99
>
> —Elaine, 29, mother of two

- have a frank discussion with your caregiver about the extent to which you would like your children to be involved in the delivery;

- make sure that your children want to be there and mentally prepare them for what they are likely to witness;

- give some thought to whether your child is old enough to handle the situation (that is, will he understand why he can't have a cuddle from mommy during the peak of a contraction?);

- bring along an extra support person for each child — someone who can take them outside for a walk if they need a break;

- talk to other families who've had their older children present at their baby's birth and see if they have any words of wisdom to share.

When to head for the hospital or birthing center

If you're planning to give birth somewhere other than at home, make sure that you and your caregiver are in agreement about when you should head for the hospital or birth center.

As with anything else in life, timing is everything. You don't want to arrive at the hospital or birth center too soon, or you will find yourself pacing the hall for hours. (Even worse, your labor could grind to an absolute halt — something that's more likely to occur if you make the move while you're still in early labor.) On the other hand, you don't want to leave things too long and risk having your picture on the front page of your local newspaper under a headline that reads: "Woman gives birth on freeway."

> 66 My contractions weren't coming at textbook intervals, so it was hard for me to know if it was time to go to the hospital. After listening to me dealing with two contractions while we were talking on the phone, my midwife decided it was time for me to go to the hospital. When I got there, I was already at 8 centimeters. 99
>
> —Tracy, 31, mother of one

Although there's an art to timing your departure, most women instinctively know when it's time to toss their labor bag in the car and go. As a rule of thumb, you should wait until you're in active labor (when your contractions are intense but not unbearable) but not until you're in transition. Your caregiver can help you to assess how far your labor has progressed and when it's time to leave home.

Here's a quick rule of thumb: If this is your first baby, you should plan to head to the hospital when your contractions are four minutes apart, lasting one minute, and occurring consistently for one hour or more; if they are so painful that you

Bright Idea

Preregistering at the hospital or birthing center will reduce the amount of paperwork you'll have to fill out when you arrive in active labor. You may even be able to complete the paperwork at your caregiver's office.

cannot talk during them or require that you use your relaxation breathing; or if you instinctively feel that it's time to go. If this is your second or subsequent baby, you may wish to head to the hospital a little sooner because your labor is likely to progress more quickly. (Just a brief footnote: One of the authors of this book waited a little too long before heading to the hospital to deliver her third child and ended up going through transition on the bumpiest road in town. Her water broke in the admitting area of the hospital, and her son was born 20 minutes later. Needless to say, she decided not to cut things quite so close the next time around!)

What to bring with you

Even if you're planning a so-called drive-through delivery (that is, you intend to be back home within 24 hours of giving birth), you should pack as if you're staying for a week. Some of those extra garments could come in handy. Checklist 18.2 contains suggestions for what you should take with you.

Checklist 18.2. What to Take to the Hospital or Birthing Center

Your labor kit:

_____ your health-insurance card and proof of insurance

_____ sponges that your partner can use to help cool you off in between contractions

(continued)

Checklist 18.2. *(continued)*

Your labor kit:

_____ snacks and drinks for your partner

_____ magazines or books to read (for both you and your partner)

_____ a picture or other object you can use as your focal point during labor (assuming that you choose to use a focal point)

_____ a camera or video camera plus spare batteries and spare film (and perhaps even a spare disposable camera in case your usual camera or video camera won't function properly). Note: Be sure to test all your camera and video equipment ahead of time. You don't want to miss out on the most exciting photo opportunity of your baby's life.

_____ pillows in colored pillowcases (so that they don't get mixed up with the hospital or birth center's pillows)

_____ a portable stereo and music to listen to during labor

_____ massage oil or lotion (or cornstarch or other nonperfumed powder, if you prefer)

_____ a hot water bottle

_____ lip balm or petroleum jelly

_____ a notebook and pens

_____ change or a prepaid phone card and a list of phone numbers

_____ your hospital preregistration forms

_____ one or more copies of your birth plan

_____ a tennis ball or rolling pin

_____ a frozen freezer pack (small) wrapped in a hand towel

_____ your partner's or labor support person's bathing suit (so that he can accompany you in the shower and help you work through contractions if that is part of your birthing plan)

_____ a change of clothes and a few basic toiletries for your partner (in case labor is particularly prolonged)

Your hospital suitcase:

Clothing

____ at least two nightgowns and two nursing bras (front-opening style if you're planning to breastfeed)

____ five or more pairs of underwear (ideally ones you don't care about in case your pad soaks through)

____ two pairs of warm socks

____ a bathrobe

____ a pair of slippers

____ a going-home outfit for you (something that fit when you were five months pregnant)

____ a going-home outfit for the baby (ideally a sleeper or newborn nightie and a cotton cap)

____ a receiving blanket

____ a bunting bag and heavy blanket if it's cold outside

____ a couple of diapers you can use when it's time to take your baby home

Toiletries

____ a hairbrush, shampoo, soap, toothbrush, toothpaste, deodorant, and other personal-care items

____ some super-absorbent sanitary pads (unless you know for a fact that the hospital will provide these free of charge)

Miscellaneous

____ small gifts for baby's siblings

____ books and magazines (including a good breastfeeding book if you intend to breastfeed your baby)

____ birth announcements

____ earplugs (so that if you are in a noisy maternity ward, you can get some rest)

Bright Idea

Bring along a bottle of witch hazel lotion to apply to your stitches or your hemorrhoids. Some women swear by this stuff.

What will happen once you arrive

Once you arrive at the hospital or birthing center, you will be taken to the birthing unit, where you will probably be asked

- when your contractions started
- how far apart they are now
- whether your membranes have ruptured (and, if so, when)
- when you last ate or drank
- whether you have a birth plan
- whether you intend to have an epidural or medications during labor

Once you've changed into your hospital nightie (or your own nightgown and housecoat, if that's your preference), the nurse will

- take your vital signs (pulse, respiration, and temperature) and record this information on your chart;
- perform an internal examination to see if your cervix has begun to dilate (unless, of course, your caregiver or an intern or a resident is on hand to perform the exam);
- monitor the frequency and duration of contractions, as well as your baby's heart rate, by using an external fetal monitor (an oversized stethoscopelike contraption that is strapped around your lower abdomen) either for a few minutes at a time or continually throughout your labor, depending on the circumstances and the hospital's policies.

What to expect during each stage of labor

Now that you've wrestled with the issue of pain relief during labor, figured out what interventions you do and do not want, and decided whom you do and do not wish to have present at the birth, it's time to consider what the experience of labor is actually like.

As you probably know, labor consists of three distinct stages:

- the first stage, which ends when the cervix is fully dilated;
- the second stage, which ends with the birth of the baby;
- the third stage, which ends once the placenta has been delivered.

The three stages of labor typically last for 12 to 14 hours for first-time mothers and 7 hours for women who have previously given birth.

The following figures illustrate what happens from prelabor through to delivery.

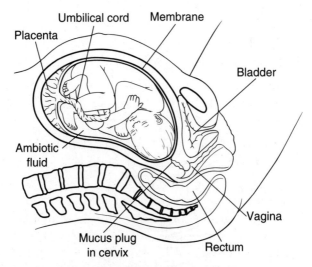

Figure 18.1. Prelabor. *Figure created by Articulate Graphics.*

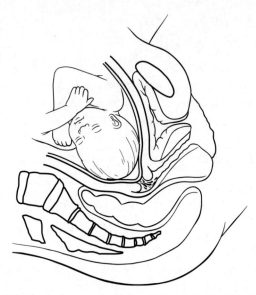

Figure 18.2. Bloody show; cervix dilating. *Figure created by Articulate Graphics.*

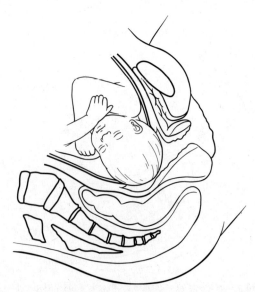

Figure 18.3. Membranes bulging; cervix effaced. *Figure created by Articulate Graphics.*

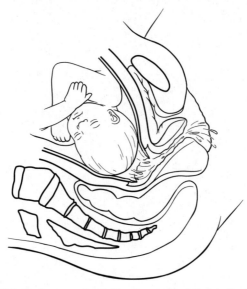

Figure 18.4. Membranes ruptured. *Figure created by Articulate Graphics.*

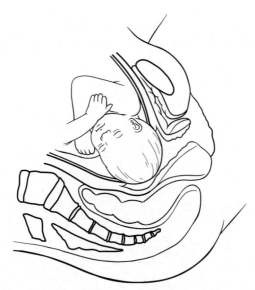

Figure 18.5. Transition; dilation complete; pushing. *Figure created by Articulate Graphics.*

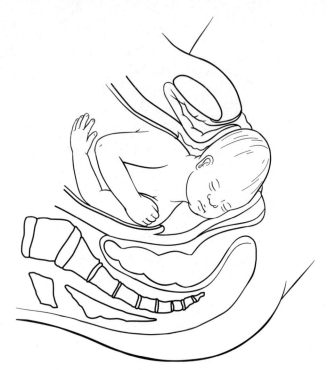

Figure 18.6. Crowning. *Figure created by Articulate Graphics.*

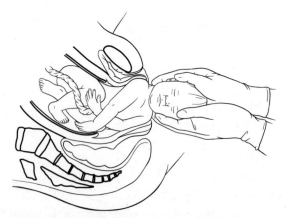

Figure 18.7. Delivery. *Figure created by Articulate Graphics.*

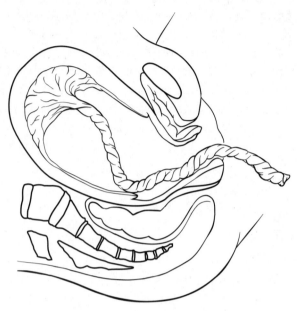

Figure 18.8. Afterbirth. *Figure created by Articulate Graphics.*

The first stage

The first stage of labor can be broken down further into three distinct phases:

- early or latent labor, when your cervix dilates from 0 to 3 centimeters;

- active labor, when your cervix dilates from 4 to 7 centimeters;

- transition, when your cervix dilates from 8 to 10 centimeters (at which point it is fully dilated).

Early labor

You are in early labor when contractions start occurring regularly and there is progressive dilation and effacement of the cervix. Any contractions you experience prior to that point are classified as false labor or prelabor (prodromal labor). By the end of early labor, your cervix will be 50 percent to 90 percent effaced (thinned out) and 3 to 4 centimeters dilated.

If you happen to go into early labor while you are asleep, you might not wake up until you are in more active labor. During early labor, your contractions can be anywhere from 5 to 30 minutes apart and will last anywhere from 30 to 45 seconds. They will probably start coming at closer intervals over time. You may be experiencing a range of physical sensations, including

- backache (either constant or just during contractions);
- menstrual-like cramping;
- indigestion;
- diarrhea;
- a feeling of warmth in the abdomen;
- bloody show (the blood-tinged discharge that occurs when your mucus plug becomes dislodged or your cervix effaces);
- a trickling or gushing sensation if your membranes have ruptured. (They may have ruptured by now, or they may remain intact until you are in more active labor, until your caregiver ruptures them, or even until the baby is being born.)

You may be feeling a range of emotions: excitement, relief, anticipation, uncertainty, anxiety, and fear. You may be tempted to phone up all your friends to let them know that you're in labor, or you may want to withdraw into yourself and prepare for the challenges that lie ahead.

During this phase of labor, you should

- eat lightly;
- either continue with your normal activities as long as you want or are able, thereby keeping your mind off the early contractions, or rest up so that you'll have some energy

reserves to call upon when it's time to face the rigors of the later stages of labor;

- ask your partner or labor support person to help you pack any last-minute things (assuming that you're going to a hospital or birth center) and to help you time contractions;

- alert your caregiver to the fact that you are in labor.

Active labor

The next phase of labor is active labor. It lasts 2 to 3 ½ hours on average, with contractions coming at 3- to 5-minute intervals and lasting from 45 to 60 seconds. By the end of the active phase, your cervix will be approximately 7 centimeters dilated.

During this stage of labor, you may experience

- increased discomfort from contractions (for example, you may no longer feel like talking or walking through them);

- pain and aching in your back and legs;

- fatigue;

- increased quantities of bloody show.

> ❝I didn't find childbirth to be painful. It was, however, overwhelmingly uncomfortable—the most intense physical experience I've ever had in my life. I remember it as powerful and amazing. Immediately after my son slid out of my body, I said to my husband, 'If childbirth is like this for every woman, I don't know why anyone uses drugs.'❞
>
> —Tracy, 31, mother of one

You may be concerned about what lies ahead, or you may be totally absorbed in what is happening right now. If labor is taking longer than you had hoped it would, you may be starting to feel discouraged.

During the active phase of labor, you should

- remain upright and active for as long as you can;

- experiment with positions until you find the one that works best for you when a contraction hits (see the following figures), since changing positions every 30 minutes or so may help the baby descend;

- rest in between contractions;

- empty your bladder at least once an hour;

- allow your partner or labor support person to help you with your labor breathing or any other relaxation techniques and ask her to apply firm counterpressure to your lower back if you're experiencing a lot of back labor;

- continue to consume light fluids (assuming that your doctor or midwife hasn't advised against this).

Figure 18.9. Laboring position (slow dancing). *Figure created by Articulate Graphics.*

Figure 18.10. Laboring position (dangling squat). *Figure created by Articulate Graphics.*

Figure 18.11. Laboring position (supported squat). *Figure created by Articulate Graphics.*

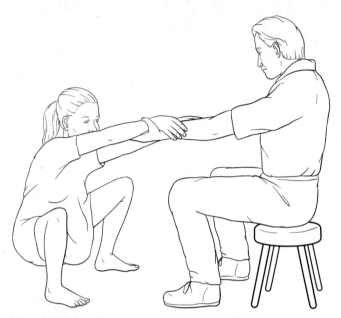

Figure 18.12. Laboring position (squatting down). *Figure created by Articulate Graphics.*

Figure 18.13. Laboring position (using a squat bar). *Figure created by Articulate Graphics.*

Figure 18.14. Laboring position (on hands and knees). *Figure created by Articulate Graphics.*

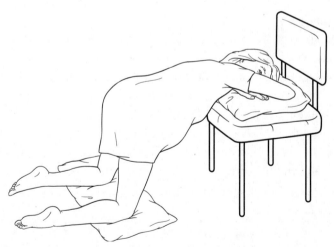

Figure 18.15. Laboring position (leaning on a chair). *Figure created by Articulate Graphics*

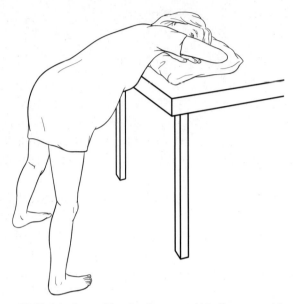

Figure 18.16. Laboring position (leaning on a table). *Figure created by Articulate Graphics.*

Transition

The third phase of labor is known as transition because it marks the end of the first stage of labor (the dilation of the cervix) and the beginning of the second stage of labor (the pushing stage). It is the most intense phase of labor, with contractions occurring 2 to 3 minutes apart and lasting for 60 to 90 seconds. The only good thing to be said about transition is that it doesn't tend to last very long: 15 minutes to an hour, on average.

During this phase of labor, you may experience

- an increased amount of show as more capillaries in your cervix burst;

- pressure in your lower back;

- perineal and rectal pressure;

- hot and cold flashes;

- shaky legs;

- an intense aching in your thighs;
- nausea or vomiting;
- belching;
- heavy perspiration.

During this stage of labor, it's common to feel as though you've reached the end of your rope. You may feel discouraged, irritable, disoriented, restless, and frustrated. You'd gladly call the whole birth off, if only you knew how to tell your uterus to stop contracting.

It's difficult to find a comfortable position during this stage of labor, but many women find that soaking in a bath or taking a shower helps ease the pain. Have your partner or labor support person hop in the shower with you so that he can provide counterpressure to your lower back, if required.

If you're having a particularly painful episode of back labor (that is, severe pain in your lower back), you might want to try one or more of these coping techniques:

- walk, crouch, squat, get down on your hands and knees, or lie on your side with your back well rounded — whatever it takes to relieve some of the pressure you are feeling in your back;
- apply a hot water bottle or a cold pack to your lower back — whichever provides the most relief;
- have your partner or labor support person apply firm counterpressure on the part of your back that is hurting by pushing with either a rolling pin, a tennis ball, or the palm of his hand;

 Watch Out!

If you experience an overwhelming urge to push during transition, have your doctor or midwife examine you to determine if your cervix is fully dilated. Pushing against a less-than-fully dilated cervix can cause swelling, something that can prolong your labor.

- put strong finger pressure below the center of the ball of
  the foot (an acupuncture technique that many laboring
  women swear by).

By the way, while you may not believe it when you're in the
heat of labor — back labor or otherwise — Mother Nature is
doing her bit to help, too. Your body releases endorphins —
natural pain relievers — while you are in labor. These endorphins are morphinelike substances that block the pain receptors in your brain.

The second stage

Just when you've reached your wit's end, your caregiver will
announce that you're fully dilated and will give you the go-
ahead to start pushing. The pushing stage typically lasts from
½ to 1 ½ hours. You'll experience a series of 60- to 90-second-
long contractions at 2- to 5-minute intervals, but these contractions will likely be much less painful than what you experienced
during transition.

Don't be alarmed if you don't feel the urge to push right
away. (You'll know you're experiencing it when you get an overwhelming desire to bear down, as if you needed to have the
world's largest bowel movement.) Some women experience a
10- to 20-minute lull between transition and the start of the second stage. The urge to bear down is triggered as the baby's head
(or buttocks, if it's a breech birth) stretches the vaginal and
pelvic-floor muscles. Microscopic receptors in the area both
trigger the Ferguson reflex (that is, the urge to push) and signal your brain that it's time to increase the production of oxytocin (the hormone that causes your uterus to contract).

 Bright Idea

Put gravity to work for you. Pushing in a semisitting or semisquatting position may make it easier for your pelvis to open up and allow your baby to be
born. Squatting widens your pelvic outlet by 20 percent to 30 percent and
provides your baby with the path of least resistance for exiting the uterus.

During this stage of labor, you may experience

- a renewed burst of energy;
- strong rectal pressure;
- an increase in bloody show;
- the desire to grunt as you bear down;
- a tingling, stretching, burning, or stinging sensation as your baby's head crowns in the vagina;
- a slippery, wet feeling as the baby suddenly emerges.

You may feel relieved that the difficult contractions of transition are now behind you and that you're finally able to start pushing your baby out, exhilarated and excited about your baby's impending birth, or discouraged and overwhelmed at how difficult it can be to push a baby out. "Pushing was a frustrating phase for me," admits Beth, a 27-year-old first-time mom. "I wasn't progressing on getting the baby out, and I was becoming angry, tired, and very upset."

During this phase of labor, you should

- allow your partner or labor support person to help you into a semisitting or semisquatting position — a position that helps gravity work for, not against, you;

- push when you feel the urge, taking several short breaths and making several short pushes during each contraction rather than trying to hold your breath and push throughout the duration of an entire contraction;

> 66 When it came time to push, I tried a variety of positions, but the most effective one was squatting on the bed while holding on to a squatting bar. 99
>
> —Tracy, 31, mother of one

- stop pushing, pant, or blow if your caregiver tells you to stop pushing in order to give your perineum a chance to stretch gradually (you might end up avoiding an episiotomy or a bad tear).

Don't be alarmed if you pass small amounts of urine or feces during the pushing stage. Many laboring women do; it kind of goes with the turf and indicates that you are pushing effectively.

Once your baby's head starts to emerge, your caregiver will

- suction the baby's nose and mouth and help the shoulders and torso to come out;

- check to see if the umbilical cord is wrapped around the baby's neck and either lift the cord over your baby's head or clamp and cut it, if necessary;

- lay the baby across your abdomen, if that's your preference (unless the baby appears to be having difficulty breathing, in which case it may be necessary to place the baby in the isolette, suction out any meconium, stimulate respiration, and give your baby some oxygen before she is returned to you);

- gently rub your baby's back to stimulate her (the days of upside-down spankings have gone the way of the dinosaur);

- cut and clamp the umbilical cord (before or after the cord has stopped pulsating or the placenta has been delivered, depending on how you and your caregiver feel about the timing of the cutting of the umbilical cord);

- perform the Apgar test (see Table 18.2);

- wrap the baby to keep her from losing too much body heat.

Table 18.2. Apgar Test

	0	1	2
Appearance (skin color); shows how well the lungs are working to oxygenate the blood	Pale or blue	Body pink, extremities blue	Pink
Pulse (heart rate); measures the strength and regularity of the heartbeat	No pulse	Below 100	Over 100

	0	1	2
Grimace (reflex irritability)	No response to grimace stimulation		Lusty cry
Activity (movements); an indication of the baby's muscle tone	No activity or weak activity	Some movement	Active movement
Respiration (breathing)	None	Slow, irregular	Crying

Note: The Apgar test is named for pediatrician Dr. Virginia Apgar, who developed it. A memory device that many caregivers find helpful when assessing a newborn is to assign the terms "appearance, pulse, grimace, activity, and respiration" to the letters of "APGAR."

The Apgar test is performed twice: once when your baby is one minute old and again when your baby is five minutes old. A baby with a one-minute combined score of seven or over is doing well; a baby with a score of five or six may require resuscitation; a baby with a score of four or less may be in serious trouble.

Because newborns are particularly alert right after birth, you might want to take advantage of this opportunity to try breastfeeding your baby. (Your baby may be much sleepier in a few hours, and you may find it difficult to get the baby to wake up enough to nurse.) There's an added bonus to breastfeeding at this stage of the game: the nipple stimulation that occurs as your baby nurses will help release oxytocin, which will help your uterus contract, expel the placenta, and stop bleeding. (Note: You will experience these contractions — so-called afterpains — each time you nurse during the first week postpartum. These contractions aren't overly uncomfortable after the birth of your first baby, but they can be downright excruciating after the birth of a subsequent child. Ask your caregiver to prescribe an analgesic if you're finding it difficult to cope with these afterpains. You went through enough during labor; there's no point in being a martyr now.)

Although you and your partner may want to spend some time alone with your new baby after the placenta has been delivered (see below), your baby may need to be taken to the nursery at some point, so that a full newborn exam can be performed. (This isn't the case in all hospitals and birthing centers, so be sure to ask about these policies ahead of time.) If you do not want to be separated from your baby, find out if you or your partner, or both of you, can accompany the baby to the nursery.

The third stage

The third stage of labor — the delivery of the placenta — will take place while you're busy admiring your new baby. You may be so distracted that you may hardly even notice the massive 1- to 2-pound placenta — your baby's life-support system for the past nine months — making its way out of your body. This stage typically lasts anywhere from five minutes to half an hour and involves mild contractions that typically last for one minute or less. These contractions tend to be so mild that you might not even feel them. If you are banking the umbilical cord blood, your caregiver will perform the collection procedure before the placenta is delivered, or right after the placenta is delivered, if the placenta is delivered before your doctor has the chance to perform the collection procedure.

In an effort to avoid any possible problems with postpartum hemorrhaging, your caregiver may give you a shot of oxytocin or methylergonovine, which will cause the uterus to contract for a prolonged period of time, minimizing bleeding from the former site of the placenta.

Once the placenta has been delivered, your caregiver will examine it to make sure that it's complete (retained placental fragments can cause hemorrhaging) and then do any stitching required to repair your perineum.

During this stage, you may feel either tired or bursting with energy, thirsty and hungry, or cold. You will be bleeding quite heavily from the vagina. This blood flow, known as lochia, tends

Bright Idea

To keep your uterus firm and minimize the amount of blood loss you experience following the birth, you should periodically attempt to feel the height of your fundus (the top of your uterus), which will be located somewhat below your navel. (If you have trouble finding it, your caregiver or nurse can help you.) It should be firm to the touch. If it is squishy rather than firm, vigorous massage will help it contract.

to be heavier than even the heaviest of menstrual periods. If the bleeding is excessive, the nurse or your caregiver may need to massage your uterus (which can be uncomfortable) to stimulate the uterus to contract. After the birth, you may even find that you gush slightly if you stand up while your uterus is contracting. You may also pass some fairly large blood clots when you go to the bathroom. You will want to alert your caregiver if they are the size of a lemon, or larger.

Why labor sometimes stops

Up until now, we've been talking about textbook labors — the kinds that follow the prenatal class handouts to the T. Unfortunately, not all labors are quite that straightforward. There are a number of reasons why labor can stop. Here are a few of the more common:

- **Failure to dilate:** If your uterine contractions are ineffective, your cervix will not be able to dilate.

- **Fetal obstruction:** If your baby is too large for your pelvis to accommodate (a problem that is medically termed cephalopelvic disproportion); is in a transverse or oblique position; has a breech, face, or brow presentation; has a congenital abnormality such as hydrocephalus; or is wrapped around another twin, your baby may not be able to be born vaginally.

- **Maternal causes of obstruction:** If you have a deformity or disproportion of the bony pelvis; pelvic tumors such as

Bright Idea

If your labor stalls during the early or latent phase, you may be able to get things going again by walking, resting, or stimulating your nipples.

exceptionally large fibroids or a very large ovarian cyst; abnormalities of the uterus, cervix, or vagina; or a tight band of muscle around your uterus that prevents a contraction from being transmitted all the way down the uterus, your labor may fail to progress.

Your caregiver will begin to suspect that there's a problem if

- during active labor, you are dilating at a rate of less than 1 centimeter per hour (if you're a first-time mom) or 1.5 centimeters per hour (if this is your second or subsequent baby) or

- the pushing stage lasts for more than two hours.

Depending on the stage at which your labor stalls and the suspected causes, your caregiver may decide to augment your labor with Pitocin, attempt to deliver your baby with forceps or a vacuum extractor, prep you for a cesarean, or wait things out a little longer to see if the problem resolves itself.

What it's really like to be induced

You've no doubt heard the horror stories about what it's like to be induced — about how the contractions come on top of one another, leaving some laboring woman gasping for air. Not all induced labors are this horrific — something you'll be glad to hear if your baby is late (or might benefit from delivery before you go into labor naturally) and your caregiver is talking induction. Here are the facts on being induced.

Reasons for an induction

The decision to induce is not made lightly. If your caregiver decides that your labor should be induced, it will likely be for one of the following reasons:

- there are signs of placental insufficiency (the placenta may not be getting sufficient nutrients and oxygen from the placenta);

- you are post-term (42 weeks plus), although recent studies suggested better outcomes and fewer cesareans if induction is done routinely at 41 weeks;

- the fetus is no longer thriving in the uterus (due to suspected postmaturity syndrome, poor placental function, maternal disease, or other problems);

- a stress test or nonstress test reveals that the placenta is no longer functioning properly, and the baby would be better off being born than remaining in the uterus any longer;

- your membranes have ruptured but labor has not yet started spontaneously within 12 to 24 hours;

- you have developed preeclampsia or another serious medical condition that cannot be controlled with bed rest and medication, and delivery is necessary for the sake of your own health as well as that of the baby.

Sometimes labor is induced for reasons that are not purely medical. Your caregiver may recommend an elective induction if

- you have a prior history of rapid labor that puts you at risk of having an unplanned home birth;

- you live a considerable distance from a hospital;

- your caregiver will be unavailable for a certain period of time (for example, if your high-risk-pregnancy specialist is about to head out of town for a conference and you're due to deliver any day);

- your family circumstances warrant it (for example, if your partner is able to get only a short period of military leave and would like to be present at the birth).

- you are within one week of an accurate established due date, your cervix is favorable (see following), and you desire a scheduled delivery for significant personal emotional reasons. Because there is always the risk that an induction may fail, necessitating a repeat attempt at induction or a cesarean section, be sure to ask your caregiver about the pros and cons of going this route before you agree to an induction. Generally, the more favorable your cervix is, the less likelihood of a failed induction. Favorable means that your cervix is already starting to soften, dilate, and efface, and the baby's head is relatively low in the pelvis.

One tool your physician may use in assessing your body's readiness for labor is the so-called Bishop scoring system, in which a score of 0 to 3 is given for each of the following five factors:

- dilatation
- effacement
- station
- consistency
- position of cervix

If your score exceeds 8 (see Table 18.3), your cervix is considered to be favorable for induction.

Table 18.3. Bishop Scoring System

	0	1	2	3
Dilatation (cm)	Cervix is closed	Cervix is 1 to 2 cm dilated	Cervix is 3 to 4 cm dilated	Cervix is more than 5 cm dilated
Effacement (%)	Cervix is 0% to 30% effaced	Cervix is 40% to 50% effaced	Cervix is 60% to 70% effaced	Cervix is more than 80% effaced
Station (an estimate of baby's the descent into the birth canal)	−3	−2	−1, 0	+1, +2

	0	1	2	3
Consistency of the cervix	Firm	Medium	Soft	
Position of the cervix	Posterior (pointing backward)	Midposition	Anterior (pointing forward)	

Note: If your labor starts but is weak, is erratic, or stops, your caregiver may augment your labor by using some of the techniques that are used to induce labor.

There are certain circumstances in which labor should not be induced, however. These include pregnancies in which either vaginal delivery is excessively risky or where additional stimulation of the uterus could add unacceptable risk, such as those pregnancies in which

- the placenta blocks the cervix (placenta previa);
- the placenta is prematurely separating from the uterine wall (placental abruption);
- there is an usual presentation of the baby that would make vaginal delivery dangerous or impossible;
- the baby is believed to be too large for your pelvis to accommodate (cephalopelvic disproportion);
- you have an active genital herpes infection;
- you are carrying multiples;
- there is evidence of fetal distress;
- the uterus is unusually large (due to the increased risk of uterine rupture if you have polyhydramnios or are carrying multiples).

Methods of induction

If your caregiver decides to induce or augment labor, he will probably use one or a combination of the following methods:

Watch Out!

Some caregivers will rupture your membranes to speed up a sluggish labor. Once your membranes have been ruptured, your labor will become faster and more intense. Make sure that you're psychologically prepared for these more intense contractions.

- **Artificial rupture of membranes (AROM):** The caregiver ruptures the membranes using a device that looks like a crochet hook. The procedure will be virtually painless if your cervix has already begun to dilate but can be quite painful if it is only 1 centimeter or less. If this procedure — known as an amniotomy — fails, your labor will have to be induced using other methods. Once your membranes have been ruptured, you've reached the point of no return: you're going to have your baby; it's simply a matter of time.

- **Prostaglandin E suppositories or gel:** Prostaglandin E suppositories or gels help ripen the cervix (make it more favorable for induction). According to the American College of Obstetricians and Gynecologists, 50 percent of women will go into labor spontaneously and deliver within 24 hours following just a single application of the gel; others will require some additional method of induction.

- **Misoprostol:** Misoprostol tablets placed high in the vagina can also help to ripen the cervix and induce labor. While this is a relatively new method of inducing labor, many caregivers are impressed by the safety, effectiveness, and ease of use of Misoprostol tablets as compared to Prostaglandin E.

- **Pitocin:** Pitocin is the synthetic form of oxytocin — a hormone that is produced naturally by your body and that is responsible for causing your uterus to contract during labor. If it is used when your cervix is already ripe, a Pitocin-induced labor won't be all that different from a natural labor. If, on the other hand, your cervix isn't ripe, it may take several hours of exposure to Pitocin in a series of separate attempts over a period of two to three days to get labor started. This is why many caregivers use Prostaglandin E or Misoprostal as a warmup to Pitocin.

When you are first hooked up to an intravenous drip, a small amount of Pitocin will be injected. This is because your caregiver will want to monitor the strength of your contractions and your baby's response to them before upping the dosage. It's very difficult to predict how a particular mother and baby will react to the drug. Sometimes, contractions caused by a Pitocin drip can be stronger, longer, and more painful than non-Pitocin-induced contractions, and there are shorter breaks between them. You may require pain medication to help you cope with the contractions, and you will probably need to be hooked up to a fetal monitor for the majority of your labor. In some cases, however, a small dose of Pitocin (especially if the membranes are ruptured) is all that is required to get labor started, and, once started, your contractions will continue on their own without any further need for Pitocin.

Despite all the scary stories you might have heard to the contrary, an induced labor does not have to be any more painful than any other labor. Since the dose of Pitocin can be precisely controlled and adjusted up or down in small increments, the contractions you experience in a labor that has been triggered with Pitocin need not be any stronger or closer together (or consequently more painful) than what would be seen in a spontaneous labor. About the only thing that is different with an induced labor in which the Pitocin is administered appropriately is that the early phase of labor may be shortened and the active phase may be reached more quickly than might otherwise have been the case.

- **Cervical dilators:** Cervical dilators are a mechanical method of dilating the cervix. Laminaria (sticks of compressed and dried seaweed or synthetic materials) are placed in the cervix. As they absorb water and swell, they force your cervix to dilate. Cervical dilators are considered to be approximately as effective as Prostaglandin E; in other words, they are able to get labor started within a 24-hour period in about 50 percent of women.

Note: Some pregnancy books may recommend nipple stimulation as a means of getting labor started. This technique is not only unproven, but it's potentially harmful in that the amount of oxytocin being released by your body when your nipples are stimulated cannot be controlled and in rare cases could lead to excessive uterine stimulation (hyperstimulation, or tetanic contractions) that could impair fetal/placental blood flow and cause distress. (If your labor has started and *stalled,* however, you can use this technique.)

Not everyone is a good candidate for induction. Your caregiver will probably suggest other alternatives (for example, a cesarean section) if

- your baby needs to be delivered quickly (for example, he is in distress or the placenta is starting to separate);
- it isn't clear whether your baby will be able to fit through your pelvis;
- you have been diagnosed with placenta previa (that is, the placenta is blocking the cervix);
- you have had five or more previous births;
- you have a vertical uterine (not skin) scar from a previous cesarean section or a deep uterine scar from other uterine surgery;
- you are carrying more than one baby;
- your baby is in the breech position.

If your caregiver believes that either you or your baby is not up to tolerating the stresses of labor, she will recommend that a cesarean be performed instead.

What to expect if you have a breech delivery

Although 97 percent of babies move into the head-down (vertex) position before labor starts, 3 percent remain in the breech position at the time labor starts. You are at increased risk of having a breech birth if

- you have had more than one pregnancy;

- you are carrying more than one baby;

- you have too much or too little amniotic fluid;

- your uterus is an abnormal shape due to a congenital anomaly;

- you have a number of large fibroids;

- the placenta partially or fully covers the opening of the uterus (placenta previa);

- your baby is premature (due to the shape of the uterus and the shape of the baby's head and body at this stage of development and the fact that premature babies are more likely to have birth defects that may predispose them to assuming the breech position).

There are three main types of breech positions, as you will see from Figure 18.17.

- the frank breech (when the baby's legs extend straight upward);

- the complete breech (when the baby is sitting cross-legged on top of the cervix);

- the footling breech (when one or both of the baby's feet are pointing downward).

Bright Idea

A bright idea or not? You be the judge. Some parents are choosing to store the blood from their child's umbilical cord and placenta in a cord blood bank so that it will be available in the event that their child someday needs a bone-marrow transplant. Cord blood banks charge approximately $1,500 for the initial deposit and $95 per year for storage—either the bargain of the century or the ultimate rip-off, according to the two sides on this controversial issue.

Assuming that your baby's presentation is detected prior to labor (and most breech babies' presentations are detected ahead of time), your caregiver may wish to try turning the baby before you go into labor. This procedure — known as external version — is typically performed after the 36th week of pregnancy. An ultrasound will be performed to assess the condition and position of the baby, locate the placenta, and measure the amount of amniotic fluid. Your caregiver will place her hands on your abdomen and try to gently coax your baby to change position — kind of like performing a slow-motion somersault in utero. You may be given a drug to relax your uterus before the procedure is attempted, and your baby will be monitored throughout the procedure in case complications arise and he goes into distress. The key drawbacks to this procedure are the fact that the procedure can be painful, it can be unsuccessful, and — even if it is successful — your baby may revert to the breech presentation between the time when the version is performed and labor commences. There's also an element of risk — which is why the American College of Obstetricians and Gynecologists states that caregivers must be prepared to do an immediate cesarean section if complications arise during a version.

If you're lucky, you may not even need a version: some babies spontaneously turn from a breech or transverse lie (sideways) into the vertex (head down) presentation after the 36th week.

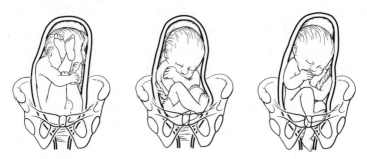

Figure 18.17. The three main types of breech presentations: frank (left); complete (middle); and footling (right). *Figure by Articulate Graphics.*

Your chances of being able to deliver a breech baby vaginally are greatest if your baby is a frank breech — but there are still no guarantees that you will be able to avoid a cesarean. Your caregiver may rule out the possibility of a trial vaginal delivery entirely if

- the baby is very large;
- your pelvis is small;
- your baby is premature;
- your baby is exhibiting signs of fetal distress;
- your caregiver feels that the risks of attempting a vaginal breech delivery outweigh the benefits and consequently he or she does not feel comfortable attempting a vaginal breech delivery. Assuming that you are able to deliver your baby vaginally, your caregiver may have to use forceps to deliver the baby's head. The baby's head is the largest part of its body, so it's possible for the baby's head to momentarily get stuck when the baby is born feet and buttocks first.

Water birth

Most caregivers agree that there are a number of advantages to laboring in warm water. Laboring in warm water promotes relaxation and a more efficient labor while reducing the perception of pain. And maternity centers have reported no increased rate of infection in women laboring in appropriately sanitized tubs after their membranes have ruptured.

Where some caregivers tend to draw the line, however, is when it comes time to actually deliver the baby. There is conflicting evidence about the safety of delivering under water, and many caregivers have particular concerns about the possibility of respiratory complications in the event that the baby inhales water.

An article in the British medical journal *Lancet* recommended that those women who do choose to give birth under water get out of the tub as soon as the baby is born and clamp the cord within a minute or two rather than delaying the clamping until after the delivery of the placenta. Staying in the warm water allows the blood vessels in the umbilical cord to stay open much longer than they normally would — something that can contribute to postdelivery complications for both the mother and the baby.

If you're planning a water birth, you will want to discuss your delivery plans with your caregiver as early on in pregnancy as possible. Not every caregiver feels comfortable attending water births and water birth will only be an option if the place where you are giving birth has it as an option.

If you feel very strongly that water birth is right for you, but your caregiver is not comfortable with your birthing choice, you will either need to start looking for an alternative caregiver or rethink your water-birthing plans.

What to expect if you have a cesarean delivery

A cesarean section involves delivering a baby through an incision in a woman's abdomen and uterus. Approximately 15 percent to 20 percent of U.S. babies are born by cesarean section — a significant increase from the 3 percent to 5 percent rate of 25 years ago. Although the media sometimes likes to put a negative spin on this increase by focusing on the number of unnecessary cesareans, what often gets left out of the discussion is the number of babies whose lives have been saved or improved because of this increase in the cesarean rate.

Bright Idea

If you know ahead of time that you will be having a cesarean section, look for childbirth classes that are tailored to couples who are planning cesareans.

This isn't to say that the 25 percent or higher cesarean rate at some institutions is something to cheer about, of course. The potential complications from a cesarean include

- infections (particularly of the uterus, the nearby pelvic organs, and the incision);
- excessive blood loss;
- complications from the anesthesia;
- blood clots due to decreased mobility after surgery;
- bowel and bladder injuries.

You may have heard a common myth about cesareans: that the baby misses out on the squeezing motion of a vaginal delivery — a process that helps clear amniotic fluid from the lungs and stimulate the circulation. There's no evidence showing that babies delivered through cesarean section are at a disadvantage because of this so-called lack of squeezing. In truth, a fair bit of squeezing does occur as the doctor guides your baby out through the incision he or she has made in your uterus.

Still, most caregivers agree that cesareans should be planned only when there's a solid medical reason for avoiding a vaginal delivery. Here are some common reasons:

- The baby is predicted to be too large to pass through your pelvis.
- The baby is in a breech or transverse position.
- You have placenta previa.
- You have an active genital herpes infection.
- You have previously had a cesarean section or certain other types of uterine surgery. Note: Not all women who have previously had a cesarean section are candidates for a

repeat cesarean. The cause of your previous cesarean (for example, a one-time emergency versus a chronic problem), the type of uterine incision used, and your obstetrical status during your subsequent pregnancy will determine whether another cesarean will be necessary. We'll be discussing this issue further on in this chapter.

What a cesarean birth is like

If your section is planned rather than the result of an obstetrical emergency, you can expect your birth to proceed something like this:

- You will be given medication to dry the secretions in your mouth and upper airway. You may also be given an antacid. (In the event that you vomit and then inhale some of the contents of your stomach, the damage that your lungs sustain will be reduced if you have taken an antacid.)

- The lower part of your abdomen will be washed and possibly shaved as well.

- A catheter will be placed in your bladder to keep it empty and to reduce the chances of injury.

- An intravenous needle will be inserted into a vein in your hand or arm to allow for the administering of fluids and medications during your surgery.

- You will be given an anesthetic (typically an epidural or spinal, but general anesthesia may be used in certain circumstances).

- Your abdomen will be washed with antiseptic solution and covered with a sterile drape.

- A screen will be placed in front of your face to keep the surgical field sterile, blocking your view of your baby's birth.

- Once the anesthetic has had an opportunity to take effect, an incision will be made through the wall of your abdomen and then the wall of your uterus. You will probably feel slight pressure at the incision site, but not any pain. Although your caregiver will attempt to use a so-called bikini cut (a horizontal cut that is low on your abdomen), a vertical skin incision is sometimes made in an emergency.

- Regardless of the type of skin incision, the uterine incision is made horizontally and low down on the uterus unless the position of your baby or the placenta demands a vertical cut instead.

- The amniotic sac will be opened and the amniotic fluid will pour out.

- Your baby will be eased out manually or, on occasion, with the aid of forceps or a vacuum extractor. You may feel a slight tugging sensation as well as feelings of pressure, if you've had an epidural. You probably won't feel anything, if you've had a spinal, except pressure on your upper abdomen if the doctor needs to apply pressure to push the baby out through the incision.

> ❝The night before our 8:00 a.m. scheduled c-section, we simply spent time hanging out in the nursery. We folded never-worn baby clothes and set up the crib. We watched the 'lullaby light show,' which attached to the baby's crib and projected little sky scenes onto the ceiling. It was a wonderful night. It felt like a closing to our life together as it had been so far.❞
>
> —Jennifer, 25, mother of one

- Your baby's nose and mouth will be suctioned. The umbilical cord will be clamped and cut, and the placenta will be removed. The doctor will hand the baby to the nurse or other caregiver responsible for suctioning the baby.

- The baby's caregiver will assess the baby and perform the Apgar test.

Watch Out!

Be sure to find out if your caregiver and the hospital allow partners or labor support people to be present at a cesarean birth—and under what circumstances. (Some hospitals won't allow anyone to be present if an emergency cesarean section needs to be performed.)

- Your uterus and abdomen will be stitched up. The stitches in your uterus will dissolve on their own. Depending on your doctor's preference, your abdominal incision will be closed with stainless-steel staples or nonabsorbent sutures, which can be removed anytime after three or four days, or absorbable sutures below the skin surface, which dissolve on their own. Another recent option is a kind of surgical "super glue" that avoids sutures and staples altogether. (Note: It's still a relatively new product, so your obstetrician may not have had a lot of experience with it yet.)

- If you feel up to it, you may have the opportunity to hold your baby in the delivery room.

- You will be taken to the recovery room, where your blood pressure, pulse rate, and respiratory rate will be monitored, and you will be watched for excessive bleeding and other potential complications. You may be given antibiotics to minimize your chances of infection and will be offered pain medication either via an IV or an injection after the anesthetic wears off.

- You will be moved to a room on the postpartum floor. If you are intending to breastfeed, your nurse will show you how to position yourself and your baby to ensure that you are as comfortable as possible, despite your incision. (You will want to either place a pillow over your incision and rest your baby on that while you sit up straight in a chair, or feed your baby when you are lying on one side.)

- Six to eight hours after your surgery, your catheter will be removed and you will be encouraged to get out of bed and move around.

- You will require intravenous fluids for a day or two until you're able to start eating and drinking.

- Your doctor will probably prescribe an analgesic to help you cope with the discomfort and pain that typically accompany a cesarean recovery.

- You will be discharged from hospital three to five days after your surgery, and you will be able to resume your normal activities four to six weeks after your baby's birth.

Emergency cesareans

Up until now, we've been talking about planned cesarean sections. An emergency cesarean section may be required if, during the course of labor,

- the baby's heart rate becomes irregular, indicating that she may be in distress and may not be able to withstand the stress of continued labor;

- the flow of blood and oxygen through the umbilical cord is being excessively restricted because of the position of the cord or the baby;

- the placenta has started to detach from the uterine wall (placental abruption);

- the baby is not moving down into the birth canal because the cervix has stopped dilating or the baby is too large for the mother's pelvis, or because of some other obstetrical complication.

Once a cesarean, always a cesarean?

Although the conventional wisdom stated that a woman who had previously had a cesarean was destined to have another cesarean during her next delivery, that is not necessarily the case. Although some women will always require cesareans, others may be good candidates for a vaginal birth after cesarean (VBAC). Your doctor or midwife may recommend that you consider a VBAC if

- you are carrying only one baby;
- your baby is vertex (head down);
- your baby is full term;
- the baby isn't too big and your pelvis isn't too small;
- you are delivering in a setting where an anesthetist is on call and a cesarean can be performed on short notice;
- your baby doesn't show any signs of distress.

Here are just a few of the benefits of trying for a VBAC:

- Vaginal deliveries are less risky than cesareans. As is the case with all major types of surgery, it's possible to develop postoperative complications, including infection, bleeding, and a reaction to the anesthetic.
- It takes less time to recover from a vaginal delivery than a cesarean.
- A woman who is having a vaginal delivery can play a more active role in the birth and, in general, has more options concerning the birth (who will be present in the delivery room and so on). This may leave you feeling more in control of your birth experience.

The primary concern posed by a trial of labor (a VBAC attempt) is the fact that it may not be successful and a cesarean will have to be performed again. Depending on the reason the first cesarean was done, the success rate for VBAC may vary by 50 percent to 80 percent. Another risk is the possibility of splitting of the uterine scar tissue from your previous incision. You're less likely to experience this rare but potentially life-threatening complication if you received a transverse uterine incision rather than a vertical incision. Note that the type of skin incision you had does not indicate what type of uterine incision you may have had. Although the vast majority of modern cesareans are done through low uterine horizontal (transverse) incisions, your caregiver will probably check your previous records to verify what type of uterine incision you had before recommending an attempt at VBAC.

How you may be feeling about having a cesarean

When you first found out you were pregnant and started thinking about the birth of your baby, you may have envisioned giving birth peacefully in the birthing suite at your local hospital or at your local birth center. Finding out midway through your pregnancy — or in the heat of labor — that you're going to require a cesarean section can be a bit of a shock.

Part of the problem stems from the fact that cesarean births are stigmatized as being less intimate and meaningful to laboring women and their partners than vaginal deliveries. This attitude angers women like Andrea, 27, a first-time mother. "Women need to realize that having a cesarean birth makes them no less of a mother than women who have vaginal deliveries," she insists.

Sometimes all that is required is a shift in mindset, says Jennifer, a 25-year-old mother of one: "I had to plan a c-section when my baby was found to be breech two weeks before my due date. I was very disappointed not to be able to experience labor and delivery as I had envisioned, but I quickly convinced myself that this could be a wonderful thing as well — to be able to relax and enjoy my baby's entrance into the world without even thinking about my performance and my breathing techniques."

If you continue to feel disappointed about your inability to deliver your baby vaginally, you may wish to share your feelings with your caregiver or talk with a therapist.

Meeting your baby

The hard work of labor and delivery are behind you, and the time has come to savor your reward. It's time to meet your baby.

You probably realize that newborns bear only a passing resemblance to those adorable eight-month-old cherubs pictured in Anne Geddes photographs. What you might not realize is how very odd newborn babies can look — particularly if you've never seen one before. Here's a brief description of what your newborn may look like:

- **Irregular head shape:** If you delivered your baby vaginally, he might have a molded or conelike shape to his head. If your baby's head was jammed against an inadequately dilated cervix, it may have an alarming lump known as a caput succedaneum. Although the molding may last for up to two weeks, the caput will likely disappear within a day or two.

- **Hair:** Some babies are born with a full head of hair; others are virtually bald. Regardless of what amount of hair your baby arrives with, her hair will soon fall out. As this newborn hair is shed, it will be replaced with new hair.

- **Vernix caseosa coating:** Vernix is the protective coating that covered your baby's skin while he was in utero. Your baby will probably have traces of vernix in his folds of skin. A premature baby may be heavily coated in vernix, whereas a postterm baby may have virtually none.

- **Lanugo:** Lanugo is the fine downy hair found on a full-term newborn baby's shoulders, back, forehead, and temples. (As is the case with vernix, lanugo is more abundant in premature babies.)

- **Genital swelling:** Your baby's genitals and breasts may be swollen as a result of maternal hormones crossing the placenta. A baby girl may even pass a milky-white or blood-tinged secretion from her vagina. These signs will disappear within a week to 10 days.

- **Birthmarks:** Reddish blotches are most common in Caucasians, whereas bluish-gray pigmentation on the back, buttocks, arms, or thighs is more common in babies of Asian, south European, or African American ancestry.

■ **Neonatal urticaria:** Your baby may have a series of red spots with yellow-white centers. These typically appear during the first day of life, but they disappear by the time your baby is one week old.

> 66 We had not learned the sex of our baby before he was born, but throughout the pregnancy, I had dreamed of a little red-haired daughter. Instead, I had just given birth to a little son with a head full of black hair. I wasn't disappointed, just surprised. I looked at him and thought, 'Well, you're not what I was expecting at all!' 99
>
> —Tracy, 31, mother of one

■ **Red marks on the skin or broken blood vessels in the skin or eye:** Your baby may have red marks on her skin or broken blood vessels in her skin or eye. These marks — which are caused by pressure during birth — typically vanish within a few days.

Note: You can find a detailed description of the characteristics of both full-term and premature newborns in *The Mother of All Baby Books* (Wiley Publishing, Inc., 2002) by Ann Douglas (one of the authors of this book).

How you may be feeling about becoming a mother

Some women experience an instant bond with their babies after they give birth; others take a little longer to warm up to the pint-sized strangers in their arms.

Suzi, a 27-year-old mother of two, recalls the feelings of joy she experienced after the births of each of her sons: "Once I had my babies, I was truly overwhelmed with joy. It was an experience and feeling that you cannot explain to anyone because it is so miraculous and beautiful."

Ann, 34, experienced similar emotions: "I was on a high from the moment my daughter was born. I was so thrilled that I was finally able to meet my baby."

Nancy, 31, couldn't believe how quickly she fell in love with her babies: "As soon as I set eyes on them, I fell head over heals for them. I couldn't get enough of them. I loved looking at those sweet little faces that I had been waiting so long to see."

Other women are surprised by their lack of emotion during those first few moments.

"I had anticipated throughout my pregnancy that holding my baby for the first time would be wondrous," admits Tracy, a 31-year-old mother of one. "I expected that I would be weeping with joy and love for my baby, that I would feel an instant connection. But when he was born and they put him, bloody and naked, up on my chest, I felt like I was being handed a stranger."

Stephanie, a 25-year-old first-time mother, echoes those feelings: "I did not feel an instant bond at all and actually remember thinking, 'What's wrong with me? I'm supposed to be loving this child right away, and all I want to do is go to sleep.'"

Marilyn, 43, who is currently pregnant with her third child, admits to feeling totally detached from her first baby immediately after the birth. "I kept thinking that her mother was about to come and fetch her at any moment and I was just minding her until then. It was perhaps a few hours later that I began to fall in love with her."

Some women gain a newfound respect for their bodies in the moments after giving birth. Heather, a 32-year-old first-time mother, describes it this way: "I felt powerfully connected to all my ancestresses down through all time. I could literally see the echoes of every woman who ever labored to give forth a new life. I felt triumphant; filled with grace; utterly humbled by my own body and by the miracle that lay wet and sweet and messy on my belly. I was full to the skin with welcome for the new life that so suddenly became real to me."

Others are surprised to find themselves experiencing feelings of regret that their pregnancy has come to an end: "I was relieved that it was all over, but also a little sad," confesses Erika, 25, a mother of two. "Being pregnant and giving birth is such a miraculous experience that part of me didn't want it to end."

Just the facts

- You may experience lightening, increased pressure in the pelvis and rectum, weight loss or reduced weight gain, fluctuating energy levels, the passage of your mucus plug, some pink or bloody show, and increasingly painful Braxton Hicks contractions in the days and weeks leading up to labor.

- It can be extremely difficult to distinguish between true and false labor. Don't be embarrassed if you experience at least one false alarm.

- While many women opt for unmediated births, epidurals have become the pain-relief option of choice among American women.

- Make sure that your caregiver knows how you feel about fetal monitoring and episiotomy and other interventions.

- You may wish to use some of the nonpharmaceutical methods of pain relief before resorting to pharmacologically based methods.

- Be sure to have an extra support person lined up for each of your children if you intend to have them present at the birth.

- Assuming that your caregiver agrees, time your departure for the birth center or hospital so that you arrive when you're in active labor rather than early labor or transition.

- Pack both a labor bag and a hospital bag at least three weeks prior to your due date. You don't want to be searching for a spare tube of toothpaste in between contractions.

- Make sure that you know what's involved in an induction, a breech delivery, and a cesarean delivery so that you'll be prepared if any of them happen to you.

- Although most caregivers will encourage you to labor in water if that's an option in the birthing facility you've chosen, the majority will encourage you to hop out of the tub when it's time to start pushing.

- Don't be concerned if you're too exhausted to bond with your baby right away. There will be plenty of time to enjoy your precious newborn during the days and weeks ahead.

GET THE SCOOP ON. . .

How you may be feeling physically ▪ Postnatal fitness ▪ How you may be feeling emotionally ▪ Sex after baby ▪ What babies are really like ▪ Getting breastfeeding off to the best possible start ▪ Caring for a premature baby or a baby with special needs

The Postpartum Survival Guide

No matter how much time you've spent reading up on babies or how much time you've spent around newborns, nothing can really prepare you for the joys and challenges of the first weeks of your baby's life. Some new moms and dads recall the early days of parenthood as a wondrous time. Others feel completely overwhelmed by the demands of caring for a tiny, helpless human being. It's impossible to predict ahead of time how the postpartum period will play out for you, so your best bet is to simply expect the unexpected!

Of course, it never hurts to arm yourself with the facts on the key challenges you're likely to face during the early weeks after your baby's birth, which is where this chapter fits in. We've made a point of zeroing in on the areas of key concern to new parents: postpartum recovery, the "baby blues" versus postpartum depression, postnatal fitness, sex after baby, newborn behavior, and so on. Here goes. . . .

Chapter 19

Your postpartum body: An owner's manual

Your body went through a remarkable series of transformations while you were pregnant. Now your body is busy reversing those changes as it begins returning to a nonpregnant state. Here's what you can expect to experience from a physical standpoint during the postpartum period.

Weight loss

Forget all those miracle diets: you'll never lose weight more effortlessly than you do during the postpartum period. (Okay, it's not quite effortless: you do have to go through labor, after all. But you get the point.) Anyway, by the time your six-week checkup rolls around, you will probably be 17 to 20 pounds lighter than you were at the time you went into labor. You will probably have at least a few extra pounds to lose — just as Mother Nature intended you to have. (Just a quick reminder: Despite what the celebrity mamas would have you believe, new mothers are *supposed* to have a bit of extra padding. The reason? So that they will have a fuel supply on hand for breastfeeding their babies. Clearly, the super-skinny movie star who manages to slip into her designer pre-pregnancy jeans for the ride home from the hospital is the exception rather than the rule. The majority of new moms look five to six months pregnant during the first week after the delivery.

> **❝**It took about three months before I could wear most of my pre-pregnancy clothing. Even though I lost all but five pounds by the time my baby was six weeks old, my weight was somehow rearranged.**❞**
>
> — Susan, 34, mother of one

Afterpains

The reason you still look six months pregnant is because your uterus is just beginning the process of returning to its pre-pregnant size (a process known as involution). During the first few weeks of the postpartum period, your uterus will alternately relax and contract. While this is happening, you may experience afterpains, which can range in intensity from virtually unnoticeable to downright painful. These afterpains tend to be more intense while you are nursing because the baby's sucking triggers the release of oxytocin, the hormone responsible for causing the uterus to contract.

Afterpains should not be confused with the symptoms of a serious infection or hemorrhage: extreme tenderness; severe, persistent cramping; or heavy bleeding. If you experience any of these symptoms, contact your doctor or midwife immediately.

Lochia

The term *lochia* refers to the discharge that occurs as the uterus sheds its lining after the birth. It typically lasts anywhere from 10 days to 6 weeks, starting out as a bright red, heavy flow, tapering down to a pinky-brown watery flow, and then becoming an almost colorless or yellowish discharge. Note: Many women find that their lochia turns bright red again if they engage in too much activity too soon.

If you notice that your discharge suddenly becomes extremely heavy (that is, you soak more than one pad over the course of an hour) or it develops an extremely unpleasant odor, contact your caregiver immediately. You could be experiencing a postpartum hemorrhage or uterine infection.

Changes to the vagina

If you had a vaginal delivery, your vagina may feel stretched and tender during the weeks after the delivery, but it will soon return to its prepregnant state. Kegel exercises can help the process along and may prevent incontinence and gynecological problems.

Perineal pain

Your perineum is likely to be tender during the first few days after a vaginal birth — particularly if you had an episiotomy or a significant tear. This is because swelling in the perineal area can cause your stitches to pull, something that can be quite painful, to say the least.

To reduce perineal pain, try one of the following techniques:

- Place ice in a washcloth or rubber glove and apply it to the swollen area (this technique is most effective during the first 12 to 24 hours after the delivery).
- Soak in a warm tub (either a bathtub or a sitz bath).
- Use a blow dryer to dry and warm your perineum.

Weakness in the pelvic floor muscles

The muscle that controls the openings of the vagina, urethra, and anus is stretched during both pregnancy and birth. If muscle tone isn't restored to the area, you may experience decreased vaginal tone; urinary incontinence; or gynecological problems such as uterine, bladder, or rectal prolapse. (These problems are typically characterized by symptoms of pelvic pressure, an uncomfortable protrusion of tissues from the vaginal opening, painful or uncomfortable intercourse, and the disruption of normal bladder and bowel function.) You can avoid many of these problems by doing your Kegel exercises religiously — something that's recommended even if you had a cesarean delivery.

Problems with urination

After months of running to the bathroom every couple of minutes, you may suddenly find yourself faced with the opposite problem: a decreased urge to urinate. There are a number of reasons why you could experience this problem after the birth:

- Drugs and anesthesia used during the delivery may temporarily decrease the sensitivity of the bladder or your alertness to its signals.

- A low fluid intake both before and during labor, combined with an excessive loss of fluids through perspiration, vomiting, or bleeding, may mean that you simply don't need to urinate.

- Perineal pain may cause reflex spasms in the urethra (the tube that carries urine from the bladder), something that can make urination difficult.

- You may be afraid to urinate, fearing that the flow of urine over your perineum will be painful. (If this is the case, you might want to try urinating while you are sitting on the toilet saddle-style, when you are standing upright in the shower, or while you are pouring water across your perineum. And here's another idea: try drinking plenty of fluids so that your urine will be highly diluted and consequently less acidic.)

You can jump-start your waterworks by contracting and relaxing the pelvic area several times to stimulate the urethral response, running water, drinking lots of fluids, and placing hot or cold packs on your perineum — whichever one triggers your urge to urinate.

 Watch Out!

If you experience internal burning after urination or an intense, painful, and unusually frequent urge to urinate, you may have a urinary tract infection. Contact your caregiver to arrange for treatment.

Bowel movements

It's not unusual to go two or three days without a bowel movement after you've given birth. This is because decreased muscle tone in the intestines, prelabor diarrhea, a lack of food during labor, perineal tenderness, and painful hemorrhoids may reduce your need (or your willingness) to have a bowel movement.

If you are having problems with constipation, increase your intake of fluids and fiber and make a point of remaining physically active. That usually takes care or the problem. (Note: If you're not up to a major workout yet, simply pop your baby into the carriage or the baby carrier and go for a walk around the block. Sometimes getting active is all that's required to get your bowels moving more regularly again.) If that doesn't work, you may want to ask your doctor or pharmacist to recommend a stool softener or a laxative to help get things moving again.

Breast changes

Even before you gave birth, your breasts were busy producing colostrum — your baby's first food. Sometime during the second or third day postpartum, your milk will come in. Your breasts can become very swollen and engorged during the 24 to 48 hours after that, regardless of whether or not you are nursing. You may also leak milk both during and in between feedings — a problem that is easily remedied by a hefty package of breast pads.

If you are breastfeeding, you can deal with engorgement by putting the baby to the breast more frequently or running warm water over your breasts and expressing just enough milk to relieve your discomfort. (If you express a lot of milk, you'll simply add to your woes by stimulating more milk production.)

If you're bottle-feeding, you should keep your breasts tightly bound in a supportive bra (or two) and use ice packs, analgesics, or both to relieve the discomfort. Resist the temptation to express milk because you'll only prolong your misery: your body will increase milk production if it thinks that the milk is needed by your baby.

Sore nipples

If you are breastfeeding, you may experience some nipple tenderness during the first few days of nursing — particularly if your baby is a particularly frequent or vigorous nurser.

The best way to treat sore nipples is to expose them to air and sunlight (or a heat lamp, if you're not into nude sunbathing). Walk around with the flaps of your nursing bra open, and stick with cotton — rather than synthetic — fabrics.

If nipple soreness doesn't disappear by the end of the first week, it's possible that a positioning problem is to blame for your discomfort. If in doubt, ask a lactation consultant, your local La Leche League leader, or an experienced breastfeeding mother to give you a second opinion on your positioning.

Cesarean recovery

If you've had a cesarean birth, you may experience tenderness around your incision site, gas pains in your upper chest and shoulders, and fatigue. It's important to give yourself time to rest and recover. You've just been through major abdominal surgery, after all.

The new you

Some of the changes your body experienced during pregnancy are permanent: your stretch marks won't fade away entirely, and your vagina may feel slacker than it did before. Other changes are temporary: your flabby abdomen will eventually tighten up (with a little work on your part), and the day will come when you won't be dripping milk wherever you go. In the meantime, when you look at yourself in the mirror, remind yourself that

 Bright Idea

Looking for some advice on dressing the part of the new mama? Download a copy of "Postpartum Diva: Fashion After Baby" from www.having-a-baby.com/ article.htm#tip_pdfs.

you're not out of shape — you're in perfect shape for someone who has just had a baby.

Postnatal fitness

Some women are eager to start a postnatal fitness program right after the birth. Others prefer to use any baby-free moments to catch up on their sleep.

If you're one of those highly motivated moms who manage to get their act together right after the delivery, be sure to take things slowly. Your body organs, system, and joints have undergone a tremendous amount of stress over the past nine months. Here are some tips on putting together an exercise program that's both safe and effective:

- Don't expect to be able to resume your prepregnancy fitness workout right away. Give yourself time to build up to your previous fitness level gradually. Stick to brisk walks and light workouts during the first two weeks postpartum. After that, you can resume moderate physical activity, provided that you listen to your body if it tells you that you're working it too hard.

- Rather than complicating things by trying to time your workout between feedings or arranging childcare, find ways to include your baby in your workout. Push your baby in his stroller while you walk or run, take a baby aerobics class (where moms and babies are given opportunities to play together while the mother works out), or pop him in the baby carrier while you ride on a stationary exercise bike. (Obviously, you'll want to keep the cycling pace relatively calm. Your newborn won't appreciate being invited to tag along to spin cycling class!)

> ❝I resumed my fitness program when my son was three months old. I simply used workout videos in my own living room while he was asleep.❞
>
> — Mary, 27, mother of one

- Wear a sports bra or two nursing bras to provide your breasts with the support they need. If you are nursing, you may be more comfortable if you breastfeed your baby right before exercising.

- If you're having problems with incontinence, hit the bathroom before you start exercising and wear a panty liner to guard against leakage during your workout. Note: Your problems with incontinence should disappear over time if you're diligent about doing your Kegel exercises.

> 66 My husband and I love running together. After our baby was born, we bought a baby jogging stroller. It was a great way to make sure that we got to exercise together. 99
>
> — Lynne, 32, mother of one

- Make sure that your exercise program includes the following components: a warm-up, a cardiovascular workout, strength training, flexibility training, and a cool-down. It should also include Kegels (to strengthen the muscles in your pelvic floor) and abdominal exercises such as curl-ups (to strengthen the muscles that support your stomach and your lower back).

- Don't overdo it. Joint laxity (looseness) can be a problem for the first few months after you give birth. To minimize the risk of injury, you'll want to perform all movements with caution and control; avoid jumping, rapid changes of direction, and bouncing or jarring motions; and eliminate deep flexion or extension of joints from your workout for now. You'll also want to avoid knee-chest exercises, full sit-ups, and double leg lifts during the postpartum period.

- Skip your workout if you're feeling particularly exhausted. Fatigue can lead to poor technique and possible injury.

- Drink plenty of fluids before, during, and after your workout.

Bright Idea

Hire a personal trainer to design a postnatal fitness program you can do in your own home. If you can afford it, arrange to have the trainer come back regularly to do your workout with you.

- Stop exercising immediately and consult with a healthcare professional if you experience any of the following symptoms: pain, faintness, dizziness, blurred vision, shortness of breath, heart palpitations, back pain, pubic pain, nausea, difficulty walking, or a sudden increase in vaginal bleeding.

- To increase your strength and endurance, make a habit of exercising regularly — ideally two to three times per week.

- Resist the temptation to diet — particularly if you're breastfeeding. You need an adequate intake of calories to cope with the demands of motherhood. Rather than drastically restricting your food intake, simply make healthier choices. (Note: See Chapter 6 for information on basic nutrition.)

What's going on with your head

As if the physical changes of new motherhood weren't enough to contend with, you may find yourself experiencing a lot of conflicting emotions during the postpartum period. One moment you may feel totally euphoric about being blessed with such a beautiful baby, and the next you may be in tears because you can't even find 10 minutes to yourself to take a shower.

You are also likely to have some other important issues to sort through at this stage of your life: your feelings about the birth, your feelings about not being pregnant anymore, your feelings about your body, and your feelings about becoming a mother. In this next section of the chapter, we touch upon each of these all-important issues.

Your feelings about the birth

If your baby's birth followed your birth plan to the letter, you're probably euphoric about the way things went. If they didn't, you may be disappointed or angry about the way things went.

Leila, a 34-year-old mother of one, initially found it hard to accept the fact that she ended up with a cesarean section rather than the natural childbirth she had hoped for: "I hated myself for having a c-section. I was disappointed with what I perceived as my failure."

Women whose babies arrive prematurely often express similar feelings of disappointment. "I was sad when my first pregnancy ended because she was nearly seven weeks early," recalls Marilyn, a 43-year-old mother of three. "Physically and emotionally, I wasn't ready to let her go so early." Therese, a 31-year-old mother of one, experienced similar feelings: "I had the baby a month early and felt like I had been 'robbed' of a month of my pregnancy."

If you are not happy about some aspect of your birth, share your feelings with your partner, your caregiver, your doula, other support people who were at the birth, a trusted friend, or a therapist. It's important to resolve your feelings about such an important event in your life.

Your feelings about not being pregnant anymore

Some women feel a certain sadness after they give birth. Although they are delighted to have their babies, they miss being pregnant: "I missed feeling the baby move inside me," explains Therese.

Not every woman feels this way, of course. Some women are positively delighted to have their pregnancies behind them: "I was so relieved not to be pregnant anymore," admits Anne, a 39-year-old mother of three. "I don't do pregnancy well."

Many women, like Mary, a 27-year-old mother of one, report a mix of emotions: "I felt both sad not to be pregnant anymore and glad to have my body back," she explains. "I missed the closeness and almost spiritual connectedness I felt while this baby was growing inside of me. I missed the warm looks I got from almost everyone, the attention, my own feeling of purpose and anticipation. But having my body back into shape and being able to wear the clothes I want, be sexy, be physically active, and even sip the occasional glass of wine is great."

Your feelings about your body

The first time you take a shower after having a baby, you may feel wonderfully slim. Gone is the huge stomach you've been carrying around for months, and you can even see your feet again.

Your feelings of svelteness are likely to last until you either try on a pair of prepregnancy pants or get a sideways glance at yourself in the mirror.

Some women find it hard to accept that they still look pregnant immediately after the delivery: "I felt very negative towards my body during the postpartum period," recalls Lisa, a 26-year-old mother of one. "It was very depressing to still have to wear those awful maternity pants when I wasn't pregnant anymore. I tried on a pair of my prepregnancy jeans a couple of days after I gave birth and almost burst into tears."

Other women — even those who have had a love-hate relationship with their bodies for much of their adult lives — finally make peace with their bodies.

> ❝The first days after my c-section, I felt this incredible, amazing love and respect and appreciation for my body and my gender. I was so proud of myself for having sustained that magnificent life in my body for nine months and given birth to her. I felt so beautiful and powerful — like I could climb Mount Everest.❞
>
> — Jennifer, 25, mother of one

"I developed the most incredible respect, admiration, and sense of awe toward my body after the birth of my first child," says Marilyn, 43, who is currently expecting her third child. "Until I had a child, I knew nothing of my body's innate capabilities and how much it could do without my help. First it conceived and nurtured a fetus; then it birthed that child; then it fed that child in a way I could not have designed — first with colostrum and then with rich, nutritious milk in just the right amounts at the right times. I no longer looked at the outward flaws of my body; what I now felt was close to worship."

Jennifer, a 21-year-old first-time mother, experienced similar feelings: "I was in total amazement with my body after I had my daughter. I couldn't believe that my body had helped produce that beautiful baby. It was the most amazing thing."

Your feelings about becoming a mother

For first-time mothers, the biggest challenge of the postpartum period is adjusting to the fact that you are now someone's mother.

Mary, a 27-year-old first-time mother, remembers wishing that she was still pregnant: "In the first weeks after he was born, I felt overwhelmed by motherhood and longed for the days when he was safely tucked inside and all I had to do was dream and plan."

Jennifer, 25, who felt so empowered by the act of giving birth, resented the way her life changed after her baby's birth. "I felt like my life was over, like a life-term prison sentence had begun, and I hated my new role as mother and housewife."

Others are stunned to discover how quickly they begin to fall in love with their babies. "I remember being consumed with love for my first baby soon after she was born," recalls 43-year-old Marilyn. "I was in awe of and terrified of her power over me. I never felt so vulnerable in my love for another human being. What if something should happen to her? Would I survive?"

With this bond came a change in focus for Marilyn, a rethinking of priorities: "The moment I gave birth to her, an unexpected, involuntary transition took place. The universe no longer centered around me and what I wanted; instead, I stepped aside and placed her life and her well-being in the forefront."

> **❝** I think the biggest thing about being a parent is how your perception of the world, yourself, and others changes. You are never able to watch a story involving a tragedy with a child without a lump in your throat, and you have sympathy for the lady in the supermarket with the child having a temper tantrum. **❞**
>
> — Jodi, 30, mother of two

Suzi, a 27-year-old mother of two, also views the moment she became a parent as a turning point in her life: "Becoming a parent has truly changed my life for the better. Everything I do has more meaning now. I work to provide for my children, I exercise so I can mentally handle being a mother and physically live longer and healthier to be here for my children. The house we bought, the neighborhood we live in, the cars we drive are all for our children. I want nothing more than to love my children and provide a nurturing environment for them to live in. I can't say one negative thing about parenting."

The baby blues versus postpartum depression

Given the massive physical and emotional challenges of the postpartum period, it's hardly surprising that some women report feeling depressed in the days following the delivery — the so-called baby blues.

"The day after giving birth — perhaps as a response to the incredible euphoria I'd experienced immediately after delivery and because of lack of sleep — I plunged into an abyss," confesses Marilyn, 43, who is currently pregnant with her third child. "I felt completely overwhelmed at the thought of taking care of a new baby — I felt completely inadequate and unprepared to do so. This feeling lasted for perhaps a week with both my babies."

If those feelings of inadequacy and depression last for longer than two weeks, leave you feeling completely exhausted or highly anxious, result in sleeping or eating disturbances, cause you to feel helpless or suicidal, or affect your ability to care for your newborn, you could be suffering from postpartum depression.

For some women, postpartum depression hits right after the birth: "I had major postpartum depression that started as soon as the baby was born," recalls Allison, 27, a mother of one. "I had to be put on antidepressants because I was so depressed that I wanted nothing to do with the baby. Thank God it finally subsided. But it lasted for about three months."

Others find that there's a delay before postpartum depression sets in: "I suffered from postpartum depression quite badly with all three pregnancies," recalls Karen, a 34-year-old mother of three. "It didn't kick in for a couple of months. I ended up getting help after my third child was born. I came to understand that I needed to drop some of my standards and accept that it was okay to use prepared foods sometimes, that I was entitled to sit with a latte for half an hour, and that, generally, I was doing a pretty good job."

"I didn't know I had postpartum depression until about eight months after the baby was born," says Anne, a 39-year-old mother of three. "I just realized I wasn't feeling spunky, happy, giggly, or sexy."

 Bright Idea

You can get a pretty clear indication of whether or not you're suffering from postpartum depression as opposed to "the baby blues" by using the Edinburgh Postpartum Depression Scale. You can find a copy of this scale online at www.childbirthsolutions.com/articles/postpartum/epds/index.php.

If you suspect that you are experiencing postpartum depression, it's important to seek help from your caregiver. You may also benefit from joining a postpartum-depression support group and sharing your experiences with other moms. You should also talk to your partner about how you are feeling. Not only will it give you a chance to express your feelings: it'll give you a chance to find out how he's doing. A study reported in the *American Journal of Psychiatry* found that 3 percent of fathers exhibit clear signs of depression after their babies are born. Men whose partners were suffering from postpartum depression were found to be at particular risk of experiencing depression themselves.

> **66** Once I realized that I was dealing with postpartum depression, I was able to blame myself less. **99**
> — Stephanie, 25, mother of one

Sex after baby

Although your caregiver will likely give you the go-ahead to resume sexual relations anywhere from two weeks until six weeks after your baby's birth, you may find that soreness in your perineal area, tenderness at the site of your cesarean incision, heavy lochia, or the mind-numbing fatigue that is so characteristic of the first few weeks postpartum serve to dampen your enthusiasm for sex at least for a while.

Here's what some of the parents we interviewed for this book had to say about sex after baby:

■ "It took my husband and me a long time to resume our sex life. At first, we were just so completely exhausted. Sex was the last thing on our minds for about two months postpartum. Finally, at three months postpartum, things started calming down. The baby was sleeping more regularly, and we both were more rested."

- "Often by the end of the day, I am 'touched out.' A nursing baby and a couple of other young children need a lot of physical contact. For my husband's sake, we began having sex again about two months after the baby was born. Once things got started, I enjoyed myself, but I had little desire to initiate things on my own."

- "To be honest, my desire for sex was absolutely nil until the baby was about nine months old. Then it finally started to return."

- "I lost my sex drive and still do not have it back fully after nine months. I love my husband dearly, but at night I just want to go to sleep and not worry about sex. We probably had sex about once a month from when our daughter was two months old until about eight months, and now it is getting better. It was really uncomfortable for about six months afterwards. We needed lots of lubrication because otherwise it was just painful."

- "Honestly, for the first year after the baby was born, I couldn't have cared less if we ever had sex again. I just didn't feel sexy."

Even when the urge does resurface, some new parents find that their initial postbaby sexual experiences are anything but satisfying: "Our first attempt at intercourse was dreadful," recalls one first-time mother. "I had two significant tears, and even though they healed perfectly, I had a lot of pain when we tried intercourse. We tried lubricants, I tried relaxing, but nothing worked. We had several abandoned attempts over the course of a few weeks. My husband was very understanding, but I was very distressed and usually ended up crying. Finally, we decided to stop trying intercourse for a while, and expressed our intimacy in different ways. This helped immensely, both emotionally and physically. We were able to resume actual intercourse by six months postpartum, and it was completely pain-free for me then."

Not all couples find that having a baby puts a crimp in their sexual style, however. Here's what one first-time mother had to say: "My husband and I started having sex again after two weeks. A little early, maybe, but we found creative ways to make it work. I've heard women say that they really had to plan for sex now that they have babies, but we found that the opposite was true: we perfected the quickie — anytime, anywhere, anyhow — because the baby slept so much."

Just because you'd rather sleep than cuddle up to your partner doesn't mean that your sex life is a thing of the past. Take it from this experienced mother: "First-time parents should realize that the frequency of sex will probably decrease significantly for the first few months. I know parents who didn't have sex for five months. However, things do get better."

> **❝**I didn't know the meaning of the word 'tired' until after the baby was born. Utter exhaustion that words cannot describe.**❞**
> — Kim, 35, mother of one

Note: Unless you're planning to hit the reproductive jackpot again right away, you'll want to give careful thought to birth control before things start getting hot and heavy in the bedroom. You can get the lowdown on postbaby contraception in "Your Next Pregnancy" (www.wiley.com/go/anndouglas).

The truth about babies

If you've never been around a newborn baby before, you may be surprised by your baby's sleeping, eating, elimination, and crying patterns. Here's a sneak peek at what you can expect to experience during the first few weeks of your baby's life.

Sleeping

A long day of parenthood is finally drawing to a close. You abandon your plans to fold that last load of laundry, heading for bed instead. You no sooner fall into a deep sleep when you're awakened by the only member of your family who seems to be getting enough rest: your baby!

If you're feeling a bit frazzled and exhausted by your baby's erratic sleep patterns, it's certainly for good reason: newborn babies typically sleep about 16 or 17 hours per day, but rarely for more than a few hours at a time. Luckily, your baby's sleep patterns will start to become a little less erratic over time. By the time your baby is three to six months old, he will have switched to a circadian rhythm and will be getting the bulk of his shut-eye at night rather than during the day.

It's at this point that most babies are ready to start sleeping through the night. According to pediatrician Dr. Alan Greene, babies are able to make this transition more easily if their parents have prepared the proper groundwork during their first weeks of life. Greene recommends that parents teach their babies the difference between night and day by exposing their babies to normal household noise during their waking hours and by engaging them in plenty of direct eye contact — something that babies find particularly stimulating.

"The most powerful wake-up activity is direct eye contact," Greene says. "When your baby locks eyes with you, it's almost like she's drinking a double latte. Her heart beat speeds up, her blood pressure rises a bit, and she becomes more awake."

Greene suggests that parents stroke their babies' feet during the daytime, because he says this stimulates the pineal gland, which helps in the regulation of the body's circadian rhythms. At night, the amount of stimulation should be kept to a minimum,

 Watch Out!

Don't lay your baby on his stomach when you tuck him into bed. The American Academy of Pediatrics recommends that babies be placed on their backs when they are sleeping — a position that has been proven to reduce the risk of Sudden Infant Death Syndrome.

and parents should rely upon a series of prebedtime rituals designed to cue the baby to the fact that the Sandman awaits.

Whereas some babies start sleeping through the night largely on their own, others seem determined to stubbornly resist their parents' attempts to encourage them to abandon their nocturnal habits. Still, although it can be exhausting to have your sleep disrupted night after night, not everyone sees parenting a night-waking baby as a problem. Some parents — particularly ones with other children who demand their time and attention by day — may actually cherish a few stolen moments alone with their baby in the wee hours of the morning. Others — although not exactly overjoyed at the prospect of losing sleep — simply accept the fact that the baby is not yet ready to sleep through the night, and resolve to make the most of the situation while they wait for their baby's sleep patterns to mature.

The secret to making it through the newborn period without turning into a total zombie is to sleep when the baby sleeps — and to remind yourself that your life won't be like this forever. Studies have shown that 90 percent of babies will sleep six to eight hours at a stretch by the time they reach three months of age.

Eating

Whether your baby is breastfed or bottle-fed, he is going to spend a lot of time eating. Babies this age need to eat frequently in order to ensure that their small stomachs receive an adequate number of calories over the course of the day. Breastfed newborns typically nurse 12 times per day, and bottle-fed newborns usually eat at least eight times per day.

When you stop to consider the fact that the entire feeding cycle (feeding, burping, and diapering) can take as long as an hour, it quickly becomes apparent that a good part of your day is going to be spent feeding and caring for your baby. If you're breastfeeding, you may want to consider taking the baby into

Bright Idea

A baby who sleeps all day needs to nurse more frequently at night. Try to encourage your baby to nurse at least every three hours during the daytime so that, over time, he will learn to reserve his longest stretch of sleep for the time of day when you need him to sleep most — the middle of the night.

bed with you for a middle-of-the-night feeding. If you're bottle-feeding, you may want to trade off middle-of-the-night feedings with your partner. If you get the midnight feeding and your partner gets the 3:00 a.m. feeding, you each have a fighting chance of getting four or five consecutive hours of sleep.

Elimination

Ever wonder why the newborn packages of disposable diapers are sold in packages of 40? It's because newborns go through a phenomenal number of diapers during the first few weeks of life. During the first six weeks of life, most babies have at least one bowel movement a day — although some may have as many as 15. What's more, a typical newborn urinates 20 to 30 times each day, which means that you'll want to change your baby's diaper at regular intervals throughout the day. (This doesn't mean you should panic if your baby only has six wet diapers each day, however. He may have urinated three or four times since you last changed him — just not enough to soak through his diaper.)

The appearance of your baby's diapers will change tremendously during the first few weeks. His first stools — made up of a greenish-black, sticky substance known as meconium — will be passed during the first day or two of life. During the next few weeks, your baby's stools will become greenish-brown and semi-liquid. Sometimes these so-called "transitional stools" are bright green and full of milk curds and mucus. When your baby gets to be about three weeks old, his stools will change again. Breastfed babies will develop orangey-yellow stools that are mustardlike in

Bright Idea

Hang an empty plastic bag off the side of your baby's change table. As he out-grows outfits, wash them and then put them in another bag. When the bag is full, tie it closed and write the size and sex of baby clothes on the bag. That way, when it comes time to sell or reuse the garments, they'll all be organized according to size.

appearance and smell faintly of sour milk. Bottle-fed babies will develop solid, pale-brown bowel movements that have a stronger odor.

By the time he reaches six weeks of age, a breastfed baby may be having as few as one bowel movement a week. This is because breast milk leaves very little solid waste to be eliminated from your baby's digestive system. Breastfed babies rarely experience problems with constipation. Any bowel movement that is looser than the consistency of peanut butter is perfectly normal for a breastfed baby.

Bottle-fed babies are more likely to experience problems with constipation than breastfed babies. As a rule of thumb, bottle-fed babies should have at least one bowel movement per day. If your baby goes for more than a day without a bowel movement or appears to be straining, he may be constipated. Call your caregiver for advice.

Don't be alarmed if you notice a pinkish stain on your baby's diaper. This stain is usually a sign of highly concentrated urine, which has a pinkish color. As long as the baby is having at least four wet diapers per day, there's probably no need for concern, but if the pinkish staining persists or you notice any bright-red blood, get in touch with your baby's doctor.

Crying

The baby who sleeps all the time in the hospital and never utters so much as a whimper often has a surprise in store for his parents a week or two down the road. Long periods of crying typically set in during the second or third week of life, peaking in duration and frequency at about the six-week mark. Many babies have at least one daily crying session of 15 to 60 minutes that cannot easily be explained. More often than not, it hits in the evening when you want nothing more than to eat your dinner in peace or to curl up in bed with a book.

Your baby's cry is designed to elicit a powerful response in you so that you will respond to his needs right away. But while colic may be an effective anthropological tool for encouraging parents to spend time with their babies, it's easy to lose sight of its advantages when you've spent the past three hours walking a baby who is inconsolable. If your baby develops full-fledged colic (crying for at least three hours per day that occurs at least three days per week and that typically lasts until the baby is three months of age), you may be desperate to find a way to soothe your baby.

Here are some techniques that have worked for other parents:

- rocking your baby (either in a rocking chair or in your arms as you sway from side to side);

- laying your baby tummy-down across your knees and gently rubbing his back (the pressure against his abdomen may help relieve his discomfort);

- gently stroking your baby's head or patting her back or chest;

- swaddling your baby snugly in a receiving blanket;

- singing or talking to your baby, or playing soft music;

- walking around with the baby in your arms, in a baby carrier (for example, a sling or Snugli), or in a stroller;

Moneysaver

Rather than purchasing a commercially manufactured baby-soother tape, make one of your own. Record "white noise" sounds that your baby finds particularly soothing: the dishwasher, the hair dryer, the vacuum cleaner, and so on.

- taking your baby for a ride in the car;
- putting your baby in a baby swing (ideally a battery-operated model that doesn't need winding);
- exposing your baby to white noise (that is, low-level background noise like the sound that a vacuum cleaner or blow dryer makes);
- burping your baby to get rid of any trapped gas bubbles;
- bathing your baby in warm water.

If none of these techniques works, it could be because your baby is exhausted. Some babies engage in "discharge crying" when they are tired. They are inconsolable until you lay them in their cribs, at which point they fall into a deep sleep within a minute or two. (If you try this and your baby doesn't settle within five minutes or so, there's probably something else bothering him.)

Food sensitivities also contribute to fussiness in some babies. If you are nursing, try eliminating any foods that could be contributing to your baby's fussiness. Perennial offenders include dairy products, caffeine, onions, and cabbage. (Note: You'll want to try eliminating one type of food at a time rather than putting yourself on starvation rations in an attempt to avoid any potentially controversial food.) If you are bottle-feeding, try switching from a milk-based formula to a soy-based formula to see if that helps with the problem. If food sensitivities are causing your baby's fussiness, you should see a marked improvement within a day or two of eliminating the problem food.

 Bright Idea

If you feel that you're reaching your wits' end, have someone else care for your baby for an hour or two so that you can have a break. Even though you may feel guilty for leaving your baby in someone else's care and worry that no one else will be able to meet his needs as you can, it's important to recharge your parental batteries on a regular basis.

Note: You can learn more about newborn behavior by reading *The Mother of All Baby Books* (John Wiley and Sons, 2002) by Ann Douglas — one of the authors of this book.

Getting breastfeeding off to the best possible start

As we mentioned in the previous chapter, newborns are particularly alert during the first hour after birth. If you're intending to breastfeed, this is the ideal time to try to establish a breastfeeding relationship.

The first time

The majority of healthy babies are born with a strong rooting reflex — a reflex that makes them open their mouth wide and move their mouth frantically in search of a nipple. You can stimulate your baby's reflex and encourage him to latch on by gently stroking his lower lip with the nipple. Your baby will then open his mouth widely, at which point you can move him toward your breast.

When your baby takes your nipple into his mouth, his jaws should close around the areola (the flat, pigmented area surrounding the nipple) rather than on the nipple itself. You can help him to latch on properly by grasping your breast with one thumb above the areola and the fingers and palms below it, and then gently compressing your breast. You can then direct your nipple into the baby's mouth. The nipple should be level or pointed slightly downward to avoid having it rub on the roof of your baby's mouth.

> 66 Nursing is so much more than a method of feeding: It's a whole way of mothering. 99
>
> — Tracy, 31, mother of one

Let the baby nurse at the first breast for as long as he likes, and then put him on the other side until he stops nursing by himself.

You can tell that your baby is nursing properly (rather than just playing with the nipple) if you

- experience the let-down reflex (a tingling or tightening in your nipple that occurs as your milk is ejected);

- hear swallowing sounds (a sign that she is engaging in vigorous "nutritive sucking" rather than the more relaxed "non-nutritive sucking" — a source of emotional comfort to young babies);

- feel uterine cramping (something you will experience only during the first few days postpartum and might not experience much at all if this is your first baby);

- notice that your baby falls asleep after nursing and appears to be satisfied with the amount of food he received.

How breastfeeding works

Your baby's sucking movements trigger a series of complex biochemical responses in your body:

- The stimulation of the nerve fibers in your nipple signals your pituitary gland that your baby needs to be fed.

- In response to this stimulation, the pituitary gland releases prolactin (a hormone that stimulates the breasts to produce more milk) and oxytocin (a hormone that stimulates contractions of the tiny muscles surrounding the ducts in your breasts, ejecting the milk into the reservoir under the areola — the so-called let-down reflex). It generally takes about two to three minutes for the let-down reflex to kick in during your first few feedings. Within a week or two, however, the reflex will speed up considerably and your milk supply will increase dramatically.

Part of the beauty of breastfeeding is the fact that it works on the basis of supply and demand. Your body knows exactly how much milk to produce to meet your baby's needs. It also knows what type of milk your baby requires at his or her particular developmental stage.

Bright Idea

If colostrum or milk flows from one breast while your baby is sucking on the other, you can feel confident that your let-down reflex is working as it should. If you want to slow the flow of milk from your other breast, gently press on it with the palm of your hand.

The food your baby will receive during the first few feedings is colostrum — a yellowish substance that contains protective white blood cells capable of attacking harmful bacteria. It is high in protein and low in sugar and fat — an ideal first food for your baby.

Within a couple of days, your milk will come in. When it comes in, your breasts may feel hot and extremely full of milk. If your breasts become overly full (that is, you experience engorgement), you can relieve some of the pressure by manually expressing a small amount of milk while you are in the shower. Sometimes the warm water from the shower will cause your milk to let down on its own. (Of course, if you are putting the baby to the breast frequently, engorgement is less likely to be a problem.)

Just one quick word of caution: Don't express too much milk or you'll simply perpetuate the problem. Your body will think it needs to produce the same vast quantity of milk in the future in order to feed your baby.

> ❝I was not prepared for the problems that sometimes occur when you are starting to breastfeed. With my first child, I got very discouraged and quit. I have always felt badly about this, and I think that if I had been better prepared, it might have worked out for us.❞
>
> — Johnna, 33, mother of three

Here are some other tips on managing engorgement:

- Wear a well-fitting nursing bra.

- Nurse your baby at least once every one to three hours —
  whenever he is hungry — and offer both breasts at each
  feeding unless your lactation consultant has recommended otherwise. Encourage your baby to nurse for 10
  to 20 minutes or longer at each breast.

- Gently massage the breast at which your baby is nursing
  in order to encourage the milk to start flowing and to
  relieve some of the tightness and discomfort you may be
  experiencing.

- If your areola is extremely firm, express a bit of milk from
  your nipple before you allow your baby to latch on. This
  will help prevent nipple soreness.

- If you are feeling particularly uncomfortable, take acetaminophen tablets or other pain-relief medications prescribed by your caregiver. (Fortunately, this type of
  discomfort tends to be relatively short-lived.)

Aches and pains

You may experience some tenderness during the early days of
breastfeeding — especially during the first minute or two of
nursing, when the baby first latches on and pulls the nipple into
his mouth. If, however, you experience extreme soreness (if you
are reluctant to put your baby to the breast because it hurts too
much), you could be positioning your baby incorrectly.

 Watch Out!

Babies who are given bottles or pacifiers before they've mastered the art of
breastfeeding sometimes experience nipple confusion — a problem that can
interfere with the establishment of breastfeeding. If you're committed to
breastfeeding your baby, talk to your caregiver about what you can do to
ensure that your baby is not inadvertently offered a bottle or a pacifier by one
of his caregivers.

Here are a few tips on troubleshooting some common positioning problems:

- If your nipples are tender, bruised, scabbed, or blistered at the tip, the tip of your nipple is probably rubbing against the roof of your baby's mouth while he is nursing.

- If your nipple is tender or cracked at or near the base, it could be because your baby's gums are closing on the nipple rather than the areola — either because he isn't opening his mouth widely enough when he first latches on, because he is slipping off the areola onto the nipple (a common problem if the breast is engorged), or because he has developed thrush (a yeast infection in the mouth that will need to be treated with antibiotics).

- If the undersides of your nipples are sore, this could be because your baby is nursing with his bottom lip tucked in. You can correct this problem by pulling the baby's bottom lip out several times during each feeding until he gets the hang of things.

- If your nipples are red, slightly swollen, and feel burning hot, you could have nipple dermatitis — a reaction to a substance that has come into contact with your nipples (for example, vitamin E preparations, lanolin, or cocoa butter). The best thing to put on sore or irritated breasts is breast milk. Just express a bit of breast milk at the end of a feeding and rub it on your nipples. Creams and lotions are unnecessary and merely contribute to other breastfeeding problems.

- If your nipples are red, swollen, itchy, tender, or cracked and you find tiny curds stuck to them, you and your baby may have a thrush infection. (You can usually confirm this diagnosis by looking inside your baby's mouth. If you find white patches on his tongue, his cheeks, the insides of his lips, and his gums, he probably has a yeast infection. A few babies don't show any symptoms in the mouth but develop a painful diaper rash that resembles a mild burn.) Some newborn babies pick up yeast infections in the birth canal during delivery — something that frequently happens if the mother is diabetic. A thrush infection can also be triggered if the mother and baby are given antibiotics during or after the delivery. If you and your baby develop problems with thrush, you will both need to be treated with an antifungal such as nystatin or gentian violet — a substance that will turn your baby's mouth, your breasts, and anything else it comes into contact with bright purple.

- If your nipples burn, itch, flake, ooze, and crust, you could be experiencing an outbreak of eczema. You will need to seek the services of a dermatologist.

Here are some general tips on coping with sore nipples:

- Express a small amount of milk just before the baby latches on. This will help reduce some of the wear and tear on your nipples.

- Offer the less sore breast to your baby when he first starts to nurse. This is the side that will receive the most vigorous sucking because baby is hungriest.

- Many lactation experts advise against using nipple shields as a means of coping with sore nipples, but if it's the only thing that's giving you any relief, you might consider using them as a temporary measure. Just be aware that they can sometimes make the soreness worse and may decrease your milk supply.

- Massage your breasts before and during each nursing session to encourage the milk to flow.

Bright Idea

If you're having difficulty with afterpains (uterine contractions stimulated by the release of oxytocin while you nurse), take a painkiller before you put your baby to the breast.

- Put your finger into the edge of your baby's mouth to break the suction before you remove him from the breast.

- Allow your nipples to air-dry after each feeding.

- Apply cold packs to your breasts for a short period after nursing. A well-positioned bag of frozen peas or corn can bring tremendous relief.

- Avoid nipple creams. They will only irritate your nipples.

- Change your nursing pads whenever they become wet. Avoid ones with plastic inserts because these increase your chances of developing a breast infection.

- Look for a cotton bra and wear cotton T-shirts while you're nursing. Other fabrics don't allow for adequate air circulation.

- Don't use soap on your nipples when you have your shower or bath.

About supplemental feedings

Most newborns don't require any fluids other than colostrum — the substance that is present in the breasts until your milk comes in about two days after the delivery. (The main exceptions are babies who have low blood sugar because their mother was diabetic, their birth weight was low, or they experienced unusual stress during labor and delivery.)

If you intend to breastfeed, it's important to avoid offering your baby a bottle during the early days of breastfeeding. Drinking from a bottle trains a baby to

- open her mouth less widely;

- wait to suck until she feels the firm bottle nipple in her mouth;

- encourage her to push her tongue forward — the opposite motion of what is required to nurse successfully.

What's more, a baby who has become accustomed to a bottle may not be willing to work at getting the milk out of a breast.

Milk flows out of a bottle right away; it takes a minute or two to get the milk to start flowing out of a breast.

Breastfeeding Q&A

Breastfeeding may be natural, but it doesn't always come naturally. Here are some answers to the most frequently asked questions about breastfeeding.

My newborn won't wake up long enough to nurse. Should I be concerned?

The bottom line is whether or not your baby is producing the number of wet or soiled diapers that is normal for a newborn baby. A minimum of five to six wet diapers, and one stool a day, is fine for babies up to the age of about six weeks.

If your baby isn't producing that many diapers, or isn't gaining weight as quickly as he should, you might want to think about waking the baby up for more frequent feeds during the day. Try for a two- to three-hour interval between feedings during the daytime, when you're awake. Feed at least once during the night.

> ❝I wish I had educated myself more on breast-feeding. I was naive to think that it would come naturally. I wish I had attended breast-feeding classes before my baby was born.❞
>
> — Kim, 35, mother of one

If you do decide to wake the baby up for more frequent feeds, don't just look at the clock — observe your baby's sleep stages. When he enters a period of light sleep (moving, eyelids flickering, and sucking), strip him down to his diaper. Do "baby sit-ups," if needed, until he is awake enough to nurse. If your baby slows down after nursing only a few minutes, gently stroking under the baby's chin or around his ears and head, or massaging your breast as he feeds, may keep him going stronger for longer.

How often should I feed my baby?

Most pediatricians recommend that breastfed babies follow a schedule of "demand feeding" — the mother feeds the baby when the baby is hungry. For breastfed babies, this typically translates into one feeding every two to three hours. Bottle-fed newborns will eat almost as often but, over time, they'll gradually require fewer feedings in a 24-hour period than their breastfed counterparts. (This is because breastmilk is digested more readily than infant formula.)

My nipples are really sore. I thought breastfeeding wasn't supposed to hurt.

Breastfeeding isn't supposed to hurt, but you might experience a bit of a tugging sensation. It should never be the kind of pain that would make you want to pull the baby off the breast immediately. If it hurts that much, there's a problem.

If your nipples are getting sore, take a look at how the baby is positioned at the breast. A lot of women will say, "It looks like he's latched on properly. He has a lot of the areola in his mouth."

However, mothers have this unique view from the top while they're nursing. You may find that the baby is simply positioned too high in the traditional cradle hold, with not enough areola on the side of his chin and jaw. Holding the baby on his side with his feet wrapped right around you makes a better angle so that you can get the nipple high against his palate, out of the way of the tongue action. His chin should be burrowing, both cheeks touching. If you have a hard time with this, move the baby down a bit so that he's "nose to nipple," and gently touch his lips to tease the mouth open into a wide gape as big as a yawn; then

> ❝ Breastfeeding is a marvel. There are no bottles or formula to prepare. It's the original 'fast food.' ❞
>
> — Melanie, 39, mother of two

bring him in close quickly. This works in all positions: cradle (when you cradle your baby in one arm and hold him across your body), football (when you put his head in your hand and tuck his body under your arm like a football), and side-lying (when you lie on one side to nurse your baby). Initially, it's trial and error, but it gets easier with practice. A good latch helps prevent 90 percent of the most common breastfeeding problems.

My sister says she leaked milk constantly when she was nursing her baby. I haven't had much problem with leaking at all. Does this mean I don't have enough milk?

Everyone is different as far as leaking goes. The bottom line, again, is your baby's weight gain. If your baby is gaining weight, it doesn't matter if you leak or don't leak. For most women, leaking is simply a laundry problem. Some women who leak constantly and copiously, even in between feedings, may have a chronic oversupply. They can improve this situation by using one side rather than two at each feeding.

My baby often falls asleep while nursing on the first side. Should I make a point of offering my baby both breasts at each feeding?

Fifteen years ago, nursing mothers were advised to feed their babies for 10 minutes on the first side and as long as the baby wanted on the second side. Today, nursing mothers are being told to nurse their baby as long as the baby wants on the first side and then switch to the second breast if the baby is still hungry. When your baby first starts to nurse on a particular side, he receives foremilk (which is low in fat), followed by hindmilk (which is high in fat). If you switch breasts before your baby finishes the hindmilk, he is obtaining fewer calories and is likely to be less satisfied than if you gave him the chance to empty the first breast thoroughly and then move on to the second breast, if necessary.

Why does my baby spit up so much?

Spitting up is rarely cause for concern. If the baby spits up large quantities of milk, you might think about feeding on only one side because the baby may be sucking for comfort and getting a whole lot more milk than he really wants.

Another reason why some babies spit up more than others is that babies have different nursing styles. Some babies are so aggressive and excited at the breast that their breathe-suck-swallow rhythm isn't very smooth or relaxed. They take in more air, and they're apt to need more burping than other babies. These babies aren't always burped as soon as they need it because they are such aggressive nursers. When they do burp, up comes all this milk.

Small amounts of spitting up in an otherwise thriving, contented baby is not a problem. On the other hand, frequent vomiting of large amounts of milk should be brought to the attention of the baby's caregiver. For babies who cry a lot and suffer from gassiness or colic, eliminating certain foods in the mother's diet may be a help. The most frequent culprit in our culture is cow's milk. A lactation consultant or your baby's caregiver can help you to pinpoint any possible food sensitivities.

Are there certain foods I should avoid while I'm nursing?

If your baby develops colicky symptoms — that is, crying, fussing, nursing more frequently, and being extremely irritable — when you eat certain foods, you might want to avoid them. Perennial offenders include "gassy" foods such as cabbage, onions, garlic, broccoli, and turnips; cow's milk; and caffeine.

 Bright Idea

If you are intending to breastfeed your baby, be sure to check with your obstetrician or pediatrician about the safely of any prescription or nonprescription drugs you may be taking.

If you eliminate the food that is causing the problem from your diet, you should see a marked improvement in your baby's temperament. If you don't see a change, the food you eliminated from your diet probably wasn't the problem.

When should I introduce a bottle?

If you want to introduce a bottle, you should be aware that some babies will develop a preference for the bottle over the breast. Try not to introduce a bottle before six weeks of age if you are firmly committed to breastfeeding. On the other hand, try not to delay introducing the bottle past four months if you want your child to accept one. If your baby won't take a bottle, use a cup or spoon. Small cups work fine for small babies if the person feeding the baby takes things slowly. Then, nurse the baby when you get home.

What can I do to avoid getting a breast infection?

You're more likely to get a breast infection (mastitis) if you're run down. Your best defense is to take things slowly during the postpartum period and to be sure that you're getting enough rest.

If you do happen to develop mastitis — which is characterized by swelling, heat, and pain in one breast (often with a fever) — notify your doctor at once so that he can prescribe antibiotics.

You should continue to breastfeed during this time because becoming engorged will only worsen the infection. The infection will not be transmitted to your baby through your breast milk, nor will the composition of your breast milk be affected. From your baby's standpoint at least, it's business as usual!

 Watch Out!

Avoid smoking and drinking alcohol while you are nursing. Cigarettes and alcohol contain substances that can interfere with your let-down, affect the content of your breast milk, and be harmful to your baby.

Breastfeeding tips for special situations

Special situations call for special breastfeeding advice. Here are some tips on breastfeeding if you give birth to multiples, if you've previously had breast surgery, if you adopt a baby, or if your baby is premature.

Breastfeeding multiples

The biggest challenge to breastfeeding multiples is logistics. Whether you intend to nurse two babies at the same time or to alternate between nursings and bottle-feedings, you will need to come up with a game plan for feeding two or more babies.

If you decide to nurse both babies simultaneously, you will want to

- find a comfortable spot to nurse (for example, a comfortable chair next to a table with a pitcher of water, the remote control for the TV, the cordless phone, and so on);
- choose a nursing position that is comfortable and that requires as few hands as possible (for example, the double football hold or the double cradle position);
- wake up the second baby when the first one wakes up to nurse and nurse both babies;
- jot down some notes about the feeding if you're worried that you'll forget important information later (for example, "Ben nursed well. Jessica kept dozing off and didn't appear to be particularly hungry.").

Here are some other tips for moms who are breastfeeding multiples:

- Drink plenty of fluids and eat plenty of nutritious foods. Breastfeeding demands approximately 500 calories per baby per day, so make sure that you're well fueled.
- Use a nursing pillow to position your babies so that you can keep one or both hands free.

- If you intend to express breast milk so that someone else can help out with feedings, rent a heavy-duty electric breast pump. Small electric and battery pumps simply aren't up to the task of pumping milk for two or more babies.

- Some mothers find it helpful to "assign" a particular breast to a particular baby rather than trying to remember which baby had which breast last.

- Remember that any amount of breast milk is better than nothing. If you're having difficulty keeping up with the breastfeeding demands of two or more babies, you may wish to consider supplementing with formula. On the other hand, if breastfeeding your babies exclusively is extremely important to you, rest assured that your breasts are almost certain to be up to the challenge.

Breastfeeding after breast surgery

Here are the facts on breastfeeding after breast surgery:

- A biopsy or removal of a lump seldom affects a woman's ability to breastfeed on the affected breast.

- A woman who has had a mastectomy can breastfeed on the remaining breast. In most cases, her remaining breast will still be able to produce more than enough milk for her baby.

- Women who have breast implants can usually breastfeed, as long as the milk ducts were not severed and there aren't any complications from the implants themselves.

- Women who have had breast reduction surgery may or may not be able to breastfeed, depending on the scope of the surgery. If, for example, the nipple was relocated, the milk ducts were probably severed and the milk supply may not be adequate. In this case, if the woman wants to breastfeed her baby, she might have to nurse with the aid of a breastfeeding supplementation device (a tubelike device that is taped to the breast and that dispenses formula in a fashion that closely mimics regular breastfeeding).

Breastfeeding after adoption

You don't have to give birth to breastfeed a baby. An infant's suck is capable of stimulating milk production. That said, the majority of adoptive mothers will need to supplement their breast milk, at least initially.

Note: Your efforts to breastfeed an adopted baby are most likely to succeed if you start nursing your baby when he is still a newborn. Mothers who adopt older babies may have difficulty introducing the breast to an infant who already has considerable experience with a bottle.

Breastfeeding a premature baby

If your baby arrives three to five weeks early, he will probably be able to breastfeed right away. If he is considerably more premature, you may need to express breast milk until the baby is healthy or mature enough to begin nursing on his own. In general, you should plan to express breast milk at least as often as your baby would normally nurse — 8 or more times in a 24-hour period.

You will need to take particular care when sterilizing your breast-pump parts and bottles. All objects that come in contact with the milk or your breasts should be scrubbed thoroughly with hot, soapy water after each use and then sterilized in boiling water or a dishwasher twice daily.

Choosing a breast pump

There are almost as many breast pumps on the market as there are automobiles, and — as is the case with cars — there's a model designed to suit every price range. If you will need to use your pump only occasionally, you can probably get away with purchasing a Chevrolet-type product. If, however, you are going to be using your pump on a daily basis and you want the best product on the market, you're best advised to invest in the Cadillac of breast pumps by renting or buying a hospital-grade machine.

When you're shopping for a breast pump, you should keep your needs in mind:

- How often will you be pumping? Will you be pumping many times each day or just occasionally?

- Where will you be pumping? Will you have access to an electrical outlet? What about a sink for rinsing the various pump components?

- How much time will you have to devote to each pump session? If you're likely to be pressed for time, should you consider renting or purchasing a double-horned unit that will enable you to pump both breasts at once?

- Will you be taking the pump back and forth to work each day? If so, how portable is the unit?

- Does the pump have continuous or intermittent pressure? (Intermittent pressure is best because it more closely imitates the suck-release pattern used by nursing babies and because it is less likely to injure your breast.)

- How easy is the unit to clean?

- How expensive is it? If it's a less-expensive machine, how well will it stand up to all the wear and tear?

 Moneysaver

Before you purchase a breast pump or sign a rental contract for an extended period of time, see if you can test-drive the unit first. There's no point in forking over a wallet full of cash only to discover that a particular model isn't going to do the job for you.

Caring for a sick or premature baby or a baby with special needs

If your baby is born prematurely or with birth-related or congenital problems, he may end up spending his first few weeks in the hospital — either in the neonatal intensive care unit or on the pediatric ward, depending on the extent of his health problems. You may find it extremely upsetting to leave the hospital without your baby, as Bridget, 36, did when her daughter, Jade, was born prematurely and with Dandy-Walker syndrome and other congenital anomalies. "You don't even feel like a mom because you don't have your baby," she recalls.

You may be worried about your baby, yet feel unsure about what questions to ask because everything about your baby's situation is utterly foreign to you. "It's like being in another country," Bridget explains. "You don't know the language or the customs."

Here are some tips on surviving your baby's hospitalization:

- Find out as much as you can about babies who are premature or who have special needs, either by talking to other parents or by having a family member do some research for you. (Note: Many hospitals have on-site pediatric reference libraries for the use of parents.) Ask someone in the unit — a parent or a nurse — to give you a crash course in NICU lingo so that you won't feel quite so intimidated.

- Bring a support person along when you're talking to the medical staff. "I didn't remember a lot of what the doctors were saying, so I made a point of having another relative there with me. It was good to have an extra set of ears to rely on," says Deirdre, 34, whose daughter experienced perinatal asphyxia and was left with multiple handicaps following the birth.

- Write down as much information about your baby's progress as you can. Note the baby's condition, medical

Bright Idea

Rather than comparing your premature baby to a full-term baby born at the same time, compare your baby to other babies who were due at the same time that he was. During the early weeks, you might want to compare your baby to photos of fetuses still in utero who are at the same gestational age as your baby. (Lennart Nilsson's book *A Child Is Born* is an excellent source of such photos.)

treatments, medications, appearance, and alert periods, as well as your own thoughts and feelings about your baby. You may find it helpful to have this record of your baby's progress to refer to during the days ahead.

■ Ask your baby's doctor if you can practice "kangaroo care." This involves laying your naked baby across your chest so that he can experience some skin-to-skin contact.

■ Talk to a social worker or counselor about any concerns you may have about the care your baby is receiving. "I mentioned to the social worker that Rebecca was always sleeping when we were there," Deirdre explains. "She said she would ask the nursery staff about cutting down her medication or altering the time at which it was given so that she would be conscious during my visits. The next day I came in and found that they had taken Rebecca right off the medication that was causing her drowsiness."

■ Ask if you can pump milk for the baby if he's unable to nurse. "Not only is it healthy for the baby; it makes you feel good to know that you are doing something that no one else can do for your baby," Deirdre explains.

■ Don't become obsessed with all the monitors and high-tech equipment. "Let the nurses worry about them," Deirdre suggests.

■ Personalize your baby's incubator by decorating it with balloons, stickers, and other items. If you want to buy a toy for your baby, however, make sure that it's made of plastic. Some hospitals won't allow stuffed animals around the incubators because they attract and hold bacteria.

- Don't beat yourself up if you aren't spending every waking moment at the hospital — particularly if your baby is hospitalized for an extended period of time. You won't be doing your baby any favors if you allow yourself to burn out.

- Ask if you can get special permission for someone other than you to spend time with your baby when you can't. "My aunt lives very close to the hospital where Rebecca was, so we made arrangements for her to visit with Rebecca as often as she wanted," says Deirdre. "It made me feel a lot better to know that she wasn't alone when we couldn't be there."

- Start preparing yourself for the day when your baby is discharged from the hospital. Participate as much as you can in your baby's day-to-day care so that it won't be quite so scary when it's time to bring him home. Play with your baby when he is alert and awake, and sing to him during diaper changes. Start getting to know this amazing little person who has just joined your family.

Just the facts

- You can expect to lose approximately 17 to 20 pounds of your pregnancy weight gain by the end of the postpartum period. You will probably still look five to six months pregnant during the first few days after you give birth because your uterus has not yet had a chance to return to its original size.

- Although your caregiver will probably give you the go-ahead to resume sexual activity within two to six weeks after the delivery, it may take a little longer for your libido to kick in.

- Don't be surprised if you experience a mix of emotions during the postpartum period. It's perfectly normal to feel this way.

- Newborn babies have erratic sleeping and eating habits and often have periods of unexplained crying.

- Be sure to lay your baby on his back when you put him to bed. According to the American Academy of Pediatrics, this is the only safe sleeping position for babies.

Glossary

active labor The period of labor in which the cervix dilates from four to seven centimeters.

afterbirth Another name for the placenta — your baby's physiological support system before birth.

Alpha-Fetoprotein (AFP) Testing A prenatal blood test performed between 15 and 18 weeks of pregnancy that is used to screen for both neural tube defects (high levels of AFP) and Down syndrome (low levels of AFP).

amniocentesis A procedure that involves inserting a needle through the abdominal wall and removing a small amount of amniotic fluid from the sac surrounding the developing baby. The amniotic fluid is then used to test for fetal abnormalities or lung maturity.

amniotic fluid The protective liquid, consisting mostly of water, that surrounds the baby inside the amniotic sac.

amniotic sac (or amnion) The thin-walled sac within the uterus that contains the baby and the amniotic fluid.

analgesic Medication for the treatment of pain. It can be given orally, by injection, or as part of an epidual or spinal procedure.

anencephaly   A neural tube defect resulting in a malformed brain and skull. Anencephaly leads to stillbirth or death soon after birth.

anesthetic   A medication that blocks the transmission of pain via nerve fibers. It can be given locally (such as in the perineum) or regionally (such as with an epidural or spinal procedure).

APGAR score   A measurement of a newborn's response to the stress of birth and life outside the womb. The test is performed at one minute and five minutes after birth.

areola   The flat, pigmented area encircling the nipple of the breast.

biophysical profile   A prenatal test that assesses the well-being of the developing baby.

bloody show   The blood-tinged mucus discharge — often — that indicates that the cervix is effacing or dilating.

Braxton Hicks contractions   Irregular contractions of the uterus that occur during pregnancy. They are felt most strongly during the late third trimester.

breech presentation   When the fetus is positioned buttocks or feet down rather than head down.

cephalopelvic disproportion   When the baby's head is too large for the mother's pelvis and birth canal (or the pelvis and birth canal is too small for the baby's head).

Certified Nurse-Midwife (CNM)   A registered nurse who has received specialized training in caring for women during pregnancy, labor, and the postpartum period.

cervical dilation   The amount the cervix has opened up prior to or during labor. Cervical dilation is measured in centimeters (from 0 to 10). Ten centimeters is fully dilated and means that you're ready to push.

cervical effacement   The thinning, shortening, or drawing up of the cervix before and during labor.

cervical incompetence   When a congenital defect or injury to the cervix causes it to open prematurely during pregnancy, causing miscarriage or a premature birth.

cervix   The entrance to the uterus.

cesarean section   The surgical procedure used to deliver a baby via an incision made in the mother's abdomen and uterus.

Chadwick's sign   A dark-blue or purple discoloration of the mucosa of the vagina and cervix during pregnancy.

chlamydia   A common sexually transmitted disease that can render a woman infertile if left untreated. Antibiotics can be used to treat the disease.

chloasma   Extensive brown patches of irregular shape and size on the face or other parts of the body that can occur during pregnancy.

chorioamnionitis   An inflammation of the membranes surrounding the fetus.

choriocarcinoma   A highly malignant cancer that can grow in the uterus during pregnancy or at the site of an ectopic pregnancy.

chorion   The outer sac enclosing the fetus within the uterus.

Chorionic Villus Sampling (CVS)   A prenatal diagnostic test in which a small amount of placental tissue is extracted via a fine hollow needle or catheter inserted into the womb. DNA extracted from this tissue is subsequently examined for genetic defects.

chromosomal abnormalities   Problems that result from errors in the duplication of the chromosomes.

chromosomes   Threadlike structures in the nucleus of a cell that transmit genetic information. The normal human chromosome number is 46, made up of 23 pairs.

circumcision   Surgical removal of the foreskin of the penis.

colostrum   The first secretion from the breasts following childbirth. Colostrum is high in protein and antibodies.

conception   When the sperm meets and penetrates the egg.

conjoined twins   Identical twins who have not separated completely. More commonly known as Siamese twins.

contraction   A painful, strong, rhythmic squeezing of the uterus that is experienced during labor.

contraction stress test   A test that assesses the baby's well-being by monitoring its response to uterine contractions.

cord prolapse   A rare obstetrical emergency that occurs when the umbilical cord drops out of the uterus into the vagina before the baby, leading to cord compression and oxygen deprivation.

cordocentesis   See Percutaneous Umbilical Cord Sampling.

Cytomegalovirus (CMV)   A virus from the herpes virus family that can infect the fetus.

D & C (Dilation and Curettage)   A surgical procedure in which the cervix is dilated and the lining of the uterus is scraped.

DES (Diethylstilbestrol)   A synthetic form of estrogen given to women between the 1940s and 1970s to inhibit miscarriage. DES was later discovered to have serious effects on women and children, including cancer, infertility, and miscarriage.

diastasis recti   Separation of the abdominal muscles resulting in a weakened area at the midline.

dizygotic twins   See fraternal twins.

Doppler (doptone)   A handheld device that uses ultrasound technology to enable the caregiver to listen to the fetal heart rate.

doula   Someone who assists a woman and her family during labor and the postpartum period.

due date   The date on which a baby's birth is expected, calculated by adding 279 days to the first day of the woman's last menstrual period (LMP) or 265 days to the date of ovulation, if known.

eclampsia   A serious and rare condition that can affect pregnant or laboring women. Eclampsia is diagnosed when seizures accompany preeclampsia. An emergency delivery may be required.

ectopic pregnancy A pregnancy that occurs outside the uterus, usually in the fallopian tube.

edema The accumulation of fluid in the body's tissues, resulting in swelling.

Electronic Fetal Monitor (EFM) An electronic instrument used to record the heartbeat of the fetus, as well as the contractions of the mother's uterus. Fetal monitors can be either external (placed on the abdomen) or internal (attached to the baby's scalp via the vagina to detect heart rate or placed into the uterus, also via the vagina, to measure the strength of contractions).

embryo A medical term for the baby during its first three months of development inside the uterus.

endometriosis The presence of uterine-lining tissue in or around other reproductive organs, particularly the ovaries and fallopian tubes.

engagement When the baby's presenting part (usually the head) settles into the pelvic cavity.

engorgement Congested or filled with fluid. This term refers to the fullness or swelling of the breasts that can occur between the second and seventh postpartum day, when a woman's breasts first start to produce milk.

epidural anesthesia/analgesia A regional anesthetic and/or analgesic injected into the epidural space near the base of the spinal cord.

episiotomy A small incision made into the skin and perineal muscle at the time of delivery to enlarge the vaginal opening and facilitate the birth of the head.

Estimated Date of Confinement (EDC) The medical term for due date.

estrogen A hormone that is produced in the ovaries and that works with progesterone to regulate the reproductive cycle.

external version   A procedure in which the doctor turns the baby or babies in the uterus (from breech to vertex) by applying manual pressure on the outside of the mother's abdomen.

face presentation   A relatively uncommon labor presentation that occurs when the baby is head down but has its neck extended, as if it were looking down the birth canal.

fallopian tube   The tube that carries eggs from the ovaries to the uterus.

false labor   When you experience regular or painful contractions that do not start to dilate or thin the cervix.

fetal monitor   See Electronic Fetal Monitor.

fetus   The medical term used to describe the developing baby from the end of the third month of pregnancy until birth.

forceps   A tonglike instrument that may be placed around the baby's head to help guide it out of the birth canal during delivery.

fraternal twins   Twins who are the result of the union of two eggs and two sperm.

fundal height   The distance from the upper rounded part of a pregnant woman's uterus to her pubic bone.

gestational diabetes   Diabetes that occurs during pregnancy.

glucose tolerance test   A blood test used to detect gestational diabetes. Blood is drawn at specified intervals following the ingestion of a sugary substance.

group B strep   A bacteria found in the vaginas and rectums of some pregnant women. Women who test positive for group B strep may require antibiotics during labor to protect their babies from picking up a serious, potentially life-threatening infection.

hemorrhoids   Swollen blood vessels around the anus or in the rectal canal that may bleed and cause pain, especially after childbirth.

Human Chorionic Gonadotropin (hCG)   The hormone produced in early pregnancy that causes a pregnancy test to be positive.

hyperemesis gravidarum Severe nausea, dehydration, and vomiting during pregnancy.

identical twins Twins that are the result of the fertilization and subsequent splitting of a single egg.

In Vitro Fertilization (IVF) When eggs are inseminated in a petri dish and then implanted in the uterus.

incomplete abortion A miscarriage in which part, but not all, of the contents of the uterus are expelled.

infertility The inability to conceive or carry a child to term.

intrathecal anesthesia/analgesia A regional anesthetic and/or analgesic given within the spinal fluid. Sometimes referred to as a spinal.

intrauterine death The death of a fetus within the uterus.

Intrauterine Device (IUD) A plastic or metal birth-control device inserted into the uterus to prevent fertilization.

Intrauterine Growth Restriction (IUGR) When the baby's growth is less than what would normally be expected.

jaundice See newborn jaundice.

Kegel exercises Exercises of the muscles of the pelvic floor, including those of the urethra, vagina, and rectum.

labor The process of childbirth, from dilation of the cervix to the delivery of the baby and the placenta.

lightening A change in the shape of the pregnant uterus a few weeks before labor that is the result of a descent of the presenting part of the baby into the pelvis.

linea nigra A dark line running from the navel to the pubic area that may develop during pregnancy.

lochia The discharge of blood, mucus, and tissue from the uterus following childbirth.

low birthweight Babies who weigh less than 5 ½ pounds at birth.

mask of pregnancy See chloasma.

mastitis   A painful infection of the breast characterized by fever, soreness, and swelling.

meconium   The greenish substance that builds up in the bowels of a growing fetus and is normally discharged shortly after birth.

miscarriage (spontaneous abortion)   Expulsion of an embryo or fetus prior to 20 weeks' gestation.

missed abortion   When the embryo dies in utero but the body fails to expel the contents of the uterus. It is typically diagnosed by ultrasound.

mittelschmerz   Pain that coincides with the release of an egg from the ovary.

molar pregnancy   A pregnancy that results in the growth of abnormal placental cells rather than a fetus.

monozygotic twins   See identical twins.

mucus plug   The plug of thick and sticky mucus that blocks the cervical canal during pregnancy, protecting the baby from infection.

neonatal death   The death of a live-born infant between birth and four weeks of age.

Neonatal Intensive Care Unit (NICU)   An intensive care unit that specializes in the care of premature, low-weight babies and seriously ill infants.

neural tube defects   Abnormalities in the development of the spinal cord and brain in a fetus, including anencephaly, hydrocephalus, and spina bifida.

newborn jaundice   The yellowish tinge of a newborn's skin that is caused by too much bilirubin in the blood. It usually develops on the second or third day of life and lasts until the baby is 7 to 10 days old. Newborn jaundice can usually be corrected by special light treatment.

nonstress test   A noninvasive test in which fetal movements are monitored and recorded, along with changes in fetal heart rate.

occiput anterior position When the baby's face is turned toward the back of the mother's pelvis in the birth canal.

occiput posterior position When the baby's face is turned toward the front of the mother's pelvis in the birth canal. This position is sometimes described as "sunny side up".

oligohydramnios A shortage of amniotic fluid.

ovulation The point in the menstrual cycle in which a mature egg is released from the ovaries into the fallopian tubes.

oxytocin The naturally occurring hormone that causes uterine contractions. A synthetic form of this hormone (Pitocin) is often used to induce or augment labor.

pelvic floor muscles The group of muscles at the base of the pelvis that help support the bladder, uterus, urethra, vagina, and rectum.

Pelvic Inflammatory Disease (PID) An infection that can affect the uterus, fallopian tubes, ovaries, and other parts of the reproductive system.

Percutaneous Umbilical Cord Sampling (PUBS) A diagnostic procedure that draws blood from the fetus's umbilical cord to test for abnormalities and genetic conditions.

perineum The muscle and tissue between the vagina and the rectum.

Phenylketonuria (PKU) A genetic disorder in which a liver enzyme is defective, possibly leading to serious retardation. This disorder is detected through a blood test done at birth and may be controlled by a special diet.

placenta The organ that develops in the uterus during pregnancy, providing nutrients for the fetus and eliminating its waste products.

placenta previa A condition in which the placenta partially or completely blocks the cervical opening.

placental abruption The premature separation of the placenta from the uterus.

placental infarction   The death of part of the placenta, which, if extensive enough, can cause stillbirth.

polyhydramnios   Also known as hydramnios. An abnormal condition of pregnancy characterized by an excess of amniotic fluid.

postmature baby   A baby who is born after 42 completed weeks gestation and who shows signs of postmaturity syndrome. Note: The terms post-term or postdates are preferred in the absence of postmaturity syndrome.

postpartum blues   Mild depression after delivery.

Postpartum Depression (PPD)   Clinical depression that can occur following the delivery. Postpartum depression is characterized by sadness, impatience, restlessness, and — in particularly severe cases — an inability to care for the baby.

postpartum hemorrhage   Loss of more than 15 ounces (450 ml) of blood at the time of delivery.

preeclampsia/toxemia   A serious condition marked by sudden edema, high blood pressure, and protein in the urine.

pregnancy-induced hypertension   A pregnancy-related condition in which a woman's blood pressure is temporarily elevated.

premature baby   A baby who is born before 37 weeks of gestation.

Premature Rupture of the Membranes (PROM)   When the membranes rupture before the onset of labor.

progesterone   A female hormone that is produced in the ovaries and works with estrogen to regulate the reproductive cycle.

prolactin   The hormone responsible for milk production that is released following the delivery of the placenta and the membranes.

psychoprophylaxis   Intellectual, physical, and emotional preparation for childbirth. The term *psychoprophylaxis* is associated with the Bradley Method of husband-coached labor.

quickening   When the pregnant woman first detects fetal movement (typically between the 16th and 20th weeks of pregnancy).

round ligament pain   Pain caused by stretching ligaments on the sides of the uterus during pregnancy.

rubella (German measles)   A mild, highly contagious viral disease that can cause serious birth defects in the developing baby.

ruptured membranes   Loss of fluid from the amniotic sac. Also described as having your water break.

sciatica   A common pregnancy-related condition. Pain in the leg, lower back, and buttock caused by pressure of the growing uterus on the sciatic nerve. Apply heat and rest to relieve the condition.

show   See bloody show.

Siamese twins   See conjoined twins.

spina bifida   A neural tube defect that occurs when the tube housing the central nervous system fails to close completely.

spinal anesthesia/analgesia   A regional anesthetic and/or analgesic that is injected into the spinal fluid.

spontaneous abortion   See miscarriage.

station   An estimate of the baby's progress in descending into the pelvis.

stillbirth   A fetal death that occurs after the 20th week of pregnancy.

stress test   A test that records the fetal heart rate in response to induced mild contractions of the uterus.

stretch marks   Reddish streaks on the skin of the breasts, abdomen, legs, and buttocks that are caused by the stretching of the skin during pregnancy.

teratogens   Agents such as drugs, chemicals, and infectious diseases that can cause birth defects in a developing baby.

terbutaline   A medication used to stop contractions in preterm labor.

threatened abortion   Bleeding during the first trimester of pregnancy that is not accompanied by either cramping or contractions.

toxoplasmosis   A parasitic infection that can cause stillbirth or miscarriage in pregnant women and congenital defects in babies.

transition   The third or final phase of the first stage of labor, when the cervix goes from 7 to 10 centimeters' dilation.

transverse lie   When the fetus is lying horizontally across the uterus rather than in a vertical position.

tubal ligation   A permanent sterilization procedure that involves tying off a woman's fallopian tubes to prevent conception.

tubal pregnancy   A pregnancy that occurs in the fallopian tube.

ultrasound   A technique that uses high-frequency sound waves to create a moving image, or sonogram, on a television screen.

umbilical cord   The cord that connects the placenta to the developing baby, removing waste products and carbon dioxide from the baby and bringing oxygenated blood and nutrients from the mother through the placenta to the baby.

vacuum extraction   A process in which a suction cup is placed on a baby's head to aid in delivery.

Vaginal Birth After Cesarean (VBAC)   A vaginal delivery after a woman has previously delivered a baby by cesarean section.

varicose veins   Abnormally swollen veins, usually on the legs.

vasectomy   A minor surgical procedure that involves cutting the vas deferens to block the passage of sperm.

VBAC   See Vaginal Birth After Cesarean.

vena cava   The major vein in the body that returns unoxygenated blood to the heart for transport to the lungs.

vernix caseosa   A greasy white substance that coats and protects the baby's skin in utero.

vertex   Head-down presentation.

Further Reading

Alban Gosline, Andrea, Lisa Burnett Bossi and Ame Mahler Beanland. *Celebrating Motherhood: A Comforting Companion for Every Expecting Mother.* Berkeley: Conari Press, 2002.

Brockenbrough, Martha. *It Could Happen to You! Diary of a Pregnancy and Beyond.* Kansas City: Andrews McMeel Publishing, 2002.

Buchanan, Andrea J. *Mother Shock: Loving Every (Other) Minute of It.* New York: Seal Press, 2003.

Cancellaro, Cecelia A. *Pregnancy Stories.* Oakland: New Harbinger Publications, Inc., 2001.

Cooke, Kaz. *The Rough Guide to Pregnancy and Birth.* London: Rough Guides, 2001.

D'Amico, Christine and Margaret A. Taylor. *The Pregnant Woman's Companion.* Minneapolis, Attitude Press, Inc., 2002.

Davis, Deborah L. *Empty Cradle, Broken Heart: Surviving the Death of Your Baby.* Golden: Fulcrum Publishing, 1996.

DiLeo, Gerard M. *The Anxious Parent's Guide to Pregnancy.* New York: Contemporary Books, 2002.

Douglas, Ann. *Choosing Childcare for Dummies.* New York: John Wiley and Sons, 2002.

Appendix B

———. *The Mother of All Baby Books.* New York: John Wiley and Sons, 2002.

———. *The Mother of All Pregnancy Books.* New York: John Wiley and Sons, 2002.

Douglas, Ann and John R. Sussman M.D. *Trying Again: A Guide to Pregnancy After Miscarriage, Stillbirth, and Infant Loss.* Dallas: Taylor Publishing Company, 2000.

England, Pam and Rob Horowitz. *Birthing From Within: An Extra-Ordinary Guide to Childbirth Preparation.* Albuquerque: Partera Press, 1998.

The Editors of *Fitness Magazine* with Ginny Graves. *Pregnancy Fitness.* New York: Three Rivers Press, 1999.

Gallo, Birgitta and Sheryl Ross. *Birgitta Gallo's Expecting Fitness.* Los Angeles: Renaissance Books, 1999.

Gaskin, Ina May. *Ina May's Guide to Childbirth.* New York: Bantam Books, 2003.

Gurevich, Rachel. *The Doula Advantage.* Roseville: Prima Publishing, 2003.

Hanson, Rick, Jan Hanson and Ricki Pollycove. *Mother Nurture: A Mother's Guide to Health in Body, Mind, and Intimate Relationships.* New York: Penguin Books, 2002.

Harris, A. Christine. *The Pregnancy Journal: A Day-to-Day Guide to a Healthy and Happy Pregnancy.* San Francisco: Chronicle Books, 1996.

Hawkins, Miranda and Sarah Knox. *The Midwifery Option: A Canadian Guide to the Birth Experience.* Toronto: HarperCollins Publishers, 2003.

Jackson, Deborah. *With Child: Wisdom and Traditions for Pregnancy, Birth and Motherhood.* San Francisco: Chronicle Books, 1999.

Klaus, Marshall H., Phyllis H. Klaus. *Your Amazing Newborn.* Reading: Perseus Books, 1998.

Louden, Jennifer. *The Pregnant Woman's Comfort Book*. New York: HarperCollins Publishers, 1995.

Luke, Barbara and Tamara Eberlein. *When You're Expecting Twins, Triplets, or Quads*. New York: HarperCollins Publishers, 1999.

Nathanielsz, Peter. *The Prenatal Prescription*. New York: HarperCollins Publishers, 2001.

Newman, Jack and Teresa Pitman. *Guide to Breastfeeding*. Toronto: HarperCollins Publishers, 2003.

Ogle, Amy and Lisa Mazzullo. *Before Your Pregnancy: A 90-Day Guide for Couples on How to Prepare for a Healthy Conception*. New York: Ballantine Books, 2002.

Reichert, Bonny. *In Search of Sleep: Straight Talk about Babies, Toddlers and Night Waking*. Sarasota: Sarasota Press, 2001.

Sears, William, Martha Sears and Linda Hughey Holt. *The Pregnancy Book: A Month-by-Month Guide*. Boston: Little, Brown and Company, 1997.

Semans, Anne and Cathy Winks. *The Mother's Guide to Sex: Enjoying Your Sexuality Through All Stages of Motherhood*. New York: Three Rivers Press, 2001.

Simkin, Penny, Janet Whalley and Ann Keppler. *Pregnancy, Childbirth and the Newborn: The Complete Guide*. New York: Meadowbrook Press, 2001.

Stone, Joanne, Keith Eddleman and Mary Murray. *Pregnancy for Dummies*. New York: Wiley Publishing, Inc., 1999.

Sullivan, Donald L. *The Expectant Mother's Guide to Prescription and Nonprescription Drugs, Vitamins, Home Remedies and Herbal Products*. New York: St. Martin's Griffin, 2001.

Sussman M.D., John R. and B. Blake Levitt. *Before You Conceive: The Complete Prepregnancy Guide*. New York: Bantam Books, 1989.

Tsiaras, Alexander and Barry Werth. *From Conception to Birth: A Life Unfolds*. New York: Doubleday, 2002.